AMERICA'S
TEST KITCHEN

ADDITIONAL COOKBOOKS AVAILABLE FROM THE PUBLISHERS OF COOK'S COUNTRY INCLUDE:

The Complete Slow Cooker

The Complete Make-Ahead Cookbook

The Complete Mediterranean Cookbook

The Complete Vegetarian Cookbook

The Complete Cooking for Two Cookbook

The Complete Cooking for Two Cookbook Gift Edition

Cooking at Home with Bridget and Julia

What Good Cooks Know

Cook's Science

The Science of Good Cooking

The Perfect Cookie

Bread Illustrated

Master of the Grill

Kitchen Smarts: Questions and Answers
to Boost Your Cooking I.Q.

Kitchen Hacks: How Clever Cooks Get Things Done

100 Recipes: The Absolute Best Way
to Make the True Essentials

The New Family Cookbook

The *America's Test Kitchen* Cooking School Cookbook

The *Cook's Illustrated* Meat Book

The *Cook's Illustrated* Baking Book

The *Cook's Illustrated* Cookbook

The *America's Test Kitchen* Family Baking Book

The Best of *America's Test Kitchen* (2007–2018 Editions)

The Complete *America's Test Kitchen*
TV Show Cookbook (2001–2018)

Food Processor Perfection

Pressure Cooker Perfection

Vegan for Everybody

Naturally Sweet

Foolproof Preserving

Paleo Perfected

The How Can It Be Gluten-Free Cookbook: Volume 2

The How Can It Be Gluten-Free Cookbook

The Best Mexican Recipes

Slow Cooker Revolution 2: The Easy Prep Edition

Slow Cooker Revolution

The Six-Ingredient Solution

The *America's Test Kitchen* Do-It-Yourself Cookbook

1993–2017 *Cook's Illustrated* Master Index

Cook's Illustrated Annual Hardbound Editions
from each year of publication (1993–2017)

The Cook's Illustrated All-Time Best Series

All-Time Best Sunday Suppers

All-Time Best Holiday Entertaining

All-Time Best Appetizers

All-Time Best Soups

Cook's Country titles

One-Pan Wonders

Cook It in Cast Iron

Cook's Country Eats Local

The Complete *Cook's Country* TV Show Cookbook,
10th Anniversary Edition

Visit our online bookstore at www.CooksCountry.com to order any of our cookbooks
listed above. You can also order subscriptions, gift subscriptions, and any of our cookbooks by calling
800-611-0759 inside the U.S., or 515-237-3663 if calling from outside the U.S.

$35.00

ISBN: 978-1-945256-37-0
ISSN: 1552-1990

To get home delivery of *Cook's Country* magazine, call 800-526-8447 inside the U.S.,
or 515-237-3663 if calling from outside the U.S., or subscribe online at www.CooksCountry.com/Subscribe.

2017 Recipe Index

Cook's Country

FEBRUARY/MARCH 2017

New Jersey Crumb Buns

It took several (sweet) weeks in the kitchen before we unlocked the secrets of crunchy crumbs and tender cake.

PAGE 20

Hearty Beef Lasagna
Two Hours, Start to Finish

Crusted Pork Tenderloin
Weeknight Favorite

Chicken Fricassee
with Apples and Cream

Cooking Class:
Chocolate Layer Cake

Texas Breakfast Tacos
Plus Homemade Tortillas

Best Immersion Blender
We Tested a Dozen

Beef Wellington for Two
Fancy and Faster

Lyonnaise Potatoes
Pan-Fried with Onions

Slow-Cooker Corned Beef and Cabbage

Sweet Potato Wedges
Five Flavor Variations

One-Pan Breakfast
You Can Have It All

CooksCountry.com
$5.95 U.S./$6.95 CANADA

LETTER FROM THE EDITOR

At left, *Cook's Country* associate editor Katie Leaird slides a pan of lasagna into a test kitchen cooling rack. Below, San Francisco's Chinatown and a San Antonio Mexican restaurant.

Hᴇʀᴇ ᴀᴛ Cᴏᴏᴋ's Cᴏᴜɴᴛʀʏ, we focus on American food. But what is American food, anyway?

There are many ways to answer that question, none of them definitive and all of them complicated.

Consider Killed Salad (page 12). It's an endemically Appalachian dish, traditionally made with ingredients foraged from the mountain woodlands, and it's wholly American. But is it any more or less American than Hearty Beef Lasagna (page 4), which has clear roots in Italy?

And what about Queso Fundido (page 18) or Mongolian Beef (page 11)? Sure, they take inspiration from the cuisines of other nations, but each is probably more common in the States than in Mexico or China.

The fact is, American cuisine is defined by its dynamic, flexible, adaptive nature. As soon as you attempt to nail it down or draw boundaries around it, it will surprise you. You just can't fence it in.

I'm not sure there's a definitive answer to the question "What is American food?" But that's OK. In fact, it's good. Because to my mind, unanswerable questions spark the best conversations, and the best conversations happen at the table. Over a supper of (French-ish) Chicken Fricassee with Apples (page 10), of course.

TUCKER SHAW

Executive Editor

Photography: Jean-Pierre Lescourret/Getty Images (middle)

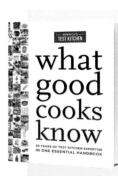

What Good Cooks Know

This indispensable wealth of information has been amassed from more than 20 years of teaching people how to cook. From foolproof techniques to invaluable product reviews, *What Good Cooks Know* promises to be your new one-stop reference, with all the authority of the test kitchen's extensive tasting, testing, and recipe development protocols behind it. This all-inclusive resource puts the answers to all your kitchen questions at your fingertips.

Order online at AmericasTestKitchen.com/goodcooks

Follow us on **Pinterest**
pinterest.com/TestKitchen

Follow us on **Twitter**
twitter.com/TestKitchen

Find us on **Facebook**
facebook.com/CooksCountry

Find us on **Instagram**
instagram.com/cookscountry

Cook's Country

Chief Executive Officer David Nussbaum
Chief Creative Officer Jack Bishop
Editorial Director John Willoughby
Executive Editor Tucker Shaw
Deputy Editor Rebecca Hays
Executive Managing Editor Todd Meier
Executive Food Editor Bryan Roof
Senior Editor Chris O'Connor
Associate Editors Morgan Bolling, Katie Leaird, Ashley Moore
Test Cooks Alli Berkey, Daniel Cellucci, Matthew Fairman, Cecelia Jenkins
Assistant Test Cook Mady Nichas
Senior Copy Editor Krista Magnuson
Copy Editor Jillian Campbell
Contributing Editor Eva Katz
Science Editor Guy Crosby, PhD, CFS
Director, Creative Operations Alice Carpenter
Hosts & Executive Editors, Television Bridget Lancaster, Julia Collin Davison

Executive Editor, Tastings & Testings Lisa McManus
Managing Editor Scott Kathan
Deputy Editor Hannah Crowley
Associate Editors Lauren Savoie, Kate Shannon
Assistant Editors Miye Bromberg, Emily Phares
Editorial Assistant Carolyn Grillo

Test Kitchen Director Erin McMurrer
Assistant Test Kitchen Director Leah Rovner
Test Kitchen Manager Alexxa Benson
Lead Senior Kitchen Assistant Meridith Lippard
Senior Kitchen Assistant Taylor Pond
Lead Kitchen Assistant Ena Gudiel
Kitchen Assistants Erick Aroche-Paz, Gladis Campos, Blanca Castanza

Design Director Greg Galvan
Photography Director Julie Cote
Art Director Susan Levin
Designer Maggie Edgar
Art Director, Marketing Melanie Gryboski
Deputy Art Director, Marketing Janet Taylor
Associate Art Director, Marketing Stephanie Cook
Senior Staff Photographer Daniel J. van Ackere
Staff Photographer Steve Klise
Assistant Photography Producer Mary Ball
Color Food Photography Keller + Keller
Styling Catrine Kelty, Marie Piraino

Senior Director, Digital Design John Torres
Executive Editor, Web Christine Liu
Managing Editor, Web Mari Levine
Senior Editor, Web Roger Metcalf
Associate Editors, Web Terrence Doyle, Briana Palma
Senior Video Editor Nick Dakoulas
Test Kitchen Photojournalist Kevin White

Chief Financial Officer Jackie McCauley Ford
Production Director Guy Rochford
Imaging Manager Lauren Robbins
Production & Imaging Specialists Heather Dube, Sean MacDonald, Dennis Noble, Jessica Voas
Senior Controller Theresa Peterson
Director, Business Partnerships Mehgan Conciatori

Chief Digital Officer Fran Middleton
VP, Analytics & Media Strategy Deborah Fagone
Director, Sponsorship Marketing & Client Services Christine Anagnostis
Client Services Manager Kate Zebrowski
Partnership Marketing Manager Pamela Putprush
Director, Customer Support Amy Bootier
Senior Customer Loyalty & Support Specialists Rebecca Kowalski, Andrew Straaberg Finfrock
Customer Loyalty & Support Specialist Caroline Augliere

Senior VP, Human Resources & Organizational Development Colleen Zelina
Human Resources Director Adele Shapiro
Director, Retail Book Program Beth Ineson
Retail Sales Manager Derek Meehan
Associate Director, Publicity Susan Hershberg

Circulation Services ProCirc

On the cover: New Jersey Crumb Buns
Keller + Keller, Catrine Kelty
Illustration: Greg Stevenson

Contents

Departments

— AMERICA'S —
TEST KITCHEN
RECIPES THAT WORK®

America's Test Kitchen is a real 2,500-square-foot kitchen located just outside Boston. It is the home of more than 60 test cooks, editors, and cookware specialists. Our mission is to test recipes until we understand exactly how and why they work and eventually arrive at the very best version. We also test kitchen equipment and supermarket ingredients in search of products that offer the best value and performance. You can watch us work by tuning in to America's Test Kitchen (AmericasTestKitchen.com) and Cooks Country from America's Test Kitchen (CooksCountry.com) on public television and listen to our weekly segments on The Splendid Table on public radio. You can also follow us on Facebook, Twitter, Pinterest, and Instagram.

Cook's Country magazine (ISSN 1552-1990), number 73, is published bimonthly by America's Test Kitchen Limited Partnership, 17 Station St., Brookline, MA 02445. Copyright 2017 America's Test Kitchen Limited Partnership. Periodicals postage paid at Boston, MA, and additional mailing offices. USPS #023453. Publications Mail Agreement No. 40020778. Return undeliverable Canadian addresses to P.O. Box 875, Station A, Windsor, ON N9A 6P2. POSTMASTER: Send address changes to Cook's Country, PO Box 6018, Harlan, IA 51593-1518. For subscription and gift subscription orders, subscription inquiries, or change of address notices, visit AmericasTestKitchen.com/support, call 800-526-8447 in the U.S. or 515-248-7684 from outside the U.S., or write to us at Cook's Country, P.O. Box 6018, Harlan, IA 51593-1518. PRINTED IN THE USA.

Ask Cook's Country

BY MORGAN BOLLING

Boiling with Curiosity

Why do recipes call for water to be at a rolling boil before dropping in the pasta? Why can't I just start it in cold water?
Elizabeth McCarthy, Albany, N.Y.

Most pasta aficionados believe there is only one way to properly cook pasta—in a large pot of boiling salted water. But is that really true? To find out, we cooked spaghetti, penne, and elbow macaroni, starting them all in cold water, and tasted them alongside batches cooked the traditional way. When drained, the pastas weighed the same, meaning that they had absorbed the same amount of water during cooking. Also, tasters could not detect a textural difference between the pastas.

We then made two batches of our Spaghetti with Pecorino Romano and Black Pepper (Cacio e Pepe), which calls for using the pasta cooking water to make the sauce. If we started with the same amount of water in each batch, the end results were nearly identical.

One word of caution if you opt to start pasta in cold water: The pasta will start cooking before the water reaches a full boil, so you have to taste the pasta for doneness rather than follow time recommendations.

THE BOTTOM LINE: It's OK to start cooking pasta in cold water, and doing so can save you a few minutes. But you'll need to taste it for doneness rather than rely on the cooking time called for on the package or in a recipe.

BREAKING THE RULES
It's fine to start pasta in cold water.

A Real Grind

Can I use "ground turkey breast" in a recipe that calls for "ground turkey"?
Tyler Joosten, Salt Lake City, Utah

Ground turkey is typically 93 percent lean and is made by grinding both light and dark meat, including the skin and fat. Ground turkey breast (which often costs twice as much) is 99 percent lean and is made from only breast meat.

To see if we could use the two products interchangeably, we made batches of our Crispy Turkey Burgers, Skillet Turkey Meatballs with Lemony Rice, and Quick Turkey Chili using each. Our tasters preferred the fattier, richer ground turkey in every application. The samples using the ultralean ground turkey breast were "dry," "chalky," and like "cardboard" in every dish.

THE BOTTOM LINE: When a recipe calls for ground turkey without specifying breast meat, do not substitute ground turkey breast—it's too lean and will result in a drier dish.

GROUND TURKEY
Moist and flavorful

GROUND TURKEY BREAST
Too lean

Heating Things Up

I like hot salsa and make a killer homemade version. But it seems to lose some of its spiciness when I refrigerate it—why is that?
Amy Triplet, Bakersfield, Calif.

To answer your question, we made a batch of fresh salsa using jalapeño chiles. We then tasted it at several different temperatures between 80 degrees and 36 degrees. We found that the colder the salsa was, the less spiciness we tasted.

Our science editor confirmed that our mouths' sensory receptors for capsaicin (the component in chiles that produces a burning sensation) are temperature-sensitive; that is, we perceive spicy heat most fully in warmer foods. So the exact same salsa can be scorching when tasted warm but mild if tasted cold.

THE BOTTOM LINE: The colder a salsa is, the less we're able to perceive its spiciness. So if you want the heat level to be readily apparent, serve a spicy salsa at room temperature. If you like it milder, chill it.

Malleable Measuring

I find measuring semisoft ingredients such as mayonnaise and peanut butter to be a challenge. Should I use a dry measuring cup or a liquid measure?
Susan Earle, Charlotte Hall, Md.

In the test kitchen, we use an adjustable measuring cup when measuring semisoft items such as honey, peanut butter, mayonnaise, and ketchup because it provides us with the most accurate and consistent results. Our favorite—the KitchenArt Adjust-A-Cup Professional Series, 2-Cup—features a plastic barrel with clear measurement markings and an easy-to-use plunger insert.

The next best option is to use a dry measuring cup. If the item you're measuring is thick, you can slide the back of a butter knife across the top

OUR CHOICE
Soft items only

of the cup to get a more accurate measurement. That said, if a weight is listed in the ingredient list and you have a scale, rely on that for the most accurate measurement.

THE BOTTOM LINE: The best way to measure semisoft foods is to use an adjustable measuring cup. If you don't have one, reach for a dry measuring cup.

Milky Matter

My grocery store sells ultrafiltered milk. How does it compare with the regular stuff?
Ellen Gaffney, Setauket, N.Y.

A few national manufacturers (The Coca-Cola Company and HP Hood LLC, for example) have started selling ultrafiltered milk. To make it, the milk is run through filters that either break down and recombine its components (eliminating the lactose and adjusting the fat levels in the process) or filter out some of the water and/or fat to concentrate the protein and calcium content. The selling points of ultrafiltered milk are that it's lactose-free and has a long shelf life. Also, manufacturers claim that the lower-fat versions are as rich and flavorful as standard whole milk.

ULTRAFILTERED
Is it any good?

To see how 2 percent ultrafiltered milk compared with 2 percent regular milk in flavor and texture, we tried each four ways: chilled straight up and in our recipes for Classic Macaroni and Cheese, Old-Fashioned Rice Pudding, and White Layer Cake. Tasters voiced preferences for one or the other but came to no consensus, deeming both milks acceptable in all applications.

THE BOTTOM LINE: We learned that ultrafiltered milk works well as a substitute for regular milk in recipes and tastes just fine chilled from a glass. It's a good option for those looking for milk with less fat and lactose.

Sour Storage

Can you freeze whole lemons?
Tessa King, Longmont, Colo.

We'd never tried this, so to find an answer to your question, we froze a dozen whole lemons in airtight containers. We found the lemons easy to juice once they had thawed because they were so soft. But the thawed lemons were nearly impossible to zest because their exteriors were too soft and soggy. However, we were able to zest the frozen lemons before we set them out to thaw.

We then tested the lemon zest and juice we harvested from the frozen fruit in our recipes for Lemon Vinaigrette, North Carolina Lemon Pie, and Roast Lemon Chicken for Two. What did we find? Tasters found that the vinaigrette, pie, and roast made with frozen lemon juice were "weak" and "less bright" than the versions made with fresh juice. The flavor of the frozen zest was still vibrant, though its color was dull.

THE BOTTOM LINE: Because freezing mutes the flavor of lemon juice, we do not recommend freezing whole lemons. Lemon zest can be frozen, but its color will be less bright than that of fresh zest.

To ask us a cooking question, visit CooksCountry.com/ask. Or write to Ask Cook's Country, P.O. Box 470739, Brookline, MA 02447. Just try to stump us!

Kitchen Shortcuts

COMPILED BY DIANE UNGER

COOL IDEA
Guac to Go
Jeremy Henderson, Birmingham, Ala.

My family loves guacamole. To make it convenient to eat at the beach, on a picnic, or while camping, I place peeled and pitted ripe avocados in a 1-gallon zipper-lock bag. Then I add lime juice, garlic, and salt and pepper and seal the bag, using my hands to smush the ingredients to the desired consistency (my 6-year-old son loves to do that part). I shape the bag into a neat, flat package that easily fits in my cooler. To serve, I just snip off the corner of the bag and squeeze the guacamole into a paper bowl.

GOOD THINKING
Rice Is Nice
Amy Robbins, Fort Wayne, Ind.

I'm superbusy during the week, and getting dinner on the table is a challenge. To make life easier, I make big batches of brown rice—which takes 45 minutes to cook—on a weekend. I spread the cooked rice out on a baking sheet to cool quickly and thoroughly and then transfer the cooled rice to zipper-lock bags, pressing out the air before sealing them and placing them in the freezer. Whenever I need a nutritious starch to round out a weeknight meal, I pull out a bag of brown rice and quickly heat it up in the microwave.

HOT TRICK Sweet Idea
Hillary Hunter, Erie, Pa.

Once you've had good hot chocolate, it's hard to go back to the supermarket packets. I've come up with a fast, easy way to make high-quality hot chocolate at home. I unwrap four chocolate truffles (Lindt dark chocolate truffles are my favorite) and put them in a mug. I then pour hot milk over them and wait a few minutes for the truffles to melt. A quick stir brings it all together for a delicious cup of rich cocoa.

NEAT IDEA Micro-Dry-It
Stephanie Sauer, Flagstaff, Ariz.

I like to make a pitcher of fresh-squeezed orange juice for Sunday brunch. One day when I was throwing away the juiced oranges, it occurred to me that I was throwing away flavorful zest, too. So now, before I cut the oranges in half for juicing, I use a vegetable peeler to remove strips of the flavorful rind. I put the strips on a paper towel–lined plate, dry them for 2 to 3 minutes in the microwave, let them cool, and then store them in a jar. I add a strip to my favorite tea or chop the dried zest and add it to muffin and cake batters and cookie dough.

THRIFTY TIP Double Duty
Joe Giordano, Taunton, Mass.

Chopped pepperoncini add a nice kick to pasta salad. For even more flavor and zesty bite, I discovered I could substitute some of the peppery brine for some of the vinegar called for in the dressing. This trick works great in potato and egg salads, too. Since the peppers (and brine) vary in heat from jar to jar, I taste both before adding them to any salad.

HANDY TRICK
One-Cup Coffee
Heather Wilson, Chico, Calif.

Before leaving on a recent ski trip, I decided to pack my favorite ground coffee and a box of filters so that I could make coffee in our rental house each morning before hitting the slopes. Naturally, the kitchen didn't have a coffee maker. I was able to improvise a pour-over contraption by using a small funnel I found in one of the drawers. It worked so well that now I use a funnel to make my cup of coffee at home every morning.

SMART TIP
Gluten-Free Coating
Beth Rooney, Dover, Md.

I'm always on the lookout for gluten-free breading alternatives to put on fried cutlets. A friend suggested I try instant potato flakes (used to make mashed potatoes). Dubious, I dipped chicken cutlets in beaten egg and then in seasoned potato flakes, pressing them firmly onto the chicken. I shallow-fried the chicken in peanut oil and was amazed at how golden, crispy, and tasty the coating was.

Hearty Beef Lasagna

Vegetarian lasagna has its place. This is not that place. BY KATIE LEAIRD

I EXPECT A LOT from lasagna. I want a crusty-topped, towering stack of noodles that tastes meaty, creamy, and cheesy all at once. I want there to be a lot more meat than tomatoes. And I don't want it to take all day or require every dish in the cupboard. With these clear goals in mind, I hit the kitchen.

At first I thought that sausage packed with Italian spices was the key to a flavorful lasagna. But after my initial tests, I found that sausage flavors varied widely from one package to the next, and I wanted more control over the spice. I tried a few combinations of ground pork and veal but ultimately committed to an all-beef lasagna. We all loved the bold and familiar flavor as well as the richness of 90 percent lean ground beef.

I amped up the meatiness by using 1½ pounds of beef and just one can of tomatoes—a much higher meat-to-tomato ratio than usual. But because of its increased presence, the beef's tendency to turn dry and pebbly was amplified. To ensure a more pleasant consistency, I stole a trick from our favorite meatball recipes and added a panade—a mixture of bread and milk—to the beef. This produced a soft-textured meat sauce that was easy to layer.

Italian lasagna traditionally includes a béchamel, a thickened milk sauce. It's easy enough to create a béchamel, but many American lasagna recipes make things even easier by calling for ricotta instead. This soft, fresh cheese loosely mimics béchamel in that it is essentially cooked (and curdled) milk. However, we noticed a slightly grainy texture in ricotta lasagna samples.

The perfect middle ground between béchamel and ricotta was a no-cook cream sauce. I used heavy cream and cottage cheese as the base. Because of its larger curd, cottage cheese baked up pillowy (rather than grainy, as ricotta did). Grated Pecorino Romano cheese, which is a little bolder and saltier than Parmesan, and a bit of cornstarch bound and thickened the sauce. And the best part about it was that it came together easily.

With time on my mind, I wondered if the meat sauce really needed a long, slow simmer. I cut it down to 30 minutes and then, feeling bold, eventually slashed the time to just 5 minutes. Since the sauce in the assembled lasagna continued to cook for nearly an hour in the oven, keeping

Underneath this cheesy topping is a pound and a half of ground beef. We use 90 percent lean ground beef for its rich flavor.

it on the stovetop just long enough to cook the meat through worked just fine. Whatever long-cooked flavor I may have sacrificed with this shortcut was easily made up for by the increased ratio of meat. In the spirit of efficiency, I cooked my meat sauce in the same pot I used to cook the noodles. Because I'd trimmed so much time from the sauce's cooking time, I decided to stick with traditional lasagna noodles rather than no-boil

noodles. To keep them from sticking together after cooking, I coated the drained noodles with oil before letting them cool on a baking sheet.

I carefully calculated how much of each component to spread on each layer and removed the traditional bottom and top layers of meat sauce. The bottom layer of sauce is there only to prevent the noodles from sticking to the dish, which can be accomplished with a quick

coating of vegetable oil spray. A top coat of sauce introduced moisture, which inhibited the bubbly browning I was after. Topping the final noodle layer with cream sauce and cheese yielded the best top crust.

After less than an hour of active prep, I was ready to bake my lasagna. And by being a little patient and letting the layers set up, I found it easy to get a perfect squared-off slice.

HEARTY BEEF LASAGNA Serves 10 to 12

We developed this recipe using dried curly-edged lasagna noodles; do not use no-boil noodles. There are about 20 individual noodles in a 1-pound box of lasagna noodles, enough for this recipe.

LASAGNA

Vegetable oil spray
17 curly-edged lasagna noodles
1 tablespoon salt
12 ounces mozzarella cheese, shredded (3 cups)
¼ cup grated Pecorino Romano cheese

MEAT SAUCE

2 slices hearty white sandwich bread, torn into small pieces
¼ cup milk
1½ pounds 90 percent lean ground beef
¾ teaspoon salt
½ teaspoon pepper
1 tablespoon extra-virgin olive oil
1 onion, chopped fine
6 garlic cloves, minced
1 teaspoon dried oregano
¼ teaspoon red pepper flakes
1 (28-ounce) can crushed tomatoes

CREAM SAUCE

8 ounces (1 cup) cottage cheese
4 ounces Pecorino Romano cheese, grated (2 cups)
1 cup heavy cream
2 garlic cloves, minced
1 teaspoon cornstarch
¼ teaspoon salt
¼ teaspoon pepper

1. FOR THE LASAGNA: Adjust oven rack to middle position and heat oven to 375 degrees. Spray rimmed baking sheet and 13 by 9-inch baking dish with oil spray. Bring 4 quarts water to boil in large Dutch oven. Add noodles and salt and cook, stirring often, until al dente. Drain noodles and transfer them to prepared sheet. Using tongs, gently turn noodles to coat lightly with oil spray. Cut 2 noodles in half crosswise.

2. FOR THE MEAT SAUCE: Mash bread and milk in bowl until smooth. Add beef, salt, and pepper and knead with your hands until well combined; set aside. Heat oil in now-empty Dutch oven over medium heat until shimmering. Add onion and cook until softened, about 5 minutes. Stir in garlic, oregano, and pepper flakes and cook until fragrant, about 1 minute.

3. Add beef mixture, breaking meat into small pieces with wooden spoon, and cook until no longer pink, about 4 minutes. Stir in tomatoes and bring to simmer, scraping up any browned bits. Reduce heat to medium-low and simmer until flavors have melded, about 5 minutes.

4. FOR THE CREAM SAUCE: Whisk all ingredients in bowl until combined.

5. Lay 3 noodles lengthwise in prepared dish with ends touching 1 short side of dish, leaving gap at far end. Lay 1 half noodle crosswise to fill gap (if needed).

6. Spread 1½ cups meat sauce over noodles, followed by ½ cup cream sauce and finally ½ cup mozzarella. Repeat layering of noodles, meat sauce, cream sauce, and mozzarella 3 more times, switching position of half noodle to opposite end of dish each time.

7. Lay remaining 3 noodles over top (there is no half noodle for top layer). Spread remaining cream sauce over noodles, followed by remaining 1 cup mozzarella. Sprinkle Pecorino over top.

8. Spray sheet of aluminum foil with oil spray and cover lasagna. Set lasagna on rimmed baking sheet. Bake for 30 minutes. Discard foil and continue to bake until top layer of lasagna is spotty brown, 25 to 30 minutes longer. Let lasagna cool for 30 minutes. Slice and serve.

TO MAKE AHEAD At end of step 7, cover dish with greased aluminum foil and refrigerate for up to 24 hours. When ready to eat, bake lasagna as directed in step 8, increasing covered baking time to 55 minutes.

For even slices that hold their shape, we let the lasagna rest for 30 minutes after baking.

Key Elements of Hearty Beef Lasagna

A great lasagna is the sum of its parts, so make the parts great. We spend less than an hour of active prep time on ours—without sacrificing structure or flavor.

NO-COOK CREAM SAUCE
Instead of simmering a traditional béchamel, we simply whisk together cottage cheese, Pecorino Romano, heavy cream, and seasonings.

TRADITIONAL NOODLES
Taking shortcuts elsewhere meant that we had time to boil traditional noodles, which are heartier than the no-boil type.

TWO CHEESES
Along with the usual mozzarella, we boost flavor with Pecorino Romano, which is slightly saltier and sharper than more-common Parmesan.

FIVE-MINUTE MEAT SAUCE
Since the sauce will cook for more than an hour in the oven, we keep it on the stovetop just long enough to cook the meat through.

TEST KITCHEN TECHNIQUE **Noodle Know-How**
Here's how to work with classic curly-edged lasagna noodles.

To prevent sticking, transfer cooked and drained noodles to prepared baking sheet, turning them to lightly coat with oil.

Use halved noodles to fill in gap at end of dish. Stagger arrangement of halved noodles to prevent lasagna from buckling.

South Texas Breakfast Tacos

We love tacos for lunch and dinner. So why not for the most important meal of the day?

BY MORGAN BOLLING

TEXANS, ESPECIALLY SOUTH Texans, love their breakfast tacos. In the Austin area alone, hundreds of spots sell these plump, egg-filled treats. And they're cheap—you can buy one for $1 or $2 at your local gas station (just one of the reasons that college students love them).

Inherent to all tacos is the tortilla—specifically a flour tortilla, the traditional choice for breakfast tacos. It should be tender and chewy yet sturdy enough to hold the substantive fillings, with a clean, slightly wheaty flavor. Unfortunately, most packaged versions fall flat of this ideal.

Homemade flour tortillas are simpler to make than you might think, and they require no special equipment. They're just a basic blend of flour, water, salt, and lard or shortening that is kneaded together, allowed to rest, shaped into flat rounds, and cooked quickly in a skillet. In testing, tasters preferred shortening, as grocery-store lard imparted a sour flavor. Letting the dough rest in the fridge after mixing made it easier to roll out and yielded more-tender tortillas. Given that I'm not a morning person, I was happy to discover that these tortillas can be made up to a couple of days ahead and stay just as pliable as fresh.

I wanted to keep the fillings for my version ultrasimple. Most breakfast tacos feature scrambled eggs with a few add-ins. Melissa Guerra (see "On the Road") told us that potato, bacon, and chorizo (all mixed with scrambled eggs) were the most popular fillings, though some menus offer mix-ins like stewed cow's cheek, cactus, or mini beef franks. (I passed on these more challenging options.) Whipping up the egg-based fillings was a breeze, even first thing in the morning.

> For the best tacos, use the best bacon. Go to **CooksCountry.com/bestbacon** to read about our favorite.

Salsas or hot sauce often live on the table at breakfast taco spots, and my recipe wouldn't be complete without one. So I made a cooked tomato salsa, similar to one found in south Texas, that came together quickly in the microwave.

Once I'd assembled all the components, my spicy, egg-stuffed tacos made an excellent breakfast. Or lunch, for that matter. Or even dinner.

It takes a bit of extra work, but soft, chewy homemade tortillas are worth the effort.

TEXAS BREAKFAST TACOS
Serves 4 to 6

It's important to follow visual cues when making the eggs, as your pan's thickness will affect the cooking time. If you're using an electric stovetop for the eggs, heat a second burner on low and move the skillet to it when it's time to adjust the heat. You can substitute store-bought tortillas for the homemade. This recipe makes enough filling for 12 (6-inch) tacos.

- 12 large eggs
  Salt and pepper
- 6 slices thick-cut bacon, cut into ½-inch pieces
- 1 small onion, chopped fine
- 1 jalapeño chile, stemmed, seeded, and minced
- 1 recipe Homemade Taco-Size Flour Tortillas (recipe follows)
- 1 recipe Salsa Roja (recipe follows)
  Shredded Monterey Jack cheese
  Thinly sliced scallions
  Lime wedges

1. Whisk eggs, ½ teaspoon salt, and ¼ teaspoon pepper in bowl until thoroughly combined and mixture is pure yellow, about 1 minute. Set aside.

2. Cook bacon in 12-inch nonstick skillet over medium heat until crispy, 8 to 10 minutes. Pour off all but 2 tablespoons fat from skillet (leaving bacon in skillet). Add onion and jalapeño and cook until vegetables are softened and lightly browned, 4 to 6 minutes.

3. Add egg mixture and, using heat-resistant rubber spatula, constantly and firmly scrape along bottom and sides of skillet until eggs begin to clump and spatula leaves trail on bottom of skillet, 1½ to 2½ minutes.

4. Reduce heat to low. Gently but constantly fold egg mixture until it has clumped and is still slightly wet, 30 to 60 seconds. Season with salt and pepper to taste. Fill tortillas with egg mixture and serve immediately, passing salsa, Monterey Jack, scallions, and lime wedges separately.

TEXAS BREAKFAST TACOS WITH CHORIZO

Substitute 8 ounces Mexican-style chorizo sausage, casings removed, for bacon. Cook chorizo in skillet over medium heat, breaking up meat with wooden spoon, until well browned, 6 to 8 minutes, before adding onion and jalapeño.

HOMEMADE TACO-SIZE FLOUR TORTILLAS

Makes 12 (6-inch) tortillas
Lard can be substituted for the shortening, if desired.

- 2 cups (10 ounces) all-purpose flour
- 1¼ teaspoons salt
- 5 tablespoons vegetable shortening, cut into ½-inch chunks
- ⅔ cup warm tap water
- 1 teaspoon vegetable oil

1. Combine flour and salt in large bowl. Using your fingers, rub shortening into flour mixture until mixture resembles coarse meal. Stir in warm water until combined.

2. Turn dough out onto counter and knead briefly to form smooth, cohesive ball. Divide dough into 12 equal portions, about 2 tablespoons each; roll each into smooth 1-inch ball between your hands. Transfer to plate, cover with plastic wrap, and refrigerate until dough is firm, at least 30 minutes or up to 2 days.

3. Cut twelve 6-inch squares of parchment paper. Roll 1 dough ball

TEXAS BREAKFAST TACOS WITH POTATO

Omit bacon. Melt 2 tablespoons unsalted butter in skillet over medium heat. Add 1 (8-ounce) russet potato, peeled and cut into ½-inch cubes, and ¼ teaspoon salt and cook until tender, 6 to 8 minutes, before adding onion and jalapeño.

into 6-inch circle on lightly floured counter. Transfer to parchment square and set aside. Repeat with remaining dough balls, stacking rolled tortillas on top of each other with parchment squares between.

4. Heat oil in 12-inch nonstick skillet over medium heat until shimmering. Wipe out skillet with paper towels, leaving thin film of oil on bottom. Place 1 tortilla in skillet and cook until surface begins to bubble and bottom is spotty brown, about 1 minute. (If not browned after 1 minute, turn heat up slightly. If browning too quickly, reduce heat.) Flip and cook until spotty brown on second side, 30 to 45 seconds. Transfer to plate and cover with clean dish towel. Repeat with remaining tortillas.

TO MAKE AHEAD

Cooled tortillas can be layered between parchment paper, covered with plastic wrap, and refrigerated for up to 3 days. To serve, discard plastic, cover tortillas with clean dish towel, and microwave at 50 percent power until heated through, about 20 seconds.

AT A GLANCE DIY Flour Tortillas

Homemade tortillas require no special equipment, and the thicker, fresher, chewier result is altogether different (and better) than store-bought.

1. Form dough into 12 equal balls.

2. Roll each ball into 6-inch circle.

3. Cook tortilla in lightly oiled skillet until browned.

Introducing Salsa Roja

Salsa roja (red sauce) is a cooked salsa common in southern Texas. We keep our recipe simple by microwaving fresh plum tomatoes and garlic, straining off excess juice, and then whizzing the mixture in the blender with jalapeño, cilantro, lime juice, and red pepper flakes. Served warm, it's the ideal topping for our breakfast tacos.

SALSA ROJA Makes about 1½ cups

This salsa is a welcome addition to our Texas Breakfast Tacos, but you can also serve it with tortilla chips or as an accompaniment to pork, chicken, or fish. To make this salsa spicier, reserve and add the jalapeño seeds to the blender before processing.

- 1 pound plum tomatoes, cored and chopped
- 2 garlic cloves, chopped
- 1 jalapeño chile, stemmed, seeded, and chopped
- 2 tablespoons chopped fresh cilantro
- 1 tablespoon lime juice
  Salt
- ¼ teaspoon red pepper flakes

1. Combine tomatoes and garlic in bowl and microwave, uncovered, until steaming and liquid begins to pool in bottom of bowl, about 4 minutes. Transfer tomato mixture to fine-mesh strainer set over bowl and let drain for 5 minutes.

2. Combine jalapeño, cilantro, lime juice, 1 teaspoon salt, pepper flakes, and drained tomato mixture in blender. Process until smooth, about 45 seconds. Season with salt to taste. Serve warm. (Salsa can be refrigerated for up to 3 days. Cover and microwave briefly to rewarm before serving.)

Early Morning, San Antonio

San Antonio is obsessed with breakfast tacos, but don't trip on the name. "Breakfast" merely denotes the time of day and doesn't necessarily confine you to an eggy filling. Stewed or grilled meat, sausage, beans, vegetables, and yes, if you insist, eggs can legitimately appear in a warmed flour tortilla. And every San Antonian has an opinion about where to find the best ones. Someone even tried to sell me on gas station tacos.

I'm an early riser with little love for traditional breakfast fare, so it was a happy coincidence that I came upon a stout stucco cantina during a 7 a.m. stroll around downtown San Antonio. Had it not been for a fellow hauling produce from a pickup through the back door of a kitchen, I might not have noticed it. Entranced by the smells of roasted pork and cumin, I entered and was greeted warmly, one of a trickle of early customers.

I ordered three (eggless) tacos and devoured them greedily. I returned at the same time the next morning and ordered three more. I was really tapping into the local food scene; surely a place like this would be considered a find, even by the most ardent restaurant hounds. When I unveiled my new dining discovery—in confidence—to local chef Melissa Guerra, her brow furrowed and a look of concern crossed her face. Her response: "Don't eat there any more. I'll make you tacos tomorrow." I said I'd meet her at 7. She was right: The tacos she made at home were even better. For more pictures of our trip to Texas, go to **CooksCountry.com/sanantonio**. –BRYAN ROOF

Early morning aromas of fresh tortillas, roasted meats, and, yes, scrambled eggs emanate from a thousand San Antonio kitchens.

Crumb-Crusted Pork Tenderloin

Bread crumbs are the key to transforming pork tenderloin. If only we could keep them in place.

BY ALLI BERKEY

INEXPENSIVE, quick-cooking, and lean, pork tenderloin is a fine choice for a weeknight supper, but it doesn't have a lot of pizzazz. I wanted to add a flavorful crust to make this cut a little more filling and a lot more exciting.

It's easy to create a crumb crust, but more difficult to make it stick. I started with an assortment of crumbs, each with a different texture: fresh bread, panko, and saltines. After trying all of them and using a variety of cooking methods, our least favorite option was saltine crumbs, which turned gray and greasy. Fresh bread crumbs took second place, but they tended to turn soggy. But crunchy-crisp panko bread crumbs were excellent, proving why they're a longtime test kitchen favorite.

Panko has a strong structure but lacks flavor, so I searched for ways to add some. Melted butter was a must and would act as my primary glue for the crumbs. Knowing that pork loves mustard, I stirred some together with the crumbs, choosing whole-grain mustard for its rustic texture. Minced garlic was another must. But something was still missing—possibly a strong herb that could withstand the roasting process? Fresh rosemary fit the bill, and I sloshed in a bit of white wine vinegar for vibrancy.

Because I was adding liquid—vinegar—to the crumbs, I knew I'd have to bake them before coating the tenderloin; otherwise they would turn soggy and slide off the meat as it cooked. Baking the panko mixture briefly on a baking sheet dried it out so that it could more easily adhere. I chose to stick to the typical flour and egg wash to coat the tenderloin and create a sticky surface for the bread crumbs.

In early tests, I experimented with pan searing, shallow frying, and even deep frying, but simply roasting the crumb-crusted pork proved to be the most successful method. By placing the pork on a wire rack and nestling this rack into a rimmed baking sheet, I was able to keep the crumbs on the bottom from turning soggy and allow airflow around the pork to ensure that it cooked evenly.

Crunchy, savory, mustardy, and meaty, my pork tenderloin delivered much more satisfaction than its simple technique would suggest.

Toasted panko bread crumbs gave us the crunchiest, best-tasting crust. The bonus: They're more convenient than homemade.

KEYS TO Preventing a Soggy, Patchy Crust

A three-pronged approach ensures a crispy crust that clings to the meat.

DIP IN FLOUR AND EGG WHITES
A traditional bound breading helps the crumbs cling to the pork.

TOAST PANKO TO DRY IT OUT
Baking the breading mixture in a hot oven before applying it helps it adhere better.

ROAST AND LET REST ON WIRE RACK
Good airflow around the meat means that the bottom stays crispy, too.

Butter-Braised Mushrooms

Why should fancy mushrooms have all the fun?

BY MORGAN BOLLING

CRUMB-CRUSTED PORK TENDERLOIN
Serves 4 to 6

Transferring the baked panko mixture to a 13 by 9-inch baking dish in step 2 provides a little extra wiggle room for coating the tenderloins in step 4.

5	tablespoons unsalted butter, melted
¼	cup whole-grain mustard
1½	tablespoons white wine vinegar
2	garlic cloves, minced
2	teaspoons minced fresh rosemary
	Kosher salt and pepper
	Pinch cayenne pepper
1½	cups panko bread crumbs
¼	cup all-purpose flour
3	large egg whites
⅓	cup grated Parmesan cheese
2	(1- to 1¼ -pound) pork tenderloins, trimmed

1. Adjust oven rack to middle position and heat oven to 350 degrees. Whisk melted butter, mustard, vinegar, garlic, rosemary, ¾ teaspoon salt, ½ teaspoon pepper, and cayenne in bowl until combined. Stir in panko until fully combined.

2. Spread panko mixture in even layer on rimmed baking sheet, breaking up any clumps. Bake, stirring every 5 minutes, until golden brown, 15 to 18 minutes. Transfer crumbs to 13 by 9-inch baking dish and let cool completely, about 10 minutes. Break up any large clumps with your fingers. Increase oven temperature to 400 degrees.

3. Set wire rack in now-empty sheet. Place flour in shallow dish. Whisk egg whites together in second shallow dish. Stir Parmesan into cooled crumb mixture. Pat tenderloins dry with paper towels and season with salt and pepper.

4. Working with 1 tenderloin at a time, dredge in flour, shaking off excess; dip in egg whites to thoroughly coat, letting excess drip back into dish; then coat with crumbs, pressing gently to adhere. Transfer tenderloins to prepared rack. Bake until pork registers 140 degrees, 25 to 30 minutes. Let tenderloins rest on rack for 10 minutes. Slice ¼ inch thick and serve.

WHITE BUTTON MUSHROOMS are the also-rans of the mushroom world, often ignored in favor of more-exotic specimens. I wanted to give them a chance at sophistication. As I flipped through cookbooks from esteemed chefs such as Alice Waters and Thomas Keller, I tagged any promising recipe, even those that starred pricey oyster or chanterelle mushrooms. I cooked my way through six, substituting humble white button mushrooms in all.

Our favorite recipe called for sautéing the mushrooms in butter with garlic and shallots before adding chicken broth and braising them, covered, until tender. It also called for removing the lid for the final minutes of cooking to let the flavorful braising liquid reduce and coat the mushrooms.

Button mushrooms are about 90 percent water. As they cook, much of this liquid seeps out into the pan. And it's flavorful, like a savory vegetable broth. Questioning whether I needed to be adding store-bought chicken broth on top of that, I omitted the broth and ended up with ultraconcentrated mushroom flavor, earthier and heartier than one would expect from mushrooms that cost just $1.99 a pack.

Stirring in ¼ cup of white wine added acidity to cut the richness. Reducing it, along with some thyme, created a flavorful glaze. Finally, a bit of butter and chopped fresh herbs (tarragon, if you like its forceful licorice flavor, or chives for a brighter note) gave them an elegant finish.

BRAISED MUSHROOMS
Serves 4

To ensure even cooking, be sure to choose mushrooms of uniform size. Medium mushrooms (1 to 2 inches in diameter) are best here. If you wash your mushrooms, blot them dry with paper towels before proceeding.

4	tablespoons unsalted butter, cut into 4 pieces
1½	pounds white mushrooms, trimmed and quartered
2	shallots, minced
4	garlic cloves, minced
	Salt and pepper
¼	cup dry white wine
1½	teaspoons minced fresh thyme
1	tablespoon minced fresh tarragon or chives

Shallots, garlic, white wine, and fresh herbs help elevate these supermarket mushrooms.

1. Melt 2 tablespoons butter in 12-inch skillet over medium-high heat. Add mushrooms, shallots, garlic, ¾ teaspoon salt, and ¼ teaspoon pepper and cook for 2 minutes. Reduce heat to medium, add wine, cover, and cook until mushrooms release their liquid and begin to soften, 6 to 8 minutes.

2. Stir in thyme and continue to simmer, uncovered, until mushrooms appear glazed and liquid is syrupy, 5 to 8 minutes. Off heat, stir in tarragon and remaining 2 tablespoons butter. Season with salt and pepper to taste. Serve.

Frugal Fungi

With the proper treatment, inexpensive button mushrooms boast a rich, earthy flavor that rivals that of hand-foraged varieties.

THRIFTY
White button:
$1.99 per pound

EXTRAVAGANT
Oyster and chanterelle:
more than $20.00 per pound

Chicken Fricassee with Apples

This old-fashioned dish of savory chicken, rich cream, and sharp apples is an exercise in balance.

BY CECELIA JENKINS

CHICKEN FRICASSEE IS an old-fashioned country dish of chicken stewed in a creamy sauce; adding vibrant apples to the mix creates a complex and delicate sweetness that enhances the savory chicken. I wanted all the parts to work in harmony: juicy chicken, tender but not mushy pieces of apple, and a balanced sauce that bridged the two.

I tested many existing recipes, and the results varied widely. One recipe contained only a few apples and was so savory it was mistaken for chicken pot pie filling; another included multiple apple products (hard cider, brandy, and apples), but tasters could barely make out any apple flavor. One had a hefty 2 cups of apple cider in it, making it too sweet overall.

With this last version in mind, I tried sautéing chicken breasts in butter until lightly browned; I then removed them and used the same pan to soften sliced Granny Smith apples—which hold their shape once cooked—with onion and thyme. I added just 1 cup of cider and returned the chicken breasts to the skillet to simmer. I finished the sauce with cream and dug in. It was disappointing. The sauce was still too sweet and, once cooked, the Granny Smiths tasted acidic and sour—plus, all that cooking left them steamed and limp.

I fine-tuned the sauce: Using equal parts cider and chicken broth created a savory balance with a fruit-forward, bright flavor and just enough acidity. Next I turned to the apples. I'd need to adjust for both flavor and texture. Apple varieties such as Fuji, Gala, and Braeburn were a marked improvement, sweeter and fruitier than the Granny Smiths. Browning them first and removing them from the pan to cook the chicken gave them a more complex, caramelized flavor and a better texture—searing set the pectin in the apples, which reinforced their structure, and less time in the pan prevented overcooking.

But my chicken was tough and my sauce too thin. Dredging the chicken breasts lightly in flour before sautéing fixed both problems. The flour protected the meat from the sear and acted as a thickening agent to give the sauce more body.

For my final version, I transferred the finished chicken from the skillet to a platter to rest and added the apples back to the skillet to warm through along with the cream. Boiling the sauce for just 2 minutes brought it to the right consistency, and a bit of cider vinegar to finish added brightness. After I spooned the creamy sauce and apples over the tender chicken, my tasters and I agreed that this old-fashioned dish is due for a comeback.

CHICKEN FRICASSEE WITH APPLES

Serves 4

Note that the apples are not peeled; their red skins contribute visual contrast to this otherwise pale dish. Cut each apple into 16 wedges; each wedge will be approximately ½ inch thick.

- 4 (6- to 8-ounce) boneless, skinless chicken breasts, trimmed
  Salt and pepper
- ¼ cup all-purpose flour
- 3 tablespoons unsalted butter
- 2 Fuji, Gala, or Braeburn apples, cored and each cut into sixteen ½-inch-thick wedges
- 1 onion, chopped
- 2 teaspoons minced fresh thyme
- ½ cup apple cider
- ½ cup chicken broth
- ½ cup heavy cream
- 2 teaspoons cider vinegar
- 1 tablespoon minced fresh chives

For fresh apple flavor, we brown the slices first and then set them aside while the chicken cooks.

1. Pat chicken dry with paper towels and season with salt and pepper. Spread flour in shallow dish. Dredge chicken in flour to coat, shaking to remove excess; transfer to plate and set aside.

2. Melt 2 tablespoons butter in 12-inch nonstick skillet over medium heat. Season apples with salt and pepper. Cook apples, cut sides down, until browned, about 5 minutes per side, moving and redistributing apples as needed for even browning. Transfer to second plate; set aside.

3. Melt remaining 1 tablespoon butter in now-empty skillet over medium heat. Add chicken and cook until lightly browned, about 2 minutes per side. Return chicken to plate.

4. Add onion, thyme, ¼ teaspoon salt, and ¼ teaspoon pepper to now-empty skillet and cook over medium heat until onion is softened and browned, 5 to 7 minutes.

5. Add cider and broth and bring mixture to boil. Return chicken to skillet. Reduce heat to medium-low, cover, and simmer until chicken registers 160 degrees, 8 to 12 minutes.

6. Transfer chicken to platter and tent with aluminum foil. Add cream and apples to skillet. Increase heat to medium-high and bring to boil. Cook until sauce has thickened slightly, about 2 minutes. Stir in vinegar and any accumulated chicken juices. Season with salt and pepper to taste. Spoon sauce and apples over chicken and sprinkle with chives. Serve.

Mongolian Beef

People love this American Chinese restaurant dish.
But could we find a way to make it from scratch at home? BY ASHLEY MOORE

SCAN THE MENU at your favorite American Chinese restaurant and you're likely to find Mongolian Beef. Though essentially unknown in Mongolia, this dish—bite-size strips of beef fried until crispy and tossed with scallions and spicy dried red chiles in a sweet-salty sauce—has become so popular stateside that you can now find packages of it in the frozen-food section of the grocery store.

But I prefer cooking from scratch to dining out or reheating prefab entrées in the microwave, so I resolved to create a recipe. To help set my course, I ordered take-out from several Boston-area Chinese restaurants, from mom-and-pop shops to well-known national chains. The results were underwhelming: soggy beef (to be fair, all the samples had traveled across town), slippery scallions, and rubbery red chiles in a drastically oversalted sauce.

I looked for home recipes and found a few. Most called for flank steak, a cut of meat we often stir-fry in the test kitchen but that in this instance was just a little too chewy. One called for beef tenderloin, an awfully expensive cut for a weeknight dish. I settled on flap meat (sometimes labeled as sirloin steak tips) because it didn't dry out or become chewy after frying.

The trick is in the slicing: For the ideal texture, the meat should be sliced ⅛ inch thick, which can be tricky even for skilled professionals. I employed a much-loved test kitchen cheat for this scenario: I froze the meat for 15 minutes to give it a firmer texture, which made slicing much easier.

I tossed the sliced beef in some cornstarch for a crispy coating and started shallow-frying it in a skillet. Talk about a hot mess: The oil splattered everywhere. A colleague suggested using a Dutch oven. Good idea: The sides of the pot were tall enough to protect the stove—and the cook—from splatters.

I stirred together a combination of water, soy sauce, and brown sugar to create a sweet-salty sauce and cooked it down to a thick but not sticky consistency, which gave me 1¼ cups. I then tossed this sauce with the fried beef just before serving.

The crunch on the beef was present and pleasant, and the sauce was just pungent enough. My tasters asked for seconds. And then thirds.

MONGOLIAN BEEF
Serves 4 to 6

Freezing the strips of beef makes them firm and allows you to slice them thin. Ask your butcher for a 1½-pound piece of flap meat instead of already-cut steak tips, which are more difficult to slice thin. You can substitute flank steak for flap meat in this recipe, if desired. For a spicier dish, use the larger number of arbols. If you can't find dried arbol chiles, you can substitute small dried Asian chiles or ¾ teaspoon of red pepper flakes.

1½	pounds beef flap meat, trimmed
½	cup cornstarch
3	cups peanut or vegetable oil
4	scallions, white parts minced, green parts cut into 1-inch pieces
2–4	dried arbol chiles (each about 2 inches long), stemmed and halved crosswise
4	garlic cloves, minced
1	tablespoon grated fresh ginger
¾	cup water
⅔	cup packed brown sugar
6	tablespoons soy sauce
4	cups cooked white rice

1. Cut beef with grain into 2½- to 3-inch-wide strips and place strips on large plate; freeze until firm, about 15 minutes. Cut strips crosswise against grain into ⅛-inch-thick slices. Toss beef with cornstarch in bowl; set aside.

2. Set wire rack in rimmed baking sheet. Heat oil in large Dutch oven over medium-high heat to 375 degrees. Add one-third of beef and fry until browned and crispy, about 4 minutes, stirring occasionally to keep pieces from sticking together. Adjust burner, if necessary, to maintain oil temperature between 350 and 375 degrees. Using spider skimmer or slotted spoon, transfer beef to prepared rack. Return oil to 375 degrees and repeat with remaining beef in 2 batches.

3. Transfer 1 tablespoon frying oil to 12-inch nonstick skillet and heat over medium-high heat until shimmering. Add scallion whites, arbols, garlic, and ginger and cook until fragrant, about 30 seconds. Stir in water, sugar, and soy sauce and bring to vigorous simmer. Cook until sauce is thickened and reduced to 1¼ cups, 6 to 8 minutes.

4. Add beef and scallion greens to sauce and cook, tossing constantly, until sauce coats beef, about 1 minute. Transfer to platter and serve with rice.

Ask the butcher for flap meat; it cooks up tender, with crispy edges.

Killed Salad

Far from "killed," this wilted mountain favorite is vibrant and lively.

BY MORGAN BOLLING

KILLED SALAD (ALSO called "kilt" salad, wilted salad, or smothered lettuce) is a traditional Appalachian side dish (see "Appalachian Salad"). At its simplest, it's made by pouring hot bacon grease over torn fresh lettuce and chopped onions to warm and barely wilt the greens. I tested this bare-bones approach alongside several more-elaborate recipes that called for mixing vinegar, lemon juice, or sugar into the dressing.

While the combination of fresh lettuce and smoky, crispy bacon was a solid one, many of these recipes called for as much as a pound of bacon. I learned that too much of a good thing (bacon) can be, well, too much. It's not called bacon salad, after all. I wanted the presence of bacon to enhance the lettuce—not destroy it.

I eventually ended up with a ratio of 6 slices of bacon to a head of greens (about 12 cups). I opted to stir in ½ cup of vinegar with the bacon fat to cut its richness, and I added some sugar to temper the vinegar's acidity. Apple cider vinegar, the traditional choice, was also our favorite, packing a tangy punch with a bit of fruity sweetness. Once the mixture hit a boil, I poured it over the lettuce and watched it wilt (a remarkably satisfying sight).

To settle on a lettuce, we sampled killed salads made with various greens. Firm greens worked best—tasters especially liked green leaf lettuce, followed closely by escarole and romaine.

I needed to make one last adjustment: When two separate tests in which I rendered equal amounts of bacon left me with ¼ cup of bacon fat in one skillet and nearly twice as much in the other, I realized it was a variable I wanted to control. The easiest way was to ditch all but a set 3 tablespoons of fat before mixing in the other ingredients.

KILLED SALAD

Serves 4

We prefer green leaf lettuce for this salad for its wilting qualities, but escarole, red leaf lettuce, or romaine can also be used, if desired.

- 1 head green leaf lettuce (12 ounces), torn into bite-size pieces
- 4 scallions, sliced thin
- 6 slices bacon, cut into ½-inch pieces
- ½ cup cider vinegar
- 3 tablespoons sugar
  Salt and pepper

1. Combine lettuce and scallions in large bowl. Cook bacon in 10-inch nonstick skillet over medium heat until crispy, 6 to 8 minutes. Using slotted spoon, transfer bacon to paper towel–lined plate. Pour off all but 3 tablespoons fat from skillet (if you don't have 3 tablespoons, supplement with vegetable oil).

2. Return skillet to medium heat. Whisk in vinegar, sugar, 1 teaspoon salt, and ½ teaspoon pepper and bring to boil.

3. Once boiling, immediately pour hot dressing over lettuce-scallion mixture and toss to combine. Season with salt and pepper to taste. Serve, sprinkled with bacon.

After rendering the fat, we set the bacon bits aside to drain before adding them to the salad.

The American Table
Appalachian Salad

Fancy a dish of chickentoe, anyone?

For centuries, people have foraged the forests of Appalachia for foods from mushrooms to tree fruits. It's a tradition that's carried on today—and not just out of desperation (or, in the case of things like ramps, trendiness). The fact is, this mountain range is dense with wild foods. Many of them are impossible to grow in gardens, which makes them more prized.

Darrin Nordahl, author of *Eating Appalachia* (2015), describes chickentoe as "a dainty vegetable . . . a member of the purslane family, the leaves are fleshier and juicier than more familiar salad greens, and they have a pleasantly crisp texture. The flavor is quite mild, however, tasting like young green lettuce."

The most common way to serve chickentoe (also called spring beauty) is to "kill" it—that is, to douse it in hot bacon grease, wilting the leaves and adding deep country flavor. But chickentoe season is fleeting—mid-March to early April—and it's next to impossible to cultivate the stuff the rest of the year. Bacon, however, knows no season, and the technique works well on other lettuces, too, as in our Killed Salad.

Lyonnaise Potatoes

Traditionally, this pan-fried dish uses leftover potatoes, but we wanted to start from scratch.

BY ASHLEY MOORE

PAN-FRIED POTATOES—tender on the inside, with slightly crispy exteriors—are always welcome on my dinner table. One version, Lyonnaise potatoes (named for Lyon, France), originated as a way to use up leftover boiled potatoes from dinner the night before; they're peeled, sliced, and pan-fried with copious amounts of butter and thin slices of onion that turn delicately brown. But who wants to wait around for leftover boiled potatoes?

I started by testing five existing recipes. Most called for precooked spuds, so I boiled and baked piles of potatoes. Then, following the recipes, I sliced some of them paper-thin and others as much as an inch thick before finishing them in a skillet with butter. I quickly nixed using baked russet potatoes, whose exteriors dried out. Boiled red potatoes were fine, but Yukon Gold potatoes were the best of all, with a deep flavor and tender texture.

A few recipes called for adding sliced onion and raw potatoes to the skillet over medium-high heat, but the cooking times of the two ingredients never completely matched up: raw potatoes and burnt onion. One recipe required me to cook the onion separately before incorporating it, but that felt too fussy.

But another recipe gave me hope: It called for placing raw potatoes and onion in a skillet and cooking them together over very low heat. This technique needed some tinkering—the cooking times of the onion and potatoes didn't quite jibe—but it was simple, and it showed me that lowering the heat would be key.

I decided to stagger the cooking, first cooking raw, thinly sliced Yukon Gold potatoes in melted butter until they were just tender. I then added the onion and cooked it until it was lightly browned. This was heading in the right direction, but the potatoes and onion still weren't cooking evenly—some tasters complained of overcooked potatoes, while others had crunchy onion. Plus, the thin potato slices were crowding the skillet and cooking down too much.

Covering the skillet would help even out the cooking, but with so many thin slices of potato, my pan was too crowded. Slicing the potatoes a bit thicker allowed everything to fit and was quicker to prep, a boon for a weeknight.

A healthy dose of butter adds richness, and a final toss of parsley freshens things up.

Now covered and over gentler heat, the potatoes cooked evenly in about 15 minutes. After adding the onion, I reduced the heat to medium-low to prevent it and the butter from getting too dark.

After 10 minutes of cooking (and occasional stirring), the onion and potatoes were soft and browned, and there was no burnt butter to be seen.

I sprinkled the potato-onion mixture with some minced fresh parsley (a traditional garnish for this dish) and called my tasters to the kitchen. Thanks to the staggered cooking and the covered skillet, we had the best of both worlds—potatoes and onion that were tender and lightly browned throughout.

LYONNAISE POTATOES
Serves 4

Use potatoes of similar size.

- 4 tablespoons unsalted butter
- 2 pounds Yukon Gold potatoes, peeled and sliced ½ inch thick
  Salt and pepper
- 1 onion, halved and sliced thin
- 1 tablespoon minced fresh parsley

1. Melt butter in 12-inch nonstick skillet over medium heat. Add potatoes and ¾ teaspoon salt and cook, covered, until just tender and golden brown, about 15 minutes, flipping potatoes occasionally to ensure even browning.

2. Reduce heat to medium-low. Add onion, ½ teaspoon salt, and ½ teaspoon pepper; cover and continue to cook until onion is tender and golden brown, about 10 minutes longer, stirring occasionally. Season with salt and pepper to taste. Transfer to serving platter and sprinkle with parsley. Serve.

TEST KITCHEN TECHNIQUE
Slice 'em Thick
Good news: There's no need for fussy thin potato slices. Cutting the potatoes a generous ½ inch thick (use the true-to-size photo below as a guide) helps the potatoes fit in the skillet so they brown evenly.

½ in

DON'T MAKE THIS MISTAKE
Raw Potatoes and Burnt Onion
Starting to cook the potatoes and onion at the same time will result in crunchy, undercooked spuds and scorched onion. Instead, we use a staggered approach, giving the potatoes a head start and a chance to soften before adding the onion to the pan.

Chicken and Pastry

This comforting Southern dish is no looker. But wait until you taste it.

BY MORGAN BOLLING

I TOOK ME a few years of living in North Carolina before I fully understood the ubiquitous phrase "Bless her heart." While the saying can, on occasion, be heartfelt, it's just as often a roundabout way to soften an otherwise devastating blow: "Bless her heart, she's no beauty queen."

It's a colloquialism I tend to avoid for fear of sending an unintended message, but I found myself leaning on a version of it recently when describing comforting chicken and pastry to non-Southern friends. To them, the recipe's name, "chicken and pastry," conjured elegance and formality: lofty images of golden, flaky puff pastry surrounding carefully, fussily cooked chicken. But, bless its heart, true Southern chicken and pastry—tender shreds of chicken and slightly chewy pastry wading in a thickened, chicken-infused broth—is no looker. Still, I truly believed that this dish's beauty was within, and I hoped to develop a straightforward recipe that, while perhaps lacking in appearance, would dazzle with its deep flavor.

To get started, I simmered my way through several existing recipes from Southern culinary icons Bill Neal and Edna Lewis (see "Southern Cooking, with Style"), as well as a few Alabama home cooks. I was delighted to discover that my best results came from the simplest recipes with the fewest ingredients. (Adding vegetables and garnishes such as carrots, peas, and parsley turned the dish into something more like chicken pot pie—tasty, but not my ultimate goal.)

Stewing chicken pieces in broth made a robust base; including celery and onion, which I would later remove once they'd given off their flavors, added even more depth

▶ A good pot makes all the difference. Go to CooksCountry.com/dutchoven to read our Dutch oven testing.

without distracting. Lean breasts dried out in tests, but bone-in chicken thighs stayed tender and moist even after simmering longer to extract more flavor. Browning the thighs beforehand made for an even more savory stew.

Base completed, I now focused firmly on pastry. Some recipes called for leftover biscuit dough or uncooked canned biscuits. But the biscuit dough dissolved,

Cutting the pastry into diamond shapes gives this simple, satisfying dish just a touch of style.

and canned biscuits turned gummy. A simple homemade dough—a mixture of flour, fat (butter, naturally), milk, and leavener—made for the most delicate, flavorful pastry.

But which leavening agent was best? After some experiments, I found that baking soda made the dumplings too tender, causing them to swell until they disintegrated. So I chose baking powder, which kept them light while

still allowing them to hold their shape. Rolling the pastry into a ⅛-inch-thick square gave me the ideal texture: more tender and fluffy than a noodle but just chewy enough.

I took Edna Lewis's suggestion and cut the pastry into diamond shapes—a rare bit of flair for this homely dish—because why not? It's just as easy as cutting squares, and a dish this deeply satisfying deserves a flourish.

The homemade pastry had another benefit, too. Adding it to the boiling broth and stirring the pot occasionally released just enough starch into the liquid to thicken its brothy consistency into something more like a stew.

The resulting supper—tender, pieces of chicken and fluffy, soft pastry cloaked in a velvety chicken broth—is rich, comforting, and simply delicious. No Southern courtesy required.

The American Table
Southern Cooking, with Style

Until Edna Lewis broke her ankle in the 1970s, she didn't have the time to write the cookbook her editor wanted—one infused with her personal story, giving texture, urgency, and humanity to the recipes she hoped to share.

A descendant of freed slaves, Lewis grew up on a subsistence farm in rural Virginia and had made a life as a farmer, a seamstress, and a celebrated New York City chef before legendary cookbook editor Judith Jones convinced her to compile her recipes and share her wisdom. After all, what else would she do with herself while her ankle was in a cast?

That book, *The Taste of Country Cooking* (1976), became a cornerstone of the American cookbook shelf; Julia Child, Alice Waters, and Craig Claiborne praised its pure recipes and intimate tone.

At Café Nicholson, the New York restaurant where she cooked in the 1950s, Lewis was known for comforting meals (roast chicken was a specialty) presented with a chic flourish (cheese soufflé on the side). It was this sense of style that inspired her to cut her dumplings into diamond shapes, as we do in our Chicken and Pastry; it's a small bit of elegance in a dish whose primary mission is to deliver deep homespun flavor.

Lewis died in 2006, having emphatically accomplished the goal she articulated to *The New York Times* in 1989: "As a child in Virginia, I thought all food tasted delicious. After growing up, I didn't think food tasted the same, so it has been my lifelong effort to try and recapture those good flavors of the past."

And to present them, of course, with a flourish.

Finding Red's

A large gentleman wearing a "Roll Tide" cap sidles up to my table and interrupts me midsentence. "You know how I know you're not from around here? 'Cause you're eating your fried chicken with a fork and knife," he says. I smile because he's right, and I happily drop the utensils.

We had driven a good way into the country before reaching the crimson clapboard Red's Little Schoolhouse in Grady, Alabama. The food there is pure Southern comfort, as is the reincarnated schoolhouse, a relic that functioned as a one-room schoolhouse from 1910 to 1960 only to be reborn as a restaurant in 1985. Inside are wide-plank floors, some with old-fashioned square-cut nails; the planks creaked beneath our feet. A dusty chalkboard, framed by portraits of ex-presidents, lists the day's offerings. Wooden tables and red checkered drapes try to hide this building's former identity, but there's no doubt that it's a restaurant worth visiting. To see more images from our trip, go to **CooksCountry.com/alabama**.

–BRYAN ROOF

CHICKEN AND PASTRY
Serves 4 to 6

Keep the root ends of the onion halves intact so the petals don't separate during cooking and the onion is easy to remove from the pot.

- 1½ cups (7½ ounces) all-purpose flour
- 2 teaspoons baking powder
- Salt and pepper
- ½ cup milk
- 2 tablespoons unsalted butter, melted, plus 1 tablespoon unsalted butter
- 2 pounds bone-in chicken thighs, trimmed
- 4 cups chicken broth
- 1 cup water
- 1 onion, peeled and halved through root end
- 1 celery rib, halved crosswise

1. Combine flour, baking powder, ½ teaspoon salt, and ½ teaspoon pepper in large bowl. Combine milk and melted butter in second bowl (butter may form clumps). Using rubber spatula, stir milk mixture into flour mixture until just incorporated. Turn dough out onto lightly floured counter and knead until no flour streaks remain, about 1 minute. Return dough to large bowl, cover with plastic wrap, and set aside.

2. Pat chicken dry with paper towels and season with pepper. Melt remaining 1 tablespoon butter in Dutch oven over medium-high heat. Add chicken, skin side down, and cook until golden brown, 3 to 5 minutes. Flip chicken and continue to cook until golden brown on second side, 3 to 5 minutes longer.

3. Add broth and water, scraping up any browned bits. Nestle onion and celery into pot and bring to boil. Reduce heat to low, cover, and simmer for 25 minutes.

4. Meanwhile, roll dough into 12-inch square, about ⅛ inch thick. Using pizza cutter or knife, cut dough lengthwise into 1-inch-wide strips, then cut diagonally into 1-inch-wide strips to form diamonds (pieces around edges will not be diamonds; this is OK).

5. Remove pot from heat. Transfer chicken to plate and let cool slightly. Discard onion and celery. Return broth to boil over medium-high heat and add pastry. Reduce heat to low, cover, and simmer, stirring occasionally, until pastry is tender and puffed, about 15 minutes. While pastry cooks, shred chicken into bite-size pieces, discarding skin and bones.

6. Stir chicken into stew and cook, uncovered, until warmed through and stew has thickened slightly, 2 to 4 minutes. Season with salt and pepper to taste. Serve.

TEST KITCHEN TECHNIQUE **Making the Pastry**
Here's how to turn a simple homemade dough into uniquely shaped pastry dumplings.

ROLL INTO SQUARE
Roll dough into 12-inch square, about ⅛ inch thick.

CUT INTO DIAMONDS
Using pizza cutter or knife, cut dough lengthwise into 1-inch-wide strips, then cut diagonally into 1-inch wide strips to form diamonds.

SIMMER IN BROTH
Add pastry to simmering broth and cook until tender and puffed.

Getting to Know Louisiana Flavors

The roots of Louisiana cuisine reach deep into the soil of a dazzling array of cultures. There's Cajun cooking, a rustic, hearty, game-heavy cuisine that has its origins in rural France via Acadia. Creole cuisine is an urban fusion of West African, Native American, French, Spanish, German, and Italian traditions. Today, Cajun and Creole traditions overlap and together comprise most of what we call Louisiana cuisine. Its multicultural influences—rooted in, but not limited by, tradition—make this cuisine uniquely American. Here are the ingredients you need to know to celebrate the brassy boldness of Louisiana cooking.

BY SCOTT KATHAN

◄ Roux
FLOUR AND FAT

Roux is a mixture of fat and flour. While lard may have been the most common fat choice a generation ago, modern Creole cooks are more apt to use butter, while their Cajun cousins are more likely to reach for vegetable oil. Roux can be cooked to white, blond, and brown stages, each of which imparts a different flavor and thickening power to the finished dish. Dark roux (pictured at left and used in most gumbos) can take hours of constant stirring to make. Try our Gumbo recipe (**CooksCountry.com/gumbo**), which uses a cool technique to cut down on the stirring and mess.

The Trinity
BUILDING BLOCK

Many Cajun and Creole dishes start with a foundation of sautéed chopped onion, green bell pepper, and celery known collectively as "the holy trinity." The standard ratio is roughly three parts onion, two parts celery, and one part bell pepper; it's important to cut the vegetables into similar-size pieces so they'll cook evenly. Once sautéed, the vegetables are often added to a roux that has been cooked to the desired color.

Cayenne Pepper
SHARP HEAT

The "red pepper" often called for in Louisiana recipes is spicy powdered cayenne. Despite what the label says, most products are made with a blend of cayenne and different chiles. The volatile oils in all chiles lose potency within a few months, so buy cayenne in small jars and replenish it regularly. We use a full 2 teaspoons in our recipe for Creole Fried Chicken (**CooksCountry.com/creolechix**).

Louisiana Seasoning
SPICE IT UP

Whether they're called Creole, Cajun, or just Louisiana spice blends, their ingredient lists include paprika, garlic,  thyme, salt, pepper, and cayenne. While we prefer our zesty home-made version to anything you can buy (go to **CooksCountry.com/laseasoning** for the recipe), our favorite supermarket product is Tony Chachere's Original Creole Seasoning, which has a salty, spicy kick.

Filé
SUFFERIN' SASSAFRASS

Filé powder is a thickening agent often used in gumbo (gumbo is traditionally thickened by either filé or okra but not both). Filé  is made by drying and grinding the leaves of the sassafrass plant and is most often added at the end of cooking, as too much time in the pot makes filé stringy. It has a woodsy flavor that some liken to root beer.

Chicory
COFFEE CUTTER

Coffee with chicory is a signature New Orleans drink. The roots of this plant, which is in the dandelion family, are  roasted, ground, and added to ground coffee to impart a distinct flavor. Although it is thought to have first been used to extend the coffee supply in Napoleonic France, chicory coffee became commonplace in New Orleans during the Civil War.

Andouille
SMOKY STAR

Pronounced "an-DOO-ee," this garlicky, peppery smoked pork sausage is used in a wide range of Louisiana dishes, including gumbo, jambalaya, and our Red Beans and Rice (**CooksCountry.com/redbeansrice**). Our favorite is smoky, spicy Jacob's World Famous Andouille, which can be ordered online.

Tasso
LOCAL SMOKED PORK

Tasso is a cured, smoked pork product of Cajun origin made from the fatty and flavorful pork shoulder. Its seasonings typically include cayenne pepper, garlic, herbs, and other spices. This intensely flavored meat is most often finely chopped and used as a component in dishes such as jambalaya.

Crayfish
HANDS-ON

These freshwater crustaceans—also called crawfish, crawdads, or mudbugs—look like mini lobsters. Most recipes, including the iconic crawfish étouffée, call for just the tails, but the whole body (including the head) is happily, messily consumed at a proper crawfish boil. Outside of Louisiana, most crayfish tails are sold frozen.

Okra
STICKY SITUATION

This oblong, ridged vegetable is African in origin and is popular throughout the South. When it's sliced and cooked, its insides turn viscous (OK, slimy), which aids in thickening soups, stews, and gumbos; the slime-averse are advised to cook whole (uncut) okra pods briefly. Breaded and fried okra is a popular appetizer in the South. We've found frozen okra to be acceptable in most dishes.

**LEMON-POACHED HALIBUT WITH
ROASTED FINGERLING POTATOES**

CHICKPEA AND KALE SOUP

STEAK AND EGGS WITH ASPARAGUS

POLENTA WITH SAUSAGE, PEPPERS, AND OLIVES

CHICKPEA AND KALE SOUP Serves 4

✓ **WHY THIS RECIPE WORKS:** Cooking the onions and fennel until they are just starting to brown gives this simple soup complex flavor.

- 2 tablespoons extra-virgin olive oil
- 1 onion, chopped
- 1 fennel bulb, stalks discarded, bulb halved, cored, and chopped
  Salt and pepper
- ¼ teaspoon red pepper flakes
- 3 garlic cloves, minced
- 4 cups chicken broth
- 1 (15-ounce) can chickpeas, rinsed
- 6 ounces kale, stemmed and chopped
  Grated Pecorino Romano cheese

1. Heat oil in Dutch oven over medium-high heat until shimmering. Add onion, fennel, ½ teaspoon salt, ½ teaspoon pepper, and pepper flakes and cook until vegetables have softened and are starting to brown, about 8 minutes. Stir in garlic and cook until fragrant, about 30 seconds.

2. Add broth, chickpeas, and kale; bring to boil. Reduce heat to medium-low, cover, and simmer until kale is tender, about 15 minutes. Season with salt and pepper to taste. Serve, passing Pecorino separately.

TEST KITCHEN NOTE: Vegetarian? No problem. Just substitute vegetable broth for the chicken broth.

LEMON-POACHED HALIBUT WITH ROASTED FINGERLING POTATOES Serves 4

✓ **WHY THIS RECIPE WORKS:** Cooking the fish in a foil packet keeps it moist and creates a flavorful broth seasoned with lemon, oregano, and tomatoes.

- 1½ pounds fingerling potatoes, halved lengthwise
- 2 tablespoons extra-virgin olive oil
  Salt and pepper
- 8 ounces grape tomatoes, halved
- 4 (6-ounce) skinless halibut fillets, 1 inch thick
- ½ teaspoon dried oregano
- 8 thin lemon slices
- 2 tablespoons minced fresh parsley

1. Adjust oven rack to lower-middle position and heat oven to 450 degrees. Toss potatoes with 2 teaspoons oil, ½ teaspoon salt, and ½ teaspoon pepper. Arrange potatoes on rimmed baking sheet, cut side down, in even layer. Roast until cut sides are starting to brown, about 10 minutes.

2. Meanwhile, lay four 12-inch-long pieces of foil on counter. Place one-quarter of tomatoes in center of each piece of foil, then place 1 fillet on each tomato pile. Sprinkle each fillet with ⅛ teaspoon oregano and season with salt and pepper, then top each with 2 lemon slices and 1 teaspoon oil. Pull edges of foil up around fish and tomatoes and crimp to form packet.

3. Place packets on top of potatoes and bake until fish is just cooked through, about 15 minutes. Divide potatoes among 4 bowls. Open 1 packet over each bowl, slide fish and tomatoes onto potatoes, then pour broth over top. Sprinkle with parsley and serve.

TEST KITCHEN NOTE: Use potatoes of a similar size to ensure consistent cooking.

POLENTA WITH SAUSAGE, PEPPERS, AND OLIVES Serves 4

✓ **WHY THIS RECIPE WORKS:** Browning the sausage on all sides provides a deep flavor base for the sauce.

- 4 cups water
- 1 cup instant polenta
- 3 tablespoons unsalted butter
  Salt and pepper
- 1½ pounds sweet Italian sausage
- 1 red bell pepper, stemmed, seeded, and sliced thin
- 1 small onion, halved and sliced thin
- 1 (14.5-ounce) can crushed tomatoes
- ¼ teaspoon red pepper flakes
- ½ cup pitted kalamata olives, halved

1. Bring water to boil in large saucepan over medium-high heat. Whisk in polenta, reduce heat to medium-low, and cook until thickened, about 3 minutes. Off heat, stir in butter, 1 teaspoon salt, and ½ teaspoon pepper. Cover to keep warm.

2. Cook sausage in 12-inch nonstick skillet over medium heat until browned on all sides, about 6 minutes. Increase heat to medium-high, add bell pepper and onion, and cook until vegetables are softened, 4 to 6 minutes. Add tomatoes, ½ teaspoon salt, ¼ teaspoon pepper, and pepper flakes. Cook until sauce has thickened slightly, about 3 minutes. Remove from heat and stir in olives.

3. Divide polenta among 4 bowls and top with sausage and sauce. Serve.

TEST KITCHEN NOTE: For a spicy kick, use hot Italian sausage.

STEAK AND EGGS WITH ASPARAGUS Serves 4

✓ **WHY THIS RECIPE WORKS:** Cracking the eggs into a bowl and pouring them into the hot pan all at once ensures quick and even cooking.

- 4 (6-ounce) blade steaks, ¾ to 1 inch thick, trimmed
  Kosher salt and pepper
- 3 tablespoons vegetable oil
- 1 pound asparagus, trimmed and sliced thin on bias
- 4 large eggs

1. Pat steaks dry with paper towels and season with salt and pepper. Heat 1 tablespoon oil in 12-inch nonstick skillet over medium-high heat until just smoking. Add steaks and cook until well browned and meat registers 125 degrees, about 6 minutes per side. Transfer steaks to individual plates.

2. Add 1 tablespoon oil, asparagus, 1 teaspoon salt, and ½ teaspoon pepper to now-empty skillet and cook over medium-high heat until asparagus is lightly browned and beginning to soften, about 4 minutes. Divide asparagus among plates.

3. Crack eggs into bowl, taking care not to break yolks. Heat remaining 1 tablespoon oil in now-empty skillet over medium-high heat until shimmering. Pour eggs into skillet and season with salt and pepper. Cook until whites begin to set, about 1 minute. Remove from heat, cover, and let sit until egg whites are cooked through but yolks remain runny, about 2 minutes. Using spatula, cut eggs into 4 portions. Top each steak with 1 egg and serve.

TEST KITCHEN NOTE: Sirloin or rib-eye steaks can be substituted for the blade steaks, if desired.

CHINESE-STYLE BEEF AND EGGPLANT

**PORK CUTLETS WITH SPINACH
AND WHITE WINE–BUTTER SAUCE**

**ROASTED CHICKEN THIGHS WITH
BRUSSELS SPROUTS AND CARROTS**

**FETTUCCINE WITH CHICKEN,
BACON, AND BROCCOLINI**

PORK CUTLETS WITH SPINACH AND WHITE WINE–BUTTER SAUCE Serves 4

✔ **WHY THIS RECIPE WORKS:** Cutting slits through the fat around the outside of each cutlet prevents curling and promotes even cooking and flavorful browning.

- 8 (3- to 4-ounce) pork cutlets, ½ inch thick, trimmed
   Salt and pepper
- 4 teaspoons vegetable oil
- 3 shallots, sliced thin
- 2 garlic cloves, minced
- ⅓ cup dry white wine
- 8 ounces (8 cups) baby spinach
- ¼ cup grated Parmesan cheese
- 2 tablespoons unsalted butter
   Lemon wedges

1. Using paring knife, cut 2 slits about 2 inches apart through fat around outside of each cutlet. Pat cutlets dry with paper towels and season with salt and pepper. Heat 1 teaspoon oil in 12-inch nonstick skillet over medium-high heat until smoking. Cook 4 cutlets until golden brown and cooked through, about 3 minutes per side. Transfer to platter and tent with foil. Repeat with 1 teaspoon oil and remaining 4 cutlets.

2. Add remaining 2 teaspoons oil, shallots, ¼ teaspoon salt, and ¼ teaspoon pepper to now-empty skillet and cook over medium heat until browned, about 3 minutes. Stir in garlic and cook until fragrant, about 30 seconds. Add wine and any accumulated pork juices and cook until almost evaporated, about 3 minutes. Stir in half of spinach and cook until just wilted, about 2 minutes. Add remaining spinach and cook until wilted, about 2 minutes. Off heat, stir in Parmesan and butter. Spoon spinach mixture and sauce over cutlets. Serve with lemon wedges.

CHINESE-STYLE BEEF AND EGGPLANT Serves 4

✔ **WHY THIS RECIPE WORKS:** Tossing eggplant with soy sauce after a thorough sauté seasons the vegetable without imparting any bitter flavor.

- ¼ cup vegetable oil
- 1½ pounds eggplant, cut into 1-inch pieces
- 2 tablespoons soy sauce
- 12 ounces 85 percent lean ground beef
- 1 red jalapeño chile, stemmed, halved, seeded, and sliced thin
- 4 garlic cloves, minced
- 1 tablespoon grated fresh ginger
- 2 tablespoons oyster sauce
- 1 tablespoon unseasoned rice vinegar
- 4 scallions, sliced thin on bias

1. Heat 3 tablespoons oil in 12-inch nonstick skillet over medium-high heat until just smoking. Add eggplant and cook, stirring frequently, until tender and browned, about 10 minutes. Stir in 1 tablespoon soy sauce and transfer to plate.

2. Heat remaining 1 tablespoon oil in now-empty skillet over medium-high heat until shimmering. Add beef, jalapeño, garlic, and ginger and cook, breaking up meat with wooden spoon and stirring occasionally, until browned, about 4 minutes.

3. Stir in oyster sauce, vinegar, and remaining 1 tablespoon soy sauce. Return eggplant to skillet with beef and continue to cook until combined and slightly thickened, about 2 minutes. Stir in half of scallions. Serve, sprinkled with remaining scallions.

TEST KITCHEN NOTE: We like to serve this dish over rice.

FETTUCCINE WITH CHICKEN, BACON, AND BROCCOLINI Serves 4

✔ **WHY THIS RECIPE WORKS:** Just ½ cup of cream plus a little pasta cooking water creates a light, not gloppy, cream sauce.

- 12 ounces fettuccine
   Salt and pepper
- 6 slices bacon, cut into ½-inch pieces
- 10 ounces broccolini, trimmed and cut into 2-inch pieces
- 2 garlic cloves, minced
- ¼ teaspoon red pepper flakes
- 1 (2½-pound) rotisserie chicken, skin and bones discarded, meat shredded into bite-size pieces (3 cups)
- 2 ounces Parmesan cheese, grated (1 cup), plus extra for serving
- ½ cup heavy cream

1. Bring 4 quarts water to boil in large pot. Add pasta and 1 tablespoon salt and cook, stirring often, until al dente. Reserve ¾ cup cooking water, then drain pasta.

2. Cook bacon in now-empty pot over medium heat until crispy, 5 to 7 minutes. Using slotted spoon, transfer bacon to paper towel–lined plate; pour off all but 1 tablespoon fat from pot. Heat fat left in pot over medium heat until shimmering. Add broccolini, garlic, and pepper flakes and cook until garlic is fragrant, about 30 seconds. Add ½ cup reserved cooking water, cover, and cook until broccolini is tender, about 5 minutes.

3. Off heat, add chicken, Parmesan, cream, pasta, and remaining ¼ cup reserved cooking water to broccolini and toss to combine. Season with salt and pepper to taste. Serve, sprinkled with bacon and extra Parmesan.

TEST KITCHEN NOTE: Our favorite thin-sliced bacon is Oscar Mayer Naturally Hardwood Smoked Bacon.

ROASTED CHICKEN THIGHS WITH BRUSSELS SPROUTS AND CARROTS Serves 4

✔ **WHY THIS RECIPE WORKS:** Searing the chicken thighs before roasting ensures crispy skin.

- 1 pound carrots, halved lengthwise
- 8 ounces Brussels sprouts, trimmed and halved
- 4 shallots, peeled and halved
- ¼ cup extra-virgin olive oil
   Salt and pepper
- 8 (5- to 7-ounce) bone-in chicken thighs, trimmed
- ½ cup plain whole-milk yogurt
- 1 tablespoon lemon juice
- 1 tablespoon minced fresh dill
- 2 garlic cloves, minced

1. Adjust oven rack to lower-middle position and heat oven to 425 degrees. Toss carrots, Brussels sprouts, shallots, 2 tablespoons oil, 1 teaspoon salt, and ¾ teaspoon pepper together in large bowl. Spread vegetables in single layer on rimmed baking sheet; roast for 8 minutes.

2. Meanwhile, pat chicken dry with paper towels and season with salt and pepper. Heat 1 tablespoon oil in 12-inch skillet over medium-high heat until just smoking. Add chicken, skin side down, and cook until well browned, about 7 minutes. Push vegetables to edges of baking sheet. Add chicken, skin side up, to middle of sheet and roast until meat registers 175 degrees and vegetables are fully tender, about 15 minutes.

3. Whisk yogurt, lemon juice, dill, garlic, and remaining 1 tablespoon oil together in small bowl. Season with salt and pepper to taste. Serve yogurt sauce with chicken and vegetables.

Sour Orange Pie

Making sour orange pie without sour oranges required a bit of imagination and a lot of moxie.

BY KATIE LEAIRD

LOCAL COOKS AND writers refer to sour orange pie as Northern Florida's answer to South Florida's Key lime pie: a prebaked crust and a custard-like interior made with sweetened condensed milk and the juice of wild sour oranges, which are otherwise thrown away since they are far too tart to eat straight from the branch. I imagined transforming this much-maligned citrus into a lush and fruity dessert, the tart tang balanced by sweetness and floral orange notes.

I started with a simple crust of crushed graham crackers and melted butter but later swapped out graham for animal crackers; the slightly sweeter cookies highlighted the sour citrus filling.

But the interior was more difficult—mostly because sour oranges aren't easy to come by in much of the country. I finally found some at a local Latin American grocer, but the variation from orange to orange proved too tricky to even out—they ranged in size from golf balls to softballs, in color from green to pale yellow to light orange, and in liquid content from dry to watery. Since good quality sour oranges were too hard to find, I'd have to make my sour orange pie . . . without sour oranges.

I started playing with combinations of (sweet) orange juice, lemon juice, lime juice, and grapefruit juice. I enlisted tasters to sip samples until we found one that accurately mimicked the flavor of true sour oranges: a mix of orange and lemon juice. But once mixed with egg yolks for structure and sweetened condensed milk for sweetness and creaminess and baked into the pie, the combination lost nuance and was too lemony—not what I was after.

I couldn't decrease the amount of lemon juice because of the crucial sour punch it added, so I had to bump up the orange. Enter frozen orange juice concentrate, a bolder, more intensely flavored product. Together with lemon, it delivered a bright, complex orange flavor balanced by a faintly bitter bite from the citrus's zest. Additional orange zest in the whipped cream gave the dessert a floral essence.

I look forward to trying an authentic sour orange pie on my next visit to Florida. But in the meantime, I'll gather these ingredients at the grocery store and imagine warm Floridian afternoons while I eat this refreshing, sunny pie.

SOUR ORANGE PIE
Serves 8

If sour oranges are available, use ¾ cup of strained sour orange juice in place of the lemon juice and orange juice concentrate. Minute Maid Original Frozen is our favorite orange juice concentrate. Depending on the brand, 5 ounces is between 80 and 90 animal crackers.

CRUST
- 5 ounces animal crackers
- 3 tablespoons sugar
  Pinch salt
- 4 tablespoons unsalted butter, melted

FILLING
- 1 (14-ounce) can sweetened condensed milk
- 6 tablespoons frozen orange juice concentrate, thawed
- 4 large egg yolks
- 2 teaspoons grated lemon zest plus 6 tablespoons juice (2 lemons)
- 1 teaspoon grated orange zest
  Pinch salt

WHIPPED CREAM
- ¾ cup heavy cream, chilled
- 2 tablespoons sugar
- ½ teaspoon grated orange zest

1. FOR THE CRUST: Adjust oven rack to middle position and heat oven to 325 degrees. Process crackers, sugar, and salt in food processor until finely ground, about 30 seconds. Add melted butter and pulse until combined, about 8 pulses. Transfer crumbs to 9-inch pie plate.

2. Using bottom of dry measuring cup, press crumbs firmly into bottom and up sides of pie plate. Bake crust until fragrant and beginning to brown, 12 to 14 minutes. Let cool completely, about 30 minutes.

3. FOR THE FILLING: Whisk all ingredients in bowl until fully combined. Pour filling into cooled crust.

4. Bake pie until center jiggles slightly when shaken, 15 to 17 minutes. Let cool completely. Refrigerate until fully chilled, at least 3 hours, or cover with greased plastic wrap and refrigerate for up to 24 hours.

5. FOR THE WHIPPED CREAM: Whisk cream, sugar, and orange zest in medium bowl until stiff peaks form, 2 to 4 minutes. Slice chilled pie and serve with whipped cream.

Our slightly sweet crust, made with crushed animal crackers, balances the sour citrus filling.

SOUR ORANGE
Intense tartness

FRESH LEMON JUICE
Provides plenty of sourness

+

FROZEN ORANGE JUICE CONCENTRATE
Adds potent orange flavor

No Sour Oranges? No Problem.
Since fresh sour oranges can be hard to find, we re-create their ultrasour, slightly bitter taste by combining fresh lemon juice with thawed frozen orange juice concentrate and bolstering the mixture with lots of orange zest and lemon zest.

Queso Fundido

We wanted to put the fun back in *queso fundido*.

BY MORGAN BOLLING

A CLAY-COLORED DISH holding hot, bubbling cheese topped with strips of smoky poblano peppers and crumbles of meaty, spicy chorizo sausage—what could be better? In northern Mexico *queso fundido* (literally "molten cheese") is appetizer fare often served in rolled tortillas. It's since become a mainstay in Mexican American restaurants as a dip; more than a few of us have finished a crockful on our own—washed down with a Mexican beer, of course.

To get started, I armed myself with a box grater and five existing queso fundido recipes I'd found in our massive cookbook library. While the queso fundido I'd eaten while in Texas was cohesive, most of the versions I made separated, leaving a plasticky ball of cheese bobbing in a pool of grease. But this test at least helped me choose a cheese. Unlike creamy *chile con queso*—the popular dip made with processed cheese and canned tomatoes and peppers—queso fundido is characterized by its gooey, string-like texture. In Mexico this is achieved by using cheeses such as *queso asadero* or *queso Chihuahua* (a cheese, not a dog). But most American recipes turn to mozzarella, cheddar, or our favorite melter in this initial test: Monterey Jack.

I started with a method I'd read about in a few recipes, whisking shredded Monterey Jack into boiling water. I topped the mixture with sautéed poblano chile, onion, and chorizo. But even after adjusting the amount of liquid, this felt more like a cheesy cream sauce than a thick-but-flowing, tortilla chip–coating queso.

A test kitchen colleague suggested I reference an uncommon offering in the *Cook's Country* arsenal: a recipe for steamed cheeseburgers. She mentioned that the steamed cheese topping was gooey and magma-like; in other words, it sounded a lot like the consistency and texture I was after for my queso fundido.

So I set a bowl of cheese atop a stovetop steamer that I'd positioned in a Dutch oven and covered it. When I opened the pot's lid 5 minutes later, I was met by clouds of steam and cheese

Go to **CooksCountry. com/besttortillachips** to find out which tortilla chips are our favorites for dipping.

Gentle cooking and a small dose of cornstarch help keep our *queso fundido* smooth and dippable.

that was perfectly soft and stringy. Our science editor confirmed that steaming heats cheese more gently and protects it from separating (See "Keys to a Gooey, Emulsified Dip.")

But bringing out a steamer to make cheese dip was awkward and ridiculous. To replicate the steamer's effect, I combined shredded Monterey Jack with ¼ cup of water, covered the mixture, and microwaved it. A few minutes later, I had a smooth and supple queso, identical to the one I'd made on the stovetop. For my next test, to add even more silkiness, I tossed the cheese with a teaspoon of cornstarch. This trick, one we use frequently in the test kitchen for cheese sauces and fondues, helps keep the cheese from breaking and leaving thick clumps of cheese swimming in oil.

What's more: Microwaving the cheese directly in its serving vessel saved me from dirtying an extra dish. And this method also heated up that serving dish so the dip would stay nice and hot.

After all this testing, we circled back to our cheese choice. We loved the way the Monterey Jack melted into a silky dip, but were we getting enough flavor out of it? After happy experiments with several cheeses, we settled on a mixture of Colby Jack (a two-fer cheese of cheddar-like Colby and Monterey Jack) and spicy pepper Jack, with its fiery flecks of hot pepper.

It'd be so easy to make a batch of this smoky, spicy, ultrastringy queso fundido next time I have a party. But then I'd have to share.

QUESO FUNDIDO Makes 3 cups

To reheat, microwave the *queso*, covered, in 30-second intervals, whisking after each, until melted. Serve with tortilla chips. Our favorite pepper Jack cheese is Boar's Head Monterey Jack Cheese with Jalapeño. You can substitute ground pork for Mexican-style chorizo sausage, if desired.

- 1 tablespoon vegetable oil
- 4 ounces fresh Mexican-style chorizo sausage, casings removed
- 1 small onion, chopped fine
- 1 poblano chile, stemmed, seeded, and chopped fine
- 8 ounces pepper Jack cheese, shredded (2 cups)
- 8 ounces Colby Jack cheese, shredded (2 cups)
- 1 teaspoon cornstarch
- ¼ cup water

1. Heat oil in 10-inch nonstick skillet over medium-high heat until shimmering. Add chorizo and cook, breaking up meat with wooden spoon, until browned, 3 to 5 minutes. Add onion and poblano and cook until vegetables are softened and lightly browned, 3 to 5 minutes. Transfer chorizo mixture to paper towel–lined plate.

2. Toss pepper Jack, Colby Jack, and cornstarch in microwave-safe 2-quart casserole dish until cornstarch lightly coats cheese. Stir in water and chorizo mixture until combined.

3. Cover with plate and microwave until cheese begins to melt around edges of dish, 1 to 2 minutes. Stir and continue to microwave, covered, until cheese is completely melted and just beginning to bubble around edges of dish, 1 to 3 minutes longer, whisking once halfway through microwaving (temperature of cheese should not exceed 180 degrees). Whisk and serve immediately.

Keys to a Gooey, Emulsified Dip

A big problem with warm cheese dips is that they can separate and turn greasy. Here's how we keep our *queso fundido* from breaking.

ADD WATER

If the cheese exceeds 180 degrees, it will break. Adding water helps reduce hot spots that can occur in the microwave.

ADD CORNSTARCH

The cornstarch and water form a gel, which coats the fat droplets in the cheese and prevents the mixture from separating.

MIX THOROUGHLY

Vigorous whisking ensures that the dip remains fully emulsified.

After extensive testing, we found that most hot dips are best at about 120 degrees.

What's the Best Way to Keep Your Dip Warm?

THE HOT DIP dilemma: Warm dips are party favorites, but most cool down and congeal after just 15 minutes on the table. No host wants to spend happy hour or the first quarter of a football game in the kitchen married to the microwave. Could we find a hands-off method for keeping a dip warm?

We gathered three of our winning small appliances that have warming settings—a mini slow cooker, a warming tray, and an electric fondue pot—and used them to keep spinach dip and our Queso Fundido warm, tracking the temperature of the dip in each. We also tried keeping the dips warm using four pieces of standard household equipment—a cast-iron skillet, a stainless-steel skillet, a glass casserole dish, and two foil-wrapped bricks—that we preheated in the oven to 200 degrees before adding the dip (for the bricks, we placed a bowl of dip on top). We then tracked how long the dips stayed above 120 degrees, the temperature at which most start to solidify.

The household hacks were mostly flops: Only the preheated glass casserole dish kept both dips warm for about 25 minutes, 10 to 15 minutes longer than dip left in an unheated bowl on the counter. The stainless-steel skillet lost heat too quickly, and pulling hot bricks from the oven was cumbersome and dangerous—plus, they looked unsightly on the table.

We had high hopes for the cast-iron skillet, but they were dashed when, after being heated in the oven for 10 minutes, the pan got so hot that it caused the queso dip to break and the spinach dip to dry out and harden. Our science editor explained that cast iron, which absorbs heat slowly and retains it well, was overheating the dip. Turning down the heat wasn't an option, as most home ovens don't go below 200 degrees.

Glass works well for this purpose because, unlike cast iron or stainless steel, it's a slow conductor of heat and transfers steady warmth to the dip. It's also the only household method that's safe to reheat in the microwave if your dip does happen to go cold at the table.

While the preheated glass dish works in a pinch, we found that two of the appliances worked much better, and one stood out as the clear winner. The fondue pot was better suited for fondue than for thick dips (even at the lowest setting, it caused dip to overheat and separate), but both the warming tray and the mini slow cooker kept dip warm and melty for more than 2 hours. They were also relatively hands-off, though it took some initial adjusting to set the warming tray to the right temperature.

In the end, the best option was our favorite mini slow cooker from Elite Cuisine, which was unobtrusive and effortless to load and set. Its lid locked moisture in so that our dips didn't dry out, and testers loved that its crock was dishwasher-safe. The biggest plus is that it kept our dips at an appropriate temperature for more than 2 hours. Dip dilemma solved.

Whether you want to rig your dips to stay warm with gear you already have or buy a specific gadget that truly lets you "set it and forget it," standing watch over your hot hors d'oeuvres will be a thing of the past.

–LAUREN SAVOIE

▶ Go to **CooksCountry.com** to see the complete testing reports for mini slow cookers, warming trays, and fondue pots.

BEST FOR DIPS

LIFE OF THE PARTY
Elite Cuisine 1.5 Quart Mini Slow Cooker
Model: MST250XW **Price:** $24.02
Kept dip warm for 2-plus hours, looked great, small footprint, and lid preserved moisture.

VERY IMPORTANT GUEST
BroilKing Professional Stainless Warming Tray
Model: NWT-1S **Price:** $126.06
Efficient but was much bigger than our winner. Bonus: can keep other apps hot, too.

SOLID BACKUP PLAN
Preheated Pyrex 8" Square Glass Baking Dish
Model: B003KZGXU8 **Price:** $9.00
Kept dip warm 10 to 15 minutes longer than an unheated vessel.

PARTY POOPER
Oster Titanium Infused DuraCeramic 3-Qt Fondue Pot
Model: FPSTFN7700W-TECO **Price:** $24.68
Great for fondue but too hot (even on lowest setting) for dip.

BOORISH GUEST
Preheated All-Clad 12-Inch Stainless Fry Pan
Model: 4112 **Price:** $154.95
Lost heat too quickly—only gained us a few minutes. And the handle was awkward.

HOT MESS
Preheated Lodge Classic Cast Iron Skillet 12"
Model: L10SK3 **Price:** $33.31
Too hot—the dips broke and dried out. Also pretty darn heavy.

BRICKS THROUGH THE WINDOW
Preheated Foil-Wrapped Bricks
Model: n/a **Price:** $1.30 each
What did you expect? They were ugly, cumbersome, and not great at holding heat.

New Jersey Crumb Buns

When it comes to crumb topping, New Jersey says go big or go home.

BY KATIE LEAIRD

I REMEMBER THE disappointment I felt upon eating my first crumb cake outside my native Garden State. "Where's the topping?" I asked, surveying what seemed like a measly sprinkling of streusel over a thick layer of coffee cake. Where I grew up, we stacked a mountain of crumbs over a thin sheet of yeasted cake and called it a crumb bun.

Bringing this favorite breakfast pastry into the test kitchen took a little explaining. Strangers to New Jersey crumb buns (also called crumb cake) guffawed when I told them about the traditional 3:1 ratio of topping to cake. They were certain it would be too sweet, too crumbly—a mess. Though my first batch wasn't perfect, my coworkers started to see the Jersey light. This pastry unapologetically magnifies the best part of crumb cake—the crumbs—so they need to be spot-on perfect.

The ingredients are simple: butter, sugar, and flour. But the ratios need to be just right. Too much butter and the topping bakes into a dense, sugary layer rather than craggy crumbs. Too little butter and the crumbs feel dry and sandy. Though sugar and flour both sound like straightforward ingredients, I was shocked by how big a difference the right type of each made.

Let's talk about sugar first. Brown sugar is actually just white sugar plus molasses (more for dark brown and less for light brown), which changes the sugar's color, flavor, and moisture content. While granulated sugar worked well in my cake base, the topping seemed dry, pale, and lacking in complexity when I used just white sugar. Using only brown sugar added too much extra moisture, rendering my crumbs too soft. A combination of half white and half brown sugar provided the best flavor and texture for the crumb topping.

Now on to the flour, which can be unexpectedly complicated. There are significant differences in protein content and absorbency among all-purpose (the variety most common in home kitchens), cake, pastry, and bread flours. Each of these factors matters.

When I used all-purpose flour in the topping, the crumbs were dry and tough and not what I remembered getting from the bakeries of my childhood. With so many crumbs in the topping, they needed to be soft enough to bite

The surprising topsy-turvy twist for tender cake and crunchy crumbs? All-purpose flour in the cake and cake flour in the topping.

through without scratching the roof of your mouth. With its lower protein and gluten content, cake flour tends to produce more delicate pastries. Cake flour (unlike our favorite all-purpose flour) is usually bleached, generally with benzoyl peroxide. This oxidizing agent reacts with the flour's starch, making cake flour easier to hydrate and thus creating a moist final product (see "Two Flours, Three Sugars"). I gave cake flour

a shot to see if it would help me produce that yielding crumb, and it worked. So I revisited my cake layer to see if I could make the swap to cake flour in that part of the recipe, too.

Nope. Changing the flour in the cake produced dramatic but dead-end results. What was yeasty and satisfyingly chewy when made with all-purpose flour turned lofty and fluffy like an angel food cake. Cake flour was the

answer to perfectly moist crumbs, but it decidedly did not work in the cake base. All-purpose flour was the way to go there.

The key to perfect crumb buns? Use all-purpose flour from the pantry for the cake and make a special trip to the store for a box of cake flour for the crumbs. You'll thank me later when you sink your teeth into a tender, sweet (mostly) crumb bun.

1. Add butter to yeasted dough 1 piece at a time, then beat until dough pulls in stretchy, web-like strands from sides of bowl.

2. Using your floured hands, press dough into even layer in greased baking dish. Cover and let rise for 1 hour.

3. To make topping, mix butter, granulated and brown sugars, cinnamon, salt, and cake flour. Let sit for 10 minutes.

4. Break crumb topping into rough ½-inch pieces and scatter in even layer over risen dough before baking.

NEW JERSEY CRUMB BUNS

Serves 12

Note that we call for both all-purpose and cake flours in this recipe. Do not substitute all-purpose flour for the cake flour (or vice versa), or the cake will be airy and fluffy and the topping will be tough and dry. We developed this recipe using Pillsbury Softasilk bleached cake flour; the topping will be slightly drier if you substitute unbleached cake flour. You can use either light or dark brown sugar in the topping.

CAKE
- 2¼ cups (11¼ ounces) all-purpose flour
- ¾ cup milk
- ¼ cup (1¾ ounces) granulated sugar
- 1 large egg
- 2¼ teaspoons instant or rapid-rise yeast
- ¾ teaspoon salt
- 6 tablespoons unsalted butter, cut into 6 pieces and softened

TOPPING
- 18 tablespoons (2¼ sticks) unsalted butter, melted
- ¾ cup (5¼ ounces) granulated sugar
- ¾ cup packed (5¼ ounces) brown sugar
- 1½ teaspoons ground cinnamon
- ½ teaspoon salt
- 4 cups (16 ounces) cake flour
  Confectioners' sugar

1. FOR THE CAKE: Adjust oven rack to middle position and heat oven to 350 degrees. Grease 13 by 9-inch baking dish. In bowl of stand mixer fitted with dough hook, combine flour, milk, sugar, egg, yeast, and salt. Knead on low speed until dough comes together, about 2 minutes.

2. With mixer running, add butter 1 piece at a time, waiting until each piece is incorporated before adding next.

Increase speed to medium-high and continue to knead until dough forms stretchy, web-like strands on sides of bowl, about 6 minutes longer (dough will be soft and sticky).

3. Using greased rubber spatula, transfer dough to prepared dish. Using your floured hands, press dough into even layer to edges of dish. Cover dish tightly with plastic wrap and let dough rise at room temperature until slightly puffy, about 1 hour.

4. FOR THE TOPPING: Ten minutes before dough has finished rising, whisk melted butter, granulated sugar, brown sugar, cinnamon, and salt together in bowl. Add flour and stir with rubber spatula or wooden spoon until mixture forms thick, cohesive dough; let sit for 10 minutes to allow flour to hydrate.

5. If dough has pulled away from sides of dish after rising, gently pat it back into place using your floured fingers. Break topping mixture into rough ½-inch pieces using your fingers and scatter in even layer over dough in dish. (Be sure to scatter all crumbs even though it may seem like too much.)

6. Bake until crumbs are golden brown, wooden skewer inserted in center of cake comes out clean, and cake portion registers about 215 degrees in center, about 35 minutes. Transfer dish to wire rack and let cake cool completely. Using spatula, transfer cake to cutting board; cut cake into 12 squares. Dust squares with confectioners' sugar and serve.

TO MAKE AHEAD

Once dough has been pressed into even layer in baking dish and dish has been wrapped tightly in plastic wrap, dough can be refrigerated for at least 4 hours (to ensure proper rising) or up to 24 hours. When ready to bake, let dough sit on counter for 10 minutes before proceeding with step 4. Increase baking time to 40 minutes.

Two Flours, Three Sugars

Trust us: It's worth pulling out multiple flours and sugars to make crumb buns. Each type makes a unique contribution, delivering just the right flavor and texture.

ALL-PURPOSE FLOUR
With a moderate amount of protein (10 to 12 percent), all-purpose flour develops enough gluten to give the yeasted cake structure and just a bit of chew.

CAKE FLOUR
Using cake flour to make the crumb topping gives it a moist, tender, delicate texture. That's because cake flour is more finely milled than all-purpose flour, making it better able to absorb fat and liquid. Cake flour is also lower in protein (6 to 8 percent) than all-purpose flour and therefore has less ability to form toughening gluten. Finally, cake flour is typically bleached to remove a yellow cast that some consumers find unappealing. This bleaching process also alters the protein structure of the flour, which makes it even less able to form gluten.

GRANULATED SUGAR
Granulated sugar is made from either sugarcane or sugar beets. Using it in the cake base preserves the traditional white color and produces the proper slightly chewy texture.

BROWN SUGAR
Brown sugar, whether light or dark, is just white sugar with a little molasses added. The addition of molasses makes the sugar soft and adds subtle flavor notes of caramel and rum. Combined with an equal amount of white sugar in the topping, brown sugar helps produce the best-textured crumbs.

CONFECTIONERS' SUGAR
Confectioners' sugar is simply pulverized granulated sugar with cornstarch added to prevent clumping. A snowy dusting on top of the crumb buns is the traditional finishing touch.

All Crumb Trails Lead to . . . Hackensack?

Since 1948, B&W Bakery in Hackensack, New Jersey, has been at the center of the crumb bun universe. At the bakery, staffers use industrial-size baking sheets to bake the cakes before sprinkling them with a thick layer of streusel (they go through 2,000 pounds of crumbs a week) and cutting them into slabs or squares, depending on your order. Fans from across northern New Jersey make it a weekly stop.

Cowboy Cookies

Hearty ingredients take a toll on texture. Could we soften this tough cookie?

BY CECELIA JENKINS

COWBOY COOKIES—PACKED with rolled oats, chocolate chips, toasted nuts, and flakes of coconut—have little to do with 10-gallon hats or gunfights at high noon. Instead they are a product of 1950s nostalgia for the American cowboy. Family recipes fondly call them hearty enough for the Western frontier.

A (home-on-the-) range of sample recipes took heartiness seriously. One version crammed in so much coconut that our jaws hurt from chewing; another had more chocolate than anything else, throwing the other ingredients off-balance. Sizes varied, but we agreed that larger cookies seemed heartier. I wanted big cookies with chewy interiors, crisp exteriors, and balanced "cowboy" ingredients.

I started with a standard cookie method: creaming butter and sugar together in a stand mixer, adding wet then dry ingredients, and finally folding in those cowboy add-ins. But the dough was stiff and hard to mix, and my tasters complained that the cookies were tough to chew.

Taking a closer look at the dough formula, large volumes of oats and coconut flakes introduced dry textures to the dough and absorbed what little moisture it contained, leading to tough cookies. Decreasing the add-ins would preserve moisture but would throw off the balance. Perhaps more moisture was the solution?

Increasing from one egg to two caused the cookies to spread too much. Adjusting to one egg plus one yolk worked better, but I still wasn't satisfied. I recalled some test kitchen cookie recipes that call for using melted butter and decided to give it a go. With the butter in liquid form, more moisture was readily available to the other ingredients, which became sufficiently hydrated such that I didn't need to add anything else. The resulting dough was easy to mix by hand—plus, now I didn't have to wait for the butter to soften.

Doubling down on my quest for a softer cookie, I deliberately underbaked the next batch, calling them done when I saw lightly browned edges and a hint of raw cookie dough showing through surface cracks. Thanks to a bit of carryover cooking, the cookies were perfect once they had cooled, with a soft chew and crisp exteriors.

Small just won't do here: We use a full ¼ cup of dough for each supersize cookie.

My dough baked evenly without any fussy portioning, rolling, or flattening—simply dropping ¼-cup portions of dough onto the sheets gave me excellent, rustic results. Staggering the portions 2½ inches apart gave them enough room to spread to the proper cowboy size.

Earthiness from the oats, sweetness from the chocolate, nuttiness from the meaty pecans, and complexity from the coconut combined for a huge hit. I knew that these cookies would never last long enough to see the inside of a saddlebag.

Don't Fence Them In

Cowboy cookies need lots of room to expand and bake evenly. To ensure that they don't spread into each other while baking, we arrange no more than 8 portions of dough on each parchment-lined cookie sheet.

COWBOY COOKIES

Makes 16 cookies

We prefer old-fashioned rolled oats in this recipe, but you can use quick or instant oats in a pinch. Do not use thick-cut oats here; the cookies will spread too much. These cookies are big and benefit from the extra space provided by a rimless cookie sheet when baking. Our favorite cookie sheet is the Wear-Ever Cookie Sheet (Natural Finish) by Vollrath.

- 1¼ cups (6¼ ounces) all-purpose flour
- ¾ teaspoon baking powder
- ½ teaspoon baking soda
- ½ teaspoon salt
- 1½ cups packed (10½ ounces) light brown sugar
- 12 tablespoons unsalted butter, melted and cooled
- 1 large egg plus 1 large yolk
- 1 teaspoon vanilla extract
- 1¼ cups (3¾ ounces) old-fashioned rolled oats
- 1 cup pecans, toasted and chopped coarse
- 1 cup (3 ounces) sweetened shredded coconut
- ⅔ cup (4 ounces) semisweet chocolate chips

1. Adjust oven rack to middle position and heat oven to 350 degrees. Line 2 rimless cookie sheets with parchment paper. Whisk flour, baking powder, baking soda, and salt together in bowl.

2. Whisk sugar, melted butter, egg and yolk, and vanilla in large bowl until combined. Stir in flour mixture until no dry streaks remain. Stir in oats, pecans, coconut, and chocolate chips until fully combined (mixture will be sticky).

3. Lightly spray ¼ cup dry measuring cup with vegetable oil spray. Drop level ¼-cup portions of dough onto prepared sheets, staggering 8 portions per sheet and spacing them about 2½ inches apart. Divide any remaining dough among portions.

4. Bake cookies, 1 sheet at a time, until edges are browned and set and centers are puffed with pale, raw spots, 15 to 17 minutes, rotating sheet halfway through baking. Do not overbake.

5. Let cookies cool on sheet for 5 minutes, then transfer to wire rack and let cool completely before serving. (Cookies can be stored in airtight container for up to 3 days.)

TO MAKE AHEAD

At end of step 3, wrap sheets tightly in plastic wrap and refrigerate for up to 2 days. When ready to bake, increase baking time to 16 to 18 minutes. To freeze, portion dough onto parchment-lined sheet and freeze until solid. Transfer frozen portions to zipper-lock bag and freeze for up to 2 months. Do not thaw before baking. Increase baking time to 17 to 19 minutes.

The American Table
Campaign Cookies

It sounds like a throwback, but the potential-First-Lady bake-off sponsored by *Family Circle* magazine every four years is a relatively new tradition. In 1992, Hillary Clinton took on Barbara Bush; after a reader vote, Clinton's oatmeal chocolate chip cookies beat out Bush's classic chocolate chip cookies, accurately forecasting the eventual election. In 1996, Clinton again prevailed; the same oatmeal chocolate chip recipe won handily over Elizabeth Dole's pecan roll sugar cookies.

But in 2000, Laura Bush avenged her mother-in-law's 1992 loss, sending her Texas cowboy cookies into the ring against Tipper Gore's gingersnaps. Her cowboy cookies won, just like her husband George.

The only year that *Family Circle* readers failed to pick the eventual winner? 2008, when Cindy McCain's butterscotch oatmeal cookies defeated Michelle Obama's shortbread cookies. Obama, however, roared back in 2012 with a batch of white and dark chocolate chip cookies that defeated Ann Romney's M&M cookies.

In 2016, Melania Trump submitted a recipe for sour cream–flavored star cookies and Bill Clinton submitted the same recipe his wife won with in the 1990s. The winner of the 2016 contest? The Clinton Family's Oatmeal Chocolate Chip Cookies.

It was no contest in 2000 when Laura Bush's version of cowboy cookies bested Tipper Gore's gingersnaps.

Cookie Carryover Baking

Just like meat, cookies continue to bake even after they are removed from the oven. To avoid overbaking, take the cookies out of the oven when they are slightly underdone and let them cool on the baking sheet for 5 minutes before transferring them to a wire rack.

Oats Are Oats, Right? Wrong.

We prefer rolled oats for baked goods, since their thin, flat shape gives cookies, bars, and toppings just the right amount of chew. In addition, they make good oatmeal relatively quickly. To find the best rolled oats, we rounded up five contenders and sampled each product as oatmeal (prepared according to package instructions) and in our recipe for Chewy Oatmeal Cookies (where we weighed the oats to ensure consistency).

In the oatmeal test, three products were nutty and hearty, but two were borderline unpalatable: one was too clumpy and dry, and the other was a gluey mass of goop. Worse, some tasters noticed a metallic, chemical taste in the gluey oats. Products that were mushy or parched in oatmeal made cookies that were a tad dense or dry. We were perplexed, too, by the appearance of cookies made with one "extra-thick" product; they spread into flat disks with crispy edges.

Some oats weigh more than others.

To find out why, we took a closer look at the oats. There wasn't a noticeable difference when we examined the raw extra-thick oats next to standard rolled oats, but when we painstakingly counted out 100 oats from each product and weighed them on a lab-grade scale (photo above), it turned out that the extra-thick oats had about 1,114 oats per ounce, while our preferred products had an average of about 1,200 oats per ounce. That may not seem like a huge difference, but when you consider that there are 9 ounces of oats in our standard cookie recipe, that adds up to more than 700 fewer oats to soak up liquid and provide structure—it's no wonder that cookies made with the extra-thick oats spread so thin.

Our new winner, Bob's Red Mill Old Fashioned Rolled Oats, makes perfectly formed cookies and hearty, creamy oatmeal in about 10 minutes. To read the full testing, go to CooksCountry.com/mar17. –LAUREN SAVOIE

RECOMMENDED		TASTERS' NOTES
BOB'S RED MILL Old Fashioned Rolled Oats **Price:** $4.59 for 32 oz ($0.14 per oz) **Oats per oz:** 1,200 **Time to Cook Oatmeal:** 10 min		★ **BEST FOR COOKIES** "This is how an oatmeal cookie should taste," said one happy taster. Our panel praised these oats' "toasty flavor" and "tender" texture, which had "just the right amount of chew." The oatmeal was "very hearty" and "tender," with a distinct "nuttiness."
BOB'S RED MILL Extra Thick Rolled Oats **Price:** $4.59 for 32 oz ($0.14 per oz) **Oats per oz:** 1,114 **Time to Cook Oatmeal:** 20 min		★ **BEST FOR BREAKFAST** These oats made a "nutty," "earthy" bowl of oatmeal in 20 minutes. But fewer oats per ounce caused the cookies to spread in the oven, producing "lacy," "crunchy" edges. While we loved the oatmeal they made, we didn't think they produced good cookies and we don't recommend them for baking.
QUAKER Old Fashioned Oats **Price:** $4.99 for 42 oz ($0.12 per oz) **Oats per oz:** 1,235 **Time to Cook Oatmeal:** 5 min	 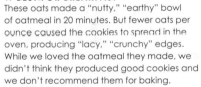	These familiar oats made oatmeal that was "tender" and "hearty," with a "clean oat flavor," in just 5 minutes, though a couple of tasters remarked that the oatmeal was "just a touch dry" when we followed the manufacturer's instructions. The oats' long, thin flakes produced cookies that were "soft," "tender," and "tall."

RECOMMENDED WITH RESERVATIONS		
COUNTRY CHOICE Oats Rolled Old Fashioned Organic **Price:** $3.59 for 18 oz ($0.20 per oz) **Oats per oz:** 1,219 **Time to Cook Oatmeal:** 3–5 min	 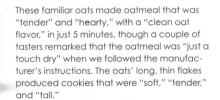	Many tasters remarked that oatmeal made with this product was "too dry" and "grainy," but most still praised its "nutty," "earthy" flavor (even though we followed the manufacturer's recipe, some tasters suggested that these oats would benefit from longer cooking). Cookies were "nicely crisp at the edges" and "chewy inside," though a few tasters deemed them "slightly on the dry side."
NOW REAL FOOD Organic Rolled Oats **Price:** $3.59 for 24 oz ($0.15 per oz) **Oats per oz:** 1,599 **Time to Cook Oatmeal:** 5–7 min		These small flakes practically disintegrated in oatmeal, making a porridge that was a bit "gummy" and reminiscent of "microwave oatmeal." Some also commented on a "metallic," "bitter" aftertaste. Since there were more oats per ounce in this product, cookies were on the "dense" side, though most tasters thought they were still "chewy" and "tender."

Cooking Class Chocolate Layer Cake with Chocolate Frosting

Making an impressive layer cake doesn't have to be intimidating. Using the right tools and our tested techniques, you can have a beautifully frosted cake in 10 steps. BY KATIE LEAIRD

Chocolate Cake 101

KEY INGREDIENTS Chocolate
This cake calls for three types of chocolate. Here's what each one brings to the table.

UNSWEETENED CHOCOLATE
Typically, unsweetened chocolate is pure chocolate liquor that has been formed into bars.
Test Kitchen Favorite: Hershey's Unsweetened Baking Bar

DUTCH-PROCESSED COCOA POWDER
Cocoa powder is chocolate liquor that has been pressed to remove most of the cocoa butter, leaving behind cocoa solids that are then finely ground.
Test Kitchen Favorite: Droste Cocoa

MILK CHOCOLATE
With only 10 percent cacao required, milk chocolate has a mild flavor. Milk fat and cocoa butter add creaminess—perfect for frosting.
Test Kitchen Favorite: Dove Silky Smooth Milk Chocolate

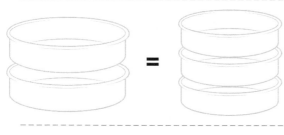

=

Two Layers or Three? You Decide.
For a two-layer cake, bake the batter in two 9-inch pans. To make a three-layer cake, use three 8-inch pans.

How the Batter Comes Together
This cake, like many, calls for creaming the butter and sugar, beating in the eggs, and then adding the flour and liquid components alternately. Does this alternation of dry and wet really make a difference in the cake's texture? To find out, we made cakes using four mixing methods: (1) following the standard dry/wet alternation technique, (2) mixing in the wet ingredients followed by the dry, (3) mixing in the dry ingredients followed by the wet, and (4) mixing in dry and wet simultaneously.

The worst cakes were made using methods 3 and 4. They were plagued by large holes and uneven crumbs—both signs that the ingredients had not been properly incorporated into the batter. The standard dry/wet alternation technique (method 1), however, made superior cakes with fewer and smaller holes and evenly fine, tender textures.

Frosting Know-How

EQUIPMENT For Easy Application

A good cake stand makes decorating faster and easier by elevating the cake for better visibility and by rotating for quick and even frosting application. Our favorite is the **Winco Revolving Cake Decorating Stand** ($29.98).

The long, narrow blade of an offset spatula is ideal for spreading frosting. We like the **OXO Good Grips Bent Icing Knife** ($9.99, above) or, for more detailed decorating, the mini **Wilton 9-inch Angled Spatula** ($4.79).

Parchment paper is essential when lining cake pans to ensure an easy release; it's also a good way to keep your cake stand clean while you frost the cake. For these jobs, we rely on our favorite brand, **Reynolds Parchment Paper** ($2.50).

TEST KITCHEN TIPS For a Professional Look

Let Cake Cool Completely
To prevent the frosting from melting, make sure to let the cake layers cool for at least 2 hours before frosting them.

Hold It Down
To keep the cake from sliding around during frosting, spoon a dollop of frosting in the center of the platter as "glue" and place one cake layer on top.

Keep It Clean
Frosting the cake right on the serving platter can be messy. To keep the platter tidy, use strips of parchment paper to cover its edges; remove the parchment before serving the cake.

Dress It Up
Here's how to give frosting a spiral finish: Set cake on turntable-style cake stand. Place tip of offset spatula or spoon at center of cake. Slowly rotate cake while dragging tip of spatula toward edge to create spiral.

STEP BY STEP Chocolate Layer Cake with Chocolate Frosting

1. PREPARE CAKE PANS
Grease pans and line with circles of parchment paper.
WHY? Many recipes call for flouring the greased pans, but we cut that step to avoid leaving white streaks on the chocolate cakes.

2. MIX DRY INGREDIENTS
Whisk flour, baking soda, baking powder, and salt together.
WHY? Whisking together the dry ingredients aerates them as effectively as sifting and ensures that there won't be pockets of leavener or salt in the batter.

3. COMBINE CHOCOLATE AND ESPRESSO
Whisk boiling water, chocolate, cocoa powder, and espresso powder together.
WHY? Boiling water melts the finely chopped chocolate and makes a smooth mixture.

4. CREAM BUTTER AND SUGAR
Beat butter and sugar until pale and fluffy.
WHY? Creaming makes butter malleable, and the tiny sugar crystals act like beaters, helping incorporate air for lift.

5. ADD WET INGREDIENTS
Mix in eggs, one at a time, until combined. Then add sour cream and vanilla.
WHY? Watery eggs and fatty butter don't mix naturally, so adding the eggs slowly gives the mixture time to emulsify.

CHOCOLATE LAYER CAKE WITH CHOCOLATE FROSTING Serves 8 to 10

For an accurate measurement of boiling water, bring a full kettle of water to a boil and then measure out the desired amount. Instant coffee can be substituted for the espresso powder, if desired. This frosting can be made with milk, semisweet, or bittersweet chocolate.

CAKE
- 1½ cups (7½ ounces) all-purpose flour
- 1 teaspoon baking soda
- ½ teaspoon baking powder
- ¼ teaspoon salt
- 1¼ cups boiling water
- 4 ounces unsweetened chocolate, chopped fine
- ½ cup (1½ ounces) Dutch-processed cocoa powder
- 1 teaspoon instant espresso powder
- 10 tablespoons unsalted butter, softened
- 1½ cups packed (10½ ounces) light brown sugar
- 3 large eggs, room temperature
- ½ cup sour cream, room temperature
- 1 teaspoon vanilla extract

FROSTING
- 20 tablespoons (2½ sticks) unsalted butter, softened
- 1 cup (4 ounces) confectioners' sugar
- ¾ cup (2¼ ounces) Dutch-processed cocoa powder
  Pinch salt
- ¾ cup light corn syrup
- 1 teaspoon vanilla extract
- 8 ounces milk chocolate, melted and cooled slightly

1. FOR THE CAKE: Adjust oven rack to middle position and heat oven to 350 degrees. Grease two 9-inch or three 8-inch round cake pans and line with parchment paper. Whisk flour, baking soda, baking powder, and salt together in bowl. In separate bowl, whisk boiling water, chocolate, cocoa, and espresso powder until smooth.

2. Using stand mixer fitted with paddle, beat butter and sugar on medium-high speed until pale and fluffy, about 3 minutes. Add eggs, one at a time, and beat until combined. Add sour cream and vanilla and beat until incorporated.

3. Reduce speed to low and add flour mixture in 3 additions, alternating with chocolate mixture in 2 additions, scraping down bowl as needed. Give batter final stir by hand.

4. Divide batter evenly between prepared pans and smooth tops with rubber spatula. Bake until toothpick inserted in center comes out clean, 15 to 20 minutes (for 8-inch pans) or 25 to 30 minutes (for 9-inch pans), rotating pans halfway through baking.

5. Let cakes cool in pans on wire rack for 10 minutes. Remove cakes from pans, discard parchment, and let cool completely on rack, about 2 hours.

6. FOR THE FROSTING: Process butter, sugar, cocoa, and salt in food processor until smooth, about 30 seconds, scraping down sides of bowl as needed. Add corn syrup and vanilla and process until just combined, 5 to 10 seconds, scraping down sides of bowl as needed. Add chocolate and process until smooth and creamy, 10 to 15 seconds. (Frosting can be held at room temperature for up to 3 hours.)

7. Using serrated knife, shave domed tops from cakes to make them all level; discard tops. Place 1 cake layer on platter or cake pedestal. Place 4 strips of parchment paper beneath edges of cake to keep platter clean.

8. Using offset spatula, spread 1 cup frosting (for 9-inch cake) or ¾ cup frosting (for 8-inch cake) evenly over top of first layer, right to edge of cake. Top with second cake layer, press lightly to adhere, then spread 1 cup frosting (for 9-inch cake) or ¾ cup frosting (for 8-inch cake) evenly over top. (For 8-inch cake, repeat with third cake layer and ¾ cup frosting.) Spread remaining frosting evenly around sides of cake. Carefully remove parchment strips before serving.

TO MAKE AHEAD
Baked, cooled cakes can be wrapped in plastic wrap and frozen for up to 1 month. Thaw at room temperature before frosting and stacking. (The frosting comes together quickly, so we recommend making it right before assembling the cake.)

6. ALTERNATE WET AND DRY
Add flour mixture in 3 additions, alternating with chocolate mixture in 2 additions.
WHY? Alternating the ingredients ensures that they will be properly incorporated, resulting in an evenly fine, tender texture.

7. DIVIDE BATTER AND BAKE
Divide batter evenly between pans. Bake until toothpick inserted in center of cakes comes out clean.
WHY? Equally dividing the batter means the layers will bake evenly and be of uniform height.

8. MAKE FROSTING IN FOOD PROCESSOR
Process butter, sugar, cocoa, and salt. Add corn syrup and vanilla, followed by melted chocolate.
WHY? The sharp blades of a food processor prevent separation that might occur in a stand mixer.

9. SHAVE DOMES
Using a serrated knife, slice the domed section off each cooled cake layer.
WHY? Layers with domed tops are difficult to stack and frost and will produce an uneven cake.

10. FROST AND ASSEMBLE
Spread measured amount of frosting on each layer. Spread remaining frosting on sides.
WHY? Measuring the frosting ensures that you will have enough to coat the top and the sides.

Slow Cooker Corned Beef and Cabbage

This traditional Irish American meal seems perfect for the slow cooker, and it is—but only if you construct it right. BY DIANE UNGER

WHEN YOU SIMMER corned beef brisket, potatoes, carrots, and cabbage for hours in herb-and-spice-seasoned water, you get a simple one-pot dish where each component is permeated with salty, beefy goodness. Accompanied by a spoonful of mustard and warm, buttered Irish soda bread, this traditional dinner can be served any time. In the United States, it is most often eaten on St. Patrick's Day. But the holiday can fall midweek, when a long-cooking meal isn't always easy to pull off. That's when the slow cooker comes in handy.

Or so I thought.

My first attempts at existing recipes—which generally called for simply throwing everything into the slow cooker and cooking until the beef was tender—gave me blown-out potatoes, disintegrated carrots, and mushy, insipid leaves of cabbage. Some recipes attempted to solve this cabbage problem by instructing you to add the cabbage to the slow cooker for only the final 1 to 2 hours of cooking time, and others suggested cooking the cabbage in a separate vessel altogether. But to my mind, these instructions defeated the promise of the slow cooker, which should be all about ease and convenience. I was determined to find a way to have this boiled dinner cook all together, with little or no work on the back end.

Another issue was the weight of the corned beef before and after cooking: The brisket lost up to 2 pounds of its weight in the 6 (or so) hours it took to cook through and become tender, so come mealtime, I was left with a depressingly small chunk of meat, hardly enough for a tableful of people.

To make sure I had enough dinner for my family and guests, I settled on a 3½- to 4-pound roast (ask for a first-cut or flat-cut brisket) to account for this inevitable shrinkage; this is just enough to serve 6 to 8 people.

In order to have every component of this meal cook at the same rate, I knew I'd have to fit everything comfortably into the slow cooker. This turned out to be easier said than done even in the large cooker; in my early experiments, I had a hard time getting the cabbage to stay put under the lid. I had a construction puzzle to solve.

Sizewise, I knew that the meat had to go into the cooker first. I sprinkled

To ensure that all the components cook through evenly, arrangement is key.

it with a tablespoon of pickling spice for flavor (this prefab blend includes warm spices such as cinnamon and allspice, along with mustard seeds and bay leaves). Then I tucked the potatoes and carrots around the meat and piled the cabbage pieces on top. The meat cooked through, the potatoes and carrots softened just enough, and the cabbage gently steamed.

But I wasn't done yet. I transferred the fork-tender beef to a carving board

to let it rest—an important step to help it maintain juiciness. Fifteen minutes later, I sliced it thin and transferred the slices to a serving platter. Using a slotted spoon, I transferred the vegetables to the platter as well and then dotted them with butter for extra flavor. Hey, it's a holiday, after all.

It turns out that despite my initial misgivings, the slow cooker really was the ideal vessel for making this St Patrick's Day feast. Erin go bragh.

SLOW-COOKER CORNED BEEF AND CABBAGE Serves 6 to 8

Be sure to buy a first-cut or flat-cut brisket, not the point cut, which is thicker and fattier. Cabbages that weigh more than 1½ pounds will be hard to fit into the slow cooker. To ensure even cooking, do not buy potatoes that are larger than 2 inches in diameter.

- 1 (3½- to 4-pound) corned beef brisket roast, about 2 inches thick, rinsed, fat trimmed to ¼ inch
- 1 tablespoon pickling spice
- 1½ pounds red potatoes, unpeeled
- 1 pound carrots, peeled and halved crosswise
- 1 small head green cabbage (1¼ pounds)
- 6 cups water
- 4 tablespoons unsalted butter, cut into ½-inch pieces

1. Set beef in slow cooker and sprinkle with pickling spice. Tuck potatoes and carrots between beef and sides of slow cooker. Cut cabbage into six 2-inch wedges through core, leaving core intact so wedges stay together while cooking. Arrange cabbage on top of beef. Add water. Cover and cook until beef is tender, 6 to 7 hours on high or 8 to 9 hours on low.

2. Turn off slow cooker. Gently push cabbage aside, remove beef from slow cooker, and transfer to carving board. Tent with aluminum foil and let rest for 15 minutes. Cover slow cooker to keep vegetables warm while beef rests.

3. Slice beef thin against grain; transfer to serving platter. Using slotted spoon, transfer vegetables to platter with beef. Dot vegetables with butter. Serve.

INGREDIENT SPOTLIGHT
Pickling Spice
Jarred pickling spice typically includes a combination of whole and coarsely crushed spices such as bay leaves, cardamom, cinnamon, allspice, mustard seeds, cloves, coriander, and ginger, offering a whole lot of flavor in just one jar. But this warm, citrusy, slightly spicy blend isn't just for making pickles. Just 1 tablespoon was all we needed to flavor our dish.

Putting It Together: Slow-Cooker Corned Beef and Cabbage
For fork-tender meat and vegetables that aren't mushy, we strategically layer the ingredients in the slow cooker.

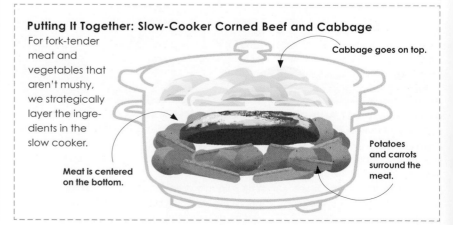

Cabbage goes on top.

Meat is centered on the bottom.

Potatoes and carrots surround the meat.

One-Pan Breakfast

What's better than breakfast any time?
Breakfast all on one pan. BY CECELIA JENKINS

BREAKFAST IS GREAT any time of day. But even greater is tucking into the works—crispy potatoes, juicy sausage links, runny egg yolks, and buttery toast—with only one pan to clean.

To make it all work, I knew I'd need a baking sheet. But even with the extra surface area, would all that food fit? I could cook components in groups and remove them to make space for the eggs at the end, but those first-cooked items would get cold and the eggs would run all over the sheet and cook unevenly. I needed a plan.

A test kitchen recipe for eggs-in-a-hole gave me a clue as to how to pull this off: I'd preheat a baking sheet, toast bread and cut holes in it, and then crack eggs into the holes and bake.

Starting the potatoes and sausages first and then moving them to one side ensured that the sheet would be hot enough to cook the eggs. But together the sausages and ½-inch potato chunks crowded the pan, steaming rather than browning. Bigger potato chunks (about 1 inch) browned much better but needed to cook for longer, which made the sausages turn dry and black.

Staggering the cooking process, I gave the potatoes a head start before adding the sausages. The sausages didn't brown much, but I didn't want them to dry out so I pressed on, moving them into a pile with the potatoes and resigning myself to lightly browned sausages. But to my surprise, the sausages in the pile browned nicely since they were slightly elevated in the circulating hot oven air, while those buried at the bottom continued to brown from contact with the sheet.

Next up: the toast. Buttering the bread and the sheet helped the toast brown and prevented the bread and eggs from sticking. To ensure that the toast and eggs finished at the same time, I pretoasted one side of the bread and then flipped it before adding the eggs.

With the oven at a very intense 500 degrees, I had been turning out an uneven mix of runny and chalky yolks. Lowering the temperature to 475 degrees still provided the initial blast of heat needed to cook the eggs through without sacrificing those luxurious runny yolks. Serving up a full breakfast (or dinner!) for four on a single pan? Mission accomplished.

ONE-PAN BREAKFAST
Serves 4

We prefer to use raw breakfast sausage links for this recipe, but fully cooked frozen links can also be used; Jimmy Dean Fully Cooked Original Pork Sausage Links are our favorite. Both types of sausage links cook in the same amount of time. The potatoes can be cut, submerged in water, and refrigerated for up to 24 hours. Dry them thoroughly with a dish towel before using.

- 2 **pounds Yukon Gold potatoes, unpeeled, cut into 1-inch chunks**
- 1 **tablespoon vegetable oil** Salt and pepper
- 4 **slices hearty white sandwich bread**
- 3 **tablespoons unsalted butter, softened**
- 12 **ounces breakfast sausage links**
- 4 **large eggs**

1. Adjust oven rack to middle position and heat oven to 475 degrees. Spray rimmed baking sheet with vegetable oil spray. Toss potatoes with oil, 1 teaspoon salt, and ¼ teaspoon pepper on prepared sheet and spread into even layer. Bake until potatoes are spotty brown on tops and sides, about 20 minutes.

2. Meanwhile, spread 1 side of bread slices evenly with 2 tablespoons butter. Using 2½-inch biscuit cutter or sturdy drinking glass of similar diameter, cut circle from center of each bread slice; reserve cut-out bread rounds.

3. Remove sheet from oven. Distribute sausages over potatoes (it's OK if

Just 3 to 4 minutes is long enough for the egg whites to set while the yolks stay beautifully runny.

some fall onto sheet), return sheet to oven, and bake until sausages are lightly browned on top, about 12 minutes.

4. Remove sheet from oven. Using metal spatula, push potatoes and sausages into pile occupying about one-third of sheet, creating enough room for bread. Place remaining 1 tablespoon butter on now-empty part of sheet and use spatula to distribute evenly. Place all bread, buttered side up, on empty part of sheet (do not

place cut-out bread rounds in holes). Bake until bread is lightly toasted on bottom, about 4 minutes.

5. Remove sheet from oven. Flip bread. Crack 1 egg into each bread hole and season eggs with salt and pepper. Bake until yolks have clouded over but still give slightly when touched, 3 to 4 minutes. Transfer sheet to wire rack and let sit until whites are completely set, about 2 minutes. Serve immediately.

AT A GLANCE One Pan, Four Steps

1. START WITH POTATOES | **2. ADD SAUSAGE** | **3. TOAST AND FLIP BREAD** | **4. FINISH WITH EGGS**

Cooking for Two Beef Wellington

We wanted a streamlined process but without sacrificing fanciness. BY ALLI BERKEY

We skip the pâté in our Beef Wellington for Two; the mushroom mixture is luxurious enough.

TEST KITCHEN TECHNIQUE **Making the Pastry Packets**

Spread ¼ cup mushroom mixture in center of pastry square, leaving 1-inch border. Place filet on top of mushrooms, then spread ½ teaspoon mustard on top of filet.

PASTRY

MUSTARD

MEAT

MUSHROOM MIXTURE

PASTRY

Stretch second pastry square over filet to meet bottom pastry square, then cup your hands around filet to create tight shape. Pinch top and bottom pastry squares together to seal. Trim excess pastry to form circle, leaving ½-inch border around filet. Crimp dough around edge using your fingers.

SAY "BEEF WELLINGTON" and what comes to mind? A grand center-cut beef tenderloin slathered in pâté, topped with finely cut mushrooms, wrapped in decadent puff pastry, and served on a silver platter. Paring this dish down to serve two required streamlining the process while stubbornly retaining the elegance.

It was an easy decision to substitute two beautiful filets mignons for the whole tenderloin. But the traditional recipe involves several steps: drying the beef overnight in the fridge, making both pâté and a mushroom mixture, and refrigerating various components between steps. Drying eliminated the meat's excess moisture, but that didn't justify the refrigeration time when cooking for two; patting the filets dry with a paper towel did the trick. And while pâté is luxurious, it is time-consuming to make (and store-bought versions are inconsistent). After side-by-side tastings, we decided to let the mushroom mixture do double duty. The meaty texture and flavor of finely chopped creminis (combined with traditional Madeira wine, thyme, and garlic to form a cooked mixture called duxelles) provided enough elegance.

Assembling and cooking the pastry packets seemed daunting. I knew I'd have to remove as much moisture as possible from the mushrooms to keep them from turning the pastry too soggy; cooking the duxelles over high heat allowed the excess moisture to escape.

I then seared the meat and layered on the rich mushroom mixture and some mustard for complexity before wrapping the stack in puff pastry, a process that proved easier than expected (see "Wrapping the Pastry Packets"). An hour-long visit to the fridge helped keep the pastry in place as the packets cooked.

Then came the biggest challenge: how to cook the meat properly in the pastry. I found that when I baked the beef to the test kitchen's preferred temperature of 120 degrees for medium-rare (this target accounts for carryover cooking), the beef was overcooked after resting. The pastry itself was insulating the beef too effectively, and the resting meat was rising much higher in temperature than I'd expected, continuing long after it had been removed from the oven.

To account for this quirk, I decided to bake the packets for a shorter time and then set them aside to allow the heat trapped inside the pastry to do the rest. Transferring the baked packets to a wire rack helped them cool evenly. I had two perfectly cooked filets in puffy pastry packages, delivering outsized elegance just for two.

BEEF WELLINGTON FOR TWO

The puff pastry packets insulate the beef, which continues to cook during the resting period. Note that we pull the packets from the oven when the meat registers about 115 degrees and give different resting times depending on desired doneness. To ensure accuracy, it's important to buy filets that are 2 inches thick. To thaw frozen puff pastry, let it sit either in the refrigerator for 24 hours or on the counter for 30 minutes to 1 hour. Do not chill the pastry packets longer than 1 hour in step 5 or the pastry will become soggy.

- 10 ounces cremini mushrooms, trimmed and halved
- 2 (8-ounce) center-cut filets mignons, 2 inches thick, trimmed Kosher salt and pepper
- 2 teaspoons vegetable oil
- 2 tablespoons unsalted butter
- 1 small shallot, minced
- 2 garlic cloves, minced
- 2 teaspoons minced fresh thyme
- 3 tablespoons Madeira
- 1 (9½ by 9-inch) sheet puff pastry, thawed
- 1 teaspoon Dijon mustard
- 1 large egg, lightly beaten

1. Adjust oven rack to upper-middle position and heat oven to 400 degrees. Line rimmed baking sheet with parchment paper. Pulse mushrooms in food processor until finely chopped, 13 to 15 pulses, scraping down sides of bowl as needed.

2. Pat filets dry with paper towels and season with salt and pepper. Heat oil in 10-inch nonstick skillet over medium-high heat until just smoking. Cook filets until well browned, about 2 minutes per side. Transfer filets to paper towel–lined plate.

3. Melt butter in now-empty skillet over medium-high heat. Add mushrooms, shallot, garlic, thyme, 1 teaspoon salt, and ¼ teaspoon pepper and cook, stirring often, until browned and nearly all moisture has evaporated, 6 to 8 minutes. Stir in Madeira and cook until no liquid remains, about 2 minutes.

Transfer to plate and let cool completely, about 20 minutes.

4. Roll puff pastry into 11-inch square on lightly floured counter. Cut pastry into 4 equal squares. Place 2 pastry squares on prepared sheet and spread ¼ cup mushroom mixture in center of each, to about same diameter as filets, leaving 1-inch border. Place 1 filet on each mushroom-coated square. Spread ½ teaspoon mustard on top of each filet. Stretch remaining pastry squares over filets to meet bottom pastry squares. Cup your hands around filets to create tight shape.

5. Pinch top and bottom pastry squares together to seal. Trim excess pastry to form circle, leaving ½-inch border around filet. Crimp dough evenly around edge using your fingers. Refrigerate pastry packets, uncovered, until cold, about 1 hour.

6. Brush tops and sides of pastry packets with egg. Bake until meat registers 110 degrees, 18 to 20 minutes. Transfer sheet to wire rack and let packets rest, 10 minutes for medium-rare or 20 minutes for medium. (Puff pastry packets act as oven and continue to cook steaks while they rest.) Serve.

KEY STEPS
Beef Wellington for Two

Follow our approach carefully for perfectly cooked filets mignons encased in crisp, flaky pastry.

ELIMINATE MOISTURE
To keep the pastry from getting soggy, cook the mushroom mixture until no liquid remains.

CHILL
Refrigerate the pastry packets before baking so the pastry firms up and the packets hold their shape.

LET REST
Remove the packets from the oven before the meat is done and let them finish via carryover cooking.

Go to CooksCountry.com/cheesestraws to see how you can put the extra sheet of puff pastry to work.

Five Easy Roasted Sweet Potato Wedges

Roasting the wedges skin side down gave us soft, tender interiors and faintly crunchy skins.

ROASTING SWEET POTATO wedges is not as easy as it seems. I thought the process would go something like this: cut potatoes into wedges, put them on a baking sheet, bake, and eat. Well, after three weeks (yes, 15 days) of testing, I found myself standing in the kitchen, surrounded by piles and piles of sweet potato wedges, with coworkers walking past, whispering, "She's still working on that recipe?"

I knew what I wanted: chunky, tender, lightly caramelized wedges of sweet potatoes. But, as I learned through trial and error, sweet potatoes release a sweet, almost syrup-like liquid as they cook. As this moisture tries to escape, the potatoes just end up stewing in their own juice. Some recipes I found called for starting the potatoes in a low oven to stem the flow and then increasing the oven temperature to caramelize the exteriors. But that method required careful monitoring of the oven temperature and several baking sheet swaps. There had to be an easier way.

The question to settle was the size of the wedges. The first few batches I made were too thin and cooked unevenly—the edges were burnt, but the centers were undercooked. I widened the wedge size to 1½ inches,

substantial and satisfying. I lined the baking sheet with parchment paper so that the wedges wouldn't stick and baked a few batches, playing around with how the potatoes were positioned on the sheet—some cut side down, others skin side down. Skin side down gave me crispy skins and soft interiors.

I tried various oven setups and landed on using the middle rack in a 450-degree oven: hot enough to brown the exteriors and cook the interiors at the same rate. Who knew? After trying everything in the book—and several things out of it—this simple method proved best. I had soft sweet potato wedges with lovely browned exteriors.

After creating a simple recipe for sweet potatoes tossed with olive oil, salt, and pepper, I looked for variations. For the first one, I went back to a childhood favorite and added some cinnamon and sugar (with just a pinch of nutmeg.) For another, I swapped in some spices for a twist featuring smoky cumin and chili powder. The next one simply adds savory curry powder. And the final variation will remind you of barbecue—full of garlic powder, onion powder, smoked paprika, and brown sugar.

Seventy pounds of sweet potatoes later, I had a solid recipe—and it used only one baking sheet. Sweet success.

After roasting more than 70 pounds of sweet potatoes, we finally got the wedges we wanted.

BY ASHLEY MOORE

ROASTED SWEET POTATO WEDGES
Serves 4 to 6
We prefer to use small potatoes, about 8 ounces each, because they fit more uniformly on the baking sheet. They should be of similar size so they cook at the same rate. Be sure to scrub and dry the whole potatoes thoroughly before cutting them into wedges and tossing them with the oil and spices.

- 2 **pounds small sweet potatoes, unpeeled, cut lengthwise into 1½-inch wedges**
- 2 **tablespoons olive oil**
- ½ **teaspoon salt**
- ½ **teaspoon pepper**

1. Adjust oven rack to middle position and heat oven to 450 degrees. Line rimmed baking sheet with parchment paper. Toss all ingredients together in bowl.

2. Arrange potatoes, skin side down, in single layer on prepared sheet. Roast until lightly browned and tender, about 30 minutes. Serve.

CINNAMON-SUGAR ROASTED SWEET POTATO WEDGES
Omit pepper. Add 2 teaspoons ground cinnamon, 2 teaspoons sugar, and pinch ground nutmeg to potato mixture in step 1.

CUMIN AND CHILI ROASTED SWEET POTATO WEDGES
Add 2 teaspoons ground cumin, 2 teaspoons chili powder, and 1 teaspoon garlic powder to potato mixture in step 1.

CURRY ROASTED SWEET POTATO WEDGES
Add 4 teaspoons curry powder to potato mixture in step 1.

SPICY BBQ ROASTED SWEET POTATO WEDGES
Add 2 teaspoons smoked paprika, 2 teaspoons packed brown sugar, 1 teaspoon garlic powder, and ⅛ teaspoon cayenne pepper to potato mixture in step 1.

Equipment Review Immersion Blenders

Manufacturers brag about speeds and power, but what really makes a good blender? We immersed ourselves in the facts to find out. BY HANNAH CROWLEY

THE TEST KITCHEN GAUNTLET
12 Blenders
10 Tests

1. Puree potato soup
2. Grind pesto
3. Blend kale and pineapple smoothies
4. Emulsify mayonnaise
5. Whip cream
6. Puree whole tomatoes
7. Have three testers evaluate each
8. Wash attachments and cups 10 times
9. Use tachometer to measure RPM
10. Make 100 smoothies with top model

WE USE IMMERSION blenders—also called stick blenders—to puree soups in their pots, eliminating the messy transfer to and from a blender or food processor. They're also designed for small blending jobs such as making mayonnaise, salad dressing, pesto, or whipped cream.

The handle of an immersion blender houses the controls and motor and trails the electrical cord. The business end is at the bottom, where the blending wand ends in an umbrella-like hood that covers the blade; the hood protects the user and has perforations that help circulate the food for even, efficient blending. Most models come with accessories such as blending cups and whisk attachments. A majority of the blenders from our last testing have been discontinued, so we tested 11 new models, priced from $14.99 to $129.99, alongside our old winner from KitchenAid.

One blender's chopping wand fell off miduse—plop, right into the soup. Another model's wand didn't detach, also a no-go (see "Safety First"). Speaking of safety, there was another deal breaker: Cuisinart recently added a safety lock to almost all its immersion blenders, including the two we tested. It requires the user to press a button to unlock the blender before it starts. This meant that every time we took our finger off the power button to shift our grip or adjust the pot, we had to stop and use our other hand (which was busy steadying the pot) to unlock it before we could start again—most inconvenient.

We noticed that manufacturers seemed to be trying to add flash to their blenders with features such as "turbo" buttons and up to 15 blending speeds. To better understand how blade speed correlates with performance, we used a tachometer to measure the blade speed

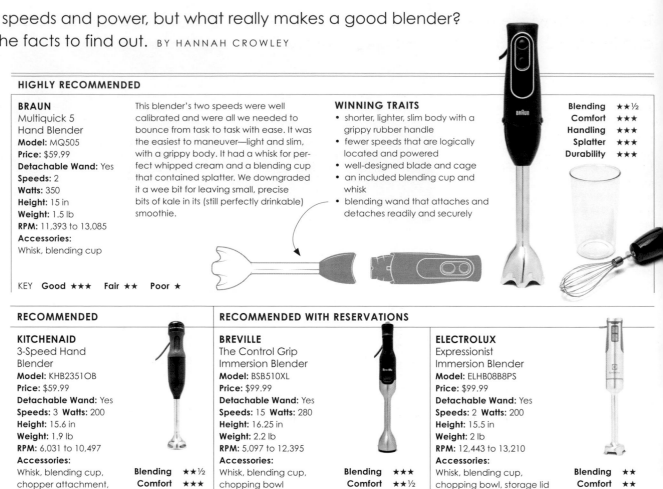

HIGHLY RECOMMENDED

BRAUN
Multiquick 5
Hand Blender
Model: MQ505
Price: $59.99
Detachable Wand: Yes
Speeds: 2
Watts: 350
Height: 15 in
Weight: 1.5 lb
RPM: 11,393 to 13,085
Accessories:
Whisk, blending cup

This blender's two speeds were well calibrated and were all we needed to bounce from task to task with ease. It was the easiest to maneuver—light and slim, with a grippy body. It had a whisk for perfect whipped cream and a blending cup that contained splatter. We downgraded it a wee bit for leaving small, precise bits of kale in its (still perfectly drinkable) smoothie.

WINNING TRAITS
- shorter, lighter, slim body with a grippy rubber handle
- fewer speeds that are logically located and powered
- well-designed blade and cage
- an included blending cup and whisk
- blending wand that attaches and detaches readily and securely

Blending	★★½
Comfort	★★★
Handling	★★★
Splatter	★★★
Durability	★★★

KEY **Good** ★★★   **Fair** ★★   **Poor** ★

RECOMMENDED

KITCHENAID
3-Speed Hand Blender
Model: KHB2351OB
Price: $59.99
Detachable Wand: Yes
Speeds: 3 **Watts:** 200
Height: 15.6 in
Weight: 1.9 lb
RPM: 6,031 to 10,497
Accessories:
Whisk, blending cup, chopper attachment, carrying bag

Blending	★★½
Comfort	★★★
Handling	★★½
Splatter	★★★
Durability	★★★

RECOMMENDED WITH RESERVATIONS

BREVILLE
The Control Grip Immersion Blender
Model: BSB510XL
Price: $99.99
Detachable Wand: Yes
Speeds: 15 **Watts:** 280
Height: 16.25 in
Weight: 2.2 lb
RPM: 5,097 to 12,395
Accessories:
Whisk, blending cup, chopping bowl

Blending	★★★
Comfort	★★½
Handling	★★
Splatter	★★★
Durability	★★½

ELECTROLUX
Expressionist Immersion Blender
Model: ELHB08B8PS
Price: $99.99
Detachable Wand: Yes
Speeds: 2 **Watts:** 200
Height: 15.5 in
Weight: 2 lb
RPM: 12,443 to 13,210
Accessories:
Whisk, blending cup, chopping bowl, storage lid

Blending	★★
Comfort	★★
Handling	★★★
Splatter	★★★
Durability	★★★

(in revolutions per minute, or RPM) of each model at various settings. Unfortunately, our results showed that faster blades don't necessarily make for better blending—a blade can move rapidly but not have a lot of power behind it. As for the blending speeds, the 15-speed Breville sounded impressive, but we found that speeds 1 to 13 varied very little, and it wasn't until speeds 14 and 15 that we started to see some action. More puzzling, speed 1 was slightly faster than speed 2, and 3 was slightly faster than 4, so these settings were superfluous *and* inaccurate. We concluded that two speeds were plenty: one low and one high, ranging in speed between 10,000 RPM on the low end and 14,000 RPM on the high end.

Some brands touted high wattage (a measure of how much electricity a motor draws), which ranged from 150 to 700 watts. But more watts didn't equal better blending. To find out why, we spoke to Professor Igor Mezic, director of the Center for Energy Efficient Design and head of UC Santa Barbara's Department of Mechanical Engineering.

Safety First

An immersion blender is a motorized, rotating blade on a stick, so safety is important when using one. Always detach the wand from the blender's body if you need to futz with the blade in any way; having a removable wand was a must for our top blenders. A good wand clicks on and off with ease and eliminates guesswork by providing visual, audible, or tactile clues to tell you when it's securely fastened.

He explained that more watts might make things go slightly faster when blending very liquid-y substances, like a big batch of thin soup. But for cutting, chopping, and pureeing more viscous foods, the design of the blade and its encircling guard is more important.

We examined the wands for common design attributes but found no pattern. Guard designs, guard vents, and distances from blade to guard varied and didn't track with performance. As

▶ Go to **CooksCountry.com/mar17** to read the full testing results, including information on the models that failed to impress us.

for the blades, some were straight and even and others were irregularly shaped, but that didn't track with performance either. At best, we can say that sharp blades with guards designed to maximize food movement into the path of the blades were very important.

What else mattered? Comfort was key, as shorter, lighter, slimmer blenders cloaked in grippy rubber were the easiest to hold and move. We preferred buttons over dials because buttons right on the grip let us hop back and forth between speeds with one hand and less fuss. Regarding accessories, we liked whisks (which whip cream more evenly and with more control than the blades) and blending cups, which minimize splatter; we found anything else extraneous.

The Braun Multiquick 5 Hand Blender ($59.99) earned our top spot. It is comfortable, secure, tidy, easy to use, and has two well-calibrated speeds.

Taste Test 100% Whole-Wheat Bread

The labels on whole-wheat bread can be perplexing. We set out to clear up the confusion and find the best sandwich bread made with 100 percent whole-wheat flour. BY JASON ALVAREZ

WHOLE-WHEAT BREAD has a flavor and nutrient profile many times more complex than that of white bread. But supermarket bakery aisles display multitudes of "whole-wheat" breads that list refined flour—regular white flour used to make white bread—as their primary ingredient. What's the deal?

Wheat kernels consist of three parts: germ, bran, and endosperm. White flour is made by grinding only the starchy endosperm; whole-wheat flour is made from all three parts. Because it includes the bran and germ, whole-wheat flour contains proteins, fats, fiber, vitamins, and minerals that refined flour lacks. But there's more to the story.

"Whole wheat" isn't a term strictly regulated by the U.S. Food and Drug Administration, but "100 percent whole wheat" is, and this is what you should seek out if you want bread with no white flour. But which bread is best?

To find out, we purchased seven widely available varieties of 100 percent whole-wheat bread and sampled them plain, in ham and cheese sandwiches, and as buttered toast. All were acceptable, but our tasters did have a preference for those with cleaner, deeper flavors. We also liked a touch of sugar. Three of the five lower rated products had 1.9 grams or less per 50-gram serving, and tasters thought the whole-grain flavors in these samples were a bit too strong. Our top two breads had 3.5 grams of sugar per serving and balanced the savory wheaty, toasty, nutty flavors with a satisfying hint of sweetness.

Tasters downgraded products for the mildly sour, bitter, or chemical notes that are all too common in store-bought bread. These unwelcome flavors can come from the host of stabilizers, emulsifiers, and preservatives found in most supermarket bread (every bread we tasted had at least some of these additives) or from the wheat itself: Whole-wheat flour is a bit bitter on its own, and it is much more prone to spoilage than white flour.

Even the worst breads we tasted—those with minor off-flavors—were passable; what really made a good bread stand out was its texture. Lower-rated products were airy, thin, and flimsy. They looked nice on the plate but became mush in the mouth. They weren't resilient enough to bear the weight of a sandwich or dense enough

to absorb butter without getting soggy. Our tasters favored moist, springy, chewy breads that were hearty enough to stand up to deli meats and butter.

To get to the heart of this distinction, we used scales and calipers to calculate the density of each bread by weighing and measuring three slices of each and averaging our results. Our winner was at least 18 percent more dense (and our runner-up was 45 percent more dense) than the five lowest-rated products. We could see the difference, too. The bottom five breads were more traditional supermarket loaves, with square slices and airy crumbs. In contrast, the top two breads featured wide, rectangular slices and dense crumbs.

With a full, clean wheaty flavor and a dense, springy texture that stood up to butter and sandwich fillings, Arnold Whole Grains 100% Whole Wheat is our top choice.

What Does "Whole Wheat" Really Mean?

Bread labels can be confusing. Here are some of the common terms you'll see on product labels and what they mean about the bread inside the bag.

100 PERCENT WHOLE WHEAT
This term can be used only for bread that uses 100 percent whole-wheat flour—no white flour allowed.

WHOLE WHEAT
Bread with this label must contain only some whole-wheat flour—thus some "whole-wheat" breads can be made with mostly refined white flour.

WHOLE GRAIN
Products must contain some whole grains.

WHOLE GRAIN WHITE
Products must contain some whole-grain flour made from a strain of white wheat that has a milder flavor than traditional wheat.

MULTIGRAIN
Must contain more than one grain, but those grains don't necessarily need to be whole grains.

WHEAT FLOUR (often listed as "unbleached" or "enriched"): Wheat flour is refined white flour—those label writers are sneaky!

RECOMMENDED

TASTERS' NOTES

ARNOLD
Whole Grains 100% Whole Wheat Bread
Price: $4.49 per 24-oz loaf ($0.19 per oz)
Sugar: 3.5 g per 50-g serving
Density: 229 mg per cm³

Our winner swept all three taste tests with its "hint of sweetness," "mild nuttiness," and "clean wheat flavor," which had "none of the bitterness" of typical bakery-aisle wheat bread. It was "tender and chewy" but not "too soft." Both crumb and crust were speckled with crunchy flecks of bulgur that were "substantial and pleasing."

PEPPERIDGE FARM
Farmhouse 100% Whole Wheat Bread
Price: $3.99 per 24-oz loaf ($0.17 per oz)
Sugar: 3.5 g per 50-g serving
Density: 281 mg per cm³

Like our winner, our runner-up "actually tastes of wheat." It was praised for its "slightly sweet" and "mild nutty" notes as well as its "dense" and "cakey" but "tender" crumb. Our only quibble was with the aftertaste, described as "very wheaty" by charitable tasters and "slightly bitter" by more critical palates.

RECOMMENDED WITH RESERVATIONS

NATURE'S OWN
100% Whole Wheat Bread
Price: $3.29 per 20-oz loaf ($0.16 per oz)
Sugar: 1.8 g per 50-g serving
Density: 195 mg per cm³

Tasters enjoyed this bread's "light wheaty sweetness," mild "nutty flavor," and "classic sandwich bread" texture. Though some perceived a faintly "sour" aftertaste, our main gripe was with its "open," "airy" crumb that "wimped out with butter" and compressed "to nothing" under the modest heft of thinly sliced ham and cheese.

WONDER
100% Whole Wheat Bread
Price: $2.99 per 16-oz loaf ($0.19 per oz)
Sugar: 0 g per 50-g serving
Density: 188 mg per cm³

Tasters deemed this product a "standard wheat sandwich bread" with "a nice sweetness" and wheat flavor that was "just assertive enough." But some noticed a "weird," "slightly sour" aftertaste. And many disapproved of the "spongy," "overly airy" texture that "collapsed from the weight of the sandwich" and seemed "mushy."

NATURE'S HARVEST
Stone Ground 100% Whole Wheat Bread
Price: $3.99 per 20-oz loaf ($0.20 per oz)
Sugar: 3.85 g per 50-g serving
Density: 198 mg per cm³

Tasters liked this bread's "wheaty but mild" taste and "nice earthy notes." However, the texture was "thin," "flimsy," and "distressingly easy to squish." It "didn't stand up to the butter" and slumped under the weight of the sandwich. But the cracked-wheat topping imparted a "slightly nutty" flavor that some tasters found pleasing.

SARA LEE
100% Whole Wheat Bread
Price: $3.99 per 20-oz loaf ($0.20 per oz)
Sugar: 1.9 g per 50-g serving
Density: 194 mg per cm³

Served plain, this bread had "almost no taste" and collapsed into a "dense wad" when chewed. It was also a bit "flimsy" for sandwiches. However, tasters enjoyed it toasted and buttered, describing it as "a good piece of toast" with a "nice crumb" that "stands up to the butter."

MARTIN'S
100% Whole Wheat Potato Bread
Price: $3.69 per 20-oz loaf ($0.18 per oz)
Sugar: 4.3 g per 50-g serving
Density: 201 mg per cm³

Although this bread includes reconstituted potato, it's still 100 percent whole wheat since it contains no white flour. Potato bread enthusiasts praised its "fluffy," "cottony" texture and "slightly sweet" flavor. But tasters expecting more conventional whole-wheat bread found its "jaundiced" hue "very off-putting" and its flavor "not wheaty at all."

Heirloom Recipe

We're looking for recipes that you treasure—the ones that have been handed down in your family for a generation or more, that always come out for the holidays, and that have earned a place at your table and in your heart through many years of meals. Send us the recipes that spell home to you. Visit CooksCountry.com/recipe_submission (or write to Heirloom Recipes, *Cook's Country*, P.O. Box 470739, Brookline, MA 02447) and tell us a little about the recipe. Include your name and mailing address. **If we print your recipe, you'll receive a free one-year subscription to *Cook's Country*.**

THREE-INGREDIENT BREAD
Makes 1 loaf
"I learned about this bread at a small restaurant in rural Maine. I love it slathered with lots of butter or dunked into a hearty beef stew."
–Alice Henderson, Concord, N.H.

Do not substitute all-purpose flour for the self-rising flour, or your bread won't rise.

- 3 cups (14¼ ounces) self-rising flour
- 3 tablespoons sugar
- 1 (12-ounce) bottle mild lager, such as Budweiser

1. Adjust oven rack to middle position and heat oven to 400 degrees. Grease 8½ by 4½-inch nonstick loaf pan.
2. Stir flour and sugar together in large bowl. Stir in beer and mix until smooth dough forms. Transfer dough to prepared pan. Bake until toothpick inserted in center of loaf comes out with no crumbs attached and top is light golden brown, 35 to 40 minutes.

3. Transfer pan to wire rack and let cool for 5 minutes. Remove loaf from pan and let cool completely on rack. Serve.

COMING NEXT ISSUE

Ready for spring? We are. We're celebrating the season with simple, springy recipes for **Spring Vegetable Pasta**, **Steak Frites**, and **Strawberry Cornmeal Shortcakes** (created by test cook Cecelia Jenkins, right). We'll show you how to impress your friends without trashing your kitchen with our one-pan **Roast Rack of Pork with Vegetables**. We'll indulge our wanderlust with a visit to North Carolina for impossibly crunchy, tangy, flavorful **North Carolina Dipped Chicken**; swing by the Gulf Coast for some **Shrimp Remoulade**; and then head up north to Worcester, Massachusetts, for a big helping of **Spinach Pie**. We'll reveal the secrets to making our foolproof **Easiest-Ever Cheesecake**. And because we just can't wait, we'll break out the grill early this year for **South Texas–Style Fajitas**. Join us!

FIND THE ROOSTER!
A tiny version of this rooster has been hidden in the pages of this issue. Write to us with its location and we'll enter you in a random drawing. The first correct entry drawn will win our winning immersion blender, and each of the next five will receive a free one-year subscription to *Cook's Country*. To enter visit **CooksCountry.com/rooster** by March 31, 2017, or write to Rooster FM17, *Cook's Country*, P.O. Box 470739, Brookline, MA 02447. Include your name and address. Jennifer Kostick of Sykesville, Maryland, found the rooster in the October/November 2016 issue on page 17 and won our favorite nonstick skillet.

WEB EXTRAS
Free for 4 months online at CooksCountry.com

Cheese Straws
Creole Fried Chicken
Gumbo
Louisiana Seasoning
Red Beans and Rice
Tasting Bacon
Tasting Rolled Oats
Tasting Tortilla Chips
Testing Dutch Ovens
Testing Fondue Pots
Testing Immersion Blenders
Testing Mini Slow Cookers
Testing Warming Trays
Vanilla Buttercream Frosting
Yellow Layer Cake

READ US ON iPAD
Download the *Cook's Country* app for iPad and start a free trial subscription or purchase a single issue of the magazine. All issues are enhanced with full-color Cooking Mode slide shows that provide step-by-step instructions for completing recipes, plus expanded reviews and ratings. Go to **CooksCountry.com/iPad** to download our app through iTunes.

Zebra Cake

Go wild with this chocolate and vanilla
striped cake, finished in a rich vanilla buttercream.

TO MAKE THIS CAKE, YOU WILL NEED:

- **3 tablespoons Dutch-processed cocoa powder**
- **3 tablespoons boiling water**
- **1 recipe yellow layer cake batter***
- **4 cups vanilla buttercream frosting***
- **1 ounce semisweet or bittersweet chocolate, chopped**

FOR THE CAKE: Adjust oven rack to middle position and heat oven to 325 degrees. Grease and flour two 8-inch round cake pans and line with parchment paper. Whisk cocoa and boiling water in medium bowl until smooth; let cool for 15 minutes. Transfer half of cake batter to bowl with cocoa mixture and stir gently to combine. Spoon 3 tablespoons chocolate batter into each prepared pan and spread into 3-inch circle. Top with 3 tablespoons yellow batter; gently press into chocolate batter without intentionally swirling batters. Repeat, alternating batters, ending with remaining chocolate batter. Gently shake pans to even out

batter but do not spread batter. Bake until toothpick inserted in center comes out clean, 30 to 35 minutes. Let cakes cool in pans for 3 minutes; using thin knife, loosen cakes from sides of pans. Invert cakes onto large plates, discard parchment, then reinvert onto lightly greased wire rack. Let cakes cool completely, about 1½ hours.

TO ASSEMBLE: Place 1 cake layer on cake plate or pedestal and spread evenly with 1 cup frosting. Invert second

layer and place on top. Frost top and sides with remaining 3 cups frosting. Melt chocolate in microwave and transfer to zipper-lock bag. Cut small hole in corner of bag and pipe chocolate in zigzag pattern across top of cake. Serve.

▶ *Go to CooksCountry.com/yellowcake and CooksCountry.com/vanillafrosting for our recipes for Yellow Layer Cake and Vanilla Buttercream Frosting, or use your own recipes.

Inside This Issue

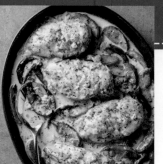

Cook's Country

APRIL/MAY 2017

Strawberry Cornmeal Shortcakes

After a few dozen batches, we fell for this rustic, down-home take on a springtime favorite.

PAGE 14

Pork Milanese
Tender, Crunchy Cutlets

Baked Ricotta Chicken
We Turn It Inside Out

Spring Vegetable Spaghetti
Pasta Primavera Simplified

Steak Fajitas
Mama Ninfa's Original

Rack of Pork with Vegetables
Bones Make the Difference

Skillet Pizza for Two
As Fast as Ordering In

**Cooking Class:
Easiest-Ever Cheesecake**

Bacon-Braised Potatoes
Crowd-Pleasing Side Dish

Pot Roast in a Bag
Mess-Free One-Pan Dinner

Carolina Dipped Chicken
Spicy Local Favorite

Slow-Cooker Coq au Vin
French Country Classic

Carrot Cake Cookies
Plus: Rating Cream Cheese

CooksCountry.com
$5.95 U.S./$6.95 CANADA

05>

7 25274 05251 6

LETTER FROM THE EDITOR

There's a catch to making our Easiest-Ever Cheesecake (left): You have to follow the recipe exactly. The same holds true for both our North Carolina Dipped Fried Chicken, which we learned about from home cook Linda Dillard (below), and our Rack of Pork with Potatoes and Asparagus (bottom).

O NE OF THE most persistent misconceptions in cooking is that if a dish is good, it must be difficult to produce. A great pasta sauce takes hours of work. A brilliant soup requires incredible diligence. And a showstopping dessert? Don't even bother—your best bet is to buy one instead.

Bunk!

Making something special in the kitchen, whether it's perfect fried chicken or a resplendent pork roast, doesn't have to be a bridge too far. Sure, it requires care and attention. It requires following directions. And yes, it requires some effort, as does anything good. But it can, and should, be done.

Just take a look at our Easiest-Ever Cheesecake (page 24). We call it "easiest-ever" not because it's particularly forgiving if you improvise but because we're confident that if you read the pages carefully, assemble the correct ingredients and equipment, make sure your oven temperature readings are accurate, and follow the instructions from beginning to end, you will make the best cheesecake that you—or any of your guests—have ever had. (No water bath necessary!)

And as anyone who's had a cheesecake disaster knows, this is a real and valuable achievement.

TUCKER SHAW

Executive Editor

One-Pan Wonders
Fuss-Free Meals for Your Sheet Pan, Dutch Oven, Skillet, Roasting Pan, Casserole, and Slow Cooker

Cooking hearty, flavorful meals on busy weeknights is a heavy lift— it's easy to be deterred by time-consuming prep before and a sink full of dirty dishes after. The test kitchen solved these challenges by creating *One-Pan Wonders*, a collection of inspired, family-friendly recipes for even the busiest home cooks. Order your copy online at **CooksCountry.com/onepan**.

Follow us on **Pinterest**
pinterest.com/TestKitchen

Follow us on **Twitter**
twitter.com/TestKitchen

Find us on **Facebook**
facebook.com/CooksCountry

Find us on **Instagram**
instagram.com/cookscountry

Cook's Country

Chief Executive Officer David Nussbaum
Chief Creative Officer Jack Bishop
Editorial Director John Willoughby
Executive Editor Tucker Shaw
Deputy Editor Rebecca Hays
Executive Managing Editor Todd Meier
Executive Food Editor Bryan Roof
Senior Editor Chris O'Connor
Associate Editors Morgan Bolling, Katie Leaird, Ashley Moore
Test Cooks Alli Berkey, Daniel Cellucci, Matthew Fairman, Cecelia Jenkins
Assistant Test Cooks Mady Nichas, Jessica Rudolph
Senior Copy Editor Krista Magnuson
Copy Editor Jillian Campbell
Contributing Editor Eva Katz
Science Editor Guy Crosby, PhD, CFS
Director, Creative Operations Alice Carpenter
Hosts & Executive Editors, Television Bridget Lancaster, Julia Collin Davison

Executive Editor, Tastings & Testings Lisa McManus
Managing Editor Scott Kathan
Deputy Editor Hannah Crowley
Associate Editors Lauren Savoie, Kate Shannon
Assistant Editors Miye Bromberg, Emily Phares
Editorial Assistant Carolyn Grillo

Test Kitchen Director Erin McMurrer
Assistant Test Kitchen Director Leah Rovner
Test Kitchen Manager Alexxa Benson
Lead Senior Kitchen Assistant Meridith Lippard
Senior Kitchen Assistant Taylor Pond
Lead Kitchen Assistant Ena Gudiel
Kitchen Assistants Gladis Campos, Blanca Castanza

Design Director Greg Galvan
Photography Director Julie Cote
Art Director Susan Levin
Designer Maggie Edgar
Art Director, Marketing Melanie Gryboski
Deputy Art Director, Marketing Janet Taylor
Associate Art Director, Marketing Stephanie Cook
Senior Staff Photographer Daniel J. van Ackere
Staff Photographer Steve Klise
Assistant Photography Producer Mary Ball
Photography Keller + Keller
Food Styling Catrine Kelty, Marie Piraino

Senior Director, Digital Design John Torres
Executive Editor, Web Christine Liu
Managing Editor, Web Mari Levine
Senior Editor, Web Roger Metcalf
Associate Editors, Web Terrence Doyle, Briana Palma
Senior Video Editor Nick Dakoulas
Test Kitchen Photojournalist Kevin White

Chief Financial Officer Jackie McCauley Ford
Production Director Guy Rochford
Imaging Manager Lauren Robbins
Production & Imaging Specialists Heather Dube, Sean MacDonald, Dennis Noble, Jessica Voas
Senior Controller Theresa Peterson
Director, Business Partnerships Meghan Conciatori

Chief Digital Officer Fran Middleton
VP, Analytics & Media Strategy Deborah Fagone
Director, Sponsorship Marketing & Client Services Christine Anagnostis
Client Services Manager Kate Zebrowski
Partnership Marketing Manager Pamela Putprush
Director, Customer Support Amy Bootier
Senior Customer Loyalty & Support Specialists Rebecca Kowalski, Andrew Straaberg Finfrock
Customer Loyalty & Support Specialist Caroline Augliere

Senior VP, Human Resources & Organizational Development Colleen Zelina
Human Resources Director Adele Shapiro
Director, Retail Book Program Beth Ineson
Retail Sales Manager Derek Meehan
Associate Director, Publicity Susan Hershberg

Director, Public Relations & Communications Becky Wisdom

Circulation Services ProCirc

On the cover: Strawberry Cornmeal Shortcakes Keller + Keller, Catrine Kelty
Illustration: Greg Stevenson

Contents

Departments

— AMERICA'S —
TEST KITCHEN
RECIPES THAT WORK®

America's Test Kitchen is a real 2,500-square-foot kitchen located just outside Boston. It is the home of more than 60 test cooks, editors, and cookware specialists. Our mission is to test recipes until we understand exactly how and why they work and eventually arrive at the very best version. We also test kitchen equipment and supermarket ingredients in search of products that offer the best value and performance. You can watch us work by tuning in to *America's Test Kitchen* (AmericasTestKitchen.com) and *Cooks Country from America's Test Kitchen* (CooksCountry.com) on public television and listen to our weekly segments on *The Splendid Table* on public radio. You can also follow us on Facebook, Twitter, Pinterest, and Instagram.

Cook's Country magazine (ISSN 1552-1990), number 74, is published bimonthly by America's Test Kitchen Limited Partnership, 17 Station St., Brookline, MA 02445. Copyright 2017 America's Test Kitchen Limited Partnership. Periodicals postage paid at Boston, MA, and additional mailing offices. USPS #023453. Publications Mail Agreement No. 40020778. Return undeliverable Canadian addresses to P.O. Box 875, Station A, Windsor, ON N9A 6P2. POSTMASTER: Send address changes to Cook's Country, P.O. Box 6018, Harlan, IA 51593-1518. For subscription and gift subscription orders, subscription inquiries, or change of address notices, visit AmericasTestKitchen.com/support, call 800-526-8447 in the U.S. or 515-248-7684 from outside the U.S. or write to us at Cook's Country, P.O. Box 6018, Harlan, IA 51593-1518. PRINTED IN THE USA.

Ask Cook's Country

BY MORGAN BOLLING

KOSHER SALT
Large crystals

SEA SALT
Irregular shapes

TABLE SALT
Very fine grains

Worth the Salt

What exactly is kosher salt, and why do you call for it in some of your recipes?
Marilyn Bergeron, Seaside, N.J.

Salt is harvested from evaporated seawater and mined from underground salt deposits. Chemically, all salt is composed of sodium chloride. But the flavor of salt can differ slightly based on the types and amounts of minerals that attach to the salt crystals. The texture and size of the crystals are determined by how the sodium chloride is processed.

Kosher salt is designed to have large, irregularly shaped crystals, which make the Jewish practice of koshering (applying salt to draw blood and juices out of just-butchered meats) more effective. Kosher salt manufacturing is done under rabbinical supervision. We often use kosher salt to season meat because it has large crystals, which make it easier to sprinkle evenly.

THE BOTTOM LINE: Kosher salt gets its name from the Jewish practice of koshering meat. We use it in some recipes because its large crystal size makes it easier to season meat uniformly.

Cast Iron Conundrum

My mother was aghast when she saw me cooking tomato sauce in a cast-iron pan, commenting that the acidic sauce will leach metal from the pan. Is there anything to this?
Sally Riggins, Wilmington, Del.

When acidic foods are cooked in cast iron for a prolonged period of time, trace amounts of metal molecules can transfer into the food. But your mother can breathe easy. These molecules are not harmful when eaten, although they can impart an unpleasant metallic taste as well as damage the pan's seasoning.

To understand the timing of this process, we simmered a tomato sauce in a well-seasoned cast-iron skillet, tasting the sauce at 10-minute intervals. Tasters were able to detect metallic flavors in the sauce after 30 minutes of cooking. We also found that the skillet's seasoning had been compromised, but that was easy to fix.

Our advice is to exercise caution when cooking acidic ingredients in cast iron. Make sure that your pan is well seasoned, as a less-seasoned pan gives off more metal molecules and therefore a stronger metallic flavor. It's OK to use cast iron when making quick-cooking foods with acidic ingredients, such as a wine pan sauce, but don't use it when making long-cooking acidic dishes. Also,

be sure to remove an acidic dish from the skillet as soon as it finishes cooking and remember to season your skillet after cooking. To learn how to season cast iron, visit **CooksCountry.com/seasoningcastiron**.

THE BOTTOM LINE: You can cook acidic ingredients in cast iron, but you should use a well-seasoned skillet and season it after cooking. Don't allow an acidic dish to cook or sit in the skillet for more than 30 minutes.

Corny Contours

The kernels in the caramel popcorn I get at the fair are much rounder and prettier than when I make it at home. Are there tricks to getting them to pop so nicely?
Carlene Murphy, St. Cloud, Minn.

There are two basic shapes of popcorn: "butterfly" (also called "snowflake") and "mushroom." Most movie theater popcorn and kernels sold in supermarkets for popping at home are the butterfly shape, which pops up light and fluffy, often with multiple appendages. What you're likely getting in your box of caramel corn at the local county fair is mushroom popcorn. It's defined by a roundish shape and a sturdy texture. Mushroom-shaped popcorn is less common than butterfly popcorn, but you may be able to find it online and at specialty stores.

We sampled both shapes plain and in our recipe for Butter Toffee Popcorn. While some people praised the "beautiful, full shape" and "hearty texture" of mushroom popcorn when tasted plain, other tasters complained about it being chewier and having more distinct pieces of kernel in each bite. This quality was lost in our Butter Toffee Popcorn, where most tasters preferred the mushroom-shaped popcorn because its large size and round shape held up better to the coating.

THE BOTTOM LINE: There are two basic shapes of popcorn, mushroom (large and round) and the more common butterfly (small and asymmetrical). Caramel corn is often made using mushroom popcorn because its heartier texture holds up better to the confectionery topping.

BUTTERFLY-SHAPED KERNEL
Asymmetrical with "wings"

MUSHROOM-SHAPED KERNEL
Round and sturdy

To Dispose or Not?

Can I reuse a disposable baking pan?
Todd Branin, Manchester, N.H.

We in the test kitchen don't typically use disposable pans for baking because they don't hold heat well and aren't as stable as metal, ceramic, or glass options, so baked goods don't brown well in them. That said, we've found that you can somewhat overcome these issues by placing your filled disposable pan directly on a preheated rimmed baking sheet in the oven.

Using this hack, we tried baking three batches each of brownies, sticky buns, and our Fudgy Tar Heel Pie in succession in the same disposable baking pan (washing it after each use). We tested with our winning disposable pan, Glad OvenWare, which is made of sturdy plastic, and with a generic aluminum disposable pan. After three rounds in the oven, the pans showed some wear and tear but didn't exhibit any significant issues. A

Glad company representative confirmed that the OvenWare pans should last for "at least three uses" on average.

THE BOTTOM LINE: You can bake in disposable baking pans and reuse them a few times as long as you wash them by hand between uses. When baking in them, we recommend placing them on a preheated rimmed baking sheet to ensure stability and optimal browning.

Hard Cheese

I have some Parmesan in my fridge that has dried out and is now rock hard. Is there a good way to revive it?
Gregory Campbell, Aurora, Colo.

The humidity inside a refrigerator is quite low, so the longer cheese sits in one, the more it dries out and hardens. Once cheese loses moisture, there's no effective way to add it back (we tried steaming, microwaving, coating it in butter, and wrapping it in wet towels). But smart storage can help prevent your cheese from drying out. The cheese should be allowed to breathe—but just a little. Our preferred method for storing Parmesan cheese is to wrap it in parchment paper (to allow it some airflow) and then wrap it in aluminum foil or place it in a small zipper-lock bag (being sure to squeeze out as much air as possible before sealing the bag).

If your Parmesan has dried out, there are plenty of good uses for it. It can be added to soups and stews for extra flavor and body. If it's not too hard, it can be cut into 1-inch pieces, processed in a food processor (no more than 1 pound at a time) for about 20 seconds, and sprinkled over pasta, salads, and the like.

THE BOTTOM LINE: There's no good way to revive dried-out Parmesan, but it still has lots of flavor. Drop a chunk into a soup or stew to add body and depth, or grate it in a food processor.

DRIED-OUT PARMESAN
Soup flavor source

▶ To ask us a cooking question, visit **CooksCountry.com/ask**. Or write to Ask *Cook's Country*, P.O. Box 470739, Brookline, MA 02447. Just try to stump us!

Kitchen Shortcuts

COMPILED BY DIANE UNGER

SMART TIP
Fast Frico
Terry Vaughn, Peekskill, N.Y.

I like to serve Parmesan crisps with cocktails, but they're ridiculously expensive to buy. I've started making my own in my microwave. I take 2 ounces of Parmesan cheese, finely shred it (for about 1 cup of shredded cheese), and spread it in an even layer on a plate.

I microwave the cheese for about 3 minutes until it's golden, let it cool for a minute, scrape it off the plate, and break it into pieces. My crisps are delicious, easy, and much more affordable than store-bought crisps.

CLEVER TIP
Bag It
Arthur Muldoon, Redmond, Wash.

My family loves marinated chicken cutlets on the grill, and—following your advice—I always buy whole boneless chicken breasts and pound them out myself. Instead of pounding the chicken between sheets of plastic wrap, I do it in a gallon-size zipper-lock bag. Once all the chicken is flattened, I add the marinade right to the bag, seal it up, and refrigerate it. The bag is handy for carrying the chicken to the grill, too.

CLEVER TRICK
Use the Leaves as a Handle
Edwin J. Westerman, San Ramon, Calif.

Peeling a fresh pineapple can turn into a slippery situation. To make things easier, I use my chef's knife to whittle away the outer leaves of the pineapple, leaving just enough so that I can use them as an easy-to-grip handle. Then I hold the pineapple by the leaves, slicing away the rind and cutting the fruit from the core with my other hand. It makes the job much easier.

Submit a tip online at CooksCountry.com/kitchenshortcuts or send a letter to Kitchen Shortcuts, *Cook's Country*, P.O. Box 470739, Brookline, MA 02447. Include your name, address, and phone number. If we publish your tip, you will receive a free one-year subscription to *Cook's Country*. Letters may be edited for clarity and length.

DOUBLE DUTY
Convenient Canister
Anne Skelton, Arlington, Texas

Flour packaging annoys me. Wrapping 5 pounds of flour in paper may be fine for shipping it from the mill to the store, but it's no good for storing and accessing flour at home. After years of frustration, I found a better way to store flour—I transfer it to an empty large (45-ounce) oatmeal container with a lid. I find it much more convenient.

NEAT IDEA
Bundt Pan Magic
Kathryn and Larry Achey, Hillertown, Pa.

We found an easy way to make stuffed peppers that don't fall over and get messy. We stuff the peppers, nestle them next to each other in a large Bundt pan, and bake them. It works great.

NEAT TRICK
Berry Good
Sarah Glidden, Middlebury, Vt.

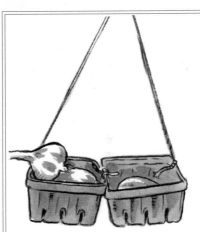

I'm always looking for ways to recycle and reuse things, and I recently came up with a neat idea for empty quart-size cardboard berry containers. I use kitchen twine to tie two together and make a hanging handle by tying a long piece of twine to either side of the baskets. I can easily hang my shallots and garlic for better air circulation and a DIY look.

DOUBLE DUTY
Blending Beans
Thomas Merrill, Stockton, Calif.

My coffee grinder broke a few years ago, and I've yet to replace it. I've been buying whole coffee beans and grinding them at the store, but once when I did that my French roast tasted like someone else's hazelnut beans—yuck. I didn't want to buy a specialized coffee grinder, but I realized I could grind a pot's worth of beans every morning at home in my blender. It takes about 45 seconds, and I get freshly ground, delicious coffee every time.

Rack of Pork with Potatoes and Asparagus

The bones in this roast don't just score points for presentation—they are the secret to its success.

BY CECELIA JENKINS

RESPLENDENT RACK OF pork—a rich, meaty roasted loin with the rib bones still attached—is just as worthy a holiday centerpiece as the celebrated prime rib roast of beef. But what makes it especially welcome at our table is its price: It costs about one-quarter as much as the beef.

The bones aren't just for show. Over the years we've learned that in the oven, heat travels more slowly through bone than through meat. In essence, the bones insulate much of the roast and keep it from cooking too quickly—a big deal considering that pork loin is so lean. Even a touch too much heat or a few too many minutes in the oven can render it unpalatably dry. So when I wanted juicy, deeply seasoned, rosy pork, along with some lovely roasted vegetables (potatoes and asparagus), I hoped the bones would help me achieve it.

To start, I rubbed a beautiful bone-in roast with brown sugar and salt and let it sit for a few hours to ensure good browning and juicy meat. Following the test kitchen's method for cooking boneless roasts, I placed the pork on a rack set in a roasting pan, tossed some Yukon Gold potatoes under it, and put the pan in a 250-degree oven. Considering that the temperature of the meat rises a few extra degrees once it's pulled from the oven (a process called carryover cooking), I removed my first roast about 5 degrees shy of my target temperature of 145 degrees.

Go to **CooksCountry.com/roastingpan** to find out which roasting pan is the best.

The undercooked potatoes were the least of my worries: The temperature of the pork rose more than 15 degrees in just 10 minutes of resting and showed no signs of stopping. When I sliced into it, I was faced with dry, gray meat. Tapping the bones with the tip of my finger revealed the reason: heat.

At such a low oven temperature, the meat really didn't need the bones for insulation while it roasted, and once it was out of the oven, the heat held in the bones was accelerating the carryover cooking. I had to figure out how to use the bones to my advantage.

A higher oven temperature would help the potatoes cook through. Perhaps I could exploit the increased carryover cooking rate and roast the pork in a hotter oven. The bones would insulate

Roasting the pork in a V-rack over a pan of potatoes gives all those flavorful juices a good place to go—right into the spuds.

the meat and help keep it juicy. And I'd remove the pork earlier, when it registered 130 degrees, relying on the heat in the bones to help it reach a perfect 145.

I tested oven temperatures of 375, 400, and 425 degrees. About 1½ hours at 400 degrees, followed by a 30-minute rest, was the best option. But my potatoes were still slightly undercooked.

These underdone potatoes proved to be less a problem than a solution for how to cook the final component, asparagus. Since the spears would need just a few minutes in the oven, I cooked the pork and seasoned potatoes together, transferred the pork to a carving board to rest, laid the asparagus over the potatoes, and returned the pan to the oven. By the time the roast was ready to carve, the potatoes were browned on the outside and creamy on the inside and the asparagus was crisp yet tender.

Running my knife between the ribs and meat, I separated the meat from the bones and carved it into thin slices. The ribs had served their purpose. There was just one thing left to do with them: Pick them clean.

RACK OF PORK WITH POTATOES AND ASPARAGUS
Serves 8
Use small Yukon Gold potatoes measuring 1 to 2 inches in diameter. The roast's bones trap heat, so the meat continues to cook during the resting period, which is why we pull it from the oven at 130 degrees; the temperature will climb to 145 degrees. Monitoring the roast with a probe thermometer is best. If you use an instant-read thermometer, open the oven door as infrequently as possible and remove the roast from the oven before taking its temperature. Serve with Quick Salsa Verde (recipe follows).

1 tablespoon packed dark brown sugar
   Kosher salt and pepper
1 (4- to 5-pound) center-cut bone-in pork rib roast, chine bone removed
2 pounds small Yukon Gold potatoes, unpeeled, halved
5 teaspoons vegetable oil
1 tablespoon minced fresh rosemary
2 pounds asparagus, trimmed

1. Combine sugar and 1 tablespoon salt in bowl. Trim fat on roast to ¼-inch thickness. Pat roast dry with paper towels and sprinkle with sugar mixture. Wrap roast in plastic wrap and refrigerate for at least 6 hours or up to 24 hours.

2. Adjust oven rack to lower-middle position and heat oven to 400 degrees. Toss potatoes with 1 tablespoon oil, rosemary, ½ teaspoon salt, and ½ teaspoon pepper in bowl, then arrange cut side down in large roasting pan.

TEST KITCHEN TIP Save the Bones
Feel free to serve the bones along with the meat for those who like to pick at them, or keep them in the kitchen as a cook's treat. Alternatively, you can save the bones and use them to make pork stock for ramen noodles or hot-and-sour soup. You can also add a single bone to chicken stock to boost its meaty flavor or to pea soup to fortify its porkiness.

To save the pork bones, wrap them tightly in aluminum foil, place them in a freezer-safe zipper-lock bag, and freeze them for up to three months.

3. Nestle V-rack among potatoes in pan. Unwrap roast and brush off any excess sugar mixture. Sprinkle roast with 1 teaspoon pepper and place fat side up on V-rack.

4. Roast until center of pork registers 130 degrees, about 1½ hours. Transfer pork and V-rack to carving board, tent with aluminum foil, and let rest for 30 minutes.

5. Meanwhile, toss asparagus with remaining 2 teaspoons oil, ⅛ teaspoon salt, and ⅛ teaspoon pepper in bowl and place on top of potatoes. Return pan to oven and cook until asparagus is bright green and potatoes are browned on bottom, 18 to 20 minutes.

6. Remove bones from roast by running sharp knife down length of bones, following contours as closely as possible. Carve meat into ¼-inch-thick slices and cut ribs between bones. Serve.

TEST KITCHEN TECHNIQUES
Monitoring the Temperature
A probe thermometer is the best tool for tracking the roast's temperature as it cooks. Our favorite is the ThermoWorks ChefAlarm. Insert the probe in the center of the roast so that the tip touches the bone, and then pull it back so the tip rests about 1 inch from the bone.

Removing the Bones
Secure the roast with one hand (using a clean dish towel to grip it). With your other hand, use a sweeping motion to run a sharp boning knife down the length of the bones, following the contours as closely as possible.

QUICK SALSA VERDE
Makes 1 cup
California Olive Ranch makes our favorite supermarket extra-virgin olive oil. The sauce can be refrigerated for up to two days. Bring to room temperature before serving.

1 cup minced fresh parsley
½ cup extra-virgin olive oil
2 tablespoons capers, rinsed and minced
4 teaspoons lemon juice
2 anchovy fillets, rinsed and minced
1 garlic clove, minced
¼ teaspoon salt

Whisk all ingredients together in bowl.

North Carolina Dipped Chicken

Dip? Hardly. We took a deep dive into this local take on fried chicken.

BY DIANE UNGER

A COWORKER FROM North Carolina, knowing that we're slightly obsessed with fried chicken, recently asked our team if we'd ever had dipped chicken—crispy, tender fried chicken doused in a spicy barbecue-like sauce. We hadn't, but after hearing a description like that, we swiftly dispatched an editor and photographer to Salisbury, North Carolina, to investigate (see "Keys to the [Fried Chicken] Kingdom").

The intel they brought back to the test kitchen was irresistible, though incomplete: They described a deeply seasoned, craggy coating that, impossibly, stayed crunchy even after the chicken's signature "dip" in a slow-burning spicy red sauce. "Amazing," they said.

But what they didn't bring was a recipe. They had gleaned a few hints about what was in the sauce (vinegar, sugar or molasses, and a hot sauce—locally produced Texas Pete) but were unable to pry a full list of ingredients from any of the secretive cooks they talked to. I'd be starting from scratch.

We often use a simple mixture of salt, sugar, and water to brine chicken destined for the fryer to keep it moist and tender, so that's where I began. After the chicken had spent about an hour in the brine, I coated it with the test kitchen's most reliable mixture: a simple combination of flour, cornstarch (which boosts crispiness), and baking powder (for volume and lightness) seasoned with salt and pepper.

After refrigerating the coated chicken for a half-hour to give the coating time to adhere, I fried it up in hot peanut oil. The chicken was well seasoned, and the coating was shatteringly crispy.

I was ready to move on to the signature component of this dish: the sweet-spicy dipping sauce. Tradition dictated that I needed to start with Texas Pete Original Hot Sauce (see "The Rise of Texas Pete"), to which I added some granulated sugar and cider vinegar. I whisked together a working recipe, dunked my fried chicken into it, and called my tasters to the kitchen. "You're on the right track," said my editor. "But it's missing something savory. And something to balance the hot sauce—it's too hot."

I tested a score or more of different combinations of ingredients (soy sauce, tomato paste, brown sugar, honey, cayenne, mustard, white vinegar, red wine vinegar, the kitchen sink) before hitting the target with Worcestershire for savoriness, deeply flavorful and sweet molasses, bright cider vinegar, and several tablespoons of peanut oil to tame the spiciness of the Texas Pete hot sauce.

Finally, I had well-seasoned chicken under a crunchy fried coating that held its crunch even when doused with the tangy-spicy red sauce.

Restaurants dunk the impossibly crispy chicken into a vat of a tangy-hot sauce before serving; we simply spoon our sauce over the top.

NORTH CAROLINA DIPPED FRIED CHICKEN Serves 4

Plan ahead: The chicken needs to brine for at least 1 hour before being coated in step 3. Do not brine the chicken longer than 4 hours or it will be too salty. Use a Dutch oven that holds 6 quarts or more. You'll need one 12-ounce bottle of Texas Pete Original Hot Sauce for this recipe.

CHICKEN

	Salt and pepper
¼	cup sugar
3	pounds bone-in chicken pieces (split breasts cut in half, drumsticks, thighs, and/or wings), trimmed
1¼	cups all-purpose flour
¾	cup cornstarch
1	teaspoon granulated garlic
1	teaspoon baking powder
3	quarts peanut or vegetable oil

SAUCE

1¼	cups Texas Pete Original Hot Sauce
5	tablespoons Worcestershire sauce
5	tablespoons peanut or vegetable oil
2	tablespoons molasses
1	tablespoon cider vinegar

1. FOR THE CHICKEN: Dissolve ½ cup salt and sugar in 2 quarts cold water in large container. Submerge chicken in brine, cover, and refrigerate for at least 1 hour or up to 4 hours.

2. Whisk flour, cornstarch, granulated garlic, baking powder, 2 teaspoons pepper, and 1 teaspoon salt together in large bowl. Add 2 tablespoons water to flour mixture; using your fingers, rub flour mixture and water together until water is evenly incorporated and shaggy pieces of dough form.

3. Set wire rack in rimmed baking sheet. Working with 1 piece at a time, remove chicken from brine, letting

To read about our first taste of North Carolina dipped fried chicken, go to CooksCountry.com/dippedfriedchicken.

How Does It Get So Crispy?

One hallmark of dipped fried chicken is its coating, which retains its crispy, craggy texture after being sauced. We've tested many fried chicken coatings over the years, and our reliable mixture of three main ingredients gave us the best results in this recipe. Here's why.

- **Flour** provides bulk and the basis for the substantial coating.
- **Cornstarch** absorbs water and helps form an ultracrispy sheath when exposed to hot oil.
- **Baking powder** leavens the mix, making the coating airy and light.

excess drip off; dredge chicken in flour mixture, pressing to adhere. Transfer to prepared rack. Refrigerate chicken, uncovered, for at least 30 minutes or up to 2 hours.

4. Set second wire rack in second rimmed baking sheet and line half of rack with triple layer of paper towels. Add oil to large Dutch oven until it measures 2 inches deep and heat over medium-high heat to 350 degrees. Add half of chicken to pot and fry until breasts register 160 degrees and drumsticks/thighs/wings register 175 degrees, 13 to 16 minutes. Adjust burner, if necessary, to maintain oil temperature between 325 and 350 degrees.

5. Transfer chicken to paper towel–lined side of prepared rack. Let chicken drain on each side for 30 seconds, then move to unlined side of rack. Return oil to 350 degrees and repeat with remaining chicken. Let chicken cool for 10 minutes.

6. FOR THE SAUCE: Meanwhile, whisk all ingredients together in bowl. Microwave, covered, until hot, about 2 minutes, stirring halfway through microwaving.

7. Transfer chicken to shallow platter. Spoon sauce over chicken. Serve.

The American Table
The Rise of Texas Pete

Thad W. Garner's initial plan was to take the money he'd put aside for college and, rather than pursue his studies, buy and run a barbecue restaurant near his family's home in North Carolina. And he did just that. But it was 1929, and within months the Great Depression killed the business. Garner was left with nothing—nothing, that is, except a recipe for a bracing, peppery hot sauce his customers loved.

Determined, Garner spent the next decade selling the sauce door to door. He called it "Texas Pete" to capitalize on the country's Hollywood-driven nostalgia for cowboy movies; even in a troubled economy, enough households could afford it for Garner to eke out a living.

By the mid-1940s, the economy was booming again, and the newly incorporated T. W. Garner Food Company was booming, too, selling hot sauce, jams, jellies, and more. But Texas Pete was—and remains—its most popular product.

Keys to the (Fried Chicken) Kingdom

I'M COMING!" YELLS Linda Dillard. She swings open the door with a wide smile, inviting me into her kitchen. A deep pot of oil heats on the stove; she flicks a few droplets of water from her wet fingertips into the oil to see if it's hot enough for chicken. It doesn't even sputter, so we turn to conversation while we wait.

Dillard delights in sharing the history of dipped chicken, made famous by her late father, Benjamin Franklin Cureton Sr. Cureton started a burger and dog business in Salisbury, North Carolina, in 1942. Fried chicken was only an afterthought. But the chicken soon proved to be the most popular thing on the menu, and the business came to be known as Frankie's Chicken Shack—"Frank's" to locals. To keep up with demand, Cureton needed to fry some chicken well before the customers arrived, and he looked for a way to keep the chicken warm. Cureton's wife, Nannie Mae Stevenson-Cureton, suggested rewarming the chicken in a sauce and developed the hot, vinegary concoction ("dip") that became their trademark. Stirred together in 5-gallon buckets, the dip, Dillard says, was called "the keys to the kingdom." So protective was the family that when it was time for Dillard's brother, Benjamin Franklin Cureton Jr., to learn the recipe himself, he grabbed a pencil and paper, but his mother was quick to tell him that the secret formula must never be written down, only memorized.

Linda Dillard with her father, Benjamin Franklin Cureton Sr., the man who first made dipped chicken popular in the 1940s at his Salisbury, N.C., restaurant.

Frankie's fame spread well beyond Salisbury. Even Duke Ellington and his musicians stopped by whenever they were in town. In 1986, Cureton Sr. handed over the business to Dillard and her brother, who ran it for another 18 years. The business eventually closed for good in 2004.

Back in her kitchen, Dillard coats pieces of chicken with seasoned flour and then drops them into the oil with the kind of confidence that only 40 years of frying chicken can produce. She needs no timer to know when it's done.

As Dillard pours the hot, spicy dip over the craggy pieces of chicken, the sharp aroma of vinegar cuts the air. I set the table, which she fills with collards, macaroni and cheese, and barbecue beans. I devour the food, and she takes great satisfaction and pride in my pleasure. –BRYAN ROOF

Easy Steak Frites

We love this classic bistro meal. We love it so much that we decided to bring it home.

BY ASHLEY MOORE

EVERY MAJOR CITY in the United States has at least one French bistro with a menu full of comforting and casual classics perfectly suited to the American palate. And no dish is more popular than steak frites. The components are simple: steak and French fries. So why don't we ever make it at home?

The answer: Restaurants employ several people at different stations—one person cooks the steak, another person cooks the fries. But at home, it's often just me. I needed to find a way to make both components simultaneously and have them ready to be served at the same time, with no sous chef.

First, I focused on the French fries, the tougher part of the equation. Most French fry recipes call for double-frying the spuds to ensure crispy exteriors and soft, fluffy interiors. But we have a favorite test kitchen method that's much easier—a cold-fry technique that goes like this: You slice the potatoes into ¼-inch-thick sticks and then place them in a large Dutch oven filled with 6 cups of room-temperature peanut oil—our preferred oil for fries thanks to its neutral flavor and ability to stay at a high heat without burning. You put the pot over high heat and cook the potatoes, without stirring, for 5 minutes, until the oil comes to a boil. Then, keeping an eye on the heat to make sure the oil continues bubbling at a constant rate, you cook the potatoes, without stirring, for 15 more minutes. By this time the exteriors of the potatoes have been set, so the potatoes need to be stirred to prevent them from sticking to each other. (Important: This method works well with Yukon Golds but not with starchy russets, which tend to fall apart. Shop accordingly.)

The usual cuts of steak for a classic bistro-style steak frites are hanger, rib eye, or New York strip. Hanger can be hard to find in most grocery stores, and while I love rib eye's rich marbling of fat, I wanted something a little bit leaner to serve with fries. New York strips are tender, flavorful, and easy to find almost everywhere.

To serve four people, I chose two gorgeous steaks, 1¼ to 1½ inches thick and about 1 pound apiece, and cut them in half. Choosing steaks this thick meant I was able to get a nice brown crust on the exterior and a rosy,

A simple mash of softened butter, shallot, parsley, and garlic makes a classic, superflavorful steak topper.

tender center after only a few minutes in the skillet. Just 4 to 7 minutes per side gave me medium-rare steaks.

Here's the tricky part: timing. The key to a successful steak frites supper is making sure everything's ready to eat at the same time—who wants cold steak or, even worse, cold fries? After a few run-throughs, I had the process down. First, start the fries on the stove. Shortly after the oil begins to bubble, place

a skillet with a tablespoon of oil over medium-high heat. Once the oil starts to smoke, add the steaks. After 4 to 7 minutes per side, the steaks will be ready to move to the cutting board to rest—just in time for you to return to the pot of oil and give the fries a stir. Once the steaks have rested (about 10 minutes), your fries will be done.

The last thing I needed to settle on was a sauce. Rather than a wine

sauce or a béarnaise (both common in restaurants), I opted for doctored-up butter—simply mashing softened butter with minced shallot, garlic, and parsley did the trick. For maximum effect, I dolloped a bit of this butter on top of the steaks while they rested.

Will I still order steak frites at a restaurant? Sure. But with this easy method, I'll be impressing my family and friends at home in the meantime.

Steak Frites Timeline

No one likes cold fries! To make sure each component of this supper comes together at the same time, have all of your ingredients and equipment ready before you begin, and put the potatoes in the oil 30 minutes before you want to eat. **Here's a sample schedule for getting dinner on the table at 7:00.** (Times will vary slightly.)

6:30 START FRIES IN COLD OIL
Place potatoes and oil in large Dutch oven; cook over high heat until oil is vigorously bubbling, about 5 minutes. Continue to cook, without stirring, about 15 minutes longer.

6:35 (oil is bubbling) **COOK STEAKS**
Meanwhile, heat oil in skillet until smoking; add steaks. Cook 4 to 7 minutes per side to reach 125 degrees for medium-rare.

6:45 LET STEAKS REST
Once steaks reach 125 degrees, transfer them to platter, top each with compound butter, tent with foil, and let rest for 10 minutes.

6:50 STIR POTATOES
Using tongs, stir potatoes, scraping up any that stick to bottom of pot, and continue to cook until golden and crispy, 7 to 10 minutes longer.

7:00 DRAIN AND SERVE FRIES
Transfer fries to paper towel-lined baking sheet, season with salt, and serve immediately with steaks.

TEST KITCHEN TECHNIQUE
Cutting French Fries

1. Cut ¼-inch-thick slice from each of potatoes' 4 long sides to square off.

2. Cut potatoes lengthwise into ¼-inch-thick planks.

3. Stack 3 or 4 planks and cut into ¼-inch-thick fries. Repeat with remaining planks.

Fresh out of the skillet, these steaks are ready for a dollop of butter and a 10-minute rest.

EASY STEAK FRITES Serves 4

For the best French fries, we recommend using large Yukon Gold potatoes (10 to 12 ounces each) that are similar in size. We prefer peanut oil for frying for its high smoke point and the clean taste it imparts to fried foods, but you can use vegetable oil, if desired. Use a Dutch oven that holds 6 quarts or more for this recipe.

- 4 tablespoons unsalted butter, softened
- 1 shallot, minced
- 1 tablespoon minced fresh parsley
- 1 garlic clove, minced
  Kosher salt and pepper
- 2½ pounds large Yukon Gold potatoes, unpeeled
- 6 cups plus 1 tablespoon peanut or vegetable oil

- 2 (1-pound) boneless strip steaks, 1¼ to 1½ inches thick, trimmed and halved crosswise

1. Mash butter, shallot, parsley, garlic, ½ teaspoon salt, and ¼ teaspoon pepper together in bowl; set compound butter aside.

2. Square off potatoes by cutting ¼-inch-thick slice from each of their 4 long sides; discard slices. Cut potatoes lengthwise into ¼-inch-thick planks. Stack 3 or 4 planks and cut into ¼-inch-thick fries. Repeat with remaining planks. (Do not place sliced potatoes in water.)

3. Line rimmed baking sheet with triple layer of paper towels. Combine potatoes and 6 cups oil in large Dutch oven. Cook over high heat until oil is vigorously bubbling, about 5 minutes. Continue to cook, without stirring, until potatoes are limp but exteriors are beginning to firm, about 15 minutes. Using tongs, stir potatoes, gently scraping up any that stick, and continue to cook, stirring occasionally, until golden and crispy, 7 to 10 minutes longer.

4. Meanwhile, pat steaks dry with paper towels and season with salt and pepper. Heat remaining 1 tablespoon oil in 12-inch skillet over medium-high heat until just smoking. Add steaks and cook until well browned and meat registers 125 degrees (for medium-rare), 4 to 7 minutes per side. Transfer steaks to platter, top each with compound butter, tent with aluminum foil, and let rest for 10 minutes.

5. Using spider or slotted spoon, transfer fries to prepared sheet and season with salt. Serve fries with steaks.

The American Table
Our First Restaurant? French.

Roadside taverns in New England served food to travelers throughout the colonial period, but it wasn't until 1793 that America got its first restaurant—complete with menus and separate prices for each item. The place, Julien's Restorator, was decidedly French.

Proprietor Jean Baptiste Gilbert Payplat, called Julien by his friends and acquaintances, cooked for the archbishop of Bordeaux before emigrating to the United States. He settled in Massachusetts and set up shop, specializing in "excellent wines and cordials, good soups and broths, pastry in all its delicious variety, . . . beef, bacon, poultry, and generally, all other refreshing viands."

After Payplat's death in 1805, his customers demanded that the business remain open, so his wife Hannah took over. She went on to manage Julien's Restorator for another decade.

Spaghetti with Spring Vegetables

Pasta primavera is easier said than made. We set out to change that.

BY KATIE LEAIRD

DON'T BE FOOLED by the Italian name. Though *nonnas* have likely been making something similar in home kitchens in Italy for centuries, what we now call pasta primavera ("springtime pasta") was actually born in New York City.

In 1975, Chef Sirio Maccioni of Le Cirque put the dish—a toss of pasta, vegetables, cream, butter, and cheese—on his menu. In 1977, *The New York Times* called it "by far, the most talked-about dish in Manhattan." With praise like that, we had to try the original. Thankfully, the newspaper published the recipe alongside its commentary.

I set the Le Cirque recipe alongside four others for a blind tasting. The newspaper's assessment held true: Le Cirque's version was the favorite. But it was also the most complicated, requiring more than a dozen individual steps (presumably accomplished at the restaurant by several people) and a huge stack of pots and pans. I wanted an equally rewarding dish without the need for a whole brigade of cooks.

My first simplifying step was to reduce the number of vegetables in the recipe. Paring down Maccioni's list, I focused on two spring vegetables, asparagus and green peas, which cook quickly and concurrently.

Every shape of pasta has its merits, but I had to choose. I tried campanelle, fettuccine, linguine, penne, and more. Thicker pastas, such as fettuccine, clobbered the vegetables and were too starchy. Small pasta shapes had to be shoveled onto my fork with the vegetables, making a satisfying bite elusive. Versatile spaghetti proved the best option; when twirled onto a fork, its long strands catch the vegetables, leading to the best eating experience.

I wanted a light and energetic sauce to highlight the spring vegetables. I tried versions with varying amounts of heavy cream, but the high-fat dairy muted and weighed down the bright flavors. Deep tomato-based sauces just didn't match the personality of this dish. Vexed, I nearly gave up. But my unlikely salvation was lurking in the produce section.

At its best, zucchini can be delicate and refreshing. At its worst, it's bland and waterlogged. But zucchini has another side that we seldom see. If you cook slices of this summer squash for a long time over gentle heat, they

A tablespoon of lemon juice and some torn fresh mint leaves amplify the vibrancy of this dish.

eventually break down into a creamy, luscious paste. Cook zucchini with garlic and a heavy dose of olive oil and it becomes a flavorful body-builder. After a few experiments adding varying amounts of water to the cooked zuke, I had a lovely sauce. I cooked my peas and asparagus directly in this liquid before tossing it with my pasta.

Just before serving, I mixed in some grated Pecorino Romano cheese, minced fresh chives, and lemon juice. But something was missing. In the original Le Cirque recipe, Maccioni garnished his pasta with sautéed cherry tomatoes. I didn't want to dirty another pan, but I longed for a sharp, acidic punctuation mark. So for my next round, I sliced and seasoned some

cherry tomatoes and let them sit with a little garlic in oil while I prepared the rest of the dish. At the last moment, I tossed the marinated tomatoes and some torn fresh mint leaves over the pasta and turned up the music. My simple pasta danced to a lively spring tempo.

TEST KITCHEN DISCOVERY
Overcooked Zucchini— on Purpose

The longer zucchini cooks, the mushier it gets. But when zucchini breaks down completely, it becomes downright silky. We embrace that trait by overcooking the squash and using it as a sauce base.

SPAGHETTI WITH SPRING VEGETABLES
Serves 4 to 6

The zucchini slices will break down as they cook and create a base for the sauce; do not be alarmed when the slices turn soft and creamy and lose their shape. The test kitchen's favorite spaghetti is De Cecco Spaghetti No. 12.

- 6 ounces cherry tomatoes, halved
- 6 tablespoons extra-virgin olive oil, plus extra for drizzling
- 1 small garlic clove, minced, plus 4 cloves, sliced thin
  Salt and pepper
- 1 pound spaghetti
- 1 zucchini, halved lengthwise and sliced ¼ inch thick
- ⅛ teaspoon red pepper flakes
- 1 pound asparagus, trimmed and cut on bias into 1-inch lengths
- 1 cup frozen peas, thawed
- ¼ cup minced fresh chives
- 1 tablespoon lemon juice
- ¼ cup grated Pecorino Romano cheese, plus extra for serving
- 2 tablespoons torn fresh mint leaves

1. Toss tomatoes, 1 tablespoon oil, minced garlic, ¼ teaspoon salt, and ¼ teaspoon pepper together in bowl; set aside.

2. Bring 4 quarts water to boil in large Dutch oven. Add pasta and 1 tablespoon salt and cook, stirring often, until al dente. Drain pasta and return it to pot.

3. Meanwhile, heat 3 tablespoons oil in 12-inch nonstick skillet over medium-low heat until shimmering. Add zucchini, pepper flakes, sliced garlic, and ½ teaspoon salt and cook, covered, until zucchini softens and breaks down, 10 to 15 minutes, stirring occasionally. Add asparagus, peas, and ¾ cup water and bring to simmer over medium-high heat. Cover and cook until asparagus is crisp-tender, about 2 minutes.

4. Add vegetable mixture, chives, lemon juice, and remaining 2 tablespoons oil to pasta and toss to combine. Transfer to serving bowl, sprinkle with Pecorino, and drizzle with extra oil. Spoon tomatoes and their juices over top and sprinkle with mint. Serve, passing extra Pecorino separately.

Baked Ricotta Chicken

Could we transform a complicated stuffed-chicken dish into a weeknight favorite?

BY ALLI BERKEY

FOR SUCH A simple yet promising idea—chicken breast stuffed with creamy ricotta cheese and topped with bread crumbs before being baked and served with a flavorful tomato sauce—so much can go wrong. I learned this after testing out a few existing, laborious recipes for ricotta-stuffed chicken that resulted in a range of disasters: broken, watery cheese oozing unappetizingly from the chicken breasts into a bland marinara sauce, for example. After all the work that was involved in carefully stuffing that cheese into the chicken, what was the point?

To get my bearings, I stepped back and looked at my list of ingredients. Nothing wrong there: chicken breasts, ricotta and Parmesan cheeses, bread crumbs, tomato sauce, and herbs and seasonings. Then it hit me: Would this lineup be any less delicious if I chose not to stuff the chicken breasts? In other words, why spend the time stuffing when I could simply stack?

I briefly parcooked the chicken breasts in a skillet on the stovetop, slathered tomato sauce and ricotta on top of each piece, sprinkled them all with bread crumbs, and baked them until the chicken was cooked through. The result? Stacking was certainly easier than stuffing, and none of my tasters minded the revamped construction. But I still had broken, grainy ricotta.

The next morning, as I sat down for a bite of breakfast and slathered some whipped cream cheese onto my bagel, it clicked. Of course: whipped. Here in the test kitchen, we often whip ricotta in a food processor before using it in a baked application or a sauce; by processing the cheese with oil and, of course, air, we achieve a smoother consistency and the cheese is less likely to break. I tried this in my next round of testing, and it worked beautifully: creamy, savory cheese with no hint of graininess.

I was happy with the dish (and so were my tasters), but I wanted it to come together even faster. So instead of toasting my bread crumbs on a baking sheet in the oven, I simply microwaved them with some olive oil, salt, and pepper for about 2 minutes until they were light golden brown. They finished browning and crisping up in the oven on top of the chicken.

Banquet-worthy dinner on any given Tuesday? Mission accomplished.

BAKED RICOTTA CHICKEN
Serves 4

Our favorite ricotta is BelGioioso Ricotta con Latte Whole Milk Ricotta Cheese. It is thicker and richer than the other products we tasted, so it stays in place when the chicken is baked. Serve the chicken with pasta or bread.

BREAD CRUMBS
- ½ cup panko bread crumbs
- 1 tablespoon extra-virgin olive oil
- ⅛ teaspoon salt
- ⅛ teaspoon pepper

CHICKEN
- 8 ounces (1 cup) whole-milk ricotta cheese
- 1½ ounces Parmesan cheese, grated (¾ cup)
- 1 teaspoon dried oregano
- Salt and pepper
- ¼ cup extra-virgin olive oil
- 4 (6- to 8-ounce) boneless, skinless chicken breasts, trimmed and pounded ½ inch thick
- 1½ cups jarred pasta sauce
- 2 tablespoons coarsely chopped fresh basil

1. FOR THE BREAD CRUMBS: Combine all ingredients in bowl. Microwave until panko is light golden brown, 1 to 2 minutes, stirring occasionally; set aside.

2. FOR THE CHICKEN: Adjust oven rack to upper-middle position and heat oven to 425 degrees. Process ricotta, Parmesan, oregano, ¼ teaspoon salt, and ¼ teaspoon pepper in food processor until smooth, about 10 seconds. With processor running, slowly add 3 tablespoons oil until incorporated; transfer ricotta mixture to bowl and set aside.

3. Pat chicken dry with paper towels and season with salt and pepper. Heat remaining 1 tablespoon oil in 12-inch skillet over medium heat until shimmering. Add chicken and cook until browned on both sides, about 6 minutes.

4. Evenly spread ¾ cup sauce in bottom of 13 by 9-inch baking dish. Transfer chicken to dish, shingling breasts in center of dish on top of sauce. Pour remaining ¾ cup sauce over chicken, then top each piece with ⅓ cup ricotta mixture. Sprinkle chicken evenly with panko mixture. Bake until chicken registers 160 degrees, about 15 minutes. Sprinkle with basil and serve.

Gently pounding the chicken to a ½-inch thickness ensures even cooking.

INGREDIENT SPOTLIGHT Ricotta

Whole-milk ricotta cheese generally offers better flavor and texture than part-skim or nonfat ricotta varieties, which often contain gums or stabilizers. Our favorite, **BelGioioso Ricotta con Latte Whole Milk Ricotta Cheese**, is made with sweet whey that is the byproduct of the company's mozzarella-making process, as well as a small amount of milk.

Ricotta can sometimes turn grainy when exposed to heat, so we give it a spin in the food processor with a bit of olive oil to break up the curds and even out the texture, leaving us with a creamy, silken consistency—just right for topping our Baked Ricotta Chicken.

Processing the ricotta with olive oil delivers a creamy consistency.

Grilled Steak Fajitas

For such a popular dish, fajitas have been treated terribly in Tex-Mex restaurants.
We set out to bring them back to glory. BY MORGAN BOLLING

IT'S AN AUTOMATIC reaction I can't be blamed for. When a table next to me orders fajitas, the wafting smells of charred meat, garlic, and chiles, often served sputtering on a hot plate, tempt me. Before I know it, I've ordered a round of my own. But restaurant fajitas are almost always a letdown, with overcooked and underseasoned meat and limp, greasy vegetables.

My eyes were opened when I made a fajita recipe inspired by the late Houston restaurateur Ninfa Laurenzo, a pillar of Tex-Mex cooking and an early champion of fajitas (see "Finding Fajitas"). Though "Mama Ninfa" never gave away her recipe, this facsimile produced tender strips of beef with charred vegetables in chewy flour tortillas. So this was what I'd been missing. I set out to make a reliable recipe for home cooks.

The word *fajita* refers to the cut of beef it's based on: skirt steak. *Faja* means "belt," and *-ito* or *-ita* added to a word means "small"; skirt steak comes from the cow's midsection, essentially where a belt would lie. This cut is perfect for fajitas because it's tender even when grilled over a piping-hot fire to medium—the perfect doneness when slicing meat thin against the grain. Also, skirt steak is wide and flat, so its ample surface area lends itself to marinating. And while our marinade doesn't have much of an effect on the steak's interior, it does help the exterior caramelize.

After much prodding, I was able to extract one piece of information from Mama Ninfa's sons: They told me that soy sauce was an important marinade ingredient. It enhances meaty flavor while seasoning with its high salt content. Adding oil and a couple of garlic cloves made for ultrasavory, succulent steak. But with such a hearty flavor, tasters craved brightness. So we tested lime, lemon, and pineapple juices before settling on ¾ cup of pineapple juice, which offered both sweetness and acidity as well as a balanced bite.

To see our recipe for homemade tortillas, go to CooksCountry.com/homemadetortillas.

Fajitas call for vegetables, usually bell peppers and onions. Grilling them in larger pieces (and holding the onion slices together with a toothpick) kept them from falling through the cooking grate. Moving them to a covered disposable aluminum pan on the cooler side of the grill to finish cooking ensured that they were tender. I tossed the finished vegetables with a couple of tablespoons of the marinade before serving.

I set out a buffet: grilled meat, grilled vegetables, and warm tortillas, along with salsa, guacamole, and other fixings. Some tasters kept things simple with just a slice or two of steak and a couple of vegetables, while others went for fully loaded fajitas. Everyone was happy.

We use pineapple juice in our marinade to give the steak a slightly fruity note, along with soy sauce to amplify its meatiness.

INGREDIENT SPOTLIGHT Skirt Steak

Long, thin skirt steak (also known as fajita or Philadelphia steak) is cut from the underside, or "plate," of the animal. It is tender, rich, fatty, and superflavorful, with such big beefiness that tasters declared it "wonderful," "beefy heaven."

SKIRT SHOPPING
Choose heavily marbled skirt steak; the fat helps keep the meat tender and adds tons of flavor.

GRILLED STEAK FAJITAS
Serves 6

Serve the fajitas with pico de gallo, avocado pieces or guacamole, sour cream, and lime wedges. One (6-ounce) can of pineapple juice will yield ¾ cup. We cook the skirt steak to between medium and medium-well so that its texture is less chewy and the steak is therefore easier to eat.

- ¾ cup pineapple juice
- ½ cup plus 1 tablespoon vegetable oil
- ¼ cup soy sauce
- 3 garlic cloves, minced
- 2 pounds skirt steak, trimmed and cut crosswise into 6 equal pieces
- 3 yellow, red, orange, or green bell peppers
- 1 large red onion, sliced into ½-inch-thick rounds
  Salt and pepper
- 12 (6-inch) flour tortillas
- 1 (13 by 9-inch) disposable aluminum pan
- 1 tablespoon chopped fresh cilantro

1. Whisk pineapple juice, ½ cup oil, soy sauce, and garlic together in bowl. Reserve ¼ cup marinade. Transfer remaining 1¼ cups marinade to 1-gallon zipper-lock bag. Add steak, press out air, seal bag, and turn to distribute marinade. Refrigerate for at least 2 hours or up to 24 hours.

2. Using paring knife, cut around stems of bell peppers and remove cores and seeds. Push toothpick horizontally through each onion round to keep rings intact while grilling. Brush bell peppers and onion evenly with remaining 1 tablespoon oil and season with salt and pepper. Remove steak from marinade and pat dry with paper towels; discard marinade. Sprinkle steak with ¾ teaspoon salt and ½ teaspoon pepper. Wrap tortillas in aluminum foil; set aside.

3A. FOR A CHARCOAL GRILL: Open bottom vent completely. Light large chimney starter filled with charcoal briquettes (6 quarts). When top coals are partially covered with ash, pour evenly over half of grill. Set cooking grate in place, cover, and open lid vent completely. Heat grill until hot, about 5 minutes.

3B. FOR A GAS GRILL: Turn all burners to high, cover, and heat grill until hot, about 15 minutes. Leave primary burner on high and turn other burner(s) to low.

4. Clean and oil cooking grate. Place bell peppers and onion on hotter side of grill and place tortilla packet on cooler side of grill. Cook (covered if using gas) until vegetables are char-streaked and tender, 8 to 13 minutes, flipping and moving as needed for even cooking, and until tortillas are warmed through, about 10 minutes, flipping halfway through cooking.

5. Remove tortillas from grill; keep wrapped and set aside. Transfer vegetables to disposable pan, cover pan tightly with foil, and place on cooler side of grill. (If using gas, cover grill and allow hotter side to reheat for 5 minutes.) Place steak on hotter side of grill and cook (covered if using gas) until charred and meat registers 135 to 140 degrees, 2 to 4 minutes per side. Transfer steak to cutting board and tent with foil. Remove disposable pan from grill.

6. Carefully remove foil from disposable pan (steam may escape). Slice bell peppers into thin strips. Remove toothpicks from onion rounds and separate rings. Return vegetables to disposable pan and toss with cilantro and reserved marinade. Season with salt and pepper to taste. Slice steak thin against grain. Transfer steak and vegetables to serving platter. Serve with tortillas.

AT A GLANCE
Steak Fajitas on the Grill
For a charcoal grill, arrange the lit coals evenly on one side of the kettle to create hotter and cooler cooking zones.

STAGE ONE
Place bell peppers and onion on hotter side of grill over coals and place tortilla packet on cooler side of grill away from coals.

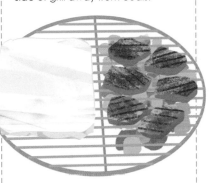

STAGE TWO
Remove tortilla packet from grill; set aside. Transfer vegetables to disposable pan, cover tightly with foil, and place on cooler side of grill. Place steak on hotter side of grill and cook until charred.

ON THE ROAD

Finding Fajitas

The waiter cuts through the crowded dining room holding a hissing black iron skillet high in the air and leaving a trail of beef smoke in his wake. There's a needle-scratch moment as all eyes turn to watch him. The fajitas have arrived.

Of all the cantinas in Texas, this is the one where, legend has it, fajitas took flight. In 1973, Ninfa Rodríguez Laurenzo, lovingly dubbed "Mama Ninfa" by Houstonians, opened a tortilla factory in this very spot on Navigation Boulevard. Looking for a way to supplement her nascent business, she took to selling fajitas, using her own fresh tortillas. Soon, tongues were wagging. With a few shabby tables and chairs and some recycled kitchen equipment, she transformed the factory into a full-blown restaurant, Ninfa's, which she ran until the late '90s. Eventually, Ninfa's blossomed into a chain.

Here, at the original location, the restaurant features a tortilla station by the front door where workers furiously slap tortillas back and forth between their hands and toss them onto a hot *plancha*. And while the rest of the menu has evolved over time, the fajitas remain. Continuity is in the fabric of this place: The current chef, Alex Padilla, first came to know Ninfa's through his own mother, who worked here when Padilla was a boy. To see more photos of our trip to Ninfa's, go to **CooksCountry.com/ninfas**. –BRYAN ROOF

A server gets a bite in before lunch service (top). The restaurant's facade is easily recognizable from the street (middle). A portrait of Mama Ninfa, the restaurant's founder and namesake, hangs in the dining room (bottom).

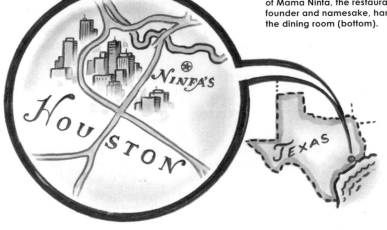

Strawberry Cornmeal Shortcakes

This Southern variation on the classic sounds charming, but getting the biscuits and filling just right was a challenge. BY ERIKA BRUCE

EVERYONE KNOWS STRAWBERRY shortcakes—light, fluffy biscuits split in half and served with sweet strawberry slices and billows of freshly whipped cream. But in the South, a version of this dessert boasts the ingenious addition of cornmeal to the biscuits. This not only gives them a sweet yet nutty flavor but also adds a delicate crunch, which nicely offsets the tender strawberry-and-cream filling.

You may think (as I did) the addition of cornmeal a straightforward technique, accomplished by simply replacing some of the flour in your favorite sweet biscuit recipe with an equal amount of cornmeal. Not so. Doing this resulted in dense, crumbly biscuits—a far cry from the lofty shortcakes they once were. I then realized that cornmeal shortcakes weren't just a variation on a classic recipe but required a recipe of their own.

I wasn't starting completely from scratch. Tucked away in our archives I found not one but two fabulous recipes for cornmeal biscuits. I made both—a roll-and-cut recipe that calls for cutting cold butter into the dry ingredients in a food processor and a drop biscuit recipe that incorporates melted butter. The drop-biscuit version was dead simple to make, and as a bonus, its lower ratio of cornmeal to flour (1:3 versus 1:2 for the other cornmeal biscuit recipes) reduced the sandiness that cornmeal can produce.

Still, I wanted more fluffiness. To get it, I added an egg to help produce a tender texture and reduced the amount of buttermilk to keep the biscuits from flattening out. A sprinkle of sugar on top of each biscuit before baking added a sweet, pleasant crunch. Once baked on a rimmed baking sheet (lined with parchment paper to prevent sticking), these tall, fluffy cornmeal shortcakes were nicely browned and ready for splitting and filling.

Strawberries for shortcakes are usually simply quartered, tossed with some sugar, and left to sit so the berries can release their juices and the sugar has time to dissolve and create a sweet syrup. But when I tried this, the quartered berries toppled right off the bis-

▶ Go to CooksCountry.com/bestcornmeal to read about our favorite cornmeal.

A bit of sugar sprinkled over each shortcake before baking provides a delicate, sweet crunch.

cuit; the few bites I did manage to catch with my fork tasted bland against the biscuit's sweet corn flavor. I tried mashing a portion of the berries and sugar and folding it back into the mix as a binder. While effective, this method was fussy. I next tried using strawberry jam as both the "glue" and the sweetener, but the cooked jam flavor canceled out the fresh berry taste. Finally, I decided on a more architectural approach—instead of quartering the berries, I sliced them thin. Now they formed a neatly stacked heap that balanced proudly on each biscuit half.

Final tweaks to the berries included a bit of lemon juice to add brightness and a small amount of salt, which amplified the sweet-tart berry flavor. Some sweetened whipped cream gave this country-style take on an American classic a final flourish.

KEY STEP **Macerating the Berries**
Tossing strawberries with sugar (along with lemon juice and a bit of salt) and leaving them to sit draws out moisture, which dissolves the sugar and creates a sweet, fruity syrup that coats the berries. To prevent the berries from tumbling off the biscuits, we slice them thin rather than halve or quarter them.

STRAWBERRY CORNMEAL SHORTCAKES

Serves 8

Because the sweetness level of strawberries can vary, taste the macerated berries and add up to 2 tablespoons of extra sugar, if needed. While the shortcakes are best served warm, the cooled cakes can be stored in a zipper-lock bag at room temperature for 24 hours. They will lose some of their crispness, but you can bring it back by warming them in a 300-degree oven for 10 minutes.

STRAWBERRIES

- 2 pounds strawberries, hulled and sliced thin (5 cups)
- ¼ cup (1¾ ounces) sugar, plus extra as needed
- 2 teaspoons lemon juice
- ⅛ teaspoon salt

SHORTCAKES

- 1½ cups (7½ ounces) all-purpose flour
- ½ cup (2½ ounces) stone-ground cornmeal
- ¼ cup (1¾ ounces) plus 1 tablespoon sugar
- 2 teaspoons baking powder
- ½ teaspoon baking soda
- ¾ teaspoon salt
- ⅔ cup buttermilk, chilled
- 1 large egg
- 8 tablespoons unsalted butter, melted and cooled

WHIPPED CREAM

- 1½ cups heavy cream, chilled
- 4 teaspoons sugar
- 1 teaspoon vanilla extract

1. FOR THE STRAWBERRIES: Gently toss all ingredients together in bowl and refrigerate for at least 30 minutes or up to 1 hour. Taste strawberry mixture for sweetness and add extra sugar if needed.

2. FOR THE SHORTCAKES: Meanwhile, adjust oven rack to middle position and heat oven to 425 degrees. Line rimmed baking sheet with parchment paper. Whisk flour, cornmeal, ¼ cup sugar, baking powder, baking soda, and salt together in large bowl. Whisk buttermilk and egg in separate bowl until combined; add melted butter and stir until butter forms clumps.

3. Add buttermilk mixture to flour mixture and stir with rubber spatula until just incorporated. Lightly spray ⅓-cup dry measuring cup with vegetable oil spray. Stagger 8 level portions of batter on prepared sheet, about 1½ inches apart. Sprinkle tops with remaining 1 tablespoon sugar. Bake until shortcakes are golden brown, about 14 minutes, rotating sheet halfway through baking. Transfer shortcakes to wire rack and let cool for at least 10 minutes.

4. FOR THE WHIPPED CREAM: Using stand mixer fitted with whisk attachment, whip cream, sugar, and vanilla on medium-low speed until foamy, about 1 minute. Increase speed to high and whip until stiff peaks form, 1 to 3 minutes.

5. Split each shortcake in half horizontally. Spoon ½ cup strawberry mixture over each shortcake bottom, followed by ⅓ cup whipped cream; top with shortcake tops. Serve, passing any remaining whipped cream separately.

The American Table
Strawberrying

"It would strengthen the social order if all men could take a two-quart lard pail on a sun-drenched, warm June day and go strawberrying. The countryman figures a two-quart pailful is a reasonable day's labor, and when he starts forth in mid-forenoon, he takes a couple slices of buttered homemade bread in his pocket. For lunch, he hulls a generous handful of berries and squeezes them between the bread slices."

–Haydn S. Pearson, *The Country Flavor Cookbook* (1956)

It's Supposed to Clump

When melted butter is added to the buttermilk mixture in step 2, it solidifies into clumps that will melt and release steam in the oven, creating light, airy biscuits.

ESSENTIAL GEAR
Parchment Paper

For this recipe, we like to line the baking sheet with parchment paper rather than grease it. The parchment guarantees that the buttery shortcakes won't stick and also makes cleanup a breeze. The test kitchen's favorite is **Reynolds Parchment Paper** (unbleached roll).

Should You Buy an Oil Mister?

Coating a muffin tin, a skillet, or a baking sheet with a spritz of our winning vegetable oil spray, PAM Original, is quick and easy. But PAM costs about $0.45 per ounce, compared with $0.07 per ounce for plain old canola oil. Refillable, manual-pump oil misters present an alternative for those who would like to avoid aerosol and additives, and you can fill them with whatever type of oil you like.

Like aerosol sprays, a good oil mister should dispense oil in a steady, fine stream that provides even coverage. We gathered seven models, priced from $9.90 to $25.99, including our former winner from Mastrad. All but one model featured a manual pumping mechanism to build the pressure that forces the oil out. The outlier looked like a bottle of cologne: a tall, thin glass cylinder that required no prepumping.

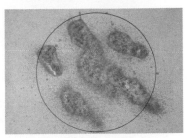

Choppy spraying means less control and uneven coverage.

We started by timing the duration and noting the quality of a single spray when each mister was full, half full, and one-third full. We then used the misters to grease our winning 12-inch skillet and 12-cup muffin tin. Next, to better understand each mister's spray, we traced a skillet onto brown butcher paper and sprayed the misters onto the outline. For comparison, we sprayed PAM alongside the misters in each test. What did we find out?

The quality of the spray was much more important than its duration. While some misters could sustain a long spray—up to 20 seconds—they sputtered and spat. So even though we held and moved each mister similarly, the butcher paper for some models looked like abstract oil paintings and didn't represent the

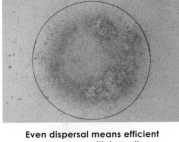

Even dispersal means efficient coverage with less oil.

even coverage we were after. The best mister sustained a shorter, 6-second spray, but it easily covered a skillet and muffin tin in just 3 seconds and covered the butcher paper with a fine, even mist. Lesser models (including the cologne-style bottle) dripped and dribbled, sprayed unevenly, or were hard to fill. The PAM sprayed beautifully every time.

Why couldn't the nonaerosol misters match PAM's perfect, even spray? Our science editor explained that aerosols contain a propellant that helps shoot out oil with more force than is possible in manual misters; the higher pressure breaks the oil into finer droplets, making it less viscous. PAM also contains soy lecithin, which coats the fine droplets of oil, making them easier to disperse to form an even coating. Without the propellant and soy lecithin, the oil is more difficult to spray and more apt to clump.

While none of the misters sprayed as evenly as the PAM, our old winner, the Mastrad Oil and Flavor Mister, came out on top again. Its full, consistent spray of oil most resembled that of an aerosol mister. Read the full story at **CooksCountry.com/may17**.

–SARAH SEITZ

KEY **Good ★★★   Fair ★★   Poor ★**

RECOMMENDED

MASTRAD Oil and Flavor Mister **Model:** A27300 **Price:** $17.29 **Dishwasher-Safe:** Top shelf only	Spray ★★½ Ease of Use ★★★	With its fine, even spray, this mister's performance came closest to that of PAM. Though its spray did not sustain a continuous stream as long as others, its wide, thorough spray quickly covered a skillet and all of the nooks and crannies of a muffin tin. It was also easy to fill and comfortable to hold.
NORPRO Hard Plastic and Stainless Steel Sprayer Mister **Model:** 793 **Price:** $10.70 **Dishwasher-Safe:** No	Spray ★★ Ease of Use ★★★	This model's thicker spray wasn't as fine or even as an aerosol can's, but it sustained a reasonably good, continuous stream for 14 seconds, giving us plenty of time to coat all types of pans. It was comfortable and easy to fill.

RECOMMENDED WITH RESERVATIONS

COLE & MASON Oil & Vinegar Mister **Model:** H103699U **Price:** $16.95 **Dishwasher-Safe:** Yes	Spray ★★ Ease of Use ★★½	Easy to fill and straightforward to use, this model sent forth a mix of medium and small droplets that left some blotches on the skillet. It lost points when its spray repeatedly dribbled down its front, dirtying our hands and making the mister slippery to hold.

Getting to Know Foraged Greens

Edible abundance is all around us, but you have to know what to look for and when and where to look. Here are some of our favorite foods that grow wild in urban, suburban, and rural environments. BY CHRISTIE MORRISON

Fiddlehead Ferns
GRASSY GOODNESS

The young, coiled shoots of several species of fern are a prized early-spring foraged food. They can be found in either your local woods or your local supermarket in the spring. No matter the source, they are delicate and highly perishable. Fiddleheads have a "grassy, nutty" flavor similar to those of asparagus and green beans. Wash them carefully before blanching them in boiling water, shocking them in an ice bath, and briefly sautéing them in butter.

Ramps
LEEKS GONE WILD

This pungent member of the onion genus (commonly known as ramps, wild leeks, or ramson) is a favorite ingredient in Appalachia, but foragers—and chefs—in temperate climates in all parts of the United States have taken notice of it as well. Both the leaves and the bulb can be eaten raw or cooked; ramps taste like a cross between a scallion and a yellow onion, with a strong, garlicky bite. We like to sauté them for soups, add them to egg dishes or stir-fries, or pickle them.

Dandelion Greens
LAWN ORNAMENT

The pesky yellow flowers of dandelion (*Taraxacum officinale*) can mar an otherwise pristine lawn, but this plant's flowers, stems, and serrated leaves are delicious (just take care not to harvest them from chemically treated lawns). The leaves, which are slightly bitter, can be cooked like other sturdy leafy greens, such as kale, or can be added to a salad as you would endive. Dandelion greens are traditionally tossed with hot bacon dressing, which softens their peppery, bitter edge.

Sea Beans
SUCCULENT SHOOTS

Sea beans are members of the genus *Salicornia* and grow in marshes and other saline environments. Also commonly known as glasswort, pickle weed, or saltwort, this plant's crunchy stems and salty flavor quickly bring to mind raw green beans or cucumbers, and like both vegetables, sea beans work well in pickled applications. The leaves and shoots of this succulent plant can be eaten raw and are also sturdy enough to stand up to stir-frying or steaming.

Nettle
VIOLENT OFFENDER

Though the nettle genus is made up of about 500 species, the variety most commonly used for culinary purposes is the stinging nettle (*Urtica dioica*). It's not hype: A network of hollow hairs on the leaves and stems really does sting. Fortunately, soaking or cooking nettles in water solves that problem. With a flavor similar to cucumber or spinach (or "an almost watermelon-like sweetness," according to one taster), nettles are often pureed into a pesto or cooked and served as a side dish. The leaves, which have a tannic quality, can be dried and brewed for tea.

Sassafras
CAJUN STAPLE

Sassafras leaves (*Sassafras albidum*) lend themselves to many applications, most notably when they're dried and ground into commercial filé powder, the ingredient commonly used in Creole and Cajun cooking to thicken dishes such as gumbo and étouffée. The raw leaves taste a bit like root beer, with a slightly sweet, candied flavor. Foragers can add young leaves and buds to salads or boil the tree's roots with some maple syrup to make sassafras tea.

Purslane
TASTY WEED

Purslane (*Portulaca oleracea*) grows all over the world but is native to Asia and is therefore a common ingredient in Indian and Middle Eastern cuisines; it is commonly known as pigweed in Australia and *verdolaga* in Mexico. Its leaves and stems are juicy and sweet with a slightly sour tang. Like those of sassafras, purslane's leaves have a slightly mucilaginous quality, so it is used to thicken soups and stews. You can find this persistent plant growing in sidewalk cracks in most parts of the United States.

Wood Sorrel
SHAMROCK IMPERSONATOR

Wood sorrel (*Oxalis acetosella*) is commonly called sourgrass for a reason: It's high in oxalic acid, which gives it a sour, tart, lemony flavor. The small, heart-shaped leaves appear in groups of three, so it's often mistaken for clover, a close relative. Wood sorrel's tang makes it a tasty complement to fish. However, because of its high concentration of oxalic acid, it can be toxic if eaten in large quantities, so go easy.

Sheep Sorrel
POINTY FELLOW

The leaves of wild sorrel (*Rumex acetosella*) look a bit like arugula—slightly elongated and pointed like a sword or spear and deep green in color. The smaller the leaf, the milder the flavor. The tender leaves lend their citrusy quality to sorrel soup, but they're also often used in omelets, salads, and herb sauces. Like wood sorrel, sheep sorrel is high in oxalic acid and should be eaten in moderation.

Lamb's Quarters
BITTER GREEN

This fast-growing plant, which is commonly known as lamb's quarters or goosefoot, belongs to the genus *Chenopodium*, which also includes plants widely used as food crops such as quinoa and spinach. It's easy to distinguish lamb's quarters from related plants, though, by the triangular leaves. Its bitter flavor can be easily mitigated by blanching; the cooked leaves are much milder.

Red Amaranth
CRIMSON CREEPER

The leaves of *Amaranthus* species range in color from green to red to gold to purple, making them popular ornamental garden plants. While it's commonly known as amaranth, this plant's other names include Chinese spinach and Joseph's coat. Used in Asian, African, and Caribbean cuisines as a leafy vegetable, red-leaved amaranth is slightly bitter; its leaves and stems can be steamed or sautéed.

Chickweed
GROUND ASSAULT

Chickweed (*Stellaria media*) grows in every corner of the world due to its tolerance of both heat and cold. The plant's flowers resemble stars, and the leaves and stems tangle into a ground cover. Add the leaves, which are soft and somewhat delicate, to salads for an earthy, grassy accent or cook the leaves and stems until just wilted—you don't want to overcook the crisp, juicy stems.

**CHICKEN THIGHS WITH GREEN BEANS
AND MUSTARD SAUCE**

FENNEL-CRUSTED PORK WITH WHITE BEANS

SESAME SALMON WITH GRAPEFRUIT SLAW

RICE NOODLE BOWL WITH PORK AND SCALLIONS

FENNEL-CRUSTED PORK WITH WHITE BEANS Serves 4

✔ **WHY THIS RECIPE WORKS:** Parmesan and full-bodied extra-virgin olive oil make these beans rich and creamy.

- 2 (12- to 16-ounce) pork tenderloins, trimmed
- 2 tablespoons fennel seeds
  Salt and pepper
- ¼ cup extra-virgin olive oil, plus extra for drizzling
- 4 garlic cloves, minced
- 2 (15-ounce) cans cannellini beans, rinsed
- 1 cup chicken broth
- 8 ounces cherry tomatoes, halved
- 2 ounces Parmesan cheese, grated (1 cup)
- 2 tablespoons chopped fresh basil

1. Adjust oven rack to middle position and heat oven to 450 degrees. Sprinkle pork with fennel seeds and season with salt and pepper, pressing to adhere. Heat 1 tablespoon oil in 12-inch skillet over medium-high heat until just smoking. Add pork and cook until browned on all sides, 5 to 7 minutes; transfer to rimmed baking sheet. Roast until pork registers 140 degrees, 14 to 18 minutes. Transfer to carving board, tent with foil, and let rest for 5 minutes.

2. Meanwhile, add 1 tablespoon oil and garlic to now-empty skillet and cook over medium-low heat until fragrant, about 30 seconds. Increase heat to medium; add beans, broth, ¼ teaspoon salt, and ¼ teaspoon pepper; and cook until slightly thickened, 5 to 7 minutes. Add tomatoes, Parmesan, and remaining 2 tablespoons oil and cook until creamy, about 2 minutes.

3. Transfer beans to shallow platter and drizzle with extra oil. Slice pork and place over beans. Sprinkle with basil and serve.

TEST KITCHEN NOTE: We recommend California Olive Ranch Everyday Extra Virgin Olive Oil.

CHICKEN THIGHS WITH GREEN BEANS AND MUSTARD SAUCE Serves 4

✔ **WHY THIS RECIPE WORKS:** We use the fat rendered from the chicken thighs as the base for a flavorful sauce.

- 8 (5- to 7-ounce) bone-in chicken thighs, trimmed
  Salt and pepper
- 3 tablespoons unsalted butter
- 1 pound green beans, trimmed
- 1 small shallot, minced
- 1 garlic clove, minced
- ½ cup dry white wine
- 3 tablespoons Dijon mustard

1. Adjust oven rack to middle position and heat oven to 450 degrees. Pat chicken dry with paper towels and season with salt and pepper. Melt 1 tablespoon butter in 12-inch skillet over medium-high heat. Add chicken and cook until browned on both sides, about 10 minutes. Transfer chicken, skin side up, to perimeter of rimmed baking sheet.

2. Add green beans to middle of sheet and sprinkle with ¼ teaspoon salt and ¼ teaspoon pepper. Bake until chicken registers 175 degrees and green beans are tender, about 15 minutes.

3. Meanwhile, pour off all but 1 tablespoon fat from skillet. Add shallot, garlic, ¼ teaspoon salt, and ⅛ teaspoon pepper and cook over medium heat until softened, about 2 minutes. Stir in wine and mustard, scraping up any browned bits, and simmer until slightly thickened, about 2 minutes. Off heat, whisk in remaining 2 tablespoons butter. Serve chicken and green beans with sauce.

TEST KITCHEN NOTE: Our favorite Dijon mustard is Trois Petits Cochons Moutarde de Dijon.

RICE NOODLE BOWL WITH PORK AND SCALLIONS Serves 4

✔ **WHY THIS RECIPE WORKS:** The sauce mixture not only adds flavor to the meat during cooking but also doubles as a vinaigrette for the noodles.

- 8 ounces rice vermicelli
- 5 tablespoons soy sauce
- 3 tablespoons toasted sesame oil
- 1½ tablespoons grated fresh ginger
- 3 garlic cloves, minced
- 1 English cucumber, cut into 2-inch-long matchsticks
- 2 tablespoons rice vinegar
- 1 pound ground pork
- 4 scallions, cut into 1-inch pieces
- ¼ cup fresh cilantro leaves

1. Bring 4 quarts water to boil in large pot. Off heat, add noodles and let sit until tender, about 5 minutes. Drain and rinse under cold water; set aside. Whisk soy sauce, 2 tablespoons oil, ginger, and garlic together in large bowl. Combine cucumber and vinegar in second bowl.

2. Heat remaining 1 tablespoon oil in 12-inch nonstick skillet over medium-high heat until shimmering. Add pork and cook, breaking up meat with wooden spoon, until browned, about 7 minutes. Stir in scallions and 2 tablespoons soy sauce mixture and cook until scallions have softened, about 2 minutes.

3. Add noodles to remaining soy sauce mixture and toss to combine. Divide noodles evenly among 4 bowls and top with pork, cucumber, and cilantro.

TEST KITCHEN NOTE: For best results, make sure to shake off all excess water from the noodles after rinsing them.

SESAME SALMON WITH GRAPEFRUIT SLAW Serves 4

✔ **WHY THIS RECIPE WORKS:** Starting the salmon in a cold pan allows the fat to render and the skin to crisp.

- 1 red grapefruit
- ½ head napa cabbage, sliced thin (5½ cups)
- 3 carrots, peeled and shredded
- 3 scallions, sliced thin
- ¼ cup vegetable oil
- 3 tablespoons rice vinegar
- 1 jalapeño, halved, seeded, and sliced thin
- 2 tablespoons sesame seeds
  Salt and pepper
- 4 (6-ounce) center-cut skin-on salmon fillets, 1¼ inches thick

1. Cut away peel and pith from grapefruit and cut into quarters. Slice quarters crosswise into ¼-inch–thick pieces.

2. Combine grapefruit, cabbage, carrots, scallions, oil, vinegar, jalapeño, 1 tablespoon sesame seeds, ½ teaspoon salt, and ¼ teaspoon pepper in large bowl; set aside.

3. Season salmon with salt and pepper. Sprinkle flesh sides of fillets evenly with remaining 1 tablespoon sesame seeds. Arrange salmon skin side down in 12-inch nonstick skillet. Place skillet over medium-high heat and cook until fat from skin renders and skin becomes crispy, about 7 minutes. Flip salmon and continue to cook until centers are still translucent when checked with tip of paring knife and register 125 degrees (for medium-rare), about 7 minutes longer. Serve salmon with slaw.

TEST KITCHEN NOTE: You can use either white or black sesame seeds or a combination of the two. Shred the carrots on the large holes of a box grater.

SPINACH-STUFFED PORTOBELLO CAPS

CHIPOTLE CHICKEN CAESAR SALAD

ROAST BEEF PANINI

STEAK TIPS WITH SPICY CAULIFLOWER

CHIPOTLE CHICKEN CAESAR SALAD Serves 4

✔ **WHY THIS RECIPE WORKS:** Lime juice brightens this southwestern-inspired Caesar.

- 3 tablespoons extra-virgin olive oil
- 2 garlic cloves, minced
  Salt and pepper
- 2 slices hearty white sandwich bread, cut into ½-inch cubes (4 cups)
- 4 (6-ounce) boneless, skinless chicken breasts, trimmed
- ¾ cup creamy Caesar salad dressing
- 2 tablespoons minced chipotle chile in adobo sauce
- 1 tablespoon lime juice
- 3 romaine lettuce hearts (18 ounces), torn into bite-size pieces
- 1 ripe avocado, halved, pitted, and cut into ½-inch cubes

1. Combine 2 tablespoons oil, garlic, and ½ teaspoon salt in large bowl. Add bread and toss to coat. Transfer bread to 12-inch nonstick skillet set over medium heat and cook, stirring often, until golden brown, about 5 minutes. Transfer to plate.

2. Pat chicken dry with paper towels and season with salt and pepper. Heat remaining 1 tablespoon oil in now-empty skillet over medium-high heat until just smoking. Add chicken and cook until golden brown and meat registers 160 degrees, about 6 minutes per side. Transfer chicken to carving board, tent with foil, and let rest for 5 minutes.

3. Stir dressing, chipotle, and lime juice together in now-empty bowl. Add lettuce and croutons and toss to coat; season with salt and pepper to taste. Transfer salad to serving dish. Slice chicken thin and arrange over salad. Sprinkle avocado over top and serve.

TEST KITCHEN NOTE: If you want a milder salad, use only 1 tablespoon of chipotle.

SPINACH-STUFFED PORTOBELLO CAPS Serves 4

✔ **WHY THIS RECIPE WORKS:** Panko bread crumbs make a quick and easy filling base.

- 8 large portobello mushroom caps, gills removed
- 5 tablespoons extra-virgin olive oil, plus extra for drizzling
  Salt and pepper
- 1½ cups panko bread crumbs
- 4 garlic cloves, minced
- 11 ounces (11 cups) baby spinach
- 7 ounces feta cheese, crumbled (1¾ cups)
- 1 teaspoon grated lemon zest
- ¼ cup fresh mint leaves, torn

1. Adjust oven racks to upper-middle and lower-middle positions and heat oven to 475 degrees. Rub mushrooms with 3 tablespoons oil and season with salt and pepper. Arrange mushrooms gill side down on rimmed baking sheet and roast on lower rack until tender, about 15 minutes.

2. Combine panko, garlic, ¼ teaspoon salt, ¼ teaspoon pepper, and remaining 2 tablespoons oil in large Dutch oven. Set pot over medium heat and cook, stirring constantly, until panko is lightly browned, about 2 minutes. Stir in spinach and cook until wilted, about 5 minutes. Off heat, stir in 1 cup feta and lemon zest.

3. Flip mushrooms gill side up and distribute filling evenly among them. Sprinkle remaining ¾ cup feta over top and bake on upper rack until feta starts to brown, about 8 minutes. Drizzle with extra oil, sprinkle with mint, and serve.

TEST KITCHEN NOTE: Use a spoon to remove the gills from the mushroom caps.

STEAK TIPS WITH SPICY CAULIFLOWER Serves 4

✔ **WHY THIS RECIPE WORKS:** We toss the still-warm cauliflower with the relish to help it better absorb the flavors.

- ½ cup jarred roasted red peppers, patted dry and chopped
- 5 tablespoons extra-virgin olive oil
- ¼ cup pickled cherry peppers, minced
- 2 tablespoons chopped fresh parsley
- 1 tablespoon capers, rinsed and minced
  Salt and pepper
- 1 large head cauliflower (3 pounds), cored and cut into 1-inch pieces
- 2 pounds sirloin steak tips, trimmed and cut into 2-inch pieces

1. Combine red peppers, 3 tablespoons oil, cherry peppers, parsley, capers, ¼ teaspoon salt, and ⅛ teaspoon pepper in large bowl; set relish aside.

2. Heat 1 tablespoon oil in 12-inch nonstick skillet over medium-high heat until shimmering. Add cauliflower and cook, covered, stirring occasionally, until browned and tender, about 10 minutes. Add cauliflower to relish and toss to combine. Season with salt and pepper to taste.

3. Pat steak dry with paper towels and season with salt and pepper. Add remaining 1 tablespoon oil to now-empty skillet and heat over medium-high heat until just smoking. Add steak and cook until browned on all sides and meat registers 125 degrees (for medium-rare), about 7 minutes. Serve steak with cauliflower.

TEST KITCHEN NOTE: Our favorite roasted red peppers are Dunbars Sweet Roasted Peppers. Sirloin steak tips are often sold as flap meat.

ROAST BEEF PANINI Serves 4

✔ **WHY THIS RECIPE WORKS:** Weighing down the sandwiches with a heavy Dutch oven makes these panini possible without a panini press.

- ¼ cup plus 4 teaspoons mayonnaise
- 1 tablespoon spicy brown mustard
- 1 tablespoon prepared horseradish, drained
  Salt and pepper
- 2 cups (5½ ounces) shredded green coleslaw mix
- ½ small red onion, sliced thin
- 8 slices hearty pumpernickel rye sandwich bread
- 8 thin slices deli smoked gouda cheese (4 ounces)
- 8 ounces thinly sliced deli roast beef
- ½ cup dill pickle chips, patted dry

1. Combine ¼ cup mayonnaise, mustard, horseradish, ¼ teaspoon salt, and ¼ teaspoon pepper in large bowl. Add coleslaw mix and onion; toss to combine and set aside.

2. Brush 1 side of each slice of bread with ½ teaspoon mayonnaise and arrange, mayonnaise side down, on cutting board. Divide gouda, roast beef, pickles, and coleslaw mixture among 4 slices of bread. Top with remaining bread, mayonnaise side up.

3. Heat grill pan or large nonstick skillet over medium heat for 1 minute. Place 2 sandwiches in pan and weigh down with Dutch oven. Cook until exteriors are golden brown and cheese is melted, about 2 minutes per side. Repeat with remaining 2 sandwiches. Serve.

TEST KITCHEN NOTE: Buy refrigerated prepared horseradish, not the shelf-stable kind, which contains preservatives and additives.

Spinach Pie

We wanted to find a quick route to this creamy, buttery, savory party favorite.

BY KATIE LEAIRD

I'VE LONG LOVED Greek spana-kopita—layers of phyllo dough wrapped around a filling of eggs, spinach, and salty feta cheese. But until recently I'd never tasted its Albanian cousin, which features a similar look but a more subtle, creamier spinach filling. Albanian-style spinach pie is common at parties and street festivals in many towns with Albanian American communities, including Worcester, Massachusetts. It's wonderful.

I started with a handwritten heirloom recipe from a coworker's collection. Following it closely, I made a dough of water, flour, and salt; rolled it out very thin; and spread on an even layer of softened butter. Then I rolled the buttered dough up into a tight log, trapping the fat inside, a process called "laminating." I chilled it, rolled it paper-thin again, and wrapped it around some spinach filling. I marveled at the impressive final product, but the process was very time-consuming.

Could I skip this lengthy process altogether by employing frozen dough from the grocery store? Unlike many prefab convenience products, dough is a true success story of the freezer chest. I bypassed phyllo because it's so delicate and fussy, instead focusing on more-forgiving puff pastry. Once thawed, rolled thin, and layered with spinach filling, it baked up with a buttery, flaky, golden-brown crust.

To create the creamy spinach filling, I first made a béchamel (a milk-based sauce thickened with cooked flour and fat). I added some shallots and garlic to boost the flavor, as well as some Parmesan cheese. I used thawed and drained frozen spinach (another freezer-section winner) to avoid cooking down masses of fresh leaves. I made sure to let the mixture cool completely before assembling the pie so as not to melt the butter-laden dough.

I wanted enough for a crowd, so I assembled my pie on a rectangular rimmed baking sheet. I marked the crust with a light cut through the top dough before baking. As the pie baked, the spinach began to peek through the slashes and the puff pastry puffed, showing off its layers.

My tasters were thrilled with the creamy, buttery, savory, thoroughly satisfying result and deemed it party-ready. All we needed now was a party.

SPINACH PIE FOR A CROWD
Serves 10 to 12

To thaw frozen puff pastry, let it sit in the refrigerator for 24 hours or on the counter for 30 minutes to 1 hour. Make sure the filling has cooled completely before assembling the pie.

- 2 tablespoons unsalted butter
- 2 shallots, minced
- 4 garlic cloves, minced
- ¼ cup all-purpose flour
- 1½ cups whole milk
- 3 ounces Parmesan cheese, grated (1½ cups)
- 20 ounces frozen whole-leaf spinach, thawed and squeezed dry
- 1 teaspoon salt
- ½ teaspoon pepper
- 2 (9½ by 9-inch) sheets puff pastry, thawed
- 1 large egg, lightly beaten

1. Melt butter in medium saucepan over medium heat. Add shallots and garlic and cook until softened, about 2 minutes. Stir in flour and cook until golden, about 30 seconds. Slowly whisk in milk and bring to simmer. Cook, stirring constantly, until thickened, about 3 minutes.

2. Off heat, stir in Parmesan until melted. Stir in spinach, salt, and pepper until combined. Transfer spinach mixture to bowl and let cool completely.

3. Adjust oven rack to lower-middle position and heat oven to 400 degrees. Grease rimmed baking sheet. Roll 1 puff pastry sheet into 14 by 10-inch rectangle on lightly floured counter. Loosely roll dough around rolling pin and unroll it onto prepared sheet. Spread spinach mixture evenly over dough, leaving ½-inch border. Brush border with egg.

4. Roll remaining puff pastry sheet into 14 by 10-inch inch rectangle on lightly floured counter. Loosely roll dough around rolling pin and unroll it over filling. Press edges of top and bottom sheets together to seal. Roll edge inward and use your fingers to crimp edge. Using sharp knife, cut top dough into 24 squares. Brush top dough evenly with egg.

5. Bake until crust is golden brown, 30 to 35 minutes. Transfer sheet to wire rack and let pie cool completely, about 30 minutes. Transfer pie to cutting board and cut along lines. Serve.

A brush of beaten egg helps this impressive pie achieve a beautifully golden-brown top.

TEST KITCHEN TECHNIQUES
Wringing out the Spinach
To dry the spinach, place the thawed leaves in the center of a clean dish towel, gather the ends of the towel, and twist firmly to remove excess moisture.

Making Cutting Guides
Once the pie is assembled, use a sharp knife to cut through the top layer of dough to create 24 pieces. When cutting to serve, use the marks as guidelines.

Pork Milanese

Our aim: crunchy, tender, perfect pan-fried pork.

BY ASHLEY MOORE

A little grated Parmesan in the crunchy coating adds extra savoriness to the cutlets.

TEST KITCHEN TECHNIQUE
Pounding the Cutlets
Be sure to use gentle, even pressure when fashioning cutlets with a meat pounder. An overly aggressive approach will result in cutlets with raggedy edges and uneven thickness.

TEST KITCHEN TIP
Keeping Cutlets Warm
Using tongs, blot the cutlets on a paper towel–lined plate to wick off any extra oil, and then transfer them to a wire rack set in a baking sheet to keep warm in a low oven while you cook the second batch.

IN ITALIAN AMERICAN restaurants, chicken, pork, or veal cutlets that are served Milanese-style are generally floured, coated with bread crumbs, and then fried until the crumbs are crispy and golden brown.

The test kitchen's tried-and-true method for breading cutlets begins with a dredge in flour and a dunk in some lightly beaten eggs before a coating of bread crumbs that have been seasoned with salt and pepper. We then shallow-fry the cutlets in a bit of oil until they're golden brown. For our Pork Milanese recipe, I added parsley, lemon zest, and Parmesan cheese to the bread-crumb mixture to give our cutlets freshness, brightness, and a bit of that unmistakable Parmesan savoriness.

I wanted pork that was easy to cut through, not the tough and leathery cutlets I have encountered so often in restaurants. After trying pounded pork chops and pork loin, I found a winner: pork tenderloin, cut into four pieces and pounded thin. It was easy to work with, handling the breading and pan frying well, and it cooked up tender. Since I couldn't fit all four pieces of tenderloin in a 12-inch skillet at once, I worked in batches and relied on a low 200-degree oven to keep the cooked pork warm.

Traditionally, pork Milanese is served with a dressed arugula salad topped with a handful of shaved Parmesan. Since I wasn't about to mess with tradition, I followed suit, tossing a bowlful of baby arugula with a vibrant lemon vinaigrette and sprinkling the salad with some shaved Parmesan. I placed the crispy, golden-brown cutlets alongside the salad and called down my team to taste. Immediately I heard comments like "I want this on a sandwich" and "imagine this with pasta." But then I heard the best, most rewarding question of all: "Can I take the rest home for my family?" Of course you can.

PORK MILANESE
Serves 4
Traditionally, this dish is served with a dressed arugula salad, but you can serve it with pasta or potatoes if you prefer.

- 1 tablespoon plus 1 cup olive oil
- ½ teaspoon grated lemon zest plus 2 teaspoons juice plus lemon wedges for serving
  Salt and pepper
- 1 (12- to 16-ounce) pork tenderloin, trimmed
- ½ cup all-purpose flour
- 2 large eggs
- 1 cup panko bread crumbs
- ¼ cup grated Parmesan cheese, plus 1 ounce shaved with vegetable peeler
- 2 tablespoons chopped fresh parsley
- 4 ounces (4 cups) baby arugula

1. Adjust oven rack to lower-middle position and heat oven to 200 degrees. Whisk 1 tablespoon oil, lemon juice, ¼ teaspoon salt, and ¼ teaspoon pepper together in bowl; set dressing aside.

2. Cut tenderloin crosswise into 4 equal pieces. Stand pieces cut side up on cutting board, cover with plastic wrap, and pound with meat pounder to even ¼-inch thickness. Pat cutlets dry with paper towels and season with pepper.

3. Place flour in shallow dish. Lightly beat eggs in second shallow dish. Combine panko, grated Parmesan, parsley, lemon zest, ½ teaspoon salt, and ½ teaspoon pepper in third shallow dish.

4. Working with 1 cutlet at a time, dredge cutlets in flour, shaking off excess; dip in eggs, allowing excess to drip off; and coat with panko mixture, pressing gently to adhere. Transfer to large plate.

5. Set wire rack in rimmed baking sheet. Line large plate with triple layer of paper towels. Heat remaining 1 cup oil in 12-inch nonstick skillet over medium-high heat until shimmering. Place 2 cutlets in skillet and cook until deep golden brown and cooked through, 2 to 3 minutes per side, gently pressing on cutlets with spatula to ensure even browning.

6. Transfer cutlets to prepared plate and let drain on each side for 15 seconds, then transfer to prepared rack and place rack in oven to keep cutlets warm. Repeat with remaining 2 cutlets.

7. Just before serving, gently toss arugula with shaved Parmesan and dressing. Serve pork with salad, passing lemon wedges separately.

TO MAKE AHEAD
At end of step 4, cutlets can be wrapped in plastic wrap and refrigerated for up to 2 hours before frying.

Bacon-Braised Red Potatoes

To get crispy bacon and soft potatoes in one pan, we had to flip the script.

BY ALLI BERKEY

BACON AND POTATOES make a happy pair. For this simple side dish, I wanted to pair faintly browned potatoes and impossibly deep bacon flavor. After roasting, boiling, and frying my way through several existing recipes claiming to have strong bacon flavor, I determined that braising—cooking in a closed, moist environment—was the way to go.

Those early tests also showed me that while Yukon Gold, fingerling, and russet potatoes had their merits, red potatoes gave me the best-tasting results. What's more, they looked great, too.

When we braise meat in the test kitchen, we usually begin by browning it over direct heat. We then add liquid, cover the pot, and finish it over a more modest heat. This method gives us soft, tender results with lovely brown edges. But when I tried it with halved red potatoes, the brown edges just turned soggy and sad. I decided to flip the script and start by braising the potatoes in a covered skillet along with cut-up bacon and sliced onion for flavor. Then, once the spuds had almost cooked through, I poured off the liquid and browned them in the same skillet with a bit of oil. Delicious—but not bacon-y enough for my tasters.

I wondered if I was sacrificing flavor by pouring off that liquid, so for my next test, once the potatoes were just tender, I removed the lid and cranked up the heat. After about 10 minutes, the water had cooked off, leaving behind plenty of flavorful bacon fat. That's when the sizzle began, and about 5 minutes later I had evenly cooked potatoes with deep bacon flavor and brown edges, plus bits of crispy bacon and browned onions. A little fresh thyme and some salt and pepper finished this dead-simple side.

Our two-step stovetop method leaves the potatoes creamy on the inside, with brown exteriors.

BACON-BRAISED RED POTATOES
Serves 4

For the best results, use potatoes that measure about 1½ inches in diameter.

- 1½ pounds small red potatoes, unpeeled, halved
- 2½ cups water
- 1 onion, halved and sliced ½ inch thick
- 2 slices thick-cut bacon, cut into 1-inch pieces
  Salt and pepper
- 2 teaspoons chopped fresh thyme

1. Arrange potatoes cut side down in single layer in 12-inch nonstick skillet. Add water, onion, bacon, ¼ teaspoon salt, and ¼ teaspoon pepper. Bring to simmer over medium-high heat. Reduce heat to medium, cover, and simmer until potatoes are just tender, 18 to 20 minutes.

2. Uncover skillet and increase heat to medium-high. Simmer vigorously until water has nearly evaporated and potatoes begin to sizzle, about 10 minutes. Continue to cook, stirring occasionally, until potatoes and onion are spotty brown and bacon has rendered completely, 5 to 7 minutes longer. Off heat, stir in thyme and season with salt and pepper to taste. Serve.

Potato Primer
Potatoes can generally be divided into three types based on their starch content.

DRY AND CRUMBLY
Russet, Idaho
Also known as "baking" potatoes, these spuds contains more total starch (from 20 to 22 percent) than other types of potatoes, which gives them a dry, mealy texture.

IN BETWEEN
Yukon Gold, Yellow Finn
With starch levels of 18 to 20 percent, these potatoes are more mealy than firm. On the plus side, they have a buttery flavor and thin skins.

FIRM AND WAXY
Red Bliss, Fingerling, Red Creamer
These potatoes contain a relatively low amount of total starch (from 16 to 18 percent) and are firm and waxy. They offer a subtly sweet flavor and thin skins.

Shrimp Rémoulade

New Orleans restaurants serve boatloads of this seafood starter. Could we re-create the dish outside the city limits? BY MORGAN BOLLING

ROAMING AROUND THE French Quarter in New Orleans, you're almost certain to come across Arnaud's Restaurant, a sprawling establishment spanning almost a full block and housing an extensive collection of Mardi Gras costumes alongside the main dining room. Arnaud's is legendary for many reasons, including its iconic version of one of the city's most beloved dishes: shrimp rémoulade, an appetizer of poached shrimp tossed with a creamy, zesty sauce and perched on a bed of lettuce.

But since I can't get to New Orleans as often as I'd like, I wanted an easy version to make at home. I started by trying out six recipes from a mix of New Orleans greats, including Paul Prudhomme and John Folse. They were delicious, but they had mile-long ingredient lists and time-consuming steps such as making homemade mayonnaise. I wanted an easier way.

My research revealed just how varied rémoulade sauces are. There are two main types: white and red (really more pink than red). The former is similar to tartar sauce, with a mayonnaise base that's amped up with herbs and pickles or capers. The more common red kind gets its color from ketchup and/or paprika. Both are boldly seasoned with vinegar or citrus, Creole mustard (a vibrant, spicy Louisiana specialty), spices, and usually the "Cajun trinity" of bell peppers, celery, and onion. It often has a pleasant—but not overwhelming—kick.

I opted to go with a red rémoulade, deciding that its potent personality would pair well with the relatively mild shrimp. To keep things simple, I started

> ▶ We had this dish in Alabama. Go to CooksCountry.com/ alabama for details.

with store-bought mayonnaise mixed with a few squirts of lemon juice; I found its citrusy punch preferable to vinegar. Since Creole mustard is hard to find outside of New Orleans, I substituted a combo of spicy brown mustard and potent horseradish. I also experimented with cayenne and hot sauce, eventually choosing the former since it contributed heat without extra acidity. In a nod to the Cajun trinity, a mix of chopped green bell pepper, scallions, and celery added vegetal crunch while ketchup and paprika contributed the traditional red color. A little Worcestershire

Our doctored mayonnaise makes a worthy stand-in for fully homemade rémoulade sauce.

and garlic offered savory depth while cornichons, though more common in white rémoulade, supplied a briny element that brought the sauce together.

To poach the shrimp (I chose jumbo shrimp since I wanted this to be an elegant, eye-catching starter), I borrowed a technique from the test kitchen's recipe for shrimp salad that eliminates any chance that the meat will turn tough. In that recipe, we start the shrimp in a pot of cold water with a handful of aromatics (like fresh thyme and black peppercorns) and bring the water to 170 degrees. Then we kill the heat and cover the pot until the shrimp turn pink and perfectly tender, which takes about 5 minutes. Finally, we shock the shrimp under cold water to stop the cooking. The result?

Perfectly tender shrimp. After testing the method myself, I ditched the aromatics from the cooking liquid, finding that my vibrant rémoulade covered up any flavor they added.

I put a batch of my shrimp rémoulade into the fridge and sampled it again an hour later with a fresh palate. It tasted even better. A subsequent side-by-side matchup confirmed that letting the shrimp hang out in the sauce for a while was the right move. It gave the bright, authentically flavored rémoulade sauce plenty of time to permeate the mild seafood, resulting in a more balanced flavor.

New Orleans, I will see you soon. But in the meantime, I'll get my "remy" at home.

SHRIMP RÉMOULADE
Serves 4

We prefer shrimp not treated with sodium or preservatives such as sodium tripolyphosphate (STPP). Most frozen E-Z peel shrimp have been treated (the ingredient list should tell you). If using treated shrimp, reduce the salt in step 1 to ½ teaspoon.

SHRIMP
- 1½ pounds jumbo shrimp (16 to 20 per pound), peeled, deveined, and tails removed
  Salt and pepper

RÉMOULADE
- ⅔ cup mayonnaise
- ¼ cup finely chopped celery
- ¼ cup finely chopped green bell pepper
- 3 tablespoons minced cornichons
- 2 scallions, sliced thin
- 1 tablespoon lemon juice
- 1½ teaspoons prepared horseradish, drained
- 1 teaspoon spicy brown mustard
- 1 teaspoon ketchup
- 1 garlic clove, minced
- ½ teaspoon paprika
- ½ teaspoon Worcestershire sauce
- ¼ teaspoon salt
- ¼ teaspoon pepper
- ⅛ teaspoon cayenne pepper

- ½ head Bibb lettuce (4 ounces), leaves separated and torn
  Lemon wedges
  Hot sauce

1. FOR THE SHRIMP: Combine 3 cups cold water, shrimp, and 1½ teaspoons salt in Dutch oven. Set pot over medium-high heat and cook, stirring occasionally, until water registers 170 degrees and shrimp are just beginning to turn pink, 5 to 7 minutes.

2. Remove pot from heat, cover, and let sit until shrimp are completely pink and firm, about 5 minutes. Drain shrimp in colander. Rinse shrimp under cold water, then pat dry with paper towels. Transfer shrimp to large bowl and refrigerate until ready to use.

3. FOR THE RÉMOULADE: Combine all ingredients in bowl.

4. Fold rémoulade into shrimp until combined. Season with salt and pepper to taste. Cover and refrigerate to let flavors blend, about 1 hour. Serve over lettuce with lemon wedges and hot sauce.

Spinach and Strawberry Salad

We wanted a satisfying but not too sweet version of this springtime classic.

BY DIANE UNGER

SPINACH AND STRAWBERRY salad has been popular for generations, served in various forms in high-end restaurants and fast food drive-throughs alike. But when I made a few versions in the test kitchen following existing published recipes, my tasters and I had a hard time understanding why. Baby spinach leaves and sliced strawberries on their own are just fine, of course, but once paired and tossed with a thick, viscous, sweet poppy seed dressing, the pairing becomes a clumpy, cloying mess. This dish needed a facelift.

To start my salad reboot, I decided to cut back on the spinach, which can verge on chalky when the leaves are eaten raw. Instead I swapped crisp, fresh chopped romaine for half the spinach. I then looked at different ways to prepare the strawberries—quartered, halved, or sliced? Sugared or salted? I settled on quartered berries, which my tasters found easiest to eat, and no salt or sugar, since good strawberries don't need either. I bumped up the berries from the usual 1 or 2 cups to a full pound so that there'd be berries in every bite.

Many of the recipes I tried featured extra ingredients, including red onion, toasted nuts, and even cucumber. We decided to skip watery cucumber, but my tasters voted to keep nuts in the mix—specifically, toasted sliced almonds. And to temper the bite of raw onion, I opted to partially soften the slices in a bit of warmed-up vinegar mixed with sugar and salt.

The real work started when I began testing the poppy seed dressing. I wanted to honor the spirit of the original (see "Department-Store Gourmet") but tone down its sweetness. Starting from scratch, I whisked together a simple vinaigrette of red wine vinegar, salt, a bit of sugar, and vegetable oil, hoping the oil's neutral, mild flavor would allow the strawberries to shine. I just needed poppy seeds. But why? Whatever flavor they have—and it isn't much—was indiscernible in the salad. To see if I could coax some flavor out of the tiny seeds, I turned to a method we often use for sesame seeds: toasting them, lightly and quickly, in a skillet. It worked. The trick brought out a nutty, pleasant flavor that subtly permeated the salad dressing.

I tossed the sweet-sour dressing with the spinach, romaine, toasted almonds, pickled onions, and quartered strawberries and called my team over for a taste. The consensus: victory. My salad had a mix of crisp, vibrant greens; softly sweet berries; the faint bite of barely pickled onion; notes of deep toasted almond flavor; and a light but flavorful dressing.

SPINACH AND STRAWBERRY SALAD WITH POPPY SEED DRESSING
Serves 4 to 6

Poppy seeds are dark, so it's hard to see when they're fully toasted. Instead, use your nose: They should smell nutty. The pickled onions can be refrigerated, covered, for up to two days.

- ½ cup red wine vinegar
- ⅓ cup sugar
- Salt and pepper
- ½ red onion, sliced thin
- 1 tablespoon poppy seeds
- ½ cup sliced almonds
- ¼ cup vegetable oil
- 1 teaspoon dry mustard
- 1 pound strawberries, hulled and quartered (2½ cups)
- 1 romaine lettuce heart (6 ounces), torn into bite-size pieces
- 5 ounces (5 cups) baby spinach

1. Whisk vinegar, sugar, and ¾ teaspoon salt together in bowl. Transfer ¼ cup vinegar mixture to small bowl and microwave until hot, about 1 minute. Add onion, stir to combine, and let sit for at least 30 minutes.

2. Meanwhile, toast poppy seeds in 8-inch nonstick skillet over medium heat until fragrant and slightly darkened, 1 to 2 minutes; transfer to bowl and set aside. Add almonds to now-empty skillet, return to medium heat, and toast until fragrant and golden, 3 to 5 minutes.

3. Whisk oil, mustard, poppy seeds, and ½ teaspoon pepper into remaining vinegar mixture. Combine strawberries, lettuce, spinach, and ¼ cup almonds in large bowl. Using fork, remove onions from vinegar mixture and add to salad. Add dressing to salad and toss to combine. Season with salt and pepper to taste. Transfer salad to serving platter and top with remaining ¼ cup almonds. Serve.

Quick-pickled red onions provide a sharp counterpoint to the sweet strawberries.

INGREDIENT SPOTLIGHT
Poppy Seeds

Tiny in size and bluish-gray in color, poppy seeds have a mild nuttiness that can be hard to detect—unless you enhance it via toasting. Although the seeds are dark, they will turn a darker shade as they toast. However, the real cue that they are done is when a nutty fragrance starts to waft up from the skillet.

WE PROPOSE A TOAST
Toast poppy seeds in a dry skillet to bring out their nutty flavor.

The American Table
Department-Store Gourmet

In the 1960s, no lunchroom in Houston, Texas, was considered more glamorous than the café at the Neiman Marcus department store, where food service director Helen Corbitt held court. It was there that she created the poppy seed dressing that inspired our recipe's version. Her version is still on the store café's menu today.

Carrot Cake Cookies

Sweet, juicy carrots are ideal for tender cakes, but their moisture hampered our quest for a chewy cookie.

BY KATIE LEAIRD

IMAGINE EVERYTHING YOU love about carrot cake: warm spices, sweet raisins, toasted walnuts, and bright orange carrots. Now imagine these ingredients in a cookie. It sounded like a great idea until I pulled my first batch out of the oven and watched smiles transform into frowns. My tasters uttered descriptors including "healthy" and "muffin-like," both of which are devastating to a pastry chef's ears.

What's more, tasters were confused by this first batch's cake-like texture. I know, "cake" is literally in the title of this recipe. But I wanted this to be unmistakably a cookie—with a discernible differentiation between a crispy edge and a yielding center—while maintaining the elements of carrot cake.

My first remedy was switching from oil, the fat traditionally called for in carrot cake, to melted butter, which promotes chewiness. And while I associate the molasses flavor of brown sugar with carrot cake, I found that using it as the sole sweetener produced a cookie that was too soft. To fix this and to give my cookies crispier edges, I substituted granulated sugar for some of the brown. I was on the right track.

My cookies were now acting more like cookies, but they still had cakey centers. Feeling like I was almost out of tricks, I researched the reasons why our fore-chefs started baking with carrots in the first place. First, you could grow them in your own garden. Second, they were naturally sweet. And third, they had plenty of moisture. Back when ingredients like sugar were scarce and prohibitively expensive, getting sweetness and moisture on the cheap from a vegetable made sense. But was all that extra moisture helping or harming my cookie recipe now?

As carrots cook, they release water, which becomes steam. This steam, much like the carbon dioxide produced by baking soda, results in an airy, cakey texture. That's just what you want in a cake, but in a cookie? It all became clear: I had to extract the excess liquid from the carrots before incorporating them into the cookie dough.

I tried cooking grated carrots in a

▶ For our Carrot Cupcakes recipe, go to CooksCountry.com/carrotcupcakes.

Tangy cream cheese frosting and crunchy chopped walnuts make these cookies a test kitchen favorite.

skillet, but they started to shrivel up and lose their flavor. When I wrung shredded carrots out in a dish towel, hardly any liquid escaped. More moisture was released when I microwaved the shredded carrots before wringing them out. But the most effective method turned out to be salting and sugaring the carrots—a test kitchen trick that draws water out of vegetables—before wringing them out. I

was happily baffled when I collected more than ¼ cup of liquid from 2 cups of shredded carrots, and I was ecstatic when the resulting cookies turned out perfectly chewy.

To my mind, the very best part of carrot cake is the sweet-tangy cream cheese frosting. Why should these cookies go without? I combined butter, sugar, cream cheese, and just a bit of vanilla in my stand mixer, beating the

ingredients until the frosting was light and fluffy. I smeared a healthy dollop of frosting over each cookie, covering them lavishly to ensure that there was frosting in every bite. I sprinkled chopped walnuts on top for a final bit of crunch and then set the cookies out in the crowded test kitchen.

Before I knew it, they'd all disappeared, and my fellow cooks were asking for more.

KEY STEPS Carrot Prep

Three simple steps enhance natural sweetness and eliminate excess moisture.

1. SHRED
Using the shredding disk of a food processor makes quick work of grating the carrots.

2. SALT/SUGAR
Tossing the carrots with salt and sugar and letting them sit helps pull out excess moisture.

3. SQUEEZE
Wringing the carrots in a dish towel (you should expel about ¼ cup of liquid) gets them as dry as possible.

CARROT CAKE COOKIES
Makes 24 cookies

Grate the carrots using the shredding disk of a food processor or on the large holes of a box grater (the Rösle Coarse Grater is our favorite). Do not use packaged preshredded carrots.

COOKIES
- 12 ounces carrots, peeled and shredded (2 cups)
- 1 teaspoon granulated sugar, plus ½ cup (3½ ounces)
- Salt
- 2 cups (10 ounces) all-purpose flour
- 1 teaspoon ground cinnamon
- ½ teaspoon baking soda
- ½ teaspoon ground nutmeg
- 1 cup packed (7 ounces) light brown sugar
- 12 tablespoons unsalted butter, melted and cooled
- 1 large egg plus 1 large yolk
- 2 teaspoons vanilla extract
- 1¾ cups walnuts, toasted and chopped coarse
- ¾ cup golden raisins

FROSTING
- 6 tablespoons unsalted butter, softened
- 1½ cups (6 ounces) confectioners' sugar
- 6 ounces cream cheese, cut into 4 pieces and softened
- 1 teaspoon vanilla extract

1. FOR THE COOKIES: Adjust oven racks to upper-middle and lower-middle positions and heat oven to 350 degrees. Line 2 baking sheets with parchment paper. Combine carrots, 1 teaspoon granulated sugar, and ½ teaspoon salt in bowl and let sit for 30 minutes. Place carrots in center of clean dish towel, gather ends of towel to form bundle, and twist to remove as much moisture from carrots as possible (you should squeeze off about ¼ cup liquid).

2. Whisk flour, cinnamon, baking soda, nutmeg, and ½ teaspoon salt together in bowl. Whisk brown sugar, melted butter, egg and yolk, vanilla, and remaining ½ cup granulated sugar in separate large bowl until fully combined. Stir flour mixture into butter mixture until just combined. Stir in carrots, 1 cup walnuts, and raisins.

3. Drop 2-tablespoon portions of dough onto prepared sheets, staggering 12 portions per sheet. (Distribute any remaining dough evenly.) Using your fingers, lightly press cookies to even ¾-inch thickness. Bake cookies until edges are set and beginning to brown, 16 to 20 minutes, switching and rotating sheets halfway through baking. Let cookies cool on sheets for 5 minutes. Transfer cookies to wire rack and let cool completely before frosting.

4. FOR THE FROSTING: Using stand mixer fitted with paddle, beat butter and sugar on medium speed until light and fluffy, about 2 minutes. Add cream cheese, 1 piece at a time, beating after each addition, until fully incorporated. Add vanilla and mix until no lumps remain.

5. Spread about 1 tablespoon frosting over each cooled cookie and sprinkle cookies with remaining ¾ cup walnuts. Serve. (Cookies can be layered between sheets of parchment paper and stored in airtight container for up to 2 days.)

Is All Cream Cheese the Same?

Cream cheese has a surprisingly interesting backstory. In the 19th century, Americans were hungry for European cheeses, but the trip across the Atlantic was expensive and the cheeses often spoiled in transit. A New York farmer named William Alfred Lawrence saw an opportunity. Mimicking creamy French Neufchâtel, he developed a smooth, rich block of cheese with more cream and salt than the original. He skirted aging by emphasizing his cheese's farm fresh flavor and branded it "Philadelphia Cream Cheese" after a city then associated with dairy farming. Lawrence's invention became hugely popular and is still the number-one cream cheese today. But how do its imitators stack up?

To find out, we gathered four nationally available full-fat cream cheeses. Three come in bricks, and one is packaged in a plastic tub. We asked 21 America's Test Kitchen staffers to blindly sample each plain, on bagels, and in frosting. Tasters appreciated pronounced tang, but one product, made by Cabot, drew criticism for its "sharp," "borderline sour" flavor.

According to Dean Sommer, cheese and food technologist at the Center for Dairy Research at the University of Wisconsin–Madison, cream cheese is an acid-set cheese, which means that the lactic acid produced by the cheese cultures coagulates the proteins in the milk (most other cheeses are coagulated with rennet). He suspects that the sour flavor of cream cheese is the result of allowing the cultures to overacidify the milk.

Another cream cheese, Organic Valley, looked yellowish and tasted superfatty; one taster wondered, "Is this butter?" We noted that the cheeses all had similar fat levels, so we turned to our science editor, who pointed out that certain strains of cheese culture can produce aroma compounds similar to those in butter. Two other manufacturers added cheese culture, too, but cultures can vary widely, and some strains are much more flavorful than others. Cow diet could also be a factor in buttery flavor; the manufacturer revealed that its cows are pastured as much as possible, resulting in more diversely flavored milk. This was distracting for some when tasted plain, but we liked it in the cream cheese frosting.

Texture mattered, too. Tasters preferred thicker samples that were creamy and dense to the one tub-style cheese, which was very tasty but had a glossy texture "like the love child of cream cheese and sour cream." Our top-rated cream cheese, a brick, and the tub-style option were from the same manufacturer, but the tub-style version is formulated with more water to give it a thinner, softer texture, and that higher water content provides more sheen; air is also mixed in to give it a lighter, fluffier texture (it is not marketed as "whipped"). Tasters still liked it, but overall we preferred our cream cheese slightly denser.

Philadelphia Cream Cheese Brick Original took the top spot. Its "classic," "fresh" flavor and "subtle tang" reminded us of farm-fresh milk, just as William Lawrence intended almost 150 years ago. –SARAH SEITZ

RECOMMENDED

PHILADELPHIA
Cream Cheese Brick Original
Price: $2.49 for 8 oz ($0.31 per oz)

Tasters appreciated our winner's "subtle," "bright but not sour" tang, which balanced its "fresh," "rich," "creamy" flavor. On a bagel, this "firm" spread was "dense enough to support lox." With 105 milligrams of salt per serving, it was "salty in a good way." One taster summed up the popular opinion: "Good balance of tang and sweetness."

PHILADELPHIA
Cream Cheese Spreads Original
Price: $4.49 for 12 oz ($0.37 per oz)

Though many tasters found this "silky" tub-packaged offering "very soft" (thanks to the addition of water, which manufacturers don't have to include on the ingredient list) and verging on "too smooth," others preferred its "light," "spreadable" consistency. It had a "nice tang" and a "sweet dairy taste."

ORGANIC VALLEY
Cream Cheese
Price: $3.79 for 8 oz ($0.47 per oz)

Tasters noticed a "grass-fed" "richness" in this product, which uses milk from cows pastured as much as possible. Its "thick texture" and "yellow tint" made a number of tasters wonder if they were eating butter. Most tasters liked the rich and creamy frosting, although a few thought it lacked assertive tang.

RECOMMENDED WITH RESERVATIONS

CABOT
Cream Cheese
Price: $1.99 for 8 oz ($0.25 per oz)

★ BEST FOR TANGY FROSTING
In our plain tasting, tasters almost unanimously commented on this product's "real sharp" tang reminiscent of "vinegar" or "white wine." On a bagel, tasters still found it "a bit too sour," but it won the frosting tasting, where it was deemed "pleasantly tangy," "smooth," and "a touch tart."

Cooking Class Easiest-Ever Cheesecake

We created an incredibly smooth and luxurious cheesecake—without using a mixer or a water bath.

BY KATIE LEAIRD

A WELL-MADE CHEESECAKE should be scented with vanilla and bolstered with a hint of tang. But when it comes down to it, the most alluring part of a perfect slice isn't really its flavor. Instead, great cheesecake is about a texture that's easy to imagine but hard to produce: a rich, dense filling that is luxuriously silky on the tongue, contrasted by a crisp, cookie-like crust.

Most recipes call for a stand mixer to whip the batter and a food processor to grind the graham crackers for the crust, but I committed to using a food processor alone. After making the crust (mixing in some flour was key to preventing sogginess) and giving the workbowl a quick rinse, I found that the blades deftly cut the cream cheese (along with eggs, sugar, cream, vanilla, and sour cream for tang) into a thoroughly smooth batter.

As for baking, I didn't want to use a *bain marie* (a water bath that helps ensure even, gentle cooking) since I always dread that precariously sloshy walk from oven to counter. Instead, I turned the oven down to 250 degrees, finding that I could successfully ditch the bath and still produce a cake with a smooth, crack-free top. I also determined that a cheesecake baked to precisely 155 degrees boasted the ideal creamy texture. A few degrees shy of that resulted in a soupy, droopy center; a higher temperature was a surefire way to get cracks. After letting the cake chill, it was time to serve up my remarkably creamy—dare I say flawless?—cake.

EASIEST-EVER CHEESECAKE
Serves 12 to 16

Reduce the oven temperature as soon as the crust is finished baking and be sure it has dropped to 250 degrees before you begin baking the cheesecake. Thoroughly scrape the processor bowl as you make the filling to eliminate lumps.

CRUST
- 6 whole graham crackers, broken into pieces
- ⅓ cup (2⅓ ounces) sugar
- ½ cup (2½ ounces) all-purpose flour
- ¼ teaspoon salt
- 6 tablespoons unsalted butter, melted

CHEESECAKE
- 2 pounds cream cheese
- 1¼ cups (8¾ ounces) sugar
- 4 large eggs
- ¼ cup heavy cream
- ¼ cup sour cream
- 2 teaspoons vanilla extract

1. FOR THE CRUST: Adjust oven rack to middle position and heat oven to 325 degrees. Process cracker pieces and sugar in food processor until finely ground, about 30 seconds. Add flour and salt and pulse to combine, about 2 pulses. Add melted butter and pulse until crumbs are evenly moistened, about 10 pulses.

2. Grease bottom and side of 9-inch springform pan. Using your hands, press crumb mixture evenly into pan bottom. Using bottom of dry measuring cup, firmly pack crust into pan. Bake until

---

STEP BY STEP **Easiest-Ever Cheesecake**

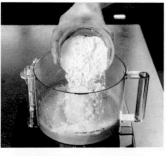

1. MAKE CRUST
Process the graham crackers and sugar in a food processor. Add the flour and salt and pulse to combine. Add the melted butter.
WHY? To ensure a crisp crust, we "waterproof" the graham cracker crumbs by coating them with flour and butter.

2. PREPARE PAN
Liberally grease the side and bottom of a springform pan with vegetable oil spray.
WHY? A well-greased pan allows for the easy release of the cheesecake once it is baked.

3. PRESS CRUMBS INTO PAN
Using the bottom of a dry measuring cup, firmly pack the crust into the pan.
WHY? A dry measuring cup with a flat bottom and perpendicular sides can rest against the side of the pan to help press and smooth all the crumbs into the bottom.

4. BAKE CRUST; LET COOL
Bake the crust at 325 degrees until fragrant and beginning to brown around the edges. Let it cool completely.
WHY? The crust and pan must be cool before the filling is added so that the bottom and sides of the cake don't cook too quickly.

5. TURN DOWN HEAT
Reduce the oven temperature to 250 degrees after baking the crust.
WHY? It may take a while, but it's worth waiting until the oven reaches 250 degrees to bake the cheesecake. If you don't, your cake will likely crack.

fragrant and beginning to brown around edges, about 13 minutes. Let cool completely.

3. FOR THE CHEESECAKE: Reduce oven temperature to 250 degrees. In clean, dry processor bowl, process cream cheese and sugar until smooth, about 3 minutes, scraping down bowl as needed. With processor running, add eggs, one at a time, until just incorporated, about 30 seconds total. Scrape down sides of bowl. Add cream, sour cream, and vanilla and process to combine, about 30 seconds.

4. Pour cheesecake mixture onto cooled crust. Gently tap pan on counter to release air bubbles. Gently draw tines of fork across surface of cake to pop any air bubbles that have risen to surface.

5. Once oven temperature has reached 250 degrees, bake cheesecake until edges are set and center jiggles slightly when shaken and registers 155 degrees, 1 hour 20 minutes to 1½ hours. Transfer pan to wire rack and let cool completely, about 2 hours. Refrigerate cheesecake, uncovered, until cold, about 6 hours. (Cake can be covered and refrigerated for up to 4 days.)

6. To unmold cheesecake, run tip of sharp paring knife between cake and side of pan and remove side. Slide thin metal spatula between crust and pan bottom to loosen, then slide cake onto serving platter. Let cheesecake stand at room temperature for 30 minutes. Using warm, dry knife, cut into wedges and serve.

Keys to Success

TEST KITCHEN TIPS FOR ANY CHEESECAKE

A perfect cheesecake is within reach if you follow our recipe to the letter, and that includes having the right equipment on hand. Temperature is paramount.

Take Your Oven's Temperature
Baking the cheesecake in an oven that is too hot or too cool can cause it to emerge dry and cracked or wet and soupy at the core. Using an oven thermometer is the best way to guarantee that your oven temperature is precisely 250 degrees, the best temp for a smooth, creamy consistency. We recommend spending a few dollars on the best model.

TEST KITCHEN FAVORITE
CDN Pro Accurate Oven Thermometer ($8.70)

Only a Springform Pan Will Do
You simply can't get a cheesecake out of a conventional cake pan. A springform allows you to remove the pan from the cake rather than the cake from the pan. Our gold-toned winning springform pan produces golden, evenly baked crusts and flawless creamy cheesecakes. Its tall side makes for easy handling.

TEST KITCHEN FAVORITE
Williams-Sonoma Goldtouch Springform Pan, 9" ($49.95)

Temp the Cake, Too
It's the only way to be sure the cake is done. Using an instant-read thermometer, carefully insert the probe halfway down into the center of the cake. The cake is done when it registers 155 degrees, at which point it will still jiggle quite a bit at the center. (The cake will set up as it cools.) The ThermoWorks ThermoPop is our winning inexpensive digital thermometer. It is fast, accurate, and easy to hold.

TEST KITCHEN FAVORITE
ThermoWorks ThermoPop ($29.00)

TEST KITCHEN TECHNIQUE
Producing a Perfect Slice

1. Run a paring knife around the edge of the cake before unlatching the springform collar.

2. Slide a metal spatula under the crust to release it, and then slide the cheesecake onto a serving platter.

3. Dip a chef's knife in hot water, and then dry it thoroughly with a clean dish towel before slicing. Clean the knife after each slice.

TEST KITCHEN DISCOVERY **Preventing a Soggy Crust**
A typical graham cracker crust turns soggy because the ground mixture is loose and porous. As a result, moisture from the heavy, wet filling seeps into the crevices and saturates the crumbs before the moisture has a chance to evaporate during baking. Our solution is to "waterproof" the crumbs, which we do by adding flour. The flour, combined with the melted butter, coats the crumbs in a waterproof sheath. The upshot: Moisture from the filling never soaks in and simply evaporates in the oven.

6. PROCESS FILLING
Process the cream cheese and sugar until smooth, and then add the eggs, one at a time. Add the cream, sour cream, and vanilla and process, about 30 seconds.
WHY? The sharp, fast processor blades are ideal for mixing a smooth batter.

7. POP AIR BUBBLES
Pour the batter into the pan. Tap the pan on the counter to release air bubbles. Draw a fork across the surface to pop air bubbles.
WHY? Air bubbles can ruin the texture of a cheesecake. Tapping the pan forces the bubbles to the surface so you can pop them.

8. BAKE LOW AND SLOW
Bake at 250 degrees until the center registers 155 degrees.
WHY? Baking to 155 degrees ensures a silky, just-set texture. Use an oven thermometer to gauge temperature and an instant-read thermometer to gauge doneness.

9. LET COOL AND CHILL
Transfer the pan to a wire rack and let the cake cool completely, about 2 hours. Refrigerate the cheesecake, uncovered, until cold, about 6 hours.
WHY? The cheesecake needs plenty of time to set up completely after it has been baked.

10. UNMOLD AND SERVE
Run the tip of a sharp paring knife between the cake and the side of the pan, and remove the side. Slide a thin spatula between the crust and the pan bottom to loosen it.
WHY? Gentle handling ensures a successful release of the cheesecake from the pan.

One-Pan Dinner Pot Roast in a Bag

Cooking in a bag is just gimmicky. Or so we thought.

BY CECELIA JENKINS

SINCE THE EARLY 1900s, Americans have been cooking food in bags. Why? For the easy cleanup. Emma Paddock Telford's 1912 book *Standard Paper-Bag Cookery* "revolutionized kitchen drudgery," relieving home cooks of unending rounds of greasy pots and pans. Nowadays, while we've been warned against cooking in paper (additives that may be used in paper bag production might have health consequences), special plastic cooking bags approved by the U.S. Food and Drug Administration still promise to make quick work of cleanup and to yield tender and juicy meat. A gimmick, or was there more to it? We needed answers.

The most ubiquitous bag-roasting recipes are for turkey and pot roast; we chose pot roast to test the method. Traditionally a tough cut of beef (we like the texture of chuck-eye best) that's been cooked in a covered pot at a gentle heat for hours, a perfect pot roast should feature beautifully tender meat—and a pot destined for a good scrubbing.

Putting the bag to the test, I started with a side-by-side comparison of simple, unadorned recipes for pot roast with potatoes and carrots, one cooked in a covered Dutch oven and one cooked in a bag set in a baking dish. Once the two pot roasts were ready, I set them out for a blind tasting. I was surprised to find that my tasters—who had no idea which roast was which—preferred the texture of the meat cooked in the bag. Because the bag creates a tighter seal than the Dutch oven, this roast was discernibly more juicy and tender. What's more, the meat wasn't drab in color; rather, it browned beautifully in the bag. A quick check with our science editor reminded me that with enough time in the oven, meat can brown (via a process called the Maillard reaction) without direct contact with a heat source.

Throwing everything into a bag, roasting it, and then emptying the beautifully tender meat into a serving dish couldn't have been simpler. What was missing was flavor, so I looked for a way to boost it. I experimented with chicken broth, soy sauce, anchovy paste, and beef broth, but these gave me either too much savoriness or slightly sour off-flavors. When a colleague suggested a packet of onion soup mix, a common midcentury pot roast addition,

I was inspired. But prefab mixes tasted off-balance. I took a cue from an earlier test kitchen recipe and made my own mix from pantry staples: onion powder, garlic powder, brown sugar, dried thyme, and celery seeds. I also added some flour to the mix, hoping that it would help thicken the braising liquid. I rubbed this mixture onto the meat before it went into the oven; once it was cooked, I had a very flavorful roast and excellent vegetables besides. But I also had too much fat.

Chuck-eye roast contains a relatively large amount of intramuscular fat that melts during braising, basting the meat and keeping it moist, but the fat has a tendency to render into the braising liquid and leave it greasy. I tried removing the meat and vegetables from the braising liquid and using a fat separator, but this left me with a sinkful of greasy dishes—exactly what I was hoping to avoid. Perhaps a leaner cut would do?

After trying a few leaner cuts (brisket, round, and sirloin) that all emerged drier than the chuck eye, it was clear that nothing compared to chuck eye. But rather than employ the fat separator, I simply snipped the bag open over the baking dish I'd used to secure it in the oven, letting the dish catch the contents. I gently tilted the dish to skim off ¼ cup of fat with a wide-bellied spoon, not worrying too much about getting every last drop of it. My tasters praised the tender roast, soft vegetables, and flavorful sauce. This one was in the bag.

POT ROAST IN A BAG Serves 6
You will need a nylon oven bag that can hold up to 8 pounds. Make sure the bag does not touch the top or sides of the oven, or it will melt. We prefer to use a ceramic, not Pyrex, baking dish, because adding liquid to a hot Pyrex dish can sometimes shock it and cause cracking.

- 4 teaspoons onion powder
- 1 tablespoon all-purpose flour
- 2 teaspoons packed light brown sugar
- 2 teaspoons salt
- 1 teaspoon pepper
- 1 teaspoon garlic powder
- 1 teaspoon dried thyme
- ½ teaspoon celery seeds
- 1 (3½- to 4-pound) boneless beef chuck-eye roast, trimmed

A bit of flour in the spice mix helps the roast create a silky sauce as it cooks.

Five Easy Pancakes

No box. No premade mix. Just as easy.

BY ASHLEY MOORE

- 1 (8-pound-capacity) oven bag
- 1½ pounds Yukon Gold potatoes, unpeeled, cut into 1½-inch pieces
- 5 carrots, peeled and cut into 2-inch lengths, thick ends halved lengthwise
- ¾ cup water
- 1 tablespoon chopped fresh parsley

1. Adjust oven rack to lower-middle position and heat oven to 300 degrees. Combine onion powder, flour, sugar, salt, pepper, garlic powder, thyme, and celery seeds in bowl.

2. Pat roast dry with paper towels. Using 3 pieces of kitchen twine, tie roast around circumference at equal intervals. Place roast in oven bag and sprinkle with spice mixture on all sides. Add potatoes, carrots, and water to bag. Tie bag closed with kitchen twine.

3. Place bag in 13 by 9-inch ceramic baking dish. Cut two ½-inch slits in top of bag. Transfer dish to oven and bake until paring knife inserted through top of bag slips easily in and out of beef, about 4 hours.

4. Remove dish from oven. Carefully cut open bag just above contents so steam releases away from you. Using tongs, transfer roast to carving board, tent with aluminum foil, and let rest for 10 minutes.

5. Carefully lift bag so vegetables and braising liquid pour into baking dish; discard bag. Push vegetables to 1 side of dish. Gently tilt dish (it will be hot) to allow braising liquid to pool on opposite side; skim ¼ cup fat from surface using large spoon.

6. Discard twine and slice beef ¼ inch thick. Transfer beef to dish with vegetables and baste with braising liquid. Sprinkle with parsley. Serve.

TEST KITCHEN FAVORITE
We recommend **Reynolds Oven Bags**, which are made of FDA-compliant heat-resistant nylon and are available in two sizes. For this recipe, use the bags sized for meats that weigh up to 8 pounds (and four to six servings).

WHAT'S BETTER THAN buttermilk pancakes? Buttermilk pancakes with some of your favorite ingredients stirred in, that's what. We wanted fluffy, tender, and slightly tangy pancakes that were as easy to make as they were to eat, and we didn't want to rely on a boxed supermarket mix.

The first thing I learned was that I needed to use two leaveners—baking soda and baking powder—to create airy, golden-brown pancakes. For flavor, I found that a mix of buttermilk and sour cream resulted in a pleasant tang.

Another crucial discovery: Do not overmix the batter. Doing so activates the flour's gluten, and too much gluten development leads to tough pancakes. For further insurance, I let the batter rest after mixing it. This gave the gluten time to relax, which in turn helped keep the pancakes tender. Finally, I found that cooking the pancakes at the right temperature is essential; otherwise they will be pale and blond or covered in uneven marks. The best time to add batter to the skillet is right after the oil starts to shimmer.

Buttermilk pancakes are good, but mix-ins make them better. Blueberries are the classic choice, but they're just the beginning. I took a poll from my tasters before settling on four more variations. The combination of apples and cinnamon was a slam dunk. For another version, I stirred together thinly sliced bananas and toasted and chopped walnuts. I added chocolate chips and shredded coconut to a third sweet, sugary option. And last, but certainly not least, some chopped ripe strawberries and a bit of vanilla extract proved a crowd-pleaser.

BLUEBERRY PANCAKES
Makes 14 pancakes
Frozen blueberries may be substituted. If using frozen berries, thaw and rinse the berries and spread them out on paper towels to dry. The pancakes can also be cooked on a 350-degree electric griddle.

- 2 cups (10 ounces) all-purpose flour
- 2 tablespoons sugar
- 1 teaspoon baking powder
- ½ teaspoon baking soda
- ½ teaspoon salt

We added chocolate chips and sweetened shredded coconut to one sweet variation.

- 2 cups buttermilk
- 2 large eggs
- ¼ cup sour cream
- 3 tablespoons unsalted butter, melted and cooled slightly
- 2 teaspoons vegetable oil
- 5 ounces (1 cup) fresh blueberries

1. Adjust oven rack to middle position and heat oven to 200 degrees. Spray wire rack set in rimmed baking sheet with vegetable oil spray; place in oven.

2. Whisk flour, sugar, baking powder, baking soda, and salt together in bowl. In second bowl, whisk buttermilk, eggs, sour cream, and melted butter together. Make well in center of flour mixture and pour in buttermilk mixture; gently stir until just combined (batter should remain lumpy, with few streaks of flour). Do not overmix. Let batter sit for 10 minutes.

3. Heat 1 teaspoon oil in 12-inch nonstick skillet over medium heat until shimmering. Using paper towels, carefully wipe out oil, leaving thin film on bottom and sides of pan.

4. Using ¼-cup dry measuring cup, portion 4 pancakes into pan. Cook until edges are set, first side is golden brown, and bubbles on surface are just beginning to break, 2 to 3 minutes. Sprinkle 1 tablespoon blueberries over each pancake.

5. Using wide spatula, flip pancakes and continue to cook until second side is golden brown, 1 to 2 minutes longer. Serve pancakes immediately or transfer to prepared rack in oven. Repeat with remaining batter and blueberries, adding remaining 1 teaspoon oil as needed.

APPLE-CINNAMON PANCAKES
Combine 2 peeled, cored, and finely chopped apples; 1 tablespoon packed brown sugar; and ½ teaspoon ground cinnamon in bowl and substitute for blueberries.

BANANA-WALNUT PANCAKES
Combine 2 ripe bananas, peeled, quartered lengthwise, and sliced thin, and ½ cup walnuts, toasted and chopped coarse, in bowl and substitute for blueberries.

CHOCOLATE CHIP–COCONUT PANCAKES
Combine 1 cup semisweet chocolate chips and ½ cup sweetened shredded coconut in bowl and substitute for blueberries.

STRAWBERRY-VANILLA PANCAKES
Combine 10 ounces hulled and finely chopped strawberries, 1 tablespoon sugar, and ½ teaspoon vanilla extract in bowl and substitute for blueberries.

Cooking for Two Skillet Pizza

We wanted pizza for two in the same time it takes to order in.

BY ALLI BERKEY

By rolling the dough slightly bigger than the skillet's surface, we get just enough golden crust.

How to Achieve an Even Pizza Crust in a Skillet
To help the dough hold its shape and to prevent large air bubbles, get out a fork.

FIRST, DOCK THE RAW DOUGH
After arranging the dough in the skillet, use a fork to prick it 10 times.

NEXT, POKE IT DURING COOKING
Halfway through cooking, use a fork to pop any air bubbles that have developed.

NO RECIPE IS easier than calling up a local pizza parlor and ordering a pie. But on a recent evening, I wanted to go one better and make a quick pizza for two at home, and I didn't want to bother heating up a pizza stone. I wanted to make this on the stovetop.

A 12-inch pizza is just about the right size to serve two, so I eyed my trusty 12-inch skillet. I rounded up a few existing recipes, but none gave me the pie I wanted. Some were still raw, others beyond burnt. Plus, most were unevenly cooked, and there was no evidence of the crisp-chewy crust I sought. What's more, some of the recipes called for pressing the dough into a hot pan, a process that left me with fresh burns on my knuckles—not my idea of a successful result.

Just like bread dough, pizza dough rises due to heat that surrounds it during cooking. But does the heat have to hit the dough in a strong initial burst? Or could I introduce it more gradually?

Hopeful, I pressed room-temperature pizza dough into an unheated skillet. I pricked the dough with a fork a few times (carefully, so as not to scratch the pan) to help it hold its shape while it cooked. I wanted it to rise some but not morph into a bulbous mess.

After about 6 minutes, the bottom was nicely cooked, but the top? Still raw and very dense. Maybe I could get a better texture if I covered the pizza while it cooked on the stovetop. I gave it a try and sure enough, when I peeked under the lid, I could see the dough beginning to rise. Score.

It was time to tackle the toppings. Hoping to keep this a stovetop recipe, I spread sauce on the crust and sprinkled cheese over the top. I re-covered the skillet and crossed my fingers. I should have known better: My pizza had steamy, unevenly melted cheese. The heat trapped in my covered skillet wasn't enough—I needed direct heat to evenly melt the cheese and create that toasty, spotty-brown top.

Because my skillet is ovensafe, I decided to slide it under the broiler. A few minutes were all I needed to get the brown, cheesy bubbles I was hoping for.

I had just what I wanted: pizza for two with a lovely crust, savory toppings, and no burnt knuckles, and it took only about 30 minutes.

SKILLET PIZZA FOR TWO
Letting the dough rest on the counter allows the gluten to relax and keeps the dough from shrinking. If you're using an electric stove, heat the burner for 3 minutes on medium heat before starting to cook.

- 2 tablespoons extra-virgin olive oil
- 12 ounces pizza dough, room temperature
- ⅓ cup jarred pasta sauce
- ⅛ teaspoon red pepper flakes
- 3 ounces whole-milk mozzarella cheese, shredded (¾ cup)
- ¼ cup grated Parmesan cheese

1. Adjust oven rack 6 inches from broiler element and heat broiler. Using pastry brush, brush bottom (not sides) of 12-inch skillet with oil.

2. Press and roll dough into 14-inch circle on lightly floured counter. Let dough rest on counter for 5 minutes. Loosely roll dough around rolling pin and gently unroll it into skillet. Using your fingertips, push dough into corners and up sides of skillet (dough should climb about 1 inch up sides of skillet). Using fork, poke bottom of dough 10 times.

3. Cover and cook over medium heat until bottom of crust is spotty brown, about 6 minutes, checking halfway through cooking and popping any air bubbles with fork. Remove from heat.

4. Spread sauce evenly over dough, leaving ½-inch border, then sprinkle with pepper flakes. Sprinkle mozzarella and Parmesan over top. Transfer skillet to oven and broil until crust and cheese are spotty brown, about 5 minutes. Using spatula, slide pizza onto cutting board and let cool for 5 minutes. Slice and serve.

Slow Cooker Coq au Vin

If ever a dish was meant for the slow cooker, this should be it. BY DIANE UNGER

COQ AU VIN ("chicken in wine") is a fancy-sounding name for a very simple dish. Julia Child put it on the American food map in the early '60s, when she introduced the American public to it through her television show, *The French Chef.* Her recipe is complicated, with the components (chicken, bacon, onions, mushrooms, and sauce) cooked separately and then reassembled. The result is a rich, comforting stew with long-cooked flavor. But I wanted an easier way—I wanted to make this iconic dish in the slow cooker.

After testing a few slow-cooker recipes, I had my doubts. The chicken was dry and rubbery, the sauces watery and bland, the mushrooms spongy, and the bacon flabby and flavorless. Undeterred, I set out to fix this recipe so that I'd end up with tender, moist chicken; firm mushrooms; crispy bacon; and a wine sauce that was concentrated and flavorful, perfect for serving with potatoes or crusty bread.

My first decision was to ditch the white meat in favor of all dark meat, specifically bone-in chicken thighs. I browned the skin side of eight thighs (5 to 7 ounces each) in a nonstick skillet to render their fat and start building flavor. After transferring the chicken to the slow cooker, I poured off (and reserved) the chicken fat. Next, I added four slices of thick-cut bacon to the skillet and cooked them until they were crispy. I transferred the bacon to a paper towel–lined plate with the idea to reserve it, refrigerated, until I was ready to serve the chicken. I combined the bacon fat with the chicken fat and added ¼ cup of the flavorful combination back to the skillet to sauté the mushrooms.

For the mushrooms, I chose cremini over white for their earthy flavor. Once I had browned the mushrooms in the fat mixture, I added tomato paste and garlic to the skillet, along with ¼ cup of flour to help create a nicely thickened sauce. I deglazed the pan with 1¾ cups of wine (red wine is traditional, but we also liked white wine for its light, brighter flavor), whisking it in slowly to prevent the flour from clumping. I brought the mixture to a simmer and cooked it until it was fairly thick, almost paste-like, knowing it would be diluted with juices from the chicken

This equal-opportunity stew works beautifully with red or white wine.

and mushrooms in the slow cooker. I poured it over the chicken, scattered 1 cup of frozen pearl onions over the top (I certainly wasn't going to peel small white onions for this), and set the cover in place.

After 6 to 8 hours on low, the chicken was supertender and the sauce had a perfect consistency. I transferred the chicken to my serving dish, microwaved the bacon I'd previously cooked to warm it up, stirred it into the sauce, and poured the lot over the chicken. It looked great (especially when sprinkled with some fresh minced parsley). And the taste? Well, I'm no French chef, but my Slow-Cooker Coq au Vin was a hit with my tasters. The sauce had a rich, deep, earthy flavor; the mushrooms were tender but not spongy; and the bacon added a smoky flavor and a welcome crunch.

SLOW-COOKER COQ AU VIN
Serves 4

Try to find chicken thighs that are within the weight specifications so they will all fit in the skillet in one batch. We like serving this dish with boiled red potatoes.

- 8 (5- to 7-ounce) bone-in chicken thighs, trimmed
  Salt and pepper
- 1 tablespoon vegetable oil
- 1 cup frozen pearl onions
- 4 slices thick-cut bacon, cut into 1-inch pieces
- 10 ounces cremini mushrooms, trimmed and quartered
- ¼ cup all-purpose flour
- 1 tablespoon tomato paste
- 2 garlic cloves, minced
- ½ teaspoon dried thyme
- 1¾ cups dry red wine
- 2 tablespoons minced fresh parsley

1. Pat chicken dry with paper towels and season with salt and pepper. Heat oil in 12-inch nonstick skillet over medium-high heat until just smoking. Add chicken, skin side down, and cook until well browned, 7 to 10 minutes. Transfer chicken, skin side up, to slow cooker. Add onions to slow cooker.

2. Pour chicken fat from skillet into bowl and set aside. Add bacon to now-empty skillet and cook over medium heat until crispy, 5 to 7 minutes. Using slotted spoon, transfer bacon to paper towel–lined plate; refrigerate until needed.

3. Pour bacon fat into bowl with chicken fat. Add ¼ cup fat mixture to now-empty skillet and heat over medium heat until shimmering. Add mushrooms and cook until well browned, 5 to 7 minutes. Stir in flour, tomato paste, garlic, and thyme and cook until fragrant, about 1 minute. Slowly whisk in wine. Bring to simmer and cook until thickened and spatula leaves trail in sauce, about 2 minutes. Pour sauce over chicken in slow cooker.

4. Cover and cook until chicken is tender, 4 to 6 hours on high or 6 to 8 hours on low. Using slotted spoon, transfer chicken to serving dish. Season sauce with salt and pepper to taste. Cover bacon with paper towel and microwave until hot, about 1 minute. Pour sauce over chicken. Sprinkle with parsley and bacon. Serve.

SLOW-COOKER COQ AU VIN WITH WHITE WINE

Substitute dry white wine for red.

Equipment Review Muffin Tins

Are gold-colored pans the new gold standard?

BY HANNAH CROWLEY

BY HANNAH CROWLEY

KEY **Good ★★★**   **Fair ★★**   **Poor ★**

THE TEST KITCHEN GAUNTLET
10 Muffin Tins
6 Tests

1. Make one batch of Basic Muffins
2. Make one batch of Easy Birthday Cupcakes
3. Make one batch of Muffin Tin Frittatas
4. Wash by hand 10 times
5. Scrub each individual cup 25 times with an abrasive sponge
6. Run a paring knife around side of each cup 25 times

DO YOU KNOW the muffin man? Well, forget him. Around these parts it's the muffin woman. Or at least that's what I've been calling myself after making 10 batches of muffins, 10 batches of cupcakes, and 10 batches of single-serve frittatas in a single week.

I was testing muffin tins. Our top two models had been discontinued, so it was time for a fresh look. We also wanted to examine a trend: Gold-colored pans have dominated our recent testings of rectangular baking pans, loaf pans, round cake pans, and square cake pans. Gold pans beat out darker and lighter pans in each category by easily releasing baked goods that had just the right amount of browning. With gold muffin tins now on the market, we wondered if the trend would continue.

To find out, we chose ten 12-cup muffin tins priced from $10.30 to $32.99. Three were gold or bronze, three were light or medium silver, and four were dark. In the past we've focused on nonstick muffin tins because easy release is key with tender muffins. But this time we included one without a nonstick coating; instead it had a very shallow snakeskin pattern etched into it, ostensibly to help with release.

We evaluated each muffin tin on its durability, release, handling, and the browning of the baked goods it produced. There were no issues with wear and tear, and only one model had a problem with release—the one without a nonstick coating. Its textured pattern left us prying out muffins with a knife. We'll stick with nonstick.

We noticed an interesting trend regarding the color of the muffin tins: In general, lighter models produced lighter-colored baked goods and darker ones made darker-colored baked goods. And the gold (or bronze) muffin tins

HIGHLY RECOMMENDED

	CRITERIA	
OXO Good Grips Non-Stick Pro 12-Cup Muffin Pan **WINNING TRAITS**	Release	★★★
Model: 11160500 • Nonstick coating	Browning	★★★
Price: $24.99 • Gold finish	Food Shape	★★★
Finish: Gold • Wide rim on all four sides	Handling	★★★

This muffin tin perfectly released its baked goods and was a dream to hold and turn. It has an oversize rim (with a lip that curls underneath) running all the way around it, so there was always a broad, secure place to grasp. Its gold finish created the most appealing baked goods, too: evenly, lightly browned and elegantly shaped.

RECOMMENDED

WILLIAMS-SONOMA Goldtouch Nonstick Muffin Pan, 12-Well	Release	★★★
	Browning	★★½
Model: 13-1984111 Price: $29.95	Food Shape	★★½
Finish: Gold	Handling	★★½

This muffin tin released its baked goods flawlessly. Its extended rim had a nice rolled edge for security but wasn't as broad as our winner's, so it was slightly fussier to maneuver. But its gold finish produced nice, mostly even browning.

ANOLON Advanced Bronze Bakeware 12-Cup Muffin Pan	Release	★★★
	Browning	★★★
Model: 57036 Price: $19.94	Food Shape	★★½
Finish: Bronze	Handling	★★

The ridge around this muffin tin's rim made it harder to hold; it dug into our hands if we didn't hold it just right. It did have two small silicone handles that worked fairly well, though we had to be a bit more precise about where we gripped. Its baked goods released perfectly and were mostly consistent.

RECOMMENDED WITH RESERVATIONS

WILTON Professional Results Non-Stick 12-Cup Muffin Pan	Release	★★★
	Browning	★★
Model: 2105-2245 Price: $13.59	Food Shape	★★½
Finish: Dark	Handling	★★

The darker finish on this muffin tin made for slightly conical muffins, but its baked goods were generally acceptable, if slightly inconsistent in color. It had two indented handles, which worked well, but it didn't have anywhere on the sides or corners for us to grab to rotate it, so we had to reach all the way into the oven every time.

produced browning that was neither too dark nor too light.

To understand why, we looked at the way heat works. In an oven, heat radiates out in waves. When the waves hit a pan, its atoms and molecules move faster, which heats everything up. But different materials absorb heat waves at different rates. In general, darker objects absorb more heat waves than lighter objects because lighter objects reflect some of the waves. You've probably

experienced this when wearing dark clothes on a sunny day—black absorbs heat waves, so you feel hotter. If you were wearing white, you'd likely feel cooler because lighter fabric reflects some of the waves and absorbs less heat.

So the muffins from darker muffin tins were darker and had thicker crusts because they'd been subjected to more heat. And muffins from lighter muffin tins were paler and softer because they had been subjected to less heat.

Muffin Quest

We learned that a muffin tin's color and shape are its most important attributes.

- Gold muffin tins heat evenly and steadily and result in more uniformly shaped baked goods because the sides set in step with the interiors.
- Gold muffin tins produce flavorful crusts and perfectly cooked interiors.
- A wide rim on all sides allows for easy maneuvering, with no smushed muffins.

▶ Visit CooksCountry.com/may17 for the full testing results, including pictures of and details on all lower-ranked models.

The gold muffin tins produced evenly browned muffins (and frittatas and cupcakes) with tender crusts.

Muffin tin color also affected the shape of the baked goods. Because dark models conduct heat faster, the sides of their baked goods set faster, leaving the rest of the batter to rise upward, sometimes into oddly conical or bulbous shapes. Light- and medium-colored models, on the other hand, made more-consistent, appealingly shaped baked goods because their sides set more slowly, in step with the rest of the batter, allowing a more controlled rise and resulting in more normal shaping.

The shape of the muffin tins was also hugely important. We included only models that had some sort of handle or extended rim, as experience has taught us that without a spot to grab, maneuvering a hot muffin tin can feel like slow dancing in middle school—you never know where to put your hands.

Muffin tins with handles seemed promising because they had clear, dedicated spots to hold on to. But the handles were often too small; we repeatedly dented the tops of muffins with our oven mitts. It became clear that oversize rims were better. Models with a broad rim on all sides were the easiest to handle and facilitated one-handed maneuvering. For models with only handles, we sometimes had to reach far into the oven, risking a burnt forearm or elbow, to grip the handle and rotate the muffin tin.

The muffin tin with the biggest rim was downright luxurious to move around. It also had a gold nonstick finish that made perfectly browned baked goods. Those factors made the OXO Good Grips Non-Stick Pro 12-Cup Muffin Pan ($24.99) our clear winner.

Taste Test Block Mozzarella

What makes the best block? It all comes down to fat, moisture, and acid. BY LAUREN SAVOIE

MOZZARELLA CONJURES UP images of Italian food, but most of what's sold as mozzarella in this country isn't actually Italian at all—it's an American invention.

Traditional Italian mozzarella is made by acidifying whole buffalo milk and heating the mixture in hot water until the solid curds separate from the liquid whey. The curds are then stretched and pulled, by hand or machine, until they form elastic balls of cheese. This type of mozzarella is packed in brine and labeled "fresh" mozzarella; we like it in uncooked applications, where its milky flavor and soft texture shine through.

The rest of the mozzarella you find in supermarkets—blocks, shredded, string cheese, and slices—is American mozzarella, invented in the early 1900s by Italian immigrants who wanted to make a cheese with a longer shelf life. It's made much like traditional mozzarella, but the curds are cooked and stirred longer before stretching, resulting in a cheese with a lower moisture content, higher acidity, and more longevity. This Americanized mozzarella is easy to grate and melts beautifully.

To find the best block mozzarella, we picked six nationally available products, three whole-milk varieties and three part-skim. We also included our winning preshredded whole-milk mozzarella. We tasted the cheeses plain and melted on our Sheet Pan Pizza.

While all of the cheeses shredded easily and melted well, our tasters preferred the fuller, more dairy-rich flavor of whole-milk cheeses to part-skim in both tastings. To get a better read on fat levels, we sent all of the cheeses to an independent lab for analysis. Our favorites, which were made from whole milk, had up to 48 percent fat in their dry solids (a measurement of how much of the cheese is fat once the water is removed), while lower-ranking part-skim cheeses were as little as 42 percent fat. According to the U.S. Food and Drug Administration (FDA), products must be labeled "part-skim" if they contain less than 45 percent fat in their dry solids. Tasters thought these cheeses had a mild flavor and a rubbery texture. We preferred products with 47 percent or 48 percent fat, which tasted milky and rich.

The one exception was the preshredded cheese, which tasters singled out for its drier, slightly powdery texture (likely from cellulose added to prevent clumping) when tasted plain. While the added starch made for drier cheese that was a tad chewier (although still pretty good) when melted on pizza, most tasters agreed that its moderate 45 percent fat content lent a creamy, rich flavor. It landed in the middle of our rankings, drawing the dividing line between the whole-milk and part-skim blocks.

But fat tells only one part of the story. According to the FDA, mozzarella can contain anywhere from 45 percent to 60 percent moisture. Wet, milky fresh mozzarella has 60 percent moisture; on the low end are the dense, firm blocks labeled "low-moisture mozzarella." We've always considered all block mozzarella to be low-moisture. But the FDA requires "low-moisture" on the labels of only mozzarellas with 45 percent to 52 percent moisture. Those with 52 percent moisture or higher can be called simply "mozzarella," regardless of whether it's a fresh ball of cheese or a denser, shreddable block.

It was telling, then, that our top two products had no mention of "low-moisture" on their labels; they were called only "mozzarella." Our lab results showed that these two samples had 53 percent and 52 percent moisture—they were dry enough to shred and melt well but had enough moisture to have a soft, smooth texture (even when melted) that approached that of fresh mozzarella.

Top-ranked mozzarellas had another thing in common: They're acidulated with vinegar—in the traditional manner of American mozzarella—rather than with cheese culture. Our tasters found these vinegar-acidulated cheeses richer and more pleasantly tangy than cheeses produced using cheese cultures.

For the best all-around texture—and especially flavor—avoid block mozzarellas labeled "part-skim" and "low-moisture" and look for those labeled simply "mozzarella," with whole milk and vinegar on the ingredient label. Our favorite of these was Polly-O Whole Milk Mozzarella Cheese. With the highest milk fat and moisture percentages of all the cheeses we tried, this whole-milk mozzarella approximated the rich, milky flavor we love in fresh mozzarella while still maintaining a springy, shreddable texture that melted effortlessly on pizza.

Go to CooksCountry.com/may17 for the full tasting results.

RECOMMENDED

	TASTERS' NOTES
POLLY-O Whole Milk Mozzarella Cheese **Price:** $5.99 for 16 oz ($0.37 per oz) **Type:** Packaged block **Fat in Dry Solids:** 48% **Moisture:** 53% **Acid:** Vinegar	This cheese was remarkably "soft" and "milky," with a "creaminess" and "hint of salt" that drew comparisons with fresh mozzarella. On pizza, its "rich" flavor "held up against the tomato sauce," and it melted into stretchy sheets that were "elastic but not gooey" and "adhered well" when we took a bite.
GALBANI Whole Milk Mozzarella Cheese **Price:** $4.99 for 16 oz ($0.31 per oz) **Type:** Packaged block **Fat in Dry Solids:** 47% **Moisture:** 52% **Acid:** Vinegar	"Classic pizza parlor cheese," said one taster about this whole-milk mozzarella, which was "tangy," "moist," and "tender." When melted on pizza, it was "chewy" and "creamy," with "a little bit of pull" that tasters loved. Though many liked its "nutty" sharpness, a few tasters thought it tasted "dull."
BOAR'S HEAD Whole Milk Low Moisture Mozzarella Cheese **Price:** $6.99 for 16 oz ($0.44 per oz) **Type:** Sliced block from deli counter, also available in packaged block **Fat in Dry Solids:** 46% **Moisture:** 45% **Acid:** Cheese culture	This mozzarella, which is sliced in fresh blocks from the deli counter, was "nutty" and "milky," with a "slight tang." It melted into a "glossy," "stretchy" sheet on pizza, with evenly browned pockets that were "buttery" but "not greasy." A few noted that this "mild" cultured cheese wasn't as punchy as vinegar-set products.
POLLY-O Whole Milk Shredded Low-Moisture Mozzarella Cheese **Price:** $2.98 for 8 oz ($0.37 per oz) **Type:** Packaged preshredded **Fat in Dry Solids:** 45% **Moisture:** 46% **Acid:** Vinegar and cheese culture	Our favorite preshredded mozzarella performed admirably on pizza, where tasters noted that it was "nutty" and "creamy," with a "bit of stretch." But most tasters detected a "powdery" chalkiness from its coating of cellulose powder (used to prevent clumping) when sampling it plain, so we'd choose a different product for snacking and salads.
GALBANI Part Skim Mozzarella Cheese **Price:** $4.99 for 16 oz ($0.31 per oz) **Type:** Packaged block **Fat in Dry Solids:** 42% **Moisture:** 53% **Acid:** Vinegar	Tasted plain, this part-skim mozzarella was "springy" and "firm," if a bit "rubbery." It melted well on pizza, where it produced "thick" and "chewy" strands that were still "buttery" and "moist." Most tasters described its flavor as "mild" and "light."
POLLY-O Part-Skim Mozzarella Cheese **Price:** $5.99 for 16 oz ($0.37 per oz) **Type:** Packaged block **Fat in Dry Solids:** 42% **Moisture:** 53% **Acid:** Vinegar	Though tasters liked the punch of this "tangy" part-skim cheese, a few remarked that its "squeaky" texture was reminiscent of "string cheese." It retained its "hearty," "milky" flavor on pizza, and its texture mellowed out to a "smooth," "stretchy" sheet when melted.

RECOMMENDED WITH RESERVATIONS

ORGANIC VALLEY Low Moisture, Part Skim Mozzarella Cheese **Price:** $4.99 for 8 oz ($0.62 per oz) **Type:** Packaged block **Fat in Dry Solids:** 45% **Moisture:** 45% **Acid:** Cheese culture	Though some tasters liked this cultured cheese's "funkier" sharpness, many were perplexed by its "yellow" color and "cheddar-y" flavor, which were likely the result of its grass-fed dairy. It performed better on pizza, where its "sharper" notes were mellowed by the sauce, and tasters liked its "fresh dairy flavor."

Good 'Rellas Here are the types of mozzarella we call for most frequently.

FRESH
This very moist, milky cheese is sold in brine so that it doesn't dry out.
Use It: Raw in salads (like caprese), on sandwiches, and as an appetizer.

BLOCK
Contains less water than fresh mozzarella, so it melts incredibly well.
Use It: Shredded and baked on pizza, in calzones, or in baked pasta. Great in panini.

SHREDDED
Block mozzarella that is preshredded and tossed with starch to prevent clumping.
Use It: In a pinch on pizza and in baked pastas.

Heirloom Recipe

We're looking for recipes that you treasure—the ones that have been handed down in your family for a generation or more; that always come out for the holidays; that have earned a place at your table and in your heart, through many years of meals. Send us the recipes that spell home to you. Visit **CooksCountry.com/magazines/home** (or write to Heirloom Recipes, *Cook's Country*, P.O. Box 470739, Brookline, MA 02447); click on Heirloom Recipes, and tell us a little about the recipe. Include your name and mailing address. **If we print your recipe, you'll receive a free one-year subscription to *Cook's Country*.**

NEIMAN MARCUS (INSPIRED) DIP
Makes about 2 cups

"When I was growing up, I hated the shopping trips my mother made me go on—except to Neiman Marcus, where we could have this dip in the department store's restaurant. I still love the dip (and I still hate to shop)."

–Colleen Martin, Sugar Land, Texas

The dip needs to sit for at least 2 hours to allow the flavors to meld. It gets better the longer it sits. We recommend using Frank's RedHot Original Cayenne Pepper Sauce in this recipe. Serve with Ritz crackers, Fritos corn chips, or apple slices.

- 8 slices bacon, cut into ½-inch pieces
- 8 ounces extra-sharp cheddar cheese, shredded (2 cups)
- 1 cup mayonnaise
- ½ cup slivered almonds, toasted
- 4 scallions, sliced thin
- 2 teaspoons hot sauce

1. Cook bacon in 12-inch nonstick skillet over medium heat until crispy, 5 to 7 minutes. Using slotted spoon, transfer bacon to paper towel–lined plate; let cool for 5 minutes.

2. Stir cheddar, mayonnaise, almonds, scallions, hot sauce, and bacon in bowl until thoroughly combined. Cover and refrigerate for at least 2 hours or up to 2 days. Serve.

COMING NEXT ISSUE

Summer's coming, and we're hitting the road. We'll pay a quick visit to Rochester, New York, for **Chicken Francese** before turning south. After digging into a dish of **Pimento Mac and Cheese**, we'll fuel up with a regional road-food specialty, **North Carolina Cheese Biscuits**, for our trip to Texas, where we'll dig into **Grilled Chuck Roast** with sides of **Braised Cabbage** and **Texas-Style Pinto Beans**. We've got your sweet tooth covered with three-layer **Cherry Streusel Bars** and supereasy, super-satisfying **Banana–Chocolate Chip Snack Cake**. And what better way to celebrate baseball season than with **Grilled Sausages with Onions and Peppers**? We'll top it off with a healthy slice of **Pig Pickin' Cake**, which you're going to have to see to believe. Come along for the ride!

FIND THE ROOSTER!
A tiny version of this rooster has been hidden in the pages of this issue. Write to us with its location and we'll enter you in a random drawing. The first correct entry drawn will win our favorite muffin tin, and each of the next five will receive a free one-year subscription to *Cook's Country*. To enter, visit **CooksCountry.com/rooster** by May 31, 2017, or write to Rooster AM17, *Cook's Country*, P.O. Box 470739, Brookline, MA 02447. Include your name and address. Margaret Barre of Seneca, South Carolina, found the rooster in the December/January 2017 issue on page 6 and won our favorite inexpensive Dutch oven.

WEB EXTRAS
Free for 4 months online at
CooksCountry.com
Carrot Cupcakes
Easy Vanilla Buttercream
Homemade Taco-Size Flour Tortillas
Pastry Cream
Tasting Block Mozzarella
Tasting Cornmeal
Tasting Cream Cheese
Testing Muffin Tins
Testing Oil Misters
Testing Roasting Pans

READ US ON iPAD

Download the *Cook's Country* app for iPad, and start a free trial subscription or purchase a single issue of the magazine. All issues are enhanced with full-color Cooking Mode slide shows that provide step-by-step instructions for completing recipes, plus expanded reviews and ratings. Go to **CooksCountry.com/iPad** to download our app through iTunes.

Pink Champagne Cake

This bubbly showstopper is the pride of the Madonna Inn in San Luis Obispo, California.

TO MAKE THIS CAKE, YOU WILL NEED:

- **6 egg whites, room temperature**
- **1 cup champagne, room temperature**
- **2 teaspoons vanilla extract**
- **6 drops red food coloring**
- **2¼ cups (9 ounces) cake flour**
- **1¾ cups (12¼ ounces) sugar**
- **4 teaspoons baking powder**
- **1 teaspoon salt**
- **12 tablespoons unsalted butter, softened but still cool**
- **3 cups pastry cream***
- **3 cups vanilla buttercream frosting***
- **Pink Chocolate Curls (recipe follows)**

FOR THE CAKE: Adjust oven rack to middle position and heat oven to 350 degrees. Grease and flour three 8-inch round cake pans and line bottoms with parchment paper. Whisk egg whites, champagne, vanilla, and food coloring together in bowl.

Using stand mixer fitted with paddle, mix flour, sugar, baking powder, and salt on low speed until combined, about 30 seconds. With mixer running, add butter, 1 piece at a time, and mix until incorporated and mixture resembles moist crumbs. Add all but ½ cup egg white mixture and beat until just combined. Increase speed to medium-high and beat until light and fluffy, about 1 minute. Add remaining ½ cup egg white mixture in slow stream. Scrape down bowl and beat batter on medium-high speed until well combined, about 15 seconds.

Divide batter evenly among prepared pans and smooth tops with rubber spatula. Bake until toothpick inserted in center comes out clean, 21 to 25 minutes, rotating pans halfway through baking. Let cakes cool in pans on wire rack for 10 minutes. Remove cakes from pans, discarding parchment, and let cool completely on rack, about 2 hours.

TO ASSEMBLE: Place 1 cake layer on cake plate or pedestal. Top with half of pastry cream. Place second cake layer on top. Top with remaining pastry cream. Place third cake layer on top. Spread buttercream in even layer over top and sides of cake. Top with pink chocolate curls. Serve.

PINK CHOCOLATE CURLS

Pink candy melts are available at most craft stores, such as Michael's.

12 ounces pink candy melts

Place candy in bowl and microwave at 50 percent power, stirring often, until melted, 2 to 4 minutes. Pour melted candy into 4 by 4-inch container at least 1 inch deep. Refrigerate until just set, 15 to 30 minutes. Let block soften slightly at room temperature, about 5 minutes. Remove block from container and run blade of vegetable peeler along width of block to form curls.

▶ *Go to **CooksCountry.com/pastrycream** and **CooksCountry.com/buttercream** for our Pastry Cream and Easy Vanilla Buttercream recipes, or use your own.

Inside This Issue

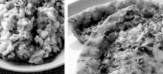

Cook's Country

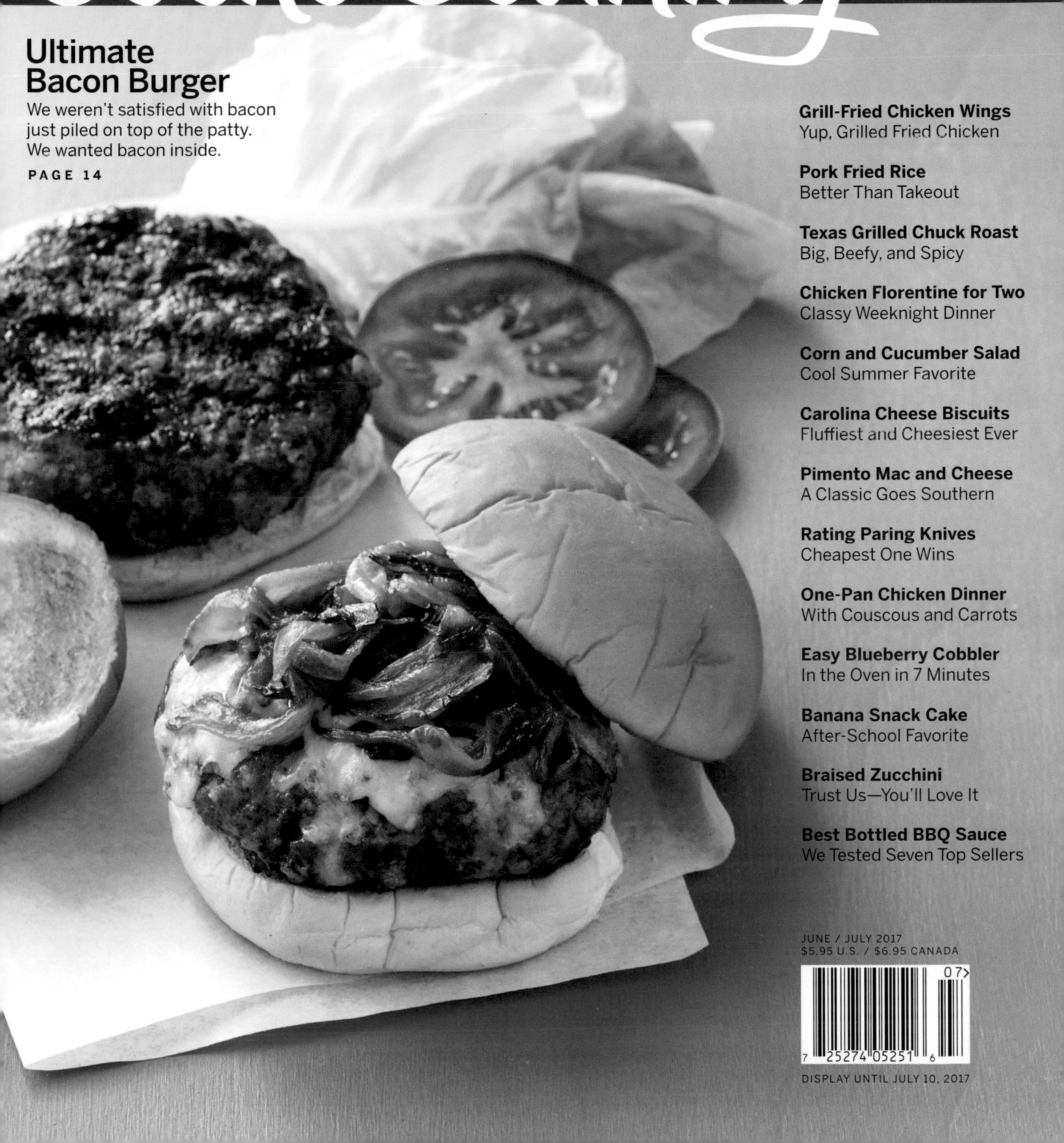

Ultimate Bacon Burger

We weren't satisfied with bacon just piled on top of the patty. We wanted bacon inside.

PAGE 14

Grill-Fried Chicken Wings
Yup, Grilled Fried Chicken

Pork Fried Rice
Better Than Takeout

Texas Grilled Chuck Roast
Big, Beefy, and Spicy

Chicken Florentine for Two
Classy Weeknight Dinner

Corn and Cucumber Salad
Cool Summer Favorite

Carolina Cheese Biscuits
Fluffiest and Cheesiest Ever

Pimento Mac and Cheese
A Classic Goes Southern

Rating Paring Knives
Cheapest One Wins

One-Pan Chicken Dinner
With Couscous and Carrots

Easy Blueberry Cobbler
In the Oven in 7 Minutes

Banana Snack Cake
After-School Favorite

Braised Zucchini
Trust Us—You'll Love It

Best Bottled BBQ Sauce
We Tested Seven Top Sellers

JUNE / JULY 2017
$5.95 U.S. / $6.95 CANADA

DISPLAY UNTIL JULY 10, 2017

LETTER FROM THE EDITOR

WHERE IS COOK'S COUNTRY? The easy answer, of course, is Boston. That's where our kitchens are, and that's where we live and work. But Boston is just a tiny speck on the map of *Cook's Country*—a massive, sprawling map. *Cook's Country* covers the entire United States, from Maine to Hawaii, Key West to Nome. We travel incessantly across the nation, from the wide-open fields of Wisconsin to the bustling streets of New Orleans, to learn who's cooking what, why, and—most important—how.

We're equally passionate about rural traditions and urban traditions, as well as the traditions of all those in-between places. We love down-home food as much as uptown food, because in our minds, it's all part of this great country we call home.

In this issue, you'll notice some exciting changes. New designs, new typefaces, new ideas. We hope you love them as much as we do.

But what hasn't changed matters even more: rigorously tested and carefully perfected recipes for everyday dishes and regional favorites that reflect the way America cooks—past, present, and future.

Where is *Cook's Country*? Right here in your hands. Take a look around! And welcome home.

TUCKER SHAW

Executive Editor

Illustration: Ross MacDonald

VEGAN FOR EVERYBODY

Let Us Help You Reimagine Mealtime

The benefits of consuming fewer animal products are many, but following a vegan diet can seem overwhelming: Will it be flavorful? Satisfying? Easy to make? In this book, the test kitchen addresses head-on what gives people pause: finding great-tasting and filling vegan protein options, cooking without dairy, preparing different vegetables and grains, and even baking. Order online at AmericasTestKitchen.com/vegan.

Find us on **Facebook**
facebook.com/CooksCountry

Find us on **Instagram**
instagram.com/CooksCountry

Follow us on **Pinterest**
pinterest.com/TestKitchen

Follow us on **Twitter**
twitter.com/TestKitchen

Cook's Country®

Chief Executive Officer David Nussbaum
Chief Creative Officer Jack Bishop
Editorial Director John Willoughby
Executive Editor Tucker Shaw
Deputy Editor Rebecca Hays
Executive Managing Editor Todd Meier
Executive Food Editor Bryan Roof
Senior Editor Chris O'Connor
Associate Editors Morgan Bolling, Katie Leaird, Ashley Moore
Test Cooks Alli Berkey, Daniel Cellucci, Matthew Fairman, Cecelia Jenkins
Assistant Test Cooks Mady Nichas, Jessica Rudolph
Senior Copy Editor Krista Magnuson
Copy Editor Jillian Campbell
Contributing Editor Eva Katz
Science Editor Guy Crosby, PhD, CFS
Director, Creative Operations Alice Carpenter
Hosts & Executive Editors, Television Bridget Lancaster, Julia Collin Davison

Executive Editor, Tastings & Testings Lisa McManus
Managing Editor Scott Kathan
Deputy Editor Hannah Crowley
Associate Editors Lauren Savoie, Kate Shannon
Assistant Editors Miye Bromberg, Emily Phares
Editorial Assistant Carolyn Grillo

Test Kitchen Director Erin McMurrer
Assistant Test Kitchen Director Leah Rovner
Test Kitchen Manager Alexxa Benson
Lead Senior Kitchen Assistant Meridith Lippard
Senior Kitchen Assistant Sophie Clingan-Darack
Lead Kitchen Assistant Ena Gudiel
Kitchen Assistants Gladis Campos, Blanca Castanza

Design Director Greg Galvan
Photography Director Julie Cote
Art Director Susan Levin
Designer Maggie Edgar
Art Director, Marketing Melanie Gryboski
Deputy Art Director, Marketing Janet Taylor
Associate Art Director, Marketing Stephanie Cook
Senior Staff Photographer Daniel J. van Ackere
Staff Photographer Steve Klise
Assistant Photography Producer Mary Ball
Photography Keller + Keller
Food Styling Catrine Kelty, Marie Piraino

Senior Director, Digital Design John Torres
Executive Editor, Web Christine Liu
Managing Editor, Web Mari Levine
Senior Editor, Web Roger Metcalf
Associate Editors, Web Terrence Doyle, Briana Palma
Senior Video Editor Nick Dakoulas
Test Kitchen Photojournalist Kevin White

Chief Financial Officer Jackie McCauley Ford
Production Director Guy Rochford
Imaging Manager Lauren Robbins
Production & Imaging Specialists Heather Dube, Sean MacDonald, Dennis Noble, Jessica Voas
Senior Controller Theresa Peterson
Director, Business Partnerships Mehgan Conciatori

Chief Digital Officer Fran Middleton
Director, Sponsorship Marketing & Client Services Christine Anagnostis
Client Services Manager Kate Zebrowski
Client Service and Marketing Representative Claire Gambee
Partnership Marketing Manager Pamela Putprush
Director, Customer Support Amy Bootier
Senior Customer Loyalty & Support Specialists Rebecca Kowalski, Andrew Straaberg Finfrock
Customer Loyalty & Support Specialist Caroline Augliere

Senior VP, Human Resources & Organizational Development Colleen Zelina
Human Resources Director Adele Shapiro
Director, Retail Book Program Beth Ineson
Retail Sales Manager Derek Meehan

Director, Public Relations and Communications Rebecca Wisdom

Circulation Services ProCirc

On the cover: Ultimate Bacon Burgers Keller + Keller, Catrine Kelty

AMERICA'S TEST KITCHEN ®

America's Test Kitchen is a real 2,500-square-foot kitchen located just outside Boston. It is the home of more than 60 test cooks, editors, and cookware specialists. Our mission is to test recipes until we understand exactly how and why they work and eventually arrive at the very best version. We also test kitchen equipment and supermarket ingredients in search of products that offer the best value and performance. You can watch us work by tuning in to *America's Test Kitchen* (AmericasTestKitchen.com) and *Cooks Country from America's Test Kitchen* (CooksCountry.com) on public television and listen to our weekly segments on *The Splendid Table* on public radio. You can also follow us on Facebook, Twitter, Pinterest, and Instagram.

8

21

22

Cook's Country magazine (ISSN 1552-1990), number 75, is published bimonthly by America's Test Kitchen Limited Partnership, 17 Station St., Brookline, MA 02445. Copyright 2017 America's Test Kitchen Limited Partnership. Periodicals postage paid at Boston, MA, and additional mailing offices, USPS #023453. Publications Mail Agreement No. 40020778. Return undeliverable Canadian addresses to P.O. Box 875, Station A, Windsor, ON N9A 6P2. POSTMASTER: Send address changes to Cook's Country, P.O. Box 6018, Harlan, IA 51593-1518. For subscription and gift subscription orders, subscription inquiries, or change of address notices, visit AmericasTestKitchen.com/support, call 800-526-8447 in the U.S. or 515-248-7684 from outside the U.S., or write to us at Cook's Country, P.O. Box 6018, Harlan, IA 51593-1518. PRINTED IN THE USA.

Primary Burners

In your grilling recipes, you often refer to a "primary burner" on a gas grill. How do I know which burner is the primary burner on my grill?

–Thomas Flynn, San Diego, Calif.

Most gas grills feature two or three burners (depending on the manufacturer and the age of the grill). In our gas-grilling recipes, we often call for adjusting the primary burner to a specific heat level and adjusting any secondary burners to a different heat level (or even turning them off) to set up hotter and cooler zones. These adjustments allow for indirect cooking (grill-roasting) in the cooler zone or cooking a variety of ingredients at different temperatures (searing steaks in the hotter zone while grilling delicate vegetables in the cooler zone, for example).

As for grill design and burner orientation, most newer gas grills—including our winning model, the Weber Spirit E-310—feature burners that run from the front of the grill to the back. Since gas grills do not typically have a default primary burner, we suggest designating either the burner on the far left or on the far right side of your grill as your primary burner. That way you have plenty of real estate on the rest of the cooking grate to place your food. If you happen to have an older gas grill with fewer burners or burners that run from side to side, you can designate either the front or back burner as your primary burner.

THE BOTTOM LINE: You choose which burner you use as the primary burner on your gas grill. We recommend using one positioned on the far left or far right side of the grill to allow the most space for cooking.

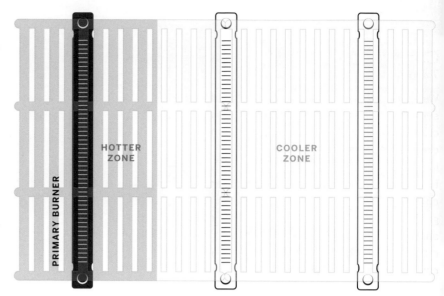

HOTTER ZONE

COOLER ZONE

PRIMARY BURNER

INDIRECT COOKING ON A GAS GRILL
Select a burner on one end of the grill as your primary burner; once the cooking grate is preheated, adjust the heat levels of the primary and secondary burners before placing the food 6 to 8 inches away from the primary burner so that it will cook gently.

Freezing Corn

There is nothing I love more than fresh, sweet summertime corn. Is there a good way to freeze it?

–Norman Gendron, North Conway, N.H.

To determine the best way to freeze fresh corn, we tried freezing whole husked cobs as well as kernels that we'd stripped from the cobs. We froze half the stripped kernels raw; we blanched and shocked (cooked them for 30 to 60 seconds in salted boiling water and transferred them to ice water to halt the cooking) the remaining kernels before freezing them. We sampled all the thawed corn plain and in our recipes for Double-Corn Cornbread and Cheesy Corn Casserole.

Our tasters preferred corn kernels that had been frozen raw—great news because you don't have to devote any time to blanching and shocking.

To cut the kernels from the cobs, remove the husks and silk from the cobs and use a chef's knife to cut the cobs in half. Stand the cobs on their cut ends (for stability) and use the knife to carefully slice the kernels from the cobs. Spread the kernels evenly (to keep them from freezing in clumps) on a rimmed baking sheet or plate and place in the freezer. Once they are frozen, transfer the kernels to a zipper-lock bag and freeze them for up to two months.

While the raw frozen kernels provide great flavor, don't expect them to have the same crisp texture as fresh kernels. They won't. That's why we use frozen corn only in recipes that specifically call for it, such as breads, soups, and casseroles.

THE BOTTOM LINE: To freeze corn kernels, cut them from the cobs and freeze them in a single layer on a plate or rimmed baking sheet. Transfer the kernels to a zipper-lock bag and freeze them for up to two months.

Remove Kernels
Cut the corn cobs in half to create a flat, stable surface, and then turn each cob on its cut end to slice off the kernels in strips.

Freeze in Even Layer
Spread the cut kernels on a baking sheet to freeze them without clumping. Transfer them to a zipper-lock bag once frozen.

Homemade Italian Seasoning

I often see Italian seasoning mixes at the grocery store. Can I make my own?

–Mary Jenkins, Waltham, Mass.

Italian seasoning mixes typically contain a combination of dried oregano, thyme, basil, rosemary, and sage.

For a make-at-home version, we tasted two common grocery store mixes, McCormick Perfect Pinch Italian Seasoning and Simply Organic Italian Seasoning, and then stirred together different amounts of each herb until we arrived at a balanced facsimile.

THE BOTTOM LINE: It's easy to make homemade Italian seasoning.

HOMEMADE ITALIAN SEASONING
Makes about ½ cup
To achieve a finer consistency, crush the dried rosemary by hand into smaller pieces or pulse it in a spice grinder (three to four pulses).

2½	tablespoons dried oregano
2½	tablespoons dried thyme
1	tablespoon dried basil
1	tablespoon dried rosemary
1	tablespoon dried sage

Combine all ingredients in bowl.

Submit questions and shortcuts at **CooksCountry.com/ask** and **CooksCountry.com/shortcuts.**

Chill Your Chips

A friend told me that storing opened bags of potato chips in the refrigerator would keep them fresher longer. Is this true?

–Laura Shea, New Orleans, La.

Stale potato chips make us sad, so we were excited to order multiple bags of our favorite chips, Lay's Kettle Cooked Original, and put this theory to the test. We removed half the chips from each bag, sealed each bag securely with a bag clip, and stored half the bags in the refrigerator and half in the pantry.

After two weeks, tasters noted that the refrigerated chips were crisp and fresh-tasting, while the chips stored in the pantry were a bit stale. Not surprisingly, after a month this difference was more pronounced. After two months, longer than most of us can make a bag of chips last, tasters noted stale flavors in both samples but strongly preferred the crunchy texture of the refrigerated chips to the softer texture of the chips from the pantry.

Why does the refrigerator help chips stay crunchy? First, its low-humidity environment means there's not as much moisture in the air for the chips to absorb and become soft. Second, potato chips are starchy; as starch molecules cool (as when refrigerated), they crystallize, becoming firm. This firmness makes for crunchier chips.

THE BOTTOM LINE: Storing opened bags of potato chips in the refrigerator can help keep them crisp.

compiled by Morgan Bolling

Corn for a Cookout
Ted McBride, Macon, Ga.

We serve a lot of corn on the cob at our backyard summer gatherings. To keep it hot and serve a crowd, I cut husked cobs in thirds, boil them, and drain. Then I melt a stick of salted butter on high in my slow cooker. Once the butter is melted, I turn the cooker to "warm" and toss in the boiled corn (and sometimes other seasonings such as garlic powder or hot sauce), give it a stir to coat, and throw on the lid. The cooker holds a lot of the mini cobs, and they're already buttered, so guests can easily grab one without stopping to doctor it.

Taco Tip
Greg Gullage, East Longmeadow, Mass.

Hard taco shells can be a challenge to fill because they don't stand up on their own. I've discovered that I can use my long grilling tongs, in the closed position, to easily hold two or three shells upright at a time for filling.

Chill Your Glasses
Shawn Tucker, Houston, Texas

Houston summers can get pretty sticky. For maximum refreshment, I keep glass tumblers in the freezer so they are frosty when my kids need some lemonade or soda to cool off. I found that the glasses get even frostier if I put them in the freezer when they're still a little wet from the dishwasher. I'm not a beer aficionado, but I suspect this would work pretty well for suds, too.

compiled by Cecelia Jenkins

Testing Ice Packs
by Lauren Savoie

SODA. BEER. SELTZER. Juice. Water. Whatever your preferred beverage, few things are better than a frosty drink on a hot summer day. A cooler loaded with loose ice is the standard way to keep your drinks cool—and your sandwiches from spoiling—in the heat of the sun, but we wondered if there was a better solution.

To find out, we selected eight ice packs priced from $3.49 to $29.99 and put them through their paces in the test kitchen, using laboratory probes and a computer to track their temperatures during a range of tests. The ice packs came in two basic styles: hard-sided packs of varying sizes and soft "ice blankets" that can be used to line the bottom of a cooler. We also tested plain ice, purchased in 5-pound bags from a local market.

Will our results surprise you? They surprised us—and made us think twice about how we'll pack our coolers.

 Go to CooksCountry.com/july17 to read the full testing results and see the complete results chart.

8 Ice Packs 5 Tests

1. Freeze the packs and track their temperatures as they thaw.
2. Submerge the frozen packs in room-temperature water and track the water temperature as it cools.
3. Fill coolers with frozen packs, add 24 cans of soda to each cooler, and monitor the temperatures for 36 hours.
4. Cut open the ice packs to extract the contents and weigh each.
5. Freeze 75 grams of each liquid and gel in identical containers and track how long each takes to reach room temperature.

Associate editor Lauren Savoie analyzed the liquids and gels she extracted from the packs.

BEST PERFORMER
Loose ice distributed its cooling power more efficiently than any of the ice packs we tested.

RUNNER-UP: BEST ICE PACK
The Arctic Ice Alaskan Series, X-Large ($20.99) was compact, contained lots of freezable liquid, and didn't bulge when frozen.

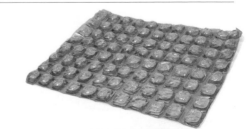

NOT UP TO SNUFF
These skimpy ice "blankets" contain lots of plastic and little liquid, so they failed to keep our food and drinks well chilled.

Deep in the Heart of Clod Country

Forks fall by the wayside at Kreuz Market in Lockhart, Texas, where the focus is on one thing only: meat.

by Bryan Roof

IN 1999, THE year Kreuz Market in Lockhart, Texas, celebrated its 99th anniversary, Roy Perez shoveled several pounds of smoldering coals from the restaurant's barbecue pit into a metal washtub. With a few media representatives in tow and a police escort to divert traffic, he and a coworker dragged the washtub down the road to the establishment's new location, where he carefully emptied the coals into a brand-new pit. The gesture was more than a photo op; this fire had been burning continuously for a century, and pit master Perez refused to allow it to go out on his watch. Superstition? Maybe, or maybe just efficiency: Kreuz's hungry regulars

expected barbecue even on moving day, and Perez, determined to serve them, needed a hot fire.

Seventeen years later, I made the trek to Kreuz Market on a quest for shoulder clod, a regional barbecue specialty. The immensity of the place engulfed me as I passed through a cavernous concrete hallway toward the barbecue pit where the mutton-chopped Perez spends most days. The stripped plywood walls held a patchwork of antique signage, black-and-white photos, and rusted butcher's tools. A menu above the counter offered promise: ribs, brisket, smoked ham, shoulder clod. Despite its magnitude, there was a warmth to the place, and wood-fire aromas perfumed the air.

Barbecued Chuck Roast

Step one: Find an easier substitute for a giant shoulder clod.

by Morgan Bolling

Barbecue fans say that Kreuz Market has some of the best shoulder clod in the country. At left, the giant pits contain flames from a fire that's been burning for more than a century. Below left, pit master Roy Perez and a coworker drag a bucket of smoldering coals from Kreuz's previous location to the new building on opening day.

I waited in line until I was called on to place my order, which I did with a mild fear of being recognized as the outsider I was. I ordered clod along with some sliced brisket and ribs, all in ½-pound increments. The cashier turned toward the pit and called out the order in a thick, rapid-fire patois that I struggled to understand.

Perez speared the meat with a large carving fork and moved it from the pit to a chunky, round butcher block well-greased from years of slicing fatty meat. Post oak logs burned in shallow craters at the ends of the sooty brick pits, and sawdust covered the surrounding floor to sop up errant drips of fat. A young man wrapped my order neatly in paper, propped a stack of sliced white bread on top, and handed it over to me as the next customers, a pair of police officers, stepped up to the counter.

I made my way to the dining room and found a seat at one of the long, unfinished wood tables, where paper towels and bottles of spice mix were stationed every few feet. I noticed a sign declaring "No Forks (They're at the end of your arm)." Empowered, I tore into the shoulder clod with my fingers, a little self-consciously at first but then with abandon as I surrendered to the primal pleasure of using my bare hands to eat meat—profoundly gratifying meat—that had been cooked over a century-old fire.

BEEF SHOULDER CLOD, a large boneless cut taken from the shoulder, delivers supremely beefy flavor underneath a dark crust spicy with black pepper and cayenne and well seasoned with salt. But shoulder clod can range from 13 to 21 pounds of meat. Twenty-one pounds!

I'm strong, but 21 pounds is a bit much for me, and besides, I couldn't find a local butcher with clod on hand. I looked instead for a more manageable cut of meat with similar characteristics. I considered top and bottom blade roasts, both cut from the shoulder, but soon settled on chuck-eye roast, a versatile piece of meat cut from a portion of the shoulder clod.

I rubbed my first roast (weighing in at 5 pounds, enough for a small crowd plus leftovers for sandwiches) with salt, cayenne, and pepper before cooking it over indirect heat on a hot grill outfitted with a packet of soaked wood chips (oak and hickory chips are the traditional choices to add smoky flavor to clod). About 2 hours later, when the roast had reached 140 degrees, I pulled it off the grill. After giving it a short rest, I sliced through the brown crust to reveal just a touch of pink in the center.

While it was deeply beefy in flavor, I found the roast chewy and underseasoned. Salting it overnight helped on both counts. Still not fully satisfied, I let my next roast cook a bit longer, until it reached 155 degrees, when the chewiness gave way to buttery tenderness. This took a little over 2 hours and was well worth the wait.

I knew that one last key to a tender serving of this roast was to slice it very thin. I let the roast rest for 20 minutes and then chose my sharpest carving knife to create thin, even slices. Tasters declared my shoulder clod—er, chuck-eye roast—tender, savory, and supremely beefy.

Perhaps the best compliment I got that day came when I asked if anyone wanted barbecue sauce. My tasters all said no, because none was needed; this showstopping clod-style chuck roast, with its richly seasoned bark and subtle smoky flavors, spoke for itself.

Go to CooksCountry.com/grills to learn which inexpensive gas grills rated highest in our testing.

Slicing the meat very thin ensures tender bites.

BARBECUED CHUCK ROAST
Serves 8 to 10

The roast must be seasoned at least 18 hours before cooking.

- 1½ tablespoons kosher salt
- 1½ teaspoons pepper
- ¼ teaspoon cayenne pepper
- 1 (5-pound) boneless beef chuck-eye roast, trimmed
- 2 cups wood chips

1. Combine salt, pepper, and cayenne in bowl. Pat roast dry with paper towels. Place roast on large sheet of plastic wrap and rub all over with spice mixture. Wrap tightly in plastic and refrigerate for 18 to 24 hours.

2. Just before grilling, soak wood chips in water for 15 minutes, then drain. Using large piece of heavy-duty aluminum foil, wrap soaked chips in 8 by 4½-inch foil packet. (Make sure chips do not poke holes in sides or bottom of packet.) Cut 2 evenly spaced 2-inch slits in top of packet.

3A. FOR A CHARCOAL GRILL: Open bottom vent completely. Light large chimney starter filled with charcoal briquettes (6 quarts). When top coals are partially covered with ash, pour evenly over half of grill. Place wood chip packet on coals. Set cooking grate in place, cover, and open lid vent completely. Heat grill until hot and wood chips are smoking, about 5 minutes.

3B. FOR A GAS GRILL: Remove cooking grate and place wood chip packet directly on primary burner. Set cooking grate in place, turn all burners to high, cover, and heat grill until hot and wood chips are smoking, about 15 minutes. Leave primary burner on high and turn off other burner(s). (Adjust primary burner [or, if using three-burner grill, primary burner and second burner] as needed to maintain grill temperature of 350 degrees.)

4. Clean and oil cooking grate. Place roast on cooler side of grill. Cover grill (positioning lid vent directly over roast if using charcoal) and cook until meat registers 155 to 160 degrees, 2 to 2½ hours. Transfer roast to carving board, tent with foil, and let rest for 20 minutes. Slice thin and serve.

Texas-Style Pinto Beans

This unfussy barbecue side dish proves that sometimes the simplest way is the best.

by Cecelia Jenkins

OFTEN, LUNCH AT barbecue spots around Texas includes a scoop of brown pinto beans on your plate. Different from mashed or refried versions, these beans are long-simmered with pork in a velvety, savory broth and are tender, flavorful, and creamy.

Dried pinto beans are the traditional choice for this dish. They are speckled, Jackson Pollock–style, until you cook them, and then the speckles disappear. They were ideal for a home on the range in the days before refrigeration: light enough to transport, packed with protein, shelf-stable for long chuck wagon journeys, and perfectly happy to bubble away unattended while home-steaders took care of other tasks.

To bring this tasty side dish to the test kitchen, I armed myself with heavy pots and several pounds of pinto beans and got to work on some existing recipes for my tasters to sample. A few called for chili powder, which over-whelmed the earthy bean flavor and subtle sweetness of the pork. Other versions tasted unpleasantly salty or totally washed-out. And most simmered into muddy-looking, starchy messes.

I tackled bean texture first. Dried beans took several hours to cook, and a quick-soak method (adding the beans to boiling water and then letting them soak for an hour off the heat before simmering them) rushed the process too much; the beans swelled unevenly and burst. The best and simplest solution? Soak the beans in water overnight, a step often taken to gradu-ally rehydrate them so that they cook relatively quickly (in about 1½ hours rather than 3 or 4 hours) and more evenly the next day.

Since I was soaking the beans, I added salt to the water to create a brine. Just as a salty brine penetrates chicken and makes it more moist, a brine simi-larly seasons beans. It also softens the beans' skins, making them more pliable so that when you boil them the next day, the skins stretch but don't burst.

When I was ready to cook the beans, I drained them and covered them with fresh water (3 quarts was just enough). I added a little salt to the cooking water; our science editor advised that this would ensure fully tender skins.

With the lid on my pot as the beans cooked, I couldn't easily monitor their progress, and I worried they'd stick to the bottom of the pot. Cooking the

beans uncovered meant that I could easily keep an eye on them. Another benefit was that the cooking liquid reduced, and I ended up with just the right amount for serving.

You'll be tempted to taste these beans before they're done, and you should. But even if you can bite through them after 30 or 45 minutes, they're likely to be unevenly cooked at that stage. Let them go for the full 1½ hours; they'll turn supremely creamy and will be infused with sweet and savory pork flavor. Plus, the re-duced sauce will take on a soft, velvety

texture, and you'll have just enough to serve with the beans.

To keep things simple, I skipped the spices and relied solely on pork for flavor. But which pork product to use? Bacon lost its flavor after simmering, and the slices turned into fatty strands that were hard to fish out. Salt pork added much better pork flavor but was much too salty—even when I tried it without any extra salt. But a smoked ham hock was the real winner. This powerhouse ingredient added smoky complexity, rich pork flavor, and meaty, buttery sweetness to the broth.

A Case for Dried Beans

We tried canned beans in this recipe and boy, were we shocked. They were sour, tinny, and pasty. Compared with the dried beans, the difference was as vast as the west Texas scrubland. Stick with dried.

WORTH THE TIME
In this three-ingredient recipe, flavorful dried beans are a must.

While traditionally served as-is, these beans are even better when garnished with chopped onion, pickles, chiles, or tomatoes.

Smothered Cabbage

Who knew such humble ingredients could be so satisfying?

by Alli Berkey

TEXAS-STYLE PINTO BEANS
Serves 8

If you can't find a ham hock, substitute 4 ounces of salt pork, omit the salt in step 2, and season to taste once finished. Monitor the water level as the beans cook: Don't let it fall below the level of the beans before they're done. If it does, add more water. Good garnishes include finely chopped onion, dill pickles, jalapeños, and/or tomatoes. Use the meat from the ham hock within a few days to flavor another dish. Plan ahead: The beans need to be brined for at least 8 hours before cooking.

    Salt
1 pound (2½ cups) dried pinto beans, picked over and rinsed
1 (10-ounce) smoked ham hock

1. Dissolve 1½ tablespoons salt in 2 quarts cold water in large container. Add beans and soak at room temperature for at least 8 hours or up to 24 hours. Drain and rinse well. (Soaked beans can be stored in zipper-lock bag and frozen for up to 1 month.)
2. Combine 12 cups water, ham hock, beans, and 1 teaspoon salt in Dutch oven. Bring to boil over high heat. Reduce heat to medium-low and simmer, uncovered, stirring occasionally, until beans are tender, about 1½ hours, skimming any foam from surface with spoon. Remove from heat and let stand for 15 minutes. Reserve ham hock for another use. Season with salt to taste. Serve.

Smoked Ham Hock

The lower portion of a hog's hind leg, a ham hock contains muscle, bone, fat, and connective tissue, which, when cooked for a long period of time over low heat, break down and add a rich, satiny texture to our beans. Most hocks, which are cut into 2- to 3-inch lengths, are cured or smoked.

THE PULLED PORK, brisket, and chicken legs offered at any given barbecue joint are only part of the story. Sides matter, too—think macaroni and cheese, coleslaw, baked beans, and fried okra. Everyone's got a favorite side dish for barbecue, and mine is smothered cabbage. This dish features roughly chopped cabbage leaves braised with onions and potatoes. When done right, the cabbage is buttery and tender, a mild counterpoint to the flavorful, spicy meat it's served with.

For the perfect texture—soft and tender, with just a hint of bite—I chose green cabbage over the savoy and napa varieties, cutting the large leaves into 1-inch pieces. And I learned that cooking the cabbage for 12 to 15 minutes in a Dutch oven with just 1½ cups of liquid gave me the perfect texture.

If cooked to the proper tenderness, cabbage retains and even deepens its sweetness, but its other flavors—the sharp, earthy notes—tend to fade. To help ensure that this dish maintained some complexity, I added some sliced onion, and for savory depth, I used chicken broth rather than water to braise it. And I added butter, of course, for a silky, rich finish.

Potatoes add bulk to this dish; plus, they soak up some of the inevitable—and delicious—meat juices that collect on your plate. Yukon Golds held up the best in the pot, and ensuring that they'd cook at the same rate as the cabbage was only a matter of cutting them into 1-inch pieces.

The final step in this recipe—removing the lid from the pot to allow the accumulated liquid to evaporate—left me with soft, tender cabbage leaves lightly coated with a savory butter sauce. Now all I needed was some 'cue.

This soft, savory side is ideal for soaking up the juices that run from barbecued meats.

Cabbage Primer

All cabbage is crisp and has a high moisture content. No matter the variety, look for tight, compact heads.

Green
Very crisp, firm texture and mellow flavor

Red
Interchangeable with regular green cabbage, though it is sweeter and more floral

Napa
More tender, milder, and slightly sweeter than green cabbage

Savoy
Loose, wrinkled leaves with mild earthy flavor and delicate texture

SMOTHERED CABBAGE *Serves 4 to 6*
We recommend buying larger Yukon Gold potatoes to ensure that you can cut 1-inch pieces. Potatoes cut smaller will overcook.

5 tablespoons unsalted butter
1 onion, sliced thin
1 large head green cabbage (3 pounds), cored and cut into 1-inch pieces
1½ cups chicken broth
10 ounces Yukon Gold potatoes, peeled and cut into 1-inch pieces
1½ teaspoons salt
½ teaspoon pepper

1. Melt butter in Dutch oven over medium heat. Add onion and cook until soft, about 4 minutes. Stir in cabbage, broth, potatoes, salt, and pepper and bring to boil. Reduce heat to medium-low, cover, and simmer until cabbage is wilted and potatoes are fork-tender, 12 to 15 minutes, stirring occasionally.
2. Increase heat to medium-high, uncover, and cook until liquid has nearly evaporated, about 12 minutes, gently stirring occasionally with rubber spatula. Serve.

Grilled Sausages with Bell Peppers and Onions

Like a walk-off home run, this ballpark favorite is all about timing.

by Ashley Moore

IT DOESN'T GET better than sitting at the stadium watching your favorite team with the sun shining on your face, an ice-cold beverage at your feet, and a plump, juicy grilled sausage, nestled in a soft roll and covered with slightly sweet onions and peppers, in your hand. But why should I have to wait for game day to have a grilled sausage sandwich in my hand? I set out to make this ballpark favorite at home.

Sausages need to be grilled over moderate heat—if the heat's too high, the casings can burst, dripping flavorful juices and causing flare-ups before the sausages are cooked through. The result: Dry, chewy sausages. I needed to find a balanced approach to achieve juicy sausages with just enough char from the grill.

After I'd experimented with a few existing recipes, one stood out. It delivered sausages ideally charred on the exteriors and perfectly cooked in the interiors, and the onions and peppers were soft and savory-sweet. This recipe started the sausages over low grill heat and then finished them on the hotter side of the grill. It also called for using a disposable aluminum pan to cook the peppers and onions, giving me the same results as if they had been cooked on the flattop grill at the ballpark. The pan provided an even surface on which they could sizzle away and develop slightly browned exteriors. The only problem was, the peppers and onions took much longer to cook through than the sausages. Nearly an hour, actually.

I wanted a faster method. Could I jump-start the cooking of the vegetables in the kitchen? I turned to the microwave. I figured I could lightly season the vegetables with a bit of vinegar, salt, pepper, and sugar before they went into the microwave and then transfer the softened vegetables to a disposable aluminum pan to finish them off on the grill.

 Still hungry? No worries. Go to CooksCountry.com/pretzels for our Ballpark Pretzels recipe.

A quick spin in the microwave ensures that the vegetables are done at the same time as the sausages.

It worked. I still had to have the parcooked vegetables on the grill for about 20 minutes to achieve the texture and browning that I wanted, but I'd saved quite a bit of time.

About that grill: I built a half-grill fire, arranging 6 quarts of lit charcoal briquettes on one side of the grill to create a hotter side. I put the disposable pan containing the vegetables directly over the coals and placed the sausages on the cooler side of the grill.

Once the sausages hit 150 degrees (I checked the temperature with an instant-read thermometer), I flip-flopped the pan of vegetables and the sausages so that both would finish cooking at the same time.

One more thing I learned: A few flare-ups are inevitable; there is no way to prevent a bit of sausage fat from dripping down onto the charcoal. But these minimal flare-ups—which last only a moment or two—are actually beneficial. They kiss each sausage link and add some color and slight char, ideal for grilled sausages.

Once the sausages' internal temperature hit 160 degrees, I knew they were done. I placed them in the pan with the tender vegetables, removed the pan from the grill, and covered it with aluminum foil for 5 minutes before spooning it all into rolls. My tasters were as happy as kids at a Saturday doubleheader—all that was missing was the crack of a bat.

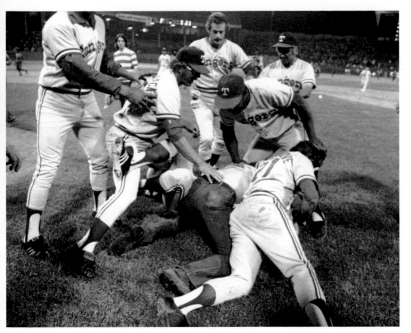
Too much cheap beer helped turn this 1974 Major League matchup into an all-out brawl.

Baseball fans go to the ballpark to watch the game, of course, but another part of the ballpark experience is the food: hot dogs, boxes of Cracker Jack, salty soft pretzels, and sausage-and-pepper subs. And to wash it all down? Beer, naturally. Nothing wrong with that.

THE AMERICAN TABLE

That is unless you're talking about the ball game played on June 4, 1974, between the Cleveland Indians and Texas Rangers at Cleveland Stadium, promoted locally as Ten-Cent Beer Night.

Other than a few well-intentioned streakers early in the game (hey, it was the 1970s, after all), the night was unremarkable until the late innings, when rowdy fans, fueled by an estimated 60,000 cups of beer sold, started pelting Texas players with hot dogs. In the ninth inning, things took an ugly turn when one Cleveland fan ran onto the field and threw a punch at a Texas right fielder. According to the *Beaver County Times*, thousands of fans followed suit, streaming onto the field for an all-out brawl. Chairs were cracked over players' heads, spectators were trampled—even game officials were bloodied before cops swarmed in to restore the peace. Umpire Nestor Chylak called a forfeit in favor of the Rangers, one of only a handful of forfeits in Major League Baseball history.

Substitutes for Sub Rolls

When we're shopping for sub rolls, we can't always locate the ideal size to serve with sausages. If you find yourself in the same predicament, consider one of these options. (It's also fine to serve the sausages with no rolls at all.)

TRY HOT DOG BUNS
Often a good fit for smaller sausages.

CUT LONG SUB ROLLS IN HALF
Place 1 sausage in each half.

HOW ABOUT A HAMBURGER BUN?
Split sausage lengthwise; lay halves side by side.

Don't Sweat the Flare-Ups

In most instances we try to avoid flare-ups by rearranging the food on the cooking grate. Here, since the sausages are on the hotter side of the grill for only 2 or 3 minutes, a few flare-ups can be beneficial, adding smoky char to their exteriors.

GRILLED SAUSAGES WITH BELL PEPPERS AND ONIONS Serves 6

You can substitute hot Italian sausages for sweet, if desired. Minimal flare-ups are to be expected when grilling the sausages on the hotter side of the grill; they give the sausages color and flavor. Our favorite instant-read thermometer is the ThermoWorks Thermapen Mk4.

- 3 red bell peppers, stemmed, seeded, and cut into ¼-inch-wide strips
- 2 onions, halved and sliced ¼ inch thick
- 3 tablespoons distilled white vinegar
- 2 tablespoons sugar
- 1 tablespoon vegetable oil
- ½ teaspoon salt
- ½ teaspoon pepper
- 1 (13 by 9-inch) disposable aluminum pan
- 2 pounds sweet Italian sausages
- 12 (6-inch) sub rolls (optional)

1. Toss bell peppers, onions, vinegar, sugar, oil, salt, and pepper together in bowl. Microwave, covered, until vegetables are just tender, about 6 minutes. Pour vegetable mixture and any accumulated juices into disposable pan.

2A. FOR A CHARCOAL GRILL: Open bottom vent completely. Light large chimney starter filled with charcoal briquettes (6 quarts). When top coals are partially covered with ash, pour evenly over half of grill. Set cooking grate in place, cover, and open lid vent completely. Heat grill until hot, about 5 minutes.

2B. FOR A GAS GRILL: Turn all burners to high, cover, and heat grill until hot, about 15 minutes. Leave primary burner on high and turn off other burner(s). (Adjust primary burner [or, if using three-burner grill, primary burner and second burner] as needed to maintain grill temperature between 375 and 400 degrees.)

3. Clean and oil cooking grate. Place disposable pan on hotter side of grill (over primary burner if using gas). Cover and cook for 20 minutes.

4. Place sausages on cooler side of grill and stir vegetable mixture; cover and cook for 8 minutes. Flip sausages and stir vegetable mixture again; cover and cook until sausages register 150 degrees and vegetables are softened and beginning to brown, about 8 minutes.

5. Transfer sausages to disposable pan with vegetables; slide disposable pan to cooler side of grill, then transfer sausages from disposable pan to hotter side of grill. Cook sausages, uncovered, turning often, until well browned and registering 160 degrees, 2 to 3 minutes (there may be flare-ups).

6. Return sausages to disposable pan with vegetables. Remove disposable pan from grill, tent with aluminum foil, and let rest for 5 minutes. Divide sausages and vegetables among rolls, if using. Serve.

A Three-Step Process

We shift the sausages and vegetables between the hotter and cooler sides of the grill to ensure even cooking.

Start microwaved bell peppers and onions in disposable pan on hotter side of grill, then arrange sausages on cooler side.

When sausages register 150 degrees, move them to hotter side of grill. Transfer pan with vegetables to cooler side of grill.

When sausages register 160 degrees, place them in pan with vegetables. Remove pan from grill, tent with aluminum foil, and let rest for 5 minutes.

Grill-Fried Chicken

We wanted the crunch of fried chicken without the frying. So we took it outside.

by Diane Unger

I HAVE A weakness for fried chicken—any sort of fried chicken. Deep-fried wings are my favorite because their small size makes it easy to get flavor all the way through the meat. And the high coating-to-meat ratio means more crunch per bite. But heating 3 quarts of oil to 350 degrees on a hot midsummer day? No thanks. I wondered if there was a way to get that deeply seasoned flavor and a thin, crispy coating using my grill.

I found very few existing recipes for this method and was disappointed by each one. The coatings failed on the grill, cooking up thick, hard, dry, and chalky and sticking to the grate.

Gnawing on a subpar drumette, I realized I was on my own—I'd have to start from scratch. So I brined 3 pounds of split chicken wings, deeply seasoning the meat so it would stay moist on the grill, and then put together a heavily seasoned flour coating. Hoping to help the coating adhere, I firmly pressed it into the chicken and put the wings in the fridge to rest (often helpful with coatings like this) before heading out to start my grill.

I knew that the wing pieces, although small, would take some time on the grill in order to render the excess fat in the skin. I loaded up my chimney starter and banked the hot coals into a mound on one side of the grill. I oiled the grate and then set the wings on the cooler side of the grill, with their fattier sides facing up.

The results? Decidedly mixed. On the positive side, the meat was juicy and flavorful, and I didn't have to flip

Brushing the chicken with oil halfway through cooking helps brown the coating.

Allowing the dredged chicken to rest before grilling helps the coating adhere.

the wings as they cooked. But the dry, dusty coating was a total letdown.

I wanted a crispy coating, but I also wanted it to glisten like deep-fried chicken. Oil is key to glistening chicken, so I tried creating a coating with some vegetable oil whisked in, but the wings cooked up greasy. I decided instead to experiment with brushing oil on the wings as they cooked.

I tested brushing the wings with oil before they went on the grill, but my results didn't improve. So I tried brushing them halfway through, at about the 30-minute mark. This gave the coating time to set up before I applied the oil. The light layer of oil soaked gently into the coating, creating a shiny exterior. Just 3 tablespoons was all I needed.

After the wings had spent another 30 minutes on the grill, I lifted the lid to discover that their coating had turned golden brown. My tasters devoured them, remarking on the satisfyingly crunchy coating and deeply seasoned meat.

GRILL-FRIED CHICKEN WINGS
Serves 4 to 6

We prefer to buy whole chicken wings and butcher them ourselves because they tend to be larger than wings that come presplit. If you can find only presplit wings, opt for larger ones, if possible. Ideally, 12 whole wings should equal 3 pounds, which will yield 24 pieces of chicken (12 drumettes and 12 flats, tips discarded) once broken down. Do not brine the chicken for longer than 3 hours in step 1 or it will become too salty. Charcoal grills tend to produce more-intense heat than gas grills do, hence the difference in cooking times.

	Salt and pepper
¼	cup sugar
3	pounds chicken wings, cut at joints, wingtips discarded
2	cups all-purpose flour
1	tablespoon granulated garlic
2	teaspoons paprika
½	teaspoon cayenne pepper
3	tablespoons vegetable oil

1. Dissolve ¼ cup salt and sugar in 2 quarts cold water in large container. Add chicken and refrigerate, covered, for at least 1 hour or up to 3 hours.
2. Set wire rack in rimmed baking sheet. Whisk flour, granulated garlic, paprika, cayenne, 1 tablespoon pepper, and 1 teaspoon salt together in large bowl. Remove chicken from brine. Working in batches of four, dredge chicken pieces in flour mixture, pressing to adhere. Place chicken on prepared rack. Refrigerate chicken, uncovered, for at least 30 minutes or up to 2 hours.
3A. FOR A CHARCOAL GRILL: Open bottom vent completely. Light large chimney starter mounded with charcoal briquettes (7 quarts). When top coals are partially covered with ash, pour into steeply banked pile against side of grill. Set cooking grate in place, cover, and open lid vent completely. Heat grill until hot, about 5 minutes.
3B. FOR A GAS GRILL: Turn all burners to high, cover, and heat grill until hot, about 15 minutes. Turn primary burner to high and turn off other burner(s). (Adjust primary burner [or, if using three-burner grill, primary burner and second burner] as needed to maintain grill temperature of 425 degrees.)
4. Clean and oil cooking grate. Place chicken, fatty side up, on cooler side of grill, arranging drumettes closest to coals. Cook chicken, covered, until lightly browned and coating is set, about 30 minutes for charcoal or about 45 minutes for gas.
5. Brush chicken with oil until no traces of flour remain (use all oil). Cover and continue to cook until coating is golden brown and chicken registers between 180 and 200 degrees, about 30 minutes longer for charcoal or about 45 minutes longer for gas. Transfer chicken to clean wire rack and let cool for 10 minutes. Serve.

BUFFALO-STYLE GRILL-FRIED CHICKEN WINGS

Add ½ cup Frank's RedHot Original Cayenne Pepper Sauce to brine in step 1. While chicken is cooling, microwave ½ cup Frank's RedHot Original Cayenne Pepper Sauce and 4 tablespoons unsalted butter in covered large bowl until butter is melted, about 1 minute. Whisk to fully combine. Add chicken and toss to coat before serving.

Pimento Mac and Cheese

Fans of creamy, tangy pimento cheese love it on sandwiches. We wanted it with macaroni.

by Alli Berkey

PIMENTO CHEESE LIVES in the hearts and the kitchens of many Americans, mostly in the South, but it's far too often relegated to sandwiches or crackers. There's nothing wrong with pimento cheese sandwiches, but why limit its range? I wanted to use this concoction—a mixture of sharp cheddar cheese, creamy mayonnaise, and tangy pimentos—in a warm, comforting macaroni and cheese casserole.

After a bit of research, I found a few recipes to try out. The worst were gloppy, chalky, greasy failures. One recipe stood out for its creamy cheese and punchy note of tanginess, but it was a bit too complicated, calling for homemade mayonnaise and a slew of different cheeses. I wanted a more straightforward route.

Many recipes for macaroni and cheese rely on a béchamel sauce for a base. This quick, flour-thickened milk sauce helps create a cheese sauce that stays silky and pliable without breaking or leaching grease—a common pitfall when using sharp cheddar (see "The Trouble with Aged Cheese"). I tested béchamel sauces made with plain milk, canned evaporated milk, and a combination of milk and cream; it was this final combination that was the creamiest, keeping the melted sharp cheddar in silky suspension. And rather than stir in mayonnaise, I added cream cheese—it provided tanginess as well as creaminess.

For a big flavor punch, I turned to pungent dry mustard and savory Worcestershire sauce, in combination with black pepper and hot sauce. And, of course, I added a cup of minced ruby-red pimentos.

I was hoping to avoid precooking the macaroni and instead simply stir everything together and bake it in a casserole dish, but the elbows were still crunchy when they came out of the oven. So I gave them a quick initial swim in boiling water (they were just short of al dente); they finished softening in the oven.

My savory, tangy pimento macaroni and cheese achieved every flavor and texture goal I was after. I may never eat plain macaroni and cheese again.

PIMENTO MAC AND CHEESE
Serves 8 to 10

We used Frank's RedHot Original Cayenne Pepper Sauce for this recipe. Barilla makes our favorite elbow macaroni.

- 1 pound elbow macaroni
  Salt and pepper
- 3 tablespoons unsalted butter
- 2 tablespoons all-purpose flour
- 1 tablespoon dry mustard
- 2 cups whole milk
- 2 cups heavy cream
- 1 pound extra-sharp cheddar cheese, shredded (4 cups)
- 2 ounces cream cheese
- 2 tablespoons hot sauce
- 1 tablespoon Worcestershire sauce
- 3 (4-ounce) jars pimentos, drained, patted dry, and minced

1. Adjust oven rack to upper-middle position and heat oven to 375 degrees. Bring 4 quarts water to boil in Dutch oven. Add macaroni and 1 tablespoon salt and cook for 5 minutes. Drain macaroni; set aside.

2. Add butter to now-empty pot and melt over medium-high heat. Stir in flour, mustard, ¾ teaspoon pepper, and ½ teaspoon salt and cook until mixture is fragrant and bubbling, about 30 seconds. Slowly whisk in milk and cream and bring to boil. Reduce heat to medium-low and simmer until sauce is thick enough to coat back of spoon, about 2 minutes, whisking frequently.

3. Remove pot from heat. Add 3 cups cheddar, cream cheese, hot sauce, and Worcestershire to sauce and whisk until cheese is melted. Add pimentos and macaroni and stir until macaroni is thoroughly coated in sauce. Transfer to 13 by 9-inch baking dish and sprinkle with remaining 1 cup cheddar. Bake until edges are lightly browned and filling is bubbling, 18 to 20 minutes. Let rest for 20 minutes. Serve.

TO MAKE AHEAD

Fully assembled casserole can be wrapped tightly in plastic wrap and refrigerated for up to 24 hours. When ready to serve, remove plastic and bake until heated through, 40 to 45 minutes.

Dry mustard and Worcestershire sauce add pungency and savory depth.

The Trouble with Aged Cheese

Aged cheeses such as cheddar are notoriously difficult to melt smoothly. That's because the aging process causes the cheese to lose a lot of water, which allows its protein clusters to move closer together and form stronger bonds. Cheddar also contains a lot of fat. This fat can melt long before the protein begins to flow, resulting in a separation of the fat and protein—a greasy, messy problem known as "breaking." Our recipe minimizes breaking by stabilizing the cheddar with flour. The starch in the flour coats the protein clusters, preventing them from coming apart and releasing droplets of fat as they melt.

What's a Pimento?

Though they look a lot like jarred roasted red peppers, jarred pimentos are made from a heart-shaped variety of red pepper that is slightly sweeter than a red bell pepper. In addition to being jarred or canned in an acidic brine, pimentos are stuffed into pitted green olives or dried and finely ground to make paprika.

Chicken Francese

A lemony, buttery pan-fried cutlet is appealing. Chicken wrapped in burnt scrambled eggs is not.

by Katie Leaird

DESPITE ITS NAME, chicken Francese is neither French nor Italian in origin. Yet this beloved egg-dipped, pan-fried chicken cutlet dressed in a tangy lemon-butter sauce—reportedly a 1970s invention from Rochester, New York—is still found on scores of Italian American restaurant menus across the United States.

Typically, when breading a cutlet (think chicken Parmesan), you use a three-step process: Dredge the cutlet in flour, dip it in eggs, and coat it in bread crumbs. For Francese you stop at the second step, sliding the egg-dipped cutlet into the skillet to cook. At its best, this creates a silky, delicate coating that absorbs the flavorful butter sauce. At its worst, you end up with an omelet-coated chicken breast.

For such a simple, ubiquitous ingredient, eggs can be vexing. Cook them too long and they scramble and burn; not long enough and they run. But after a few experiments, I realized that heat and time weren't my only challenges here—the real key to success was using the right cut of chicken. A breast proved far too thick to cook through before the eggs burned. Cutlets were much more promising. But precut chicken cutlets varied too much in size, and I couldn't control the outcome. I found that slicing boneless, skinless chicken breasts in half horizontally and then gently pounding them to a ¼-inch thickness was the most reliable and successful technique; throughout all my testing, my cutlets cooked through evenly in just a few minutes—before the coating could burn.

Now, about that coating. On my first try, I simply dredged my cutlets in flour and then in beaten eggs, but I ended up with a gloppy, gluey mess. Whisking some milk into the

eggs made the coating more fluid and easier to manage, but there was still a pasty quality to the dish that wasn't quite right. I switched from flour to cornstarch and found that it helped keep the egg coating in place and also eliminated the pastiness.

I wanted the right balance of butter and lemon for a velvety, slightly tangy sauce. So once all the chicken was fried and set aside, I added garlic, capers, chicken broth, and lemon juice to the skillet and reduced the mixture to concentrate the flavors before adding butter to thicken it. But this method cooked all the brightness out of the lemon, leaving me with a dull, one-note sauce.

I added a splash of white wine to my next batch for a bit of acidity and let it simmer with the chicken broth. I saved the lemon juice to stir in at the very end, with the butter, to preserve its fresh tang. The egg-coated chicken cutlets absorbed the silky sauce, making each bite lemony and luscious.

Briny capers provide a sharp counterpoint to the deeply savory sauce.

Cutting Chicken Breasts into Cutlets

Place one hand on top of the chicken breast. Position a sharp chef's knife parallel to the cutting board at the thick end of the breast and slice through the middle of the breast horizontally. Pound the pieces between two sheets of plastic wrap into ¼-inch-thick cutlets.

CHICKEN FRANCESE WITH LEMON-CAPER SAUCE
Serves 4

Freezing the chicken breasts for just 15 minutes makes them easier to slice into cutlets. To help keep the fragile egg coating in place, use a fork instead of tongs to flip the cutlets. Reese Non Pareil Capers are our favorite capers.

- 4 (6- to 8-ounce) boneless, skinless chicken breasts, trimmed
- ½ cup plus 1 teaspoon cornstarch
- 2 large eggs
- 2 tablespoons milk
- 1 cup chicken broth
- ½ cup dry white wine
  Salt and pepper
- 6 tablespoons unsalted butter, cut into 6 pieces
- 2 tablespoons capers, rinsed
- 1 garlic clove, minced
- 2 tablespoons lemon juice
- 1 tablespoon chopped fresh parsley

1. Adjust oven rack to middle position and heat oven to 200 degrees. Set wire rack in rimmed baking sheet. Place chicken breasts on large plate and freeze until firm, about 15 minutes.

2. Meanwhile, place ½ cup cornstarch in shallow dish. Whisk eggs and milk together in second shallow dish. Whisk broth, wine, ¼ teaspoon salt, and remaining 1 teaspoon cornstarch together in bowl.

3. Working with 1 breast at a time, starting at thick end, cut breasts in half horizontally. Using meat pounder, gently pound each cutlet between 2 pieces of plastic wrap to even ¼-inch thickness. Pat cutlets dry with paper towels and season with salt and pepper. Working with 1 cutlet at a time, dredge cutlets in cornstarch, shaking off excess; dip in egg mixture to coat, letting excess drip off; then place on large plate in single layer.

4. Melt 2 tablespoons butter in 12-inch nonstick skillet over medium-high heat. Transfer 4 cutlets to skillet and cook until golden brown and cooked through, 2 to 3 minutes per side, using fork to flip. Transfer to prepared rack and place in oven to keep warm. Repeat with 2 tablespoons butter and remaining 4 cutlets.

5. Add capers and garlic to now-empty skillet and cook until fragrant, about 30 seconds. Add broth mixture to skillet and bring to boil. Cook until reduced by half, about 5 minutes. Off heat, stir in lemon juice and remaining 2 tablespoons butter.

6. Transfer chicken to serving platter. Spoon sauce over chicken and sprinkle with parsley. Serve.

Pork Fried Rice

The fastest route to this Chinese American favorite is the phone. But the better route is your stovetop. *by Matthew Fairman*

Its ingredient list is a little long, but this dish comes together quickly.

WHEN THE DELIVERY driver's peeling out of our driveway and we're prying open the paper boxes from the Chinese restaurant a few blocks away, pork fried rice is always in one of them. And for good reason. Fried white rice makes a simple, texture-rich backdrop for flavorful pork and scrambled egg; the savory sauce brings it all together.

But can it be better—fresher, hotter, more delicious—at home? If you follow the traditional rule prohibiting the use of freshly cooked rice, then the answer is no. But I get ornery waiting for rice to cool down and dry out, so I took to the kitchen to see if I could test my way to a better, faster pork fried rice.

It was easy to choose a cut of pork. After rejecting loin and chops, I settled on widely available country-style pork ribs. Chopped and marinated briefly in soy sauce, brown sugar, baking soda (for tenderness and browning), and cornstarch (to help create a velvety texture), the pork cooked up juicy, tender, and beautifully browned.

The sauce took some doing. I began with a simple combination of soy sauce and brown sugar, but the rice just tasted monotonously salty. Traditional recipes call for hard-to-find ingredients such as Shaoxing wine (a Chinese rice wine) and fermented shrimp paste to punch up savoriness, so I opted for substitutes. Dry sherry is the test kitchen's go-to sub for rice wine, and it worked here, adding a pleasing nutty complexity. In place of the shrimp paste, I turned to more commonly available oyster sauce. For a little extra sweetness and brightness to bring this sauce home, I chose a surprising ingredient: ketchup. The blend of tomato, vinegar, and sugar acts as a three-in-one ingredient, adding depth and tang.

Ketchup? What Gives?

The ketchup called for in this recipe isn't as out of place as it might seem. Besides contributing a wide variety of flavors—sweetness, sharpness, savoriness, and more—it actually has deep roots in Asian cuisine. In Hokkien Chinese, the word *kê-tsiap* refers to a (tomato-free) condiment of fermented fish that made its way to Malaysia and Indonesia and proved very popular with 17th-century British and Dutch adventurers. Over time, *kê-tsiap* became *ketchup*, a catchall term for a wide range of multi-ingredient condiments, eventually including the tomato ketchup we know today. Our favorite supermarket ketchup is Heinz Organic Ketchup, which we love for the well-rounded range of flavors it provides—it's not just a hamburger topping.

With my sauce done, I was now ready to tackle the rice. It turns out there's a good reason not to fry freshly cooked rice: You create mushy clumps of steamy rice instead of distinct grains. But there's another way of cooking rice that I hoped might work here: the pasta method. Cooking rice like pasta helps ensure that it won't stick together, since the abundance of water sloughs away excess starch.

Skeptical yet hopeful, I tried it. I was delighted when the cooked rice hit the pan with a satisfying sizzle, broke up easily into individual grains when pressed with a spatula, and began frying just as the leftover stuff had. In minutes, I served up the fastest (and tastiest) pork fried rice I'd ever made.

Bringing Pork Fried Rice Home

Boil and Drain the Rice
There's no need for leftover rice. Cooking and draining rice like pasta rids it of starch, so it won't clump when you stir-fry it.

Use a Skillet, Not a Wok
Woks are designed to be used in an open cooking pit. A nonstick skillet provides better contact with a flat Western burner.

SIMPLE PORK FRIED RICE
Serves 4

The stir-fry ingredients can be prepped while your rice cooks, but be sure to have all the ingredients ready and close by before step 3 so you're equipped for fast cooking. We preferred the slightly higher fat content and heartiness of country-style pork ribs, but pork blade chops can be substituted with similar results (be sure to account for the weight of the bone when purchasing, though).

- 8 ounces boneless country-style pork ribs, cut into ½-inch pieces
- 4 teaspoons soy sauce
- 1 tablespoon packed brown sugar
- 1 teaspoon cornstarch
- ¼ teaspoon baking soda
- 2 tablespoons oyster sauce
- 1 tablespoon dry sherry
- 1 tablespoon ketchup
- 1 teaspoon salt
- ¼ teaspoon pepper
- 2 cups long-grain white rice
- 3 tablespoons vegetable oil
- 2 large eggs, lightly beaten
- 6 scallions, white and green parts separated and sliced thin
- 2 garlic cloves, minced
- ¼ cup frozen peas, thawed

1. Combine pork, 2 teaspoons soy sauce, sugar, cornstarch, and baking soda in bowl. Let pork mixture sit for at least 15 minutes, or cover and refrigerate for up to 1 hour. In separate bowl, combine oyster sauce, sherry, ketchup, salt, pepper, and remaining 2 teaspoons soy sauce; set aside.

2. Meanwhile, bring 3 quarts water to boil in large saucepan over high heat. Add rice and cook, stirring occasionally, until just cooked through and tender, about 12 minutes. Drain rice in fine-mesh strainer or colander.

3. Heat 1 tablespoon oil in 12-inch nonstick skillet over high heat until just smoking. Add pork in single layer and cook, without stirring, until browned, about 2 minutes. Stir pork and continue to cook, stirring frequently, until dark brown on all sides, about 3 minutes longer. Transfer to clean bowl.

4. Heat 1 tablespoon oil in now-empty skillet over high heat until shimmering. Add eggs and stir with rubber spatula until set but still wet, about 15 seconds. Push eggs to 1 side of skillet. Add remaining 1 tablespoon oil, scallion whites, and garlic to empty side and cook until fragrant, about 15 seconds.

5. Add rice and stir to break up clumps and any large egg curds. Cook until rice begins to sizzle and pop loudly, about 3 minutes. Stir in peas, oyster sauce mixture, pork, and scallion greens and cook, stirring constantly, until thoroughly combined, about 2 minutes. Serve.

Ultimate Bacon Burgers

Why put bacon on your burger when you can put bacon *in* it?

by Cecelia Jenkins

PERFECTLY CRISPED strips of salty bacon teeter atop a meaty burger piled high with your favorite toppings. You circle it, strategizing the perfect bite. Sound familiar?

Topping a burger with crispy strips of bacon is nothing new, but what about incorporating bacon into a burger? Now there's a wacky idea. Changing the bacon from an add-on to an add-in promised savory, bacony bliss in every bite, no plan of attack required. Now, how to execute it?

I found a few recipes that called for mixing chopped-up strips of bacon (raw in some recipes, cooked in others) with ground beef, shaping the mixture into patties, and grilling the patties. It sounded simple enough, so I got to work. Assembling batches of patties with different amounts of bacon and beef prepared in different ways, I eagerly anticipated a range of flavorful bacony samples.

I was sorely disappointed. Most of the bacon burgers were bland, and some cooked up tough, dry, and crumbly. How could an idea with so much potential be so underwhelming?

I felt robbed.

Determined to have tender, juicy, supremely bacony burgers, I zeroed in on the star ingredient. Though it seemed logical to mix raw chopped or ground bacon with raw ground beef before forming and grilling the patties, I soon discovered that combining sticky minced bacon and sticky ground beef led to overworked, compressed patties and tough, dry burgers despite the bacon fat that should have kept them juicy. (When we make meatloaf or meatballs, we avoid this problem by using a panade, a mixture of bread and liquid that adds moisture and guards against toughness. But I wanted bacon burgers, not meatloaf burgers.)

For the next batch, I tried mixing cooked bacon that I'd crumbled by hand into the ground beef. It was easier to form patties with this mixture than it was when working with raw bacon,

To take the bacon flavor over the top, we use the excess rendered bacon fat to cook the onion.

and spreading the beef out on a baking sheet, sprinkling the cooked crumbles on top, and combining the two with a fork helped distribute the bacon more evenly and made the mixture harder to overwork.

At eight slices of cooked and crumbled bacon, I'd reached the threshold; any more bacon tempted a grease fire on the grill. I wondered if I could achieve more bacon flavor throughout by processing the raw bacon in the food processor before cooking it to render out some of the excess fat. This step would also create even smaller bits of bacon, which were easier to incorporate into the meat mixture.

This worked but created an almost crunchy consistency, so for my next round I undercooked the bacon, rendering some fat but not taking it to a fully crispy texture.

Finally, I'd hit on the delicious bacon flavor and juiciness I wanted, and with 85 percent lean ground beef (15 percent fat), the burgers were tender but not delicate or crumbly (as they were when I tried using leaner 90 percent lean ground beef).

To take this burger to new heights, I topped it with crumbled blue cheese (a classic pairing) and onion that I'd sautéed in some of the leftover bacon fat. These additions took this already ambitious burger right over the top.

Just where I wanted it.

Bacon in Every Bite

For bacony goodness in every bite, we fold tiny pieces of partially cooked bacon into the ground beef. Grind eight slices of bacon to a paste in a food processor, and cook the paste gently in a nonstick skillet for just 5 minutes. Strain off the fat (reserve it for cooking the onion) before incorporating the cooled bacon into the beef.

FLAVOR FLECKS
We mix bacon bits deep into each patty.

Making a Good Impression

When we make burgers, we always form a shallow indentation in the center of each patty before cooking it. That's because the collagen, or connective tissue, in ground meat shrinks when heated. This causes the bottom and sides of the meat to tighten like a belt, which forces the surface of the burger to expand. To prevent a bulging burger, press a ¼-inch-deep divot into the center of each patty. When the collagen tightens, it will cause the divot to fill out so that it is level with the rest of the patty.

Shopping for Burger Buns

Ultimate burgers deserve top-notch buns. Our favorites are **Martin's Sandwich Potato Rolls**: They boast a mild sweetness that pairs well with a rich, salty beef burger. They also have a particularly light, tender, moist texture. That's because instead of hydrating the dough with water, Martin's uses a mixture of potato flakes, milk, and butter (essentially mashed potatoes). Mashed potatoes are hefty and substantial, but in potato rolls, the milk protein and butterfat weaken the structure of the dough, leaving the rolls softer, moister, and more tender.

BEST BUNS: LIGHT, TENDER, MOIST

GRILLED BACON BURGERS WITH CARAMELIZED ONION
Serves 4

Martin's Sandwich Potato Rolls are our favorite hamburger buns, and Oscar Mayer Naturally Hardwood Smoked Bacon is our favorite thin-sliced bacon. Be gentle when shaping the patties, taking care not to overwork the meat, or the burgers will become dense. Serve the burgers with lettuce and tomato, if desired.

- 8 slices bacon
- 1 large onion, halved and sliced thin
  Salt and pepper
- 1½ pounds 85 percent lean ground beef
- 4 ounces blue cheese, crumbled and chilled (1 cup) (optional)
- 4 hamburger buns, toasted

1. Process bacon in food processor to smooth paste, about 1 minute, scraping down sides of bowl as needed. Cook bacon in 12-inch nonstick skillet over medium heat until lightly browned in spots but still pink (do not cook until crispy), about 5 minutes, breaking up pieces with spoon. Drain bacon in fine-mesh strainer set over bowl. Transfer bacon to paper towel–lined plate and let cool completely. Reserve bacon fat.

2. Add 2 tablespoons reserved fat to now-empty skillet and heat over medium heat until shimmering. Add onion and ¼ teaspoon salt and cook until well browned, about 20 minutes. Transfer to bowl and set aside.

3. Spread beef in even layer in rimmed baking sheet. Sprinkle bacon, 1 teaspoon pepper, and ⅛ teaspoon salt over beef. Gently toss with 2 forks to combine. Divide beef mixture into 4 equal mounds. Gently shape each mound into ¾-inch-thick patty about 4½ inches in diameter. Using your fingertips, press center of each patty down until about ½ inch thick, creating slight divot. (Patties can be covered and refrigerated for up to 24 hours.)

4A. FOR A CHARCOAL GRILL: Open bottom vent completely. Light large chimney starter filled with charcoal briquettes (6 quarts). When top coals are partially covered with ash, pour evenly over grill. Set cooking grate in place, cover, and open lid vent completely. Heat grill until hot, about 5 minutes.

4B. FOR A GAS GRILL: Turn all burners to high, cover, and heat grill until hot, about 15 minutes. Leave all burners on high.

5. Clean and oil cooking grate. Season patties with pepper. Cook patties divot side down, uncovered, until browned, about 3 minutes. Flip patties and top each with ¼ cup blue cheese, if using. Cover and continue to cook until burgers register 125 degrees (for medium-rare) or 130 degrees (for medium), about 2 minutes longer. Transfer burgers to buns, top with onion, and serve.

Is Crumbled Blue Cheese Any Good?

by Hannah Crowley

FOR MANY KITCHEN tasks—dips, dressings, salads, sauces—crumbled blue cheese is an easier alternative to the stinky, sticky task of crumbling a wedge yourself. In search of the best crumbled blue cheese, we chose five products carried in national supermarkets and tasted them in a series of blind taste tests: plain, in blue cheese dressing, and toasted on crostini. The goal was a rich, creamy cheese with an unmistakably pungent (but balanced) blue-cheese funk.

PRODUCT TASTING

We noticed right away that tasters preferred the amplified funk of cheeses that were bluer in color to whiter cheeses, which they thought tasted more like "feta" or "cheddar." The trend held for dressing, too; those made with whiter cheeses lacked blue cheese's signature "blue" flavor and thus tasted more like ranch or mayonnaise. Not surprisingly, the "blue" flavor in blue cheese comes from the blue mold. Why do some blue cheeses have more blue mold?

To produce blue cheese, mold spores are added to the milk early in the cheese-making process. Like seeds in soil, the mold spores germinate and grow in the cheese as it ages. We assumed that the bluer cheeses simply had more mold spores added, but according to Dean Sommer, cheese and food technologist at the Center for Dairy Research at the University of Wisconsin–Madison, that's not the case. Mold needs oxygen to grow, and how much flavorful blue mold develops depends largely on how much oxygen the spores are exposed to. Cheese makers can control this by making cheese with more natural air pockets or by piercing the developing cheeses with metal rods to create airflow. The sharper blue cheeses in our lineup were exposed to more oxygen during production.

Two other keys to success: using raw milk, which makes for a more complex, nuanced cheese, and the addition of potato starch—not the cellulose many manufacturers use—to prevent clumping. Our winner, Roth Buttermilk Blue Crumbles, hit all the marks and impressed tasters with its moist texture and bold but balanced funk.

RECOMMENDED	TASTERS' NOTES
Our Favorite  **Roth** Buttermilk Blue Crumbles **Price:** $3.99 for 4 oz ($1.00 per oz)	"Now that's blue cheese!" wrote one taster about this top-rated product. It was "assertive yet dignified." Or, as another taster put it, this cheese had a "good amount of funk without tasting like feet." Its "clear, clean blue cheese" flavor had a "well-balanced" acidity, and its "lush" crumbles were "soft and creamy" both cooked and uncooked.
Boar's Head Creamy Blue All Natural Cheese Crumbles **Price:** $6.49 for 6 oz ($1.08 per oz)	This "creamy" cheese had a nice smooth texture both cooked and raw. With a "sharp, punchy tang," it was "ripe," "intense," and "assertively funky," with some "savory" and "floral" notes. Most blue-cheese lovers liked this "mega blue," but it was too assertive for a few: "Packs a punch." "Too strong for me."
Athenos Crumbled Blue Cheese **Price:** $4.29 for 4.5 oz ($0.95 per oz)	This product uses cellulose to keep its crumbles separate but was not as dry as other cheeses with cellulose added. Tasters noted that the crumbles were slightly dry when tasted plain but deemed them fine in the dressing and "mostly melty and smooth" on the crostini.

 Go to **CooksCountry.com/july17** to see the full results of our crumbled blue cheese tasting.

Broiling the stuffed tomatoes for just 5 minutes unlocks their deepest flavors.

HASSELBACK TOMATOES
Serves 4 to 6
For the best results, we recommend buying ripe tomatoes of similar weight and size. We developed this recipe with tomatoes that averaged 3 ounces in weight and 2½ inches in length.

- 8 ripe plum tomatoes, cored
- 7 ounces Gruyère cheese, shredded (1¾ cups)
- 1½ cups fresh basil leaves
- 6 tablespoons extra-virgin olive oil
- ¼ cup panko bread crumbs
- 1 garlic clove, minced
  Salt and pepper

1. Line rimmed baking sheet with aluminum foil and set wire rack in sheet. Using serrated knife, cut ¼-inch-thick slice from 1 long side of each tomato. Turn tomatoes onto cut sides so they sit flat, then slice crosswise at ¼-inch intervals, leaving bottom ¼ inch of each tomato intact.
2. Process ¾ cup Gruyère, basil, oil, panko, garlic, ½ teaspoon salt, and ½ teaspoon pepper in food processor until smooth, scraping down sides of bowl as needed, about 10 seconds.
3. Adjust oven rack 6 inches from broiler element and heat broiler. Combine ¾ teaspoon salt and ¾ teaspoon pepper in bowl. Carefully open tomato slices and sprinkle with salt-pepper mixture. Using small spoon, spread basil mixture evenly between tomato slices (about 2 tablespoons per tomato).
4. Arrange tomatoes on prepared wire rack. Sprinkle remaining 1 cup Gruyère over tomatoes. Broil until cheese is golden brown, about 5 minutes. Serve.

Prepping the Tomatoes

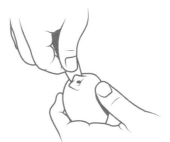

Using paring knife (see our favorite model on page 30), remove core.

Using serrated knife, cut ¼-inch-thick slice from 1 long side of each tomato. Turn tomatoes onto cut sides so they sit flat, then slice crosswise at ¼-inch intervals, leaving bottom ¼ inch intact.

Hasselback Tomatoes

This trendy side dish made us skeptical—until we tried it. *by Ashley Moore*

YOU MAY HAVE heard of Hasselback potatoes, the accordion-like, sliced-yet-still-in-one-piece potatoes covered in butter, topped with cheesy bread crumbs, and baked. You may have seen Hasselback squash or even eggplant. But what about tomatoes?

"Hasselbacking" is nothing new. Back in the 1950s, cooks at the Hasselbacken Hotel in Stockholm, Sweden, were peeling and partially slicing large potatoes, brushing them with butter, sprinkling them with bread crumbs, and baking them. Customers took to them for their striking look but also for the range of textures this process creates. They are still on the hotel's menu today.

But I was focused on tomatoes, not potatoes. I wondered if a similar technique would have an equally big impact. After consulting with my test kitchen coworkers, I decided to double down on summery flavors, stuffing the tomatoes with vibrant pesto and soft, flavorful cheese.

I started by making a homemade pesto of basil leaves, garlic, Parmesan cheese, and olive oil in the food processor, adding some crunchy panko bread crumbs. I set this aside and sliced several slits into some cored plum tomatoes, almost to their bottoms, leaving about ¼ inch intact (see "Prepping the Tomatoes"). I seasoned the tomatoes with salt and pepper, spread the pesto mixture evenly throughout the tomatoes, and sprinkled them with Parmesan cheese. I baked them until

the cheese was bubbling and called down my team to taste.

The consensus? These were OK, but they lacked punch. I knew the basil was powerful, so for my next test I swapped out the Parmesan for more pungent, flavorful Gruyère cheese. By the time they'd baked long enough for the cheese to melt, the tomatoes were soggy and unappetizing.

I decided to ditch the baking in favor of broiling; this switch would limit the amount of time the tomatoes spent in the oven and allow them to hold on to some summery freshness. I was right: A short blast under the broiler did the trick. Now I had warm but fresh-tasting tomatoes, melty cheese, and crunchy crumbs. Just right.

Tuna Steaks with Cucumber-Peanut Salad

30-MINUTE SUPPER

Spiced Beef Pitas

30-MINUTE SUPPER

Smoked Salmon Niçoise Salad

30-MINUTE SUPPER

Hash Brown Frittata

30-MINUTE SUPPER

Spiced Beef Pitas *Serves 4*

WHY THIS RECIPE WORKS: Pumpkin pie spice takes the place of the usual assortment of warm spices to simplify preparation while keeping the depth of flavor.

- ¼ cup tahini
- 3 tablespoons lemon juice
- 3 tablespoons water
- Salt and pepper
- 1 (14-ounce) bag green coleslaw mix
- ½ cup fresh parsley leaves
- 1 pound 85 percent lean ground beef
- 2 garlic cloves, minced
- 1 teaspoon ground cumin
- ½ teaspoon pumpkin pie spice
- 2 (8-inch) pita breads, halved

1. Whisk tahini, lemon juice, water, and ½ teaspoon salt together in medium bowl. Add coleslaw mix and parsley and toss to combine. Combine beef, garlic, cumin, pie spice, 1 teaspoon salt, and ½ teaspoon pepper in separate bowl. Shape beef mixture into four 6 by 3-inch oval patties.
2. Place patties in 12-inch nonstick skillet and cook over medium-high heat until browned on bottom, about 4 minutes. Flip patties and continue to cook until browned on second side and just cooked through, about 2 minutes longer. Stuff each pita half with 1 patty, then divide cabbage mixture evenly among pita halves. Serve.

TEST KITCHEN NOTE: Garnish with diced tomatoes and plain yogurt.

Tuna Steaks with Cucumber-Peanut Salad
Serves 4

WHY THIS RECIPE WORKS: Peanuts give the cucumber salad a crunchy contrast, and the fish sauce and lime juice in the dressing complement the tuna.

- 1 English cucumber, halved lengthwise and sliced thin
- ⅓ cup unsalted dry-roasted peanuts, chopped coarse
- ¼ cup fresh cilantro leaves
- ¼ cup fresh mint leaves, torn
- 2 tablespoons vegetable oil
- 1 tablespoon lime juice
- 1 tablespoon fish sauce
- 1 teaspoon Asian chili-garlic sauce
- Kosher salt and pepper
- 4 (8-ounce) tuna steaks, 1 inch thick

1. Toss cucumber, peanuts, cilantro, mint, 1 tablespoon oil, lime juice, fish sauce, chili-garlic sauce, and ¼ teaspoon salt together in bowl. Set aside.
2. Pat tuna dry with paper towels. Sprinkle each side of each steak with ¼ teaspoon salt and ¼ teaspoon pepper. Heat remaining 1 tablespoon oil in 12-inch nonstick skillet over medium-high heat until just smoking. Cook tuna until well browned on each side (but centers remain red), about 2 minutes per side. Serve with cucumber salad.

TEST KITCHEN NOTE: To cook the tuna to medium-well, increase the cooking time in step 2 to about 4 minutes per side.

Hash Brown Frittata *Serves 4*

WHY THIS RECIPE WORKS: Lining the pan with shredded potatoes creates a unique crunchy crust and a potato side dish all in one.

- 12 large eggs
- ⅓ cup whole milk
- Salt and pepper
- 8 ounces asparagus, trimmed and cut into ¼-inch pieces
- ¼ cup minced fresh chives
- 3 tablespoons unsalted butter
- 1 pound Yukon Gold potatoes, unpeeled, shredded and squeezed dry
- 4 ounces Gruyère cheese, shredded (1 cup)

1. Whisk eggs, milk, ¾ teaspoon salt, and ½ teaspoon pepper together in large bowl. Stir in asparagus and chives and set aside.
2. Melt butter in 12-inch nonstick skillet over medium-high heat. Add potatoes, ½ teaspoon salt, and ¼ teaspoon pepper. Cook, stirring occasionally, until potatoes begin to brown, about 4 minutes. Using rubber spatula, spread and pack potatoes into even layer in bottom of pan. Pour egg mixture over top and sprinkle with Gruyère.
3. Reduce heat to medium-low, cover, and cook until egg mixture has set, 12 to 14 minutes. Remove from heat and let rest, covered, for 5 minutes. Transfer to cutting board, slice into wedges, and serve.

TEST KITCHEN NOTE: To remove the moisture from the potatoes, squeeze them in a clean dish towel.

Smoked Salmon Niçoise Salad *Serves 4*

WHY THIS RECIPE WORKS: Starting the potatoes first and adding the green beans later ensures that both vegetables finish cooking at the same time.

- 1 pound small red potatoes, unpeeled, halved
- Salt and pepper
- 8 ounces green beans, trimmed
- ⅔ cup sour cream
- 2 tablespoons lemon juice
- 1 tablespoon chopped fresh dill
- 10 ounces (10 cups) mesclun
- 4 hard-cooked large eggs, halved
- 8 ounces sliced smoked salmon
- ½ cup pitted kalamata olives, halved

1. Bring 2 quarts water to boil in large saucepan over medium-high heat. Add potatoes and 1½ tablespoons salt; return to boil and cook for 10 minutes. Add green beans and continue to cook until both vegetables are tender, about 4 minutes longer. Drain.
2. Combine sour cream, lemon juice, 2 tablespoons water, dill, ¼ teaspoon salt, and ⅛ teaspoon pepper in small bowl. Toss mesclun and ¼ cup sour cream mixture together in large bowl. Divide dressed mesclun, potatoes, green beans, and eggs evenly among 4 bowls. Divide salmon and olives evenly among bowls. Drizzle salads with remaining dressing. Serve.

TEST KITCHEN NOTE: Use small red potatoes measuring 1 to 2 inches in diameter.

Jalapeño Chicken Quesadillas

30-MINUTE SUPPER

Teriyaki Chicken Kebabs with Grilled Bok Choy

30-MINUTE SUPPER

Orzo with Sausage and Broccoli Rabe

30-MINUTE SUPPER

Grilled Pork Chops with Plums

30-MINUTE SUPPER

Teriyaki Chicken Kebabs with Grilled Bok Choy *Serves 4*

WHY THIS RECIPE WORKS: We brush the teriyaki sauce on the chicken toward the end of grilling so that it stays bright and sweet rather than burning and turning bitter.

- 4 heads baby bok choy (4 ounces each), halved
- 1 tablespoon vegetable oil
  Salt and pepper
- 1½ pounds boneless, skinless chicken breasts, trimmed and cut into 1-inch pieces
- ½ pineapple, peeled, cored, and cut into 1-inch pieces
- ½ red onion, cut into 1-inch pieces
- ½ cup teriyaki sauce
- 2 teaspoons toasted sesame seeds

1. Toss bok choy, oil, ½ teaspoon salt, and ¼ teaspoon pepper together in bowl. Cover and microwave until beginning to soften, about 5 minutes.
2. Thread 1 chicken piece, then 1 pineapple piece, then 1 onion piece onto each of eight 12-inch metal skewers. Repeat pattern 2 more times on each skewer. Season all over with salt and pepper.
3. Grill bok choy and kebabs over hot fire until bok choy is char-streaked and tender and chicken registers 160 degrees, about 10 minutes, flipping halfway through cooking. Brush ¼ cup teriyaki sauce onto kebabs and continue to cook until lightly charred, about 2 minutes longer. Transfer kebabs and bok choy to platter, brush chicken with remaining ¼ cup teriyaki sauce, and sprinkle with sesame seeds. Serve.

TEST KITCHEN NOTE: You will need eight 12-inch metal skewers for this recipe. Serve with rice.

Jalapeño Chicken Quesadillas *Serves 4*

WHY THIS RECIPE WORKS: Weighing the quesadillas down with a heavy pot evens out the cooking and promotes crispy tortillas.

- 1 (2½-pound) rotisserie chicken, skin and bones discarded, meat shredded into bite-size pieces (3 cups)
- 8 ounces Monterey Jack cheese, shredded (2 cups)
- ¾ cup jarred pickled jalapeños, chopped fine
- ½ cup fresh corn kernels
- 4 scallions, sliced thin
- ¼ teaspoon pepper
- 4 (10-inch) flour tortillas
- 3 tablespoons vegetable oil

1. Combine chicken, Monterey Jack, jalapeños, corn, scallions, and pepper in bowl. Spread 1 heaping cup chicken mixture over half of each tortilla, leaving ½-inch border at edge. Fold tortillas over filling, pressing firmly to seal.
2. Heat 2 tablespoons oil in 12-inch nonstick skillet over medium heat until shimmering. Place 2 quesadillas in skillet, weigh down with large saucepan, and cook until browned and cheese has melted, about 2 minutes per side. Transfer to cutting board. Repeat with remaining 1 tablespoon oil and remaining 2 quesadillas. Cut into wedges and serve.

TEST KITCHEN NOTE: Serve with sour cream and salsa.

Grilled Pork Chops with Plums *Serves 4*

WHY THIS RECIPE WORKS: Thin-cut chops grill up in a flash, and the brown sugar in the rub aids in browning.

- 2 tablespoons extra-virgin olive oil
- 1 tablespoon lemon juice
- 4 plums, halved and pitted
- 2 tablespoons packed brown sugar
- 1½ teaspoons ground coriander
- ½ teaspoon ground ginger
  Salt and pepper
- 4 (6-ounce) bone-in pork rib or center-cut chops, ½ inch thick, trimmed
- 3 ounces (3 cups) baby arugula

1. Whisk oil and lemon juice together in medium bowl; set aside dressing. Rub cut sides of plums with 1 tablespoon sugar. Combine coriander, ginger, 1 teaspoon salt, ¼ teaspoon pepper, and remaining 1 tablespoon sugar in small bowl. Pat pork dry with paper towels and sprinkle all over with spice mixture.
2. Cook pork over hot fire until browned and meat registers 140 degrees, 2 to 3 minutes per side. Transfer to platter, tent with foil, and let rest for 10 minutes. Cook plums over hot fire until caramelized and tender, about 3 minutes per side.
3. Add plums and arugula to bowl with dressing and toss to combine. Transfer to platter with pork and serve.

TEST KITCHEN NOTE: Peaches can be substituted for the plums, if desired.

Orzo with Sausage and Broccoli Rabe *Serves 4*

WHY THIS RECIPE WORKS: Sweet, spicy, salty Peppadew peppers liven up this sausage-studded dish.

- 2 tablespoons extra-virgin olive oil
- 8 ounces broccoli rabe, trimmed and cut into 1½-inch pieces
- ¼ teaspoon salt
- 4 garlic cloves, sliced thin
- 1 pound sweet Italian sausage, cut into 1-inch pieces
- 2¼ cups chicken broth
- 1¼ cups orzo
- ¼ cup dry white wine
- ½ cup thinly sliced jarred hot Peppadew peppers
- ⅓ cup grated Parmesan cheese

1. Heat 1 tablespoon oil in 12-inch nonstick skillet over medium-high heat until shimmering. Add broccoli rabe and salt, cover, and cook until wilted, about 2 minutes. Stir in half of garlic and continue to cook, uncovered, until broccoli rabe is tender, about 2 minutes longer. Transfer to plate and tent with foil.
2. Heat remaining 1 tablespoon oil in now-empty skillet over medium-high heat until shimmering. Add sausage and cook until browned, about 3 minutes. Add remaining garlic and cook until fragrant, about 30 seconds.
3. Stir in broth, orzo, and wine and bring to boil. Reduce heat to medium, cover, and cook until orzo is al dente and nearly all liquid has been absorbed, 6 to 8 minutes. Sprinkle broccoli rabe, peppers, and Parmesan over top. Serve.

TEST KITCHEN NOTE: For a spicy kick, use hot Italian sausage.

Smoke

Smoke is a fragrant, visible suspension of particles in air that rises from burning materials. Along with drying and salting, smoking is one of the oldest known methods of preserving and flavoring foods: Archaeologists think our ancestors of more than 3,000 years ago were using this technique. Here is what you need to know to add smoke to your culinary arsenal.

by Scott Kathan

Making Smoke Work for You

Most of our recipes for smoking call for food to stay on the grill for anywhere from 2 to 6 hours—so why do we use smoke only at the start? It's because the flavor compounds in smoke are water-soluble, and meat contains more water when it is cooler and uncooked. Since smoke doesn't penetrate much beyond the surface of meat, it is mostly the meat's exterior that absorbs smoke flavor. The cleanest, easiest way to smoke food on a backyard grill is to use wood chips (soaked in water to make them burn slower and smoke longer) wrapped in aluminum foil. The foil packet further ensures a slower burn and thus more smoke.

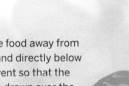

TOP VENT
This vent controls the draw of air through the grill. Position it directly over the food and open it fully, adjusting (in tandem with the bottom vent) as necessary.

FOOD
Place the food away from the fire and directly below the top vent so that the smoke is drawn over the food as it leaves the grill.

FOIL PACKET
Position the packet with the vent holes facing upward so that you can better direct the flow of smoke.

WATER PAN
A pan of water helps maintain a low temperature inside the grill. The water also creates humidity, which moistens the surface of the food to allow for better absorption of smoke's flavor compounds (which are water-soluble).

BOTTOM VENT
This vent governs the airflow so that there's just enough oxygen to promote slow, controlled combustion. We typically keep this vent fully open, but you can adjust it if you find that your charcoal is burning too hot.

Key to a Slow Burn

To make a foil packet, place soaked wood chips on a large piece of aluminum foil and fold the foil into a packet that measures roughly 8 by 4½ inches; then cut two evenly spaced 2-inch slits in the top of the packet so the smoke can escape. Place the packet on the fire and wait 5 minutes for the smoke to build before starting to cook.

Can You Smoke on Gas?

We prefer to use a charcoal grill for smoking because the vents allow for better control of the flow of air and smoke, but you can get good results on a gas grill. The trick is to preheat all burners, and then turn off the all but the primary burner and place the foil packet directly on it (under the cooking grate). Once the smoke starts wafting, place the food on the grill 6 to 8 inches away from the lit burner. Note that the smoke vents out the back of gas grills, so placing your food toward the back of the grate will expose it to more smoke.

Smoke Varieties

MAPLE
While we liked maple smoke on every meat we tried, some of our tasters found it "resin-y" on smoked salmon.

APPLE AND CHERRY
These relatively "mild" and "sweet" smokes are versatile but are especially good with mild foods such as whitefish, pork, and chicken.

HICKORY
We found this "balanced," "intense" smoke to be a strong all-around choice for chicken, fish, beef, and pork.

OAK
This "nutty," "mild" smoke is very well balanced and is the traditional choice in much of American barbecue.

ALDER
Its notes of "coriander" and "juniper" were great with fish.

MESQUITE
Mesquite smoke's strong flavor matches well with stronger-tasting cuts of beef, pork, lamb, and game.

Smoke Without Fire

The test kitchen is fond of two pantry ingredients that can add great smoke flavor without having to fire up the grill.

Liquid smoke is a potent flavoring agent made by channeling wood smoke through a condenser. The resulting liquid is great in barbecue sauces, dressings, and glazes. Our favorite is Wright's Liquid Smoke, which has a heady smokiness.

Chipotle chiles are smoked and dried jalapeños; they are commonly sold canned in a vinegary tomato-based adobo sauce. We like to mince the chiles and add them to all manner of Mexican and Tex-Mex dishes for a bold hit of smoke and heat. Leftover chipotles will keep in the refrigerator (in a nonreactive container) for up to three weeks.

North Carolina Cheese Biscuits

What makes a better biscuit? In some parts of the Tar Heel State, cheese.

by Christie Morrison

A light-colored cake pan helps us achieve the perfect golden color—not too light and not too dark.

Filling the Biscuits with Cheese

1. Using your hands, squeeze ⅓ cup shredded cheese into firm ball. Repeat to form 5 more balls.

2. Using greased ½-cup dry measuring cup, transfer 6 portions of dough to prepared sheet. Dust top of each with flour.

3. Flatten each dough ball into 3½-inch circle and coat with flour. Enclose cheese ball in center of dough and pinch to seal.

THE CATHEAD BISCUITS found in the region around Rocky Mount, North Carolina, are big, golden, and stuffed with molten, gooey cheese (see "Lining up for Biscuit Love"). These giant buttermilk biscuits, described as "big as a cat's head," are fluffy rather than flaky, partly due to the lower-protein Southern flour (such as White Lily) or self-rising flour traditionally used. The structure helps them keep their shape even when stuffed with cheese.

To develop a recipe here in my New England kitchen, I started with more commonly available all-purpose flour. And instead of lard, I chose butter for its rich flavor and because it's so much easier to find.

While experienced biscuit makers can cut fat into flour without thinking twice, I used a food processor instead, pulsing the chilled butter into the flour until the texture was like crumbly cornmeal. I used a lighter hand to incorporate some buttermilk, knowing that if I worked the dough too hard, I'd overdevelop the gluten in the flour and end up with tough, not tender, biscuits. I then greased a ½-cup dry measuring cup and divided the dough into 6 equal portions.

Regional cheese biscuit recipes call for hoop cheese, a yellow cheese common in North Carolina but hard to find elsewhere. After tasting a few more widely available options, I settled on yellow sharp cheddar cheese for its tangy flavor and meltability. And while cheese biscuit pros easily stuff a loose handful of shredded cheese into a wad of wet dough in a messy dance perfected by years of practice, I found that first pressing the cheese into more firmly packed balls made assembly much easier and didn't sacrifice meltability. (Experiments with just a wedge or slice of cheese led to unmelted middles.) I placed a cheese ball in the center of each slightly flattened circle of dough and gently pulled the edges up and around to seal the cheese inside.

Baking the biscuits in a round cake pan helped give them structure and kept most of the cheese from escaping, but the biscuits' texture was slightly gummy. So I took a cue from a favorite test kitchen recipe for mile-high biscuits, which called for twice as much buttermilk as I was using; the theory was that a wet dough would have a

Carolina hoop cheese can be hard to find, so we stuff our biscuits with sharp cheddar.

higher rise and a more tender, fluffy texture due to the increase in trapped steam. I gave it a shot, dusting my hands with a bit of flour to keep the dough from sticking as I shaped and stuffed the biscuits. Once they were nestled into a cake pan, I slid them into a hot oven to bake.

As the soft biscuits rose in the pan, their flexible structure expanded outward, building tender but still impermeable walls around the cheese. After about 20 minutes, my biscuits had turned a beautiful golden brown. I let them cool briefly before tearing one open and biting into the cheesiest, fluffiest biscuit I'd ever tasted.

NORTH CAROLINA CHEESE BISCUITS
Makes 6 biscuits

Look for sharp or mild yellow cheddar cheese; extra-sharp cheddar doesn't melt as smoothly. The biscuit dough will be very wet and soft. Keep your hands well floured and don't be afraid to sprinkle extra flour on the biscuits to keep them from sticking. To keep the biscuits tender and prevent overbrowning, use a light-colored cake pan; our favorite is the Nordic Ware Naturals Nonstick 9-Inch Round Cake Pan.

8	ounces yellow sharp cheddar cheese, shredded (2 cups)
3½	cups (17½ ounces) all-purpose flour
1	tablespoon sugar
1	tablespoon baking powder
½	teaspoon baking soda
1	teaspoon salt
4	tablespoons unsalted butter, cut into ¼-inch pieces and chilled, plus 2 tablespoons melted
1½	cups buttermilk

1. Adjust oven rack to middle position and heat oven to 500 degrees. Grease light-colored 9-inch round cake pan. Working with ⅓ cup cheese, use your hands to squeeze cheese tightly into firm ball. Repeat with remaining cheese to form 5 more balls; set cheese balls aside.

2. Pulse 2¼ cups flour, sugar, baking powder, baking soda, and salt in food processor until combined, about 6 pulses. Add chilled butter and pulse until mixture resembles pebbly, coarse cornmeal, 8 to 10 pulses. Transfer mixture to large bowl. Stir in buttermilk until just combined. (Dough will be very wet and slightly lumpy.)

3. Spread remaining 1 cup flour in rimmed baking sheet. Using greased ½-cup dry measuring cup, transfer 6 portions of dough to prepared sheet. Dust top of each portion with flour from sheet.

4. Using your well-floured hands, gently flatten 1 portion of dough into 3½-inch circle and coat with flour. Pick up dough and place 1 cheese ball in center. Gently pull edges of dough over cheese to enclose and pinch together to seal. Shake off excess flour and transfer to prepared pan. Repeat with remaining dough and cheese, placing 5 biscuits around edge of pan and one in center. (Biscuits will be soft and will spread slightly as they sit.)

5. Brush biscuit tops with melted butter. Bake for 5 minutes, then reduce oven temperature to 450 degrees. Continue to bake until biscuits are deep golden brown, 15 to 20 minutes longer. Let biscuits cool in pan for 2 minutes, then invert onto plate. Break biscuits apart and turn right side up. Let cool for 5 minutes; serve warm.

Lining up for Biscuit Love

by Bryan Roof

ON THE ROAD

IT'S 8:30 ON a Thursday morning in Wilson, North Carolina, and the line of cars for the drive-through window at Flo's Kitchen trails around the building and back out onto the street, where it stretches for several blocks. The traffic jam is a reliable morning occurrence as Flo's regulars line up for massive cathead biscuits stuffed with local hoop cheese. Waitresses approach cars, notepads in hand, to take orders. It's an efficient process; biscuits are churned out with such speed that many patrons get their food before they even pull up to the window to pay.

I have to dodge cars to get to the front door, but once inside I spy a stack of 5-gallon buckets of lard under the counter, a sure sign that I'm in the right place. The hustle in the air makes the place feel bigger than its tiny footprint should allow. Behind the counter, it's controlled chaos—two focused women work the griddle and deep fryer, preparing the eggs, bacon, and fried chicken patties that they'll tuck into split cheese biscuits. Behind them are two more employees on nonstop biscuit duty: shape, fill, bake, and repeat. Presiding over it all is the matriarch of Flo's, Linda Brewer, who works the cash register and delivers fresh biscuits and sandwiches to her customers, all of whom, first-timers and regulars alike, are named "sweetie," "honey," or "sugar."

Flo's isn't the only game around. Sixty miles to the east in Washington, North Carolina, you can find Alice Matthews churning out equally large—and no less cheesy—biscuits at Mom's Grill. While the pumps at this bright yellow gas station have long since emptied, customers still swing by religiously to fuel up on biscuits.

At Flo's Kitchen in Wilson, above, patrons entering or exiting on foot have to dodge the line of cars waiting for service at the drive-through window. Alice Matthews of Mom's Grill in Washington, below, stuffs and shapes dozens of cheese biscuits each morning. Just as at Flo's, most regulars use the drive-through window to pick up their daily biscuit.

Corn and Cucumber Salad

The key to coaxing the most from these subtle summer players was supplying the right supporting cast. *by Ashley Moore*

CUCUMBER AND CORN, two iconic farmstand ingredients, can be refreshing and lovely on their own. But exciting? Well, let's just say their charms are understated. Subtle. I wanted to create a salad that gave these two ubiquitous midsummer stalwarts a chance to be surprising.

A handful of existing recipes for corn and cucumber salad gave me poor results—some were tossed (or doused) in creamy dressings, others in tangy, vinegary ones. A few came off more like salsa than salad, with long lists of add-ins. None allowed the corn or the cukes to shine.

I took a step back and looked at the two primary components. First, corn. Should it be cooked? Raw? I nixed blanching the loose kernels cut from four ears of corn—corralling those kernels in simmering water took too much effort, and they overcooked quickly. Raw corn was too . . . raw. The best option was to lightly sauté the kernels in some olive oil for about 7 minutes, which turned them ever-so-slightly brown and deepened their sweetness.

Next, cukes. I chose an English cucumber, which has minimal seeds and less water than the American variety and delivers lots of crunch and a clear, clean flavor. I halved the cucumber lengthwise and sliced it into half-moons.

I whisked together a simple vinaigrette of lime juice, olive oil, salt, and pepper and added some sharp sliced red onion and minced jalapeño to this mixture; after it sat for a minute, the vegetables' sharp flavors and crisp textures softened slightly. I tossed the cooled corn, the sliced cucumbers, and the dressing together and sprinkled some salty feta cheese on top along with some torn fresh basil leaves. The restrained but still punchy dressing played well with the corn and cucumber, but the salad needed one final touch.

After a quick discussion with my team, I decided to introduce a creamy element to provide a soft, silky counterpoint. I stirred together a portion of the lime vinaigrette with a bit of tangy sour cream. I made the salad again and, after tossing it all together, drizzled this sour cream mixture over the top. Instead of covering up the vegetables' sweet, refreshing flavors, this creamy finish served as a launching pad, boosting the pop of sweet corn and the crunch of crisp, fresh cucumber.

A tangy lime and sour cream mixture, spooned over the top, adds a punch of flavor.

Which Cukes Are Best?

Long, slender English cucumbers are our top choice for salads. They have tiny seeds and more-tender skins, while American cucumbers have large seeds and thick skins that are typically coated in wax.

AMERICAN CUCUMBER
Too wet and seedy

ENGLISH CUCUMBER
Less water, tiny seeds, and an appealing crunch

CORN AND CUCUMBER SALAD
Serves 4 to 6

To make this dish spicier, reserve the jalapeño seeds and add them to the lime vinaigrette. For the best results, use the freshest corn you can find and do not substitute frozen corn.

- ½ cup extra-virgin olive oil
- 4 ears corn, kernels cut from cobs
  Salt and pepper
- 5 tablespoons lime juice (3 limes)
- ¼ cup sour cream
- ½ red onion, sliced thin
- 1 jalapeño chile, stemmed, halved, seeded, and sliced thin
- 1 English cucumber, halved lengthwise and sliced thin
- 3 ounces feta cheese, crumbled (¾ cup)
- ¼ cup fresh basil leaves, torn

1. Heat 1 tablespoon oil in 12-inch nonstick skillet over medium-high heat until shimmering. Add corn and ¼ teaspoon salt and cook, stirring occasionally, until tender and spotty brown, 7 to 9 minutes; transfer to large bowl. Refrigerate corn until completely cool, about 45 minutes.

2. Meanwhile, whisk lime juice, remaining 7 tablespoons oil, ¾ teaspoon salt, and ½ teaspoon pepper together in bowl. Transfer ¼ cup lime vinaigrette to separate bowl and whisk in sour cream; set aside. Add onion and jalapeño to remaining lime vinaigrette; let sit while corn is cooling, at least 15 minutes.

3. Add cucumber and onion-jalapeño mixture (including vinaigrette) to bowl with corn and toss to coat. Season with salt and pepper to taste and transfer to serving platter. Drizzle with sour cream mixture. Sprinkle with feta and basil. Serve.

CORN AND CUCUMBER SALAD WITH RED BELL PEPPER AND CILANTRO

Add 1 red bell pepper, cut into ¼-inch pieces, to skillet with corn in step 1. Substitute 1 tablespoon minced canned chipotle chile in adobo sauce for jalapeño. Top salad with 1 ripe avocado, cut into ½-inch pieces, and substitute fresh cilantro leaves for basil.

Got more corn? Go to **CooksCountry. com/huskgrilledcorn** for our grilled corn recipe.

Braised Zucchini

We've all been scarred by slimy zucchini. We think it's time to heal.

by Alli Berkey

YOU CAN'T ESCAPE zucchini at the height of summer. The little green squashes (and some not so little) are piled high at the farmers' markets and supermarkets. If you haven't got it growing in your backyard, you've got a neighbor trying to unload the extra zukes as a "gift."

Unfortunately, more often than not, after dutiful prepping and cooking, zucchini shows up at the table slimy and dull. I wanted to rewrite this script so that the final scene featured a fresh and summery but still warm side dish of gently cooked zucchini that was filled with vibrant vegetable flavor—hold the slime.

After cooking through several recipes, I learned a few things. Lesson number one: Always choose small to medium zucchini (less than 8 ounces each) for the best flavor. Like many seeded vegetables, when zucchini grow too large, their flavor fades and their texture becomes mealy.

Lesson number two: Even with the right size zucchini, if the pieces you cut are too small or if you cook them for too long, the flavor all but disappears, and you've got nothing but sad, stewed chunks.

Lesson number three (and this is the good news): Both of these obstacles are easy to clear if you shop and cook carefully.

Most methods for braising vegetables call for cooking them through in a very small amount of liquid before or after you've browned them. In this case, I wanted a cooking liquid that would allow the natural flavor of zucchini to shine rather than cover it up. After auditioning chicken stock and vegetable stock, I settled on the easiest possible cooking liquid: water. I doctored it with a bit of olive oil for flavor, two sliced cloves of garlic for a bracing counterpoint, a couple of sprigs of basil for freshness, and just enough red pepper flakes to contribute a restrained prick of heat.

I experimented with different-size pieces of squash. I found that when cut too small (½-inch cubes), the zucchini would cook into flavorless mush way too quickly. And when cut too big, it would turn a sad, muddy green before it cooked through. Two-inch pieces proved perfect; after 8 minutes on the stovetop, they were tender but still held their structure.

The flavorful cooking liquid makes for a fresh, satisfying sauce.

Braised zucchini benefits from a couple of finishing touches. I introduced some halved cherry tomatoes to the skillet near the end of cooking, tossing them in for just the last minute or two so that they'd brighten in color and not release too much juice. And I served lemon wedges alongside; a spritz of lemon added a final burst of fruity freshness.

Vibrant, supersummery, and flavorful, this was a cooked zucchini dish that even squash haters could love. Served warm, it's perfect for al fresco midsummer suppers.

Next time the neighbors come around with armfuls of zucchini from their overproductive garden, maybe I won't hide in the basement.

BRAISED ZUCCHINI

Serves 4

Zucchini no larger than 8 ounces are best. Larger zucchini have more seeds and moisture and are blander. Stir with a rubber spatula because it's gentle on the zucchini, which has a tendency to break apart. Zucchini skin can be sandy, so scrub it well when washing.

- 4 zucchini (8 ounces each), quartered lengthwise and cut crosswise into 2-inch pieces
- ¼ cup extra-virgin olive oil
- ¼ cup water
- 2 sprigs fresh basil
- 2 garlic cloves, sliced thin
  Salt and pepper
- ¼ teaspoon red pepper flakes
- 3 ounces (½ cup) cherry tomatoes, halved
  Lemon wedges

1. Bring zucchini, oil, water, basil sprigs, garlic, 1 teaspoon salt, ¼ teaspoon pepper, and pepper flakes to boil in 12-inch nonstick skillet over medium-high heat. Reduce heat to medium, cover, and simmer until zucchini is fork-tender, about 8 minutes, stirring with rubber spatula every 2 minutes.

2. Gently stir in tomatoes and cook, uncovered, until tomatoes are just softened, about 2 minutes. Discard basil sprigs. Transfer zucchini mixture to platter. Serve with lemon wedges.

THE AMERICAN TABLE

An Embarrassment of Squashes

The good news for home gardeners is this: Zucchini are very easy to grow, and they thrive in many different climates and soil conditions. The bad news for gardeners is also this: Zucchini are very easy to grow. So easy, in fact, that come midsummer, backyard botanists across the nation find themselves faced with a surfeit of this vegetable that doesn't take well to canning or freezing. What to do with that bounty? Give it away, of course.

According to *The Old Farmer's Almanac*, August 8 is National Sneak Some Zucchini onto Your Neighbor's Porch Day. As writer Doreen G. Howard explains, "To celebrate it, you simply wait until the dead of night and quietly creep up to your neighbors' front door, leaving plenty of zucchini for them to enjoy."

Your other option is to let them grow, and grow they will. *Guinness World Records* lists the longest zucchini ever measured as 8 feet, 3 inches long, grown by Giovanni Scozzafava in Niagara Falls, Ontario, Canada.

Cherry Streusel Bars

We wanted a three-layer cookie bar without three times as much work.

by Katie Leaird

EATING A BATCH of three-layer cookie bars can be a joy. But making a batch? Intimidating. Because really, does a baked good with triple the components yield a final product that is truly three times better than a standard dump-and-stir option? And would it take three times the work? After tasting a three-layer cherry streusel bar—featuring a crisp cookie base, a jammy filling, and a delicious streusel topping—I was determined to find out.

I started in the middle, with the cherry filling. I can imagine a similar three-layer bar with raspberry, apricot, or nearly any other kind of fruit, but I picked cherries for their multidimensional, sweet-tart flavor. The filling needed to be juicy but not runny; it needed to stay put in the bar. To start, I threw some pitted cherries into a saucepan with sugar and let them stew into a homemade jam, hoping to find just the right texture (I had to take into account the fact that the filling would also bake in the oven and would therefore thicken further). I boiled the jam down to my best guess and then waited for it to cool. And waited.

I couldn't risk melting the crust and sacrificing its structure by dumping boiling cherry liquid over it, but a saucepan full of hot, sugary jam takes its sweet time cooling down. As I waited, frustrated, I pondered whether I could bypass cooking the filling by using another cherry product.

There are many cherry products to choose from: frozen cherries, canned cherries, dried cherries, cherry liqueur, cherry preserves, cherry pie filling, and maraschino cherries. I tried them all, but the winning move was mixing chopped frozen cherries into jarred cherry preserves. With a squeeze of lemon for brightness, a pinch of salt, and a few drops of almond extract to deepen the flavor (almond and cherry are famously friendly), I had a delicious no-cook

cherry filling. To further simplify things, I threw it all together in the food processor, which took about 10 seconds.

On to the cookie base and streusel topping. The base ingredients are simple: flour, sugar, butter, and salt. Streusel ingredients are pretty much the same, so I decided to streamline the work. I made a big batch of crust in the food processor and set aside a portion of it as the beginning of my streusel before pressing the rest of the buttery crumbs into a baking pan. I stirred some oats and almonds into the reserved mixture for some crunch, added a little more sugar and butter, and . . . streusel.

I baked the crust on its own to ensure a crisp bottom. Then I spread the cherry filling over the still-warm crust and sprinkled the streusel over the top. In the end, I had three delicious layers with distinct flavors and textures, but I had made only one dough and hadn't cooked anything on the stovetop. Streamlined, yes. Fussy, no. Three times better? Absolutely.

CHERRY STREUSEL BARS
Makes twenty-four 2-inch squares
Measure the cherries while they are still frozen, and then transfer them to a paper towel–lined baking sheet to thaw. One 12-ounce jar of cherry preserves is more than enough preserves for this recipe.

CRUST
- 2½ cups (12½ ounces) all-purpose flour
- ⅔ cup (4⅔ ounces) granulated sugar
- ½ teaspoon salt
- 16 tablespoons unsalted butter, cut into ½-inch pieces and chilled

CHERRY FILLING
- 2 cups (9 ounces) frozen sweet cherries, thawed
- 1 cup cherry preserves
- 2 teaspoons lemon juice
- ¼ teaspoon almond extract
  Pinch salt

STREUSEL
- ½ cup (1½ ounces) old-fashioned rolled oats
- ½ cup slivered almonds, chopped
- ¼ cup packed (1¾ ounces) brown sugar
- 2 tablespoons unsalted butter, cut into ½-inch pieces and softened

A tiny bit of almond extract enhances the cherry flavor in these bars.

1. FOR THE CRUST: Adjust oven rack to middle position and heat oven to 375 degrees. Make foil sling for 13 by 9-inch baking pan by folding 2 long sheets of aluminum foil; first sheet should be 13 inches wide and second sheet should be 9 inches wide. Lay sheets of foil in pan perpendicular to each other, with extra foil hanging over edges of pan. Push foil into corners and up sides of pan, smoothing foil flush to pan. Spray foil lightly with vegetable oil spray.
2. Process flour, sugar, and salt in food processor until combined, about 5 seconds. Add butter and pulse until mixture resembles wet sand, about 15 pulses.
3. Transfer 1¼ cups dough to medium bowl and set aside. Transfer remaining dough to prepared pan and use your hands to evenly distribute it over bottom of pan (dough will be slightly dry). Using bottom of dry measuring cup, firmly press dough into even

layer. Bake until light golden brown, 16 to 18 minutes, rotating pan halfway through baking.
4. FOR THE CHERRY FILLING: Meanwhile, wipe processor bowl clean with paper towels. Pulse all ingredients in food processor until finely chopped, about 7 pulses; set aside.
5. FOR THE STREUSEL: Add oats, almonds, and sugar to reserved dough and toss to combine. Add butter and rub mixture between your fingers until butter is fully incorporated and mixture forms small clumps. Set aside streusel.
6. Transfer filling to pan and spread evenly over crust (crust needn't be cool). Sprinkle streusel evenly over filling (do not press streusel into filling). Bake until filling is bubbling and streusel is deep golden brown, 24 to 28 minutes, rotating pan halfway through baking. Transfer pan to wire rack and let bars cool completely. Using foil overhang, lift bars out of pan. Cut into 24 squares and serve.

Banana–Chocolate Chip Snack Cake

Dense, moist banana bread is great. But tender, fluffy banana snack cake is something else again.

by Cecelia Jenkins with Diane Unger

WHEN I WAS growing up, snack cake was a one-layer affair cut into squares and packed into my lunchbox or ready to eat when I got home from school. It was simple to make, it didn't require decoration (aside from perhaps a smear of frosting), and—most important—I didn't need a special occasion to enjoy it. It was approachable and welcome anytime, whenever hunger struck.

I hadn't thought about snack cake in a while, but then a friend shared a recipe for banana snack cake from her trove of family recipes. Banana cake? Wasn't that just banana bread?

Easy answer: No. The ingredients are nearly the same, but the outcome is entirely different. A slice of banana bread has a dense, heavy crumb and a crusty exterior. Banana cake, on the other hand, is baked in a shallow cake pan rather than a loaf pan, and you don't eat a slice, you eat a piece. It is crustless and has a fluffier, more tender, less moist crumb than banana bread.

One of the biggest differences between the two lies in the fat. Banana bread recipes call for combining wet and dry ingredients by hand and often contain oil, which contributes to a denser texture. To achieve a lighter, cake-like crumb, I drew on many years of test kitchen knowledge and reached for a stick of butter and my stand mixer.

Beating a stick of softened butter with sugar, a process called creaming, incorporates more air into the mixture, which helps create the lighter structure a cake needs. Once the batter was light and fluffy, I added two large eggs, one at a time, mixing between additions; I then alternated adding the dry and wet ingredients, including 1 cup of mashed bananas (from two or three speckled bananas). The result was just the cakey texture I wanted.

About those mashed bananas: Ripeness proved critical to creating a strong banana flavor in the cake. Out of three batches of cake—one made with slightly green, underripe bananas; one made with speckled, ripe bananas; and one made with completely brown bananas—tasters noted that the underripe bananas yielded cake with bland, somewhat bitter banana flavor, whereas the other two cakes had strong banana flavor (see "Ripe Bananas Are Key").

To really make my tasters happy, I added a cup of chocolate chips to the

mix. As the kitchen around me filled with the aroma of freshly baked banana cake, I was suddenly very popular. Tangy cream cheese frosting paired deliciously with the sweetness of the bananas, so I polled the eager crowd: To frost or not to frost? Their answer: This cake's a hit no matter how you slice it.

BANANA–CHOCOLATE CHIP SNACK CAKE *Serves 8*

Ripe bananas contain nearly three times as much sugar as unripened bananas. Don't use anything less than speckled bananas in this recipe, or your cake will be bland. If you like, serve this cake frosted with Cream Cheese Frosting (recipe follows). Be sure to let the cake cool completely before frosting.

- 2 **cups (10 ounces) all-purpose flour**
- ¾ **teaspoon salt**
- ½ **teaspoon baking soda**
- 8 **tablespoons unsalted butter, softened**
- 1½ **cups (10½ ounces) sugar**
- 2 **large eggs**
- 1 **cup mashed ripe bananas (2 to 3 bananas)**
- 1 **teaspoon vanilla extract**
- ½ **cup whole milk**
- 1 **cup (6 ounces) semisweet chocolate chips**

1. Adjust oven rack to middle position and heat oven to 350 degrees. Grease and flour 8-inch square baking pan. Whisk flour, salt, and baking soda together in bowl.

2. Using stand mixer fitted with paddle, beat butter and sugar on medium-high speed until pale and fluffy, about 3 minutes. Add eggs, one at a time, and beat until combined. Add bananas and vanilla and beat until incorporated.

3. Reduce speed to low and add flour mixture in 3 additions, alternating with milk in 2 additions, scraping down bowl as needed. Using rubber spatula, stir in ½ cup chocolate chips. Transfer batter to prepared pan and smooth top with rubber spatula. Sprinkle remaining ½ cup chocolate chips evenly over top. Bake until toothpick inserted in center comes out clean, 45 to 50 minutes, rotating pan halfway through baking.

4. Let cake cool completely in pan on wire rack. Serve. (Cooled cake can be wrapped in plastic wrap and stored at room temperature for up to 2 days.)

A full cup of semisweet chips ensures the best chocolate flavor.

CREAM CHEESE FROSTING

Makes about 1 cup

Use softened cream cheese to avoid lumps in the finished frosting.

- 4 **tablespoons unsalted butter, softened**
- 1 **cup (4 ounces) confectioners' sugar**
- 4 **ounces cream cheese, cut into 4 pieces and softened**
- ¾ **teaspoon vanilla extract**

Using stand mixer fitted with paddle, beat butter and sugar on medium speed until light and fluffy, about 2 minutes. Add cream cheese, 1 piece at a time, beating after each addition until fully incorporated. Add vanilla and mix until no lumps remain.

Ripe Bananas Are Key

We recommend using ripe bananas for this recipe. Because bananas sweeten as they ripen, speckled bananas are sweeter than unspeckled. To hasten their ripening, place bananas in a loosely closed paper bag. The bag will trap the ethylene gas produced by the fruit, which triggers ripening. Since ripe fruit emits the most ethylene, placing an already-ripe banana in the bag will further speed up the process.

NOT READY YET   **RIPE AND READY**

Grilled Vegetable Salad

Too often vegetables come off the grill crunchy and scorched or watery and soggy.
Here's how to cut and cook them for perfectly tender, lightly charred results. *by Katie Leaird*

Prepping Vegetables and Herbs

(TEST KITCHEN TIPS FOR PRODUCE)

To loosen their skins, cover hot bell peppers with plastic wrap for 5 minutes.

Bell Peppers: Use Steam to Remove Skins

To make their skins easier to remove, place grilled bell peppers in a bowl, cover it with plastic wrap, and let the bell peppers sit for 5 minutes. The steam created by the heat in the sealed bowl loosens the skins from the flesh, making them easier to separate. Slip the loosened skins off and discard.

Eggplant: Brush with Oil Last

Eggplants are filled with both air pockets and water, which means they can absorb large amounts of oil, resulting in a greasy mess. For this reason, we brush all the other vegetables with oil first and use only what is left to oil the eggplants.

Herbs: Chop Them Like a Pro

To chop fresh leafy herbs, some home cooks make thin, loose piles of leaves on their cutting boards and then run their knives back and forth over the piles. But this isn't the most efficient approach, and often the leaves are chopped inconsistently. Here's the best way to chop leafy herbs.

Gather the washed, dried leaves into a tight pile and hold them with your nonknife hand. Using your chef's knife in a rocking motion, slice the leaves thin, working your way through the pile. Turn the slices about 90 degrees, gather them tightly again, and repeat cutting to form small pieces.

Making Vinaigrette

Use the Right Ratio

Many modern recipes call for a 4:1 ratio of oil to acid (vinegar or citrus juice), but the test kitchen generally prefers the classic ratio of 3 parts oil to 1 part acid for a well-balanced, pleasantly vibrant flavor.

3:1
OIL   VINEGAR

How Emulsification Works

Vinaigrette relies on the principle of emulsification. An emulsion is a combination of two liquids that don't ordinarily mix—for example, oil and an acidic liquid such as vinegar or lemon juice. The only way to mix them is to whisk strenuously so that one of the two ingredients breaks down into tiny droplets—eventually so tiny that they remain separated by the other liquid. The two liquids are now effectively one. Many vinaigrettes contain mustard, which acts as an emulsifying agent, helping the oil and vinegar combine into a unified sauce and stay that way.

Great vinaigrette starts with high-quality ingredients. Here are some of our favorites:

Extra-Virgin Olive Oil

A good extra-virgin olive oil will provide fresh, fruity flavor to a vinaigrette, but since olives are highly perishable, the oil can degrade quickly. It's important to seek out a reputable product.

California Olive Ranch Extra-Virgin Olive Oil
($9.99 for a 500 ml bottle) Our favorite supermarket extra-virgin olive oil is "fruity" with a "complex finish." In fact, its flavor rivaled that of our favorite high-end extra-virgin olive oil.

Dijon Mustard

Mustard helps emulsify a vinaigrette. The best Dijon versions are creamy, with more body than conventional yellow mustard, and pack a good amount of heat.

Trois Petits Cochons Moutarde de Dijon
($6.99 for a 7-ounce jar) This Dijon's heat "kicks in gradually" and "builds."

Maille Dijon Originale
($4.49 for a 7.5-ounce jar) This "well-rounded" Dijon was "fairly spicy but not too sharp."

Ten Simple Steps

1. Make vinaigrette
Whisk lemon juice, mustard, garlic, salt, and pepper together in large bowl. Slowly whisk in oil, then stir in basil.
Why? Adding mustard to the mixture and slowly whisking in the oil emulsifies the vinaigrette so that it won't break.

2. Prep bell peppers
Slice off tops and bottoms of bell peppers and remove cores. Make slit down 1 side of each bell pepper, then press flat into 1 strip, removing ribs and remaining seeds as needed. Halve strips crosswise.
Why? Long, flat strips are easy to handle on the grill.

3. Score eggplant and zucchini
Using sharp paring knife, cut ½ inch crosshatch pattern in flesh of eggplant and zucchini, being careful not to cut through skin.
Why? Cutting through the flesh of these watery vegetables helps them release excess moisture during grilling.

4. Keep onions intact
Push toothpick horizontally through each onion round.
Why? The toothpicks keep the onion rounds intact, making them easier to flip.

5. Oil and season vegetables
Brush vegetables with oil. Season with salt and pepper.
Why? A generous coating of oil ensures that the vegetables won't stick to the cooking grate. Seasoning the vegetables well ensures a flavorful salad.

GRILLED VEGETABLE SALAD
Serves 4 to 6

Serve as a side dish to grilled meats and fish; with grilled pita as a salad course; or with hard-cooked eggs, olives, and premium canned tuna as a light lunch.

VINAIGRETTE
- 1 **tablespoon lemon juice**
- 2 **teaspoons Dijon mustard**
- 1 **garlic clove, minced**
- ¼ **teaspoon salt**
- ⅛ **teaspoon pepper**
- 3 **tablespoons extra-virgin olive oil**
- 2 **tablespoons chopped fresh basil, mint, chives, or parsley**

VEGETABLES
- 2 **red bell peppers**
- 1 **eggplant, halved lengthwise**
- 1 **zucchini (8 to 10 ounces), halved lengthwise**
- 1 **red onion, cut into ½-inch-thick rounds**
- 4 **plum tomatoes, cored and halved lengthwise**
- 3 **tablespoons extra-virgin olive oil Salt and pepper**

1. FOR THE VINAIGRETTE: Whisk lemon juice, mustard, garlic, salt, and pepper together in large bowl. Whisking constantly, slowly drizzle in oil. Stir in basil and set aside.

2. FOR THE VEGETABLES: Slice ¼ inch off tops and bottoms of bell peppers and remove cores. Make slit down 1 side of each bell pepper, then press flat into 1 long strip, removing ribs and remaining seeds with knife as needed. Cut strips in half crosswise (you should have 4 bell pepper pieces).

3. Using sharp paring knife, cut ½-inch crosshatch pattern in flesh of eggplant and zucchini, being careful to cut down to but not through skin. Push toothpick horizontally through each onion round to keep rings intact while grilling. Brush tomatoes, bell peppers, zucchini, and onion all over with oil, then brush eggplant with remaining oil (it will absorb more oil than other vegetables). Season vegetables with salt and pepper.

4A. FOR A CHARCOAL GRILL: Open bottom vent completely. Light large chimney starter filled with charcoal briquettes (6 quarts). When top coals are partially covered with ash, pour evenly over grill. Set cooking grate in place, cover, and open lid vent completely. Heat grill until hot, about 5 minutes.

4B. FOR A GAS GRILL: Turn all burners to high, cover, and heat grill until hot, about 15 minutes. Turn all burners to medium-high.

5. Clean and oil cooking grate. Place vegetables on cooking grate, cut sides down, and cook until skins of bell peppers, eggplant, and tomatoes are well browned and interiors of eggplant and zucchini are tender, 10 to 16 minutes, flipping and moving vegetables as necessary to ensure even cooking and transferring vegetables to baking sheet as they finish cooking. Place bell peppers in bowl, cover with plastic wrap, and let steam to loosen skins, about 5 minutes.

6. When cool enough to handle, peel bell peppers and tomatoes, discarding skins. Using spoon, scoop eggplant flesh out of skin; discard skin. Chop all vegetables into 1-inch pieces, transfer to bowl with vinaigrette, and toss to coat. Serve warm or at room temperature.

6. Prepare grill
Pour single layer of hot coals into charcoal grill or turn all burners of gas grill to high.
Why? A hot grill imparts flavorful char to vegetables quickly and ensures that they won't stick to the cooking grate.

7. Grill cut side down
Arrange vegetables on cooking grate with their cut sides facing down and cook, turning occasionally, until well browned and tender.
Why? Grilling cut side down browns the flesh first. Finish on the skin side, which can withstand longer exposure to heat.

8. Peel away skins
When tomatoes and bell peppers are cool, remove charred skins.
Why? Blistering the skins makes removing them easier. Simply slip the grilled tomato skins off with your fingers. Use our steam method (see "Prepping Vegetables and Herbs") for the bell peppers.

9. Scoop eggplant
Using spoon, scoop eggplant flesh out of skin.
Why? The eggplant flesh becomes tender during grilling, but the skin toughens. Discard the charred skin and use only the soft eggplant flesh.

10. Cut and toss
Chop all vegetables into 1-inch pieces, transfer to bowl with vinaigrette, and toss to coat.
Why? Dressing the vegetables soon after they come off the grill causes them to absorb more vinaigrette.

Chicken with Couscous and Carrots

Our goal: Juicy chicken plus vegetables and starch, all in one skillet. *by Cecelia Jenkins*

THE BEST SUMMERTIME meals are on the lighter side, but all too often "lighter" means no starch. This sounds fine in theory—a piece of chicken served alongside a bunch of vegetables can be gorgeous—but without a starchy component to round out the meal, I'm often left wanting more. I set out to create a simple skillet chicken supper that cut a bright flavor profile but was filling and complete, too.

I grabbed a skillet and got to work. After searing eight chicken thighs on both sides to maximize the flavorful browned bits in my skillet (my tasters preferred the richer flavor of chicken thighs to that of breasts), I moved them to a plate and discarded the excess fat. Then I added an onion and a few handfuls of sliced carrots; the vegetables contributed lovely sweet-savory flavors, and their moisture helped me release the browned bits from the skillet into the dish. Next I added aromatic garlic and earthy paprika and cumin, followed by 2 cups of water and 1 cup of dry couscous.

Couscous (often mistaken for a grain because of its tiny size) is actually a pasta made from semolina. Traditionally used as a sauce absorber beneath North African stews and braises, it cooks in a fraction of the time required for rice, potatoes, or larger pasta shapes. After placing the chicken back atop the other ingredients, I covered the skillet and slid it into the oven for a few minutes so the couscous could absorb all the liquid and the chicken could cook through.

One pitfall of couscous: With too much liquid, it can turn gummy. Lifting the lid to see a soupy mess, I immediately knew that 2 cups of water (plus the juices released from the chicken thighs) was too much. I tried 1 cup—still too much. I scaled back the water to just ½ cup, but this resulted in some stray crunchy bits of couscous. Three-quarters of a cup of water turned out to be the perfect amount in which to cook the couscous so that once I had taken it out of the oven, I could fluff it with a fork into separate "grains" before adding some last-minute lemon juice to brighten it.

For a bit of textural interest, I stirred in a can of drained and rinsed chickpeas; they added a touch of creaminess to the dish. With a handful of fresh parsley tossed in as a finishing touch, I had a satisfying, superflavorful one-pot meal.

Plenty of minced parsley and a healthy dose of lemon juice give this dish a final lift.

What Is Couscous?

Although it is often mistaken for a grain because of its tiny, granular shape, couscous is, in fact, a pasta made of durum semolina—the same wheat flour used to make Italian pasta. Even in its homeland of North Africa, couscous is rarely made from scratch anymore; the laborious process of dampening semolina and then rolling it gently beneath your fingertips until it forms tiny balls is too laborious. Instead, most cooks turn to packaged, precooked couscous that simply needs to be rehydrated in hot water or broth.

One-Pan Process

Once the chicken has been browned and set aside, we cook carrots and onion with aromatics and spices in the residual fat. Chickpeas, water, and couscous are added, and then the chicken is returned to the skillet (along with any accumulated juices) to cook through.

NORTH AFRICAN FLAVORS
We cook the vegetables in a skillet until they're softened before adding minced garlic, paprika, and ground cumin.

ONE-PAN CHICKEN WITH COUSCOUS AND CARROTS *Serves 4*
The chicken will crowd the skillet in step 2 but, if left undisturbed, will still brown well. Don't worry if the skillet lid does not fit snugly in step 4; it will still trap enough heat.

  8 (5- to 7-ounce) bone-in chicken thighs, trimmed
      Salt and pepper
  1 teaspoon vegetable oil
  1 pound carrots, peeled and cut into 2-inch lengths, thin pieces halved lengthwise, thick pieces quartered lengthwise
  1 onion, chopped
  4 garlic cloves, minced
  1 teaspoon paprika
  ½ teaspoon ground cumin
  1 (15-ounce) can chickpeas, rinsed
  ¾ cup water
  1 cup couscous
  ⅓ cup minced fresh parsley
  2 tablespoons lemon juice, plus wedges for serving

1. Adjust oven rack to middle position and heat oven to 450 degrees. Pat chicken dry with paper towels and season with salt and pepper.

2. Heat oil in 12-inch ovensafe skillet over medium-high heat until just smoking. Add chicken, skin side down, and cook until skin is crispy and golden, 7 to 9 minutes. Flip chicken and continue to cook until golden on second side, 7 to 9 minutes longer. Transfer chicken to plate, skin side up.

3. Pour off all but 1 tablespoon fat from skillet, then heat over medium heat until shimmering. Add carrots, onion, 1 teaspoon salt, and ½ teaspoon pepper and cook until onions are softened, about 5 minutes. Add garlic, paprika, and cumin and cook until fragrant, about 30 seconds. Stir in chickpeas and water and bring to boil, scraping up any browned bits.

4. Stir in couscous, scraping down any that sticks to sides of skillet. Return chicken, skin side up, and any accumulated juices to skillet, pressing chicken into couscous mixture. Cover, transfer to oven, and bake until chicken registers 175 degrees, about 18 minutes.

5. Transfer chicken to clean plate. Add parsley and lemon juice to couscous mixture and fluff with fork. Season with salt and pepper to taste. Return chicken to skillet, skin side up. Serve with lemon wedges.

Pineapple Salsas

To cut down on the cutting, we leaned on the food processor. *by Ashley Moore*

ON A RECENT steamy summer afternoon at a local restaurant, a friend ordered a fruity salsa. Tangy, slightly spicy, a bit sweet, and totally refreshing—it contained pineapple, jalapeño, red onion, lime juice, and cilantro—the salsa collected perfectly in the curve of a tortilla chip, a refreshing bite that cooled me down even as it pricked my tongue with mild peppery heat. I decided to make my own at home.

I started with a few existing recipes. Most used sturdy pineapple as a base, a flavorful choice that I loved, so I started by dicing pineapple into ¼-inch pieces. I'm pretty handy with a chef's knife, but by the time I'd chopped the pineapple, red onion, and other salsa ingredients, my hand hurt. So for my next round I ditched my knife and turned to my food processor.

I now needed only to cut the fruit and vegetables into rough chunks. I tossed some pineapple pieces, a big handful of cilantro leaves, some jalapeño slices, a roughly chopped red onion, lime juice, and salt and pepper into the processor and pulsed it all together. The result? Watery and way too oniony.

I reduced the amount of onion and tried again. This salsa was more balanced but still too wet. A colleague wondered whether adding the lime juice and salt for that initial round of processing was causing the fruit to break down and exude too much liquid; she recommended waiting until everything else was chopped up before adding the lime and salt. She was right: Waiting kept the salsa from turning too watery.

After a few more flavor tweaks, my sweet-hot, chip-ready pineapple salsa was exactly what I wanted and was ripe for variations. For my first variation, I replaced the cilantro with mint and stirred in some diced cucumber with the wet ingredients. To add sweetness to another version, I incorporated chunks of ripe mango along with mild chives. A third salsa was made both savory and colorful by the addition of chopped roasted red peppers. For my final iteration, I substituted fresh basil for the cilantro and half a habanero for the jalapeño and, once everything was processed, stirred in some diced watermelon. (Processing the watermelon made things much too runny.)

My salsas were a hit and not just on chips: I spotted coworkers spooning them over chicken breasts, into a fish taco, and even atop a turkey burger.

PINEAPPLE SALSA
Makes about 2 cups

Do not use canned pineapple in this recipe. For a spicier salsa, reserve and add the jalapeño seeds.

- 2 cups (12 ounces) 1-inch pineapple pieces
- 3 jalapeño chiles, stemmed, seeded, and cut into ½-inch pieces
- 1 cup fresh cilantro leaves
- ¼ cup coarsely chopped red onion
- 2 garlic cloves, smashed and peeled
- 1 tablespoon fresh lime juice
- 1 tablespoon extra-virgin olive oil
- ½ teaspoon salt
- ½ teaspoon pepper

Pulse pineapple, jalapeños, cilantro, onion, and garlic in food processor until coarsely chopped, about 6 pulses, scraping down sides of bowl as needed. Transfer to serving bowl. Stir in lime juice, oil, salt, and pepper. Serve.

PINEAPPLE-CUCUMBER SALSA
Decrease pineapple to 1½ cups. Substitute ½ cup fresh mint leaves for cilantro. Add 1 cup (6 ounces) ¼-inch English cucumber pieces to bowl with lime juice.

PINEAPPLE-MANGO SALSA
Decrease pineapple to 1½ cups. Substitute ¼ cup chopped fresh chives for cilantro. Add 1½ cups (9 ounces) 1-inch mango pieces to processor with pineapple.

PINEAPPLE–ROASTED RED PEPPER SALSA
Add ¼ cup rinsed and patted dry jarred roasted red peppers to processor with pineapple.

PINEAPPLE-WATERMELON SALSA
Decrease pineapple to 1½ cups. Substitute ½ habanero chile for jalapeños and ½ cup fresh basil leaves for cilantro. Add 1 cup (8 ounces) ¼-inch watermelon pieces to salsa with lime juice.

These salsas are delicious on tacos. Go to CooksCountry.com/fishtacos for our California Fish Tacos recipe.

Above: the makings of Pineapple Salsa before being processed. Below, clockwise from top left: Pineapple-Cucumber Salsa, Pineapple-Mango Salsa, Pineapple–Roasted Red Pepper Salsa, Pineapple-Watermelon Salsa.

Ropa Vieja

Some dishes need extensive adaptations to work in a slow cooker. This one is tailor-made for it.

by Matthew Fairman

ROPA VIEJA, CUBA'S national dish and a favorite in Cuban neighborhoods throughout the United States, is elemental and beautifully simple—a beefy braise of flank steak in a sauce that balances tomato and white wine with sweet peppers, onions, and garlic. Cumin and oregano add warmth while briny olives and bright vinegar cut the richness of the meat and make the flavors pop. Served over rice, it's a comforting meal.

The backstory goes like this: A man, too broke to afford meat for his family, stirred some old clothes ("ropa vieja" in Spanish) into a pot of broth. He then prayed over the pot and later, after some divine assistance, ladled out a rich stew of beef and vegetables. It's a fitting story for a satisfying dish made with humble ingredients.

Traditional recipes require that you cut up and sauté vegetables twice, once for a homemade beef broth and once for the finished stew. The method takes time and the results are worth it, but I wanted an easy recipe that was ready when I came home and still had the complexity of old-school versions. So I turned to the slow cooker.

A few tests of existing recipes identified my top problems: meat that was too difficult to shred and a final stew that was too soupy. Choosing the cut of beef was easy: Flank steak, the traditional choice, won out over chuck (greasy and hard to shred), skirt (mushy after long cooking), and brisket (a little fibrous and not always easy to find). Flank, with its lean, large muscle fibers all running in one direction, not only was the easiest cut to shred but also stood up best to long, slow cooking without turning greasy.

I set out to address the other issue: soupiness. The versions I'd tested produced a watery broth rather than a rich stew. So I ditched the beef broth altogether—in the closed environment of the slow cooker, I didn't need the added liquid. Soy sauce and tomato

A quarter-cup of tomato paste adds deep flavor and color to this Cuban American favorite.

paste added back the savoriness I'd lost. But the dish still had too much liquid.

Traditionally, ropa vieja gets its complex sweetness from a *sofrito*—a mixture of onions, peppers, garlic, and tomato—that is cooked down and concentrated. I'd been adding the raw sofrito ingredients straight into the slow cooker, but it was clear they were exuding too much liquid. So I tried making a sped-up version of a sofrito by sautéing the vegetables and aromatics for just 10 minutes. Doing so not only drove off that excess moisture but also began to caramelize and faintly sweeten the vegetables. I added them to the meat and other ingredients.

When I lifted the lid 5 hours later, I was heartened by the heady aroma. The shredded beef was tender; the sauce that clung to it was intricate and substantial. My teammates loved it. The old clothes were transformed.

Speedy Sofrito

Cubans cook a *sofrito*—onions, peppers, garlic, tomato—over a low flame for a long time to evaporate moisture and concentrate flavor. We shorten the process by sautéing the mixture quickly in a skillet until it softens and browns. We then transfer it to the slow cooker to simmer with the meat.

SLOW-COOKER ROPA VIEJA
Serves 4 to 6

The contents of the slow cooker will look dry at the start, but the ingredients will release moisture after a couple of hours of cooking. Our favorite tomato paste is from Goya. Serve this dish with steamed white rice.

- 3 tablespoons vegetable oil
- 2 onions, halved and sliced thin
- 2 red bell peppers, stemmed, seeded, and sliced into ½-inch-wide strips
- ¼ cup tomato paste
- 4 garlic cloves, minced
- 2 teaspoons ground cumin
- 1½ teaspoons dried oregano
    Salt and pepper
- ½ cup dry white wine
- 2 tablespoons soy sauce
- 2 bay leaves
- 1 (2-pound) flank steak, trimmed and cut crosswise against grain into 4 equal pieces
- ¾ cup pitted green olives, sliced
- 1 tablespoon distilled white vinegar

1. Heat oil in 12-inch nonstick skillet over medium-high heat until shimmering. Add onions and bell peppers and cook, covered, until softened and spotty brown, 8 to 10 minutes, stirring occasionally.

2. Push vegetables to sides of skillet. Add tomato paste, garlic, cumin, oregano, and ½ teaspoon salt to center and cook until fragrant, about 1 minute. Stir vegetables into tomato paste mixture. Add wine and cook until nearly evaporated, about 2 minutes. Transfer vegetable mixture, soy sauce, and bay leaves to slow cooker. Season steak with salt and pepper and nestle into vegetable mixture. Cover and cook until meat is very tender, 6 to 7 hours on low or 5 to 6 hours on high.

3. Transfer steak to cutting board. Discard bay leaves. Using 2 forks, shred steak into bite-size pieces, then return it to slow cooker. Stir in olives and vinegar. Season with salt and pepper to taste. Serve.

No Liquid Needed

Most slow-cooker recipes call for added liquid, but our version doesn't need any. As the meat cooks, it will exude plenty of liquid, producing a saucy dish.

Chicken Florentine

This buffet-line favorite was due to be freshened up. Not to mention sped up.

by Alli Berkey

HIT THE BUFFET at any given fund-raiser or corporate function and you'll likely run into chicken Florentine. A riff on cordon bleu or other chicken breast dishes, this one features spinach in a mild cream-and-Parmesan sauce—sometimes stuffed inside, sometimes stacked on top. But for all its potential, chicken Florentine so often disappoints: dry chicken, soggy spinach, and a stodgy sauce. I love each of these three components individually, so I knew I could make this dish better and do it faster—and scale it back to serve just two people.

My first decision was to nix stuffing the breasts: too much work for a weeknight supper. I started with spinach, which, as anyone who's recently shopped for spinach knows, isn't as straightforward as it sounds. After sampling curly-leaf spinach, frozen spinach, and bagged baby spinach, my tasters and I decided to stick with baby spinach for its delicate texture. A simple sauté in a large skillet with a bit of oil and salt was all it needed. I transferred it to a colander to drain—no need to hang on to the grassy-tasting runoff. On to the chicken.

Because I wanted a speedy supper, I gently pounded two chicken breasts ½ inch thick. I knew these thin cutlets would cook quickly in the same skillet I'd used for the spinach (wiped clean with a paper towel). About 4 minutes on each side over medium-high heat gave me golden-brown cutlets without drying them out. The bonus of a relatively thin cut? More browning and more flavor. I set the chicken aside under an aluminum foil tent to stay warm while I made my sauce.

I returned the skillet to the heat, eyeing the browned bits left behind by the chicken; I knew that they'd add savory depth to the sauce. After quickly cooking some garlic and a shallot, I deglazed the pan with chicken broth, scraping up the browned bits. Next came heavy cream, which I whisked in before bringing it all to a simmer to reduce. After 10 minutes, I removed the skillet from the heat, whisked in 2 tablespoons of Parmesan cheese (I'd add a bit more later for garnish), and hit the mixture with some lemon juice and zest for vibrancy. I placed the chicken on plates, whisked the accumulated juices into the sauce, tasted it for seasoning, and returned the spinach to

the sauce to warm through. I covered the chicken with the saucy spinach, sprinkled on a little more Parmesan, and rang the dinner bell.

Bad buffet food? No more. This redo was better, and faster, than that.

CHICKEN FLORENTINE FOR TWO

Draining the wilted spinach in a colander rids it of excess moisture that would water down the sauce.

- 2 (6- to 8-ounce) boneless, skinless chicken breasts
  Salt and pepper
- 2 tablespoons vegetable oil
- 6 ounces (6 cups) baby spinach
- 1 small shallot, minced
- 1 garlic clove, minced
- ½ cup chicken broth
- ½ cup heavy cream
- ¼ cup grated Parmesan cheese
- ¼ teaspoon grated lemon zest plus 1 teaspoon juice

1. Place chicken between 2 sheets of plastic wrap and pound to even ½-inch thickness. Pat chicken dry with paper towels and season with salt and pepper; set aside.

2. Heat 1 tablespoon oil in 12-inch nonstick skillet over medium-high heat until shimmering. Add spinach and ⅛ teaspoon salt and cook, stirring occasionally, until wilted, about 2 minutes. Transfer spinach to colander set in sink and allow any excess liquid to drain off. Wipe skillet clean with paper towels.

3. Heat remaining 1 tablespoon oil in now-empty skillet over medium heat until just smoking. Cook until chicken is golden brown and registers 160 degrees, about 6 minutes per side. Transfer chicken to plate and tent with aluminum foil.

4. Add shallot and garlic to skillet and cook until fragrant, about 30 seconds. Whisk in broth and cream, scraping up any browned bits, and bring to boil. Cook until reduced to about ⅔ cup, about 7 minutes. Off heat, stir in 2 tablespoons Parmesan and lemon zest and juice.

5. Transfer chicken to individual plates and stir any accumulated chicken juices into sauce. Season sauce with salt and pepper to taste. Stir spinach into sauce to warm through. Top chicken with spinach and sauce and sprinkle with remaining 2 tablespoons Parmesan. Serve.

A bit of lemon—juice and zest—adds a light note to this deeply flavorful dish for two.

BACKSTORY

Why do we use the term "Florentine" to describe dishes that feature spinach (eggs Florentine and chicken Florentine quickly come to mind)? Legend suggests it's a carryover from the 16th century, when Catherine de' Medici, an Italian noblewoman from Florence, married Henry II of France and moved to Paris.

What's in a name? Just a bit of spinach.

There, she overhauled the royal kitchen, installing her own Italian cooks and refining the traditional court menus to suit her tastes.

Among Catherine's favorite ingredients was spinach. Though it was already widely used in France, she heightened its popularity, and many spinach-based dishes have since been named "Florentine" to indicate Catherine's, and Florence's, influence.

Paring Knives

For precision cuts, call on the (cheap) little guy.

by Hannah Crowley

Our winner hulled strawberries with ease.

8 Knives 8 Tests

1. Test initial sharpness by slicing copy paper
2. Slice cheddar cheese
3. Peel and slice fresh ginger
4. Peel, quarter, and core apples
5. Section oranges
6. Hull strawberries
7. Have multiple users test and evaluate
8. Test final sharpness by slicing copy paper

HIGHLY RECOMMENDED   CRITERIA

Victorinox
Swiss Army Fibrox Pro 3¼" Spear Point
Paring Knife
Model: 47600 or 40600, depending on packaging   **Price:** $9.47
Weight: 17.52 g
Usable Blade Length: 3.25 in
Spine Thickness: 1.12 mm

Comfort ★★½
Sharpness ★★★
Agility ★★★

This knife was "superadept"; its sharp, flexible blade nimbly hugged curves, so we could surgically remove peels or cores without plunging too deeply. It was the lightest knife we tested, with a slim handle that a few testers found insubstantial but most praised for its ability to disappear in your palm and become an extension of your hand: "There's no disconnect between my brain and the blade."

Winning Traits:
- Sharp
- Lightweight
- Slightly flexible blade
- Comfortable, secure handle
- Blade between 3 and 3.25 inches long
- Spine thickness of about 1.3 millimeters or less

RECOMMENDED

Wüsthof
Classic 3½" Paring Knife
Model: 4066-7/09   **Price:** $39.99
Weight: 61.98 g
Usable Blade Length: 3.25 in
Spine Thickness: 1.59 mm

Comfort ★★★
Sharpness ★★½
Agility ★★½

Zwilling J.A. Henckels
Four Star 3" Paring Knife
Model: 31070-083   **Price:** $49.95
Weight: 44.79 g
Usable Blade Length: 3 in
Spine Thickness: 1.10 mm

Comfort ★★½
Sharpness ★★★
Agility ★★½

RECOMMENDED WITH RESERVATIONS

OXO Good Grips
Pro 3.5" Paring Knife
Model: 11191100
Price: $11.46
Weight: 69.25 g

KitchenAid
Professional
3½" Paring Knife
Model: KKFTR3PRWM
Price: $44.84
Weight: 74.01 g

Mercer Culinary
Millennia 3"
Slim Paring Knife
Model: M23900P
Price: $8.76
Weight: 28.16 g

Dexter Russell
Sani-Safe 3¼"
Cook's Style
Paring Knife
Model: 15303 S104
Price: $9.20
Weight: 31.44 g

Shun Sora
Paring Knife
Model: VB0700
Price: $31.95
Weight: 58.36 g

A GOOD PARING knife is a small but mighty addition to any knife collection. We choose this diminutive blade over a chef's knife for three primary tasks where control is paramount. One: poking things without stabbing too widely or deeply, as when scoring chicken skin to help the fat render, piercing boiled potatoes to gauge doneness, or nipping into salmon fillets to see if they're cooked through. Two: incisions, such as splitting open dates to fill with blue cheese for our Devils on Horseback, slicing pockets into pork chops to stuff them with herbs and cheese, hulling strawberries, or coring tomatoes. Three: peeling fruits and vegetables such as apples, oranges, ginger, or stubborn celery root.

To find the best paring knife, we tested eight models priced from $8.76 to $49.95, including our previous winner from Wüsthof and our previous Best Buy from Victorinox. We limited our testing to knives with blades that were between 3 and 4 inches long, as we knew from past testing that shorter blades can't reach through the food and longer blades are difficult to control.

While all the knives we tested were at least decent, we did find an awesome new favorite. But I'd bet you $100.00 that if you stopped strangers on the street and asked them to choose one of the knives we tested to take home, they would choose the wrong one. That's because—there's no other way to say it—our winning paring knife looks cheap. And it is cheap, selling for less than $10.00. It's light and small with a plastic handle and none of the heft, snazzy looks, or authoritative air some of the other knives have. But it was the best performer nonetheless.

What separated this small, unassuming blade from the pack? For one, the slight, no-frills plastic handle was comfortable, a quality that might be more important for a paring knife than for any other knife. That's because, unlike chef's knives, paring knives are often used in the air, off a cutting board: You hold a strawberry in one hand and hull it with the knife held in your other hand. Thus, using a paring knife often requires the user to cut in different directions on different planes, swerving around, say, bumps on a piece of ginger root or the curved exterior of an orange. When we made these cuts with heavier paring knives or with those that had larger handles, our hands got tired. Fatigue wasn't an issue with our light, slim winner.

We also liked its blade, which was sharp and felt particularly smooth in use: "I'm not pushing, just guiding," said one tester. All the knives were sharp out of the box; a few were less so at the end of testing, possibly due to the lower quality of their metal. Sharp knives are easy to work with and safe—the risk of injury increases when using a dull blade because you have to push harder.

Flexibility was important. With a chef's knife a firm, rigid blade inspires confidence, but with paring knives you want some flex so the blade can worm

Go to **CooksCountry.com/july17** to read the full story and the see the expanded testing chart.

its way into tight spaces or conform to curves for cleaner cuts. Knives with stiffer blades were harder to turn and took off a bit more fruit with their peels.

Spine thickness also impacted our preferences. The spine is the top of the blade, opposite the sharp edge. When peeling apples and oranges, we noticed that knives with thicker spines, around 1.5 millimeters, felt duller because we had to pull more metal through the fruit than we did with blades with slimmer spines of about 1.3 millimeters or less. Finally, we preferred knives with pointy tips. One knife had a notably dull, rounded tip, and it cored strawberries like a shovel.

The knife from Victorinox edged out the competition to take the top spot. "I think it's giving me better knife skills," said one tester. What more could you ask for?

Bottled Barbecue Sauce

Last year Americans spent more than $700 million on supermarket barbecue sauce. Did any of those bottled sauces earn a spot on our grocery list? *by Emily Phares*

THE BIRTHPLACE OF barbecue sauce is shrouded in mystery—one theory is that Christopher Columbus discovered a version in the Caribbean during his travels. Regardless of its origin, this centuries-old condiment is now an American staple. Today there are many styles of barbecue sauce, each with its own regional riff, but the most ubiquitous of the bunch hails from Kansas City. Most supermarket sauces are modeled after this thick, sweet, and tangy tomato-based style.

Since we last tasted supermarket barbecue sauces, our former favorite product, Bull's-Eye Original BBQ Sauce, changed its recipe to include high-fructose corn syrup (HFCS) instead of sugar. So we rounded up the seven top-selling national barbecue sauces, including the new version of Bull's-Eye, and tasted again to see how the supermarket sauces stacked up. We like our bottled sauce to be versatile, so we sampled each sauce plain, stirred into pulled pork, and as a dip for chicken fingers.

Sweetness had a big impact on our preferences. The sauces we fully recommend all list either HFCS or cane sugar as their primary ingredient, and the two products with the most sugar (each with 16 grams per 2-tablespoon serving) both landed in that category. The two sauces with the least sugar (one with only 4 grams per 2-tablespoon serving) dropped to the bottom

THE AMERICAN TABLE

Styles of American barbecue sauce vary widely not just by region but also by city, neighborhood, or even from house to house. But while sauce aficionados in Kansas City might take umbrage, most Americans, and certainly most national retailers, associate "Kansas City style" with the sweet, smoky, tomato-based style of barbecue sauce commonly sold in supermarkets. Why? Some point to the rise of KC Masterpiece Original Barbecue Sauce, which in the 1980s became a top-selling supermarket barbecue sauce across the country. Other companies followed suit, creating similar sauces that customers would find familiar while tweaking minor flavor notes (spiciness or smokiness, for example) to stand apart.

of our rankings. However, while the sauces with the most sugar scored well, neither one was our winner, as the true sweet spot was a slightly lower sugar level. Our winner had 11 grams of sugar per serving, about 30 percent less than the runner-up.

We wondered if the type of sugar played a role in determining which sauces we liked best. To find out, we contacted Dr. Jean-Xavier Guinard, a sensory scientist in the University of California–Davis's Food Science and Technology department. We asked Dr. Guinard if some sugar sources—such as HFCS, the main sweetener in more than half the products—taste inherently sweeter than others. He explained that different sweeteners do have different potencies, but the intensity of what we taste is usually a reflection of the volume of sweetener and not the type. Overall, tasters didn't prefer one sugar source to another—our winning product used HFCS as its primary sweetener, whereas the runner-up used cane sugar.

Aside from preferring moderate sweetness, our tasters liked sauces that had a pronounced tomato flavor as well as smoke, spice, and tang. In other words, they liked sauces that were complex and balanced rather than having one dominant flavor. All seven products contained tomato in some form, either paste or puree, but there was no clear reason why some sauces tasted more "tomato-forward." Products that ranked lower in tomato flavor played up smoke and spice instead and weren't as well-rounded.

Consistency was also important. Products ranged from watery to gelatinous, with most tasters preferring a middle-of-the-road ketchupy thickness. Our least favorite barbecue sauce was runny and thin; water was its first ingredient. This product walloped us with tomato but skimped significantly on sugar; the resulting lack of sweetness was another reason it finished in last place.

In the end, our winner once again was the aptly named Bull's-Eye Original BBQ Sauce. This moderately sweet, tomatoey sauce offered just enough spice and smoke, producing a well-balanced medley of flavors and exhibiting a texture that was neither too thick nor too thin. It will remain our go-to bottled sauce.

RECOMMENDED | TASTERS' NOTES

Bull's-Eye
Original BBQ Sauce
Price: $2.59 for 18 oz
($0.14 per oz)
Our Favorite
Sugars: 11 g

This "all-purpose" product won over tasters with its "balanced sweetness," "tomatoey" flavor, "subtle smoke," and "nice tang," all "without any of the flavors overwhelming each other." This "straightforward" barbecue sauce was "immediately pleasing to the palate" and "not as gloppy" as some others.

Heinz
Classic Sweet & Thick BBQ Sauce
Price: $2.79 for 21.4 oz
($0.13 per oz)
Sugars: 16 g

Though some tasters found this product "a tad too sweet," others enjoyed this "bold" barbecue sauce's "very sweet" and "peppery" flavor combo, as well as the "bit of tang" and "nice smoky aftertaste." This "viscous" product's "smooth" texture and "addictive flavor" led one taster to declare, "The more I eat, the more I like it."

Sweet Baby Ray's
Barbecue Sauce
Price: $2.69 for 18 oz
($0.15 per oz)
Sugars: 16 g

This pleasantly "sugary" and "robust" product's "instant hit of flavor" and "tangy bite" added up to "pretty perfect" flavor for some tasters, even though it seemed "supersweet" to others. This product's "ketchupy" texture made it an "excellent barbecue sauce for dipping" while the "good spiciness" lent a "touch of heat."

RECOMMENDED WITH RESERVATIONS

KC Masterpiece
Original Barbecue Sauce
Price: $1.69 for 18 oz
($0.09 per oz)
Sugars: 12 g

Most tasters enjoyed this product's "pleasantly smoky" and "supersweet" flavor; its "good cling" and "thick" texture further won over tasters. A few took issue with the sauce's "unassuming" taste, saying the flavor was "too weak" and "needed a little more of a kick."

Kraft
Original Barbecue Sauce & Dip
Price: $1.99 for 18 oz
($0.11 per oz)
Sugars: 13 g

This "candy-like" sauce's "unique flavor" reminded tasters of "pumpkin-spiced barbecue" and "roasted fruit." Even though this "very sweet" product was overwhelming for some and the "almost plummy" flavor "may not be mainstream enough," the sauce was lauded for its "nice heat" and "hint of smoke."

Jack Daniel's
Original No. 7 Recipe Barbecue Sauce
Price: $2.99 for 19 oz
($0.16 per oz)
Sugars: 9 g

"It tastes exactly like a campfire," noted one taster, describing this product's "woodsy" and "liquid smoke" flavor. The "deep and smoky" sauce was "delicious," "pure barbecue flavor" to some, but others found it "artificial" and thought this "meaty and savory" sauce "could use a pinch more sweetness."

NOT RECOMMENDED

Stubb's
Original Legendary Bar-B-Q Sauce
Price: $4.49 for 18 oz
($0.25 per oz)
Sugars: 4 g

Tasters likened this Texas-style (rather than Kansas City-style) product to "spicy, watery ketchup" that "was not sweet at all." The "tart" and "sour" flavor reminded one taster of "old tomato puree," while others took issue with the "metallic aftertaste" and "very thin" texture.

Go to CooksCountry.com/july17 to read the full story and the see the expanded tasting chart.

Sugar amounts based on 2-tablespoon serving size.

Easy Blueberry Cobbler

EASY BLUEBERRY COBBLER
Serves 8 to 10
Serve with vanilla ice cream.

1. (14-ounce) can sweetened condensed milk
1¼ cups (6 ounces) self-rising flour
½ cup whole milk
8 tablespoons unsalted butter, melted
10 ounces (2 cups) blueberries
¼ cup (1¾ ounces) sugar

1. Adjust oven rack to middle position and heat oven to 350 degrees. Grease 13 by 9-inch baking dish. Whisk condensed milk, flour, milk, and melted butter together in bowl. Pour batter into prepared baking dish. Sprinkle blueberries and sugar evenly over surface.
2. Bake until deep golden brown and toothpick inserted in center comes out clean, about 35 minutes. Transfer cobbler to wire rack; let cool for 10 minutes. Serve warm.

Dessert is never a tough sell for my kids. Fresh fruit, on the other hand, can be hit or miss. Luckily we've reached a compromise with this fresh blueberry "cobbler," passed on from a family friend.
—BRYAN ROOF
Executive food editor and Cook's Country TV presenter

We're celebrating the 10th season of *Cook's Country from America's Test Kitchen,* which airs this autumn on PBS and features a great cast, including hosts Bridget Lancaster and Julia Collin-Davison. Check your local PBS listings for details. In the meantime, to revisit earlier seasons and find your favorite Cook's Country recipes, visit CooksCountry.com. You may also submit a favorite family recipe (or write to Heirloom Recipes, Cook's Country, P.O. Box 470739, Brookline, MA 02447). Include your name and mailing address. If we print your recipe, you'll win a one-year subscription to Cook's Country.

COMING NEXT ISSUE

We love backyard cooking in *Cook's Country.* Next month, we'll hit the grill with recipes for big **Grilled Porterhouse Steaks**, **Grilled Butterflied Chicken**, and a superflavorful **Grilled Sweet Potato Salad**. Peak summer produce will find its way into our **Simple Tomato Salad** and **Easy Summer Fruit Tart**, and we'll hit the road to uncover the secrets to **Detroit Pizza**, North Carolina **Lazy Strawberry Sonker**, and Gulf Coast **Shrimp Po' Boys**. For dessert? The best **Coconut Cream Pie** ever.

RECIPE INDEX

FIND THE ROOSTER!

A tiny version of this rooster has been hidden in the pages of this issue. Write to us with its location, and we'll enter you in a random drawing. The first correct entry drawn will win our favorite paring knife, and each of the next five will receive a free one-year subscription to Cook's Country. To enter, visit CooksCountry.com/rooster by July 31, 2017, or write to Rooster JJ17, Cook's Country, P.O. Box 470739, Brookline, MA 02447. Include your name and address. Joy Nakfoor of Lansing, Michigan, found the rooster in the February/March 2017 issue on page 6 and won our favorite immersion blender.

WEB EXTRAS

Free for four months online at CooksCountry.com

Ballpark Pretzels
California Fish Tacos
Husk-Grilled Corn
Lightly Sweetened Whipped Cream
Tasting Bottled Barbecue Sauce
Tasting Crumbled Blue Cheese
Testing Gas Grills Under $500
Testing Ice Packs
Testing Paring Knives
Yellow Layer Cake Batter

READ US ON IPAD

Download the Cook's Country app for iPad and start a free trial subscription or purchase a single issue of the magazine. All issues are enhanced with full-color Cooking Mode slide shows that provide step-by-step instructions for completing recipes, plus expanded reviews and ratings. Go to CooksCountry.com/iPad to download our app through iTunes.

RC=Recipe Card

PIG PICKIN' CAKE

In some states, this light, fruity cake is served at a whole-hog roast, or "pig pickin'" party.
But we think it would be a hit at any barbecue.

TO MAKE THIS CAKE, YOU WILL NEED:

1 (15-ounce) can mandarin oranges in light syrup, drained
1 recipe yellow cake batter*
2 tablespoons cake flour
1 teaspoon orange extract
1 (20-ounce) can pineapple rings in syrup, drained
3 cups lightly sweetened whipped cream*
1 cup store-bought vanilla pudding (about 3 snack cups)

FOR THE CAKE:

Adjust oven rack to middle position and heat oven to 350 degrees. Grease and flour two 9-inch round cake pans and line with parchment paper. Set aside 19 orange segments for topping. Using stand mixer fitted with paddle, beat cake batter, flour, orange extract, and remaining oranges on medium-high speed until oranges have broken down, about 1 minute. Divide batter evenly between prepared pans. Bake until toothpick inserted in center comes out clean, 25 to 30 minutes, rotating pans halfway through baking. Let cakes cool in pans on wire rack for 10 minutes. Remove cakes from pans, discarding parchment, and let cool completely on rack, about 2 hours.

FOR THE FILLING AND FROSTING:

Cut 4 pineapple rings into quarters and set aside. Chop remaining pineapple fine and place in bowl (you should have about 1 cup). Fold whipped cream into pudding. Gently fold 1 cup pudding mixture into chopped pineapple.

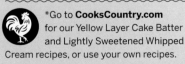 *Go to **CooksCountry.com** for our Yellow Layer Cake Batter and Lightly Sweetened Whipped Cream recipes, or use your own recipes.

TO ASSEMBLE:

Place 1 cake layer on plate or pedestal. Spread pineapple mixture in even layer over top. Top with second cake layer. Spread top and sides of cake with remaining pudding mixture. Alternate reserved pineapple quarters and 16 reserved orange segments around outside edge of top of cake. Place remaining 3 orange segments in center of cake. Serve.

INSIDE THIS ISSUE

Cook's Country

Summer Fruit Tart

Our easy step-by-step instructions ensure fresh flavors in a flaky shell every time.

PAGE 24

AUGUST / SEPTEMBER 2017
$5.95 U.S. / $6.95 CANADA

0 74470 02742 3

09>

DISPLAY UNTIL
SEPTEMBER 11, 2017

LETTER FROM THE EDITOR

R ECENTLY, WHEN I was assigned to bring a dessert for a potluck, a friend suggested a recipe for a simple dump-and-stir sheet cake, saying it was as "easy as pie." She was wrong. It was much easier than pie. Pie, for all its alleged ease, isn't always a cinch to make. But that doesn't mean it's not worth doing.

It's this idea of "worth doing" that drives our decisions about which recipes to feature in *Cook's Country*. We look for a wide range of recipes: Some are simple, a breeze to create on a weeknight; others are more involved but deliver an outsize return on your invested effort. Such is the case with our splendid Coconut Cream Pie (page 22). It's a project, but it's doable if you're willing. Be willing, because boy, does this gorgeous construction of cookie crumb–crust, coconut-infused custard, and mile-high whipped topping deliver.

But if pie's not in your sights today, turn to page 20. There you'll find our Lazy Strawberry Sonker, a little-known Appalachian dessert with a rich history that requires very little effort to put together. It may cut a more modest profile on the table, but it's every bit as satisfying and is full of lively summertime flavor. It's not easy as pie—it's easier. And who wouldn't love calling friends and family to the table for a serving (or a few) of lazy sonker?

TUCKER SHAW

Executive Editor

Associate editor Cecelia Jenkins checks her sonker for doneness (above). Below, two sonker contest hopefuls—sisters Rosa Elaine Opoulos (left) and Emma Jean Tucker (right)—at the annual Sonker Festival in Surry County, North Carolina.

Photography: Sara Brennan (bottom)

Cook's Country

Chief Executive Officer David Nussbaum
Chief Creative Officer Jack Bishop
Editorial Director John Willoughby
Executive Editor Tucker Shaw
Executive Managing Editor Todd Meier
Executive Food Editor Bryan Roof
Deputy Editor Scott Kathan
Associate Editors Morgan Bolling, Cecelia Jenkins, Katie Leaird, Ashley Moore
Lead Cook, Photo Team Daniel Cellucci
Test Cooks Alli Berkey, Matthew Fairman
Assistant Test Cooks Mady Nichas, Jessica Rudolph
Senior Copy Editor Krista Magnuson
Copy Editor Jillian Campbell
Contributing Editor Eva Katz
Science Editor Guy Crosby, PhD, CFS
Director, Creative Operations Alice Carpenter
Hosts & Executive Editors, Television Bridget Lancaster, Julia Collin Davison

Executive Editor, Tastings & Testings Lisa McManus
Deputy Editor Hannah Crowley
Associate Editors Miye Bromberg, Lauren Savoie, Kate Shannon
Assistant Editor Emily Phares
Editorial Assistant Carolyn Grillo

Test Kitchen Director Erin McMurrer
Assistant Test Kitchen Director Alexxa Benson
Test Kitchen Manager Meridith Lippard
Test Kitchen Facilities Manager Sophie Clingan-Darack
Lead Kitchen Assistant Ena Gudiel
Kitchen Assistants Gladis Campos, Blanca Castanza

Creative Director John Torres
Photography Director Julie Cote
Art Director Susan Levin
Designer Maggie Edgar
Art Director, Marketing Melanie Gryboski
Deputy Art Director, Marketing Janet Taylor
Associate Art Director, Marketing Stephanie Cook
Senior Staff Photographer Daniel J. van Ackere
Staff Photographers Steve Klise, Kevin White
Photography Producer Mary Ball
Photography Keller + Keller
Food Styling Catrine Kelty, Marie Piraino

Executive Editor, Web Christine Liu
Managing Editor, Web Mari Levine
Senior Editors, Web Roger Metcalf, Briana Palma
Associate Editor, Web Terrence Doyle
Senior Video Editor Nick Dakoulas

Chief Financial Officer Jackie McCauley Ford
Production Director Guy Rochford
Imaging Manager Lauren Robbins
Production & Imaging Specialists Heather Dube, Dennis Noble, Jessica Voas
Senior Controller Theresa Peterson
Director, Business Partnerships Mehgan Conciatori

Chief Digital Officer Fran Middleton
Director, Sponsorship Marketing & Client Services Christine Anagnostis
Client Services Manager Kate Zebrowski
Client Service and Marketing Representative Claire Gambee
Partnership Marketing Manager Pamela Putprush
Marketing Director, Social Media & Content Strategy Claire Oliverson
Senior Social Media Coordinators Kelsey Hopper, Morgan Mannino
Director, Customer Support Amy Bootier
Senior Customer Loyalty & Support Specialists Rebecca Kowalski, Andrew Straaberg Finfrock

Senior VP, Human Resources & Organizational Development Colleen Zelina
Human Resources Director Adele Shapiro
Director, Retail Book Program Beth Ineson
Retail Sales Manager Derek Meehan

Circulation Services ProCirc

On the cover: Easy Summer Fruit Tart
Keller + Keller, Catrine Kelty

AMERICA'S TEST KITCHEN ®

America's Test Kitchen is a real 2,500-square-foot kitchen located just outside Boston. It is the home of more than 60 test cooks, editors, and cookware specialists. Our mission is to test recipes until we understand exactly how and why they work and eventually arrive at the very best version. We also test kitchen equipment and supermarket ingredients in search of products that offer the best value and performance. You can watch us work by tuning in to *America's Test Kitchen* (AmericasTestKitchen.com) and *Cooks Country from America's Test Kitchen* (CooksCountry. com) on public television and listen to our weekly segments on *The Splendid Table* on public radio. You can also follow us on Facebook, Twitter, Pinterest, and Instagram.

12

9

22

Cook's Country magazine (ISSN 1552-1990), number 76, is published bimonthly by America's Test Kitchen Limited Partnership, 17 Station St., Brookline, MA 02445. Copyright 2017 America's Test Kitchen Limited Partnership. Periodicals postage paid at Boston, MA, and additional mailing offices, USPS #023453. Publications Mail Agreement No. 40020778. Return undeliverable Canadian addresses to P.O. Box 875, Station A, Windsor, ON N9A 6P2. POSTMASTER: Send address changes to *Cook's Country*, P.O. Box 6018, Harlan, IA 51593-1518. For subscription and gift subscription orders, subscription inquiries, or change of address notices, visit AmericasTestKitchen.com/support, call 800-526-8447 in the U.S. or 515-248-7684 from outside the U.S., or write to us at *Cook's Country*, P.O. Box 6018, Harlan, IA 51593-1518. PRINTED IN THE USA.

The Amount of Water in Your Water Pan

Your grill-roasting recipes often call for a disposable pan filled with a specific amount of water to be placed inside the grill. Does it really matter how much water is in the pan? –*Jim Sullivan, Des Moines, Iowa*

Some of our low-and-slow grill-roasting recipes call for placing a disposable aluminum pan filled with water in the bottom of the grill adjacent to the hot coals. Both the pan and the water absorb heat, which helps moderate the temperature inside the grill and ensure gentler, more controlled cooking. The water also creates steam and moisture to help keep foods such as ribs, brisket, and chicken from drying out.

To determine how much the amount of water in the pan mattered, we built small charcoal fires (using 4½ quarts of briquettes) in three grills and placed a 13 by 9-inch disposable aluminum pan opposite the coals in each of them. One pan we left empty, one we filled with our standard 3 cups of water, and one we filled with 9 cups of water. We noted the temperatures in the grills every 10 minutes for 1 hour.

The amount of water had a big impact. The starting temperature in all three grills was about 430 degrees. The temperature in the grill with no water fell to 400 degrees after 1 hour. The temperature in the grill with 3 cups of water fell to 360 degrees after 1 hour. And the temperature in the grill with 9 cups of water dropped to 345 degrees after 1 hour.

THE BOTTOM LINE: Pay attention to how much water you add to the disposable pan in the bottom of a grill. Too much water can moderate the grill temperature more than intended.

by Morgan Bolling

EMPTY WATER PAN: The grill was too hot.

PAN WITH 9 CUPS OF WATER: The grill was too cool.

PAN WITH 3 CUPS OF WATER: The grill temperature was just right.

Advance Brining

Can you brine boneless chicken breasts, take them out of the brine, and refrigerate them the day before cooking them? –*Richard Trammel, Birmingham, Ala.*

We often suggest brining or salting chicken (and other lean meats) to add deep seasoning and provide a buffer against dry meat. Our recipes—including brining ratios and times—are carefully engineered to work every time.

But to see if it's possible to brine in advance, we brined one batch of four chicken breasts for 1 hour (using our standard brine formula of ¼ cup of salt dissolved in 2 quarts of water), removed them from the brine, and left them on a plate, covered in plastic, in the refrigerator overnight. The next day, we cooked them along with some chicken breasts that we'd just brined. We cooked both batches of chicken to 160 degrees.

Tasters noted that both batches of chicken breasts were moist and juicy but found that the chicken brined and stored in the refrigerator was a bit saltier than the just-brined chicken. This is because the salt on the surface of the stored chicken continued to penetrate the meat and was less easily expelled during cooking. Many tasters preferred these breasts to the just-brined breasts, but if you're salt-sensitive, you may not.

THE BOTTOM LINE: For convenience's sake, it's OK to brine chicken breasts, remove them from the brine, and refrigerate them for up to 24 hours before using them. Keep in mind that the chicken will be slightly saltier than just-brined chicken. *–MB*

A Fine Line(r)

It says on the package of the aluminum baking cups I bought that they're sturdy enough to fill and use directly on a baking sheet—no muffin tin required. Is this true? –*Praveen Subraman, San Francisco, Calif.*

Excited about potentially easy cleanup, we put this claim to the test by baking two batches each of our Ultimate Chocolate Cupcakes and Mackinac Lemon-Blueberry Muffins (see page 15)—one batch of each baked in foil cups set in muffin tin cups and the other batch of each baked in foil cups placed, unsupported, on a baking sheet.

The chocolate cupcakes, which are made from a loose batter, varied slightly between the two batches, but both versions were acceptable—although the ones baked in the muffin tin baked up higher and more uniformly round.

The muffins, which are made from a thick batter, were starkly different. Those baked in the muffin tin were tall, with distinct, domed tops. The muffins not baked in a tin were not acceptable, as the batter weighed down the foil cups and spread and sprawled to form wide, flat muffins with sides that were pale and wan because they lacked contact with the beneficial heat conductivity of a metal pan.

THE BOTTOM LINE: It's worth investing in a muffin tin if you want to make muffins or cupcakes that are tall and nicely domed. Our favorite muffin tin is the OXO Good Grips Non-Stick Pro 12-Cup Muffin Pan ($24.99). *–MB*

LIGHT CUPCAKE BATTER
Results are OK but not as tall as we usually like.

HEAVY MUFFIN BATTER
Results are unacceptable.

Counterfeit Crab

Imitation crab is much cheaper than lump crabmeat. Is it worth buying? –*Emily Josephs, Somerville, Mass.*

Imitation crab is made by grinding pollock or other whitefish and adding seasonings (including sugar), food coloring, small amounts of real crabmeat or crab flavoring, and binders such as starch or egg whites. Its sold shredded, in chunks, or as sticks.

To see how it compared to the real McCoy, we made two batches of our Maryland Crab Cakes—one using real lump crab and the other using imitation crab. Tasters strongly preferred the real stuff, commenting that the imitation crab was "oddly sweet," "bouncy," and wet. "No amount of tartar sauce could cover that up," bemoaned one less-than-enthused taster.

We also tasted the imitation crab in our Light and Creamy Hot Crab Dip and our Crab Louis Salad. Again, tasters strongly preferred the versions made with real crab. In the salad—the only uncooked application we tried—some tasters found the imitation crab acceptable. It didn't fool anyone into thinking it was real crab, but it had an inoffensively sweet, seafoody flavor.

THE BOTTOM LINE: We didn't like imitation crab in cooked applications, but in a pinch you can use it as a stand-in for crab in seafood salads. *–MB*

Submit questions and shortcuts at CooksCountry.com/ask and CooksCountry.com/shortcuts.

Perfect Pit Removal

Nancy Jones, Plano, Texas

I find removing the pit from a halved avocado awkward, so I was happy to discover another way to prep avocados. First, I run my knife around the pit from pole to pole. Then, I run the knife around the pit along the avocado's equator to quarter it. The pieces separate easily; the skin often peels right off (sometimes I need to use a spoon), and the pit is easy to remove from the flesh. I then use the avocado chunks in mashed applications such as guacamole.

Worry-Free Straining

Rita Foran, Endicott, N.Y.

I am a recent convert to quinoa. The instructions on the package say to rinse it to get rid of bitterness, but a lot of quinoa heads down my drain since the holes in my strainer are too big. A large French press comes in handy here—just dump in your measured quinoa, add water, plunge, pour off the water, and you're ready to cook.

Measuring Charcoal

Scott Flaherty, Saginaw, Mich.

Many recipes call for charcoal fires made with a specific amount (usually measured in quarts) of charcoal. But how do you measure charcoal when your biggest measuring cup holds only 2 cups? I found an easy solution: Save 1-quart containers from your local deli or takeout place, and keep one near your grill for easy, accurate measuring of charcoal.

compiled by Cecelia Jenkins

Tasting Chocolate Ice Cream

by Emily Phares

LITTLE IS MORE satisfying than a scoop of chocolate ice cream—but which one is best? To find out, we gathered seven nationally available chocolate ice creams and asked 21 tasters to sample them plain and in cones.

An ice cream's texture was very important to our tasters, so we contacted industry experts to learn more about how commercial ice cream is made. Though not listed on the package, air is a defining ingredient in ice cream; it is churned into the base ingredients to increase texture, volume, and, since air is free, the manufacturer's bottom line. The percentage of air added is called "overrun," so "100 percent overrun" means the base ingredients are inflated with air to double their original volume. A high overrun percentage makes for light, airy ice cream.

However, manufacturers may add certain ingredients to counter the airiness of high-overrun ice cream. Our winner, from Turkey Hill, has relatively high overrun, but the inclusion of corn syrup contributes to the "creamy," "silky" texture our tasters loved. Other producers use ingredients such as buttermilk, tapioca starch, and pectin to alter texture and mask the airiness of high-overrun products.

A balanced yet prominent chocolate flavor was important, too. Cocoa powder is the sole source of chocolate flavor in all the ice creams we tasted, and experts told us that the quality and acidity of the cocoa had a big impact on how the ice creams tasted. In the end, we liked most products, with the great flavor and texture of our winner, Turkey Hill Premium Dutch Chocolate Ice Cream, earning it the top ranking. We also loved that it was the least expensive product in our lineup.

Our taste-test winner had a "silky," "velvety" texture that our tasting panel loved.

 Go to **CooksCountry.com/sept17** to read the full story and see the complete results chart.

Our Favorite
Turkey Hill Premium Dutch Chocolate Ice Cream
Price: $2.99 for 1.5 qt ($0.06 per fl oz)
Overrun Percentage: 103
Comments: Tasters raved about this ice cream's "fabulous" texture, which was "creamy," "very smooth," and "velvety." It boasted an "accessible" "milk chocolate" flavor with a "great aftertaste." The combination of "silky" texture and "friendly" chocolate flavor proved irresistible.

Breyers Chocolate Ice Cream
Price: $4.99 for 1.5 qt ($0.10 per fl oz)
Overrun Percentage: 99.8
Comments: This ice cream's "very chocolaty" flavor was the "perfect balance between sweet and bitter." This product seemed "a bit airy," but ultimately its "clean chocolate richness" and "delicious aftertaste" earned it high marks.

Edy's Chocolate Ice Cream (sold as Dreyer's in the western United States and Texas)
Price: $5.99 for 1.5 qt ($0.12 per fl oz)
Overrun Percentage: 99.2
Comments: Tasters favored this "pleasantly light" and "frothy" ice cream for its "robust," "deep dark chocolate flavor" and "smooth texture." They thought it had "the right amount of sweetness."

ON THE ROAD

IT COULDN'T HAVE happened anywhere but in Detroit.

As a child in Sicily, Connie Piccinato grew up eating squared-off wedges of focaccia studded with leftover meats. As an adult in 1946, while working as a waitress at Buddy's in Detroit, she found herself craving the pies of her youth. But she faced a dilemma. Food-grade rectangular pizza pans simply didn't exist at the time, so "square pizza" wasn't known in the States.

But Piccinato found inspiration in a discarded rectangular "blue steel" pan used for collecting errant nuts and bolts in the string of automobile-related factories along Six Mile Road. She and Buddy's owner August "Gus" Guerra pressed a batch of dough into one of the pans, nudging it into the sharp corners; topped it with cheese and sauce; and baked it off. The square pizza was a hit, and it gave Buddy's, originally a "blind pig" speakeasy selling contraband booze during Prohibition, a new lease on life.

The rectangular pans, then made by a company named Dover Parkersburg, were "blued" at high temperatures to resist rust and came in two sizes, just right for small and large pizzas. After repeated use, the deeply seasoned pans gave the crusts an extra kick of flavor and a noticeably lacy, cheesy crunch, similar to the crusty edge of a baked lasagna.

"The pans became part of the folklore as to why this pizza tastes the way it does," says Wesley Pikula, vice president of operations for Buddy's. "Everything about it was contrary to what the current pizza styles were."

Pikula describes Buddy's pizza as "a Neapolitan-style dough, with a Sicilian assembly, baked in Detroit scrap-metal pans." Back then, the pans were cheap and readily available. Nowadays, Buddy's Pizza pays five to six times the price they once did to have the pans specially made.

The city has changed over the years, but the pizza, popular as ever, remains the same. The folks at Buddy's care deeply for their product; for them, it's personal. "There's only one way to make a great thing," Pikula says.

Old World Pie, New World Pan

How an unassuming factory fixture made this squared-off Motor City staple possible.

by Bryan Roof

Buddy's operations chief Wesley Pikula (top) had many stories to share, including how his pizza parlor's famous pie came to be and the origin of the steel pans in which the pizzas are made (middle). Today the company doesn't have to rely on discarded steel pans—they're made to order for the chain. At right, a crew of regulars gathers for a card game over pizza and beer at Buddy's in the 1960s.

Detroit-Style Pizza

We hit the streets and then hit the kitchen to uncover the secrets of this topsy-turvy Michigan favorite. *by Ashley Moore*

DETROIT PIZZA, A deep-dish local favorite, is light and airy, with a crunchy, buttery crust. It's topped with soft, stretchy cheese and a slightly sweet tomato sauce full of herbs and spices. But aficionados will tell you that the best part is the crispy, lacy fried edges.

The pizza starts familiarly enough, with mixing and kneading the dough, which is then transferred to a 13 by 9-inch seasoned steel pan and left to rise and fill the pan. Cooks then flip the traditional pizza script, evenly spreading shredded brick cheese—a mild, slightly tangy semisoft cheese hard to find outside Michigan—from the dough's middle to its edges before draping ladle-fuls of the sweet tomato sauce over the cheese. In the oven, the dough bakes into a soft base with crispy, brown, cheesy edges.

While this style of pizza originated at a Detroit bar named Buddy's in the 1940s (see "Old World Pie, New World Pan"), there are now many local experts. I reached out to Shawn Randazzo of Detroit Style Pizza Co. to learn what goes into his dough and how to best reproduce the flavor and texture of brick cheese. After picking his brain for tips, I compiled some recipes and put them to work, producing five pizzas that were purportedly Detroit-style. I fed them to my coworkers, including a few Detroit natives. The results? Well, the optimistic take was "promising, but not quite."

I experimented with different types of flour for my dough, ultimately landing on ubiquitous all-purpose flour for its easy availability. To create that soft interior, Randazzo warned me, I'd need a rather wet and sticky dough, so I let the stand mixer do most of the hard work of bringing it together. After a quick 1-minute knead on the counter, I eased the dough into a 13 by 9-inch baking pan that I'd lightly greased. After it proofed for a few hours, the silky dough tripled in volume, nearly filling the pan, and I noticed many large bubbles, a sign that this dough was going to be tender and airy but still chewy.

This was the point at which, if I were making another style of pizza, I'd add sauce. But Detroit pizza takes cheese first, sauce later. I first had to find a good substitute for mild, melty brick cheese. To do so, I held a grand tasting, pitting thirteen types of cheese against brick cheese, which I had mail-ordered. The tasters had a clear preference for

Monterey Jack. It was slightly tangy, melted beautifully, and had just enough fat in it to fry those essential crispy edges as it baked.

In Detroit, pizza chefs use canned tomatoes and dried spices for the sauce. I settled on a mixture of canned crushed tomatoes, fresh garlic, fresh basil, dried basil (I needed both to mimic the trademark complexity of the herb mixture), dried oregano, sugar, salt, and pepper.

After baking dozens of pizzas, I was proud to serve my Detroit-born colleagues big squares of their hometown favorite with soft interiors, tangy sauce, melty cheese, and those trademark lacy, crispy edges.

The sauce, which sits in rows on top of the cheese, caramelizes a bit in the hot oven.

DETROIT-STYLE PIZZA
Serves 4

When kneading the dough on medium speed, the mixer can wobble and move on the counter. Place a towel or shelf liner under the mixer to keep it in place, and watch it closely. To add more toppings, such as pepperoni or sausage, to your pizza, press them into the dough before adding the cheese.

PIZZA
- 1 tablespoon extra-virgin olive oil
- 2¼ cups (11¼ ounces) all-purpose flour
- 1½ teaspoons instant or rapid-rise yeast
- 1½ teaspoons sugar
- 1 cup water, room temperature
- ¾ teaspoon salt
- 10 ounces Monterey Jack cheese, shredded (2½ cups)

SAUCE
- 1 cup canned crushed tomatoes
- 1 tablespoon extra-virgin olive oil
- 1 tablespoon chopped fresh basil
- 1 garlic clove, minced
- 1 teaspoon dried oregano
- 1 teaspoon dried basil
- ½ teaspoon sugar
- ½ teaspoon pepper
- ¼ teaspoon salt

1. FOR THE PIZZA: Spray 13 by 9-inch nonstick baking pan with vegetable oil spray, then brush bottom and sides of pan with oil. Using stand mixer fitted with dough hook, mix flour, yeast, and sugar on low speed until combined, about 10 seconds. With mixer running, slowly add room-temperature water and mix until dough forms and no dry flour remains, about 2 minutes, scraping down bowl as needed. Cover with plastic wrap and let stand for 10 minutes.

2. Add salt to bowl and knead on medium speed until dough forms satiny, sticky ball that clears sides of bowl, 6 to 8 minutes. Turn dough onto lightly floured counter and knead until smooth, about 1 minute.

3. Transfer dough to prepared pan, cover with plastic, and let rest for 15 minutes. Using your well-oiled hands, press dough into corners of pan. (If dough resists stretching, let it rest for another 10 minutes before trying again to stretch.) Cover with plastic and let dough rise at room temperature until nearly tripled in volume and large bubbles form, 2 to 3 hours. Adjust oven rack to lowest position and heat oven to 500 degrees.

4. FOR THE SAUCE: Combine all ingredients in bowl. (Sauce can be refrigerated for up to 24 hours.)

5. Sprinkle Monterey Jack evenly over dough to edges of pan. Spoon three 1-inch-wide strips of sauce, using ⅓ cup sauce for each, over cheese evenly down length of pan.

6. Bake until cheese is bubbly and browned, about 15 minutes. Let pizza cool in pan on wire rack for 5 minutes. Run knife around edge of pan to loosen pizza. Using spatula, slide pizza onto cutting board. Cut into 8 pieces and serve.

Grill-Roasted Butterflied Chicken

Grilling a whole chicken can produce uneven results. We wanted a level playing field.

by Cecelia Jenkins with Diane Unger

COME SUMMER, I'D rather fire up the grill than heat up my oven. So when I found myself craving roasted chicken—a craving that spans seasons—I wanted a simple outdoor method that would yield juicy, tender meat and crispy, lightly charred skin.

Removing the chicken's backbone (aka butterflying or spatchcocking) allows the bird to lay flat, creating a more uniform thickness to promote even cooking and browning, and it's much easier than you might think—a few snips with a pair of kitchen shears on either side of the backbone do the trick. I quickly prepped a few chickens and headed out to the grill.

Seven quarts of charcoal generate enough heat to roast whole birds in other test kitchen recipes. But when I spread the same amount of lit coals across the bottom of the grill in an even layer, my chicken's underside and drumsticks ended up blackened. For my next test, I created a half-grill fire, arranging the lit coals on one side of the grill to create two heat zones, one hotter and one cooler. I placed the chicken on the cooler side of the grill, skin side up, until it was almost cooked through before flipping it and placing it directly over the coals to finish cooking and, I figured, to crisp the skin. The skin did crisp up, but after losing one of the chicken's legs, ripping the skin on the breast with my tongs, and making an overall mess, I looked for a way to skip the flip.

I carefully skewered a butterflied chicken (see "Skewering the Bird") to help it hold together, placed it on the cooler side of the grill, covered the grill, and walked away. About an hour later, the meat was tender and moist, but the skin was still too blond. For my next round, I applied a simple rub of brown sugar, salt, and pepper to the skin, hoping the sugar would caramelize and turn the skin a beautiful bronze. It worked perfectly and imparted only a faint sweetness to the meat—many tasters never picked up on it.

While the chicken cooked, I whipped up a bold chimichurri-style sauce with smoky paprika, tangy red wine vinegar, garlic, and fresh herbs. I had a beautiful grill-roasted whole chicken that required minimal attention—and no flipping—on the grill. And the bonus: Because I'd butterflied it, it was a breeze to carve.

A little brown sugar helps create nicely browned skin without adding much sweetness.

Skewering the Bird

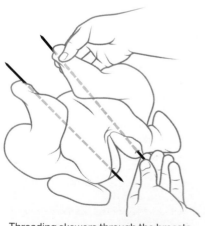

Threading skewers through the breasts and legs keeps the chicken intact. Insert 1 skewer down length of chicken through thickest part of breast and into and through end of drumstick. Repeat with second skewer on other half of chicken.

EASY GRILL-ROASTED BUTTERFLIED CHICKEN
Serves 4
Threading two wooden skewers through the breasts and drumsticks keeps the chicken intact during cooking. Serve the chicken with Red Chimichurri Sauce (recipe follows).

- 1 (4-pound) whole chicken, giblets discarded
- 2 (12-inch) wooden skewers
- 1 tablespoon packed light brown sugar
- 2 teaspoons kosher salt
- 2 teaspoons pepper

1. Place chicken, breast side down, on cutting board. Using kitchen shears, cut through bones on either side of backbone; discard backbone. Flip chicken over and press on breastbone to flatten. Tuck wingtips underneath.

Insert 1 skewer down length of chicken through thickest part of breast and into and through drumstick. Repeat with second skewer on other half of chicken.
2. Combine sugar, salt, and pepper in bowl. Rub mixture evenly over skin side of chicken. Transfer chicken, skin side up, to plate and refrigerate, uncovered, for at least 1 hour or up to 24 hours.
3A. FOR A CHARCOAL GRILL: Open bottom vent completely. Light large chimney starter mounded with charcoal briquettes (7 quarts). When top coals are partially covered with ash, pour evenly over half of grill. Set cooking grate in place, cover, and open lid vent completely. Heat grill until hot, about 5 minutes.
3B. FOR A GAS GRILL: Turn all burners to high, cover, and heat grill until hot, about 15 minutes. Leave primary burner on high and turn off other burner(s). (Adjust primary burner [or, if using three-burner grill, primary burner and second burner] as needed to maintain grill temperature around 400 degrees.)
4. Clean and oil cooking grate. Place chicken, skin side up, on cooler side of grill with skewers parallel to fire. Cover (position lid vent over chicken if using charcoal) and cook until breasts register 160 degrees and thighs register 175 degrees, about 1 hour, rotating chicken halfway through cooking.
5. Transfer chicken, skin side up, to carving board; tent with aluminum foil; and let rest for 15 minutes. Remove skewers and carve chicken. Serve.

RED CHIMICHURRI SAUCE
Makes about ½ cup
Our favorite supermarket olive oil is California Olive Ranch Everyday Extra Virgin Olive Oil. The sauce can be refrigerated for up to 48 hours.

- ¼ cup minced fresh parsley
- ¼ cup red wine vinegar
- ¼ cup extra-virgin olive oil
- 1 shallot, minced
- 1½ teaspoons paprika
- 1 garlic clove, minced
- ¼ teaspoon kosher salt
- ⅛ teaspoon red pepper flakes

Whisk all ingredients together in bowl. Let stand at room temperature for at least 30 minutes to allow flavors to blend. Whisk to recombine before serving.

Honey-Mustard Coleslaw

We were after a simple slaw with big flavor.

by Cecelia Jenkins

SWEET AND PUNGENT honey mustard is a welcome addition to sandwiches and barbecue sauces and a perfect dip for chicken nuggets or pretzels. Why not toss it into a slaw? The challenge would lie in balancing aggressively sweet honey and aggressively bold mustard. I wanted sharp mustard flavor tamed with just the right amount of sweetness in a creamy-yet-crisp slaw.

Drawing on the knowledge we've gleaned from dozens of slaw recipes over the years, I knew I had to pull some liquid out of the cabbage before I dressed it to ensure a crunchy, not soggy, slaw. The answer seemed simple: Toss the shredded cabbage with a bit of salt, which draws out moisture, and then drop it into a colander and let it drain. But the result was too salty. I could rinse away the lingering salt, of course, but rinsing and drying were extra steps I was trying to avoid. Swapping out some salt in favor of sugar, which also has water-extracting properties, proved to be the solution (and meant that I could make the slaw a day or two ahead with less risk of serving it soggy).

I started with a dressing of equal parts mustard and honey, but the supersweet honey was overpowering. Doubling the amount of mustard got the slaw back on track. Tasters favored complex spicy brown mustard over yellow mustard (too acidic) or Dijon mustard (too sharp). For a bit of creaminess, I added 2 tablespoons of mayonnaise. A sprinkling of chives added subtle onion flavor and a fresh burst of color.

HONEY-MUSTARD COLESLAW
Serves 6 to 8

Our favorite spicy brown mustard is Gulden's. Do not use bagged shredded cabbage here. To save time, slice the cabbage in a food processor fitted with a slicing disk. If you don't have a food processor, slice the cabbage wedges crosswise about ⅛ inch thick.

- 1 head green cabbage (2 pounds), quartered, cored, and sliced thin (12 cups)
  Salt and pepper
- 1½ teaspoons sugar
- ½ cup spicy brown mustard
- ¼ cup honey
- 3 tablespoons minced fresh chives
- 2 tablespoons mayonnaise

1. Toss cabbage, 1½ teaspoons salt, and sugar together in large bowl. Transfer to colander and set colander in now-empty bowl. Let stand until cabbage has wilted and released about 2 tablespoons water, about 1 hour, stirring and pressing on cabbage occasionally with rubber spatula.
2. Discard liquid and wipe bowl clean with paper towels. Whisk mustard, honey, chives, mayonnaise, ½ teaspoon pepper, and ⅛ teaspoon salt in now-empty bowl until combined. Stir in cabbage and refrigerate, covered, until chilled, about 1 hour. Season with salt and pepper to taste. Serve. (Coleslaw can be refrigerated for up to 2 days.)

Grilled Sweet Potato Salad

Could we create this summery side dish by cooking only on the grill? *by Alli Berkey*

SUMMER IS THE season of potato salads and grilling. I decided to combine these two traditions, with a little twist—sweet potatoes.

The first step was cutting the tubers down to size; they're dense and would take a long time to cook through if left whole. After experimenting with chunks and rounds, I found that rounds took on more charred flavor. Still, it wasn't easy to get them to grill evenly. By the time the centers cooked through, the exteriors looked like coal.

The answer was to drop the rounds into a disposable aluminum pan, cover the pan tightly with aluminum foil, set it over the fire, and let the water in the potatoes steam them through. I then transferred the steamed potatoes from the pan to the cooking grate to char. At this point, they were good, but not great. For a flavor boost, I tossed the rounds with a sweet-smoky vinaigrette of lime juice, honey, cumin, and chipotle chile before grilling.

I also grilled a red onion, sliced into rounds that I skewered to help them hold together on the grill. To assemble the salad, I tossed the charred spuds and onions with a bit more vinaigrette and topped it all with salty feta, sliced scallions, and fresh cilantro.

GRILLED SWEET POTATO SALAD
Serves 4 to 6

Buy medium-size sweet potatoes, 2 to 3 inches in diameter, because they'll fit neatly in the disposable aluminum pan.

- 1 small red onion, sliced into ½-inch-thick rounds
- 3 tablespoons lime juice (2 limes), plus lime wedges for serving
- 2 tablespoons honey
- 1 teaspoon minced canned chipotle chile in adobo sauce
- ½ teaspoon ground cumin
  Salt and pepper
- ⅓ cup vegetable oil
- 2½ pounds sweet potatoes, peeled and cut into ½-inch-thick rounds
- 1 (13 by 9-inch) disposable aluminum pan
- 2 ounces feta cheese, crumbled (½ cup)
- 3 scallions, sliced thin on bias
- ¼ cup coarsely chopped fresh cilantro

1. Thread 1 toothpick horizontally through each onion round. Whisk lime juice, honey, chipotle, cumin, ½ teaspoon salt, and ¼ teaspoon pepper together in bowl. Slowly whisk in oil.
2. Toss potatoes, onion rounds, ¼ cup vinaigrette, ½ teaspoon salt, and ½ teaspoon pepper together in separate bowl. Place onion rounds in bottom of disposable pan, layer potatoes over top, then pour in any remaining liquid from bowl. Cover disposable pan tightly with aluminum foil.
3A. FOR A CHARCOAL GRILL: Open bottom vent completely. Light large chimney starter filled with charcoal briquettes (6 quarts). When top coals are partially covered with ash, pour evenly over grill. Set cooking grate in place, cover, and open lid vent completely. Heat grill until hot, about 5 minutes.
3B. FOR A GAS GRILL: Turn all burners to high, cover, and heat grill until hot, about 15 minutes. Turn all burners to medium. Adjust burners as needed to maintain grill temperature around 400 degrees.
4. Clean and oil cooking grate. Place disposable pan on grill. Cover grill and cook until vegetables are tender, 20 to 25 minutes, shaking disposable pan halfway through cooking to redistribute potatoes. Remove disposable pan from grill.
5. Place vegetables on cooking grate. Cook (covered if using gas) until lightly charred and tender, 2 to 4 minutes per side. Transfer vegetables to platter. Remove toothpicks from onion rounds and separate rings. Pour remaining vinaigrette over vegetables and toss to coat. Sprinkle feta, scallions, and cilantro over top. Serve with lime wedges.

Grilled Thick-Cut Porterhouse Steaks

This giant special-occasion steak can vex even experienced grillers.
We wanted a simple route to perfect medium-rare. *by Cecelia Jenkins*

THE RESPLENDENT THICK-CUT porterhouse: a fat-marbled, flavorful strip steak and a generous portion of buttery tenderloin attached to a single bone. At an impressive 1½ to 2 inches thick and nearly 3 pounds, this doubled-up cut is both exciting and intimidating. And it's far from cheap.

With stakes (steaks?) this high, I needed a foolproof grilling method that would yield a rosy interior and a crusty exterior—on both sides of the beast. To get that crust, I knew I'd need plenty of heat. But simply blasting the meat would burn the outsides of the steaks before the insides were cooked through. I needed more control.

Drawing on test kitchen knowledge, I built a half-grill fire, piling 6 quarts of coals on one side of the grill and leaving the other side empty. After trimming excess fat from the meat to keep flare-ups to a minimum, I grilled the steaks directly over the coals to char their exteriors. I then moved them to the cooler side of the grill and covered the grill to finish cooking the steaks while limiting any further charring.

I had mixed results. While the strip side of the steak fared well, the leaner tenderloin portion overcooked and dried out. It was clear that I needed to protect it from too much direct heat.

But how? Orientation. For my next test, I positioned the steaks so that the tenderloins faced the cooler side of the grill. Then, once I moved the steaks to the cooler side, I used the T-bone as a shield (see "Orienting the Steaks on the Grill"). These minor but important tweaks to the process proved fruitful.

The only way to know when a steak this big is done is to take its temperature. But you can't just stick that thermometer anywhere. After many experiments, I found the prime probing spot to be the area near the tapered tip of the strip, the narrowest part of the steak. When this zone registered medium-rare (115 to 120 degrees), it was time to pull the steaks off the fire; the thicker parts would reach medium-rare as the steaks rested.

After I carved the rosy meat off the bone and sliced the strip and tenderloin portions, the luxurious steaks were excellent on their own. But in the spirit of celebration, I gilded the lily with the old-fashioned addition of melted butter drizzled over the top for an even richer flavor.

After slicing the steaks, we reassemble the slices around the bones so that it's easy to identify strip and tenderloin pieces when serving.

GRILLED THICK-CUT PORTERHOUSE STEAKS
Serves 6

Flare-ups may occur when grilling over charcoal. If the flames become constant, slide the steaks to the cooler side of the grill until the flames die down.

- 2 (2½- to 3-pound) porterhouse steaks, 2 inches thick, fat trimmed to ¼ inch
  Kosher salt and pepper
- 4 teaspoons olive oil (if using gas)
- 3 tablespoons unsalted butter, melted

1. Pat steaks dry with paper towels and sprinkle each side of each steak with 1 teaspoon salt. Transfer steaks to large plate and refrigerate, uncovered, for at least 1 hour or up to 24 hours.

2A. FOR A CHARCOAL GRILL: Open bottom vent completely. Light large chimney starter filled with charcoal briquettes (6 quarts). When top coals are partially covered with ash, pour evenly over half of grill. Set cooking grate in place, cover, and open lid vent completely. Heat grill until hot, about 5 minutes.

2B. FOR A GAS GRILL: Turn all burners to high, cover, and heat grill until hot, about 15 minutes. Leave primary burner on high and turn off other burner(s). (Adjust primary burner [or, if using three-burner grill, primary burner and second burner] as needed to maintain grill temperature of 450 degrees.)

3. Pat steaks dry with paper towels. If using gas, brush each side of each steak with 1 teaspoon oil. Sprinkle each side of each steak with ½ tea-spoon pepper.

4. Clean and oil cooking grate. Place steaks on hotter side of grill, with tenderloins facing cooler side. Cook (covered if using gas) until evenly charred on first side, 6 to 8 minutes. Flip steaks and position so tenderloins are still facing cooler side of grill. Continue to cook (covered if using gas) until evenly charred on second side, 6 to 8 minutes longer.

5. Flip steaks and transfer to cooler side of grill, with bone side facing fire. Cover and cook until thermometer inserted 3 inches from tip of strip side of steak registers 115 to 120 degrees (for medium-rare), 8 to 12 minutes, flipping halfway through cooking. Transfer steaks to wire rack set in rimmed baking sheet, tent with aluminum foil, and let rest for 10 minutes.

6. Stir ¼ teaspoon salt into melted butter. Transfer steaks to carving board. Carve strips and tenderloins from bones. Place bones on platter. Slice steaks thin against grain, then reassemble sliced steaks around bones. Drizzle with melted butter and season with salt and pepper to taste. Serve.

Orienting the Steaks on the Grill

Tenderloins Face the Cooler Side
Char steaks on hotter side of grill for 6 to 8 minutes on each side with tenderloins facing cooler side of grill, then flip and turn steaks so tenderloins are still facing cooler side.

Bones Face the Fire
Flip steaks and cook for 8 to 12 minutes on cooler side of grill, with bone sides positioned so that they are facing fire. To check temperatures, insert thermometer 3 inches from tips of strip sides of each steak (see arrow above).

Simple Tomato Salad

When tomatoes are at their peak, don't stand in their way.

by Morgan Bolling

TOMATO SALAD IS the It Girl of summer—stylish, great taste, effortlessly cool, with just enough accessories to amplify the attention it attracts.

Making a handful of existing recipes I'd found for tomato salad taught me a few things. First, a great tomato salad doesn't start in the kitchen but rather at your local farmers' market or at the grocery store—nothing sinks a salad faster than an underripe tomato. You want to select tomatoes that feel heavy for their size and smell fruity. In the salads I made, some of the most oddly shaped tomatoes were the most flavorful, from some tender yet wrinkly heirloom varieties to supermarket options such as Kumato or Campari. Using a mix of colors and sizes added allure (see "A Few Tomato Types").

After settling on my tomato lineup, I made a simple dressing, following the test kitchen's standard 3:1 ratio of oil to acid. I whisked together high-quality extra-virgin olive oil and freshly squeezed lemon juice (which added more freshness than vinegar would), plus some salt and pepper, and poured this mixture over a platter of sliced tomatoes.

Because tomatoes are already fairly acidic, we found the dressed salad way too sharp. I tried cutting the lemon juice from the dressing altogether, but tasters missed its vibrancy. After some experimenting, I found that a 9:1 ratio (3 table-spoons of oil to 1 teaspoon of lemon juice) tasted much more balanced. A minced shallot completed the dressing, adding just a bit of sweetness and crunch.

As a finishing touch, I sprinkled some toasted pine nuts and fragrant torn basil leaves over the dressed salad. And because my tomatoes were so juicy, I served some crusty bread on the side to sop up the tasty tomato-flavored liquid. Summer.

A mix of various tomato types and sizes provides a range of colors and textures.

SIMPLE TOMATO SALAD *Serves 4*
For the best results, use peak-of-the-season tomatoes. Serve this salad with crusty bread to sop up the dressing.

- 1½ pounds mixed ripe tomatoes, cored and sliced ¼ inch thick
- 3 tablespoons extra-virgin olive oil
- 1 tablespoon minced shallot
- 1 teaspoon lemon juice
- ½ teaspoon salt
- ¼ teaspoon pepper
- 2 tablespoons pine nuts, toasted
- 1 tablespoon torn fresh basil leaves

Arrange tomatoes on large, shallow platter. Whisk oil, shallot, lemon juice, salt, and pepper together in bowl. Spoon dressing over tomatoes. Sprinkle with pine nuts and basil. Serve immediately.

SIMPLE TOMATO SALAD WITH CAPERS AND PARSLEY
Add 1 tablespoon rinsed capers, 1 rinsed and minced anchovy fillet, and ⅛ teaspoon red pepper flakes to dressing. Omit pine nuts. Substitute coarsely chopped fresh parsley for basil.

SIMPLE TOMATO SALAD WITH PECORINO ROMANO AND OREGANO
Add ½ teaspoon grated lemon zest and ⅛ teaspoon red pepper flakes to dressing. Omit pine nuts and sprinkle salad with 1 ounce shaved Pecorino Romano cheese. Substitute 2 teaspoons coarsely chopped fresh oregano for basil.

A Few Tomato Types
The best-tasting tomatoes always come from your own garden. But if the supermarket's your source, here's a guide to the most commonly available options.

Vine-Ripened: "Vine-ripened" toma-toes are left on the plant until at least 10 percent of their skin has turned red. They are sweeter and juicier than regular supermarket tomatoes.

Heirloom: Any variety that is not as-sociated with large-scale commercial production may be labeled "heir-loom." Because heirloom varieties generally can't withstand the rigors of long-distance shipping, most are lo-cally grown and can be readily found at farmers' markets.

Roma: The firm texture of these plum tomatoes makes them great for cooked sauce. But when eaten fresh, most supermarket Roma tomatoes underdeliver on flavor.

Campari: Often sold with a portion of the vine attached, these deep-red, relatively compact tomatoes are prized for their sweet, juicy flesh.

Kumato: These green-brown beau-ties have more fructose than most conventional tomatoes, so they taste sweeter, with a hefty, meaty texture.

Fried Pork Chops with Milk Gravy

We knew there was a secret to keeping the coating crunchy even under the gravy. We just had to unlock it. **by Alli Berkey**

A bit of black pepper and a little cayenne pepper add punch to the crunchy coating.

I GREW UP in the Midwest, so when I hear "gravy," I automatically think of the standard brown, broth-based version. It wasn't until a friend introduced me to Southern-style milk gravy—a pale, flour-thickened, pepper-flecked, milk-based sauce that's used to smother chicken-fried steak, biscuits, or other dishes—that I realized I'd been missing out. The soft, comforting stuff was a lovely counterpoint to a crunchy fried pork chop. I wanted to make my own versions of both at home.

As I read through different existing recipes, I found that the ingredient lists rarely overlapped and techniques varied dramatically. I started by experimenting with different cuts of pork. While loin chops and blade chops fared well enough, rib chops stood out for their even cooking and moist meat.

To achieve a perfect crunchy exterior, I knew I'd need a healthy amount of oil. But did I really want to pull out all the stops and set up a deep-frying station for what should be a quick weeknight dinner? Instead, I committed to shallow-frying the chops in a skillet with just 1 cup of oil.

Our usual coating procedure involves a dredge in flour (seasoned, in this case, with a bit of garlic powder and cayenne) to help create a dry surface on the meat's exterior, a dunk in beaten egg, and another dredge in flour. Following this method, I achieved a nice crispy coating on my chops. But I wanted a supercraggy, supercrunchy coating that could stand up to a smothering of gravy. After experimenting with variations on this theme, I discovered that adding a bit of milk to the flour used in the coating process helped create a sort of shaggy dough that readily stuck to the chops. A short rest in the refrigerator helped ensure that the coating stayed put. Once fried, these chops were as crunchy as I'd hoped they'd be, with tender, moist meat inside.

The gravy came together easily. Taking advantage of some of the fat left in the skillet, I whisked in a bit more flour for thickness, added 1½ cups of milk, and let the mixture simmer and thicken for just a couple of minutes. A heavy hand with the pepper grinder added the perfect smattering of flecks and pushed this gravy over the finish line.

The true test of this dish was whether those chops would stay crunchy under gravy. And thanks to that superthick coating, they did. My Carolina- and Georgia-raised coworkers devoured the dish before granting me honorary Southerner status.

Creating a Substantial, Crunchy Coating

We put a twist on the usual breading process by turning the flour into a shaggy dough. Add 2 tablespoons of milk to a seasoned flour mixture, rubbing it with your fingers until the milk is fully incorporated and ragged pieces of dough form.

TRIPLE-DIP FOR A SUPERTHICK CRUST
Dip the chops into the flour mixture, then into beaten egg, and then back into the flour.

PAN-FRIED PORK CHOPS WITH MILK GRAVY
Serves 4

Use pork chops no more than ½ inch thick to ensure that the meat cooks through before the breading begins to burn. If you can find only chops that are slightly thicker than ½ inch, thin them with a meat pounder.

- 1 cup plus 2 tablespoons all-purpose flour
- 2 teaspoons garlic powder
  Salt and pepper
- ½ teaspoon cayenne pepper
- 2 tablespoons plus 1½ cups whole milk
- 2 large eggs
- 4 (5- to 7-ounce) bone-in pork rib chops, ½ inch thick, trimmed
- 1 cup vegetable oil

1. Whisk 1 cup flour, garlic powder, 1½ teaspoons salt, 1 teaspoon pepper, and cayenne together in shallow dish. Add 2 tablespoons milk to flour mixture; using your fingers, rub flour and milk together until milk is fully incorporated and shaggy pieces of dough form. Whisk eggs together in second shallow dish.

2. Set wire rack in rimmed baking sheet. Pat chops dry with paper towels and season with salt and pepper. Working with 1 chop at a time, dredge chops in flour mixture, shaking off any excess; dip into eggs to thoroughly coat, letting excess drip back into dish; and dredge again in flour mixture, pressing gently to adhere. Transfer to prepared wire rack. Refrigerate coated chops for at least 15 minutes or up to 2 hours.

3. Line large plate with triple layer of paper towels. Heat oil in 12-inch nonstick skillet over medium-high heat to 375 degrees. Add 2 chops and cook until golden brown and meat registers 140 degrees, 2 to 3 minutes per side. Transfer to prepared plate. Repeat with remaining 2 chops.

4. Carefully pour off all but 2 tablespoons fat from skillet and place skillet over medium heat. Whisk in remaining 2 tablespoons flour, 1 teaspoon pepper, and ½ teaspoon salt and cook until bubbly and fragrant, about 30 seconds. Whisk in remaining 1½ cups milk, bring to boil, and cook until slightly thickened, about 2 minutes. Serve gravy with chops.

Bacon-Wrapped Chicken Breasts

Our mission: to make this restaurant favorite at home. *by Ashley Moore*

IT SOUNDS LIKE a good idea: moist, tender chicken breasts encased in savory, crispy bacon. I've seen this dish in restaurants and have always assumed there was some complicated magic involved—how else would you be able to avoid overcooking the chicken before the bacon was rendered and crispy? I set out, with measured optimism, to decipher the magic.

I started with five recipes to test. One called for cooking the wrapped chicken breasts in a moderate oven. But when the chicken was done (and it was done perfectly—well-seasoned and juicy), the bacon wrapping was still flabby and underdone. Another recipe called for browning the bacon-wrapped chicken breasts in a skillet, flipping them once or twice, before finishing them in the oven. This gave me over-cooked, bordering-on-burnt bacon by the time the chicken cooked through, and I lost a slice or two of bacon during flipping. The rest of the recipes gave me mixed results, none perfect.

What I'd learned: Relatively gentle heat leads to the juiciest chicken, but the bacon would need high heat for at least a portion of the cooking time to crisp properly. What's more, I'd have to cook the chicken on both sides to ensure crispy bacon all around.

I mused about the heat sources at my disposal as I wrapped four chicken breasts in bacon, and then I eyed my broiler. I lined up the chicken on a baking sheet, slid it into a 350-degree oven until it reached an internal temperature of 150 degrees, and then turned on the broiler, hoping that a blast of heat would crisp the bacon.

And it did. But only on the tops; the bacon underneath the breasts was still squishy and fatty.

I thought back to the chicken I'd cooked in the skillet, which sported nicely rendered bacon on both sides. Could I achieve similar results without all that flipping? I rendered the bacon on the bottoms of the breasts in the skillet on the stovetop, transferred the skillet to the oven to almost cook the chicken through, and then hit it with the broiler heat. But it took several minutes for the bacon on top to achieve the deep brown color I wanted.

Maybe I could boost the color with a bit of sugar, which would caramelize into a brown, crispy coating and add a bit of pleasant sweetness. For my

A stint on the stovetop followed by a visit to the oven ensures crispy bacon and moist chicken.

next test, after cooking the chicken on the stovetop until the bottom bacon was crispy and rendered, I sprinkled a little brown sugar over each breast and transferred the skillet to the oven. When the chicken was nearly cooked through, I turned on the broiler. Thanks to the sugar, the bacon-wrapped breasts emerged deeply browned and crispy in just 4 minutes.

My tasters loved the results but wanted one more flavor note: rosemary, a beautiful match for the slightly sweet bacon.

Magic? Nope. All this dish took was a bit of attention and ingenuity.

That's a Wrap

For maximum bacon flavor, we wrap each breast with two slices. Starting at the fatter end of the breast, wrap the bacon around, stretching it as you go and making sure it doesn't overlap itself. Continue wrapping with the second slice until the breast is completely covered.

Start wrapping bacon on the fatter end of the chicken breast.

BACON-WRAPPED CHICKEN BREASTS
Serves 4

Do not use thick-cut bacon here; it won't render and crisp as well as thin-cut bacon. Oscar Mayer Naturally Hardwood Smoked Bacon is our winning thin-sliced bacon. For even cooking, be sure to use chicken breasts that are consistent in size and weight.

- 1 teaspoon minced fresh rosemary
- 1 teaspoon salt
- ¾ teaspoon pepper
- 4 (6- to 8-ounce) boneless, skinless chicken breasts, trimmed
- 8 slices bacon
- 1 tablespoon vegetable oil
- ¼ cup packed brown sugar

1. Adjust oven rack 6 inches from broiler element and heat oven to 350 degrees. Combine rosemary, salt, and pepper in bowl. Sprinkle chicken all over with rosemary mixture.

2. Wrap each chicken breast with 2 pieces of bacon: Starting with 1 piece of bacon on underside of wide end of breast, stretch and wrap bacon around breast, spiraling down toward middle. Continue wrapping with second piece of bacon until breast is completely wrapped and bacon seams end up on underside of breast.

3. Heat oil in 12-inch skillet over medium-high heat until shimmering. Add chicken, bacon seam side down, and cook, without moving it, until bacon is golden brown, about 3 minutes. (Do not flip chicken.)

4. Sprinkle top of each breast with 1 tablespoon sugar. Transfer skillet to oven and roast until chicken registers 155 degrees, 15 to 20 minutes. Remove skillet from oven and heat broiler. Broil until bacon is well browned and chicken registers 160 degrees, 4 to 5 minutes. Let chicken rest for 5 minutes. Serve.

Shrimp Po' Boys

This street-food sandwich has been a workday favorite in Louisiana for generations. We wanted it at home. *by Alli Berkey*

THE FIRST SO-CALLED poor boy sandwiches served in New Orleans (see "The American Table") were made with sliced beef and gravy, but the idea was ripe for improvisation—not just with the name (it was soon shortened to "po' boy") but with the fillings, too. One version, stuffed with crunchy, flavorful fried shrimp and tons of fixings, became especially popular.

I set out to create a sandwich that would deliver a satisfying range of spicy-savory New Orleans flavors. The first trick was to nail the shrimp. Simply coating the shrimp using the typical three-step method (first tossing them in a bit of seasoned flour to create a dry surface, then dunking them in beaten egg, and then adding another layer of seasoned flour) before frying them in hot peanut oil gave me tender shrimp with lightly crispy exteriors. But I didn't want lightly crispy, I wanted crunchy. We've added cornmeal to similar seasoned-flour coatings on chicken in the past, so I gave it a try here. And it worked—sort of. The shrimp were crunchier, but the coating was now sliding off the shrimp like a jacket at the end of a long day.

A colleague suggested bolstering the beaten egg with a bit of the seasoned flour to create a slightly more paste-like mixture. Doing so—and then giving the fully coated shrimp a 30-minute rest in the refrigerator before frying them—helped the coating adhere to the shrimp. And jazzing up the flour dredge with a Creole spice mix added an extra flavor punch.

No shrimp po' boy is complete without a superflavorful dressing, so I created a simple rémoulade by stirring mayonnaise together with sharp horseradish, savory Worcestershire sauce, some piquant hot sauce, and ground pepper. I slathered fresh sub rolls with sauce on both sides and piled them high with shrimp, lettuce, tomatoes, and briny pickle chips: These sandwiches won't leave any po' boy hungry.

We pack flavor into every element of this sandwich, from the Creole-seasoned breading to the pungent rémoulade dressing.

Strikers take to the New Orleans streets, 1929.

THE AMERICAN TABLE

The Birth of a Sandwich

Nineteen twenty-nine was a bumpy year for New Orleans—and not just because of that year's famous October stock market crash. Several months earlier, streetcar workers with the Amalgamated Association of Street and Electric Railway Employees of America, Division 194, went on strike to protest the creation of a rival company-sponsored union. They took to the streets on July 1, stomachs growling. Bennie Martin and his brother Clovis, former streetcar workers who'd since opened their Martin Brothers' Coffee Stand and Restaurant, came along to feed the picketers with their "poor boy" sandwiches, distributed free of charge. The sometimes-violent strike lasted in varying degrees for several years, and the sandwiches, originally filled with beef, became a signature New Orleans lunch. Eventually variations on po' boys—shrimp, for one—caught on and spread to other Gulf Coast towns, from Galveston, Texas, to Pensacola, Florida.

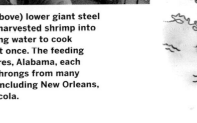

Shrimp by the Ocean

by Bryan Roof

A line of boisterous festival-goers stretches from the shaded window of a steel-clad food truck, where a woman exchanges platters of giant glistening, freshly boiled shrimp for cash. Inside, cooks use an industrial-looking pulley system to lower deep baskets of the shrimp into massive pots of heavily seasoned water, where they cook for just moments before being hauled out in a fog of spice and steam, mixing with the saline aroma of the sea wafting in off the beach.

I'm in Gulf Shores, Alabama, for the Annual National Shrimp Festival, known locally as "Shrimp Fest." Started in 1971 as a bid to extend the summer tourist season, the festival attracts 250,000 people with a common love of shrimp, live music, and the stunning cotton-white sand beaches of coastal Alabama.

Amid a constant chant of "Roll Tide!" from the innumerable University of Alabama fans in attendance, bright food stalls and trucks sell everything from paella to Cajun Pistols: deep-fried rolls filled with a cheesy shrimp and crawfish étouffée. And, of course, overstuffed shrimp po' boys, best paired with cold beer and sandy toes.

Shrimp vendors (above) lower giant steel baskets of locally harvested shrimp into seasoned simmering water to cook dozens of orders at once. The feeding frenzy in Gulf Shores, Alabama, each October attracts throngs from many Gulf Coast cities, including New Orleans, Mobile, and Pensacola.

SHRIMP PO' BOYS *Serves 4*

Use refrigerated prepared horseradish, not the shelf-stable kind, which contains preservatives and additives. Frank's Red Hot Original Cayenne Pepper Sauce is best here. Use a Dutch oven that holds 6 quarts or more. Do not refrigerate the breaded shrimp for longer than 30 minutes, or the coating will be too wet. It may seem like you're spreading a lot of rémoulade on the rolls, but it will be absorbed by the other ingredients.

RÉMOULADE

- ⅔ cup mayonnaise
- 2 tablespoons prepared horseradish
- 1 tablespoon Worcestershire sauce
- 1 tablespoon hot sauce
- ¼ teaspoon pepper

SHRIMP

- 2 cups all-purpose flour
- ¼ cup cornmeal
- 2 tablespoons Creole seasoning
- 4 large eggs
- 1 pound medium-large shrimp (31 to 40 per pound), peeled, deveined, and tails removed
- 2 quarts peanut or vegetable oil
- 4 (8-inch) sub rolls, toasted
- 2 cups shredded iceberg lettuce
- 2 large tomatoes, cored and sliced thin
- 1 cup dill pickle chips

1. FOR THE RÉMOULADE: Whisk all ingredients together in bowl. Set aside.
2. FOR THE SHRIMP: Set wire rack in rimmed baking sheet. Whisk flour, cornmeal, and Creole seasoning together in shallow dish. Whisk eggs and ½ cup flour mixture together in second shallow dish.
3. Place half of shrimp in flour mixture and toss to thoroughly coat. Shake off excess flour mixture, dip shrimp into egg mixture, then return to flour mixture, pressing gently to adhere. Transfer shrimp to prepared wire rack. Repeat with remaining half of shrimp. Refrigerate shrimp for at least 15 minutes or up to 30 minutes.
4. Line large plate with triple layer of paper towels. Add oil to large Dutch oven until it measures about 1½ inches deep and heat over medium-high heat to 375 degrees. Carefully add half of

Creole Seasoning

Recipes for Louisiana spice blends vary in name, but whether called Cajun or Creole (the terms are often used interchangeably), most contain paprika, garlic, thyme, salt, pepper, and cayenne. In taste tests, we preferred saltier, spicier products and those that stuck to traditional paprika-heavy and garlic-forward notes. Our favorite is **Tony Chachere's Original Creole Seasoning.** It's "vibrant" and "zesty," with strong notes of garlic and red pepper, a "punch of heat," and a "slightly sweet" aftertaste.

shrimp to oil. Cook, stirring occasionally, until golden brown, about 4 minutes. Using slotted spoon or spider skimmer, transfer shrimp to prepared plate. Return oil to 375 degrees and repeat with remaining shrimp.
5. Spread rémoulade evenly on both cut sides of each roll. Divide lettuce, tomatoes, pickle chips, and shrimp evenly among rolls. Serve.

For a crispy coating that won't fall off, refrigerate the shrimp for 15 to 30 minutes after dipping them in the flour and egg mixtures. Transfer the shrimp to a paper towel–lined plate after frying.

Lemon-Blueberry Muffins

We baked more than 300 muffins before we found the perfect balance of sweet and tart.

by Morgan Bolling

LEMON AND BLUEBERRY are a power couple in the baking world. That's because the vibrant freshness of lemon plays well with the tart sweetness of blueberries. For many years, the Hotel Iroquois in Mackinac Island, Michigan, has capitalized on this fruity affinity with its signature mini lemon-blueberry muffins. Full of rich, buttery flavor; ample amounts of both lemon and blueberries; and a crunchy top resulting from a quick dip in a mixture of melted butter and sugar right after baking, these muffins have earned legions of fans.

I was inspired to make a similar recipe for home cooks, so I turned first to the test kitchen's archive of blueberry muffin recipes. After making a few, I put together a basic lineup of dry ingredients: flour, salt, and baking powder (testing has shown us that baking soda can turn blueberries green). I mixed in melted butter, milk, eggs, sugar, and 1 teaspoon of lemon zest before folding in frozen wild blueberries—a test kitchen favorite for year-round quality. Instead of mini muffins, I opted for full-size, using a scoop to portion the batter into my muffin tin. Twenty minutes later I had beautiful muffins, but they barely tasted of lemon, and dipping full-size muffins in the butter-sugar mixture was a messy affair.

For the next batch, I amped up the lemon flavor by tripling the amount of zest incorporated into the batter. And I switched out the milk for sour cream, which made the muffins more tender and enhanced their lemony tang. These flavor tweaks helped, but I needed that crunchy sugar top.

Rather than dip each muffin in melted butter and sugar, I took an easier route: I brushed the tops of the uncooked muffins with melted butter and sprinkled them with sugar. In the oven, the sugar gently caramelized into a sweet, crunchy shell. Adding an extra helping of lemon zest to this topping gave it even more flavor.

For my final batch, I measured out my dry ingredients the night before and baked the muffins in the morning before my coworkers had finished their first cups of coffee. A warm, lemony aroma filled the kitchen as we gathered around to taste. The cozy, comforting flavors were almost as good as crawling back into bed for a snooze.

For refreshing lemon flavor throughout, we add freshly grated zest to both the batter and the crunchy sugar topping.

The Best Muffin Tin

We recently evaluated 10 muffin tins, rating them on their durability, release, handling, and the browning of the baked goods they produced. Our favorite had the biggest rim of those we tested, providing a broad, secure place to grasp when wearing oven mitts. Its gold nonstick finish produced impressively golden-brown, nicely domed muffins and cupcakes that released with ease.

GOLD STAR
The **OXO Good Grips Nonstick Pro 12-Cup Muffin Pan** ($24.99) perfectly browned and released muffins.

MACKINAC
LEMON-BLUEBERRY MUFFINS
Makes 12 muffins

To prevent streaks of blue in the batter, leave the blueberries in the freezer until the last possible moment. Frozen blueberries make this a year-round recipe; fresh blueberries may be substituted, if desired. If your lemons are small, buy an extra one to ensure that you're able to get 5 teaspoons of zest.

1½	cups (10½ ounces) sugar
5	teaspoons grated lemon zest (2 lemons)
2½	cups (12½ ounces) all-purpose flour
4	teaspoons baking powder
¾	teaspoon salt
1½	cups sour cream
7	tablespoons unsalted butter, melted
2	large eggs
7½	ounces (1½ cups) frozen blueberries

1. Adjust oven rack to middle position and heat oven to 400 degrees. Generously spray 12-cup muffin tin, including top, with vegetable oil spray. Combine ¼ cup sugar and 2 teaspoons lemon zest in small bowl; set aside.

2. Whisk flour, baking powder, and salt together in bowl. Whisk sour cream, 5 tablespoons melted butter, eggs, remaining 1¼ cups sugar, and remaining 1 tablespoon lemon zest together in large bowl.

3. Using rubber spatula, fold flour mixture into sour cream mixture until just combined. Fold in blueberries until just evenly distributed; do not overmix. Using greased ⅓-cup dry measuring cup or #12 portion scoop, portion batter among cups in prepared muffin tin; evenly distribute any remaining batter among cups. Brush batter with remaining 2 tablespoons melted butter and sprinkle with sugar-zest mixture (about 1 teaspoon per muffin cup).

4. Bake until muffins are golden brown and toothpick inserted in center comes out with few crumbs attached, 20 to 25 minutes, rotating muffin tin halfway through baking. Let muffins cool in muffin tin on wire rack for 10 minutes. Transfer muffins to rack and let cool for 5 minutes. Serve warm.

THE AMERICAN TABLE

Mackinac Island, situated in Lake Huron between Michigan's Upper and Lower Peninsulas, was an idyllic summertime vacation spot for the 19th-century well-to-do from Detroit, Chicago, Buffalo, and other Great Lakes ports. Horses drew carriages along the island's few roads, delivering daytime strollers to wading beaches and evening party-hoppers to the ballrooms of the great hotels that lined the bluffs.

But at the turn of the 20th century, a newfangled mode of transportation appeared on the island: the automobile. Mackinac natives rose up in protest—the revving engines startled one too many local horses that first season—and the island's governing council banned all automobiles.

The burgeoning automobile industry wasn't happy with that decision; after all, many of Mackinac's most well-heeled visitors were entrepreneurs from Detroit. But the islanders stayed stubborn and held fast to the ban. It was a prescient decree, preserving not just the horses' nerves but also the island's quiet character. Today, the only motorized vehicles allowed on Mackinac are emergency vehicles and service trucks.

Do you have some berries left over? Put them to use in pancakes. Go to **CooksCountry.com/pancakes**.

A New Way to Zest

We usually brace our rasp-style grater on a cutting board and swipe the fruit across it. But recently we spied a test cook in our kitchen who keeps the fruit stationary instead, sliding the upside-down grater across the fruit. She finds it easier to see how deep the blades are cutting, and because the zest accumulates in full view, she can see how much she's harvested.

Testing Rasp-Style Graters

by Hannah Crowley

WE USE RASP-STYLE graters to zest citrus fruits and to grate hard cheeses, ginger, shallots, garlic, nutmeg, and more. One product has ruled the roost for years. Grace Manufacturing, the parent company of Microplane, pioneered and patented a special photographic etching process that creates razor-sharp grating teeth. The company initially produced long metal rasps for woodworking but found that consumers were using them in the kitchen, too, so they added a culinary line. But their patent on this process expired in 2011, freeing other manufacturers to create their own versions of this tool.

The one small gripe we've had with the Classic model is that its 1-inch-wide grating surface cuts a trench in blocks of cheese as we grate. We hoped that graters with wider surfaces would fix this problem, so we rounded up three wider models and tested them against our old favorite and four other newcomers, using them all to zest lemons and to grate Parmesan cheese, garlic, nutmeg, and ginger. We learned that—in addition to the width of the grating surface—the shape and size of the grating teeth still matter: One model with small teeth didn't dig deeply enough into food, forcing us to make more passes to get the job done. Graters with bigger teeth—and yes, we measured—cut too deeply, harvesting too much bitter pith when zesting citrus. Unfortunately, the three models with wider grating surfaces had larger teeth, and we can't fully recommend them. Products with medium-size (between 3 and 4 millimeters) teeth were best.

Comfort and durability also played into our rankings. In the end, we found two models that we really liked. Our old winner, the Microplane Classic Zester/Grater, grated like a dream, but it was usurped by the Microplane Premium Classic Zester/Grater. The two models performed identically, but the Premium model offers a cushier handle—making it worth the extra few bucks. To read the full testing results, go to **CooksCountry.com/sept17**.

KEY **Good** ★★★ **Fair** ★★ **Poor** ★

RECOMMENDED

CRITERIA

Microplane Premium Classic Zester/Grater
Model: 46220, turquoise
Price: $14.95
Average Hole Size: 3.25 sq mm
Cutting Edge Dimensions: 7.25 x 1 in

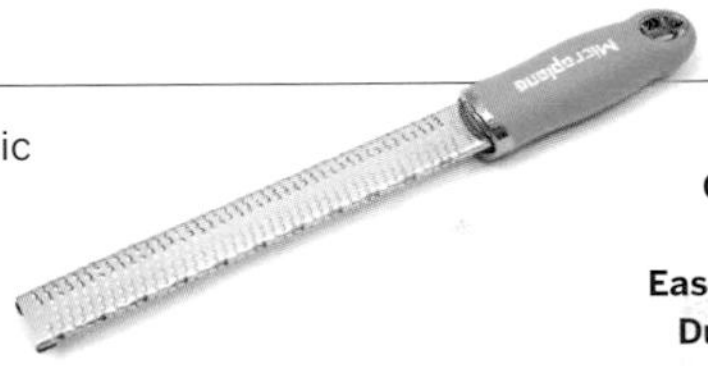

Grating	★★½
Comfort	★★★
Speed	★★★
Ease of Use	★★½
Durability	★★★

Comments: This model grabbed the top spot thanks to its great performance and grippy rubber handle that was slightly more comfortable and secure than that of our old winner. It zested lemons and grated cheese, nutmeg, garlic, and ginger with ease. It stayed sharp and looked as good as new after testing. We wish it had a wider surface so it didn't form trenches in the cheese, but it's still the best option.

Microplane Classic Zester/Grater
Model: 40020
Price: $12.95
Average Hole Size: 3.25 sq mm
Cutting Edge Dimensions: 7.25 x 1 in

Grating	★★½
Comfort	★★½
Speed	★★★
Ease of Use	★★½
Durability	★★★

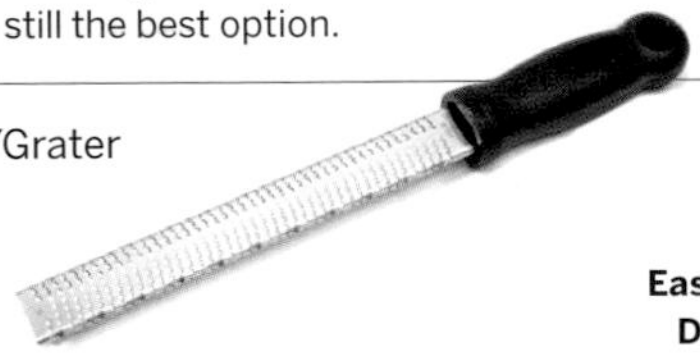

Comments: Our old winner turned in an admirable performance. Its medium-size teeth bit into cheese, lemons, and whatever else we used it on with speed and ease. It was as sharp at the end of testing as it was at the beginning. Its rounded plastic handle was comfortable, though harder and not as grippy as that of our winner, so we docked a few points. Its width still resulted in trenches, but it remains a great choice.

RECOMMENDED WITH RESERVATIONS

OXO Good Grips Zester
Model: 1122180V2
Price: $9.99
Average Hole Size: 4.36 sq mm
Cutting Edge Dimensions: 5.8 x 1.55 in

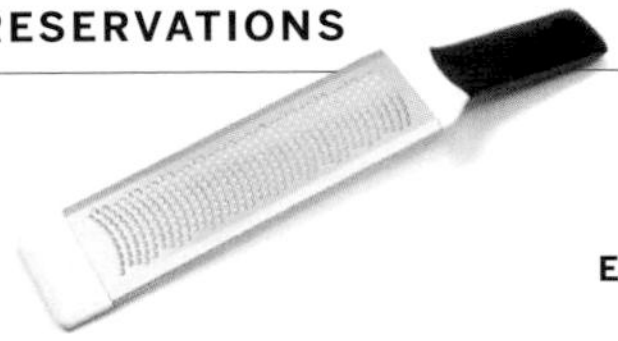

Grating	★★½
Comfort	★★½
Speed	★★★
Ease of Use	★★
Durability	★★½

Comments: This grater's wide teeth dug into Parmesan with gusto but were too wide for lemons, sinking deeply into the skin and removing too much bitter pith. Its soft, grippy handle was too small, and its rectangular shape felt awkward to some. Its wide 2-inch grating surface wore down the cheese more evenly (no gouged trenches).

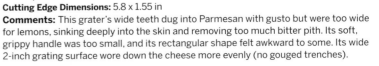

Greek Layer Dip

To get the most out of this multilayered snack, we focused on its architecture.

by Ashley Moore

YOU'RE AT A party, and you've aimed your chip at a bowl of a multilayered dip with the goal of bringing a little bit of everything back to your mouth. But on the way in, the chip breaks, leaving your best intentions buried in the dip. We wanted to spare partygoers this feeling of frustration and construct our Greek Layer Dip in a way that would welcome any chip.

A play on Greek salad, this party dip is built on a base of savory hummus and layered with tangy yogurt, salty crumbled feta cheese, pieces of fresh cucumber and roasted red peppers, and chopped briny kalamata olives. With so many elements, I decided to streamline the process by letting convenience products (store-bought hummus and jarred roasted red peppers) do some of the heavy lifting—giving me more time to get ready for the party.

But after making several layered dips of differing quantities and proportions, my tasters and I were vexed by broken chips and incomplete bites. After trying different chips and different constructions, I'd resorted to using a spoon to scoop dip onto chips. Not the solution I had in mind.

I reached out to a caterer friend, who suggested I construct a shallower dip on a wide platter, allowing guests to drag chips through it rather than plunge them in from above. This technique, she said, would yield fewer broken chips and a more equal distribution of elements onto each chip.

After spooning a generous, sturdy base of hummus onto the platter, I spread a creamy sheet of plain Greek yogurt over the top (we chose Greek yogurt for its rich texture and tangy flavor). Next, I stirred together a few recognizable elements of Greek salad—kalamata olives, cucumbers, and roasted red peppers—along with chopped fresh mint and sliced scallions, adding a few tablespoons of extra-virgin olive oil to help bind the ingredients together. I spread this vegetable mixture evenly on top of the yogurt. Finally, because a Greek salad isn't complete without feta cheese, our Greek Layer Dip wasn't either. I crumbled a good portion of feta over top of everything.

I now had a superflavorful layered dip suitable for a backyard gathering or a fancier evening fete. And because I'd built it on a platter, my broken-chip problem was long gone.

Building and serving this dip on a shallow platter makes dipping, or swiping, much easier.

GREEK LAYER DIP
Serves 8 to 10

We prefer the thick texture of Greek yogurt to the thinner texture of regular yogurt for this recipe. Our favorite hummus, from Sabra, comes in a 17-ounce family size; two of these containers will equal 4¼ cups. For added flavor, you can substitute store-bought tzatziki sauce for the yogurt. For best results, be sure to assemble this dip shortly before serving, because it doesn't store well. Serve the dip with pita chips or sliced vegetables.

- 4¼ cups hummus
- 1½ cups plain Greek yogurt
- 1 cup ¼-inch English cucumber pieces
- ½ cup jarred roasted red peppers, patted dry and chopped
- ⅓ cup pitted kalamata olives, chopped
- 4 scallions, sliced thin
- 3 tablespoons extra-virgin olive oil, plus extra for drizzling
- 2 tablespoons chopped fresh mint
- ¼ teaspoon salt
- ¼ teaspoon pepper
- 2 ounces feta cheese, crumbled (½ cup)

1. Spread hummus in single layer on large, shallow serving platter. Carefully spread yogurt in even layer over hummus.

2. Combine cucumber, red peppers, olives, scallions, oil, mint, salt, and pepper in bowl. Spoon vegetable mixture in even layer over yogurt. Sprinkle with feta and drizzle with extra oil. Serve.

Our Picks For the Best Dip

Our dip's base layer is easy to make using two convenience foods, whereas we prefer homemade pita chips.

Sabra Classic Hummus
Our winning hummus could pass for homemade: It has a clean tahini flavor and a consistency that's hearty but not dense.

Fage Total Classic Greek Yogurt
Our top-rated Greek yogurt boasts a fresh, mildly tangy dairy taste and a luxuriously thick, creamy consistency.

Pita Chips
Homemade pita chips are dead simple to make, and their taste and texture are worlds apart from the store-bought kind.

 We've got you covered. For our pita chip recipe, go to **CooksCountry.com/homemadepitachips.**

Thai-Style Red Curry Chicken with Vegetables

30-MINUTE SUPPER

Spiced Pork Lettuce Wraps

30-MINUTE SUPPER

Grilled Pork Tenderloin with Broccolini and Hazelnut Browned Butter

30-MINUTE SUPPER

Queso Fundido Burgers

30-MINUTE SUPPER

Spiced Pork Lettuce Wraps

Serves 4

WHY THIS RECIPE WORKS: To avoid sogginess and ensure crisp wraps, we serve them deconstructed on a platter so each person can build their own wrap when and how they like.

- ½ cup sour cream
- 2 tablespoons chopped fresh mint
- 2 tablespoons water
- 1 teaspoon ground cumin
  Salt and pepper
- 1 pound ground pork
- 1 tablespoon Sriracha sauce
- 2 garlic cloves, minced
- 1 head Bibb lettuce (8 ounces), leaves separated
- 1 avocado, halved, pitted, and sliced thin
- 1 mango, peeled, pitted, and chopped fine

1. Whisk sour cream, mint, water, ¼ teaspoon cumin, ½ teaspoon salt, and ¼ teaspoon pepper together in bowl. Set aside.

2. Cook pork in 12-inch nonstick skillet over medium-high heat until no longer pink, about 4 minutes, breaking up meat with spoon. Stir in Sriracha, garlic, remaining ¾ teaspoon cumin, 1 teaspoon salt, and ½ teaspoon pepper and cook until fragrant, about 2 minutes. Transfer to 1 side of large serving platter. Arrange lettuce, avocado, and mango on empty side of platter. Serve, passing sour cream mixture separately.

TEST KITCHEN NOTE: For the best results, be sure to use a ripe avocado and mango here. You can tell when each is ripe if it yields to gentle pressure when squeezed.

Thai-Style Red Curry Chicken with Vegetables *Serves 4*

WHY THIS RECIPE WORKS: A combination of fish sauce and brown sugar gives the chicken a complex sweet and savory flavor.

- 1½ pounds boneless, skinless chicken thighs, trimmed and cut into 1½-inch pieces
- 3 tablespoons fish sauce
- 2 tablespoons packed brown sugar
- 2 tablespoons vegetable oil
- 2 red bell peppers, cored, seeded, and cut into 1-inch pieces
- 1 red onion, cut into 1-inch pieces
- 2 tablespoons red curry paste
- 1 (14-ounce) can coconut milk
- 2 tablespoons lime juice, plus lime wedges for serving
- ¼ cup chopped fresh cilantro

1. Combine chicken, 2 tablespoons fish sauce, and sugar in bowl. Heat 1 tablespoon oil in 12-inch nonstick skillet over high heat until shimmering. Add chicken and cook until well browned on all sides and cooked through, 8 to 10 minutes. Transfer chicken to plate and wipe skillet clean with paper towels.

2. Add bell peppers and onion to skillet and cook over high heat until crisp-tender and lightly charred, about 7 minutes. Stir in curry paste and remaining 1 tablespoon oil and cook until fragrant, about 1 minute. Stir in coconut milk, bring to boil, and cook until slightly thickened, about 4 minutes. Stir in lime juice, chicken, and remaining 1 tablespoon fish sauce and cook until heated through, about 1 minute. Transfer to platter and sprinkle cilantro over top. Serve, passing lime wedges separately.

TEST KITCHEN NOTE: Serve with rice. Our favorite fish sauce is Red Boat 40° N Fish Sauce.

Queso Fundido Burgers

Serves 4

WHY THIS RECIPE WORKS: Frying the chorizo, poblano, and onion directly into the burger creates a boldly flavored, caramelized crust.

- 1½ pounds 85 percent lean ground beef
  Salt and pepper
- 4 ounces fresh Mexican-style chorizo sausage, casings removed
- 1 cup water
- 1 poblano chile, stemmed, seeded, and sliced thin
- 1 small onion, halved and sliced thin
- 4 ounces Colby Jack cheese, shredded (1 cup)
- 4 hamburger buns, toasted and buttered
- 1½ cups shredded iceberg lettuce
- ¼ cup jarred sliced jalapeños

1. Shape beef into four ¾-inch-thick patties and make shallow indentation in center of each. Season with salt and pepper. Combine chorizo, water, poblano, onion, and ½ teaspoon salt in 12-inch nonstick skillet and cook, covered, over high heat until chorizo is cooked through and vegetables are softened, 8 to 10 minutes, uncovering occasionally to break meat into small pieces with spoon. Uncover and cook until water is completely evaporated and mixture begins to brown, 1 to 3 minutes.

2. Reduce heat to medium and divide chorizo mixture into 4 even piles in skillet. Press 1 beef patty, indentation side down, firmly into each pile. Cook until well browned, about 4 minutes. Flip patties and cook until beef registers 125 degrees (for medium-rare), about 2 minutes. Top burgers with Colby Jack, cover, and cook until cheese is melted, about 1 minute. Place burgers on buns and top with lettuce and jalapeños. Serve.

TEST KITCHEN NOTE: If you don't have a tight-fitting lid for your skillet, pay attention to make sure all the water doesn't evaporate early in step 1, or the vegetables may scorch. Add more water if necessary.

Grilled Pork Tenderloin with Broccolini and Hazelnut Browned Butter

Serves 4

WHY THIS RECIPE WORKS: Adding the basil after browning the butter allows its flavor to bloom without burning the delicate herb.

- 2 (1-pound) pork tenderloins, trimmed
  Salt and pepper
- 1 pound broccolini, trimmed
- 2 tablespoons extra-virgin olive oil
- 8 tablespoons unsalted butter
- ½ cup blanched hazelnuts, chopped
- 3 tablespoons shredded fresh basil
- 1 tablespoon lemon juice

1. Season pork with salt and pepper. Toss broccolini with oil, ¼ teaspoon salt, and ¼ teaspoon pepper. Place pork and broccolini on grill over hot fire. Cook broccolini until charred and tender, 8 to 10 minutes; cook pork, turning occasionally, until browned all over and meat registers 140 degrees, about 15 minutes. Transfer broccolini to serving platter and pork to cutting board and tent both with foil.

2. Cook butter, hazelnuts, and ¼ teaspoon salt in 10-inch skillet over medium heat until nuts are toasted and butter is lightly browned, about 4 minutes. Remove from heat and stir in basil and lemon juice. Slice pork and transfer to platter with broccolini. Spoon sauce over pork and broccolini and serve.

TEST KITCHEN NOTE: If the broccolini stems are thicker than ½ inch, cut them in half lengthwise to ensure that they cook at the same rate as the smaller florets.

Tortellini in Broth with Spinach

30-MINUTE SUPPER

Steak Salad with White Beans and Rosemary Vinaigrette

30-MINUTE SUPPER

Grilled Chicken and Potatoes with Sun-Dried Tomato Relish

30-MINUTE SUPPER

Pan-Seared Salmon with Lentil Salad

30-MINUTE SUPPER

Steak Salad with White Beans and Rosemary Vinaigrette

Serves 4

WHY THIS RECIPE WORKS: The combination of hearty romaine and fragrant rosemary stands up well to steak.

- 1½ pounds sirloin steak tips, trimmed
-     Salt and pepper
- ⅓ cup extra-virgin olive oil
- 3 tablespoons lemon juice
- 1 tablespoon Dijon mustard
- 1 teaspoon minced fresh rosemary
- 3 romaine lettuce hearts (18 ounces), halved and sliced thin
- 1 (15-ounce) can cannellini beans, rinsed
- 6 ounces grape tomatoes, halved
- 3 ounces Pecorino Romano cheese, shredded (1 cup)

1. Pat steak dry with paper towels and season with salt and pepper. Heat 1 tablespoon oil in 12-inch nonstick skillet over medium-high heat until just smoking. Add steak and cook until well browned all over and meat registers 125 degrees (for medium-rare), 8 to 10 minutes. Transfer steak to cutting board, tent with foil, and let rest for 5 minutes.

2. Whisk lemon juice, mustard, rosemary, ½ teaspoon salt, and ¼ teaspoon pepper together in large bowl. Gradually whisk in remaining oil. Add lettuce, beans, tomatoes, and ½ cup Pecorino and toss to combine. Transfer salad to serving platter. Slice steak thin against grain and arrange over salad. Sprinkle with remaining ½ cup Pecorino. Serve.

TEST KITCHEN NOTE: You can substitute sage or thyme for the rosemary in the vinaigrette, if desired. Sirloin steak tips are often sold as flap meat.

Tortellini in Broth with Spinach

Serves 4

WHY THIS RECIPE WORKS: For a rich, satisfying stock, we doctored store-bought broth with umami-rich soy sauce and Parmesan cheese.

- 3 tablespoons unsalted butter
- 1 small onion, minced
-     Salt and pepper
- 1 garlic clove, minced
- 6 cups chicken broth
- 1 tablespoon soy sauce
- 6 ounces cheese tortellini
- 3 ounces (3 cups) baby spinach
- 2 ounces Parmesan cheese, grated (1 cup)

1. Melt butter in large saucepan over medium heat. Add onion, ½ teaspoon salt, and ¼ teaspoon pepper and cook until softened but not browned, about 5 minutes. Add garlic and cook until fragrant, about 30 seconds.

2. Add broth and soy sauce and bring to boil over high heat. Stir in pasta and cook until al dente. Off heat, stir in spinach and Parmesan. Serve.

TEST KITCHEN NOTE: Our favorite supermarket tortellini is Barilla Three Cheese Tortellini.

Pan-Seared Salmon with Lentil Salad

Serves 4

WHY THIS RECIPE WORKS: The bright red wine vinegar dressing on the lentil salad contrasts with the rich salmon.

- ¼ cup extra-virgin olive oil
- 1 shallot, minced
- 3 tablespoons red wine vinegar
- 2 teaspoons honey
- 2 teaspoons Dijon mustard
- 1 garlic clove, minced
-     Salt and pepper
- 2 (15-ounce) cans lentils, rinsed
- ½ cup fresh parsley leaves
- 4 (6- to 8-ounce) skin-on salmon fillets, 1 to 1½ inches thick

1. Combine 3 tablespoons oil, shallot, vinegar, honey, mustard, garlic, ½ teaspoon salt, and ¼ teaspoon pepper in large bowl. Stir in lentils and parsley. Season with salt and pepper to taste. Set aside.

2. Pat salmon dry with paper towels and season with salt and pepper. Heat remaining 1 tablespoon oil in 12-inch nonstick skillet over medium-high heat until just smoking. Add salmon, skin side up, and cook until well browned, 4 to 6 minutes. Flip and continue to cook until fish registers 125 degrees (for medium-rare), 4 to 6 minutes longer. Serve salmon with lentil salad.

TEST KITCHEN NOTE: Our favorite red wine vinegar is Laurent du Clos Red Wine Vinegar. If you can't find it, we recommend our second-place vinegar: Pompeian Gourmet Red Wine Vinegar.

Grilled Chicken and Potatoes with Sun-Dried Tomato Relish

Serves 4

WHY THIS RECIPE WORKS: Microwaving the potatoes allows them to cook through on the grill at the same rate as the chicken.

- 1½ pounds small red potatoes, unpeeled, halved
- 2 tablespoons water
-     Salt and pepper
- ½ cup oil-packed sun-dried tomatoes, drained and chopped fine
- 3 tablespoons extra-virgin olive oil
- 3 tablespoons red wine vinegar
- 1 small shallot, minced
- 2 tablespoons capers, rinsed and minced
- 2 tablespoons chopped fresh oregano
- 4 (6- to 8-ounce) boneless, skinless chicken breasts, trimmed

1. Combine potatoes, water, 1 teaspoon salt, and ½ teaspoon pepper in large bowl. Microwave, covered, until almost tender, about 4 minutes, stirring halfway through microwaving. Combine tomatoes, oil, vinegar, shallot, capers, oregano, ½ teaspoon salt, and ¼ teaspoon pepper in second bowl. Set aside.

2. Season chicken with salt and pepper. Place chicken and potatoes on grill over hot fire. Cook potatoes, turning often, until tender and char-streaked, about 8 minutes, and cook chicken until meat registers 160 degrees, about 6 minutes per side; transfer potatoes and chicken to platter as they finish cooking. Serve with tomato relish.

TEST KITCHEN NOTE: The sun-dried tomato oil can be used to flavor vinaigrettes and relishes. Use small red potatoes measuring 1 to 2 inches in diameter.

Heat

Whether you crave the spicy burn of hot chile peppers or want to avoid it, it pays to know the ins and outs of chiles' incendiary qualities. Chile peppers get their fire from a class of spicy compounds called capsaicinoids, the most prominent of which is **capsaicin**. This compound binds to receptors on our skin and tongues and causes that familiar burning sensation. Here's what you need to know to cook with chile peppers.

by Scott Kathan

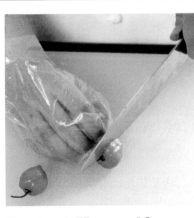

PITH
512 mg
capsaicin/kg

SEEDS
73 mg
capsaicin/kg

FLESH
12 mg
capsaicin/kg

Where Is the Heat in a Hot Chile?

Most of a chile's heat is found not in its flesh but in its white pith—including the ribs. In fact (according to lab tests we conducted on jalapeño chiles), the pith contains more than 40 times as much capsaicin as the flesh, while the seeds contain six times more. So if you want the flavor of a jalapeño but not its full burn, remove the pith and seeds and use just the flesh.

How Hot Is That Chile?

In 1912, pharmacist Wilbur Scoville invented the scale of spiciness that bears his name. Scoville scores are computed by diluting pepper extract until it no longer registers heat; a sweet pepper has a Scoville rating of zero, while a weapons-grade chile such as the ghost pepper has a score of more than 1,000,000—the larger the number, the spicier the pepper. Scoville scores are often presented as ranges; the numbers below are the average of ranges collected from several sources. And remember, even within the same types of chiles, some will be hotter than others.

HABANERO
400,000

CAYENNE
40,000

SERRANO
18,000

JALAPEÑO
5,000

POBLANO
1,200

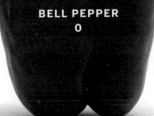
BELL PEPPER
0

SCOVILLE UNITS ←hotter milder→

Heat up Your Spice Cabinet

Red Pepper Flakes

We often use a small amount of red pepper flakes to add flavor and depth—but not necessarily burn—to a dish. The flakes lose their potency over time, so don't buy a big jar unless you use a lot of them.

Cayenne

This pepper powder has enough kick that we often call for just a pinch in recipes. It's the go-to heat in Louisiana cooking.

Chipotle Powder

This smoky, hot powder packs lots of flavor—use it sparingly.

Hot Sauces

You likely know Tabasco, the peppery Louisiana sauce that clocks in at 2,500 Scoville units, and Frank's RedHot Original Cayenne Pepper Sauce, the vinegar-heavy sauce that's much milder at 450 Scoville units. But there is a world of choices beyond those two supermarket staples. One test kitchen favorite is Sriracha sauce, a Thai hot sauce that packs 2,200 Scoville units into every drop.

Storing Chiles

Fresh chiles dry and wither relatively quickly in the refrigerator, so we ran a series of tests to find the best way to preserve their flavor, texture, and heat. To keep chiles in peak condition for the longest time, halve them lengthwise, submerge them in a brine of 1 tablespoon of salt per 1 cup of water in a nonreactive container (a clean jelly jar works great), and refrigerate them. Chiles stored this way retain their flavor and crunch for up to one month. Rinse the chiles before using.

BEST METHOD
Store the chiles in brine.

Protect Yourself

When handling hot chiles, we recommend wearing rubber gloves, as capsaicin can get on your hands and be readily—and painfully—spread to your face and eyes if you unwittingly scratch an itch. Don't have rubber gloves? Try putting plastic sandwich bags over your hands instead.

REMEDY: How do you find relief when your mouth is on fire? We found that two of the most common purported remedies—drinking ice water or drinking cold beer—don't work at all. Milk is a much better bet, as its fats bind with and thus absorb the capsaicin.

Carne Guisada

This Texas take on beef stew deserves to be on every table in the country.

by Matthew Fairman

IF YOU'VE EATEN *carne guisada* before, you know it as a bold and intensely satisfying stew that punches up the familiar braise of beef and potatoes with energetic Mexican ingredients. In Texas, it's commonly served either as a taco filling—our favorite way to eat it—or as a stew, with beans, rice, and tortillas on the side.

Recipes for carne guisada (the term is Spanish for "stewed meat") can vary wildly, but they nearly always include a few core ingredients: beef, broth, chiles, cumin, oregano, bell pepper, and potatoes. My challenge was to find the right combination of these to make the best stew without overcomplicating it.

For the beef I turned to a favorite for low, slow braising: beef chuck roast. Though I tried everything from sirloin to short ribs, nothing compared to rich, tender, inexpensive chuck.

Beef broth seemed like an obvious choice for my braising liquid, and nearly all recipes I found called for it. But surprisingly, in a side-by-side test pitting beef broth against chicken broth, we agreed that bold beef broth overpowered the other ingredients, while the more restrained chicken broth allowed the other flavors to come forward.

I tested many combinations of fresh and dried chiles, but I found that the flavor of fresh chiles nearly disappeared with cooking, and the more dried chiles I added to the mix, the muddier the dish became. I ditched both in favor of chili powder. We surprised ourselves by liking it more, and using it saved me the trouble of buying several varieties of dried chiles. Ground coriander's citrusy notes and cumin's earthy flavor balanced the warmth of the chili powder.

After browning some of the beef and developing a flavorful fond in a Dutch oven on the stovetop, I added my liquid and other ingredients, scraped up the browned bits, and finished the stew in the sustained heat of the oven to produce tender meat. Adding green bell pepper and Yukon Gold potatoes partway through the cooking time guaranteed tender but not disintegrated vegetables.

After much tinkering, I was happy to offer a version of carne guisada that any home cook could proudly serve should a discerning Texan stop by for supper.

CARNE GUISADA
Serves 8 to 10

Note that you are browning only half the beef in step 1. If your Dutch oven holds less than 6 quarts, you may need to brown the beef in batches to avoid overcrowding the pot. This recipe yields enough filling for about 24 tacos.

- 3 pounds boneless beef chuck-eye roast, trimmed and cut into 1-inch pieces
  Salt and pepper
- 2 tablespoons vegetable oil
- 2 onions, chopped
- 2 tablespoons tomato paste
- 4 garlic cloves, minced
- 1 tablespoon chili powder
- 1 tablespoon dried oregano
- 2 teaspoons ground coriander
- 1½ teaspoons ground cumin
- 1 tablespoon all-purpose flour
- 1 (14.5-ounce) can diced tomatoes, drained
- 1 cup chicken broth
- 1 pound Yukon Gold potatoes, peeled and cut into ½-inch pieces
- 2 green bell peppers, stemmed, seeded, and cut into ¼-inch strips
- 24 flour tortillas, warmed
  Fresh cilantro leaves
  Lime wedges

1. Adjust oven rack to lower-middle position and heat oven to 325 degrees. Pat beef dry with paper towels and season with salt and pepper. Heat oil in Dutch oven over medium-high heat until just smoking. Add half of beef and cook until browned on all sides, 7 to 10 minutes; transfer to plate.

2. Reduce heat to medium-low, add onions and 1 teaspoon salt to pot, and cook until softened, about 5 minutes. Stir in tomato paste, garlic, chili powder, oregano, coriander, and cumin and cook until fragrant, about 30 seconds. Stir in flour and cook for 1 minute. Stir in tomatoes and broth and bring to simmer, scraping up any browned bits. Stir in all of beef and any accumulated juices. Cover, transfer pot to oven, and cook for 1½ hours.

3. Remove pot from oven and stir in potatoes and bell peppers. Cover, return pot to oven, and continue to cook until beef and potatoes are tender, about 45 minutes longer.

4. Season with salt and pepper to taste. Spoon small amount of stew into center of each tortilla, top with cilantro, and serve with lime wedges.

Is it a stew? Yes. Is it a taco filling? Yes. In summertime, we like it best on flour tortillas with cilantro and lime.

Calabacitas

Too often, this Mexican mix turns out muddy. We set out to return its vibrancy.

by Katie Leaird

A KISSING COUSIN to succotash, *calabacitas* is a popular side dish and taco filling in Texas, New Mexico, and other Southwest locales. If you use the season's best, brightest green zucchini and sweetest golden-yellow corn, calabacitas can be a colorful, vibrant addition to a summer meal. But all too often the vegetables arrive at the table overcooked into a mushy, unrecognizable mess. I wanted my calabacitas to showcase the vibrant flavors of these high-summer vegetables, not smother them.

Digging through southwestern cookbooks, I found some recipes that called for heavy cream and cheese and some made with just stock or water. Those with added dairy masked the vegetables' flavors entirely, so I eliminated them from consideration. Some recipes, including a 1947 classic from Josefina Velázquez De León, called for lard, pork spareribs, or meat stock. It was very good, but I was committed to a strictly vegetarian take. Though recipes commonly called for poblano chiles, some versions also included anchos, jalapeños, or bell peppers. Poblano and red bell peppers made the cut.

Zucchini is delicate, and when I stewed it slowly, its flavor all but vanished and it became slightly slimy. So I decided to take a different approach and crank up the heat, cooking the vegetables more quickly to maintain a bit of fresh flavor and to give them a little char.

To rev up the colors, I added yellow summer squash to the traditional mix of zucchini, corn, red bell peppers, and poblano chiles. Things were looking and tasting good, but the dish was a little too lean. Adding a restrained amount of heavy cream at the very end helped tie everything together without rendering the dish too heavy.

Though it's rooted in Mexican cuisine, there's no need to wait for a Mexican meal to make this dish. It's as easy to love next to a straightforward grilled steak as it is in a taco.

What's in a Name?

In Mexico, the word *calabacita* can refer to a tender-skinned, young summer squash that is similar but not identical to zucchini. The two behave very similarly and are all but interchangeable in most recipes.

Easy Vegetable Prep

Zucchini and Summer Squash
Cut off ends, then cut lengthwise into planks. Cut planks lengthwise into strips, then turn strips crosswise and cut into pieces.

Red Bell Pepper
Slice off top and bottom and remove seeds and stem. Slice down through side. Unfurl, lay flat on counter, and trim away any remaining ribs and seeds before cutting into strips. Turn strips crosswise and cut into pieces.

Corn
Use chef's knife to cut cobs in half. Stabilize cobs by standing them on flat cut ends before slicing kernels from cobs.

A quarter-cup of heavy cream helps balance the flavors without turning the dish cloudy.

CALABACITAS
Serves 4

Cotija is a semihard Mexican cheese. If you can't find it at your local market, you can substitute feta.

- 3 tablespoons unsalted butter
- 1 onion, chopped fine
- 1 poblano chile, stemmed, seeded, and cut into ½-inch pieces
- ½ cup chopped red bell pepper
- 2 garlic cloves, minced
  Salt and pepper
- 1 zucchini (8 ounces), cut into ½-inch pieces
- 1 yellow summer squash (8 ounces), cut into ½-inch pieces
- 3 ears corn, kernels cut from cobs
- ¼ cup heavy cream
- 2 ounces Cotija cheese, crumbled (½ cup)
  Lime wedges

1. Melt butter in 12-inch nonstick skillet over medium-high heat. Add onion, poblano, bell pepper, garlic, 1 teaspoon salt, and ½ teaspoon pepper and cook until vegetables are softened, about 4 minutes.

2. Stir in zucchini and summer squash and cook until just tender, about 6 minutes. Stir in corn and cream. Using spatula, pat vegetables into even layer and cook, without stirring, until liquid has evaporated and vegetables are lightly browned, 5 to 7 minutes. Season with salt and pepper to taste. Transfer to platter and sprinkle with Cotija. Serve, passing lime wedges separately.

Lazy Strawberry Sonker

Sonker has spent too much time in the shadows. We wanted to give this Appalachian original its due.

by Cecelia Jenkins

IN THE SHADOW of North Carolina's Blue Ridge Mountains lies Surry County, where, if you're lucky, you'll cross paths with a fruit sonker. Not quite a pie, not quite a cobbler, and not quite a betty, crisp, or pandowdy (see "Is It a Slump? A Grunt? A Buckle? Depends Who You Ask."), the sonker is a sweet, juicy, comforting, fruit-filled North Carolina dessert rarely found farther afield. So beloved is the stuff in Surry County that the annual Sonker Festival in Mount Airy draws thousands of celebrants (see "The American Table").

Supremely juicy, with a cakey, sweet crust on top, sonkers are traditionally made deep-dish style to feed crowds and use up surplus summertime fruit on its way out. This is simple country cooking, and my research uncovered more family heirloom recipes than formally published ones.

What's more, each recipe was bewilderingly different from the next. Most of the variance lay in the top crust. Some versions were rectangular variations on pie, with bottom and top crusts, the top sometimes latticed to allow for evaporation. Others dolloped the filling with spoonfuls of biscuit dough, which baked into a pleasing, cobbler-like topping.

But I was most intrigued by a subset of sonker recipes made with a batter topping instead, called "lazy" sonkers. In these, the fruit is cooked into a sweet stew and topped with a pancake batter that bakes into a distinct, lightly crisp layer of cake with juice bubbling up around the edges. I loved the idea of this style most of all. My tasters helped me settle on strawberries for the filling, for their ruby-red color and summery sweetness.

It wasn't long before I realized that the lane I'd picked was full of potholes. In some instances, the batter sank into and mixed with the cooked strawberries, preventing the top layer from baking properly. This left soggy pockets of batter and turned the filling into a chalky, Pepto-pink gravy. I tried an even lazier method, simply pouring batter over raw berries, but this version was bereft of the signature juice, and because the surface was bumpy, the batter flowed into spaces between the fruit, giving me gummy spots throughout.

I needed a filling that was superjuicy but still capable of supporting the

A small amount of cornstarch adds just enough body to the filling without sacrificing its juiciness.

batter on top as it baked. Rather than cook the berries in a pot, I tossed them with sugar and put them in the baking dish to stew. Stewed berries would give the batter a uniform, level surface on which to bake (eliminating crevices of raw batter), and their heat would help bake the batter from underneath. To give the filling just a bit of structure to help it support the batter, I added cornstarch to the berries once they had stewed. The cornstarch thickened the

juice a bit as the filling baked, helping it withstand the batter's weight without sacrificing too much moisture.

For further insurance against a sinking top, I looked for ways to create a lighter, more floatable batter. The answer was fat. Fat floats (think about how oil floats above vinegar), and since there's more fat in butter than in milk, I swapped out some of the milk in my batter in favor of melted butter. As a bonus, there was, of course, the obvious

flavor boost butter always provides.

I poured my new batter over a pan of cooked fruit and, to my relief, it floated happily on top of the bubbling berries. Once it had baked into a beautiful layer of golden cake, I gathered my tasters. Their response to this sweet, fruity, juicy dessert was enthusiastic. And with a few more fruit filling variations to sample, it felt like we were having a little Sonker Festival of our own.

LAZY STRAWBERRY SONKER

Serves 6

If you're using frozen strawberries in this recipe, there's no need to let them thaw. In steps 2 and 3, be sure to stir the strawberry filling as directed, scraping the bottom of the dish to incorporate the cornstarch so that it evenly and thoroughly thickens the mixture. In step 3, add the butter to the batter while it is still hot so it remains pourable, and be sure to mix the batter only right before pouring it over the filling. Serve with vanilla ice cream.

- 2 pounds fresh strawberries, hulled (6½ cups), or 2 pounds (7 cups) frozen whole strawberries
- 1 cup (7 ounces) sugar
  Salt
- ¼ cup water
- 3 tablespoons cornstarch
- 1 cup (5 ounces) all-purpose flour
- 1 teaspoon baking powder
- ½ cup whole milk
- 8 tablespoons unsalted butter, melted and hot
- ¼ teaspoon vanilla extract

1. Adjust oven rack to middle position and heat oven to 350 degrees. Line rimmed baking sheet with parchment paper. Combine strawberries, ¼ cup sugar, and ¼ teaspoon salt in bowl. Whisk water and cornstarch together in second bowl; add to strawberry mixture and toss until strawberries are evenly coated.

2. Transfer strawberry mixture to 8-inch square baking dish and place dish on prepared sheet. Bake until filling is bubbling around sides of dish, 35 to 40 minutes (1 hour if using frozen strawberries), stirring and scraping bottom of dish with rubber spatula halfway through baking.

3. Remove sheet from oven and stir filling, scraping bottom of dish with rubber spatula. Whisk flour, baking powder, remaining ¾ cup sugar, and ¼ teaspoon salt together in bowl. Whisk in milk, melted butter, and vanilla until smooth. Starting in corner of dish, pour batter evenly over filling.

4. Bake until surface is golden brown and toothpick inserted in center comes out with no crumbs attached, 35 to 40 minutes, rotating dish halfway through baking. Let sonker cool on wire rack for 15 minutes. Serve.

LAZY BLUEBERRY SONKER

Substitute 2 pounds (6½ cups) fresh or frozen blueberries for strawberries.

LAZY PEACH SONKER

Substitute 2½ pounds peaches, peeled, halved, pitted, and cut into ½-inch-thick wedges or 2 pounds frozen sliced peaches (break up any slices that are frozen together) for strawberries.

THE AMERICAN TABLE

Mount Airy, North Carolina, isn't just the home of the fruit sonker: It's also the hometown of Andy Griffith and the inspiration for the characters featured in *The Andy Griffith Show* and *Mayberry R.F.D.*, the long-running 1960s sitcoms. Besides a museum dedicated to Griffith, Mount Airy is also home to the Snappy Lunch Diner, where the town's favorite son ate fried pork chop sandwiches as a child.

Over the years, more-familiar fruit pies have nudged sonker off the menu at many local restaurants, so the very best time to sink a spoon into the stuff is at the annual Mount Airy Sonker Festival, an autumn gathering hosted by the Surry County Historical Society. There's bluegrass music and flat-foot dancing all afternoon, but the centerpiece, of course, is sonker, offered up in a slew of styles based on heirloom family recipes.

Using frozen berries makes our Lazy Blueberry Sonker a year-round dessert.

Our Lazy Peach Sonker can be prepared with fresh or frozen fruit.

Is It a Slump? A Grunt? A Buckle? Depends Who You Ask.

We can all agree: Rustic fruit desserts are great to make and eat. But what we can't agree on is what to call them. One cook's cobbler is another cook's buckle. Sounds like fun and games! And it is, until you walk into the wrong barbecue joint and call their prized cobbler a pie. Here is a short list of our favorites in the test kitchen and the names we use for them.

Betty (also known as Brown Betty): Sweetened fruit, usually apples but also rhubarb or bananas, layered with bread crumbs and butter and baked.

Buckle: Cake batter poured over fruit, often berries, and baked. Buckle sometimes resembles a streusel-topped coffee cake.

Cobbler*: Biscuit dough dolloped over fruit, often peaches or berries, and baked to resemble cobblestones. But tread lightly.

Crisp and Crumble: Fruit, often apples or peaches, baked under a crunchy, streusel-like topping, which often contains oats.

Grunt and Slump: Fruit, usually berries, cooked underneath dollops of dumpling dough on the stovetop. Dumplings "grunt" under heat.

Sonker: Syrupy cooked fruit topped with a thin, pancake-like batter and baked.

Pandowdy: Fruit baked under pie dough or sliced stale bread; topping is pressed into fruit while it cooks.

* "Cobbler" is perhaps the most controversial moniker used to describe a fruit dessert. In some corners of the United States, a cobbler can be a double-crust rectangular pie. In others, it's the same thing as a buckle.

Frozen Berries Work Just Fine

While the test kitchen's preference is usually for fresh fruit and produce, the hour-plus cooking time for the filling in our sonker recipe means that versions made with fresh and frozen fruit are virtually indistinguishable. The frozen fruit doesn't even need to be thawed, though it does take a little longer in the oven to reach the desired consistency. Our favorite frozen strawberries are **Cascadian Farm Frozen Premium Organic Strawberries**, which won our taste test by virtue of their plump texture, clean flavor, and a "sweetness (that) didn't override the berry taste."

Coconut Cream Pie

How do you improve a retro classic? Start with the crust and work your way up, packing each component with maximum flavor.

by Katie Leaird

I CAN STILL feel the magnetic pull of the rotating glass dessert displays that drew me into diners as a kid growing up in New Jersey. I found just about any greasy spoon's voluminous, over-the-top, mile-high cakes and pies mesmerizing. The coconut cream pie, with its lofty profile, billowing cream topping, and shaggy coconut garnish, especially called to me. Sometimes I requested a slice before placing my lunch order because I just couldn't wait.

Fast forward to the present day. When I started developing this recipe, I was dead set on building my pie in a traditional flaky crust because that is what I remembered about the pies from my childhood. But I loyally followed our test kitchen process, which entails testing a diverse range of recipes. Surprisingly, we all fell in love with the pie baked in one particular cookie crust. Nilla Wafers, shredded coconut, and an unconventionally hearty dash of salt added up to a clear winner. Plus, it was supereasy to work with. Prebaking the crust until it was golden brown and aromatic ensured that it was crisp and snappy—a texture that nicely contrasted with the creamy custard filling.

With my crust set, I turned my attention to the filling. Coconut is a versatile ingredient: Coconut milk gives Southern Indian curry its earthy creaminess, shredded coconut flakes make macaroons sweet and chewy confections, coconut cream is used in many tropical mixed drinks, and coconut extract finds its way into cookies and cakes. With so many coconut products to choose from, I had to try them all to find the coconut flavor I craved.

Subtlety is not the name of the game with this pie, so I quickly dismissed coconut milk, as it delivered muted coconut flavor. And my team of tasters revolted when I snuck a few drops of coconut extract into the custard filling, reacting negatively to its artificial tinge.

Our favorite filling was fairly straightforward: a standard milk-based custard with sweetened shredded coconut stirred in once the custard had thickened. It had the light but stable texture I was after. For added richness, I used egg yolks, forgoing the egg whites, which can cause a custard to turn grainy (because whites coagulate faster than yolks when cooked).

It's customary to thicken a custard pie filling with a starch to make it sliceable, and I quickly ruled out flour because it made a stodgy filling. I ultimately chose cornstarch, which thickened the filling without announcing its presence. A thick custard also safeguarded against a soggy bottom crust. A dash of vanilla helped enhance the filling's overall flavor.

No coconut cream pie would be complete without a heavy-handed pile of whipped cream on top. I did not shy away from tradition as I spread 3 cups of lightly sweetened, vanilla-scented whipped cream over my coconut custard. And then, to really dress it up, I sprinkled some toasted shredded coconut over the creamy white mountain. This final maneuver meant that all three components of this pie—crust, filling, and topping—contained forthright coconut flavor. My pie was ready for the diner dessert case—if only I could keep it away from my tasters.

Vanilla and coconut make a happy pair, so we use crushed Nilla Wafers for the crunchy press-in crust.

Two Ways to Toast

A sprinkle of toasted coconut tops our pie. But there's more than one way to toast those flakes. Spread them evenly on a rimmed baking sheet and bake at 325 degrees for about 5 minutes, stirring frequently, until golden brown. Or zap 'em! Spread the flakes in an even layer on a microwave-safe plate and microwave on high for 2 to 3 minutes, stirring every 15 to 30 seconds, until golden brown. In both cases, keep an eagle eye on that coconut to make sure no flakes burn.

Custard 101:
The custard filling for our coconut cream pie is easy to prepare—if you pay careful attention.

1. Whisk
Whisk ¼ cup of milk, egg yolks, cornstarch, and salt together so that the dry ingredients are thoroughly dissolved. The cornstarch will help the custard set into a sliceable filling.

2. Heat
Slowly bring the remaining 2¾ cups of milk and the sugar to a simmer in a saucepan over medium heat. Take care not to boil the milk too rapidly.

3. Temper
You want custard, not scrambled eggs. Gradually increasing the temperature of the yolk mixture helps guard against curdling. It's easy: Slowly whisk half the hot milk mixture into the eggs.

4. Cook
Carefully pour the egg mixture back into the saucepan and cook over medium heat, whisking constantly, until the custard is thickened and registers 180 degrees. This should take 30 to 90 seconds. Remove it from the heat right away.

ADD FLAVORINGS LAST
Off the heat, whisk in the coconut and vanilla.

COCONUT CREAM PIE
Serves 8 to 10
Be sure to let the cookie crust cool completely before you begin making the filling—at least 30 minutes. Plan ahead: For the filling to set completely, this pie needs to be refrigerated for at least 3 hours or up to 24 hours before serving.

CRUST
- 2 cups (4½ ounces) Nilla Wafer cookies (34 cookies)
- ½ cup (1½ ounces) sweetened shredded coconut
- 2 tablespoons sugar
- 1 tablespoon all-purpose flour
- ¼ teaspoon salt
- 4 tablespoons unsalted butter, melted

FILLING
- 3 cups whole milk
- 5 large egg yolks
- 5 tablespoons cornstarch
- ¼ teaspoon salt
- ½ cup (3½ ounces) sugar
- ½ cup (1½ ounces) sweetened shredded coconut
- ½ teaspoon vanilla extract

TOPPING
- 1½ cups heavy cream, chilled
- 3 tablespoons sugar
- 1 teaspoon vanilla extract
- ¼ cup (¾ ounce) sweetened shredded coconut, toasted

1. FOR THE CRUST: Adjust oven rack to middle position and heat oven to 325 degrees. Process cookies, coconut, sugar, flour, and salt in food processor until finely ground, about 30 seconds. Add melted butter and pulse until combined, about 6 pulses. Transfer mixture to 9-inch pie plate. Using bottom of dry measuring cup, press crumbs firmly into bottom and up sides of plate. Bake until fragrant and set, 18 to 22 minutes. Transfer plate to wire rack and let crust cool completely.

2. FOR THE FILLING: Whisk ¼ cup milk, egg yolks, cornstarch, and salt together in large bowl. Bring sugar and remaining 2¾ cups milk to simmer in large saucepan over medium heat. Slowly whisk half of hot milk mixture into yolk mixture to temper.

3. Return milk-yolk mixture to remaining milk mixture in saucepan. Whisking constantly, cook over medium heat until custard is thickened and registers 180 degrees, 30 to 90 seconds. Remove from heat and stir in coconut and vanilla. Pour filling into cooled crust and spread into even layer.

4. Spray piece of parchment paper with vegetable oil spray and press flush onto surface of custard to cover completely and prevent skin from forming. Refrigerate until cold and set, at least 3 hours or up to 24 hours.

5. FOR THE TOPPING: Using stand mixer fitted with whisk attachment, whip cream, sugar, and vanilla on medium-low speed until foamy, about 1 minute. Increase speed to high and whip until stiff peaks form, 1 to 3 minutes. Spread whipped cream evenly over pie. Sprinkle coconut over top. Serve.

One Ingredient, Three Ways
We found that sweetened shredded coconut was the only form of coconut necessary to give our pie the bold coconut flavor we wanted. We use it in each of the three components.

Crust: Processing sweetened shredded coconut with Nilla Wafers forms a coconutty crumb crust.

Filling: Folding sweetened shredded coconut into the custard adds tropical flavor and sweetness.

Garnish: Toasted sweetened shredded coconut creates a crunchy, colorful topping for the whipped cream.

SWEETENED SHREDDED COCONUT
One form of coconut flavors the entire pie.

BACKSTORY
After auditioning traditional graham cracker and pastry crusts for our coconut cream pie recipe, we came upon an even better option: a Nilla Wafer crumb crust. With their crunchy yet lightly cakey texture and vanilla-forward flavor, these slender, airy cookies turned out to be a terrific choice. When ground with sweetened shredded coconut and mixed with a little flour, sugar, and melted butter, they produced an ideal tropical base for our pie.

The original recipe for the cookies was cooked up by German-born inventor and confectioner Gustave Mayer in Staten Island, New York. Mayer sold his recipe to Nabisco in 1929. At the time, Nabisco marketed the cookies as Vanilla Wafers; they shortened the name to Nilla Wafers in 1967. Since their introduction, the cookies have been eaten straight from the box as well as used as an ingredient in many desserts.

Easy Summer Fruit Tart

With no top crust and no fussy crimping, making this rustic tart is easier than pie. *by Katie Leaird*

EASY PEACH AND BLACKBERRY TART
Serves 6
Taste the fruit before adding sugar; use less if it is very sweet, more if it is tart. Do not toss the sugar with the fruit until you are ready to form the tart. If using frozen peaches, reduce the amount to 14 ounces, thaw them completely, and pat them dry before tossing them with the berries.

1½	cups (7½ ounces) all-purpose flour
½	teaspoon salt
10	tablespoons unsalted butter, cut into ½-inch pieces and chilled
6–7	tablespoons ice water, plus 1 tablespoon water
1	pound peaches, halved, pitted, and cut into ½-inch-thick wedges
5	ounces (1 cup) blackberries
6	tablespoons sugar

1. Process flour and salt in food processor until combined, about 3 seconds. Scatter butter over top and pulse until mixture resembles coarse crumbs, about 10 pulses. Transfer to bowl. Sprinkle 6 tablespoons ice water over mixture. Using rubber spatula, stir and press dough until it sticks together, adding up to 1 tablespoon more ice water if it will not come together.
2. Turn dough onto lightly floured counter, form into 4-inch disk, wrap tightly in plastic wrap, and refrigerate for 1 hour. (Wrapped dough can be refrigerated for up to 2 days or frozen for up to 1 month.)
3. Adjust oven rack to lower-middle position and heat oven to 375 degrees. Line rimmed baking sheet with parchment paper. Let chilled dough sit on counter to soften slightly, about 10 minutes, before rolling. Roll dough into 12-inch circle on lightly floured counter, then transfer to prepared sheet.
4. Gently toss peaches, blackberries, and 5 tablespoons sugar together in bowl. Mound fruit in center of dough, leaving 2-inch border around edge. Carefully grasp 1 edge of dough and fold up 2 inches over fruit. Repeat around circumference of tart, overlapping dough every 2 inches; gently pinch pleated dough to secure, but do not press dough into fruit.
5. Brush dough with remaining 1 tablespoon water and sprinkle remaining 1 tablespoon sugar evenly over dough and fruit. Bake until crust is deep golden brown and fruit is bubbling, 45 to 50 minutes. Transfer sheet to wire rack and let tart cool for 10 minutes. Using metal spatula, loosen tart from parchment and slide onto wire rack; let cool until warm, about 30 minutes. Cut into wedges and serve.

EASY APRICOT AND BLUEBERRY TART
Substitute apricots for peaches and blueberries for blackberries.

EASY PLUM AND RASPBERRY TART
Substitute plums for peaches and raspberries for blackberries. (Do not use frozen raspberries in this recipe.)

 Bourbon whipped cream on top? Yup. Go to **CooksCountry.com/ bourboncream** for the recipe.

Step by Step

1. Combine dry ingredients
Process the flour and salt in a food processor until combined, about 3 seconds.
Why? Processing the salt and flour together ensures that there will be no pockets of salt in the finished dough.

2. Pulse butter into flour
Scatter the butter and pulse until the mixture forms coarse crumbs.
Why? Pulsing cold butter into flour creates a dough with tiny pieces of butter. During baking, the water in the butter turns to steam, creating pockets that develop into flaky layers.

3. Stir in ice water
Add the ice water, and use a rubber spatula to stir and press the dough.
Why? If you overwork the dough, too much gluten will develop and it will be tough. Using ice water keeps the dough cold so the butter doesn't liquefy.

4. Refrigerate dough
Turn the dough onto a lightly floured counter, form it into a 4-inch disk, wrap it tightly in plastic wrap, and refrigerate it.
Why? Letting the dough rest and chill allows the flour to fully hydrate and the dough to become more pliable for easy rolling.

5. Prep oven and baking sheet
Adjust the oven rack to the lower-middle position and heat the oven to 375 degrees. Line a rimmed baking sheet with parchment.
Why? To keep the bottom of the tart from becoming soggy, we bake it on the lower-middle rack.

Prepping Fruit

How to Remove Pits from Peaches, Plums, and Apricots

1. Locate the crease on the fruit that marks the pointed edge of the pit. Following the crease, cut the fruit in half, pole to pole.

2. Grasp both halves of the fruit and gently twist them apart to expose the pit, which can then be popped out easily.

FIRST TRY

LAST RESORT

Dealing with Stubborn Pits

It can be hard to separate the pits from cling peaches and nectarines. There are a couple of strategies that can be employed. The first is to use a paring knife to cut the flesh into wedges. You then reinsert the blade of the knife into one of the cuts and, using your thumb to steady the wedge against the flat of the blade, pry the wedge free of the pit. If you find that the fruit is intractable, then resort to strategy number two, which incurs some waste and will give you imperfect slices: With the fruit sitting stem-side down for stability, cut the flesh from the pit with vertical swipes of a chef's knife.

Cleaning Berries

Gently wash the berries in a bowl filled with three parts water and one part white vinegar. Drain the liquid, rinse the berries with tap water, and then spin them dry in a salad spinner lined with paper towels. In our tests, this method removed 98 percent of the surface bacteria.

Making the Pastry

TEST KITCHEN TIPS FOR ANY PASTRY DOUGH

Eliminating Sticking

Start with very cold dough, work quickly, and make sure to lift and turn the dough as you roll. Add flour to the counter each time you lift the dough to turn it. If the dough still sticks, transfer it to a rimmed baking sheet and refrigerate it for 15 minutes.

Achieving an Even, Round Shape

Start with a flat, even disk, and check the shape often as you roll it out. Use your hands or a bench scraper to help maintain a round shape.

Avoiding Off-Flavors

Wood absorbs and holds on to odors, so don't roll out dough on a butcher-block counter. If necessary, roll the dough between two pieces of parchment paper or waxed paper.

Helpful Tools

Rolling Pin

The long, straight shape of our winning rolling pin, the **J.K. Adams Plain Maple Rolling Dowel** ($13.95), makes it easy to roll dough evenly.

Bench Scraper

The beveled edge of the **Dexter-Russell 6" Dough Cutter/Scraper—Sani-Safe Series** ($7.01) makes it the perfect tool for scraping a counter clean and halving balls of dough.

Why Is Hydration Important?

Gluten, the protein that gives dough structure and strength, develops when water is mixed with flour. When pastry dough rests in the refrigerator, the flour hydrates fully and evenly, making the dough less prone to cracking when it's rolled. At the same time, natural proteins in the dough break down gluten proteins, allowing them to relax. These two processes make the dough less likely to shrink and easier to roll.

6. Roll out dough
Let the chilled dough sit on the counter to soften slightly before rolling it, about 10 minutes. Roll it into a 12-inch circle, and then transfer it to the prepared sheet.
Why? Giving the chilled dough some time to soften slightly makes it easier to work with.

7. Add sugar to fruit
Gently toss the fruit and sugar together in a bowl. Mound the fruit in the center of the dough, leaving a 2-inch border.
Why? Sugar pulls liquid out of fruit. To ensure that the filling doesn't become too soupy, mix it just before assembling the tart.

8. Fold and pleat
Fold 1 edge of the dough 2 inches over the fruit. Repeat around the edge of the tart, overlapping the dough every 2 inches; pinch the pleated dough to secure it.
Why? Folding the dough over the filling holds the fruit in place and gives the tart its signature look.

9. Brush and sugar
Brush the dough with the remaining water, and sprinkle the remaining sugar evenly over the dough and fruit.
Why? Adding sugar to the top of the dough creates a sweet crunch; a little water helps the sugar adhere to the dough.

10. Bake
Bake until the crust is deep golden brown and the fruit is bubbling, 45 to 50 minutes. Transfer the sheet to a wire rack and let the tart cool for 10 minutes.
Why? Once the dough turns deep golden brown, it is fully baked and will have a crisp, flaky texture.

Ratatouille with Chicken

Juicy roast chicken and a warm, velvety summer-vegetable stew, all on a baking sheet? It was a tall order. *by Cecelia Jenkins*

Fresh thyme and lemon zest amplify the bright, summery flavor of the cooked vegetables.

RATATOUILLE CAN BE a disappointing, overcooked, mushy mess. But it shouldn't be. This rustic stew of late-summer produce should be full of fresh flavor. I set out to create a ratatouille with all the vibrancy its components promise, as well as some juicy bone-in chicken breasts with crispy, golden skin—all on one pan.

I started not with a pan but with a large Dutch oven, the traditional choice when making ratatouille. I cooked the vegetables in batches to keep them from turning to mush. But then what? Trying to roast chicken parts in an almost-finished pot of ratatouille was an exercise in futility—it required both stovetop and oven work, and the steep walls of the pot kept the chicken from browning.

But who says a stew has to be made in a pot anyway? What if, instead of bringing the chicken to the vegetables, I brought the vegetables to the chicken and cooked everything on a rimmed baking sheet? I decided to give it a try.

I evenly spread bite-size chunks of eggplant, summer squash, and red bell peppers, plus grape tomatoes and sliced shallots, on a baking sheet and placed the chicken on top of the vegetables so that everything roasted together. The result? Promising but problematic: While the chicken was juicy, with lovely golden-brown skin, the vegetables released liquid that collected in a puddle on the overcrowded sheet.

I aimed to control the runoff by cooking the components in stages. I tossed the vegetables with some oil and a little salt and pepper, spread them evenly on a baking sheet, and cooked them partway through (they wilted and shed some liquid, which quickly evaporated) before pushing them to one side of the sheet. I then arranged the chicken in the clearing to roast while the vegetables continued to cook. The results were promising, but I wanted deeper color on the chicken. To that end, I increased the oven temperature to 450 degrees. The chicken was gorgeous: crispy-skinned and beautifully browned. But the pan now harbored a puddle of chicken drippings.

After transferring the chicken to a cutting board, I followed my instincts and stirred the drippings into the vegetables with my rubber spatula. To my delight, the spongy eggplant absorbed the rich juices. Just a few swipes were all that was needed.

Although the chicken drippings had added a savory note to the dish, it still needed some final touches to brighten it up. Minced fresh basil and ½ cup of halved briny kalamata olives stirred into the vegetables, plus some lemon zest and fresh thyme sprinkled over the chicken, livened up the flavors.

A delicious, satisfying meal that produced only one pan to clean, this combination won many adoring fans in the test kitchen.

Parcook the Vegetables; Then Add the Chicken

To produce beautifully browned chicken and tender vegetables, first spread the vegetables evenly on a rimmed baking sheet and roast them in a 450-degree oven for about 25 minutes, until they're slightly softened, giving them a quick stir halfway through to encourage evaporation and even cooking. Next, remove the sheet from oven, push the vegetables to one side, arrange the chicken breasts skin side up on the empty side of the sheet, and return the sheet to the oven. Continue roasting until the vegetables have softened and the chicken registers 160 degrees, about 25 minutes longer.

ONE-PAN RATATOUILLE WITH CHICKEN
Serves 4

Be sure to use a heavyweight rimmed baking sheet; flimsy sheets can warp in a hot oven. Our favorite is the Nordic Ware Baker's Half Sheet. Serve with crusty bread.

- 1 pound eggplant, peeled and cut into 1-inch pieces
- 12 ounces yellow summer squash, cut into 1-inch pieces
- 2 red bell peppers, stemmed, seeded, and cut into 1-inch pieces
- 10 ounces grape tomatoes or 12 ounces cherry tomatoes
- 6 shallots, sliced thin
- ¼ cup extra-virgin olive oil
- 3 garlic cloves, sliced thin
  Salt and pepper
- 4 (10- to 12-ounce) bone-in split chicken breasts, trimmed
- ½ cup pitted kalamata olives, halved
- ¼ cup minced fresh basil
- 2 teaspoons grated lemon zest, plus lemon wedges for serving
- 2 teaspoons minced fresh thyme

1. Adjust oven rack to middle position and heat oven to 450 degrees. Toss eggplant, squash, bell peppers, tomatoes, shallots, oil, garlic, 1 teaspoon salt, and 1 teaspoon pepper together on rimmed baking sheet and spread into even layer. Roast until vegetables are slightly softened and charred in spots, about 25 minutes, stirring halfway through roasting.

2. Pat chicken dry with paper towels and season with salt and pepper. Remove sheet from oven. Using rubber spatula, push vegetables to 1 side of sheet. Arrange chicken, skin side up, on now-empty side of sheet. Roast until chicken registers 160 degrees and vegetables are completely softened, about 25 minutes, stirring vegetables and rotating sheet halfway through roasting.

3. Remove sheet from oven, tent with aluminum foil, and let rest for 5 minutes. Transfer chicken to cutting board, carve chicken from bones (discard bones), and slice chicken ½ inch thick. Stir vegetables and pan juices until juices are almost completely absorbed, about 1 minute. Stir in olives and basil and top with chicken. Combine lemon zest and thyme in small bowl and sprinkle over chicken. Serve with lemon wedges.

Chicken Tortilla Soup

We wanted a savory bowlful with deep corn flavor. *by Matthew Fairman*

WITH RICH BROTH, tender chicken pieces, a little smoky heat, bright lime, and crisp tortilla strips, a vibrant chicken tortilla soup makes a lovely dinner. But what sets it apart from other chicken soups is the toasty corn flavor that comes from steeping tortillas in the broth while it simmers. For a slow-cooker version, I wanted to keep all the best elements of this delicious dish while minimizing the hands-on cooking time.

Many slow-cooker chicken soup recipes produce watery, washed-out versions, because the closed environment of the slow cooker doesn't allow for evaporation or concentration of flavors. I knew I'd be layering flavors into this broth, but I wanted it to stand on its own and not rely completely on loads of garnishes to give it interest. To get there, I started with a mixture of tomatoes, onion, garlic, minced jalapeño, and some smoky chipotle chile in adobo, which I cooked on the stovetop to drive off extra moisture and concentrate the flavors. This short step paid big dividends, and by adding an ample amount of chicken to the slow cooker, I achieved a rich broth.

Tortilla soup incorporates torn-up corn tortillas, which simmer along with the other ingredients for the last bit of cooking time, thickening the broth and introducing its signature toasted-corn flavor. But when I added the tortillas late in the game to my slow-cooker version, that toasted-corn note was missing. I decided to add the tortillas up front, giving them 4 to 6 hours to steep in the slow cooker. Success: All it took was a little whisking to completely break down the tortillas and distribute that lovely toasted-corn flavor throughout the soup.

I could have slurped down this soup straight from the slow cooker, but I knew that a few garnishes would take it over the top. The best restaurant versions of this soup boast freshly fried, supercrisp tortilla chips. Supermarket chips proved a poor, overly salty stand-in, so I quickly shallow-fried some strips of soft corn tortilla in the skillet I'd used for the vegetables. With just a cup of oil and 5 minutes on the stove, I was able to produce tortilla strips that stayed crisp. With a few more fixings, this savory corn-flavored soup surprised my tasters with its comforting complexity. Seconds all around.

SLOW-COOKER CHICKEN TORTILLA SOUP *Serves 6*

For a spicier soup, add some of the jalapeño seeds in step 4. You can substitute Monterey Jack for the Cotija.

- 1 tablespoon plus 1 cup vegetable oil
- 2 tomatoes, cored and chopped
- 1 onion, chopped fine
- 2 jalapeño chiles, stemmed, seeded, and minced
- 6 garlic cloves, minced
- 1 tablespoon tomato paste
- 1 tablespoon minced canned chipotle chile in adobo sauce
   Salt and pepper
- 10 (6-inch) corn tortillas
- 6 cups chicken broth
- 1½ pounds boneless, skinless chicken thighs, trimmed
   Crumbled Cotija cheese
   Fresh cilantro leaves
   Diced avocado
   Sour cream
   Lime wedges

1. Heat 1 tablespoon oil in 12-inch nonstick skillet over medium-high heat until shimmering. Add tomatoes, onion, half of jalapeños, garlic, tomato paste, 2 teaspoons chipotle, and ½ teaspoon salt and cook, stirring often, until onion is softened, 8 to 10 minutes. Transfer to slow cooker and wipe skillet clean with paper towels.

2. Tear 4 tortillas into ½-inch pieces. Add broth and tortilla pieces to slow cooker. Season chicken with salt and pepper and nestle into slow cooker. Cover and cook until chicken is tender, 4 to 6 hours on low.

3. Meanwhile, halve remaining 6 tortillas, then cut halves crosswise into ½-inch-wide strips. Heat remaining 1 cup oil in now-empty skillet over medium-high heat until shimmering. Add tortilla strips and cook, stirring occasionally, until golden brown, 4 to 6 minutes. Using slotted spoon, transfer strips to paper towel–lined plate. Season with salt to taste and let cool completely.

4. Transfer chicken to cutting board and shred into bite-size pieces with 2 forks. Whisk soup vigorously until tortillas are broken down, about 30 seconds. Stir in chicken, remaining jalapeños, and remaining 1 teaspoon chipotle. Season with salt and pepper to taste. Serve, passing tortilla strips, Cotija, cilantro, avocado, sour cream, and lime wedges separately.

Besides the tortilla strip garnish, we also steep tortillas in the soup for rich corn flavor.

Homemade Tortilla Chips

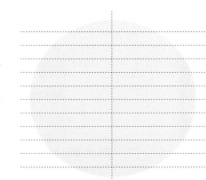

Cut the tortillas into strips.
Halve six 6-inch tortillas, then cut halves crosswise into ½-inch-wide strips.

Fry the strips and let them drain.
Fry strips in 1 cup oil until golden brown. Transfer strips to paper towel–lined plate and let cool before using.

Steak Teriyaki

The key to this Japanese American favorite? Make your own teriyaki sauce.   *by Alli Berkey*

Just ¼ teaspoon of red pepper flakes adds a pleasant hit of heat.

TERIYAKI, A COMPLEX sweet-savory sauce familiar to fans of Japanese cooking, is often poorly represented by store-bought versions. Too often it's simply sugary or syrupy rather than balanced and restrained. I wanted a toned-down but still exciting version of steak teriyaki for a quick dinner for two at home.

I chose strip steaks, thick enough (about 1 inch) to take on a nice exterior sear in a nonstick skillet without over-cooking on the inside—an easy choice.

To avoid the syrupy supermarket style of teriyaki, I decided to make my own sauce from scratch. After stirring together several versions based on existing recipes, I was struck by how different they were. One was overly sweet, another oily, a third too thick. I identified the common ingredients—sugar, soy sauce, and mirin (see "Homemade Teriyaki Sauce")—and set off to improvise.

I found that brown sugar gave the sauce a deeper caramel flavor than granulated sugar did. Soy sauce lent all the saltiness required, as well as a bit of savory depth. And after experimenting with alternatives to mirin (I tried white wine and various vinegars), I realized that there's no good substitute for its bright, faintly sour flavor.

To keep the sauce from being cloying, I added rice vinegar to the mix. Though it's not a traditional ingredient, its acidity helped provide balance. Red pepper flakes kicked up the spice level, and a little cornstarch thickened the sauce nicely.

But my teriyaki still lacked some savoriness. After trying various fixes,

I realized that the answer was right under my nose: the drippings left in my skillet after cooking the steaks. What if I added my other ingredients to the skillet and then stirred them together over a bit of heat to let them reduce to just the right consistency? Bingo.

I found that I could stir the sauce together and simmer it during the few minutes that I let the steaks rest—a necessary step for juicy steaks. I then sliced the meat, poured the warm sauce over the top, and finished the dish with a sprinkling of sliced scallions. My teriyaki was savory, sweet, and lively, and it was ready to eat in a flash.

STEAK TERIYAKI FOR TWO

Be sure to use unseasoned rice vinegar here. Both rice vinegar and mirin can be found in your supermarket's Asian foods section. Serve the steak with rice.

- 5   tablespoons packed light brown sugar
- ¼   cup soy sauce
- ¼   cup mirin
- 2   tablespoons rice vinegar
- 2   tablespoons water
- 2   teaspoons cornstarch
- ¼   teaspoon red pepper flakes
- 1   (1-pound) boneless strip steak, 1 inch thick, trimmed and halved crosswise
    Pepper
- 2   teaspoons vegetable oil
- 2   scallions, sliced thin on bias

1. Whisk sugar, soy sauce, mirin, vinegar, water, cornstarch, and pepper flakes together in bowl.
2. Pat steaks dry with paper towels and season with pepper. Heat oil in 10-inch nonstick skillet over medium heat until just smoking. Cook steaks until well browned and meat registers 125 degrees (for medium-rare), about 5 minutes per side. Transfer to plate, tent with aluminum foil, and let rest for 5 minutes.
3. Reduce heat to medium-low and add sugar–soy sauce mixture to skillet. Bring to simmer, scraping up any browned bits, and cook until slightly thickened, about 2 minutes.
4. Slice steaks thin and top each with 3 tablespoons sauce. Sprinkle with scallions and serve, passing remaining sauce separately.

Homemade Teriyaki Sauce

Store-bought teriyaki sauce has a tendency to be cloying, with little depth. To create our own more balanced and complex yet quick-to-make version, we combined an ingredient from the American pantry—light brown sugar—with three stand-bys from the Asian pantry: soy sauce, rice vinegar, and mirin. We whisked these ingredients together right in the skillet we used to cook the steaks, making good use of the fond (flavorful browned bits) left behind in the skillet.

Soy Sauce

Soy sauce adds characteristic saltiness, umami depth, and a deep brown color to teriyaki sauce. Kikkoman makes our favorite soy sauce. (Tamari is a gluten-free alternative.)

Rice Vinegar

This vinegar has both malty sweetness and mild acidity. You can buy seasoned and un-seasoned versions; we prefer the unseasoned type because it's more versatile.

Mirin

Japanese rice wine has a subtle salty sweetness that simply can't be replicated by regular white wine. Mitoku Organic Mikawa Mirin Sweet Rice Seasoning is our favorite.

Our nonstick skillet testing is available for free for 4 months. Go to **CooksCountry.com/nonstick.**

Fresh Tomato Sauces

Long-cooked tomato sauce offers great depth, but we wanted a midsummer sauce with fresh-off-the-vine tomato flavor. *by Ashley Moore*

RECENTLY, A FRIEND served me a dish of pasta tossed with a simple fresh tomato sauce made with only a handful of ingredients chosen to enhance the tomatoes' flavor, including extra-virgin olive oil, garlic, salt, pepper, a bit of sugar to temper the acidity, and some fresh basil. After a very short simmer, the sauce was lively and flavorful.

Inspired, I took this idea into the test kitchen and came up with my own version. I started by setting a saucepan over medium heat and briefly cooking minced garlic in extra-virgin olive oil until its fragrance reached my nose. I stirred in some blanched and peeled plum tomatoes along with salt, pepper, and sugar and simmered this mixture for about 10 minutes.

We loved this sauce's bright flavor, but some of my colleagues questioned if peeling the tomatoes was necessary. Wouldn't the skins of fresh tomatoes be tender and soft? After a few tests, we found that to be true. Fresh tomatoes simply cut up and added to the saucepan were just fine, their skins tender enough to go unnoticed in the sauce. One step eliminated.

I tinkered with the seasonings and was pleased with how easy, quick, and refreshing this tomato sauce was. I didn't want the fun to stop there, though, so I created four variations. I added a savory note to one by cooking the tomato sauce in rendered pancetta fat to mimic Italian *amatriciana* sauce. To a second variation I added some crushed red pepper flakes and minced anchovies for a sauce akin to an Italian *arrabbiata*. My next version was a pungent *puttanesca*, full of briny olives and capers, and my final variation was a creamy vodka sauce, enriched with a handful of grated Parmesan cheese for salty, savory flavor.

The Best Way to Store Basil

We stored fresh basil, both wrapped in damp paper towels and unwrapped, in unsealed zipper-lock bags in the refrigerator. After three days, both samples were still green and perky. But after one week, only the towel-wrapped basil still looked and tasted fresh. Don't be tempted to rinse the basil until just before you need to use it; when we performed the same tests after rinsing, the shelf life was decreased by half.

There's no need to peel fresh, ripe tomatoes. Their tender skins go unnoticed in the sauce.

AMATRICIANA

ARRABBIATA

VODKA

PUTTANESCA

FRESH TOMATO SAUCE

Makes 4 cups; enough for 1 pound pasta

Be sure to choose the ripest tomatoes you can find. While this sauce is best when eaten right away, it can be frozen for up to one month. If you plan to freeze it, hold off on adding the basil until right before serving. If you're using exceptionally sweet in-season tomatoes, omit the sugar.

- 3 tablespoons extra-virgin olive oil
- 2 garlic cloves, minced
- 2 pounds plum tomatoes, cored and cut into ½-inch pieces
  Salt and pepper
- ½ teaspoon sugar
- 2 tablespoons chopped fresh basil

Heat oil and garlic in large saucepan over medium heat until garlic is fragrant but not browned, 1 to 2 minutes. Stir in tomatoes, ¾ teaspoon salt, ½ teaspoon pepper, and sugar. Increase heat to medium-high and cook until tomatoes are broken down and sauce is slightly thickened, about 10 minutes. Stir in basil and season with salt and pepper to taste. Serve.

FRESH TOMATO AMATRICIANA SAUCE

Reduce oil to 1 tablespoon. Cook oil and 4 ounces finely chopped pancetta in saucepan over medium heat until pancetta is rendered and crispy, 5 to 7 minutes, before adding garlic.

FRESH TOMATO ARRABBIATA SAUCE

Add 3 rinsed, minced anchovy fillets and ¾ teaspoon red pepper flakes with garlic.

FRESH TOMATO PUTTANESCA SAUCE

Add ¼ cup coarsely chopped pitted kalamata olives and ¼ cup rinsed capers to saucepan with tomatoes.

FRESH TOMATO VODKA SAUCE

Add ½ cup heavy cream and ¼ cup vodka to saucepan with tomatoes. Stir in ¼ cup grated Parmesan cheese with basil.

Following a gluten-free diet? Go to **CooksCountry.com/gfpasta** to read about our winning pasta.

Paper Towels

It took 96 rolls—88,608 sheets—to find one phenomenal paper towel.

by Lauren Savoie

12 Towels 20+ Tests

- Scrub six different surfaces
- Drain bacon
- Blot steaks dry
- Rip sheets with wet and dry hands
- Pass sheets numerous times across rough-surfaced cutting board
- Count number of sheets on each roll
- Measure thickness and dimensions
- Calculate absorbency by weighing each sheet dry and wet
- Place 30-, 200-, and 500-gram weights on dry and wet sheets and lift
- Have 36 home testers use towels in everyday kitchen applications

One sheet of our favorite towel (left) held almost ¼ cup of liquid. A poor performer (right) couldn't absorb that much liquid.

COLORFUL DUTCH OVENS, turbocharged blenders, and flashy knives may hog the spotlight, but the most essential piece of equipment in our test kitchen might be the humble paper towel. We use paper towels to sop up grease, water, and other messes; to blot meat and dry herbs; to clean gritty stovetops and counters; to oil grill grates; to wipe out cast-iron skillets; and simply to dry our hands. A good paper towel is tough, absorbent, and versatile.

While many shoppers just buy whichever paper towels are on sale, we decided to conduct tests to find out which product performs best. We focused on the smallest rolls sold by the top seven national manufacturers. Since people have very strong opinions on paper-towel size, we included five full-sheet and seven variable-sheet rolls, for a grand total of 12 products priced from $0.87 to $2.49 per roll.

Towels and cleaning supplies in hand, we put the towels through a barrage of tests. We weighed and measured all the towels. We used the towels to scrub all-purpose cleaner off a variety of surfaces—plastic, wood, metal, granite, marble, and glass before examining the towels for tears, the surfaces for lint, and our hands for excessive wetness. We used folded towels to blot steaks dry and to drain cooked bacon, checking to see if any meat juices or greases soaked through. We also asked 36 testers to try out the rolls at home over the course of four weeks. What did we learn?

First, there was no difference in performance difference between full- and variable-sheet towels. Though the variable sheets were about half the width of full-size sheets, they were equally as strong and absorbent per square inch. Testers were split over which style of sheet they favored, so we agreed that style is a matter of preference, not performance. But sheet style aside, most towels completely bombed our tests, and in the end, we found only two products we liked.

What set these two towels apart? Though manufacturers wouldn't tell us anything about how they made their products, we noted that our favorites were twice as thick as lower-ranked towels—0.4 versus 0.2 millimeters. In most cases, the added thickness was due to the towel's ply. The 12 products we tested were made from either a single sheet of paper (single ply) or two layers of paper bonded together (double ply). Nearly all the low-ranked products were made from just a single ply; they consistently soaked through and ripped, leaving our hands and our counters wet.

Perhaps not surprisingly, double-ply paper towels held twice as much liquid as single-ply towels—0.4 versus 0.2 grams of water per square inch, or about ¼ cup versus just 2 tablespoons of water for a full-size sheet. They were also much stronger: After passing our top two products across the surface of a cutting board 300 times, we still hadn't broken through the second ply.

There were exceptions, however; two single-ply products from Viva were luxuriously soft and 1 millimeter thicker than all the other towels. But while

HIGHLY RECOMMENDED

Bounty Paper Towels
Available in: Full sheet and Select-A-Size
Price: $2.49 for 1 roll (full sheet, regular and Select-A-Size, regular)
Price per Square Foot: $0.07 (full sheet and Select-A-Size)
Number of Sheets: 48 (full sheet), 84 (Select-A-Size)
Water Absorbency: 0.4 g per sq in
Ply: 2
Thickness: 0.4 mm

Comments: Every tester who tried these towels gave a positive review. The sheets were thick, soft, and sturdy, and a single full-size towel could hold nearly ¼ cup of water—about twice as much as lower-ranked towels. Thanks to their double-ply thickness, the sheets were unscathed after 300 passes across a semiabrasive cutting board—and we detected nary a hair of lint, even on glass.

	CRITERIA
Absorbency	★★★
Strength	★★★
Linting	★★★
Ease of Use	★★★

Winning Traits
- Soft, plush sheets that are also sturdy
- Available in full-sheet and variable-sheet styles
- Two-ply sheets that are 0.4 millimeters thick
- Full-size sheets absorb up to ¼ cup of liquid
- Sheets stay intact after 300 passes across a semiabrasive surface
- Full-size sheets hold more than 1 pound of weight when wet and dry
- Minimal linting
- White, unpatterned sheets

RECOMMENDED

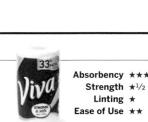

Brawny Paper Towels
Available in: Full sheet and Pick-A-Size
Price: $1.99 for 1 roll (full sheet, regular), $3.16 for 2 (Pick-A-Size, big)
Price per Square Foot: $0.05 (full sheet), $0.03 (Pick-A-Size)
Number of Sheets: 48 (full sheet), 117 (Pick-A-Size)
Water Absorbency: 0.4 g per sq in
Ply: 2   **Thickness:** 0.4 mm

Absorbency	★★★
Strength	★★★
Linting	★★½
Ease of Use	★★½

RECOMMENDED WITH RESERVATIONS

Viva Towels
Available in: Full sheet and Choose-A-Sheet
Price: $3.83 for 2 rolls (full sheet, regular), $2.29 for 1 (Choose-A-Sheet, regular)
Price per Square Foot: $0.04 (full sheet) and $0.05 (Choose-A-Sheet)
Number of Sheets: 68 (full sheet), 102 (Choose-A-Sheet)
Water Absorbency: 0.4 g per sq in   **Ply:** 1   **Thickness:** 0.5 mm

Absorbency	★★★
Strength	★½
Linting	★
Ease of Use	★★

Viva Vantage Towels
Available in: Choose-A-Sheet
Price: $2.19 for 1 roll
Price per Square Foot: $0.05
Number of Sheets: 88
Water Absorbency: 0.3 g per sq in
Ply: 1   **Thickness:** 0.4 mm

Absorbency	★★
Strength	★★
Linting	★★
Ease of Use	★½

NOT RECOMMENDED

Bounty Basic Paper Towels
Available in: Full sheet and Select-A-Size
Price: $6.98 for 8 rolls (full sheet, regular), $17.99 for 12 (Select-A-Size, regular)
Number of Sheets: 40 (full sheet), 89 (Select-A-Size)

Sparkle Paper Towels
Available in: Full sheet and Pick-A-Size
Price: $14.90 for 8 rolls (full sheet, regular), $12.05 for 6 (Pick-A-Size, big)
Number of Sheets: 44 (full sheet), 102 (Pick-A-Size)

Scott Towels
Available in: Choose-A-Sheet
Price: $2.29 for 1 roll
Number of Sheets: 102

Shredded Mozzarella

We found a shredded cheese that's (almost) as good as fresh from the block.

by Lauren Savoie

these single-ply towels were very absorbent, they couldn't hold even ½ pound of pressure when wet—no good when drying and lifting heavy produce such as grapes—and they often tore when we used them to scrub various surfaces.

We also looked at ease of use, taking note of how the towels felt in our hands and how much lint they left behind when used to dry glasses or blot moisture from steaks. One towel was so linty that we thought it had snowed on our expensive steaks after just a few dabs. Other towels were too abrasive or uncomfortable to grip. Our favorites were plush and not at all linty.

While the towels' performance was clear-cut, prices were not. Many of the lower-ranked towels, such as Viva Vantage and Bounty Basic, bill themselves as budget-friendly versions of higher-rated products, but something about these towels seemed suspect—the rolls were loosely wound and had deep embossing that made them look deceptively thick. We did some sleuthing and discovered something sneaky: Budget paper towels have about 17 percent fewer sheets than premium products. While they might be cheaper if you're looking solely at the price per roll, a deeper truth becomes evident when you calculate the price per square foot. Most of these budget products cost between $0.03 and $0.05 per square foot—on par with prices for the premium versions of the same products.

Our favorite product was also the national top seller: Bounty Paper Towels. The two-ply sheets were thick, ultrastrong, and highly absorbent. We tested both plain and patterned versions and noticed that the patterned towels tended to rub dye onto light-colored surfaces, so we recommend buying white paper towels to avoid this issue. Though the Bounty towels are slightly more expensive than others—$2.49 for a regular-size roll, or about $0.07 per square foot—every tester who tried these plush, durable towels was impressed with their performance.

Go to **CooksCountry.com/sept17** to read the full testing story and see the complete results chart.

IT'S A TEMPTING shortcut: Spend a few more dollars for a bag of shredded cheese and save time—and potentially skinned knuckles—by not having to grate the cheese yourself. We usually prefer to shred our own mozzarella since most shredded cheeses contain anticaking agents, such as cellulose powder (minuscule pieces of plant fiber), that can make the cheese stiff and dry. But we wondered if there was a shredded option that could work in a pinch.

To find out, we gathered 21 staff members and asked them to try seven shredded mozzarellas plain and melted on pizza. We also sent the cheeses to an independent lab to get a read on their fat and sodium contents.

Texture was the most glaring problem for most of the cheeses. None were great when eaten raw—the anticaking agents made their strands gritty and powdery, and there was no fooling tasters into thinking this was freshly shredded mozzarella. But while tasters said "*No, grazie*" to the idea of eating these cheeses for a snack or sprinkled on a salad, most agreed that texture was less of an issue when the cheese was melted on pizza. Though many of the cheeses were still unacceptably rubbery and stiff when melted, a handful emerged from the oven perfectly stretchy and chewy.

Why were some cheeses better than others when melted? The nutritional labels didn't reveal any differences in the amounts of cellulose powder or potato starch coating the products. Instead, lab tests pointed to fat as the culprit. Our winner—the only cheese in our lineup made from whole milk—contained 45 percent fat in its dry solids (a measurement of how much of the cheese is fat once water is removed). Lower-scoring cheeses (all made from part-skim milk) were significantly leaner, with between 36 percent and 41 percent fat in their dry solids. Fat helps cheese retain a tender, milky texture when melted, which explains why leaner products turned dense and rubbery while fattier cheeses were more stretchy.

Fat also contributes to flavor, so it was no surprise that lower-fat cheeses lacked the buttery, rich flavor we expect from mozzarella. It didn't help that some of these products were also under- or oversalted; we found the sweet spot to be between 210 and 230 milligrams of sodium per serving—just enough

Stringiness when melted is a good thing.

to add a savory complexity. One other factor contributed to flavor: Our winner was the only cheese that contained vinegar, and our tasters appreciated the tang it added.

Tasters also noticed that a few very finely shredded cheeses easily balled up into dense clumps that left the cheese splotchy and unevenly melted. When we measured individual strands with calipers, our favorite shreds were two to three times thicker than lower-ranked products—about 2.8 millimeters compared to 0.9 millimeters. Larger strands were easier to sprinkle over pizza, didn't clump in our hands, and melted in uniformly browned sheets.

Our winner, Polly-O Low Moisture Whole Milk Shredded Mozzarella, contained the most fat and a moderate amount of salt and had the thickest strands. Its superior flavor and higher fat level can be attributed to the fact that it's the only cheese in our lineup made with whole milk and vinegar, just like our favorite block mozzarellas. The shreds made with part-skim milk didn't have the same bouncy, springy texture and rich tang as the Polly-O whole-milk shreds.

Polly-O also makes our winning block-style mozzarella, and while it was clear from the lab results that the shredded product is a different cheese from the block mozzarella, we decided to sample them side by side. The Polly-O block mozzarella was clearly superior when tasted plain, but the two cheeses were pretty close when melted. So if you're tossing mozzarella into baked pasta or on top of a pizza, you can go ahead and buy our "classic," "creamy" shredded winner in a pinch.

Go to **CooksCountry.com/sept17** to read the full tasting story and see the complete results chart.

RECOMMENDED

Our Favorite
Polly-O Low Moisture Whole Milk Shredded Mozzarella
Price: $2.98 for 8 oz ($0.37 per oz)
Milk: Whole   **Fat in Solids:** 45%
Sodium: 210 mg
Average Thickness: 2.8 mm
Comments: These "chunky" strands were easy to spread over pizza dough and were "stringy," "evenly browned," and "chewy" when melted. Tasters praised their "classic," "creamy" milkiness and "tang," which added a "rich" sharpness to pizza.

Sargento Off the Block Shredded Low Moisture Part-Skim Mozzarella Cheese
Price: $4.29 for 8 oz ($0.54 per oz)
Milk: Part-skim   **Fat in Solids:** 38%
Sodium: 229 mg
Average Thickness: 1.8 mm
Comments: These "big, fat shreds" had a relatively "rich" flavor and melted into a nicely "pliable," "soft" sheet on the pizza.

Kraft Shredded Low-Moisture Part-Skim Mozzarella Cheese
Price: $3.99 for 8 oz ($0.50 per oz)
Milk: Part-skim   **Fat in Solids:** 41%
Sodium: 207 mg
Average Thickness: 1.1 mm
Comments: Nicely "stretchy" and "chewy" when melted, these shreds had a "mild," familiar "string cheese" flavor.

RECOMMENDED WITH RESERVATIONS

Kraft With a Touch of Philadelphia Mozzarella Shredded Cheese
Price: $3.99 for 8 oz ($0.50 per oz)
Milk: Part-skim   **Fat in Solids:** 40%
Sodium: 253 mg
Average Thickness: 1.4 mm
Comments: Tasters liked this cheese's "nutty," "tangy" flavor, but some deemed it a "tad salty" or found its coating "powdery." When melted, it was a bit "rubbery."

Horizon Organic Shredded Mozzarella Cheese
Price: $4.49 for 6 oz ($0.75 per oz)
Milk: Part-skim   **Fat in Solids:** 39%
Sodium: 231 mg
Average Thickness: 1.5 mm
Comments: We liked this cheese's "tangy," "sharp" flavor when tasted plain, but it was the "greasiest" of the bunch when melted.

Polly-O Low Moisture Part Skim Shredded Mozzarella
Price: $2.98 for 8 oz ($0.37 per oz)
Milk: Part-skim   **Fat in Solids:** 36%
Sodium: 175 mg
Average Thickness: 2.8 mm
Comments: This cheese was "too lean," and its big shreds were "dry" when melted.

Artichoke–Green Chile Dip

My family huddles around a dish of this warm, gooey artichoke dip at gatherings of all kinds. Sure, there's some conversation in the first few moments after everyone arrives, but it quickly dies down once everyone spots this dip. Be sure to serve it hot—no one wants a cold cheesy artichoke dip. (OK, I would still eat it.)

–ASHLEY MOORE
*Associate editor
and Cook's Country TV presenter*

ARTICHOKE–GREEN CHILE DIP
Serves 6
Be sure to dry the artichokes thoroughly with paper towels; excess water can cause the dip to look soupy. Serve with tortilla chips, pita chips, or vegetables.

- 4 ounces Parmesan cheese, grated (2 cups)
- 4 ounces mozzarella cheese, shredded (1 cup)
- 1 cup canned whole artichoke hearts, rinsed, patted dry, and chopped
- 1 cup mayonnaise
- ¼ cup canned chopped green chiles, drained
- ¼ teaspoon garlic powder

Adjust oven rack to middle position and heat oven to 350 degrees. Combine all ingredients in bowl and transfer to 9-inch pie plate. Bake until golden brown and bubbling around edges, about 30 minutes. Let cool for 10 minutes before serving.

We're celebrating the tenth season of Cook's Country from America's Test Kitchen, which airs this autumn on PBS and features a great cast, including hosts Bridget Lancaster and Julia Collin-Davison. Check your local PBS listings for details. In the meantime, to revisit earlier seasons and find your favorite Cook's Country recipes, visit CooksCountry.com. You can also submit a favorite family recipe (or mail it to Heirloom Recipes, Cook's Country, P.O. Box 470739, Brookline, MA 02447). Include your name and mailing address. If we print your recipe, you'll win a one-year subscription to Cook's Country.

COMING NEXT ISSUE

*We traversed the map for recipes to share in the upcoming October/November issue of Cook's Country, from Texas for German-style **Potato Pancakes** to Minnesota for **Tater Tot Hotdish** to Baltimore for superchocolaty **Bergers Cookies**. And if you've got a crowd coming for Thanksgiving, we'll show you the best way to roast a hefty turkey and fill your table with sides from **Sweet Potato Casserole** to **Green Bean Casserole**. Be sure to save room for Pennsylvania-style **Dutch Apple Pie**.*

RECIPE INDEX

FIND THE ROOSTER!

A tiny version of this rooster has been hidden in the pages of this issue. Write to us with its location, and we'll enter you in a random drawing. The first correct entry drawn will win our favorite paper towels, and each of the next five will receive a free one-year subscription to Cook's Country. To enter, visit CooksCountry.com/rooster by September 30, 2017, or write to Rooster AS17, Cook's Country, P.O. Box 470739, Brookline, MA 02447. Include your name and address. Dan Phillips of Anchorage, Alaska, found the rooster in the April/May 2017 issue on page 8 and won our favorite muffin tin.

WEB EXTRAS

Free for four months online at
CooksCountry.com
Blueberry Pancakes
Bourbon Whipped Cream
Chocolate Layer Cake Rounds
Crab Louis Salad
Salt and Olive Oil Pita Chips
Tasting Chocolate Ice Cream
Tasting Gluten-Free Spaghetti
Tasting Shredded Mozzarella
Testing Nonstick Skillets
Testing Paper Towels
Testing Rasp-Style Graters

READ US ON IPAD

Download the Cook's Country app for iPad and start a free trial subscription or purchase a single issue of the magazine. All issues are enhanced with full-color Cooking Mode slide shows that provide step-by-step instructions for completing recipes, plus expanded reviews and ratings. Go to CooksCountry.com/iPad to download our app through iTunes.

RC=Recipe Card

CHOCOLATE MALTED CAKE

To get that nostalgic ice cream parlor flavor in every bite, we added malted milk powder to the chocolate frosting and sprinkled crushed malted milk balls between the cake layers.

TO MAKE THIS CAKE, YOU WILL NEED:

- 1 cup malted milk powder
- ⅓ cup heavy cream
- 1 teaspoon vanilla extract
- 24 tablespoons (3 sticks) unsalted butter, softened
- ¼ teaspoon salt
- 3 cups (12 ounces) confectioners' sugar
- 6 ounces milk chocolate, melted and cooled
- 2 (5-ounce) boxes malted milk balls
- 3 (8-inch) chocolate layer cake rounds*

FOR THE FROSTING: Stir malted milk powder, cream, and vanilla in bowl until thoroughly combined. Using stand mixer fitted with whisk attachment, whip butter and salt on medium-high speed until smooth, about 1 minute. Reduce speed to medium-low, slowly add sugar, and mix until smooth, 1 to 2 minutes. Add malted milk mixture, increase speed to medium-high, and whip until light and fluffy, about 3 minutes. Add chocolate and whip until thoroughly combined.

TO ASSEMBLE: Place 1 cup malted milk balls in 1-gallon zipper-lock bag and crush coarse with rolling pin. Place 1 cake layer on cake plate or pedestal. Spread 1 cup frosting evenly over top. Sprinkle ½ cup crushed malted milk balls evenly over frosting. Repeat with second cake layer, 1 cup frosting, and remaining ½ cup crushed malted milk balls. Place third cake layer on top and frost top and sides of cake with remaining frosting. Arrange whole malted milk balls around top and bottom edges of cake. Arrange 5 malted milk balls in center of cake. Serve.

*Go to **CooksCountry.com /chocolatelayercake** for our Chocolate Layer Cake recipe, or use your own recipe.

INSIDE THIS ISSUE

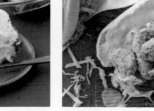

Cook's Country

Big Thanksgiving

Turkey for a Crowd, Fully Loaded
Sweet Potatoes, Step-by-Step Stuffing,
Crunchy Green Bean Casserole,
and More

Easy Mashed Potatoes
Five Flavor Variations

Dutch Apple Pie
Plus: We Rate Pie Plates and
Ready-Made Pie Crusts

Roast Pork Tenderloin
Brown Sugar–Citrus Glaze

Indoor BBQ Chicken
Endless Summer Flavor

Slow-Cooker Gumbo
Stress-Free Stew

Spice-Crusted Steak
Big Flavor in a Hurry

Crispy Potato Pancakes
Texas Festival Favorite

OCTOBER / NOVEMBER 2017
$5.95 U.S. / $6.95 CANADA

DISPLAY UNTIL NOVEMBER 6, 2017

0 74470 02742 3

1 1>

LETTER FROM THE EDITOR

I'M GOING TO say something shocking.

Ready?

The food is not the most important part of Thanksgiving.

There. I said it. And I swear it's true. The more Thanksgivings I experience, the more I believe it.

Sure, your guests will gush over your turkey and its crispy, brown skin and juicy meat. They'll ask for seconds of that soft, savory stuffing with a crunchy golden top. And who doesn't go weak in the knees for a perfect slice of holiday pie?

With the recipes featured in this issue, you'll have all of the above and then some at your table this year. We hope they'll add something memorable to the holiday.

But when you give thanks, remember the people—friends, family, and even strangers—who bring richness to your life.

I remember one Thanksgiving when I was much younger. I spent it by myself, in a booth at a diner on 6th Avenue in New York City, where I dined on an open-faced turkey sandwich doused in gravy and a bottomless cup of coffee. My company was a server in squeaky shoes, the only waitress on the clock that sleepy day. I was alone, but I was anything but lonely because Squeaky Shoes smiled at me every time she walked by. And when she bid me "Happy Thanksgiving" on my way out the door, it was perhaps the sincerest holiday wish I've ever received. She wasn't a stranger anymore. "Thank you," I said, and I meant it.

Would I have been happier with a gorgeous meal at the family table instead of a soggy sandwich? Maybe so. But I am still thankful for Squeaky Shoes. In my memory, that simple 6th Avenue supper has transformed into a kingly feast, and I wouldn't trade it for anything.

TUCKER SHAW

Executive Editor

EVERYONE'S FAVORITE TREAT

The Perfect Cookie

Our test kitchen has learned a thing or two about making perfect cookies over the last 25 years. In this book, we break down key steps and recipe techniques to help you bake your way through 250 foolproof recipes. There is also an extensive introduction to get you started, with insight into everything from essential equipment to what makes a cookie chewy versus crispy. Order your copy at **AmericasTestKitchen.com/cookie.**

Find us on **Facebook**
facebook.com/CooksCountry

Find us on **Instagram**
instagram.com/CooksCountry

Follow us on **Pinterest**
pinterest.com/TestKitchen

Follow us on **Twitter**
twitter.com/TestKitchen

Cook's Country

Chief Executive Officer David Nussbaum
Chief Creative Officer Jack Bishop
Editorial Director John Willoughby
Editor in Chief Tucker Shaw
Executive Managing Editor Todd Meier
Executive Food Editor Bryan Roof
Deputy Editor Scott Kathan
Associate Editors Morgan Bolling, Cecelia Jenkins, Katie Leaird, Ashley Moore
Photo Team & Special Events Manager Tim McQuinn
Lead Cook, Photo Team Daniel Cellucci
Test Cooks Alli Berkey, Matthew Fairman
Assistant Test Cooks Mady Nichas, Jessica Rudolph
Senior Copy Editor Krista Magnuson
Copy Editor Jillian Campbell
Contributing Editor Eva Katz
Science Editor Guy Crosby, PhD, CFS
Hosts & Executive Editors, Television Bridget Lancaster, Julia Collin Davison

Executive Editor, Tastings & Testings Lisa McManus
Deputy Editor, Tastings & Testings Hannah Crowley
Associate Editors, Tastings & Testings Miye Bromberg, Lauren Savoie, Kate Shannon
Assistant Editor, Tastings & Testings Emily Phares
Editorial Assistant, Tastings & Testings Carolyn Grillo

Executive Editor, Web Christine Liu
Managing Editor, Web Mari Levine
Senior Editors, Web Roger Metcalf, Briana Palma
Associate Editor, Web Terrence Doyle
Assistant Editor, Web Molly Farrar

Creative Director John Torres
Photography Director Julie Cote
Art Director Susan Levin
Designer Maggie Edgar
Senior Staff Photographer Daniel J. van Ackere
Staff Photographers Steve Klise, Kevin White
Photography Producer Mary Ball

Director, Creative Operations Alice Carpenter
Test Kitchen Director Erin McMurrer
Assistant Test Kitchen Director Alexxa Benson
Test Kitchen Manager Meridith Lippard
Test Kitchen Facilities Manager Sophie Clingan-Darack
Senior Kitchen Assistant Receiver Kelly Ryan
Senior Kitchen Assistant Shopper Marissa Bunnewith
Lead Kitchen Assistant Ena Gudiel
Kitchen Assistants Gladis Campos, Blanca Castanza

Chief Financial Officer Jackie McCauley Ford
Director, Customer Support Amy Bootier
Senior Customer Loyalty & Support Specialists Rebecca Kowalski, Andrew Straaberg Finfrock
Customer Loyalty & Support Specialist J.P. Dubuque
Production Director Guy Rochford
Imaging Manager Lauren Robbins
Production & Imaging Specialists Heather Dube, Dennis Noble, Jessica Voas

Chief Revenue Officer Sara Domville
Director, Special Accounts Erica Nye
Director, Sponsorship Marketing & Client Services Christine Anagnostis
Client Services Manager Kate Zebrowski
Client Service and Marketing Representative Claire Gambee
Director, Business Partnerships Mehgan Conciatori
Partnership Marketing Manager Pamela Putprush

Chief Digital Officer Fran Middleton
Marketing Director, Social Media and Content Strategy Claire Oliverson
Senior Social Media Coordinators Kelsey Hopper, Morgan Mannino

Senior VP, Human Resources & Organizational Development Colleen Zelina
Human Resources Director Adele Shapiro

Public Relations & Communications Director Brian Franklin
Public Relations Coordinator Lauren Watson

Photography Keller + Keller
Food Styling Catrine Kelty, Marie Piraino
Circulation Services ProCirc

On the cover: Turkey and Gravy for a Crowd, Loaded Sweet Potato Casserole, and Simple Holiday Stuffing

America's Test Kitchen is a real kitchen located in Boston. It is the home of more than 60 test cooks, editors, and cookware specialists. Our mission is to test recipes until we understand exactly how and why they work and eventually arrive at the very best version. We also test kitchen equipment and supermarket ingredients in search of products that offer the best value and performance. You can watch us work by tuning in to **America's Test Kitchen** (AmericasTestKitchen.com) and **Cooks Country from America's Test Kitchen** (CooksCountry.com) on public television and listen to our weekly segments on *The Splendid Table* on public radio. You can also follow us on Facebook, Twitter, Pinterest, and Instagram.

12

5

8

Cook's Country magazine (ISSN 1552-1990), number 77, is published bimonthly by America's Test Kitchen Limited Partnership, 21 Drydock Avenue, Suite 210E, Boston, MA 02210. Copyright 2017 America's Test Kitchen Limited Partnership. Periodicals postage paid at Boston, MA, and additional mailing offices, USPS #023453. Publications Mail Agreement No. 40020778. Return undeliverable Canadian addresses to P.O. Box 875, Station A, Windsor, ON N9A 6P2. POSTMASTER: Send address changes to *Cook's Country*, PO Box 6018, Harlan, IA 51593-1518. For subscription and gift subscription orders, subscription inquiries, or change of address notices, visit AmericasTestKitchen.com/support, call 800-526-8447 in the U.S. or 515-248-7684 from outside the U.S., or write to us at *Cook's Country*, P.O. Box 6018, Harlan, IA 51593-1518. PRINTED IN THE USA.

Buttermilk Substitute

I love the tang of buttermilk in biscuits and pancakes, but my husband can't eat dairy. What's the best substitute?
–*Emily Hughes, Missoula, Mont.*

Buttermilk adds a tangy flavor to foods such as pancakes and biscuits. But its high acidity also influences texture; it helps give baked goods lift when combined with a basic (or alkaline) ingredient such as baking soda. The acidity also helps tenderize baked goods.

To find a good substitute, we tested several unflavored nondairy milks (rice, oat, soy, almond, and coconut) to which we added lemon juice, white vinegar, and cream of tartar—all acidic ingredients meant to mimic the natural tang and pH of buttermilk. We tried these substitutes in our recipes for buttermilk biscuits, buttermilk pancakes, and Boston brown bread. For good measure, we also tried them in a savory application: buttermilk mashed potatoes.

In the baked applications, oat milk mixed with lemon juice provided the best combination of flavor and texture and was our favorite (some other combinations had off-flavors or just tasted wrong). It was followed closely by soy milk (which is a bit easier to find) mixed with lemon juice. In the savory mashed potatoes, the oat milk was too sweet, making the soy milk–lemon juice combination the tasters' favorite.

To make buttermilk substitute, stir 1 tablespoon of lemon juice into 1 cup of oat or soy milk. Let the mixture sit for a few minutes if you're using soy milk (soy milk will thicken to a buttermilk-like consistency, but oat milk won't). Then use it as you would buttermilk. ***by Morgan Bolling***

1 cup soy milk or oat milk + 1 tablespoon lemon juice = 1 cup buttermilk

THE BOTTOM LINE: For a tangy nondairy buttermilk substitute for sweet applications, we suggest reaching for oat milk or soy milk mixed with lemon juice. For savory recipes, use a mixture of soy milk and lemon juice.

Salting Pasta Water

I saw on your television show that you always salt the water when you boil pasta. Does it really make a difference?
–*Valerie Graham, Port St. Lucie, Fla.*

We call for adding 1 tablespoon of table salt to 4 quarts of water when cooking 1 pound of pasta (of any size or shape) so that the pasta is seasoned throughout.

To see if we could instead season pasta after cooking, we prepared two batches of pasta: one cooked in salted water and one cooked in unsalted water and salted after cooking and draining. We then tossed batches of pasta prepared each way with marinara and pesto sauces and sampled them all.

All the salted-after-cooking samples had problems. Some tasters got salty pieces of pasta, while others commented that the pasta was underseasoned. With so much surface area on a pound of cooked pasta, it's difficult to season it all evenly. Conversely, tasters thought the samples cooked in salted water were nicely seasoned throughout.

We know from lab tests that pasta cooked in salted water absorbs little sodium—about ¼ teaspoon of salt per pound of pasta—but the salt is evenly distributed.

THE BOTTOM LINE: Cooking pasta in salted water results in evenly seasoned noodles. *–MB*

Chile Chile Bang Bang

There are lots of chile powders at my supermarket. Can ancho chile powder, chipotle chile powder, and regular chili powder be used interchangeably in recipes?
–*Hilary Oakes, Annapolis, Md.*

Traditional chili powder is a blend of dried, ground chiles and spices, typically cumin, oregano, garlic, paprika, and salt. Depending on the chiles used, it can range from mild to hot and is labeled accordingly. The other two powders—ancho and chipotle—consist solely of those dried, ground peppers: Anchos are dried poblanos, and chipotles are jalapeños that have been smoked and then dried.

We tasted the three powders three ways: sprinkled on white rice, in our Two-Bean Chili, and on our Chili-Lime Spiced Nuts. Not surprisingly, our tasters noted major flavor differences among the batches. The regular chili powder was more complex and saltier than other samples, with bold notes of cumin and oregano. The ancho powder was earthy, bitter, and fragrant. The chipotle powder had a spicier kick with rich, smoky flavor.

THE BOTTOM LINE: Ancho chile powder, chipotle chile powder, and regular chili powder can all add depth to recipes, but each has a distinctive flavor that recipes employing it account for, so we don't recommend using them interchangeably. *–MB*

Parsing Pears

I recently saw Asian pears at the grocery store, but I've never tried them. How do they compare with other kinds of pears?
–*Mark Geddes, Keene, N.H.*

There are dozens of pear varieties, but the most common grocery store types are Asian, Anjou, Bartlett, and Bosc. We tasted each raw in our Spinach Salad with Gorgonzola and Pear (which uses pear slices in the salad and processed pear in the dressing), roasted, and in our Pear-Walnut Upside-Down Cake. Our notes on each variety follow.

THE BOTTOM LINE: Asian pears are more crisp, less juicy, and have a milder flavor than other common pears, so they are not really suitable for cooked applications. But they're good for snacking or to add texture to salads. *–MB*

ASIAN

Also known as "pear-apples," Asian pears are rounder and squatter than other varieties. They are crunchy, as they do not soften as they ripen. Tasters noted that they "lack pear flavor," with one taster asking, "Is this a pear or an apple?" They add crisp texture to salads or slaws.

ANJOU

Available with red or green skin, Anjou pears are squat and plump, with wider necks than other varieties. Their flesh is creamy, tender, and incredibly juicy when ripe. Tasters described them as having "classic pear flavor."

BARTLETT

Green when underripe, these pears take on a yellowish hue when ripe. They have a floral, sweet flavor and thin, delicate skin. Bartletts are the most widely grown pear in America and are the variety typically used for canned pears.

BOSC

Easy to recognize by their brownish skin and elongated necks, Bosc pears are very sweet and fragrant when ripe and are our favorite pears for baking. They're naturally firmer than other varieties, which keeps their flesh from turning mushy when cooked.

 Submit questions and shortcuts at CooksCountry.com/ask and CooksCountry.com/shortcuts.

Smashing Results

Anya Sadler, Buffalo, N.Y.

I mistakenly bought a tub of unpitted olives at the grocery store. I quickly found pitting them with a paring knife to be tedious and messy. Luckily, I came up with a better way to pit them: I put a handful of olives on my cutting board, covered them with a lid from a plastic storage container, and pressed firmly on the lid to flatten the olives. The pits cleanly released from the flesh so I could easily pick them out. As a bonus, the flattened olives stayed put while I chopped them.

Better Shredder

Ben Golden, Woodstock, Ill.

Tacos made with poached chicken breasts are a weeknight staple in our house. To take the work out of shredding the meat, I transfer the four poached breasts from the pan to the bowl of my stand mixer, let them rest for 5 minutes, and then mix with the paddle on low for about 30 seconds. It couldn't be easier, and any juices released during resting are reincorporated into the shredded chicken.

Cutting Crab Cakes

Marcy Vaughn, Clearwater, Fla.

Forming and breading crab cakes by hand can be a messy task, but I found an easier way to shape them. After portioning the crab mixture into balls, I roll each ball in bread crumbs. Then, working with one ball at a time, I place them in a greased cookie or biscuit cutter (without handles) and tamp them down with a flat-bottomed glass. This method presses in the bread crumbs while perfectly molding the cakes for even cooking.

Compiled by Cecelia Jenkins

Do Electric Knives Really Work?

by Emily Phares

4 Electric Knives 7 Tests

1. Slice 1 loaf of challah bread ½ inch and ¼ inch thick
2. Slice 1 loaf of Japanese milk bread ½ inch and ¼ inch thick
3. Slice 1 loaf of Francese bread ½ inch and ¼ inch thick
4. Slice 1 rotisserie chicken ¼ inch and ⅛ inch thick
5. Carve 1 whole roasted turkey into ¼-inch-thick and ⅛-inch-thick slices
6. Use top-rated model to slice 10 loaves of Francese bread ½ inch and ¼ inch thick to test durability
7. Measure noise level using decibel meter

EQUIPMENT REVIEW

ELECTRIC KNIVES MAY seem like relics of the past, but some home cooks (and professional chefs) swear by their ability to effortlessly carve poultry without ripping the skin and to slice delicate breads without crushing them. These gizmos have two identical serrated blades, riveted together, which are snapped into a motorized base that doubles as the knife's handle. The blades shimmy in opposite directions to create a sawing motion that cuts food with minimal downward pressure.

To see if we could find a model we liked, we bought four top-selling electric knives, priced from $19.92 to $122.00, and tested them by slicing a variety of breads and carving both turkeys and chickens. It quickly became clear that, aside from slicing ability, in-hand comfort and noise level were important factors. We preferred models with start buttons on the undersides of the handles, as start buttons on tops of the handles were sometimes painful to press. We also look at how loud a product was. One model was so loud that it drowned out all conversation in the room; while this could be an advantage at some family gatherings, we downgraded this knife for excessive noise.

Only one knife, the Black + Decker ComfortGrip 9" Electric Knife, offered good slicing ability—especially when carving a roast—comfort, and a tolerable noise level. This product made us appreciate how useful an electric knife can be. There's another plus: It was the least expensive model we tested. So even if you use it only once a year to carve a turkey, this knife is a worthwhile investment.

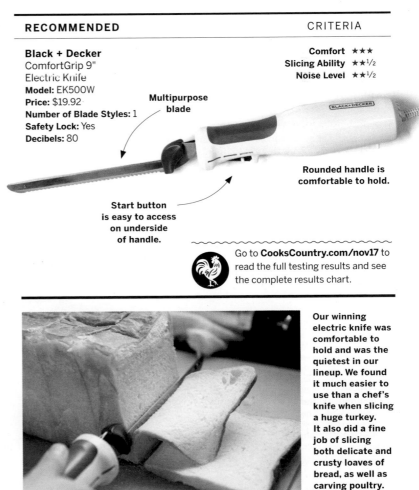

RECOMMENDED   CRITERIA

Black + Decker
ComfortGrip 9"
Electric Knife
Model: EK500W
Price: $19.92
Number of Blade Styles: 1
Safety Lock: Yes
Decibels: 80

Comfort ★★★
Slicing Ability ★★½
Noise Level ★★½

Multipurpose blade

Rounded handle is comfortable to hold.

Start button is easy to access on underside of handle.

Go to **CooksCountry.com/nov17** to read the full testing results and see the complete results chart.

Our winning electric knife was comfortable to hold and was the quietest in our lineup. We found it much easier to use than a chef's knife when slicing a huge turkey. It also did a fine job of slicing both delicate and crusty loaves of bread, as well as carving poultry.

HOLLY RICCIARDI GAZES lovingly at a slightly imperfect shoofly pie on the counter. The molasses filling has bubbled up and broken through the top crust. "Shoofly, she has a mind of her own." Ricciardi refers to her pies as "she," like a doting mother, and she's not upset with this pie; she's just remarking on its quirks. She knows it'll be delicious.

Growing up in a Pennsylvania Dutch household in the rolling countryside west of Philadelphia, Ricciardi watched closely as her mother baked pies year-round from scratch—shoofly, butterscotch, mixed berry, Dutch apple.

Decades later, after building a successful design business, Ricciardi felt the tug of the apron strings drawing her back to the kitchen. "I wanted to bake."

Ricciardi also wanted to share those childhood memories with her adopted city of Philadelphia, so she enrolled in a year-long course at a pastry school with the goal of opening a bakery after graduating. And she did just that: Magpie Artisan Pie Boutique opened in a revitalized neighborhood on South Street in 2012.

Customers soon lined up for Ricciardi's rustic pies, and Magpie has become something of a local touchstone for longtime residents and newcomers alike.

Ricciardi is known for her small, innovative recipe tweaks: sweetened milk in place of cream in Dutch apple pie, ground oats in crumb toppings to absorb excess moisture—the kind of fine-tuning that only endless tinkering can produce. She now shares her collage of knowledge—gleaned from her mother, tempered by cooking school, and ever-evolving through experimentation—with students of her own, creating the next generation of pie makers.

As Ricciardi assembles ingredients for another pie, she grabs a fork and, with a stern look, declares, "You mix this pie with a fork. Because that's what my mom did." Her expression softens into a warm, reassuring smile as another customer walks through the door.

Called Back to a Life of Pie

A career change returned this entrepreneurial baker to her Pennsylvania Dutch roots, much to the delight of her Philadelphia neighbors.

by Bryan Roof

Magpie Artisan Pie Boutique proprietor Holly Ricciardi (above right) refers to the look of her pie shop as "granny chic," with patterned wallpaper, kitschy-but-stylish appointments, and clean lines. She swears that most pies benefit from an overnight rest, so most Magpie pies (right) are a day old. Above, a seven-slice cutting tool creates perfect-size wedges.

Dutch Apple Pie

This rustic holiday pie boasts a subtly creamy filling. The key ingredient was hiding in plain sight.

by Cecelia Jenkins

WHAT IS DUTCH apple pie? For starters, it is not Dutch. (It's sometimes called Pennsylvania Dutch apple pie—still not Dutch but getting warmer.) The name comes from a modern-day misnomer for the early German settlers of Pennsylvania and their descendants; the word "Dutch" most likely grew out of *Deutsch*, the German word for "German."

Now about this pie. It has a bottom crust only and is topped with a generous sprinkling of sweet streusel. The filling (apples, sugar, lemon juice, cinnamon) contains vanilla, cream, and sometimes raisins, and the result is a pie that holds its shape when sliced.

Some existing recipes I tried overdid the cream, so the filling looked curdled. Others called for thickeners such as flour or cornstarch to set the filling quickly, but tasters found these pies gummy. Too many warm spices (cinnamon, nutmeg, allspice, clove) clobbered the sweet apple flavor. I wanted a simple method for a pie bursting with bright apple and creamy vanilla flavors, with a flaky crust and crunchy crumble on top.

Many recipes for Dutch apple pie call for sour cream in the crust for a bit of tang, a quality I love, so I decided to make my own crust. It came together quickly in the food processor.

Moving on to the filling, I sliced 2½ pounds of Golden Delicious apples, which I love for their versatility and strong apple flavor. Precooking the apples, which many recipes recommend, turned the filling mushy. But simply slicing the apples and piling them into the pie crust made an unevenly cooked pie. The answer was tossing the sliced apples with sugar and a bit of lemon juice and letting them sit for an hour to soften, making it easier to press and flatten the slices neatly into the shell.

This pie traditionally has cream in the filling, and after experimentation I found that ½ cup provided just the right amount of creaminess. But later, as I scooped vanilla ice cream to go with my finished slice of pie, it came to me: If the pie tastes so good with ice cream on top, why not put it inside as well? I melted enough ice cream to

equal ½ cup and used it in place of the cream. This added not just extra creaminess but also more of the rich vanilla flavor that's a hallmark of this pie.

The final task? The crumble topping. A mixture of melted butter, flour, brown sugar, and a good dose of salt made a crumble that tasted supremely buttery. A short rest in the refrigerator helped it harden enough to crumble easily. Once I'd sprinkled it over the top, I baked the pie for 1 hour and 10 minutes at 350 degrees, with a midbake rotation to ensure even cooking.

Giving in to anticipation, I sliced into the still-warm pie. It tasted fantastic, but I didn't have the clean slice I wanted. Giving the pie a few hours (or even overnight) to set up was the answer. Then I had a gorgeous, multilayered apple pie just right for the holidays.

DUTCH APPLE PIE *Serves 8 to 10*
We prefer Golden Delicious or Gala apples here, but Fuji, Braeburn, or Granny Smith varieties also work well. You may substitute ½ cup of heavy cream for the melted ice cream, if desired. This pie is best when baked a day ahead of time and allowed to rest overnight. Serve with vanilla ice cream.

CRUST
- ¼ cup ice water
- 4 teaspoons sour cream
- 1¼ cups (6¼ ounces) all-purpose flour
- 1½ teaspoons granulated sugar
- ½ teaspoon salt
- 8 tablespoons unsalted butter, cut into ¼-inch pieces and frozen for 15 minutes

FILLING
- 2½ pounds apples, peeled, cored, halved, and sliced ¼ inch thick
- ½ cup melted vanilla ice cream
- ½ cup raisins (optional)
- ½ cup (3½ ounces) granulated sugar
- 1 tablespoon lemon juice
- 1 teaspoon vanilla extract
- 1 teaspoon ground cinnamon
- ½ teaspoon salt

TOPPING
- 1 cup (5 ounces) all-purpose flour
- ½ cup packed (3½ ounces) light brown sugar
- 6 tablespoons unsalted butter, melted
- ½ teaspoon salt

To find out which vanilla ice cream is our favorite, go to **CooksCountry.com/vanillaicecream**.

A scoop on the side echoes the vanilla ice cream we use in the apple filling.

1. FOR THE CRUST: Combine water and sour cream in bowl. Process flour, sugar, and salt in food processor until combined, about 5 seconds. Scatter butter over top and pulse until butter is size of large peas, about 10 pulses. Add sour cream mixture and pulse until dough forms clumps and no dry flour remains, about 12 pulses, scraping down sides of bowl as needed.

2. Turn dough onto sheet of plastic wrap and form into 4-inch disk. Wrap tightly in plastic and refrigerate for 1 hour. (Wrapped dough can be refrigerated for up to 2 days or frozen for up to 1 month. If frozen, let dough thaw completely on counter before rolling.)

3. FOR THE FILLING: Toss all ingredients in large bowl until apples are evenly coated. Let sit at room temperature for at least 1 hour or up to 2 hours.

4. Adjust oven rack to lower-middle position and heat oven to 350 degrees. Let chilled dough sit on counter to soften slightly, about 10 minutes, before rolling. Roll dough into 12-inch circle on lightly floured counter. Loosely roll dough around rolling pin and gently unroll it onto 9-inch pie plate, letting excess dough hang over edge. Ease dough into plate by gently lifting edge of dough with your

hand while pressing into plate bottom with your other hand.

5. Trim overhang to ½ inch beyond lip of plate. Tuck overhang under itself; folded edge should be flush with edge of plate. Crimp dough evenly around edge of plate using your fingers. Wrap dough-lined plate loosely in plastic and refrigerate until dough is firm, at least 30 minutes.

6. FOR THE TOPPING: Stir all ingredients in bowl until no dry spots remain and mixture forms clumps. Refrigerate until ready to use.

7. Place dough-lined plate on parchment paper–lined rimmed baking sheet. Working with 1 large handful at a time, distribute apple mixture in plate, pressing into even layer and filling in gaps before adding more. Take care not to mound apple mixture in center of plate. Pour any remaining liquid from bowl into pie. Break topping (it will harden in refrigerator) into pea-size crumbs and distribute evenly over apple mixture. Pat topping lightly to adhere.

8. Bake pie on sheet until top is golden brown and paring knife inserted in center meets no resistance, about 1 hour 10 minutes, rotating sheet halfway through baking. Let pie cool on wire rack for at least 4 hours or preferably overnight. Serve.

Turkey for a Crowd

We wanted moist meat, beautiful brown skin, and enough turkey to feed the (entire extended) family.

by Alli Berkey

After carving the turkey, we drizzle it with a mixture of melted butter, thyme, and rosemary for a fancy finish.

WHENEVER IT'S MY turn to host Thanksgiving, the size of the guest list inevitably strikes fear into my heart. Twelve people? That's not a dinner party, that's a baseball team—plus umpires. For an event of this magnitude, I was in need of a foolproof recipe for an extra-large bird that was moist and beautifully browned and didn't hog the oven for half the day.

Roasting a whole turkey is an annual challenge. And when the turkey is gigantic, it's even more challenging. The bird takes a long time to cook, and the longer it's in the hot oven, the more likely it is to dry out. But I love a challenge, and I was determined to find the best way.

I made several trial runs in the test kitchen, following existing big-turkey recipes that called for a wide range of temperatures, times, and techniques. Some used high heat to achieve beautiful browning but gave me dry breast meat. Others used gentler temperatures but took upwards of 6 hours to cook through. Still others called for frequent basting or even starting the bird breast side down and flipping it halfway through cooking. This method holds promise for more modestly sized turkeys, but turning over a hot, half-baked, giant 20-pounder was a recipe for Thanksgiving disaster.

But one method stood out. It called for roasting the seasoned turkey in an ovensafe plastic bag for just about 3 hours. Really? Sure, we've used the bag in the past for more forgiving meats, such as pot roast—which, for all its appeal, is not a looker of a dish. But turkey is a holiday centerpiece that has to be beautiful. I had my doubts. The bag might help me get moist meat. But browning? And so fast?

I figured I had nothing to lose, so I dusted the inside of the bag with flour (a step manufacturers recommend to help prevent the bag from bursting; see "Cooking in an Oven Bag: What You Need to Know"), set the bag in a roasting pan, put my turkey inside, sealed the bag, and slipped the whole lot into the oven.

My pessimism transformed into elation when my timer went off some 3 hours later. I pulled the roasting pan from the oven and cut the bag away from the turkey to reveal a gorgeous, golden-brown showstopper of a bird. And the meat? Juicy.

Despite my misgivings about browning, the bag actually worked in my favor. The trapped steam created even heat, ensuring uniform rendering of fat and consistent browning, too. In fact, the biggest challenge I had with the bag was getting the bird out of it. A bit of muscle and a pair of trusty kitchen shears solved my problem (see "Remove the Bag; Leave the Turkey").

What's turkey without gravy? Not much. While some recipes suggest loading carrots, celery, and onion into the bag with the turkey and then creating a gravy with the contents of the bag, I found that this method gave me subpar gravy lacking in flavor. Instead, I took a cue from more-traditional recipes for smaller birds and loaded the bottom of the roasting pan with onion, carrots, celery, herbs, chicken stock, white wine, and for even more flavor, the turkey neck. I then positioned a V-rack over the mixture and placed the bagged turkey in it.

Sure enough, this setup gave me deeply browned vegetables and a caramel-colored fond in the bottom of the pan that was just right to scrape up and incorporate into the juices the turkey had released in the bag. With these, I was able to create a rich, unctuous gravy.

It's a holiday! So after carving the turkey, I decided to gild the lily by drizzling it with melted butter that I'd stirred together with thyme, rosemary, salt, and pepper. Sure, my bird was moist enough, but this simple, buttery gesture made it even more special. I called over my coworkers to taste and talk about this turkey. But among the twelve of us, we had very little to say. Our mouths were full.

TURKEY AND GRAVY FOR A CROWD

Serves 12, with leftovers

Since different-size turkeys exude varying amounts of juices, buy a full quart of broth so you'll be sure to have enough liquid when making the gravy. We recommend using a "self-basting" or prebrined turkey. You will need a turkey-size oven bag here; this recipe was developed using Reynolds Oven Bags. Before putting the turkey in the oven, make sure all sides of the bag are tucked into the roasting pan to prevent them from touching the oven walls. Fresh sage can be substituted for the rosemary, if desired.

- 1 (18- to 20-pound) prebrined turkey, neck reserved, giblets discarded
- 1 large onion, chopped
- 6 carrots, peeled and chopped
- 3 celery ribs, chopped
- 2 cups chicken broth, plus extra as needed
- 1 cup dry white wine
- 3 sprigs fresh thyme plus 1 tablespoon minced
- 1 sprig fresh rosemary plus 1 tablespoon minced
- 2 bay leaves
- 10 tablespoons unsalted butter Kosher salt and pepper
- 1 tablespoon plus ⅔ cup all-purpose flour
- 1 turkey-size oven bag

1. Adjust oven rack to lowest position and heat oven to 350 degrees. Place turkey neck, onion, carrots, celery, 2 cups broth, wine, thyme sprigs, rosemary sprig, and bay leaves in large roasting pan. Set V-rack in pan.

2. Pat turkey dry with paper towels. Tuck wings behind back and tie legs together with kitchen twine. Microwave 2 tablespoons butter in bowl until melted, about 30 seconds. Brush turkey with melted butter and season with salt and pepper.

3. Add 1 tablespoon flour to oven bag, then hold bag closed and shake to distribute flour. Place turkey in bag. Tie bag closed with kitchen twine or included bag tie. Place turkey in V-rack and cut four 1-inch slits in top of bag to allow steam to escape. Roast until breasts register 160 degrees and thighs register 175 degrees, 2¾ to 3¼ hours.

4. Remove pan from oven. Using paring knife, poke holes in underside of bag to release liquid into pan. (Be careful of escaping steam.) Using kitchen shears, cut bag around perimeter of turkey and remove top of bag. Holding tied end, pull bottom portion of bag from underneath turkey, using tongs to tilt turkey as needed. Discard bag. Transfer V-rack with turkey to rimmed baking sheet, tent with aluminum foil, and let rest for 1 hour.

5. Using wooden spoon, scrape up any browned bits from bottom of pan. Discard turkey neck. Strain contents of pan through fine-mesh strainer set over large bowl. Using spoon, press on vegetables to extract as much liquid as possible; discard vegetables. Let juices sit to allow fat to rise to top, about 5 minutes. Using ladle, skim fat from top of juices and reserve ½ cup; discard remaining fat.

6. If necessary, add enough extra broth to defatted juices to measure 6 cups. Combine reserved fat and remaining ⅔ cup flour in medium saucepan and cook over medium heat until mixture is color of peanut butter, about 10 minutes, stirring occasionally. Slowly whisk in defatted juices and bring to simmer. Cook until gravy is slightly thickened and coats back of spoon, about 5 minutes. Season with salt and pepper to taste. Cover and keep warm.

7. Carve turkey and transfer to serving platter. Microwave remaining 8 tablespoons butter with minced thyme, minced rosemary, ¾ teaspoon salt, and ¼ teaspoon pepper until melted, about 1 minute. Pour herb butter over turkey. Serve, passing gravy separately.

To find out which chicken broth won our testing, go to **CooksCountry.com/chickenbroth**.

Remove the Bag; Leave the Turkey

Here's how to safely remove the cooked turkey from the bag.

1. Use a paring knife to carefully poke holes in the bottom of the bag; let the flavorful juices drain into the roasting pan. You'll need these juices for gravy.

2. Use kitchen shears to cut the bag around the perimeter of the turkey; discard the top portion of the bag.

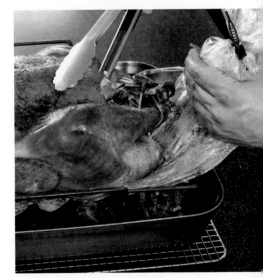

3. While tilting the bird with tongs, hold the knotted end of the bag and gently pull to remove the bag bottom from beneath the turkey. Discard the bag bottom.

Cooking in an Oven Bag: What You Need to Know

The purpose of an oven bag is to trap heat and steam to accelerate cooking and the rendering of fat. But what about browning? Can the Maillard reaction—the chemical reaction that creates flavor when foods are browned—occur in the relatively moist environment of an oven bag? It sure can; our turkeys came out with beautifully browned skin. Here are a few additional tips to add to your, ahem, bag of tricks.

BIG BAGS ARE A MUST
Oven bags are available in many sizes. Be sure to buy bags sized for large turkeys.

Mind the temperature.
Because the bag traps heat and steam, the heat energy in the bag will be greater than the heat energy of the dry air in the oven. The higher heat energy in the bag contributes nice browning. Never use plastic oven bags in an oven set to a temperature above 400 degrees.

Add flour to the bag.
Bag manufacturers claim that adding flour helps prevent the bag from bursting. While the slits cut into the bag likely do most of that work, the flour does absorb some moisture and thus reduces the pressure in the bag a bit.

Seal the bag well.
Reynolds Oven Bags—the product seen most in markets—come with zip ties to seal the bag. Use them, as a poorly sealed bag will not trap heat and steam as effectively as a tightly sealed bag.

Put the bagged turkey on a V-rack.
Turkey skin will not turn crispy if it cooks in its own juices. Elevating the bagged turkey on a V-rack allows the juices exuded by the turkey to accumulate away from the bird in pockets that form along the bottom of the bag.

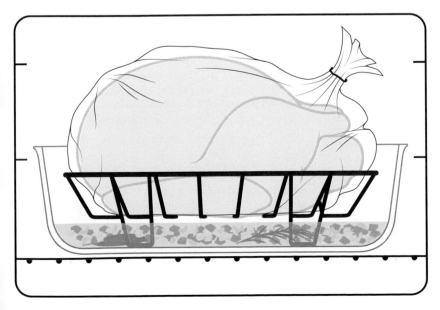

Fully Loaded Sweet Potatoes

Swapping out russets for sweet potatoes in a gratin? Not so fast. We had a better idea.

by Katie Leaird

Scallions, bacon, extra-sharp cheddar, and sour cream make this casserole "fully loaded."

THIS YEAR I wanted a new way to bring sweet potatoes, with their vibrant hue and sweet flavor, to the holiday table. I had my doubts about simply swapping them in for regular spuds in a bacon-studded potato gratin, and my first test confirmed my fears: When I pulled my gratin from the oven, all I had was a mushy mess.

Sweet potatoes and more-familiar russet or yellow potatoes are from completely different botanical families and behave differently under heat. Whereas slices of standard potatoes simply soften when cooked, sweet potato slices exude water. In a gratin, this means that instead of a thick, luxurious sauce, you get a stewy, watery puddle. Not exactly festive.

A consultation with our science editor gave me hope. He told me about an enzyme in sweet potatoes that, when activated by gentle heat (in this case, between 120 and 160 degrees), helps the slices hold their shape and keeps much of their water trapped. The slices eventually soften completely, without falling apart into mush.

After fiddling around on the stovetop, I found the microwave to be the best method for this step. Just a few minutes did the trick. I also tossed the sliced sweet potatoes with some paprika and garlic powder before microwaving them for an early flavor boost.

Once the sweet potatoes were baked into a gratin, however, I realized that my dish was suffering from an identity crisis. Their sweetness didn't sit comfortably with the traditional gratin ingredients (chicken stock, white wine, and heavy cream). I was trying to wedge a square peg into a round hole. So I decided to take my sweet potatoes, and the knowledge I'd gained, in a new direction: fully loaded.

Nixing the creamy, winey sauce base, I instead focused on a suite of crowd-pleasing add-ins, starting with 2 cups of shredded extra-sharp cheddar distributed between the layers of sweet potato. The cheese bound the slices into cohesive layers as the casserole baked and provided a pungent, cheesy counterpoint to the sweet roots.

To round out the dish, I added some crispy bits of bacon (there was no way I was going to lose this component), a sprinkle of fresh scallions, and a dollop of sour cream for a tangy finish. Fully loaded? Oh yes. And fully dressed for a holiday dinner.

LOADED SWEET POTATO CASSEROLE *Serves 6 to 8*

Any shallow baking dish of similar size will work for this recipe. A mandolin makes quick work of evenly slicing the sweet potatoes.

- 3 pounds sweet potatoes, peeled and sliced ¼ inch thick
- 2 tablespoons extra-virgin olive oil
- 1 tablespoon smoked paprika
- 1 tablespoon garlic powder
- 1¼ teaspoons salt
- ½ teaspoon pepper
- 8 ounces extra-sharp cheddar cheese, shredded (2 cups)
- 4 slices bacon, cut into ½-inch pieces
- 3 scallions, sliced thin on bias
  Sour cream

1. Adjust oven rack to middle position and heat oven to 400 degrees. Grease 13 by 9-inch baking dish.

2. Toss potatoes, oil, paprika, garlic powder, salt, and pepper together in large bowl. Microwave, covered, until potatoes are just tender, 10 to 12 minutes, stirring halfway through microwaving. Uncover and let sit until cool enough to handle, about 15 minutes.

3. Shingle one-third of potatoes in prepared dish, then sprinkle with ½ cup cheddar. Repeat with half of remaining potatoes and ½ cup cheddar. Shingle remaining potatoes in dish and pour any remaining liquid from bowl over top. Sprinkle with remaining 1 cup cheddar. Bake until tip of paring knife inserted into potatoes meets no resistance and cheese is spotty brown, about 30 minutes.

4. Meanwhile, cook bacon in 10-inch nonstick skillet over medium heat until crispy, 6 to 8 minutes. Using slotted spoon, transfer bacon to paper towel–lined plate.

5. Transfer dish to wire rack and let cool for 15 minutes. Sprinkle bacon and scallions over top and serve, passing sour cream separately.

Quit Your Yam-mering

The terms "yam" and "sweet potato" are often used interchangeably, but they technically don't refer to the same vegetable. True yams have woolly, fibrous skins and white flesh and are bland, with relatively little sweetness. Yams are common in tropical and African cooking. Sweet potatoes come in a variety of colors, but the most common is the bright orange variety most supermarkets carry. As their name implies, they are very sweet.

SWEET POTATO
Call it what it is.

Key Ingredient

Smoked paprika might seem like an odd seasoning for our Loaded Sweet Potato Casserole, but we found that it enhanced the bacon's smoky presence while also adding depth. Our favorite is **Simply Organic Smoked Paprika**, which is made from peppers smoked over oak fires in Spain. It can add smoky complexity to a variety of dishes: Try it in soups, rubbed into meats before roasting, or mixed into mayonnaise for an easy, deeply flavorful sauce.

Extra-Crunchy Green Bean Casserole

Our latest take on this holiday stalwart is like an old friend in a new suit.

by Alli Berkey

THE THANKSGIVING TABLE seems incomplete without green bean casserole—that well-loved combination of tender green beans coated in a savory, creamy mushroom sauce (er, canned cream of mushroom soup) and topped with crunchy fried onions. I love it, too. But this year, I wanted a crunchier topping, a sauce with an extra note of complexity, and a slightly more streamlined process.

Most recipes for green bean casserole, including some of ours, follow a similar routine: Precook the green beans, create a silky cream sauce, stir it all together in a casserole dish, top with crunchy onions, and bake until bubbly. Easy, right? Yes. And delicious. But I wanted it to be even easier.

The first order of business was the sauce. Besides cream and chicken broth, I settled on cremini mushrooms for their meaty flavor; by browning them first, I got rid of any liquid that might dilute the sauce. Garlic, thyme, salt, pepper, butter, and white wine rounded out the flavors. By adding flour, I created a creamy, flavorful sauce that was far better than the canned stuff.

Simply stirring raw green beans into this sauce before baking didn't allow the beans to cook through. Blanching the beans to give them a head start was one option, but the microwave was even easier. About 8 minutes produced the best texture.

To me, the best part of this casserole is the fried-onion topping, and early tests proved that prefab fried onions straight from the can just can't be beat. To add even more crunch, I cooked some panko bread crumbs in butter (again in the microwave) to stir into the onions before topping my casserole and sending it to the oven.

This worked beautifully, but a fellow test cook wondered why the crunchy topping had to be baked at all. She was right: Simply spooning the fried-onion mixture over the baked casserole kept it supercrunchy. This meant that I could prepare the topping while the casserole baked, streamlining the process even further.

My tasters and I agreed: This soft, creamy, flavorful casserole with a supercrunchy top was on the fast track to my Thanksgiving table.

We bump up store-bought fried onions with butter-enriched panko bread crumbs.

THE AMERICAN TABLE

Among the displays at the National Inventors Hall of Fame, visitors will find some familiar names: George Washington Carver, Thomas Edison, the Wright Brothers. But they'll also find a less-familiar name: Dorcas Reilly.

In the early 1950s, Reilly, one of the first test cooks employed by the Campbell's Soup Company, was tasked with creating new recipes calling for Campbell's cream of mushroom condensed soup. The soup was already a common pantry staple, particularly in the Midwest, where home cooks used it in casseroles (earning it the nickname "Lutheran binder"), and Campbell's wanted to sell even more.

In 1955, after a few misfires, Campbell's released Reilly's recipe, called "Green Bean Bake," to almost immediate success. Today, Campbell's estimates that nearly 30 million homes serve the stuff each holiday season.

Dorcas Riley (above) created the beloved casserole in the 1950s.

EXTRA-CRUNCHY GREEN BEAN CASSEROLE

Serves 6 to 8

White mushrooms can be substituted for the cremini, if desired.

TOPPING
- ½ cup panko bread crumbs
- 1 tablespoon unsalted butter, melted
- 2½ cups canned fried onions

CASSEROLE
- 2 pounds green beans, trimmed and cut into 1-inch pieces
- 3 tablespoons unsalted butter
- 1 pound cremini mushrooms, trimmed and sliced thin
- 1 tablespoon minced fresh thyme
- 2 garlic cloves, minced
- 1½ teaspoons salt
- ½ teaspoon pepper
- ¼ cup all-purpose flour
- 1½ cups chicken broth
- 1½ cups heavy cream
- ½ cup dry white wine

1. FOR THE TOPPING: Combine panko and melted butter in bowl. Microwave, stirring occasionally, until panko is golden brown, about 2 minutes. Let cool completely, then stir in fried onions; set aside.

2. FOR THE CASSEROLE: Adjust oven rack to middle position and heat oven to 400 degrees. Combine green beans and ½ cup water in large bowl. Cover and microwave until green beans are just tender, about 8 minutes, stirring halfway through microwaving. Drain green beans in colander; set aside.

3. Melt butter in 12-inch nonstick skillet over medium-high heat. Add mushrooms, thyme, garlic, salt, and pepper and cook until liquid is nearly evaporated, 6 to 8 minutes.

4. Stir in flour and cook for 1 minute. Slowly whisk in broth, cream, and wine and bring to boil. Cook, stirring occasionally, until sauce has thickened, 4 to 6 minutes. Transfer green beans to 13 by 9-inch baking dish. Pour sauce over green beans and toss to combine.

5. Bake until bubbling and green beans are completely tender, about 25 minutes. Remove from oven, top with fried-onion mixture, and let cool for 10 minutes. Serve.

TO MAKE AHEAD
At end of step 4, let casserole cool completely. Cover dish with aluminum foil and refrigerate for up to 24 hours. To serve, bake, covered, until green beans are heated through and completely tender, about 40 minutes. Uncover and continue to bake until edges begin to brown, about 10 minutes longer.

Radicchio Salad

For variety in our fall salad rotation, we turned to the unique flavor and texture of radicchio.

by Ashley Moore

RADICCHIO IS OFTEN reserved for braises or pasta dishes, but that's a shame: The sharp, pleasantly bitter flavor of this vibrant purple and white, softball-size sphere can be a welcome addition to many dishes. For this recipe, I wanted to highlight radicchio in its crisp, raw form by simply tossing it with a handful of ingredients to make a refreshing, flavorful, and brightly colored salad.

I began by making a handful of the recipes that I found for radicchio salads. Some salads were surprisingly delicate, combining the radicchio with assorted fruit and nuts and finishing with sweet vinaigrettes. Others were more aggressive, featuring strong cheeses and spicy dressings. I set out to find a sweet spot somewhere in the middle; I also wanted to find a way to tone down the hearty chew of this vegetable's somewhat fibrous leaves.

My tasters loved how sweet vinaigrettes played off the radicchio's bitterness in the delicate versions we tried, so I whisked together honey, white wine vinegar, olive oil, and potent Dijon mustard. For added interest and a pop of green, I tossed in a few handfuls of peppery baby arugula. Parmesan cheese—thinly shaved with a vegetable peeler, a fancy-looking touch that couldn't be easier to produce—added salty depth. Finally, a generous handful of toasted and chopped almonds and some crisp sliced apple added even more crunch.

As for the radicchio, one recipe dealt with the chewiness issue by calling for finely shredding the leaves, but that seemed like a lot of work for a simple salad. Instead, I found that simply coring the radicchio, chopping it into 1-inch pieces, and letting it sit in the vinaigrette for about 15 minutes before adding the other ingredients softened its fibrous texture and made for more pleasant eating.

This salad was so good that I decided to create another version with the flavor pumped up a bit. I substituted rich balsamic vinegar for the white wine vinegar and used pear instead of apple. Whole parsley leaves replaced the baby arugula, and I swapped in crumbled blue cheese for the Parmesan shavings and toasted and chopped pistachios for the almonds.

RADICCHIO SALAD WITH APPLE, ARUGULA, AND PARMESAN
Serves 4

Letting the radicchio sit in the dressing for 15 minutes softens its fibrous texture. The easiest way make thin Parmesan shavings is with a sharp vegetable peeler.

- 5 tablespoons extra-virgin olive oil
- 3 tablespoons honey
- 2 tablespoons white wine vinegar
- 1 teaspoon Dijon mustard
  Salt and pepper
- 1 head radicchio (10 ounces), halved, cored, and cut into 1-inch pieces
- 1 apple, cored, halved, and sliced thin
- 2 ounces (2 cups) baby arugula
- 2 ounces Parmesan cheese, shaved with vegetable peeler
- ¼ cup almonds, toasted and chopped

1. Whisk oil, honey, vinegar, mustard, 1 teaspoon salt, and ½ teaspoon pepper together in large bowl. Fold in radicchio and let sit until slightly softened, about 15 minutes.

2. Add apple, arugula, and Parmesan to radicchio mixture and toss to combine. Season with salt and pepper to taste. Transfer to platter, sprinkle with almonds, and serve.

RADICCHIO SALAD WITH PEAR, PARSLEY, AND BLUE CHEESE

Substitute balsamic vinegar for white wine vinegar, 1 ripe pear for apple, 1 cup fresh parsley leaves for arugula, ½ cup crumbled blue cheese for Parmesan, and pistachios for almonds.

We balance boldly bitter radicchio with sweet honey and apple in this satisfying salad.

Radicchio Prep Is as Easy as Halve, Core, and Chop

Halve Radicchio
Use a chef's knife to halve the radicchio through the core.

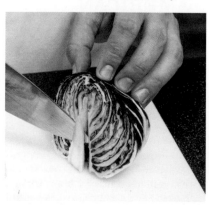

Cut Out Core
Use the tip of your knife to cut out the tough, woody core.

Chop into Pieces
Place each half cut side down; cut it into strips and then into 1-inch pieces.

Jalapeño-Cheddar Cornbread

This Thanksgiving, we're saving a place at the table for this cheesy, spicy side.

by Cecelia Jenkins

I GREW UP believing cornbread could come only from a box; in my house, it was the same flavor, texture, and color every time. We made it this way for ease, we thought. But cornbread from scratch really isn't much harder to make, and starting from scratch opens up a vast world of cornbread varieties. Plain and simple, I grew up missing out. So I jumped at the chance to create a method and flavor combination to get beyond the box: jalapeño-cheddar cornbread.

My goal was a vibrant jalapeño kick balanced by savory cheesy tang and subtly sweet corn flavor. Experimenting with existing recipes, I learned that this balance wasn't easy to achieve. One version, which called for a can of creamed corn, was much too sweet, and the corn added so much moisture that the bread turned out gummy. Some versions were sandy, dry, and flavorless, while others were too spicy, too cheesy, or peppered with distracting corn kernels that overshadowed the chile and cheese.

My first challenge was to nail down the bread's texture. I needed a dense, moist, tender cornbread that was sturdy enough to handle the add-ins. Most cornbreads are made with cornmeal and flour; the ratio of those ingredients determines how dense or fluffy the cornbread will be. After some tests, I settled on 1½ cups cornmeal to 1 cup flour for optimal texture. Two tablespoons of sugar added just enough sweetness to enhance the corn flavor.

I had many jalapeño options to consider. Canned? Pickled? Fresh? Testing these variables side by side, I found that canned jalapeños were so mild we could barely taste them, while just 1 tablespoon of minced pickled jalapeños sent us scrambling for water (their heat intensifies in the vinegar brine). Fresh jalapeños, seeded to control their burn, were the answer. Four minced chiles studded the cornbread with beautiful emerald-green flecks and provided enough, but not too much, heat.

Now for the cheese. I couldn't use any old cheddar because I wanted strong flavor—that meant extra-sharp, the most pungent variety. I stirred most of the shredded cheese into the batter to distribute the flavor throughout, reserving ½ cup to sprinkle over the top, which baked into a beautiful cheesy crust.

JALAPEÑO-CHEDDAR CORNBREAD
Serves 8

We developed this recipe using fine-ground cornmeal. Our favorite is Arrowhead Mills Organic Yellow Cornmeal; however, more commonly available Quaker Yellow Cornmeal will work just fine here. Do not use coarse-ground cornmeal. Do not use mild or regular sharp cheddar cheese in this recipe, as its flavor doesn't stand out like that of extra-sharp cheddar. You can use an 8-inch square baking pan instead of a 9-inch round cake pan. If you use a dark-colored cake pan, reduce the baking time in step 3 to 30 to 35 minutes.

- 1½ cups (7½ ounces) yellow cornmeal
- 1 cup (5 ounces) all-purpose flour
- 2 tablespoons sugar
- 1½ teaspoons baking powder
- ½ teaspoon baking soda
- 1½ teaspoons salt
- 1¼ cups whole milk
- 2 large eggs
- 6 tablespoons unsalted butter, melted
- 6 ounces extra-sharp cheddar cheese, shredded (1½ cups)
- 4 jalapeño chiles, stemmed, seeded, and minced (¾ cup)

1. Adjust oven rack to middle position and heat oven to 400 degrees. Grease light-colored 9-inch round cake pan, line with parchment paper, and grease parchment.

2. Whisk cornmeal, flour, sugar, baking powder, baking soda, and salt together in large bowl. Whisk milk, eggs, and melted butter together in second bowl. Stir milk mixture into cornmeal mixture until just combined. Stir in 1 cup cheddar and jalapeños until just combined. Transfer batter to prepared pan, smooth top with spatula, and sprinkle with remaining ½ cup cheddar.

3. Bake until cornbread is deep golden brown, top is firm to touch, and paring knife inserted in center comes out clean, 35 to 40 minutes, rotating pan halfway through baking. Let cornbread cool in pan on wire rack for 10 minutes. Remove cornbread from pan, discarding parchment, and let cool completely, about 1 hour. Serve.

To learn which 9-inch cake pan won our testing, go to **CooksCountry.com/cakepan**.

We stir most of the extra-sharp cheddar into the batter, saving ½ cup to sprinkle on top.

Building a Bold Cornbread

You can't just dump extra ingredients into cornbread and expect the recipe to work; you have to select the ingredients carefully and make sure they work together to create a balanced result that maintains the proper texture.

For this recipe, we found that just 2 tablespoons of sugar reinforced the sweet corn flavor and enhanced exterior browning, while 1½ cups of extra-sharp cheddar provided dual wallops of richness and tang. Four minced fresh jalapeños provided a bright counterpoint to the earthiness of the cornmeal and the richness of the cheese.

Working together, these ingredients make a perfectly balanced cornbread with big, bold flavor.

Easy Fish and Chips

For the crispiest coating, we needed just four ingredients.

by Ashley Moore

IN DETROIT, PEOPLE have been flocking to Scotty Simpson's restaurant for crispy, golden-brown fish and chips since the 1950s. After hearing about executive food editor Bryan Roof's trip to the restaurant (see "Old-School Fish and Chips"), I wanted to find a way to make this light, perfectly crunchy version of fish and chips at home. A tall feat, sure. But I was up for a challenge.

I began my research with a phone call to Harry Barber, the owner of Scotty Simpson's. Barber began working at the restaurant as a dishwasher on his first day of high school decades ago; he purchased the restaurant, as well as the recipe for its famous fish and chips, in 2002. I asked Barber how he made the batter for the fish, but I didn't get very far (trust me—I tried all the tricks up my sleeve to get the information out of him). The recipe is a closely guarded secret. Instead, I needed to rely on Roof's excellent food memory, the pictures from the trip, and the various videos I found online to try to re-create this dish.

As the restaurant does, I chose to use cod because of its firm texture and wide availability. After trying precut fillets from the fish counter at the grocery store, which tended to be inconsistently sized, I found that I got better results when I bought a large fillet and portioned it myself.

I knew that the coating needed to be light and crispy, and after making six batches using existing fish and chips recipes, I narrowed my ingredient list to include just beer, flour, cornstarch, and a leavener. The beer not only provided a subtle sweetness that tasters preferred but also made the coating slightly more acidic, which helped prevent it from getting too tough. (If you prefer, you can substitute seltzer for the beer; it, too, provides the right balance.)

Equal parts all-purpose flour and cornstarch produced the ideal light, golden-brown, shell-like coating I was after. I found that letting the batter rest for 20 minutes before coating the fish helped it adhere better. And a bit of baking powder in the mix helped give the coating a light, airy texture.

For the French fries, I relied on our almost hands-off test kitchen method, which is a cold-fry technique. I simply put my sliced Yukon Gold potatoes into room-temperature oil in a large Dutch oven, brought the oil up to temperature, and cooked the fries, stirring just once,

A bit of baking powder added to the batter helps create a seriously crispy coating.

until they were done. Then I realized that to get the hot fish and chips on the table at the same time, I'd need to tweak this method slightly. I cooked the potatoes until they were just golden, removed them to make room for the fish, and then returned them to the hot oil for just 1 minute to finish cooking after the fish was ready.

I called over my coworkers for one final taste. We were thrilled with the crispy, tender, savory results.

Pro Tip for Frying

To keep the pieces of fish from sticking together in the hot oil, spear one piece of battered fish with a fork, let the excess batter drip off, and then drag the fish along the oil's surface before releasing it to sink. This gives the batter a chance to set up and harden so that it won't adhere to other pieces it touches in the oil.

Order of Operations

This recipe comes together easily if you follow this simple sequence.
1. Make the tartar sauce.
2. Make the batter, portion the fish, and cut the potatoes.
3. Start the fries in cold oil, and cook them until they're almost done.
4. Batter and fry the fish in two batches.
5. Return the fries to the oil for just 1 minute to finish cooking them.
6. Serve the fries with the fish and sauce.

FISH AND CHIPS

Serves 4

Try to find large Yukon Gold potatoes, 10 to 12 ounces each, that are similar in size. We prefer peanut or vegetable oil for frying and do not recommend using canola oil since it can impart off-flavors. Use a Dutch oven that holds 6 quarts or more. A light-bodied American lager, such as Budweiser, works best here. If you prefer to cook without alcohol, substitute seltzer for the beer. We prefer to use cod for this recipe, but haddock and halibut will also work well. Serve with Tartar Sauce (recipe follows), if desired.

- 1 cup (5 ounces) all-purpose flour
- 1 cup (4 ounces) cornstarch
  Salt and pepper
- 1 teaspoon baking powder
- 1½ cups beer
- 1 (2-pound) skinless cod fillet, about 1 inch thick
- 2½ pounds large Yukon Gold potatoes, unpeeled
- 8 cups peanut or vegetable oil
  Lemon wedges

1. Whisk flour, cornstarch, 1½ teaspoons salt, and baking powder together in large bowl. Add beer and whisk until smooth. Cover with plastic wrap and refrigerate for at least 20 minutes.

2. Cut cod crosswise into 8 equal fillets (about 4 ounces each). Pat cod dry with paper towels and season with salt and pepper; refrigerate until ready to use.

3. Square off each potato by cutting ¼-inch-thick slice from each of its 4 long sides. Cut potatoes lengthwise into ¼-inch-thick planks. Stack 3 to 4 planks and cut into ¼-inch fries. Repeat with remaining planks. (Do not place potatoes in water.)

4. Line rimmed baking sheet with triple layer of paper towels. Combine potatoes and oil in large Dutch oven. Cook over high heat until oil has reached rolling boil, about 7 minutes. Continue to cook, without stirring, until potatoes are limp but exteriors are beginning to firm, about 15 minutes longer. Using tongs, stir potatoes, gently scraping up any that stick, and continue to cook, stirring occasionally, until just lightly golden brown, about 4 minutes longer (fries will not be fully cooked at this point). Using spider skimmer or slotted spoon, transfer fries to prepared sheet. Skim off any browned bits left in pot.

5. Set wire rack in second rimmed baking sheet. Transfer fish to batter and toss to evenly coat. Heat oil over medium-high heat to 375 degrees. Using fork, remove 4 pieces of fish from batter, allowing excess batter to drip back into bowl, and add to hot oil, briefly dragging fish along surface of oil to prevent sticking. Adjust burner, if necessary, to maintain oil temperature between 350 and 375 degrees.

6. Cook fish, stirring gently to prevent pieces from sticking together, until deep golden brown and crispy, about 4 minutes per side. Using spider skimmer or slotted spoon, transfer fish to prepared rack and skim off any browned bits left in pot. Return oil to 375 degrees and repeat with remaining 4 pieces of fish.

7. Return oil to 375 degrees. Add fries to oil and cook until deep golden brown and crispy, about 1 minute. Using spider skimmer or slotted spoon, transfer fries back to prepared sheet and season with salt. Transfer fish and chips to platter. Serve with lemon wedges.

TARTAR SAUCE

Makes about 1 cup

The test kitchen's favorite mayo is Blue Plate Real Mayonnaise, which is not available in all areas of the country. Hellmann's Real Mayonnaise, which is available nationwide, was a close second and is a great option.

- ¾ cup mayonnaise
- ¼ cup dill pickle relish
- 1½ teaspoons distilled white vinegar
- ½ teaspoon Worcestershire sauce
- ½ teaspoon pepper
- ⅛ teaspoon salt

Combine all ingredients in small bowl. Cover with plastic wrap and refrigerate until flavors meld, about 15 minutes.

Old-School Fish and Chips

by Bryan Roof

ON THE ROAD

AS YOU CARVE your way through the quiet side streets of the Brightmoor neighborhood in northwest Detroit, the last dining option you expect to find is a faded brick seafood shack. Detroit, after all, is known more for pizza and Coney Island dogs than for fried saltwater fish. But Scotty Simpson's has been selling traditional fish and chips on this corner since 1950, building a loyal following that crosses generations.

Harold "Harry" Barber took a dishwashing job at Scotty Simpson's on his first day of high school in 1966 and has been there ever since. He "didn't know it was gonna be an 'ever since' kinda thing," but about 15 years ago, as Simpson made plans to retire, Barber asked him, "Can I buy a job?" So Simpson sold him the business. Even though he's the boss now, most days Barber can still be found behind the counter, tending to frying fillets of cod.

The menu is simple, well suited to the wood-paneled dining room. Model ships give a nod to the nautical, and a fog of fryer exhaust has yellowed some of the old photos and press clippings on the walls. It's a well-used space, filled with stories.

Barber is a man of few words, and when he comes around to my table to check on my meal, I tell him with all sincerity that it's wonderful. "As it should be," he responds, and walks back to the fryer.

Cutting French Fries Made Easy

Square Off Sides
Slicing off the four long sides of each potato eliminates the need for peeling and creates a stable base for the next cuts.

Cut into Planks, Then Fries
Cut the potatoes lengthwise into ¼-inch-thick planks, then cut the stacks of planks into fries. You're ready to fry!

Harry Barber (top), who is the owner of Scotty Simpson's as well as the fry cook, could fry fish to perfection in his sleep. The restaurant's decor is a combination of 1950s Detroit working-class charm (middle) and nautical kitsch, as evidenced by the model ships (bottom) and the numerous fish decoys hanging on the walls.

Texas Potato Pancakes

To do justice to the *Kartoffelpuffer* of Texas, we were after fluffy interiors surrounded by maximum crunch.

by Morgan Bolling

EVERY NOVEMBER, THE small town of New Braunfels, Texas, hosts one of America's best kept secrets: Wurstfest, a "Ten-Day Salute to Sausage." But the festival is not all sausages and polka dancing: Some say the stars of the event are the Texas-size potato pancakes.

Known as *Kartoffelpuffer* in German, these pancakes, sold from a booth run by the local Rotary Club, consist of shredded potatoes mixed with onion, egg, and salt and then fried. The cakes feature moist, fluffy interiors surrounded by supremely crispy, lacy exteriors. Also, they're huge—up to 10 inches across. Some festival-goers dollop sour cream on them while others eat them with applesauce and powdered sugar.

I decided to create a home version of these pancakes. To get started, I scoured cookbooks for potato pancake (and latke) recipes and made several different versions. My early tests showed that russet potatoes, with their high starch content, were the best choice for producing crispy pancakes. But, like other potatoes, they have a very high water content, which can inhibit crispiness. I needed to lose some liquid.

I had a few test kitchen tricks up my sleeve. Wringing out the shredded potatoes in a clean dish towel drove off a lot of moisture, but I still had some liquid to banish. The answer: absorbent starch. But which starch? I tested flour, cornstarch, and instant potato flakes. The potato flakes added great flavor, but those pancakes fell apart in the oil. Though cornstarch produced structurally sound pancakes, it introduced a faint off-flavor. Flour was our favorite, turning the pancakes from soft and greasy to French-fry crispy.

The pancakes at Wurstfest are gigantic, but the folks making the great big cakes have a massive griddle to accommodate them. I chose a more modest (but still ample) size: 4 inches across. This allowed me to fit three at a time in my 12-inch skillet and to fry in batches, holding the cooked pancakes on a rack in a low oven to keep them

These crunchy cakes are traditionally served with tangy sour cream or sweet applesauce, but they're just as good on their own.

Shaping the Cakes
These crispy, lacy-edged pancakes are easy to make if you follow our simple steps.

Portion Mixture
Use a ⅓-cup dry measuring cup to ensure pancakes of the same size.

Flatten Pancakes
Press the mounds with the back of a spoon to flatten them.

Flip Gently
Use two spatulas to flip the pancakes to minimize splashing oil.

crispy until serving time. The smaller cakes were also easier to flip than the dinner plate–size versions. As I sprinkled salt and pepper on my final golden-brown pancake, I called my tasters. Some chose sour cream, others applesauce, but all agreed that these spuds were spot-on.

TEXAS POTATO PANCAKES
Serves 4 to 6
Shred the potatoes and onion on the large holes of a box grater or with the shredding disk of a food processor. The potato shreds may take on a red hue if left to sit out for a few minutes before cooking. This does not affect their flavor.

- 2 pounds russet potatoes, peeled and shredded
- ½ cup all-purpose flour
- 2 large eggs, lightly beaten
- ⅓ cup shredded onion
  Salt and pepper
- 1¼ cups vegetable oil, plus extra as needed
  Sour cream
  Applesauce

1. Adjust oven rack to middle position and heat oven to 200 degrees. Set wire rack in rimmed baking sheet and place in oven. Line large plate with triple layer of paper towels.
2. Place half of potatoes in center of clean dish towel. Gather ends together and twist tightly to squeeze out as much liquid as possible. Transfer to large bowl and repeat with remaining potatoes.
3. Stir flour, eggs, onion, and 1¼ teaspoons salt into potatoes until combined. Heat oil in 12-inch skillet over medium heat to 325 degrees. Using ⅓-cup dry measuring cup, place 3 portions of potato mixture in skillet and press into 4-inch disks with back of spoon.
4. Cook until deep golden brown, 3 to 4 minutes per side, carefully flipping pancakes with 2 spatulas. Transfer pancakes to paper towel–lined plate to drain, about 15 seconds per side, then transfer to prepared wire rack in oven.
5. Repeat with remaining potato mixture in 3 batches, stirring mixture, if necessary, to recombine and adding extra oil to skillet as needed to maintain ¼-inch depth. Season pancakes with salt and pepper to taste. Serve immediately, passing sour cream and applesauce separately.

Migas
This Tex-Mex scramble loaded with chiles, onion, and fried tortillas often falls short on flavor. We set out to change that.

by Morgan Bolling

SOME SAY THE breakfast of champions is a bowl of Wheaties. But after a trip to Austin, Texas, I call shenanigans. There, I ate a plate of *migas*—fluffy scrambled eggs cooked with chiles and onion and studded with pleasantly chewy strips of corn tortillas. The tortilla pieces infused the eggs with a deep, sweet toasted-corn flavor that made the dish a knockout. I set out to make a great homemade version.

Most recipes for migas (its name translates literally as "crumbs") call for either store-bought tortilla chips or fresh corn tortillas that are cut into strips, deep- or pan-fried, and stirred into scrambled eggs. I made a couple of versions with each. The chips added mostly saltiness and very little corn flavor. The fresh corn tortillas that I fried myself, on the other hand, took me right back to Texas.

As I cobbled together a working recipe, the first order of business was to make frying the tortilla strips as easy as possible. Deep frying was a little much at breakfast time. A shallow fry in a skillet, with just 3 tablespoons of oil, was much easier. I set the strips aside, willing myself not to eat them all before I got my eggs going.

After sautéing onion, red bell pepper, and fresh jalapeños, I followed our tried-and-true company method for scrambled eggs, starting them in a hot pan and quickly reducing the heat while gently folding the eggs to ensure fluffy curds. I added my tortilla strips during the final seconds of cooking and dug in. Disappointment: The tortillas added precious little flavor.

For my next batch, I fried the tortilla strips and then, instead of removing them, left them in the skillet, adding the vegetables to soften and then scrambling the eggs. A win. The crispy strips (and the oil they were fried in) offered tons of toasted-corn flavor to the eggs.

Briny jarred jalapeños (an easy substitute for fresh) added welcome heat and acidity, and ⅓ cup of shredded Monterey Jack helped create a creamy, cohesive scramble.

The fried tortilla strips add deep toasted-corn flavor and pockets of crunch.

MIGAS *Serves 4*
It's important to follow the visual cues when making the eggs, as your pan's thickness will affect the cooking time. If you're using an electric stove, heat a second burner on low and move the skillet to it when it's time to adjust the heat. For a spicier dish, use the larger amount of jarred jalapeños.

- 8 large eggs
  Salt and pepper
- 3 tablespoons vegetable oil
- 6 (6-inch) corn tortillas, cut into 1- by ½-inch strips
- 1 onion, chopped fine
- 1 small red bell pepper, stemmed, seeded, and chopped fine
- 1–2 tablespoons minced jarred jalapeños
- 1½ ounces Monterey Jack cheese, shredded (⅓ cup), plus extra for serving
- 1 tablespoon chopped fresh cilantro
  Salsa

1. Whisk eggs, ¼ teaspoon salt, and ¼ teaspoon pepper in bowl until thoroughly combined, about 1 minute; set aside.
2. Heat oil in 12-inch nonstick skillet over medium-high heat until shimmering. Add tortillas and ¼ teaspoon salt and cook, stirring occasionally, until golden brown, 4 to 6 minutes. Add onion, bell pepper, and jalapeños and cook, stirring occasionally, until vegetables are softened, 5 to 7 minutes.
3. Add egg mixture and, using heat-resistant rubber spatula, constantly and firmly scrape along bottom and sides of skillet until eggs begin to clump and spatula leaves trail on bottom of skillet, 30 to 60 seconds.
4. Reduce heat to low and gently but constantly fold egg mixture until clumped and still slightly wet, 30 to 60 seconds. Off heat, gently fold in Monterey Jack and cilantro. Serve immediately, passing salsa and extra Monterey Jack separately.

Browning Tortilla Strips
When frying the tortilla strips, it's important to take them to a nice golden brown; the browning develops flavor and ensures the right crisp-chewy texture in the finished dish.

PROPER BROWNING
For the best flavor and texture

Pumpkin Spice Muffins

This trendy spice mix was missing one thing: actual pumpkin flavor. Not anymore.

by Katie Leaird

PUMPKIN SPICE HAS proven to be a more pervasive and longer-lasting flavor trend than most. Case in point: I recently emerged from a local grocery store with bags filled with a range of products, from granola, energy bars, frozen waffles, and chai to spreadable cheese, all sporting a "pumpkin spice" profile. Curious to know how the pumpkin spice flavor was represented in these products, I returned to the test kitchen and laid out a grand tasting of these supermarket finds. We learned that "pumpkin spice," in most cases, simply meant sweet and slightly cinnamony, with the occasional soft note of nutmeg or ginger—more the flavor of the spices in pumpkin pie than of actual pumpkin.

This wasn't a huge surprise. Pumpkin on its own has a very mild, faintly earthy flavor similar to that of winter squash, which likely wouldn't translate to most of these products. But I love pumpkin, and I was dead set on packing it into my muffins alongside the spices. I knew there'd be a beneficial side effect: Pumpkin can add moisture and body to baked goods, and it's not the only vegetable to do so—think carrot cake or zucchini bread.

One thing I was certain of, though, was that I didn't want my muffins to taste like health food. Some muffin recipes employ pumpkin as a low-fat substitute for butter or oil, but I wasn't willing to ditch the fat. After experimenting with both options, I ultimately chose butter for its superior flavor.

Pumpkin pie spice, which is a pre-mixed combination of ground spices including cinnamon, ginger, nutmeg, allspice, and cloves, has been sold in the United States for more than a century. Home cooks depend on it to streamline pie making each Thanksgiving. I tested different products and, for due diligence, made my own blend. Once we'd tasted batches of muffins made with each, we came to a conclusion rarely reached in the test kitchen: My spice blend and store-bought blend versions didn't taste much different. With flavor being relatively equal, the store-bought blend won out for its convenience.

The batter was easy to prepare: I whisked together the dry ingredients (flour, sugar, baking powder, salt, and the spice mix) and combined this mixture with the whisked wet ingredients (canned pumpkin, melted butter, eggs,

A spice-infused streusel topping makes these beautiful muffins irresistibly good.

milk, and a bit of vanilla). I was then ready to scoop the relatively stiff batter into my well-greased muffin tins.

Once baked, my muffins were satisfyingly pumpkin spice–flavored and moist. But to make them just a measure more special, I added a crunchy, sweet, spicy streusel topping. The muffins were delicious the same morning they were baked, but thanks to that moisture-holding pumpkin, they were just as good a day or two later.

Go to **CooksCountry.com/muffintin** to find out which muffin tin took the top spot in our testing.

HOMEMADE PUMPKIN PIE SPICE

Makes 4 teaspoons

We found supermarket pumpkin pie spice acceptable in these muffins, but if you'd like to make your own, here's our formula.

- **2 teaspoons ground cinnamon**
- **1 teaspoon ground ginger**
- **½ teaspoon ground nutmeg**
- **½ teaspoon ground allspice**

Thoroughly combine all ingredients in small bowl.

PUMPKIN SPICE MUFFINS

Makes 12 muffins

Our favorite canned pumpkin puree is made by Libby's. One 15-ounce can of pumpkin puree is more than enough for this recipe. You can transfer the leftover pumpkin to a zipper-lock bag and freeze it for up to a month.

TOPPING

- **½ cup (2½ ounces) all-purpose flour**
- **5 tablespoons (2¼ ounces) sugar**
- **1 teaspoon pumpkin pie spice**
  Pinch salt
- **4 tablespoons unsalted butter, melted**

MUFFINS

- **2½ cups (12½ ounces) all-purpose flour**
- **2 cups (14 ounces) sugar**
- **1 tablespoon pumpkin pie spice**
- **2 teaspoons baking powder**
- **¾ teaspoon salt**
- **1 cup canned unsweetened pumpkin puree**
- **8 tablespoons unsalted butter, melted**
- **2 large eggs**
- **¼ cup milk**
- **2 teaspoons vanilla extract**

1. Adjust oven rack to middle position and heat oven to 375 degrees. Generously spray 12-cup muffin tin, including top, with baking spray with flour.
2. FOR THE TOPPING: Combine flour, sugar, pumpkin pie spice, and salt in bowl. Add melted butter and stir until evenly moistened and mixture resembles wet sand; set aside.
3. FOR THE MUFFINS: Whisk flour, sugar, pumpkin pie spice, baking powder, and salt together in bowl. Whisk pumpkin, melted butter, eggs, milk, and vanilla together in separate bowl. Stir flour mixture into pumpkin mixture until just combined.
4. Using greased ⅓-cup dry measuring cup, portion heaping ⅓ cup batter into each muffin cup (cups will be filled to rim). Sprinkle topping evenly over batter, about 1 tablespoon per muffin.
5. Bake muffins until golden brown and toothpick inserted in center comes out with few crumbs attached, 22 to 25 minutes, rotating muffin tin halfway through baking. Let muffins cool in muffin tin on wire rack for 10 minutes. Remove muffins from muffin tin and let cool on rack for 5 minutes. Serve.

Cumin Chicken and Winter Squash Salad

30-MINUTE SUPPER

Spicy Linguine with Olives and Garlic

30-MINUTE SUPPER

Moroccan Steak Tips and Couscous

30-MINUTE SUPPER

Portobello Mushroom Sandwiches

30-MINUTE SUPPER

Spicy Linguine with Olives and Garlic

Serves 4

WHY THIS RECIPE WORKS: Cooking garlic with relatively gentle heat allows it to soften while infusing the oil with its flavor.

- 1 **pound linguine**
  Salt and pepper
- 1 **tablespoon plus ½ cup extra-virgin olive oil**
- ½ **cup panko bread crumbs**
- 6 **garlic cloves, sliced thin**
- 1 **teaspoon red pepper flakes**
- 1 **cup pitted green olives, halved**
- ¼ **cup chopped fresh parsley**
- 2 **tablespoons lemon juice**

1. Bring 4 quarts water to boil in large pot. Add pasta and 1 tablespoon salt and cook, stirring often, until al dente. Reserve ¼ cup cooking water, then drain pasta and return it to pot.

2. Meanwhile, combine 1 tablespoon oil, panko, and ¼ teaspoon salt in 12-inch nonstick skillet. Cook over medium heat, stirring often, until panko is lightly toasted, about 3 minutes. Transfer to bowl.

3. Add remaining ½ cup oil, garlic, pepper flakes, ½ teaspoon salt, and ¼ teaspoon pepper to now-empty skillet and cook over medium heat until garlic begins to brown, about 4 minutes. Add olives, parsley, lemon juice, oil-garlic mixture, and reserved cooking water to pasta and toss to combine. Sprinkle with panko and serve.

TEST KITCHEN NOTE: You can substitute spaghetti, angel hair, or another strand pasta for the linguine, if desired.

Cumin Chicken and Winter Squash Salad

Serves 4

WHY THIS RECIPE WORKS: Covering the squash on the stovetop traps steam inside the skillet and shortens the overall cooking time.

- 6 **tablespoons extra-virgin olive oil**
- 1 **pound butternut squash, peeled, seeded, and cut into 1-inch pieces (3 cups)**
- 2 **teaspoons ground cumin**
  Salt and pepper
- 4 **(6- to 8-ounce) boneless, skinless chicken breasts, trimmed**
- 3 **tablespoons lemon juice**
- 1½ **tablespoons tahini**
- 6 **ounces (6 cups) baby kale**
- 6 **ounces seedless red grapes, halved (1 cup)**
- 3 **ounces goat cheese, crumbled (¾ cup)**

1. Heat 1 tablespoon oil in 12-inch nonstick skillet over medium-high heat until shimmering. Add squash, ½ teaspoon cumin, ¾ teaspoon salt, and ¼ teaspoon pepper and cook, covered, until tender, about 15 minutes, stirring occasionally. Transfer to plate.

2. Pat chicken dry with paper towels, sprinkle with remaining 1½ teaspoons cumin, and season with salt and pepper. Heat 1 tablespoon oil in now-empty skillet over medium-high heat until just smoking. Add chicken and cook until well browned and meat registers 160 degrees, about 6 minutes per side.

3. Meanwhile, whisk lemon juice, tahini, remaining ¼ cup oil, ½ teaspoon salt, and ¼ teaspoon pepper together in large bowl. Add kale, grapes, goat cheese, and squash and toss to combine. Slice chicken and serve over salad.

TEST KITCHEN NOTE: Cold goat cheese is easier to crumble, so be sure to keep it chilled before trying to crumble it.

Portobello Mushroom Sandwiches

Serves 4

WHY THIS RECIPE WORKS: Classic antipasti ingredients piled high atop a roasted portobello cap make a hearty, flavor-packed sandwich.

- 4 **large portobello mushroom caps, gills removed**
- ¼ **cup extra-virgin olive oil**
- 3 **garlic cloves, minced**
  Salt and pepper
- 8 **ounces fresh mozzarella cheese, sliced into ¼-inch-thick rounds**
- ½ **cup pesto**
- 4 **ciabatta sandwich rolls, split**
- 1 **cup marinated artichoke hearts, patted dry and chopped coarse**
- ½ **cup chopped jarred hot Peppadew peppers**

1. Adjust oven rack to upper-middle position and heat oven to 400 degrees. Toss mushrooms, oil, garlic, 1 teaspoon salt, and ½ teaspoon pepper together on rimmed baking sheet. Flip mushrooms gill side up and bake until tender and beginning to brown, about 20 minutes.

2. Remove sheet from oven and top mushrooms with mozzarella. Divide pesto among cut sides of rolls. Sandwich 1 mushroom, ¼ cup artichokes, and 2 tablespoons peppers in each roll. Serve.

TEST KITCHEN NOTE: Use a spoon to remove the mushroom gills.

Moroccan Steak Tips and Couscous

Serves 4

WHY THIS RECIPE WORKS: We add meaty flavor to the couscous by cooking it in the same skillet used to sear the steak tips.

- 2 **teaspoons ground cumin**
  Salt and pepper
- 1½ **teaspoons ground cinnamon**
- 1½ **pounds sirloin steak tips, trimmed and cut into 2-inch chunks**
- 1 **tablespoon vegetable oil**
- 1¼ **cups water**
- 1 **(15-ounce) can chickpeas, rinsed**
- ¾ **cup couscous**
- ½ **cup golden raisins**
- 2 **ounces (2 cups) baby spinach, chopped**

1. Combine cumin, 2 teaspoons salt, cinnamon, and ¼ teaspoon pepper in bowl. Pat steak dry with paper towels and season with 1 tablespoon spice mixture.

2. Heat oil in 12-inch nonstick skillet over medium-high heat until just smoking. Add steak and cook until browned on all sides and meat registers 125 degrees, 6 to 8 minutes. Transfer steak to plate and tent with foil.

3. Add water, chickpeas, couscous, raisins, and remaining spice mixture to now-empty skillet and bring to boil over medium-high heat. Remove from heat, cover, and let sit until couscous is tender, about 5 minutes. Stir in spinach, then serve with steak.

TEST KITCHEN NOTE: Serve with lemon wedges, if desired.

Skillet Bratwurst with Apples and Brussels Sprouts

30-MINUTE SUPPER

Pan-Seared Scallops with White Bean–Salami Salad

30-MINUTE SUPPER

Stir-Fried Chicken and Chestnuts

30-MINUTE SUPPER

Filet Mignon with Pecorino Potatoes and Escarole

30-MINUTE SUPPER

Pan-Seared Scallops with White Bean–Salami Salad *Serves 4*

WHY THIS RECIPE WORKS: Mild, sweet sea scallops pair nicely with this tangy, meaty bean salad.

- 2 (15-ounce) cans cannellini beans, rinsed
- 2 ounces thinly sliced genoa salami, halved, then cut crosswise into thin strips
- 5 tablespoons extra-virgin olive oil
- ¼ cup fresh parsley leaves
- 1 shallot, halved and sliced thin
- 2 tablespoons sherry vinegar
- 2 teaspoons Dijon mustard
  Salt and pepper
- 1½ pounds large sea scallops, tendons removed

1. Combine beans, salami, 3 tablespoons oil, parsley, shallot, vinegar, mustard, 1 teaspoon salt, and ¼ teaspoon pepper in bowl. Divide salad among 4 bowls.

2. Pat scallops dry with paper towels and season with salt and pepper. Heat 1 tablespoon oil in 12-inch nonstick skillet over medium-high heat until just smoking. Add half of scallops in single layer, flat side down, and cook, without moving them, until well browned, 1½ to 2 minutes per side. Transfer scallops to plate and tent with foil. Repeat with remaining 1 tablespoon oil and remaining scallops. Divide scallops evenly among bowls. Serve.

TEST KITCHEN NOTE: Our favorite sherry vinegar is Napa Valley Naturals Reserve Sherry Vinegar.

Skillet Bratwurst with Apples and Brussels Sprouts *Serves 4*

WHY THIS RECIPE WORKS: A cup of water hastens the cooking of the sausages and onions and helps the onions caramelize evenly.

- 2 pounds bratwurst
- 2 onions, halved and sliced thin
- 1 cup water
- ¼ cup extra-virgin olive oil
- 2 tablespoons honey
  Salt and pepper
- 1 pound Brussels sprouts, trimmed and quartered
- 3 Gala apples, cored and quartered
- ⅓ cup dried cranberries
- 1 tablespoon cider vinegar
- 1 tablespoon Dijon mustard

1. Combine bratwurst, onions, water, 1 tablespoon oil, 1 tablespoon honey, ½ teaspoon salt, and ¼ teaspoon pepper in 12-inch nonstick skillet. Cover and cook over medium-high heat until bratwurst is nearly cooked through, about 10 minutes, flipping bratwurst halfway through cooking. Uncover and continue to cook, stirring frequently, until water has evaporated and bratwurst and onions are well browned, 7 to 10 minutes longer. Transfer to platter and tent with foil.

2. Wipe skillet clean with paper towels. Heat remaining 3 tablespoons oil in now-empty skillet over medium-high heat until just smoking. Add Brussels sprouts, ¼ teaspoon salt, and ¼ teaspoon pepper and cook, covered, until browned, about 4 minutes, stirring often. Stir in apples, cranberries, vinegar, mustard, and remaining 1 tablespoon honey and cook until apples are browned and Brussels sprouts are tender, about 5 minutes. Serve with bratwurst and onions.

TEST KITCHEN NOTE: Honeycrisp, Granny Smith, and Braeburn apples will also work in this recipe.

Filet Mignon with Pecorino Potatoes and Escarole *Serves 4*

WHY THIS RECIPE WORKS: We sear the filets while the potatoes cook and sauté the escarole in the flavorful fond while the filets rest.

- 1½ pounds small Yukon Gold potatoes, unpeeled
- ¼ cup extra-virgin olive oil
  Salt and pepper
- 2 ounces Pecorino Romano cheese, grated (1 cup)
- 1 teaspoon grated lemon zest plus 1 tablespoon juice
- 4 (6- to 8-ounce) center-cut filets mignons, 1½ inches thick
- 2 garlic cloves, sliced thin
- ⅛ teaspoon red pepper flakes
- 1 head escarole (1 pound), trimmed and cut into 1-inch pieces

1. Combine potatoes, 1 tablespoon oil, and ½ teaspoon salt in large bowl. Microwave, covered, until paring knife inserted into potatoes meets no resistance, about 15 minutes, stirring halfway through microwaving. Add ½ cup Pecorino, lemon zest, and ½ teaspoon pepper and toss to coat.

2. Meanwhile, pat steaks dry with paper towels and season with salt and pepper. Heat 2 tablespoons oil in 12-inch skillet over medium-high heat until just smoking. Cook steaks until well browned and meat registers 125 degrees (for medium-rare), 4 to 6 minutes per side. Transfer to platter and tent with foil.

3. Add garlic, pepper flakes, and remaining 1 tablespoon oil to now-empty skillet and cook over medium-high heat until fragrant, about 30 seconds. Stir in escarole and lemon juice and cook until tender, about 3 minutes. Sprinkle remaining ½ cup Pecorino over potatoes. Serve steaks with escarole and potatoes.

TEST KITCHEN NOTE: Look for potatoes that measure 1 to 2 inches in diameter.

Stir-Fried Chicken and Chestnuts *Serves 4*

WHY THIS RECIPE WORKS: Sweet chestnuts, amplified by honey, add a new twist to this classic chicken stir-fry.

- 1½ pounds boneless, skinless chicken thighs, trimmed and cut into 1-inch pieces
- 2 tablespoons honey
- 2 tablespoons vegetable oil
- 6 scallions, white parts sliced thin, green parts cut into 2-inch pieces
- 3 garlic cloves, minced
- 2 teaspoons grated fresh ginger
- 1 yellow bell pepper, stemmed, seeded, and cut into ½-inch-wide strips
- 5 ounces peeled, cooked chestnuts, cut into ½-inch pieces
- 3 tablespoons soy sauce
- 1 tablespoon oyster sauce

1. Pat chicken dry with paper towels and toss with honey in bowl until coated. Heat oil in 12-inch nonstick skillet over medium-high heat until just smoking. Add chicken and cook, stirring frequently, until well browned, about 6 minutes.

2. Add scallion whites, garlic, and ginger and cook until fragrant, about 30 seconds. Add bell pepper and cook until crisp-tender, about 7 minutes. Stir in chestnuts, soy sauce, oyster sauce, and scallion greens and cook until sauce is slightly thickened, about 1 minute. Serve.

TEST KITCHEN NOTE: Serve with steamed rice. Chestnuts are sold jarred or vacuum-packed in many supermarkets.

Braising

Braising is perhaps the most transformative of all cooking methods: A tough, gnarly cut goes into a pot with some liquid, and hours later, without any hands-on work, you have tender, succulent meat. Some braises start with a sear to build flavor, while others get straight to the moist cooking, but all braises involve long, gentle simmering in a liquid that, once the fat has been strained out, can become a flavorful sauce. We present you with a primer on this invaluable technique.

by Scott Kathan

What's in a Name?

Braising, stewing, pot roasting, and slow cooking all share common ground: Cooking protein with liquid in a closed, moist environment to help break down the protein and achieve soft, tender meat. But where stewing usually involves completely submerging small pieces of meat with liquid, braising generally calls for much less liquid. And the resulting dish is more often eaten with a fork, not a spoon.

Low and Slow

Tough cuts come from well-used muscles that have lots of chewy collagen. Slow, moist cooking transforms the tough collagen into tender gelatin. The sweet spot for this conversion is between 140 and 200 degrees; larger cuts need to stay in this range for several hours to fully tenderize.

LIQUID

Most braising recipes use broth, but water, milk, and wine are also common mediums. Meats release juices as they cook, thereby increasing the volume of liquid in the pot.

AROMATICS

Ingredients such as onions, garlic, ginger, carrots, celery, herbs, and spices flavor both the meat and the liquid.

What to Braise?

Technically speaking, you can braise a carrot or a tender fish fillet. But usually, braising means starting with cuts of meat that are laden with fat and tough connective tissue. Here are a few of our favorites:

BRISKET

BEEF SHORT RIBS

BEEF CHUCK ROAST

CHICKEN THIGHS

PORK BUTT (SHOULDER) ROAST

PORK BLADE CHOPS

The Best Tool For the Job

Our favorite braising vessel is a heavy Dutch oven that retains heat well. We highly recommend the **Cuisinart 7 Qt. Round Covered Casserole** ($121.94); this pot is sturdy, heats evenly, has comfortable handles, works great both on the stovetop and in the oven, and features a light enameled interior that makes it easy to monitor browning.

 Our website has a new look! And it is stocked with fantastic braising ideas for a variety of dishes. Visit **CooksCountry.com/nov17** for foolproof recipes for Braised Beef Short Ribs and Cider-Braised Pork, free for a limited time.

Indoor Barbecued Chicken

We discovered how to get outdoor grill flavor without leaving the kitchen. *by Matthew Fairman*

FIRE-KISSED, TANGY barbecued chicken is one of the purest delights of summertime. Must we give it up in the fall when we cover our grills and pull them inside for the colder months? And what of those without a grill? Don't they deserve that saucy, smoky, charred-yet-still-juicy chicken experience? Enter indoor barbecued chicken.

Most of the existing recipes I found for "oven-barbecued" bone-in chicken pieces were poor imitations of the delicious stuff that comes off the grill. They served up chicken parts with soggy, floppy skin that had been braised in a bath of sauce. I wanted indoor chicken with the best qualities of the grilled version: juicy meat; beautifully rendered, browned skin; and heady smoke flavor.

To make the chicken really sing, I decided to apply a potent dry spice rub to the pieces before cooking them and brushing on a sauce during cooking. I imagined that the spice rub would provide a base of barbecue flavor and, since it would contain sugar, hasten browning. Brushing the chicken with a quick from-scratch barbecue sauce while it was cooking would allow the sauce to thicken into an intensely flavored, glossy glaze.

After rubbing the spice mix onto the chicken, I quickly seared the pieces in an ovensafe skillet on the stovetop to jump-start cooking, develop flavorful browning, and render the fat in the skin to help it crisp. After removing the seared (but not fully cooked) chicken, I whipped up a quick barbecue sauce in the same skillet, returned the chicken to the skillet, tossed it to coat it with sauce, and slid the whole thing into the oven to finish cooking.

At this point the results were already superior to the flabby, stewed chicken I had made previously. The chicken was juicy, the skin was nicely rendered, and the rub and sauce imparted the signature bold, sweet, and tangy barbecue flavor I was after. But the chicken was missing the mouthwatering charred bits and smokiness that develop when it's cooked over the high heat of the grill. Adding just ½ teaspoon of good-quality liquid smoke—the kind that contains only water and concentrated hickory smoke (see "A Smoky Solution")—and finishing the chicken under the broiler gave it the requisite char and smoke flavor it was missing.

Finally, I had no-grill barbecued chicken to satisfy my cravings through the longest and bleakest of winters.

A Smoky Solution

You can use bottled barbecue sauce here, but our simple homemade sauce—made from ingredients you likely have in your kitchen—is worlds better. The one sauce ingredient you may not stock in your pantry (but should) is liquid smoke. Our sauce recipe calls for just ½ teaspoon to lend that "tastes like it was cooked outdoors" essence. Our favorite liquid smoke is Wright's, which contains nothing more than smoke and water; avoid products that list "smoke flavor" as an ingredient, as they can have off-flavors.

A quick finishing stint under the broiler gives this chicken a tasty char.

INDOOR BARBECUED CHICKEN
Serves 4

We call for using either all white meat or all dark meat chicken in this recipe because they cook at different rates. This roughly comes out to either 4 breasts or 8 thighs, but use overall weight as your guide. If you choose to use a combination of both, you may have to remove some pieces from the oven before all the pieces are done to avoid overcooking. If you don't feel like making your own barbecue sauce, you can substitute 1 cup of your favorite store-bought barbecue sauce in step 3. Just pour off all remaining fat from the skillet and omit the onions.

- 2½ teaspoons chili powder
- 1½ teaspoons packed brown sugar
- 1 teaspoon garlic powder
- 1 teaspoon salt
- 1 teaspoon pepper
- ½ teaspoon ground cumin

- 3 pounds bone-in chicken pieces (either split breasts or thighs), trimmed
- 2 tablespoons vegetable oil
- ½ cup finely chopped onion
- ¼ cup water
- ⅔ cup ketchup
- 3 tablespoons molasses
- 1 tablespoon Worcestershire sauce
- 1 tablespoon Dijon mustard
- 2 teaspoons cider vinegar
- ½ teaspoon liquid smoke

1. Adjust oven rack to middle position and heat oven to 350 degrees. Combine chili powder, sugar, garlic powder, salt, pepper, and cumin in bowl. Sprinkle chicken all over with spice mixture.

2. Heat oil in ovensafe 12-inch skillet over medium heat until shimmering. Add chicken, skin side down, and cook until browned, about 5 minutes. Flip chicken and continue to cook until browned on second side, about 3 minutes longer. Transfer to plate.

3. Pour off all but 1 tablespoon fat from skillet and return to medium heat. Add onion and 2 tablespoons water and cook until onion is softened, 3 to 5 minutes, scraping up any browned bits. Stir in ketchup, molasses, Worcestershire, mustard, vinegar, liquid smoke, and remaining 2 tablespoons water and bring to simmer.

4. Return chicken to skillet and turn to coat with sauce. Flip chicken skin side up. Transfer skillet to oven and cook until breasts register 155 degrees or thighs register 170 degrees, 30 to 40 minutes for breasts or 20 to 25 minutes for thighs.

5. Remove skillet from oven and heat broiler. Broil until chicken is charred in spots and breasts register 160 degrees or thighs register 175 degrees, 2 to 5 minutes. Transfer chicken to platter and let rest for 5 minutes. Whisk sauce in skillet to recombine. Serve, passing sauce separately.

Brown Sugar-Citrus Pork Tenderloin

Our goal was tender meat with a flavorful, gently sweet exterior. Would we get burned in our pursuit?

by Matthew Fairman

A PORK TENDERLOIN holds the promise of delivering an appealingly tender roast to the table with a minimal investment of time, effort, and expense. But how do you add pizzazz to this mild-tasting cut? How about pairing it with brown sugar, an ingredient that our test kitchen matchmakers have proven goes exceedingly well with many cuts of pork? The combination of brown sugar and quick-cooking pork tenderloin seemed like it would result in a blissful union.

But when I experimented with existing recipes for brown sugar pork tenderloin, it was a dysfunctional marriage at best. Most of these recipes called for seasoning the pork with salt and brown sugar, searing it on the stovetop, and then moving it to the oven to finish cooking. Almost without fail, the pork was overcooked and the sugar burnt.

Fixing the first problem—overcooked pork—was a simple matter of adjusting the target temperature. Recipes suggested roasting the seared tenderloins until they reached between 145 and 160 degrees, but this gave me dense, chewy meat. I lowered that bar to 135 degrees, knowing that carryover cooking (the cooking that happens while the meat rests after coming out of the oven) would bring it to about 145 degrees, just the right temperature for perfectly cooked pork.

As for the acrid, burnt sugar crust, I knew that both searing and roasting with the crust in place was too much. But how could I avoid burning while still cooking the roast quickly? For my next test, I tried something unusual and seasoned the pork with only salt and pepper before searing it. Once the exterior was nicely browned, I spooned the brown sugar on top of the pork and placed it in the preheated 375-degree oven. In the relatively gentle heat, the sugar that sat atop the tenderloins didn't burn; instead, it was transformed into a crunchy, flavorful, faintly sweet crust.

With this success under my belt, I turned to the task of adding extra flavor to the brown sugar topping. After experimenting, I landed on a simple mixture of minced fresh thyme, grated orange zest, salt, and a pinch of cayenne pepper stirred together with the brown sugar, which gave the dish a savory complexity and a balanced sweetness that accentuated but didn't overwhelm the pork. Adding a touch of orange juice to the pan while the pork rested dissolved the sugary fond left behind, creating a luscious sauce that made a happy match with the tender pork. A couple of teaspoons of apple cider vinegar kept the sweetness in check.

At our final tasting of this juicy, brightly flavored, and supereasy dish, we knew: Pork and brown sugar belong together. On our plates.

We complement our brown sugar–topped pork with a bright and citrusy pan sauce.

Parade of Flavors

Mild pork tenderloin is a blank canvas that takes incredibly well to the sweet and sour flavors we chose for this recipe.

ORANGE
We featured the fragrant zest as part of the brown sugar seasoning for the pork and then used the juice to echo that flavor in the easy sauce.

APPLE CIDER VINEGAR
This sweet-sharp vinegar contributed a bright, fruity flavor to our quick pan sauce.

LIGHT BROWN SUGAR
Molasses-enriched brown sugar provides depth to the mild pork.

THYME
This fragrant herb is an old friend to pork and for good reason—its potent woodsy flavor plays beautifully with pork's gentle sweetness.

BROWN SUGAR–ORANGE PORK TENDERLOIN *Serves 4*

The Microplane Premium Classic Zester/Grater is our winning zesting tool. Do not use dark brown sugar here, as it is too strong-tasting for this sauce.

- ¼ cup packed light brown sugar
- 2 teaspoons minced fresh thyme
- ½ teaspoon grated orange zest plus 1 tablespoon juice
  Kosher salt and pepper
- ⅛ teaspoon cayenne pepper
- 2 (1-pound) pork tenderloins, trimmed
- 2 tablespoons vegetable oil
- 2 tablespoons water
- 2 teaspoons cider vinegar

1. Adjust oven rack to upper-middle position and heat oven to 375 degrees. Combine sugar, thyme, orange zest, ⅛ teaspoon salt, and cayenne in bowl; set aside. Pat tenderloins dry with paper towels and sprinkle with 1 tablespoon salt and ½ teaspoon pepper.

2. Heat oil in 12-inch nonstick skillet over medium-high heat until just smoking. Add tenderloins and cook until browned on all sides, 5 to 7 minutes.

3. Off heat, sprinkle sugar mixture evenly over tops of tenderloins, pressing to adhere (it's OK if some falls off). Transfer skillet to oven and roast until meat registers 135 degrees, 10 to 14 minutes. Transfer tenderloins to plate, tent with aluminum foil, and let rest for 10 minutes.

4. Add water, vinegar, orange juice, and any accumulated pork juices to liquid left in skillet. Place skillet over medium heat (skillet handle will be hot) and cook until sauce is slightly thickened, about 2 minutes, pressing on any solid bits of sugar with spatula to dissolve. Slice tenderloins ½ inch thick and serve with sauce.

Tater Tot Hotdish

This hearty, creamy casserole is crowned with its namesake crispy potato nuggets. Our challenge? Get the tots to brown, not drown. *by Cecelia Jenkins*

HOTDISH (ONE WORD, not two) is to Minnesotans what a casserole is to the rest of the country. But Minnesotans do it better—they top theirs with tater tots. When tater tot hotdish is done right, the bottoms of the tots meld with the bubbling casserole base and the tot tops brown into the ultimate crispy, tasty, golden topping.

The dish's base traditionally features a mixture of browned ground beef, a can or two of condensed cream of mushroom soup, and plenty of frozen vegetables (often green beans, carrots, corn, and/or peas). It's all topped, of course, with the signature golden-brown tots. But the recipes I gathered all disappointed, especially when it came to the tots. Most were too pale in color, and some were so swamped in sauce (and, in one recipe, cheese) that they ate more like mashed potatoes, which is fine for shepherd's pie but certainly not for hotdish. As for the base, the condensed soup was overly salty, too pasty, and generally uninspired. The frozen green beans and carrots were troublesome, too: They threw off excess moisture that turned the tots soggy.

My goal was to keep this dish simple but to elevate and freshen the flavors and, above all, to turn out crispy, browned tots. First on the chopping block was the canned-soup base. Luckily, the test kitchen has years of experience making white sauces, so I

had a lot of knowledge at my disposal. After precooking beef, mushrooms, and onion (a necessary step to extract water and create flavorful browning) in a Dutch oven, I stirred in 3 tablespoons of flour. I then added chicken broth and milk and cooked the mixture for a few minutes until it thickened. A bit of Parmesan cheese contributed depth, and frozen peas and corn studded the hotdish with color and pleasant pockets of vegetable flavor (without adding excess moisture). I poured the lot into a 13 by 9-inch baking dish and smoothed the top.

Next up was the most important component: the tots. When cooked on their own on a baking sheet, tots brown where they come in contact with the sheet. Since I wasn't relying on a sheet for browning, I knew I'd have to provide a little extra heat to get the tots to brown on top. After a few trial runs, I found that adjusting the oven rack to the upper-middle position allowed the oven's heat to reflect off the ceiling, producing optimum browning.

As I pulled the hotdish from the oven, incredible aromas instantly drew a small horde of my colleagues to my side. After letting the casserole cool, I scooped out hearty, crispy-tot-topped portions for everyone to try, and they were impressed. Run-of-the-mill casserole? Hardly. This hotdish does Minnesota proud.

THE AMERICAN TABLE

In 1925, the Minnesota Valley Canning Company was having a difficult time marketing its newest product, a large variety of wrinkly, tender pea. This new variety was confusing to American consumers, who were accustomed to much smaller peas. Rather than ditch the crop, however, corporate bosses took a gamble, choosing to emphasize the pea's large size by naming it the Green Giant—and creating a mascot with the same name.

For about a decade, the Green Giant was a menacing presence draped in bearskin, but in 1935 advertising executive Leo Burnett gave him a makeover, dressing him in a leafy suit and adding "Jolly" to his name. In 1979, a 55-foot-tall fiberglass Jolly Green Giant statue was unveiled in Blue Earth, Minnesota; today, he attracts more than 10,000 visitors a year.

Grated Parmesan cheese stirred into the creamy base boosts the savory flavor.

TATER TOT HOTDISH
Serves 6 to 8
Be sure to buy cylinder-shaped frozen tater tots (not crispy crowns or coins). Do not thaw the tots or the vegetables; they go into the hotdish frozen. Serve with ketchup.

- 1½ pounds 85 percent lean ground beef
- 1 pound white mushrooms, trimmed and sliced thin
- 1 onion, chopped
- 4 garlic cloves, minced
- 1 tablespoon minced fresh thyme
  Salt and pepper
- 3 tablespoons all-purpose flour
- 1½ cups whole milk
- 1½ cups chicken broth
- 3 ounces Parmesan cheese, grated (1½ cups)
- 1 cup frozen peas
- 1 cup frozen corn
- 1 (2-pound) bag frozen tater tots

1. Adjust oven rack to upper-middle position and heat oven to 450 degrees. Combine beef, mushrooms, onion, garlic, thyme, 1½ teaspoons salt, and 1½ teaspoons pepper in Dutch oven. Cook over medium-high heat until

nearly all liquid has evaporated, 25 to 28 minutes, stirring occasionally and breaking up meat with spoon.
2. Stir in flour until fully incorporated and cook for 1 minute. Stir in milk and broth and bring to simmer, scraping up any browned bits. Cook until mixture is slightly thickened, about 3 minutes. Off heat, stir in Parmesan. Transfer mixture to 13 by 9-inch baking dish.
3. Sprinkle peas and corn evenly over beef mixture. Lightly arrange tater tots in even layer over top, but do not press into mixture (you may have extra tater tots). Bake until tater tots are deep golden brown and filling is bubbling, 35 to 38 minutes, rotating dish halfway through baking. Let cool for 15 minutes before serving.

TO MAKE AHEAD
At end of step 2, let beef mixture cool completely, then cover with aluminum foil and refrigerate for up to 24 hours. To serve, bake beef mixture, covered, until hot in center, 15 to 20 minutes. Remove foil, stir beef mixture, sprinkle with peas and corn, arrange tater tots on top, and bake as directed in step 3.

Spice-Crusted Steaks

We wanted a crust that was superflavorful, not superburnt. *by Alli Berkey*

I'VE HAD MY share of steakhouse dinners of peppercorn-crusted steak, with a deeply colored, flavorful crust surrounding a perfectly cooked, tender interior. But a visit to a steakhouse can break the bank. I was looking to create a recipe that I could make at home, only better—building on the idea of a peppercorn crust but welcoming a wider range of flavors to the mix. This crust needed to feature a balanced blend of spices that didn't overwhelm me or the beef, and it had to be easy enough to pull off using my stove.

To get started, I gathered a handful of existing recipes, which called for coating various cuts of beef with a slew of spices and herbs (including ancho chiles, coriander seeds, mustard seeds, white and black peppercorns, five-spice powder, dried or fresh rosemary, and more) before cooking them to the desired doneness in a hot skillet. More often than not, the spices overpowered the beef flavor—if they didn't end up burning first. Why waste the beef?

Still, I learned some things. Coriander seeds, mustard seeds, and fresh rosemary landed on our short list of favorite flavors. I'd hoped to use the coriander and mustard seeds for a bit of crunch, but the whole seeds promptly burned in the pan, so I turned to ground versions of both. Combining these powders with some coarsely crushed black peppercorns gave me a winning mix of flavors and just enough crunch to satisfy.

Next up: Finding the right cut of beef. I tried flank, rib-eye, strip, blade, and skirt steaks as well as flap meat. The tender, tasty rib-eye steak won in a landslide, as it had two things going for it that no other cut could match: It was rich and beefy enough to stand up to the bold (but not overly aggressive) spice crust and thick enough—at a hefty 1½ inches—to provide the perfect ratio of interior meat to exterior spice, ensuring the right mix of flavors and textures in every bite.

Up to this point, I'd been using a cast-iron skillet. And while we loved the results, I was leaving behind a lot of crust, which stuck to the surface of the pan both when I flipped the steaks and when I pulled them out at the end

of cooking. I wondered if a nonstick skillet would solve the problem: Would a less sticky cooking surface encourage more spices to stay put on the steaks? Answer: Yes. And as a bonus, my cleanup was much easier.

One last trick helped seal the deal: turning the steaks every 2 minutes. This helped keep the spice crusts from burning, and while I was concerned that all this flipping would make the spices fall off, the nonstick pan—and using a fork, not tongs, to turn the steaks—helped keep it all in place.

My spice-crusted steaks were now juicy and tender on the inside, with lovely crusts full of bold flavor. And after cooking at home, I had plenty left in my wallet for a nice bottle of wine.

SPICE-CRUSTED STEAKS
Serves 4

A rasp-style grater is the best tool for zesting lemons. Turning the steaks every 2 minutes helps prevent the spices from burning.

- 1   tablespoon black peppercorns
- 2   tablespoons chopped fresh rosemary
- 1   tablespoon kosher salt
- 2   teaspoons ground coriander
- 2   teaspoons grated lemon zest
- 1½ teaspoons dry mustard
- 1   teaspoon red pepper flakes
- 2   (1-pound) boneless rib-eye steaks, 1½ inches thick, trimmed
- 1   tablespoon vegetable oil

1. Place peppercorns in zipper-lock bag and seal bag. Using rolling pin, crush peppercorns coarse. Combine peppercorns, rosemary, salt, coriander, lemon zest, mustard, and pepper flakes in bowl. Season steaks all over, including sides, with spice mixture, pressing to adhere. (Use all of spice mixture.)
2. Set wire rack in rimmed baking sheet. Heat oil in 12-inch nonstick skillet over medium heat until just smoking. Add steaks and cook, flipping steaks with fork every 2 minutes, until well browned and meat registers 125 degrees (for medium-rare), 10 to 13 minutes. Transfer steaks to prepared rack, tent with aluminum foil, and let rest for 5 minutes. Slice and serve.

The spice crust adds potent seasoning and a satisfying crunch to juicy rib-eye steaks.

Key Steps to Better Spice-Crusted Steaks
It's a simple recipe, so the details matter. Here are two tips that really work.

'Corn Crushing
Coarsely crushing the peppercorns results in big, bold pepper flavor. We like to put the peppercorns in a zipper-lock bag and have at 'em with a rolling pin.

Fork Flipping
Use a fork—not a pair of tongs—to turn the steaks in the skillet. Tongs could scrape off the spice coating.

Bergers-Style Cookies

After cooking our way through 38 pounds of chocolate, we came up with a recipe that honors the Baltimore original.

by Morgan Bolling

UNTIL THIRD GRADE, I was as picky as kids come. So my mother—who is a doctor but, more important, is also a mom who was afraid that her tiny daughter would shrivel away—fed me a steady diet of the only foods I would eat: breakfast cereal, plain hot dogs (no ketchup or bun), and, because we were in Baltimore, Bergers cookies.

Those who aren't from Baltimore may not be familiar with the glorious Bergers cookie. Its base is a lightly sweet, softly crumbly, dome-shaped vanilla cookie. But the real draw is the ½-inch layer of fudgy chocolate frosting that sits proudly on top. The cookie gets its name from Henry Berger, a German immigrant who opened his bakery in Baltimore in the 1800s (see "Backstory"). The bakery still churns out cookies by the truckload, and true Baltimoreans know that the *s* in "Bergers" is silent.

Though I've since left Baltimore, I've never stopped loving these treats from my youth. Since they're rarely found outside of Maryland, I decided to make them myself.

To get my bearings, I ordered a batch of Bergers cookies directly from the bakery to share and discuss with my team in the test kitchen. After some recipe research, the few existing recipes I found left me unsatisfied—they tried to clean up the cookie and make it fancy, which it's not—so I baked a handful of similar-sounding vanilla cookies, as well as five options for chocolate frosting and ganache.

The closest cookie replica came from a simple recipe for grocery store–style sugar cookies: It called for butter and sugar to be creamed together before adding an egg, some cream, plenty of

The addition of cocoa powder to the superfudgy milk chocolate frosting gives it dark color and complex flavor.

vanilla, cake flour (for a softer texture), baking powder, and salt. The cookies were simple in flavor, with just a hint of vanilla, but they were a bit too tender to hold up to the heavy helmet of fudgy frosting. Switching to all-purpose flour wasn't the answer, as it made the cookies too tough.

Egg yolks contain fat, which can add tenderness to cookies. Because I was after a sturdier cookie, I decided to nix the yolk and just use the egg white. The resulting batch of cookies was

firm but still fluffy. Plus, this change amplified the cookies' vanilla flavor; the rich yolk had been muting it. With the cookie part of my recipe settled, I turned my attention to the chocolate.

I knew that the topping should be thicker than cake frosting but softer than fudge; it should be just supple enough that you leave teeth marks when you bite through it. I started with a ganache recipe that called for melting semisweet chocolate chips and cream together and then whisking in

confectioners' sugar. My tests proved that as long as I spread this mixture while it was warm, it would naturally cascade over the cookies and set up into a smooth, dense frosting as it cooled. Now the topping was the right texture, but it was a tad too bitter.

A switch to milk chocolate chips was the answer, especially after I figured out that I also could swap some of the confectioner's sugar for cocoa powder to maintain the frosting's texture while adding a smidge of complexity. With some vanilla and salt to intensify the chocolate flavor, I had a dead ringer for the original Bergers frosting.

Flipping the cookies over before spooning the chocolate onto their flatter bottom sides made it easier to pile it on thick and create their signature domed tops. Until I can make it back to Baltimore, I have a cookie to tide me over.

BACKSTORY

When German-born Henry Berger arrived in Baltimore in 1835, he found German spoken on the streets nearly as much as English. Soon the enterprising baker was selling breads and pastries at open-air markets across town; by the end of the 19th century, increased access to sugar and chocolate allowed Berger (and eventually, his sons) to focus almost exclusively on his best-selling fudge-topped cookie. Today, the bakery turns out 36,000 cookies daily, each one frosted by hand.

BERGERS-STYLE COOKIES

Makes 24 cookies

The consistency of the frosting should resemble that of a thick brownie batter. It should mound and slowly spread over the cookies. It's OK if some of the frosting drips down the sides of the cookies. If the frosting's temperature drops below 90 degrees, it may become too thick to spread. To bring it back to its proper consistency, simply microwave it at 50 percent power in 5-second intervals, whisking after each interval. Our favorite Dutch-processed cocoa powder is Droste Cocoa.

COOKIES

- 2 cups (8 ounces) cake flour
- 1½ teaspoons baking powder
- ¼ teaspoon salt
- 8 tablespoons unsalted butter, softened
- ¾ cup (5¼ ounces) granulated sugar
- 1 large egg white
- 1½ tablespoons heavy cream
- 1½ teaspoons vanilla extract

FROSTING

- 3 cups (18 ounces) milk chocolate chips
- 1¼ cups heavy cream
- ¼ teaspoon salt
- 1⅔ cups (5 ounces) Dutch-processed cocoa powder
- 1¼ cups (5 ounces) confectioners' sugar
- 1½ teaspoons vanilla extract

1. FOR THE COOKIES: Adjust oven rack to middle position and heat oven to 350 degrees. Line 2 baking sheets with parchment paper. Whisk flour, baking powder, and salt together in bowl; set aside. Using stand mixer fitted with paddle, beat butter and sugar on medium-high speed until pale and fluffy, about 3 minutes.
2. Add egg white, cream, and vanilla and beat until combined. Reduce speed to low and add flour mixture in 3 additions until incorporated, scraping down bowl as needed.
3. Working with 1 heaping tablespoon dough at a time, roll into balls and space 2 inches apart on prepared sheets, 12 per sheet. Using your moistened fingers, press dough balls to form disks about ¼ inch thick and 2 inches in diameter. Bake, 1 sheet at a time, until cookies are just beginning to brown around edges, 8 to 10 minutes, rotating sheet halfway through baking. Let cookies cool completely on sheet.
4. FOR THE FROSTING: Once cookies have cooled, combine chocolate chips, cream, and salt in large bowl. Microwave chocolate mixture at 50 percent power, stirring occasionally, until melted and smooth, 1 to 3 minutes. Whisk cocoa, sugar, and vanilla into chocolate mixture until smooth. (Frosting should be texture of thick brownie batter and register about 95 degrees.)
5. Flip cookies on sheets. Spoon 2 tablespoons frosting over flat side of each cookie to form mound. Let cookies sit at room temperature until frosting is set, about 3 hours. Serve. (Cookies can be stored in airtight container at room temperature for up to 2 days.)

Spreadable Frosting

The temperature and consistency of the frosting are important: It should register between 90 and 100 degrees and should resemble thick brownie batter when you spoon it onto the cookie. If the frosting is too thick, that means it is too cool. To make it spreadable, microwave it in 5-second intervals, whisking after each interval, until it registers between 90 and 100 degrees. If it gets too hot, it will be thin and run off the cookies; in this case, simply let it cool a bit.

Tasting Milk Chocolate Chips
by Lauren Savoie

CHOCOLATE CHIPS, LIKE bar chocolate, are available in many varieties besides semisweet. Although decadent dark chocolate chips may take center stage, we think creamy milk chocolate chips deserve some of the spotlight, too. So for this tasting, we decided to focus on milk chocolate chips, which are made from four key ingredients: sugar, cocoa butter, cocoa solids (the part of the cacao plant left over once the cocoa butter is extracted), and milk. Contrary to popular belief, chocolate chips don't contain any wax or special stabilizers other than lecithin, which is also present in bar chocolate. Instead, they usually contain a lower percentage of cocoa butter (i.e., fat) than bar chocolate does, which helps the chips hold their shape during baking. For this reason, we usually prefer to melt chopped bar chocolate rather than chocolate chips when we want smooth melted chocolate in recipes. We save the chips for cookies, muffins, and bars, where we want distinct morsels of chocolate speckled throughout.

A good milk chocolate should be creamy and sweet, with a melt-in-your-mouth smoothness. To find the best, we rounded up four nationally available milk chocolate chip products, trying each plain, in our Perfect Chocolate Chip Cookies, and in our Chocolate Pudding, which is formulated to work with chocolate chips. The pudding was a wash; once melted and chilled into pudding, all the chips were perfectly rich and milky, with only minor differences in texture.

But tasters had clear preferences in the plain tasting. Although milk chocolate is typically mild and creamy, we gave the edge to products that tasted more complex, with fruity and floral notes.

While tasters liked the flavor of all the chips in the cookie tasting, they found that chip size was important. Bigger chips either overwhelmed each bite of cookie or left large patches where there wasn't a single chip to be found. We preferred smaller chips that were dotted all throughout the cookie, for the perfect balance of chocolate and cookie in each bite.

Our favorite product was Hershey's Kitchens Milk Chocolate Chips; at $0.27 per ounce, it was also one of the least expensive options in our lineup. These chips were the smallest of the bunch, and tasters loved that they made perfectly balanced cookies with a classic milky flavor.

Go to CooksCountry.com/nov17 to read the full tasting results and see the complete results chart.

PRODUCT REVIEW

RECOMMENDED

Hershey's Kitchens Milk Chocolate Chips
Price: $3.29 for 12 oz ($0.27 per oz)
Fat per 15-g Serving: 4.5 g
Number of Chips per 1 Cup: 394

Guittard Milk Chocolate Chips
Price: $4.49 for 12 oz ($0.37 per oz)
Fat per 15-g Serving: 4.5 g
Number of Chips per 1 Cup: 139

Ghirardelli Milk Chocolate Chips
Price: $4.49 for 11.5 oz ($0.39 per oz)
Fat per 15-g Serving: 3.5 g
Number of Chips per 1 Cup: 192

Nestlé Toll House Milk Chocolate Morsels
Price: $3.29 for 12 oz ($0.27 per oz)
Fat per 15-g Serving: 4 g
Number of Chips per 1 Cup: 330

TASTERS' NOTES

Our Favorite

These "smaller" chips sure packed a punch with their "deep cocoa flavor," "fruity" notes, and "classic" creaminess. Pudding made with these chips was "thick" and "milky," and cookies were flawlessly "tall" and "tender," with dots of chocolate speckled throughout for a "perfect balance of chips and cookie in every bite."

Creamy "butter" notes and a "caramel-y" richness lent these "melt-in-your-mouth" chips a "subtle" decadence that tasters loved plain and in pudding. When baked into cookies, these chips were "fudgy," with "just the right amount of sweetness," but a few tasters thought that their "big" size made for slightly unbalanced bites.

These "oversize" morsels were "very sweet" and "floral," with a "creamy" flavor that was reminiscent of "hot cocoa" or "chocolate milk." A few tasters noted that these "large" chips didn't disperse as well in cookies, but most loved their "caramel-like" butteriness.

These chips from the original makers of the chocolate chip were "classic" and "familiar," with strong notes of "vanilla" and "cocoa." Cookies had "well-balanced" pockets of chocolate and dough and a "substantial," chewy texture. A few tasters remarked that these chips tasted "one note," like "Easter chocolate."

Simple Holiday Stuffing

Though it has just a handful of ingredients and is supereasy to make, this casserole-style stuffing delivers big, buttery, savory flavor. *by Katie Leaird*

Key Ingredients

Bread

Insubstantial, flavorless bread will make a mushy, muddy stuffing. Our taste test winner—and our top choice for stuffing—is **Arnold Country Classics White Bread**, which our tasters praised for its "perfect structure" and "subtle sweetness."

Chicken Stock

Chicken stock is a workhorse ingredient in our kitchen, so it's important to use one that has clean, potent chicken flavor. The test kitchen's favorite is **Swanson Chicken Stock**, which our tasting panel called out for its "rich," "meaty" flavor.

Poultry Seasoning

Invented by William G. Bell in Boston in

1867, **Bell's Poultry Seasoning** combines several herbs and aromatics—rosemary, oregano, sage, ginger, and marjoram—for bold flavor, complexity, and depth in just one ingredient. You can find it in the herb and spice section of the supermarket.

Core Techniques

How to Dice an Onion Like a Pro

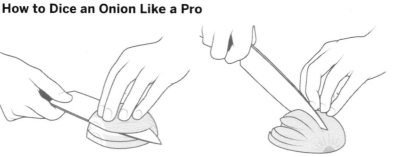

1. Halve onion through root end, then remove peel from onion and trim top. Make several horizontal cuts from cut end of onion to root end, taking care not to cut through root end.

2. Make several vertical cuts into onion from root end to cut end. Again, be sure to keep root end intact as it holds cut pieces in place.

3. With root end of onion facing toward you, make thin slices across previous cuts. As you slice, onion will fall apart into chopped pieces.

Browned Butter = More Flavor

Butter cooked until the water evaporates and the solid milk proteins turn brown adds deep, nutty flavor to recipes. We recommend making it in a light-colored pan so that you can easily judge the color; it can quickly go from browned to burnt. Foaming, which happens when the water evaporates, is your clue that the butter is nearly done. Once the foaming subsides, start paying close attention. Almost immediately, you'll see tiny specks settling to the bottom of the pan. These are the milk solids—particles of protein and carbohydrate— that give the browned butter its characteristic color and flavor. As soon as the butter turns chestnut brown and smells toasty, it's ready.

PROPERLY BROWNED BUTTER
Dark brown color, rich flavor

Toast Bread with a Light Touch

Some recipes call for toasting fresh bread cubes until they turn a deep golden brown, but we found that bread goes very quickly from brown to burnt. All you really need to do is dry out the bread cubes and lightly brown them so they can keep their shape and absorb the flavorful broth.

Step by Step

1. Preheat low oven
Adjust the oven rack to the middle position and heat the oven to 300 degrees.
Why? A low temperature ensures that the bread doesn't scorch as it dries out.

2. Dry bread
Arrange the bread evenly on a rimmed baking sheet. Bake it for 25 minutes, stir it, and continue to bake it until light golden brown, 25 to 30 minutes longer.
Why? Stirring the bread cubes halfway through baking ensures that they dry evenly.

3. Increase oven temperature
Increase the oven temperature to 375 degrees.
Why? Baking the stuffing at a higher temperature encourages browning and crisps the top.

4. Brown butter
Melt the butter in a skillet over medium-low heat. Cook, swirling the pan, until the butter is golden brown and has a nutty aroma, 5 to 7 minutes. Set aside 3 tablespoons of the browned butter.
Why? Browned butter imparts rich, complex flavor.

5. Cook vegetables
Add the onions and celery, increase the heat to medium, and cook until they are soft and beginning to brown, 10 to 13 minutes.
Why? A long sauté over medium heat ensures that the aromatic vegetables cook evenly and thoroughly to become soft and sweet.

SIMPLE HOLIDAY STUFFING
Serves 10 to 12
Use a hearty white sandwich bread, such as Arnold Country Classics White Bread (our taste test winner). You will need one loaf for this recipe. We developed this recipe using Bell's Poultry Seasoning.

1½	pounds hearty white sandwich bread, cut into ½-inch pieces (16 cups)
12	tablespoons unsalted butter, cut into 12 pieces
2	onions, chopped fine
2	celery ribs, chopped fine
1	tablespoon poultry seasoning
1½	teaspoons salt
¾	teaspoon pepper
2½	cups chicken broth

1. Adjust oven rack to middle position and heat oven to 300 degrees. Arrange bread evenly on rimmed baking sheet. Bake for 25 minutes. Remove sheet from oven and stir bread to redistribute. Return sheet to oven and continue to bake until bread is light golden brown, 25 to 30 minutes longer. Let cool completely, then transfer to large bowl. (Cooled bread can be stored in zipper-lock bag for up to 2 days.) Increase oven temperature to 375 degrees.

2. Melt butter in 12-inch skillet over medium-low heat. Continue to cook, swirling pan occasionally, until butter is dark golden brown and has nutty aroma, 5 to 7 minutes. Transfer 3 tablespoons browned butter to small bowl and set aside.

3. Add onions and celery to skillet, increase heat to medium, and cook until vegetables are soft and beginning to brown, 10 to 13 minutes. Stir in poultry seasoning, salt, and pepper and cook until fragrant, about 30 seconds. Add vegetable mixture to bowl with bread.

4. Add broth to bread mixture and fold to combine. Let sit for 10 minutes. Fold again until broth is fully absorbed. Transfer stuffing to 13 by 9-inch baking dish and distribute evenly but do not pack down. Drizzle reserved butter evenly over top. Bake until golden brown and crisp on top, 30 to 35 minutes. Transfer dish to wire rack and let cool for 15 minutes. Serve.

TO MAKE AHEAD
Before drizzling butter over stuffing in step 4, cover dish with aluminum foil. Refrigerate stuffing and reserved butter for up to 24 hours. To serve, microwave reserved butter until melted. Remove foil, drizzle butter over stuffing, re-cover dish with foil, and bake for 15 minutes. Uncover and continue to bake until stuffing is heated through and top is golden brown, 30 to 35 minutes longer.

SIMPLE HOLIDAY STUFFING WITH MUSHROOMS AND HERBS
Add 12 ounces white mushrooms, trimmed and quartered, to skillet with onions and celery in step 3 and increase cooking time to about 15 minutes. Add 2 tablespoons chopped fresh parsley and 2 teaspoons minced fresh thyme with broth. Sprinkle 1 tablespoon chopped fresh parsley over top before serving.

SIMPLE HOLIDAY STUFFING WITH SAUSAGE
Decrease butter to 8 tablespoons. Add 8 ounces bulk pork sausage to skillet with onions and celery in step 3, breaking up meat with spoon. Decrease salt to 1 teaspoon.

The best stuffings—like this one—feature a contrast between a crisp top and a tender interior.

6. Add seasonings
Stir in the poultry seasoning, salt, and pepper and cook until fragrant, about 30 seconds.
Why? Using poultry seasoning is a quick and easy way to add complexity to stuffing. Cooking it briefly helps bring out its flavor.

7. Combine and let rest
Add the vegetable mixture to the bread, and then add the broth to the bread mixture and fold to combine. Let the mixture sit for 10 minutes.
Why? The resting period gives the bread a chance to absorb the broth.

8. Transfer to baking dish
Fold the mixture again until the broth is fully absorbed. Distribute the stuffing evenly in a baking dish, but do not pack it down.
Why? You want to fold and transfer the stuffing gently so as not to compress the bread cubes, which would result in dense stuffing.

9. Drizzle with butter
Drizzle the reserved browned butter evenly over the top.
Why? Extra butter on top ensures a flavorful, crisp topping.

10. Bake
Bake until the stuffing is golden brown and crisp on top, 30 to 35 minutes.
Why? Since there are no eggs in this stuffing and the vegetables are already tender, you need to bake it only until it's heated through and crisped.

Chicken Saltimbocca

The dish's Italian name promises flavors that "jump in the mouth." We didn't want to jump through hoops to get there. *by Katie Leaird*

We put an exclamation point on this dish with a simple—but rich and vibrant—pan sauce.

IT SOUNDS FANCY, but chicken saltimbocca is really just a pretty package of simple staples: chicken, ham (prosciutto), and sage. The challenge is that these last two ingredients have big, bold personalities that need to be carefully balanced with the demure poultry lest they overwhelm the dish.

I decided to start with the sage. I wanted a soft but discernible herbal presence. After researching a few existing recipes, I started my testing by sandwiching some chopped fresh sage between a chicken cutlet and a layer of prosciutto and searing it off in a skillet. But because it steamed between the meats, the sage took on a slightly soggy texture and a grassy flavor—not the result I sought.

I decided on a different tack, one we've used before in the test kitchen: I'd fry whole sage leaves and introduce them to the dish later. I heated a few tablespoons of olive oil in a skillet and then slipped in the sage leaves. As their distinctive aroma filled the kitchen, their hue transformed from mossy to hunter green, their texture became crisp, and their flavor went from piney and harsh to delicate and nutty. I set the leaves aside to drain on paper towels. The oil left behind now had a rich sage flavor, which I could use to my advantage.

But first I had to deal with the chicken. We've found that store-bought cutlets are often ragged and uneven, so we prefer to make our own by slicing boneless, skinless breasts in half horizontally (this is easier to do if you briefly freeze them first) and gently pounding them out. As for the prosciutto, most recipes call for just a small amount, but I love the stuff, so I wrapped liberally sized salty, porky slices around the chicken cutlets and cooked them in the sage-infused oil. Turns out that the recipes were right: This heavy hand with the potent pork turned the dish far too salty.

Since wrapping the prosciutto around the chicken was out, I tried gluing a thin slice to one side of each cutlet with a bit of flour, which worked—but I wondered if I needed the flour at all.

Instead, I gently pressed the prosciutto slices onto the pounded cutlets and found that they stuck together just fine with no assistance.

I carefully assembled a row of four chicken and ham stacks and lowered them into the skillet to fry in the sage-infused oil. But when it came time to flip them to cook the second side, I pulled up a naked chicken cutlet with my tongs and frowned at the prosciutto left sizzling in the pan. To solve this problem, I didn't need to change the recipe, just the pan. Moving to a nonstick skillet encouraged the ham to stick to the chicken instead.

The beauty of cooking this dish for two is that you're done after you cook one batch—there's no need to keep cutlets warm while frying another round. This opened the door for a quick sauce. After removing the chicken from the skillet, I added a bit of sliced garlic and minced sage, followed by a little chicken broth. Once this mixture had cooked down a bit, I finished it with butter and lemon juice. Now I had a rich, tangy sauce to pour over the prosciutto-wrapped chicken. Topped with glistening fried sage leaves, this simple dish was in perfect balance and had impressive payoff.

King of Domestic Hams

While you can spend a king's ransom on imported Italian prosciutto in specialty food stores, you can find great North American prosciuttos at most supermarkets. Our favorite domestic option is **Volpi Traditional Prosciutto** ($5.75 for 3 ounces), which is made in Missouri using traditional Italian methods. Our tasters were wowed by its "silky," "ultrasupple," "buttery" texture; "sweet," "porky" flavor; and "salty punch."

CHICKEN SALTIMBOCCA FOR TWO

Freezing the chicken breasts for 15 minutes makes it easier to slice them into cutlets. Our favorite boneless, skinless chicken breasts are from Bell & Evans.

- 2 (6- to 8-ounce) boneless, skinless chicken breasts, trimmed
  Salt and pepper
- 4 thin slices prosciutto (2 ounces)
- 2 tablespoons extra-virgin olive oil
- 4 large fresh sage leaves, plus
  1 teaspoon minced
- 1 garlic clove, sliced thin
- ½ cup chicken broth
- 2 tablespoons unsalted butter, cut into 2 pieces and chilled
- 2 teaspoons lemon juice

1. Place chicken on plate and freeze until firm, about 15 minutes. Working with 1 breast at a time, starting on thick side, cut breasts in half horizontally. Using meat pounder, gently pound each cutlet to even ¼-inch thickness between 2 sheets of plastic wrap.

2. Pat cutlets dry with paper towels and season lightly with salt and pepper. Place 1 prosciutto slice on top of each cutlet, pressing to adhere and folding ends of slice as needed to prevent overhang.

3. Heat oil in 12-inch nonstick skillet over medium-high heat until shimmering. Add sage leaves and cook until leaves begin to change color and become fragrant, 15 to 20 seconds. Using slotted spoon, transfer sage leaves to paper towel–lined plate.

4. Add cutlets to skillet, prosciutto side down, and cook until lightly browned, about 2 minutes. Flip cutlets and cook until second side is light golden brown and cutlets are cooked through, about 2 minutes. Transfer to platter and tent with aluminum foil.

5. Reduce heat to medium; add garlic and minced sage to now-empty skillet and cook until fragrant, about 30 seconds. Stir in broth and bring to simmer; cook until reduced by half, about 2 minutes. Reduce heat to low and whisk in butter, 1 piece at a time, until incorporated. Stir in lemon juice and season with salt and pepper to taste. Spoon sauce over chicken. Top each cutlet with 1 fried sage leaf. Serve.

Chicken and Sausage Gumbo

This New Orleans stew can take all day. That's fine with us—as long as the slow cooker does the work.

by Matthew Fairman

NEW ORLEANS MAY be the most beloved food destination in the United States, and gumbo may be its most sought-after dish. Its quintessential component, a dark roux of flour toasted in hot oil, adds body and deep savory notes to the broth and takes gumbo out of everyday stew territory to something remarkable. Perhaps that's why Louisiana natives (including my wife and her family) take such fierce pride in doting over their slowly browned batches of flour and fat, patiently stirring for sometimes an hour or more; they know the result will be worth it.

This extreme effort makes traditional gumbo an hours-long affair. And some days that's fine. But other days, I'd rather fill the house with the rich smell of chicken, smoky and peppery andouille sausage, and toasted flour without quite as much effort and sweat. I'd rather put my slow cooker to work.

The thing is, you can't make a good, proper roux in a slow cooker—it just doesn't get hot enough. So I set out to make an easy, quick, stress-free roux that I could then add to the slow cooker with the other gumbo ingredients. After trying to make a roux using superhigh heat (too much splatter), the microwave (too hard to monitor), and the oven (too slow), I settled on heating the oil in a nonstick skillet over medium-high heat before adding the flour and stirring for a few minutes, adjusting the burner to medium once the roux turned the color of peanut butter. The skillet, while less traditional than a saucepan, worked well because the larger cooking surface meant more efficient browning, and its shallow shape meant I could stir with a long-handled spatula and not have to hold my hands directly above a pot. After just about 10 minutes of stirring, I had a nice brown roux.

With the roux handled, finishing my recipe was a simple matter: a few more minutes on the stove to soften the holy trinity of onion, celery, and bell pepper; a healthy addition of Creole spices; some meaty chicken thighs and spicy andouille sausage; and the traditional okra for added body and texture and an extra vegetal flavor note.

The final step was zeroing in on the right amount of chicken broth to give the finished gumbo the ideal texture: not gravy, not really even stew, but not

soup either. Four cups of stock was perfect; I stirred half into the skillet with the roux and vegetables to guard against lumps and added the rest after I'd transferred everything to the slow cooker. I then covered the cooker and set it to low.

A little more than 4 hours later, I ladled my fragrant gumbo over white rice in a bowl, adorned it with sliced scallions, splashed on a little vinegary hot sauce, and offered it to my wife, among the most discerning of NOLA natives. Her brow furrowed as she contemplated her second bite, and finally she said, "This can't be from the slow cooker. This tastes like my gumbo!"

SLOW-COOKER CHICKEN AND SAUSAGE GUMBO
Serves 6 to 8
The test kitchen's favorite Creole seasoning is Tony Chachere's Original Creole Seasoning. Trimming the fat from the raw chicken thighs reduces the amount of fat you'll need to skim off the finished gumbo.

- ½ cup vegetable oil
- ¾ cup all-purpose flour
- 2 onions, chopped
- 1 green bell pepper, stemmed, seeded, and chopped
- 1 celery rib, chopped fine
- 4 garlic cloves, minced
- 1 tablespoon Creole seasoning
- 4 cups chicken broth
- 1½ pounds boneless, skinless chicken thighs, trimmed
- Salt and pepper
- 12 ounces andouille sausage, sliced ½ inch thick
- 10 ounces frozen cut okra
- 2 bay leaves
- 4 scallions, white and green parts separated and sliced thin
- 4 cups cooked white rice
- Hot sauce

1. Heat oil in 12-inch nonstick skillet over medium-high heat until just smoking. Using rubber spatula, stir in flour and cook until mixture is color of peanut butter, about 3 minutes, stirring constantly. Reduce heat to medium and continue to cook, stirring constantly, until roux is slightly darker and color of ground cinnamon, 5 to 10 minutes longer.
2. Stir in onions, bell pepper, celery, garlic, and Creole seasoning and cook

until vegetables are softened, 7 to 10 minutes. Stir in 2 cups broth and bring to simmer over high heat; transfer to slow cooker.
3. Season chicken with salt and pepper and transfer to slow cooker. Stir in andouille, okra, bay leaves, and remaining 2 cups broth. Cook on low until chicken is tender, 4 to 5 hours.
4. Transfer chicken to plate. Using 2 forks, shred chicken into bite-size pieces. Skim any excess fat from surface of gumbo and discard bay leaves. Stir in scallion whites and chicken. Serve over rice, sprinkled with scallion greens, passing hot sauce separately.

Don't be tempted to skip the scallions: They add color and a signature burst of fresh flavor.

Frozen Okra Is A-OK
While fresh okra is typically available year-round in the South, it can be hard to find in other parts of the country. That's why we turned to frozen okra, which has the added advantage of being sold already cut. When okra is cooked, it releases a viscous substance that helps thicken the gumbo.

Ramen Noodle Bowls

Could we find a way to cook the meat, noodles, and vegetables all in the same pan?

by Cecelia Jenkins

AN ASIAN-STYLE NOODLE bowl—a mound of steaming noodles tossed with deeply seasoned meat and vegetables—holds plenty of culinary appeal. The challenge of making this dish at home is that you have to cook the noodles, meat, and vegetables separately, which translates into many dirty pots and pans. Or do you? I set out to make tasty, satisfying noodle bowls using a single skillet.

Any recipe for Asian-style noodle bowls has to start with—you guessed it—Asian noodles. But which type? Not every supermarket stocks fresh lo mein noodles, but there is one type of Asian noodle every supermarket (and even many convenience stores) carries: instant ramen. I'm no fan of the salty seasoning packets that accompany these inexpensive noodles, but the noodles themselves are consistently good. Acknowledging them as an unusual choice, I forged ahead with widely available ramen noodles. A bonus: They are precooked and thus require only a quick simmer to be ready to eat.

I started laying the flavor foundation for this one-pan dish by browning sliced white mushrooms in a nonstick skillet over medium-high heat. I then added aromatic minced garlic and grated ginger before pouring in some chicken

Instant ramen noodles—sans the salty flavor packets—help this dish come together quickly.

broth and bringing it to a boil. Next I added the noodles—three packages to make sure I'd have enough for four servings—and covered the skillet. After about 3 minutes, I uncovered the skillet, flipped and stirred the wavy strands to separate them, added bite-size pieces of broccoli, and covered the skillet again so the broccoli would steam through while the noodles finished cooking, which took about 3 more minutes. The noodles absorbed all the liquid, taking in the flavors of the broth, garlic, ginger, and mushrooms.

I was nearly there. I transferred the noodles to serving bowls to await the final component: quick-cooking, thinly sliced pork tenderloin. I wiped my skillet clean and added the pork, which cooked through in about 2 minutes. There was just one problem: The pork was gray, leathery, and bland. I tried again, but this time I coated the pork in a mixture of soy sauce and hoisin sauce for flavor, plus a bit of cornstarch to encourage the sauce to cling to the meat. This did the trick. The pork had much better flavor and color. A sprinkle of scallions finished the dish. One-pan noodle bowls: Mission accomplished.

ONE-PAN NOODLE BOWLS
Serves 4

It doesn't matter which flavor of ramen noodles you buy since you won't be using the seasoning packets sold with the noodles. Don't discard the packets; you can use them to flavor freshly popped popcorn. Serve the noodle bowls with Sriracha hot sauce.

- ¼ cup hoisin sauce
- 3 tablespoons soy sauce
- 2 teaspoons cornstarch
- 1 (12-ounce) pork tenderloin, trimmed, halved lengthwise, and sliced crosswise ¼ inch thick
- 2¼ cups chicken broth
- 2 tablespoons vegetable oil
- 4 ounces white mushrooms, trimmed and sliced thin
- 1 tablespoon grated fresh ginger
- 2 garlic cloves, minced
- 3 (3-ounce) packages ramen noodles, seasoning packets reserved for another use
- 12 ounces broccoli florets, cut into 1-inch pieces
- 3 scallions, sliced thin on bias

1. Whisk 1 tablespoon hoisin, 1 tablespoon soy sauce, and cornstarch together in bowl. Add pork and toss to coat; set aside. Whisk broth, remaining 3 tablespoons hoisin, and remaining 2 tablespoons soy sauce together in second bowl; set aside.

2. Heat 1 tablespoon oil in 12-inch nonstick skillet over medium-high heat until shimmering. Add mushrooms and cook until browned, about 5 minutes. Add ginger and garlic and cook until fragrant, about 30 seconds.

3. Add broth mixture and bring to boil. Arrange noodles in skillet in single layer; cover and reduce heat to medium. Cook until noodles have softened on bottoms (tops will still be dry), about 3 minutes.

4. Uncover skillet and, using tongs, flip noodles and stir to separate. Spread noodles in even layer and scatter broccoli over top. Cover and cook until noodles and broccoli are tender, about 3 minutes, tossing halfway through cooking. Divide noodle mixture evenly among individual bowls; tent with aluminum foil.

5. Wipe skillet clean with paper towels. Heat remaining 1 tablespoon oil in now-empty skillet over high heat until just smoking. Add pork in single layer, breaking up any clumps, and cook without stirring until browned on bottom, about 1 minute. Stir and continue to cook until pork is no longer pink, about 1 minute longer. Divide pork among bowls. Sprinkle with scallions and serve.

Step-by-Step Noodle Bowls
These flavorful noodle bowls take less than 30 minutes of cooking. Here's how we do it:

1. Sear the mushrooms to concentrate their flavor.

2. Cook the noodles in the enhanced chicken broth.

3. Steam the broccoli on top of the noodles.

4. Brown the pork in the now-empty skillet.

Mashed Potatoes

Great mashed potatoes aren't complicated, but you need to pay attention to the details.

by Ashley Moore

WE ALL HAVE our own way of making mashed potatoes. But the more versions I eat, the more I notice that many of them, despite all the different tricks and techniques people use, could be so much better. Why settle for a mediocre mash?

My goal was to make delicious, deeply seasoned, creamy potatoes via a streamlined cooking method that didn't require special equipment such as a ricer or a steamer basket. I chose to rely solely on basic equipment that nearly all home cooks have in their kitchens: a saucepan, a potato masher, and a microwave.

The first thing I had to settle on was the type of potato to use; I chose Yukon Gold potatoes because they're less starchy than russets and therefore produced a creamier mash (though I did determine that russets will work if they're all that's available). After testing different types of dairy, I settled on half-and-half, which was less fatty than heavy cream but richer than milk. To make sure that the mash made it to the table nice and hot, I microwaved the half-and-half and butter before adding them to the cooked spuds.

Lastly, I focused on the seasoning. When I make mashed potatoes, I'm always amazed by how much salt I need to add right before serving to make them taste fully seasoned. This time, however, I tried adding the salt in two stages, first while the potatoes cooked and then again just before serving. This method ensured even, thorough seasoning. All they needed was an additional ½ teaspoon of pepper, and these potatoes were so luscious, creamy, and delicious that I would happily serve them at my holiday table.

Because I was so pleased with the master recipe, I decided to jazz things up with some variations. For a decidedly Italian-inspired take, I added nutty and salty grated Parmesan cheese, minced fresh garlic, and earthy rosemary. For a tribute to the loaded baked potato, I stirred in crispy bacon, crumbled blue cheese, and sliced scallions. I added pungent prepared horseradish and peppery minced fresh chives to the mash for another option. And I took an unexpected approach for my final variation, stirring in bright minced fresh parsley and lemon zest. Mashed potatoes were never so easy—or so good.

EASY MASHED POTATOES
Serves 4
We prefer Yukon Gold potatoes here, but russet potatoes will work in a pinch.

    2   pounds Yukon Gold potatoes, peeled
        and sliced ½ inch thick
        Salt and pepper
    ¾   cup half-and-half
    6   tablespoons unsalted butter

1. Place potatoes and 1 tablespoon salt in large saucepan, add water to cover by 1 inch, and bring to boil over high heat. Reduce heat to medium and simmer until potatoes are tender and paring knife can be easily slipped in and out of potatoes, 18 to 22 minutes.
2. Meanwhile, combine half-and-half and butter in 2-cup liquid measuring cup and microwave, covered, until butter is melted and mixture is warm to touch, about 2 minutes.
3. Drain potatoes and return them to saucepan. Cook over low heat, stirring, until potatoes are thoroughly dried, about 30 seconds. Remove from heat and, using potato masher, mash potatoes until smooth and no lumps remain. Stir in half-and-half mixture, ¾ teaspoon salt, and ½ teaspoon pepper until fully incorporated. Season with salt and pepper to taste. Serve.

EASY MASHED POTATOES WITH PARMESAN, GARLIC, AND ROSEMARY
Stir ½ cup grated Parmesan cheese, 1 minced garlic clove, and 1 teaspoon minced fresh rosemary into potatoes after dairy is incorporated.

EASY MASHED POTATOES WITH BACON, BLUE CHEESE, AND SCALLIONS
Stir ¼ cup crumbled cooked bacon, ¼ cup crumbled blue cheese, and 2 thinly sliced scallions into potatoes after dairy is incorporated.

EASY MASHED POTATOES WITH HORSERADISH AND CHIVES
Stir ¼ cup drained prepared horseradish and ¼ cup minced fresh chives into potatoes after dairy is incorporated.

EASY MASHED POTATOES WITH PARSLEY AND LEMON
Stir ¼ cup minced fresh parsley and 1 tablespoon grated lemon zest into potatoes after dairy is incorporated.

Our variation featuring Parmesan, garlic, and rosemary has a flavorful Italian flair.

EASY MASHED POTATOES

BACON, BLUE CHEESE, AND SCALLIONS

PARSLEY AND LEMON

HORSERADISH AND CHIVES

Pie Plates

Ingredients are important, but the real secret to a perfect pie may be the dish you bake it in.

by Emily Phares

7 Pie Plates
5 Tests

- Bake chocolate pudding pie with graham cracker crust in each plate
- Bake blueberry pie with double pastry crust in each plate
- Bake quiche Lorraine with single pastry crust in each plate
- Heat each plate empty, tracking time and temperature
- Measure dimensions, including thickness

IT'S DIFFICULT TO make a great pie without a great pie plate. Pie plates come in a variety of styles, and the differences aren't just aesthetic—a pie plate's material, thickness, and color all affect the final product.

The Pyrex Basics 9" Pie Plate won our last testing; we liked its overall solid performance, its see-through bottom (for monitoring the bottom crust), and the good (if not great) browning of crusts baked in it. Since then, new and different pie plates have become available, including one made of gold-colored aluminized steel, a material that's won several of our recent bakeware testings with its optimal browning capability and easy release.

It was time to retest. We selected seven widely available pie plates priced from $7.59 to $39.95: two metal, two ceramic, and three glass models, including our former winner. All were close to the standard 9 inches in diameter. To make sure they were truly versatile, we baked three pies per plate, each with a different type of crust: chocolate pudding pie with a graham cracker crust, blueberry pie with a homemade double pastry crust, and a single-crust quiche using a store-bought pastry crust.

Several days and many pies later, we concluded that while all the pie plates produced nicely cooked fillings, the quality of the crusts varied wildly. The two big problems: poor crust release and pale bottom crusts.

All three glass pie plates struggled with the chocolate pudding pie's graham cracker crust. This crust stuck to the glass, requiring extra muscle to slice and remove pie pieces. Our previous winner was especially egregious here. We had to pry the blueberry pie's pastry crust from its glass surface, too. None of the metal or ceramic plates had release

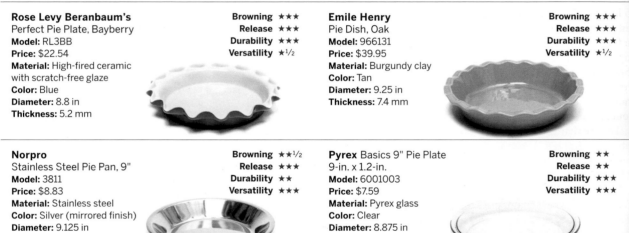

HIGHLY RECOMMENDED

CRITERIA

Williams-Sonoma
Goldtouch Nonstick Pie Dish
Model: 5-1978204
Price: $18.95
Material: Commercial-grade aluminized steel with Goldtouch ceramic nonstick coating
Color: Gold
Diameter: 9 in   **Thickness:** 0.8 mm
Comments: This golden-hued metal plate baked crusts beautifully without overbrowning; even bottom crusts emerged crisp and flaky. Additionally, we liked this plate's nonfluted lip, which allowed for maximum crust-crimping flexibility. One minor drawback: The metal surface is susceptible to scratches and nicks, but we found that this didn't affect its performance.

Criteria	Rating
Browning	★★★
Release	★★★
Durability	★★
Versatility	★★★

WINNING TRAITS
- Produced crisp, golden-brown top and bottom crusts
- Produced evenly cooked, nicely set fillings
- Produced pies that were easy to cut and released cleanly from plate
- Unfluted lip allowed for maximum crust-crimping flexibility

Our winning pie plate consistently produced evenly browned bottom crusts.

RECOMMENDED

Rose Levy Beranbaum's
Perfect Pie Plate, Bayberry
Model: RL3BB
Price: $22.54
Material: High-fired ceramic with scratch-free glaze
Color: Blue
Diameter: 8.8 in
Thickness: 5.2 mm

Criteria	Rating
Browning	★★★
Release	★★★
Durability	★★★
Versatility	★½

Emile Henry
Pie Dish, Oak
Model: 966131
Price: $39.95
Material: Burgundy clay
Color: Tan
Diameter: 9.25 in
Thickness: 7.4 mm

Criteria	Rating
Browning	★★★
Release	★★★
Durability	★★★
Versatility	★½

Norpro
Stainless Steel Pie Pan, 9"
Model: 3811
Price: $8.83
Material: Stainless steel
Color: Silver (mirrored finish)
Diameter: 9.125 in
Thickness: 0.4 mm

Criteria	Rating
Browning	★★½
Release	★★★
Durability	★★
Versatility	★★★

Pyrex Basics 9" Pie Plate
9-in. x 1.2-in.
Model: 6001003
Price: $7.59
Material: Pyrex glass
Color: Clear
Diameter: 8.875 in
Thickness: 4.3 mm

Criteria	Rating
Browning	★★
Release	★★
Durability	★★★
Versatility	★★★

RECOMMENDED WITH RESERVATIONS

OXO
Good Grips Glass 9" Pie Plate
Model: 11175900
Price: $8.99

Criteria	Rating
Browning	★★
Release	★★
Durability	★★★
Versatility	★★½

NOT RECOMMENDED

Pyrex Easy Grab 9.5"
Pie Plate
Model: 1085800
Price: $10.44

Criteria	Rating
Browning	★★
Release	★★
Durability	★★★
Versatility	★

issues—all crusts released effortlessly.

Crust color was an important factor. All the double-crust pies had nicely browned top crusts, but the real challenge was getting the bottom crusts similarly browned and crisp. While the metal and ceramic plates produced picture-perfect bottom crusts, the glass plates disappointed, as their bottom crusts were soft and pale. And we learned that the see-through bottom of a glass plate wasn't a huge advantage, as monitoring the color of the top crust and adhering to a recipe's stated baking times was enough to ensure success.

Why did the metal and ceramic plates brown better than the glass plates? First, metal (both metal plates we tested were steel) is generally a

better conductor of heat than ceramic or especially glass, which heats slowly. Second, since steel is so strong, the metal plates can be made thinner than plates of other materials, which helps them heat faster. The main advantage of ceramic plates was their color: Both ceramic models we tested have dark-colored exteriors, and dark colors absorb more heat than light colors. Overall, the gold-colored metal plate did the best job of browning—crusts emerged beautifully golden and crisp.

Versatility was also important. Most of the plates had flat rims, but our two ceramic contenders had fluted edges. We were impressed by these plates' overall performance, but they just weren't as versatile; while a wavy edge

Go to **CooksCountry.com/nov17** to see the details of all the pie plates in our testing.

is a helpful fluting guide for some bakers, it limits crust styling.

In the end, the Williams-Sonoma Goldtouch Nonstick Pie Dish ($18.95) outshone the rest. It made evenly baked pies with beautifully browned crusts on both top and bottom, and its slices were easy to cut and remove. The plate is also dishwasher-safe and cools down quickly for easy handling. One minor drawback: We noticed scratches on its surface after using metal utensils on it, but these didn't affect its performance. In this case, a gold-colored plate again takes the cake—or rather, the pie.

Ready-Made Pie Crusts

We have high standards for pastry pie crust. Is there a supermarket option that lives up to them?

by Lauren Savoie

GOOD HOMEMADE PIE crust has better flavor and texture than store-bought ready-made versions. But sometimes you don't have the time to make your own pie dough and you need to trade a little quality for convenience. Is there a supermarket crust that will work in a pinch?

Supermarket pie crusts come in two styles: rolled crusts that you unroll and press into your own pie plate and crusts prefitted into aluminum pie plates. We've learned from experience that the prefitted crusts are trouble: They're too small to hold all the filling for most pies, their thin pie plates heat and bake unevenly, and making an attractive double-crust pie is next to impossible—you have to pry a crust out of its pie plate and wrestle with it to form a top crust. To find the best supermarket rolled pie crust, we tasted three top-selling national products three ways: plain (after blind-baking them), in single-crust quiche, and in double-crust blueberry pie.

To our dismay, problems emerged with some crusts before we even got them into the oven. A supermarket crust should be, above all, easy to use, but two of the three crusts weren't large enough to fit in our standard-size 9-inch pie plate. We had to use a rolling pin to stretch them another couple of inches to fit. Only one crust, made by Pillsbury, was large enough to use straight out of the package. What's more, the Wholly Wholesome crust cracked and tore when we unrolled the dough or crimped its edges. We tried everything the company recommends to make the dough workable, but it still cracked. The other two crusts needed only 15 to 30 minutes out of the refrigerator or about 1 hour out of the freezer to reach room temperature and become workable.

On to the oven, where the Pillsbury crust was the only product that fared well. In the blueberry pie test, the Pillsbury crust emerged tender, flaky, and evenly browned after the 1½-hour baking time, but the other two crusts started to burn about halfway through baking. One crust, by Immaculate Baking Co., began to char at the edges after 10 minutes, and we had to pull it from the oven with 40 minutes left on the timer. Another, by Wholly Wholesome, was evenly browned but done 20 minutes early. Why? The Wholly

Our winning crust bakes up light and flaky.

Wholesome and Immaculate Baking Co. crusts contain a small amount of sugar, while the Pillsbury crust has none. Our science editor explained that even a tiny amount of sugar—typically added for flavor—can accelerate browning by the Maillard reaction. The Pillsbury crust tasted great and browned in sync with our recipes.

As for texture, pie crust should be pleasantly flaky, but again only the Pillsbury crust hit the mark. In test after test, the Pillsbury crusts were crisp and flaky, while the other two products were dense and mealy. Here, fat was the issue. As a general rule, pie dough is made with solid fats—butter, shortening, or lard—because these fats never fully disperse within the flour during

mixing; the resulting pockets of fat melt in the oven and release steam that creates flaky layers. (Liquid fats, such as oils, on the other hand, fully saturate the flour during mixing and create dense, tough crusts with no layering.)

All three crusts use a solid fat as their primary fat, so why were their textures so different? The Wholly Wholesome and Immaculate Baking Co. crusts are made with palm oil (Immaculate Baking Co. also adds canola oil), while the Pillsbury crust is made with lard. Though lard and palm oil are both solid fats, their molecular structures affect the textures of the baked crusts. Lard has a very stable molecular structure similar to that of shortening and forms pockets of fat that melt slowly in the oven, producing tender, flaky layers. The fat crystals in palm oil, however, are less stable and begin to melt as the dough is handled and prepared, so fewer of the desired pockets of fat are created, resulting in denser, less flaky crusts.

In the end, one product stood out. Pillsbury Refrigerated Pie Crusts were simple to unroll, fit in our 9-inch pie plate without extra stretching, and baked up golden and flaky. Though we still prefer homemade pie dough, we'll reach for a Pillsbury crust when we're pressed for time.

We Tasted Graham Cracker Crusts, Too: Our Winner Is Made by Elves

Like store-bought pastry crusts, supermarket graham cracker crusts can be big timesavers. To find the best one, we tasted four top-selling national products (including one gluten-free crust) both plain and in our Icebox Lemon Pie. In the end, we found two products we liked; our winner, from Keebler (the same company that makes our winning graham crackers), took top honors for its "sugary" and "buttery" flavors and "crisp" yet "tender" texture. To see the full tasting and results chart, go to CooksCountry.com/grahamcrusts.

KEEBLER READY CRUST GRAHAM PIE CRUST

Go to CooksCountry.com/nov17 to read the full testing results for both types of ready-made pie crusts.

RECOMMENDED
TASTERS' NOTES

Pillsbury
Refrigerated Pie Crusts
Price: $3.99 for 2 crusts ($2.00 per crust)
Fat: Lard and modified lard
Sugar: 0 g per 25-g serving

"Flaky," "buttery," and "user-friendly," this product met all our requirements for an ideal supermarket crust. It fit perfectly in our pie plate right out of the package, with "plenty of overhang" that allowed us to make "picture-perfect" crimped edges. Tasters loved its "light," "crispy" texture and "clean," "toasty" flavor that "allowed the filling to shine."

RECOMMENDED WITH RESERVATIONS

Wholly Wholesome
Bake At Home Organic Pie Dough
Price: $6.99 for 2 crusts ($3.50 per crust)
Fat: Palm oil
Sugar: <1 g per 25-g serving

Though most testers liked the "savory" nuttiness of this "thick," "shortbread"-like crust, some thought the texture was a bit "dense" and "dry." It was also difficult to use: The dough cracked when we tried to unroll it, had to be rolled further to fit in our pie plate, and browned quickly in the oven. While it required more work than we prefer in a supermarket crust, this product makes a decent pie if you prefer a vegetarian crust.

NOT RECOMMENDED

Immaculate Baking Co.
Ready to Bake Pie Crusts
Price: $3.99 for 2 crusts ($2.00 per crust)
Fat: Palm fruit oil and canola oil
Sugar: <1 g per 25-g serving

There was little to like about this crust: It tasted "fishy," "vegetal," and "sour" even though it was well within its sell-by date, and its texture was "tough" and "dense," like "plywood" or "cardboard." Though it unrolled easily, we had to stretch it paper-thin for it to fit in our pie plate, so the bottom crust baked up "soggy." Added sugar made the flavor "oddly sweet" and caused the crust to burn halfway through a 1½-hour bake.

Pine Nut Macaroons

"This recipe comes from my maternal grandmother, Katherine Pizzarello, who taught me more about cooking than anyone else."
– JACK BISHOP
Chief Creative Officer and Cook's Country TV presenter

PINE NUT MACAROONS
Makes 18 large cookies
If desired, the cookies can be dusted with confectioners' sugar just after they come out of the oven.

- 1²/₃ cups slivered almonds
- 1¹/₃ cups (9¹/₃ ounces) sugar
- 2 large egg whites
- 1 cup pine nuts

1. Adjust oven racks to upper-middle and lower-middle positions and heat oven to 375 degrees. Line 2 rimmed baking sheets with parchment paper.
2. Process almonds and sugar in food processor until finely ground, about 30 seconds. Add egg whites and process until smooth, about 20 seconds. (Dough will be sticky.) Transfer dough to large bowl. Place pine nuts in separate shallow bowl.
3. Spray 1-tablespoon measuring spoon with vegetable oil spray. Working with 1 rounded tablespoon dough at a time, shape into balls and roll balls in pine nuts until evenly coated. Place 9 balls on each prepared sheet, spaced 2 inches apart.
4. Bake cookies until light golden brown, 14 to 16 minutes, switching and rotating sheets halfway through baking. Let cookies cool completely on sheets. Serve. (Cookies can be stored in airtight container for several days.)

We're celebrating the tenth season of Cook's Country from America's Test Kitchen, starring Bridget Lancaster and Julia Collin-Davison. Check your local listings for details. In the meantime, to revisit earlier seasons and find your favorite recipes, visit CooksCountry.com. There, you can also submit a favorite family recipe (or write to Heirloom Recipes, Cook's Country, 21 Drydock Avenue, Suite 210E, Boston, MA 02210). Include your name and mailing address. If we print your recipe, you'll receive a free one-year subscription to Cook's Country.

COMING NEXT ISSUE

*We're gearing up for the holidays. This year, we'll share the secrets to perfect **Roasted Beef Tenderloin** and a supersimple **Spice-Roasted Butternut Squash** side dish. For something sweet, we'll serve **Rum Balls** and **Chocolate Chip Panettone**. We'll also visit Moss Landing, California, to sample a famous **Cioppino**; New York City for **Cheese Blintzes**; and Fall River, Massachusetts, for savory **Pork Pies**. Come along!*

RECIPE INDEX

RC=Recipe Card

FIND THE ROOSTER!

A tiny version of this rooster has been hidden in a photo in the pages of this issue. Write to us with its location, and we'll enter you in a random drawing. The first correct entry drawn will win our favorite p plate, and each of the next five will receive a free one-year subscription to Cook's Country. To enter, visit CooksCountry.com rooster by November 27, 2017, or write to Rooster ON17, Cook's Country, 21 Drydock Avenue, Suite 210E, Boston, MA 02210. Include your name and address. Corey Pollack of Forest Grove, Oregon, found the rooster in the June/July 2017 issue on pa 11 and won our favorite paring knife.

WEB EXTRAS

Free for four months at
CooksCountry.com
Braised Beef Short Ribs
Cider-Braised Pork
Coffee Whipped Cream Frosting
Lemon Chiffon Layer Cake
Tasting Chicken Broth
Tasting Milk Chocolate Chips
Tasting Ready-Made Graham Cracker Crusts
Tasting Ready-Made Pie Crusts
Tasting Vanilla Ice Cream
Testing Cake Pans
Testing Electric Knives
Testing Muffin Tins
Testing Pie Plates

READ US ON IPAD

Download the Cook's Country app for iPad and start a free trial subscription or purchase a single issue of the magazine. issues are enhanced with full-color Cook Mode slide shows that provide step-by-step instructions for completing recipes, plus expanded reviews and ratings. Go to CooksCountry.com/iPad to download or app through iTunes.

BLUM'S COFFEE CRUNCH CAKE

Crushed bits of homemade coffee candy adorn the outside of this delicious cake.

In the 1970s, no shopping excursion to San Francisco's I. Magnin department store was complete without a stop at their in-house bakery, Blum's, for a slice of cake. Their signature concoction featured light-as-a-feather lemon cake frosted with coffee-flavored whipped cream and studded with bits of light, crunchy coffee candy. The bakery has been closed for decades, but the iconic cake lives on.

TO MAKE THIS CAKE, YOU WILL NEED:

- 1½ cups (10½ ounces) sugar
- ¼ cup brewed coffee
- ¼ cup light corn syrup
- 1 tablespoon baking soda
- 1 (9-inch) Lemon Chiffon Layer Cake round*
- 4 cups Coffee Whipped Cream Frosting*

FOR THE COFFEE CRUNCH:

Grease 8-inch square baking pan and line with parchment paper, allowing excess to overhang pan edges; grease parchment. Heat sugar, coffee, and corn syrup in large saucepan over medium-high heat, stirring occasionally, until mixture registers 310 degrees. Stir in baking soda until incorporated, about 20 seconds (mixture will puff up significantly). Pour mixture into prepared pan and let cool completely, about 1 hour. Once cooled, remove coffee crunch block from pan, place in large zipper-lock bag, and seal. Using rolling pin, crush into bite-size pieces.

TO ASSEMBLE:

Using long serrated knife, cut 1 horizontal line around sides of cake; then, following scored line, cut cake into 2 even layers. Place 1 cake layer on cake plate or pedestal. Spread 2 cups frosting evenly over top right to edge of cake. Top with second cake layer and press lightly to adhere, then spread remaining 2 cups frosting over top and sides of cake. Lightly press crushed coffee crunch all over cake. Slice and serve.

 *Go to **CooksCountry.com** for our Lemon Chiffon Layer Cake and Coffee Whipped Cream Frosting recipes.

INSIDE THIS ISSUE

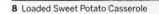

Cook's Country

Perfect Sugar Cookies

This year, we want cozy, sweet, and simple. Our foolproof recipe takes the guesswork out of these deceptively tricky holiday treats.

PAGE 24

Roast Beef Tenderloin
Holiday Classic, Decoded

Foil Potatoes
Easiest-Ever Method

Spice-Roasted Squash
Big Flavor, Little Work

Potent Rum Balls
Dessert for Grown-Ups

Mini Pork Pies
Flaky Crust, Juicy Filling

Monterey Bay Cioppino
West Coast Favorite

Extra-Sharp Cheddar
Supermarket Showdown

Ricotta Gnocchi
Easier Than You Think

Ground Beef Stroganoff
Weeknight Special

DECEMBER / JANUARY 2018
$5.95 U.S. / $6.95 CANADA

01>

0 74470 02742 3

DISPLAY UNTIL JANUARY 8, 2018

LETTER FROM THE EDITOR

THE HOLIDAY SEASON represents the best opportunity all year for a home cook to show off. The guest lists are long and the stakes high. Roasts are grand, side dishes are special, desserts are exciting. It's a wonderful time to surprise and delight family and friends with a festive feast.

But let's face it: It's also the best opportunity all year for a home cook to fall flat. Get distracted for a moment and that roast can overcook, that side dish can go south, that cake can collapse.

It's a high-wire act, wobbly and uncertain.

At *Cook's Country*, we believe the answer is balance. Construct your holiday menu not just with an eye to how the food will taste but with a strict eye to how you'll achieve it. Be realistic. Don't shy away from the high-impact dishes that require care and attention (see our resplendent Classic Roast Beef Tenderloin on page 18), but offset these with simple, homey favorites such as Foil-Roasted Potatoes (page 21). Look for things you can make ahead—for example, our perfect Chewy Sugar Cookies (page 24)—and don't forget that you are your own toughest critic.

After all, the goal is to celebrate, not to sweat.

TUCKER SHAW

Editor in Chief

CELEBRATIONS CALL FOR MEALS THAT IMPRESS

All-Time Best Holiday Entertaining

The experts in the test kitchen are no strangers to pulling off a great holiday meal. In this book, we've gathered the absolute best dishes for making your next celebration memorable. Plus, we've included tips and make-ahead instructions to help you plan ahead and reduce stress, Order your copy online at **AmericasTestKitchen.com/holidayentertaining**.

Find us on **Facebook**
facebook.com/CooksCountry

Find us on **Instagram**
instagram.com/CooksCountry

Follow us on **Pinterest**
pinterest.com/TestKitchen

Follow us on **Twitter**
twitter.com/TestKitchen

Chief Executive Officer David Nussbaum
Chief Creative Officer Jack Bishop
Editor in Chief Tucker Shaw
Executive Managing Editor Todd Meier
Executive Food Editor Bryan Roof
Deputy Editor Scott Kathan
Associate Editors Morgan Bolling, Cecelia Jenkins, Katie Leaird, Ashley Moore
Photo Team & Special Events Manager Tim McQuinn
Lead Cook, Photo Team Daniel Cellucci
Test Cooks Alli Berkey, Matthew Fairman
Assistant Test Cooks Mady Nichas, Jessica Rudolph
Senior Copy Editor Krista Magnuson
Copy Editor Jillian Campbell
Contributing Editor Eva Katz
Science Editor Guy Crosby, PhD, CFS
Hosts & Executive Editors, Television Bridget Lancaster, Julia Collin Davison

Executive Editor, Tastings & Testings Lisa McManus
Deputy Editor, Tastings & Testings Hannah Crowley
Associate Editors, Tastings & Testings Miye Bromberg, Lauren Savoie, Kate Shannon
Assistant Editor, Tastings & Testings Emily Phares
Editorial Assistant, Tastings & Testings Carolyn Grillo

Executive Editor, Web Christine Liu
Managing Editor, Web Mari Levine
Senior Editors, Web Roger Metcalf, Briana Palma
Associate Editor, Web Terrence Doyle
Assistant Editor, Web Molly Farrar

Creative Director John Torres
Photography Director Julie Cote
Art Director Susan Levin
Designer Maggie Edgar
Senior Staff Photographer Daniel J. van Ackere
Staff Photographers Steve Klise, Kevin White
Photography Producer Mary Ball

Director, Creative Operations Alice Carpenter
Test Kitchen Director Erin McMurrer
Assistant Test Kitchen Director Alexxa Benson
Test Kitchen Manager Meridith Lippard
Test Kitchen Facilities Manager Sophie Clingan-Darack
Senior Kitchen Assistant Receiver Kelly Ryan
Senior Kitchen Assistant Shopper Marissa Bunnewith
Lead Kitchen Assistant Ena Gudiel
Kitchen Assistants Gladis Campos, Blanca Castanza

Chief Financial Officer Jackie McCauley Ford
Director, Customer Support Amy Bootier
Senior Customer Loyalty & Support Specialists Rebecca Kowalski, Andrew Straaberg Finfrock
Customer Loyalty & Support Specialist J.P. Dubuque
Production Director Guy Rochford
Imaging Manager Lauren Robbins
Production & Imaging Specialists Heather Dube, Dennis Noble, Jessica Voas

Chief Revenue Officer Sara Domville
Director, Special Accounts Erica Nye
Director, Sponsorship Marketing & Client Services Christine Anagnostis
Client Services Manager Kate Zebrowski
Client Service and Marketing Representative Claire Gambel
Director, Business Partnerships Mehgan Conciatori
Partnership Marketing Manager Pamela Putprush

Chief Digital Officer Fran Middleton
VP, Marketing Natalie Vinard
Marketing Director, Social Media and Content Strategy Claire Oliverson
Senior Social Media Coordinators Kelsey Hopper, Morgan Mannino

Senior VP, Human Resources & Organizational Development Colleen Zelina
Human Resources Director Adele Shapiro

Public Relations & Communications Director Brian Franklin
Public Relations Coordinator Lauren Watson

Photography Keller + Keller
Food Styling Catrine Kelty, Sally Staub
Circulation Services ProCirc

On the cover: Chewy Sugar Cookies

Cook's Country magazine (ISSN 1552-1990), number 78, is published bimonthly by America's Test Kitchen Limited Partnership, 21 Drydock Avenue, Suite 210E, Boston, MA 02210. Copyright 2017 America's Test Kitchen Limited Partnership. Periodicals postage paid at Boston, MA, and additional mailing offices, USPS #023453. Publications Mail Agreement No. 40020778. Return undeliverable Canadian addresses to P.O. Box 875, Station A, Windsor, ON N9A 6P2. POSTMASTER: Send address changes to *Cook's Country*, PO Box 6018, Harlan, IA 51593-1518. For subscription and gift subscription orders, subscription inquiries, or change of address notices, visit AmericasTestKitchen.com/support, call 800-526-8447 in the U.S. or 515-237-3663 from outside the U.S., or write to us at *Cook's Country*, P.O. Box 6018, Harlan, IA 51593-1518. PRINTED IN THE USA.

FLAT-LEAF PARSLEY
Vibrant flavor

Parsley 101

Are curly- and flat-leaf parsleys interchangeable in recipes?
Carina Sorenson, Ada, Mich.

In the test kitchen, we almost always call for flat-leaf parsley because we prefer its flavor to that of curly-leaf parsley. A bonus is that it's easier to chop than its curly-leafed cousin. But we're never content to rest on our laurels, so we decided to revisit this preference with a series of blind taste tests. We bought multiple bunches of both flat-leaf and curly-leaf parsley, chopped them fine so there was no visual difference, and used both in three of our recipes: Real Tabbouleh, Salsa Verde, and Herbed Croutons. Tasters were asked to try both versions of each side by side.

The crouton recipe calls for just a small amount of parsley, and tasters couldn't tell a difference between the two. But parsley plays a starring role in the salsa and the tabbouleh. Tasters much preferred the flat-leaf versions, commenting that they had a "fresh," "vibrant," "lemon-pepper" astringency, whereas the curly-leaf batches were more "mild" and "vegetal."

THE BOTTOM LINE: If you're just sprinkling a little chopped parsley over a dish to add color, it doesn't matter which kind you use. But if parsley is a major player in a recipe, we recommend using the flat-leaf variety (unless a recipe specifies otherwise). **by Morgan Bolling**

CURLY-LEAF PARSLEY
Best for garnishes

 Submit questions and shortcuts at CooksCountry.com/ask and CooksCountry.com/shortcuts.

Cracking the Cream Code

Can I whip light cream instead of heavy cream to avoid excess fat?
Barbara Blakelock, Missoula, Mont.

With so many options in the dairy aisle, it's hard to keep all the creams straight. At its most basic, cream is the fat-rich layer skimmed off the top of unhomogenized milk. From there, creams are categorized based on their milk fat content: Light cream is 18 to 30 percent milk fat, whipping cream is 30 to 36 percent milk fat, and heavy cream is 36 to 40 percent milk fat. Half-and-half, which weighs in between 10.5 and 18 percent milk fat, is a combination of cream and milk (whole milk is 3.5 percent milk fat).

To see how the creams compare, we first tried whipping each. Since cream needs to be 30 percent milk fat or higher to hold enough air to solidify, light cream and half-and-half remained liquid no matter how long we whipped them. Whipping cream reached the same volume as heavy cream and reached stiff peaks faster. It was airier and less creamy than whipped heavy cream but was still acceptable.

We also sampled each product in our Cream Biscuits and our Classic Tomato Soup, which is finished with ½ cup of heavy cream. The biscuit batters made with light cream and half-and-half were too thin and impossible to form or cut. The biscuits made with whipping cream were a touch less rich but were comparable to those made with heavy cream. In the tomato soup, heavy cream was, again, the favorite, but the whipping cream came in a close second. Both the light cream and the half-and-half broke when added to the acidic soup. The soups tasted fine but were visually unappealing and lacked the body of the heavy-cream sample. **–M.B.**

THE BOTTOM LINE: Go ahead and swap whipping cream for heavy cream if you're trying to cut calories, but don't try to substitute light cream or half-and-half for heavy cream.

PRODUCT	FAT CONTENT	WILL IT WHIP?
Heavy Cream	36 to 40%	Yes
Whipping Cream	30 to 36%	Yes
Light Cream	18 to 30%	No
Half-and-Half	10.5 to 18%	No

LIGHT CREAM
Not enough fat to hold air and solidify

WHIPPING CREAM
Airier than heavy cream but still acceptable

Reheating Rice

I often have leftover white rice in the refrigerator. What's the best way to reheat it?
Sylvia Ahmet, Alpharetta, Ga.

Reheating white rice can be a tricky proposition—especially if you want it to be as light and fluffy as freshly cooked rice. To find the best method, we made a batch of white rice and also ordered in rice from a local take-out spot. We let both rices cool completely and then tried reviving them using a few different techniques.

Reheating the rice in a covered baking dish in the oven for 25 minutes or in a saucepan on the stovetop for nearly 15 minutes took too long. And both methods required adding significant amounts of water to avoid burning the grains, which caused some of them to become soggy.

We next turned our attention to the microwave, reheating batches of the rices at different power levels, covered and uncovered, and with and without water. We finally landed on a method that worked surprisingly well. Simply microwave up to 4 cups of cold cooked rice and 1 tablespoon of water, covered, until the rice is steaming and heated through, stirring once halfway through microwaving. This method took about 5 minutes total; smaller amounts of rice will heat more quickly. We found that it works well with rice that has been refrigerated for up to three days.

THE BOTTOM LINE: To revive refrigerated rice, combine up to 4 cups of the rice with up to 1 tablespoon of water and microwave, covered, until heated through. **–M.B.**

Freezing Ricotta

Ricotta spoils quickly. Can I freeze it if I don't use the whole tub?
Amy Carrera, Springfield, Mo.

To see how fresh ricotta cheese would fare once frozen and thawed, we bought a couple of tubs and froze the cheese two ways: directly in the tub and in a zipper-lock bag with the air pressed out. A week later, we thawed the samples and tried both, along with a sample of fresh ricotta, plain and in our recipes for Simple Lasagna with Hearty Tomato Meat Sauce and Ricotta Crostini with Cherry Tomatoes and Basil.

Tasters noticed visual differences in the plain samples right away. The frozen batches looked separated, with a pool of milky liquid surrounding gritty cheese specks (freezing ruptures cell walls in the cheese, causing the liquid and fat to separate). Both frozen samples were noticeably less smooth and creamy.

When it came to taste, tasters slightly preferred the sample frozen in a sealed zipper-lock bag because it was less separated. In the crostini recipe, where the ricotta is blitzed in the food processor until smooth, the differences were less evident, but both frozen samples were looser, making it hard to smear them

on bread. The frozen samples fared the best in the lasagna. While some tasters preferred the fresh ricotta for its smoother texture, some tasters could not tell a difference, deeming both fresh and frozen samples acceptable.

THE BOTTOM LINE: We don't recommend freezing ricotta, as it negatively affects the cheese's texture. But if it comes down to throwing it out or freezing it, place it in a zipper-lock bag, remove all the air, seal the bag, and freeze it. Thaw it in the refrigerator and use it only in applications where it is not the star of the dish. **–M.B.**

Ice Is Nice
Bill Wall, Hawkinsville, Ga.

I use a rasp grater a lot for grating citrus zest, hard cheese, garlic, and ginger. But often food clings to the back of the blade even after I've tapped it and wiped it out. I found that grating a large ice cube pushes out any stuck-on bits. All I need to do after that is give the grater a quick blast under the faucet.

All Bundled Up
Regan Langley, Chino, Calif.

Following your advice, I store fresh chives rolled in a damp paper towel in the crisper drawer of my refrigerator—this really does keep them fresh for longer. I realized that the paper towel, when peeled back a bit, can also be a great help while chopping. It helps secure the long strands and keeps them in a tight bundle as I chop.

Peeler in Disguise
Chris Dillon, Alexandria, Va.

I recently bought a silicone handle protector for my cast-iron pans. One day I realized how much it looks like one of those garlic-peeling tubes, so I tried peeling garlic in it and it worked great! Just put the garlic cloves inside the handle protector and use the heel of your hand to roll them around on the counter. The skins come off easily, and the tube rinses right out for easy cleanup.

Compiled by Cecelia Jenkins

Your Nonstick Skillet: The surprising rules for using, cleaning, and—yes—seasoning this go-to kitchen workhorse. *by Hannah Crowley*

Use It For:

- **Eggs:** Fried and scrambled eggs and omelets can stick and tear in regular skillets.
- **Stir-fries:** Most stir-fries start with searing protein, but we don't want to lose any flavorful browning; with nonstick, the browning sticks to the meat, not to the skillet.

EQUIPMENT

- **Pan-frying breaded foods:** We want the breading to stick only to the food.
- **Pancakes:** Batter can stick to traditional skillets and burn, but it easily releases from nonstick models.

Don't Use It For:

- **Pan sauces:** Nonstick skillets discourage the development of fond.
- **Browning butter and toasting nuts:** The dark nonstick surface makes it hard to see important visual cues that signal when the food is done.
- **Searing foods over very high heat:** Steel or cast-iron skillets give better results when searing, and there's no danger of damaging the nonstick coating or emitting toxic fumes at high temperatures.

Test Kitchen Winner
Our winning skillet, the **OXO Good Grips Non-Stick 12-inch Open Frypan** ($32.02), features three layers of nonstick coating applied to a hard-anodized aluminum core. Its slick, durable surface cooks and releases food perfectly.

Handle Hack
The surfaces of most nonstick skillets are ovensafe up to about 500 degrees, but their plastic handles will melt before temperatures get that high. To get around this problem, we wrap the handle in a layer of wet paper towels and then a double layer of aluminum foil, which we've found keeps the handle at a safe temperature for more than an hour in a 425-degree oven.

Tips for Preserving the Nonstick Surface

- **Utensils:** Use plastic, wood, and silicone utensils—and try to avoid using metal ones. Even if your skillet is labeled "scratch resistant," it's still susceptible to scratches, which compromise its nonstick ability.

- **Storage:** To minimize scratches, avoid stacking other pans in a nonstick skillet. If you need to, layer paper plates or paper towels over its surface to protect it.

- **Cleaning:** The surface of a nonstick skillet can get damaged during cleaning, too. We recommend avoiding abrasive sponges and cleaners. Use soft sponges and regular dish soap instead. Fortunately, hard scrubbing is rarely necessary because the slick surfaces of nonstick skillets are notably easy to clean.

Seasoning Nonstick Skillets
Seasoning isn't just for cast-iron and carbon-steel skillets. In our recent nonstick skillet testing, we learned that a few manufacturers suggest seasoning their nonstick skillets before use to enhance and maintain nonstick ability. We tried it and noticed a marked improvement. We suggest seasoning new nonstick skillets and any nonstick skillets that seem to be getting a little sticky.

To season a nonstick skillet, warm the empty skillet over low to medium-low heat for 30 seconds, remove it from the heat, and use a paper towel to rub it with 1 tablespoon of vegetable oil. Wipe it out with a clean paper towel before using it.

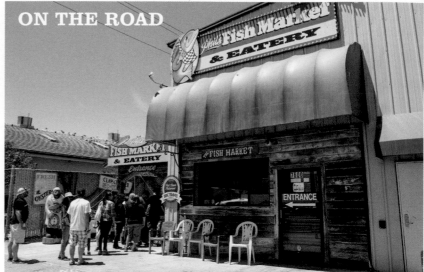

Phil's Fish Story

A childhood by the bay led to a life of chipping in. *by Bryan Roof*

IF IT WEREN'T for the line of people snaking through the parking lot to the front door of Phil's Fish Market & Eatery in Moss Landing, California, you could easily drive right by it. The tin-sided combination of seafood market and restaurant blends into its industrial port surroundings, camouflaged by stacks of wooden pallets, rusted shipping containers, and dry-docked boats. The building was once a squid processing plant, one of many now-defunct fish processing facilities in the area (John Steinbeck's famous novel *Cannery Row* was set in Monterey, just a short drive down the coast from Phil's).

Crowds from a rodeo and a motorcycle rally taking place in nearby Salinas mix with local sightseers fresh from the Monterey Bay Aquarium. DiGirolamo expected to feed 3,500 customers on the day that I arrived. The place is loud, owing in part to the polished concrete floor, intended for high traffic and easy cleanup. "It's not for everybody," DiGirolamo explains. "I play to families."

DiGirolamo is a stout man with a salt-and-pepper beard and warm eyes.

He grew up along this stretch of coast, one of 13 kids who pitched in at the family seafood restaurant. "We wanted to be managers, but my uncles had those jobs." Instead, DiGirolamo stuck to the kitchen, where he learned his grandmother's cooking secrets, measuring her handfuls of ingredients so he could re-create the recipes.

The most popular item on the menu is cioppino, which DiGirolamo claims gets its name from everyone "chipping in" to the pot depending on what came in from the sea that day. His version contains an astonishing amount of seafood—scallops, prawns, calamari, mussels, fish, clams, and a cluster of Dungeness crab legs poking out of the top. Servers deliver gadgets for cracking shells and prying meat along with cheap plastic bibs that, while not stylish, do keep your clothes safe from stains.

Some years back, DiGirolamo began giving cioppino cooking demonstrations. He recalls, "One day, a guy comes in, looks at the cioppino in the electric wok, and says, 'I want that.' He gave me a $100 bill, I gave him the cioppino and the wok . . . and then I went out and bought five more woks."

Phil DiGirolamo (above) can serve thousands of customers a day at his cavernous market, where newbies order by the bowl but regulars order by the tub to take home. He views his business as a community touchstone as much as a restaurant, and he makes a point of wandering through the room regularly. Also on the menu: Phil's famous artichoke cupcakes.

Monterey Bay Cioppino

This stew is famous in San Francisco. But just down the coast, we found a version we like even better.

by Matthew Fairman

CIOPPINO IS AN Italian American fish stew from San Francisco featuring an abundance of seafood in a garlicky broth of tomatoes, stock, and wine. It's a treasured dish, a staple in Bay Area restaurants. But on a recent visit to Phil's Fish Market in Moss Landing, a 90-minute drive away, we were inspired by a slightly sweeter, more herby version that locals and visitors alike line up for (see "Phil's Fish Story").

Phil DiGirolamo's cioppino is built on a tomato-based broth, which is traditional. But then DiGirolamo sets his cioppino apart from others: He makes a basil pesto and sautés mussels and clams in that pesto, along with a few other surprising ingredients—Worcestershire sauce, saffron, cinnamon, brown sugar for sweetness, and a healthy dose of Sauternes, a white dessert wine. These additions make DiGirolamo's cioppino sweeter and more complex and aromatic than the standard version. He then brings the dish together by incrementally adding the rest of the seafood—sea bass, calamari, shrimp, scallops, and Dungeness crab—along with the tomatoey broth and a long pour of clam juice.

To create a home recipe inspired by this variation, I needed to make some strategic adjustments. The marinara base stayed straightforward, relying on pantry staples and coming together quickly. And while DiGirolamo makes a separate pesto for cooking the seafood, I decided to skip the food processor and simply add pesto's key ingredients (olive oil, basil, and garlic) to the mix. My tasters approved.

It's easy enough for a seaside restaurant to have access to such a wide range of seafood, but for a home version, I wanted to tighten the roster. I ditched the clams and calamari, leaving me with easy-to-find shrimp, scallops, sea bass, and mussels. (Rest assured, this stew is delicious even if you decide to leave out one or more of these ingredients; see "Seafood Substitutions.") DiGirolamo also adds Sauternes, an expensive choice to use as a cooking wine. When I tried a few cheaper substitutes, dry sherry stood out as a clear favorite, adding a comparable complex sweetness.

When I brought out my simplified version of DiGirolamo's cioppino, it drew raves. But I had my eyes on only one taster, our executive food editor

Bryan Roof, who had tried the real thing in Moss Landing. He didn't rave; he was too busy spooning cioppino into his mouth.

MONTEREY BAY CIOPPINO
Serves 6 to 8

We recommend buying "dry" scallops, which don't have chemical additives and taste better than "wet" scallops. Dry scallops will look ivory or pinkish; wet scallops are bright white. If you can't find fresh dry scallops, you can substitute thawed frozen scallops. If you can't find sea bass, you can substitute cod, haddock, or halibut fillets.

MARINARA

- 3 tablespoons extra-virgin olive oil
- 1 large onion, halved and sliced thin
- 3 garlic cloves, sliced thin
- ¾ teaspoon salt
- 1 (15-ounce) can tomato sauce
- 1 cup canned tomato puree
- ½ cup chopped fresh basil
- 1 tablespoon packed light brown sugar
- 1½ teaspoons Worcestershire sauce
- ¼ teaspoon ground cinnamon

CIOPPINO

- 1½ pounds skinless sea bass fillets, 1 to 1½ inches thick, cut into 1½-inch pieces
- 12 ounces extra-large shrimp (21 to 25 per pound), peeled, deveined, and tails removed
- 12 ounces large scallops, tendons removed, cut in half horizontally Salt and pepper
- 3 tablespoons extra-virgin olive oil
- 1 pound mussels, scrubbed and debearded
- ½ cup chopped fresh basil
- ¼ cup dry sherry
- 3 garlic cloves, minced
- 1 teaspoon Worcestershire sauce
- ½ teaspoon saffron threads, crumbled
- 2 (8-ounce) bottles clam juice
- 1 (12-inch) baguette, sliced and toasted Lemon wedges

1. FOR THE MARINARA: Heat oil in large saucepan over medium heat until shimmering. Add onion, garlic, and salt and cook until onion is softened and just beginning to brown, about 8 minutes. Add tomato sauce, tomato puree, basil, sugar, Worcestershire, and cinnamon and bring to boil. Reduce heat to medium-low and

This cioppino is richer, darker, and more complex than more-common renditions.

simmer until marinara is slightly thickened, 10 to 12 minutes. Remove from heat, cover, and set aside.

2. FOR THE CIOPPINO: Season sea bass, shrimp, and scallops with salt and pepper; set aside. Heat oil in Dutch oven over medium-high heat until shimmering. Add mussels, basil, sherry, garlic, Worcestershire, saffron, and ½ teaspoon salt. Cover and cook until mussels start to open, about 2 minutes.

3. Stir in clam juice and marinara until combined. Nestle sea bass and scallops into pot and bring to boil. Reduce heat to medium, cover, and simmer until seafood is just turning opaque, about 2 minutes. Nestle shrimp into pot and return to simmer. Cover and cook until all seafood is opaque, about 3 minutes. Remove from heat and let sit, covered, for 5 minutes. Serve with baguette slices and lemon wedges.

Seafood Substitutions

Our version of Phil's cioppino uses a carefully considered collection of seafood, but that doesn't mean you can't make it if you can't find everything on the ingredient list. For instance, sea bass is our first choice, but you can also use cod, haddock, or halibut fillets of a similar size. Here are a few more options:

- Double the amount of shrimp or scallops if you can't find one or the other.
- Use small clams in place of the mussels, or use half clams and half mussels.
- Garnish the stew with cooked crabmeat—or, for the full Phil's effect, cooked crab legs—before serving.

Oven-Roasted Jerk Ribs

Move over, chicken; jerk makes for some fine swine. *by Morgan Bolling*

THE FOUNDATION OF most great jerk recipes is the combination of fiery Scotch bonnet chiles, warm allspice, and fragrant thyme; these elements combine to create a flavor that's bold, yes, but also deeply complex—hot, sweet, savory, herbal, and fruity. Although Americans may know jerk best as a spicy coating for grilled chicken, in Jamaica it was originally used to season pork. As a nod to this history—and, to be honest, because I love ribs—I set out to develop a recipe for oven-cooked jerk ribs that could brighten up any table with big flavors and a little Jamaican heat.

The first order of business was to determine what type of ribs to use. I tried coating St. Louis–style spareribs, baby back ribs, and country-style pork ribs with store-bought jerk paste and roasted them in a low 275-degree oven. About 4 hours later, I pulled out the now-tender ribs and called my team to taste. We liked the St. Louis–style ribs best; their meaty, almost sweet flavor was a perfect vehicle for the bold jerk seasoning.

The next order of business was improving on the jarred jerk paste. I prepared six promising jerk recipes I'd found in various Caribbean and barbecue cookbooks. They all had their merits, but some called for as many as 23 ingredients—excessive for what should be a simple dish. After several days of trial and error, I created my own version using the most essential ingredients: habanero chiles (a close relative of Scotch bonnets, which can be hard to find), ground allspice, dried thyme, scallions, garlic, ginger, brown sugar, salt, and—to create the right consistency—vegetable oil. I roasted a few racks that I'd slathered with this homemade jerk paste and called the troops in to taste. "Pretty good," my colleagues opined, "but not yet great."

I headed back into the test kitchen and set about tweaking the recipe. Letting the ribs marinate for a few hours in the intense jerk paste made them more flavorful. Using molasses in place of the brown sugar added more depth to the mix. But the ribs were still missing something, and my tasters helped me pinpoint it: acid. Following the lead of a few recipes I'd seen, I tried both brushing the ribs with cider vinegar and squeezing some lime juice over them before serving, but the raw acids were too sharp and masked the nuanced jerk flavor. Instead, I mixed a little vinegar with some reserved marinade and brushed it over the ribs for the last 10 minutes of cooking. This created a bright, fresh, deeply flavorful crust that took the ribs from good to great.

We suggest serving these spicy, punchy ribs with a reggae soundtrack and plenty of ice-cold Red Stripe beer.

What a Jerk!

Jerk is the spicy Jamaican seasoning paste based on Scotch bonnet peppers, allspice, and thyme. But it's also a verb—you can "jerk" chicken, ribs, fish, and the like if you coat them in the paste and grill them.

The heat will make you sit up straight, but these ribs also have an herby, fruity depth.

Which Ribs Work Best for Jerk?

Three cuts of pork ribs are commonly offered at supermarkets: St. Louis–style, baby back, and country-style ribs. Country-style ribs aren't ribs at all but are more like long, irregular chops cut from where the loin meets the shoulder; they contain a mix of dark and light meat. Baby back ribs are cut from the loin area and are smaller and leaner than St. Louis–style spareribs. For this recipe, we opted for St. Louis–style, as their big flavor (they're cut from near the belly, where bacon comes from) stood up to the jerk's bold spices. If you see spareribs not called "St. Louis–cut," they probably have extra meat and bone attached—this gives them an irregular shape and makes them hard to cook evenly.

St. Louis–style ribs: meaty flavor, uniform shape

JERK PORK RIBS
Serves 4 to 6

Plan ahead: This recipe requires letting the coated ribs sit for at least 1 hour. We recommend wearing rubber gloves when handling the habaneros—they're hot! If you are spice-averse, remove the seeds and ribs from the habaneros or substitute jalapeños, which are less spicy.

- 8 scallions, chopped coarse
- ¼ cup vegetable oil
- ¼ cup molasses
- 3 tablespoons chopped fresh ginger
- 2 tablespoons ground allspice
- 1–2 habanero chiles, stemmed
- 3 garlic cloves, peeled
- 1 tablespoon dried thyme
- 1 tablespoon salt
- 2 (2½- to 3-pound) racks St. Louis–style spareribs, trimmed
- 3 tablespoons cider vinegar
  Lime wedges

1. Process scallions, oil, 3 tablespoons molasses, ginger, allspice, habaneros, garlic, thyme, and salt in blender until smooth, 1 to 2 minutes, scraping down sides of blender jar as needed. Transfer ¼ cup jerk paste to bowl, cover, and refrigerate until needed. Place ribs on rimmed baking sheet and brush all over with remaining paste. Cover sheet tightly with plastic wrap and refrigerate for at least 1 hour or up to 24 hours.

2. Adjust oven rack to middle position and heat oven to 275 degrees. Line second rimmed baking sheet with aluminum foil and set wire rack in sheet. Unwrap ribs and place, meat side up, on prepared wire rack. Roast until tender and fork inserted into meat meets no resistance, 4 to 4½ hours.

3. Stir vinegar and remaining 1 tablespoon molasses into reserved jerk paste. Brush meat side of racks with vinegar mixture. Return ribs to oven and roast until sauce sets, about 10 minutes. Transfer ribs to carving board, tent with foil, and let rest for 20 minutes. Slice racks between ribs. Serve with lime wedges.

Glazed Roast Chicken

Even the tastiest glaze becomes useless if it runs off the bird. For a glaze that stays put and looks incredible, paint it on in stages. *by Alli Berkey*

A BIG PART of a roast chicken's appeal is the high reward—beautiful presentation, juicy meat, and tasty skin—for minimal effort. Adding a flavorful glaze to the mix sounded like a worthwhile goal that wouldn't take much extra work.

My end goal was a straightforward recipe with a simple stir-together, no-cook glaze. The recipes I found that met these criteria employed a range of oven temperatures, a variety of timings for applying the glaze, and an assortment of flavors—soy sauce, molasses, jams and jellies, hoisin sauce, honey, citrus, and even bacon fat.

After sampling a half-dozen glazed chickens, my tasters and I arrived at a starting point of a 400-degree oven for efficient roasting and a jelly-based glaze: Jelly brings flavor, sweetness (which helps in browning), and a sticky texture that aids in adherence. Recipes we tried called for apple, apricot, and red pepper jellies, and the red pepper jelly stood out for its savory-sweet flavor. A little balsamic vinegar added punch and color. Potent Dijon mustard lent a sharp kick and helped thicken the glaze so that it stayed put on the chicken's skin—as long as I applied it at the right time.

My test recipes taught me that even the thickest glazes have little chance of staying on a roasting chicken if they're applied too early; the combination of the oven's heat melting the glaze and the mechanics of chicken juices and fat coming out of the bird makes the glaze run off the skin, pool at the bottom of the roasting vessel, and burn—and a smoky kitchen was definitely not part of my master plan. It was much better, I found, to let the chicken roast without a glaze until it was approaching doneness; with the skin rendered and dried out a bit, I could brush on the glaze in a few stages to ensure that it stuck and created layers of flavor.

After a good bit of trial and error, I found that the best timing for building a layered, lacquered, showstopping glaze was to brush it on after about 50 minutes in the oven, again 10 minutes later, and one final time once the chicken came out of the oven.

The glaze tasted great and my method was solid, but I wanted the chicken to taste as good as it looked—and it looked incredible. To take the

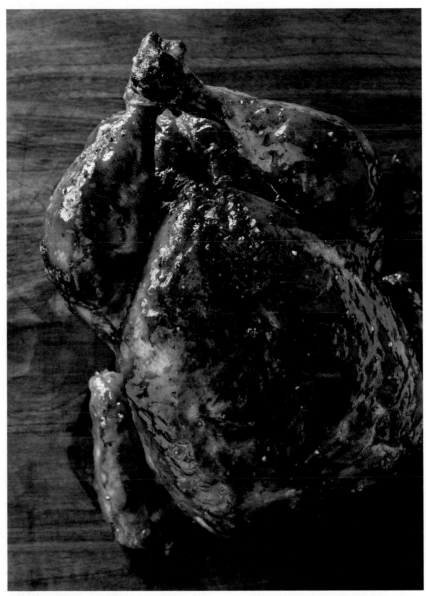

We apply the glaze three times to build up a deeply flavored, beautifully lacquered exterior.

chicken from good to great, I added a seasoning mix to the chicken—just salt, pepper, granulated garlic, and dry mustard (to echo the mustard in the glaze). Continuing with the "layers of flavor" theme, I sprinkled it on once before roasting (after brushing the chicken with oil to help it stick) and then again on top of my first application of glaze. This way, the seasoning mix and glaze combined to create deep flavor.

This beautifully lacquered chicken delivers a satisfying wallop of bright, savory-sweet flavor and juicy meat without much additional work for the cook. And while it's plenty easy for a weeknight, it has the look of a special-occasion masterpiece.

Layering Flavor

Rub First
Sprinkle chicken with spices, then roast partway.

Then Glaze
Brush chicken with glaze, then . . .

Sprinkle
Coat chicken with more spice rub; continue roasting.

Glaze Again
Apply another coat of glaze; continue roasting.

Glaze to Finish
Apply final coat of glaze when bird is done.

GLAZED ROAST CHICKEN
Serves 4

Other jellies and preserves can be substituted for the red pepper jelly, if desired (apple and apricot both work well here). Preserves will have to be strained of their solid fruit before using. Note that the chicken is brushed with the glaze three separate times, and we divide the glaze into thirds so as not to double-dip after brushing the partially cooked chicken; be sure to wash and dry your brush between glaze applications.

- 1 (3½- to 4-pound) whole chicken, giblets discarded
- 1 tablespoon dry mustard
- 2 teaspoons granulated garlic
  Kosher salt and pepper
- 1 tablespoon vegetable oil
- ¾ cup red pepper jelly
- 1½ tablespoons Dijon mustard
- 1 tablespoon balsamic vinegar
- 1 tablespoon ketchup

1. Adjust oven rack to lower-middle position and heat oven to 400 degrees. Pat chicken dry with paper towels. Tuck wingtips behind back and tie legs together with kitchen twine. Transfer chicken, breast side up, to 12-inch ovensafe skillet.

2. Combine dry mustard, granulated garlic, 1 teaspoon salt, and ½ teaspoon pepper in bowl. Brush chicken with oil and evenly sprinkle with 1 tablespoon spice mixture. Whisk jelly, Dijon mustard, vinegar, ketchup, ½ teaspoon salt, and ¼ teaspoon pepper together in separate bowl (you will have about 1 cup). Divide glaze evenly among 3 small bowls, about ⅓ cup each.

3. Roast chicken until thickest part of breast registers 135 degrees, 40 to 50 minutes. Remove chicken from oven. Using pastry brush, gently brush chicken evenly with ⅓ cup glaze. Sprinkle top and sides of chicken with remaining spice mixture. Return chicken to oven and roast for 10 minutes.

4. Remove chicken from oven. Gently brush chicken evenly with ⅓ cup glaze. Return chicken to oven and roast until breasts register 160 degrees and thighs register 175 degrees, 10 to 15 minutes.

5. Remove chicken from oven and transfer to carving board. Gently brush chicken evenly with remaining ⅓ cup glaze; let rest for 15 minutes. Discard twine, carve, and serve.

Easy Ricotta Gnocchi

These cheesy pasta pillows look like fancy restaurant food, but they're simple enough to add to your weeknight repertoire. *by Matthew Fairman*

RICOTTA GNOCCHI ARE light, flavorful dumplings that taste even better than they look. Not to be confused with finicky potato gnocchi (which can turn dense and rubbery in even the most careful hands), these luscious clouds are more forgiving, light, and tender; they far surpass any fresh pasta you can buy at the supermarket.

I wanted a stress-free, foolproof home recipe that turned out impressive dumplings every time. Traditional recipes call for hand-rolling long ropes of dough on a floured counter and cutting the ropes at 1-inch intervals. It's a time-honored method, but it's not infallible: Rolling neat ropes of soft, sticky dough isn't an easy task, especially on the first try.

But how could I achieve the classic shape without the rope-rolling method? After fiddling with fragile ropes, clumsily cutting the gnocchi like tiny biscuits, and scooping sticky dough blobs into hot water with spoons, I landed on a simple method that produced consistent results. I used a pastry bag or, alternatively, a plastic zipper-lock bag with a small hole cut in one corner to pipe the dough onto a baking sheet, using a knife to cut the raw dumplings as I went. When the sheet was full, I popped it into the freezer for about 2 hours to firm up the delicate puffs. To cook the gnocchi, I just dropped them into boiling water for a few minutes.

Now that I had perfectly shaped gnocchi, I was ready to whip up a few quick sauces to showcase them. We found that the combination of

browned butter and sage is classic for good reason—it was utterly delicious. A buttery tomato sauce was equally good and gave us an option for a brighter profile. Lastly, these dumplings tasted like summer when tossed with a fragrant basil pesto and fresh cherry tomatoes. With a sauce for every whim and the easiest technique yet for the gnocchi, you should plan on having these tonight.

EASY RICOTTA GNOCCHI WITH SAGE-BROWNED BUTTER SAUCE
Serves 4
We developed this recipe using our winning whole-milk ricotta, Belgioioso Ricotta con Latte Whole Milk Ricotta Cheese. If you can't find it, look for a ricotta without stabilizers. If you don't have a pastry bag, you can use a large zipper-lock bag with a ¾-inch opening cut from one corner.

GNOCCHI
- **1 pound (2 cups) whole-milk ricotta cheese**
- **¼ cup grated Parmesan cheese, plus extra for serving**
- **1 large egg**
- **Salt and pepper**
- **⅛ teaspoon ground nutmeg**
- **1 cup (5 ounces) all-purpose flour**

SAUCE
- **4 tablespoons unsalted butter**
- **1 shallot, minced**
- **2 teaspoons minced fresh sage**
- **¼ teaspoon salt**
- **¼ cup water**
- **1 teaspoon lemon juice**

Pipe Down
Pipe the gnocchi onto a prepared baking sheet, using a greased butter knife to cut the dough at the pastry bag tip. Take care not to let them touch.

1. FOR THE GNOCCHI: Pour off any water on top of ricotta in container. Whisk ricotta, Parmesan, egg, 1 teaspoon salt, ½ teaspoon pepper, and nutmeg in large bowl until combined. Using rubber spatula, stir in flour until thoroughly combined. Transfer dough to pastry bag with ¾-inch opening.
2. Line rimmed baking sheet with parchment paper and spray with vegetable oil spray. Pipe evenly spaced 1-inch lengths of dough onto prepared sheet, using greased butter knife to cut dough at tip of bag. Cover sheet with plastic wrap and freeze until gnocchi are completely firm, at least 2 hours. (Gnocchi can be transferred to zipper-lock bag and frozen for up to 1 month.)

Ricotta cheese lends richness and a light texture to this easy homemade pasta.

3. FOR THE SAUCE: Melt butter in 12-inch skillet over medium-high heat. Cook, swirling pan occasionally, until butter is dark golden brown and has nutty aroma, about 2 minutes. Stir in shallot, sage, and salt and cook until fragrant, about 1 minute. Off heat, stir in water and lemon juice.
4. Bring 4 quarts water to boil in large pot over high heat. Add 1 tablespoon salt and gnocchi. Gently stir gnocchi once. When all gnocchi have floated to surface, continue to cook 2 minutes longer. Using slotted spoon, transfer gnocchi to skillet with sauce.
5. Cook gnocchi and sauce over medium-high heat, stirring gently, until sauce is heated through, about 2 minutes. Serve, passing extra Parmesan separately.

EASY RICOTTA GNOCCHI WITH TOMATO SAUCE *Serves 4*
We developed this recipe using our winning whole-milk ricotta, Belgioioso Ricotta con Latte Whole Milk Ricotta Cheese. If you can't find it, look for a ricotta without stabilizers. If you don't have a pastry bag, you can use a large zipper-lock bag with a ¾-inch opening cut from one corner.

GNOCCHI
- **1 pound (2 cups) whole-milk ricotta cheese**
- **¼ cup grated Parmesan cheese, plus extra for serving**
- **1 large egg**
- **Salt and pepper**
- **⅛ teaspoon ground nutmeg**
- **1 cup (5 ounces) all-purpose flour**

Broccoli Rabe with White Beans

Most recipes for this boldly flavored green call for softening its edges by blanching it. But we wanted to embrace its flavor, not tamp it down.

by Morgan Bolling

1. FOR THE GNOCCHI: Pour off any water sitting on top of ricotta in container. Whisk ricotta, Parmesan, egg, 1 teaspoon salt, ½ teaspoon pepper, and nutmeg in large bowl until combined. Using rubber spatula, stir in flour until thoroughly combined. Transfer dough to pastry bag with ¾-inch opening.

2. Line rimmed baking sheet with parchment paper and spray with vegetable oil spray. Pipe evenly spaced 1-inch lengths of dough onto prepared sheet, using greased butter knife to cut dough at tip of bag. Cover sheet with plastic wrap and freeze until gnocchi are completely firm, at least 2 hours. (Gnocchi can be transferred to zipper-lock bag and frozen for up to 1 month.)

3. FOR THE SAUCE: Melt butter in 12-inch skillet over medium-high heat. Add shallot, garlic, and oregano and cook until fragrant, about 1 minute. Add tomatoes, sugar, ½ teaspoon salt, and ¼ teaspoon pepper and bring to boil. Reduce heat to medium-low and cook until slightly thickened, about 10 minutes.

4. Bring 4 quarts water to boil in large pot over high heat. Add 1 tablespoon salt and gnocchi. Gently stir gnocchi once. When all gnocchi have floated to surface, continue to cook 2 minutes longer. Using slotted spoon, transfer gnocchi to skillet with sauce.

5. Increase heat to medium-high, add ¼ cup water, and cook, stirring gently, until sauce is heated through, about 2 minutes. Sprinkle gnocchi with basil and serve, passing extra Parmesan separately.

Our recipe for Easy Ricotta Gnocchi with Pesto and Cherry Tomato Sauce is available online at CooksCountry.com/jan18.

BROCCOLI RABE HAS a big personality. Once cooked, it looks beautiful, yes—it features brilliant jade stalks, spiky leaves, and baby florets—but what makes this vegetable really stand out is its bright, faintly bitter flavor that shocks the palate awake. Italian cookbooks often pair broccoli rabe with cannellini beans; the mellow, creamy beans and the pleasantly sharp greens complement each other incredibly well. I decided to develop my own version of this pairing.

Almost all the recipes I found for this combination of beans and greens called for blanching the broccoli rabe to remove some of its bite before sautéing it. One recipe called for microwaving it, which turned it an unfortunate shade of army green and gave it a dulled, grassy flavor. But I didn't want to take the bite out of broccoli rabe—I wanted to celebrate its boldness.

I found that the best technique was also the simplest: Chop the broccoli rabe into 1-inch pieces and simply sauté it, with no precooking, in olive oil. This method turned it tender while highlighting—not hiding—its vibrant flavor. Garlic and red pepper flakes best infused the dish when I added them to the cold oil before bringing it up to temperature and then threw in the chopped greens.

Canned beans were the obvious choice to keep this dish an easy weeknight option. Stirring in the beans early in the cooking process gave them time to soften and to absorb the flavors of the oil. A little chicken broth tied the dish together while adding savory depth—plus, it created extra rich, garlicky liquid to soak up with crusty bread. To give these strong greens a strong finish, I served the dish with lemon wedges to brighten the flavors and a sprinkling of potent Parmesan cheese for a savory grounding.

A spritz of lemon juice just before serving brings the vibrant flavors into focus.

BROCCOLI RABE WITH WHITE BEANS *Serves 4*

Do not mince the garlic here. Broccoli rabe is also sold as rapini at the supermarket. Vegetable broth may be substituted for the chicken broth.

- ¼ cup extra-virgin olive oil
- 3 garlic cloves, sliced thin
- ¼ teaspoon red pepper flakes
- 1 pound broccoli rabe, trimmed and cut into 1-inch pieces
- 1 (15-ounce) can cannellini beans, rinsed
- ¼ cup chicken broth
- Salt and pepper
- Grated Parmesan cheese
- Lemon wedges

1. Combine 2 tablespoons oil, garlic, and pepper flakes in Dutch oven. Cook over medium heat until garlic is golden brown, 2 to 4 minutes.

2. Stir in broccoli rabe, beans, broth, and ½ teaspoon salt and cook, stirring occasionally, until broccoli rabe is tender, 4 to 6 minutes. Off heat, stir in remaining 2 tablespoons oil and season with salt and pepper to taste. Transfer mixture to shallow platter and serve, passing Parmesan and lemon wedges separately.

To find out which cannellini beans are our favorite, go to **CooksCountry.com/cannellini**.

New England Pork Pies

Could we create a home version of these beloved New England treats? *by Cecelia Jenkins*

THE STOUT LITTLE pies from Hartley's Original Pork Pies (see "Pies by the Million") cut charming figures with their straight, sturdy sides and golden crimped crowns. The crumbly crusts contain a deeply seasoned, savory, juicy filling of ground pork and gravy.

Translating the pies to a home kitchen, though, was a tall order. First, I needed a baking vessel to mimic Hartley's 100-year-old individual cast-iron pie tins. Muffin tins were too small and the wrong shape. Larger 6-ounce ceramic ramekins proved perfect in both size and shape, yielding evenly golden-brown sides and bottoms.

For the dough, I processed flour with melted butter to create the crumbly crust I wanted. Sour cream added richness and flavor without compromising texture, and an egg provided structure.

Simply pressing portions of dough into the ramekins didn't work well. Rolling and cutting the dough to fit was a better route. For the bottoms and sides, I measured ⅓ cup of dough for each pie, rolled each portion into a circle of even thickness, and then fit each one into a ramekin. For the tops, I rolled out the remaining dough and stamped out circles with an inverted ramekin. Once the pies were filled, I placed the circles on top and rolled up the overhanging dough to seal the pies.

Grinding my own pork was off the table, but because preground pork is relatively lean, I suspected I'd need a panade (a mixture of bread or bread crumbs and liquid, usually milk) to help it hold on to moisture. After a few unsuccessful tests, a colleague suggested ditching the panade for buttery crushed Ritz Crackers. The extra fat in the crackers helped the meat stay supple.

At Hartley's, cooks pour flavorful pork gravy through the pie's vent holes for a juicy finish. To mimic this step, I thickened our favorite beef broth with a bit of cornstarch.

My pork pies released easily from the greased ramekins. When these proud little packages of ultrasavory, supermoist filling in a buttery crust impressed my tasters, I knew I'd done Hartley's justice.

 To see which beef broth won our tasting, go to **CooksCountry.com/ beefbroth**.

NEW ENGLAND PORK PIES
Serves 6

You will need six 6- to 7-ounce ramekins, measuring 3½ inches wide and about 2 inches deep, for this recipe.

DOUGH
- 12 tablespoons unsalted butter, melted and cooled
- ½   cup sour cream
- 1   large egg, plus 1 lightly beaten large egg for brushing
- 3   cups (15 ounces) all-purpose flour
- ½   teaspoon salt

FILLING
- 22 Ritz Crackers
- 1½ pounds ground pork
- 1¼ teaspoons salt
- 1¼ teaspoons pepper

GRAVY
- 1½ cups beef broth
- 1   tablespoon cornstarch

1. FOR THE DOUGH: Whisk melted butter, sour cream, and 1 egg in bowl until combined. Process flour and salt in food processor until combined, about 3 seconds. Add butter mixture and pulse until dough forms, about 10 pulses, scraping down sides of bowl as needed. Turn out dough onto counter and form into 4-inch disk. Wrap disk tightly in plastic wrap and refrigerate for at least 30 minutes or up to 24 hours. (If chilling longer than 30 minutes, allow dough to soften on counter for 30 minutes before rolling.)

2. FOR THE FILLING: Meanwhile, adjust oven rack to middle position and heat oven to 400 degrees. In clean, dry workbowl, process crackers until finely ground, about 20 seconds. Combine pork, salt, pepper, and cracker crumbs in bowl and knead with your hands until fully combined. Refrigerate until ready to use.

3. Using ⅓ cup dry measuring cup, portion out 6 pieces of dough (3½ ounces each); set aside and cover with plastic. Roll remaining dough into 11-inch circle on well-floured counter. Using inverted 6- to 7-ounce ramekin as guide, cut 6 circles for tops of pies, rerolling scraps if necessary. Set tops aside and cover with plastic.

4. Spray six 6- to 7-ounce ramekins

with vegetable oil spray. Roll each ⅓-cup dough portion into 7-inch circle on well-floured counter. Line ramekins with 7-inch dough circles, letting excess dough hang over rims. As dough pleats along insides of ramekins, press pleats flat to even out thickness.

5. Divide filling among dough-lined ramekins, about heaping ½ cup each. Place reserved dough circles over filling. Roll overhanging bottom dough inward and crimp together with top dough.

6. Brush tops of pies generously with beaten egg. Using paring knife, poke

hole in center of each pie to create ½-inch-wide vent. Place ramekins on parchment paper–lined rimmed baking sheet. Bake until tops of pies are deep golden brown, 40 to 45 minutes, rotating sheet halfway through baking. Let pies cool for 10 minutes.

7. FOR THE GRAVY: Whisk broth and cornstarch in small saucepan until cornstarch is dissolved. Bring to boil over medium-high heat and cook until thickened, about 30 seconds. Remove from heat and transfer to 2-cup liquid measuring cup.

8. Lift pies out of ramekins, loosening edges with paring knife if necessary (do not invert; juices inside are hot). If vent holes have shrunk during baking, widen with paring knife so gravy can be poured in. Pour gravy into vent hole of each pie until pie is filled (you will have extra gravy for serving). Let pies cool for 20 minutes. Serve, passing remaining gravy separately.

TO MAKE AHEAD
At end of step 5, poke vent holes in pies but do not brush with egg. Wrap pies tightly in plastic wrap and freeze for up to 1 month. When ready to bake, do not thaw pies. Unwrap frozen pies and proceed with step 6, extending baking time to about 1¼ hours.

Ground Ritz Crackers added to the pork filling give it richness and help keep it tender. For the finishing touch, we pour gravy into the pies right through the vent holes in their crusts.

Pies by the Million

by Bryan Roof

ON THE ROAD

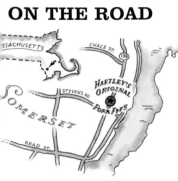

AS YOU APPROACH the counter of Hartley's Original Pork Pies in Somerset, Massachusetts, you notice a faint, rhythmic squeaking coming from deep inside the building. Owner Don Setters tells me he's caught kids peeking into the kitchen to uncover the source of the noise. I'm curious, too, so he waves me back, conspiratorially. "Usually, no one is allowed to see the kitchen."

The source of the squeaking is a cast-iron pie press forcing dough into miniature steel ramekins that Setters tells me are 100 years old. The candy apple–red machine isn't alone—the kitchen is full of antiques, including a 1920s-era belt-driven mixer, a meat grinder with an oversize switch, and an old coal-fired oven that now houses the cash drawer. The relics make Setters' flip phone seem cutting-edge.

It's the first day of Lent, and a customer walks in to order five salmon pies—plus two pork pies, just in case. Hartley's also makes a pie filled with *chouriço*, a Portuguese sausage. Most days they make about 200 pies, but they've sold as many as 800 on a Super Bowl Sunday. Don tells me proudly, "I've made millions of pies. Millions! And I never get sick of them."

Thomas Hartley opened Hartley's in Somerset in 1902 to feed the influx of English immigrants who came to work in the local mills. According to Setters, Mr. Hartley originally wanted to open a fish and chips shop but likely changed his plans after realizing that pies were better suited for the rigors of mill work. Pies were the ideal lunch food of the time—sturdy, filling, and compact—and Mr. Hartley used to say they were the original fast food. The shop opened early in the morning so customers could buy pies on the way to work.

The Setters family was one of Hartley's best customers, and Setters' father said that if he were ever interested in selling, they'd be interested in buying. "Mr. Hartley sold us the business because he knew we'd keep the tradition alive. I like the tradition of the thing. It's what keeps me here. That and the smiles on people's faces."

Regulars make stops at Hartley's Original Pork Pies, sometimes for lunch, sometimes just for a snack. Owner Don Setters (left) uses a cast-iron pie press, nicknamed "Little Champion," to fill ramekins with dough and then to imprint a small H in the center of each pie's top crust. On most days, Hartley's turns out as many as 800 pies.

Will Any Old Ramekin Do? Not Exactly.

by Lauren Savoie

EQUIPMENT REVIEW

THOUGH NOT ESSENTIAL equipment, ramekins are surprisingly versatile. They're perfect for individually portioned desserts and soufflés or for using as mini prep bowls or salt cellars. Though the straight-sided, fluted ramekin is the classic design, they come in many sizes, shapes, and materials.

We tested eight ramekins, priced from $1.98 to $16.00 per ramekin, focusing on ceramic and glass models with advertised capacities of about 6 ounces. We made chilled berry puddings, sticky crème caramels that bake in a water bath, delicate chocolate soufflés, and quick-cooking baked eggs in each model. We preferred thick, heavy ceramic ramekins, which provided the insulation needed to produce perfect baked eggs.

Since each manufacturer uses a different benchmark for its advertised capacity, we measured the capacity of each ramekin when it was filled to the brim. The ramekins' true capacities ranged from 6 to 8 ounces—slightly larger than advertised. Those with a true capacity of 7.5 or 8 ounces performed best, as they easily held all the fillings with room to spare.

The width and shape of the ramekins also affected performance. We preferred ramekins with classic straight sides and a rim-to-rim width of about 3.7 inches; they fit comfortably in a 13 by 9-inch baking dish, were easy to fill, and produced the most attractive food. Stackability was a nice bonus.

Le Creuset Stackable Ramekins, our favorites, were the heaviest and thickest in the bunch. Everything we cooked in them emerged evenly baked, and they're stackable—but they're expensive. Our Best Buy ramekins don't bake quite as evenly and don't stack, but they work well and are a great value. To read the full story and complete results chart, including the losers, go to **CooksCountry.com/jan18.**

KEY **Good** ★★★ **Fair** ★★ **Poor** ★

HIGHLY RECOMMENDED   CRITERIA

Our Favorite

Le Creuset Stackable Ramekin
Model: PG1627-09
Price: $16.00 for 1 ramekin
Material: Ceramic
Capacity: 7.5 oz
Width: 3.7 in
Thickness: 0.3 in

Ease of Use ★★★
Cooking ★★★
Durability ★★★

Comments: Thick walls provided gentle insulation for perfect baked eggs. A bonus: They're stackable.

RECOMMENDED

Best Buy

Mrs. Anderson's Baking Souffle
Model: 98005
Price: $22.52 for set of 6 ($3.75 per ramekin)
Material: Ceramic
Capacity: 7.8 oz
Width: 3.7 in
Thickness: 0.3 in

Ease of Use ★★★
Cooking ★★½
Durability ★★★

Comments: Moderate heft and thick edges provided slow, gentle heat for great cooking. Unlike our winner, they don't stack.

Emile Henry Ramekin, Set of 4
Model: 794028 (Charcoal)
Price: $36.00 for set of 4 ($9.00 per ramekin)
Material: Ceramic
Capacity: 7 oz
Width: 3.7 in
Thickness: 0.2 in

Ease of Use ★★½
Cooking ★★½
Durability ★★★

Comments: Though smaller than our favorites, these ramekins were wide enough to fill cleanly and maneuver easily. A few eggs overbaked in them.

Chicken Sauce Piquant

This homey, spicy Louisiana dish deserves a wider audience.

by Matthew Fairman

This simple recipe overdelivers on rich, slightly spicy, and totally satisfying flavor.

SAUCE PIQUANT IS a beloved Cajun dish featuring meat braised in a cayenne-spiked, brown roux–thickened tomato sauce and served over white rice. The dish is most commonly made with chicken, although native cooks are likely to employ wild game or even alligator tail. It's bold, satisfying, and economical, yet sauce piquant isn't often made outside Louisiana. I think that's a culinary crime, so I got to work developing a bulletproof recipe to help spread the word.

To see how other cooks put this dish together, I gathered and prepared a handful of cookbook recipes, most of them from Louisiana natives. The least impressive versions offered up dry, overcooked chicken suspended in a stodgy, muted tomato gravy. More promising recipes produced either juicy, tender chicken or a bright, full-bodied tomato sauce with a healthy dose of acidic heat—but never both in the same dish. Nearly all of them, however, took an unnecessarily long time to prepare. I wanted tender chicken and a lively sauce, and I wanted a process that was easier and more efficient than those of the recipes I'd sampled.

I knew from the get-go that I wanted to use boneless chicken in my version so it would be easy to eat. My initial tests confirmed one thing that I had suspected would be true: Chicken thighs, which are more flavorful and less apt to dry out than chicken breasts, were the way to go.

I started by sprinkling boneless chicken thighs with Louisiana seasoning, dredging them in flour, and shallow-frying them in a Dutch oven until golden. At this point, the recipes I'd tested called for pulling the chicken from the pot and starting on the roux, a mixture of fat (oil, in this case) and flour that can take the better part of an hour—or longer—to cook. But I wondered if I could skip the roux here, as I'd already developed browned-flour flavor when I seared the flour-coated chicken thighs. Instead of making a roux, I tossed in onion, bell pepper, celery, and the rest of the flour left over from coating the chicken. After softening the vegetables over medium-high heat, I added crushed tomatoes, chicken broth, a bay leaf, and the browned chicken; dropped on the lid; and popped the whole thing into a preheated oven for the sauce to thicken and the chicken to gently cook through.

After about 45 minutes, the chicken thighs had turned perfectly tender and the tomato sauce had just enough body (thanks to the flour in the mix) to evenly coat the pieces without being too thick or gloppy. Happily, the sauce had that signature cooked-flour background flavor and was so nicely thickened that my tasters didn't even notice I had skipped the arduous process of making the roux.

But my colleagues did think the sauce was too tame for a dish with "piquant" in the name. I jazzed up my next batch with a splash of Worcestershire sauce for salty, punchy depth and a glug of Tabasco sauce for a bright, peppery heat. And since so many beloved Louisiana dishes employ some form of cured pork for flavor, I tossed in a couple of bacon slices, which perfumed the sauce with their rich, meaty smokiness (I removed the bacon before serving).

I ladled out bowlfuls of the dish and called my tasters to the table with a proud grin. The lively, spicy sauce perfectly napped the tender chicken pieces, and the combination of rich, spicy flavors was spot-on. This was Louisiana food at its best—bright and fiery yet comforting and satisfying.

To read our tasting of Worcestershire sauces, go to **CooksCountry.com/worcestershire**.

CHICKEN SAUCE PIQUANT
Serves 6 to 8

Louisiana seasoning is typically a mix of paprika, garlic powder, thyme, cayenne, celery salt, oregano, salt, and black pepper. The test kitchen's taste test winner is Tony Chachere's Original Creole Seasoning.

- ½ cup all-purpose flour
- 2 pounds boneless, skinless chicken thighs, trimmed and quartered
- 3½ teaspoons Louisiana seasoning
- 5 tablespoons vegetable oil
- 1 onion, chopped
- 1 green bell pepper, stemmed, seeded, and chopped
- 1 celery rib, chopped
- 2 garlic cloves, minced
- 1 (28-ounce) can crushed tomatoes
- 3 cups chicken broth
- 2 slices bacon
- 2 tablespoons Worcestershire sauce
- 1 bay leaf
- 1 teaspoon Tabasco sauce, plus extra for serving
  Salt and pepper
- 4 cups cooked rice
- 4 scallions, sliced thin

1. Adjust oven rack to lower-middle position and heat oven to 350 degrees. Place flour in large bowl. Season chicken with 1 tablespoon Louisiana seasoning. Transfer chicken to bowl with flour and toss to coat.

2. Heat ¼ cup oil in Dutch oven over medium-high heat until shimmering. Shaking off excess flour, add half of chicken to pot and cook until golden brown, 3 to 5 minutes per side; transfer to plate. Repeat with remaining chicken. Reserve remaining flour.

3. Add onion, bell pepper, celery, garlic, remaining ½ teaspoon Louisiana seasoning, remaining 1 tablespoon oil, and reserved flour to now-empty pot. Cook, stirring often, until vegetables are just softened, about 5 minutes.

4. Stir in tomatoes, broth, bacon, Worcestershire, and bay leaf, scraping up any browned bits. Nestle chicken into pot and add any accumulated juices. Bring to simmer, cover, and transfer to oven. Cook until chicken is tender, about 45 minutes.

5. Remove pot from oven. Discard bacon and bay leaf, stir in Tabasco, and season with salt and pepper to taste. Serve over rice, sprinkled with scallions, passing extra Tabasco separately.

Ground Beef Stroganoff

Wouldn't it be great to make this creamy, comforting weeknight meal even easier?

by Ashley Moore

MANY UPSCALE VERSIONS of beef Stroganoff call for slices of pricey beef tenderloin. On the other end of the spectrum sits the weeknight version of this recipe, featuring ground beef with canned cream of mushroom soup and served over egg noodles. While the test kitchen has developed great beef Stroganoff recipes that call for tenderloin and steak tips, I was surprised to find that we've never tackled the ground beef version. I set out to change that by creating a ground beef version—minus the canned soup—that was inexpensive and came together quickly.

Since I was kicking the can to the curb, I'd use fresh mushrooms in my homemade sauce. I began by sautéing thinly sliced button mushrooms (we've found that they have plenty of flavor in dishes like this) in a skillet; when they were browned, I transferred them to a bowl and began to soften some onions and garlic. I added the ground beef—I settled on 85 percent lean because it provided strong beefy flavor in the finished dish—and cooked it until it was no longer pink. I sprinkled the beef with a few tablespoons of flour for thickening, cooked it slightly, and then added chicken broth (see "Why Not Beef Broth?") and a little white wine. I simmered the sauce for a few minutes, took the skillet off the heat, and stirred in the cooked mushrooms and some sour cream to enrich the sauce. I scooped portions over egg noodles I'd boiled in another pot; my tasters were smiling, but I had one last trick up my sleeve.

I made another batch, but this time I switched from a skillet to a Dutch oven and upped the amounts of chicken broth and wine so I could stir the raw egg noodles right into the sauce to cook (instead of boiling them in a separate pot). Ten minutes later, the noodles were tender and the flavors had melded. After stirring in the browned mushrooms and sour cream, I sprinkled a small handful of bright green, mildly oniony minced chives over the top. Then I summoned my tasters to see if they could tell the difference between this beef Stroganoff and prior batches where the noodles were cooked separately.

They couldn't. My Beef Stroganoff was satisfying, comforting, and rich—and definitely easy and affordable enough for a weeknight.

GROUND BEEF STROGANOFF
Serves 4
Pennsylvania Dutch Wide Egg Noodles are our favorite.

- 2 **tablespoons vegetable oil**
- 8 **ounces white mushrooms, trimmed and sliced thin**
  Salt and pepper
- 1 **onion, chopped fine**
- 2 **garlic cloves, minced**
- 1 **pound 85 percent lean ground beef**
- 3 **tablespoons all-purpose flour**
- 4 **cups chicken broth**
- ¼ **cup dry white wine**
- 8 **ounces (4 cups) egg noodles**
- ½ **cup sour cream, plus extra for serving**
- 2 **tablespoons minced fresh chives**

1. Heat 1 tablespoon oil in Dutch oven over medium-high heat until shimmering. Add mushrooms and ¼ teaspoon salt and cook until liquid has evaporated and mushrooms begin to brown, 5 to 7 minutes; transfer to bowl.
2. Add remaining 1 tablespoon oil to now-empty pot and return to medium-high heat until shimmering. Add onion, garlic, ½ teaspoon salt, and ½ teaspoon pepper and cook, stirring occasionally, until onion begins to soften, about 5 minutes. Add beef, ¼ teaspoon salt, and ¼ teaspoon pepper and cook, breaking up meat with spoon, until no longer pink, 5 to 7 minutes.
3. Add flour and stir until beef is well coated; cook for 1 minute. Stir in broth and wine and bring to simmer, scraping up any browned bits. Cook until mixture is slightly thickened, about 3 minutes. Stir in noodles, reduce heat to medium, and cook, uncovered, until noodles are tender, 10 to 12 minutes, stirring occasionally.
4. Off heat, stir in sour cream and mushrooms until fully combined. Season with salt and pepper to taste. Transfer to shallow platter and sprinkle with chives. Serve, passing extra sour cream separately.

Why Not Beef Broth?
We often prefer the lighter, cleaner, and more versatile flavor of chicken broth to that of beef broth—which we found to be too meaty in this recipe. Our favorite chicken broth is Swanson Chicken Stock.

We use ground beef and cook the noodles right in the sauce for an easy weeknight meal.

BACKSTORY

Picture him with his knee-high riding boots, tousled hair, and piercing eyes: Count Pavel Stroganov cut a striking figure in 18th-century Russia. At that time, members of the Russian court were Francophiles, speaking French and turning to Paris for cultural inspiration. Beef Stroganoff was likely created by a French chef in honor of the Count. As was often the case when cooking for a patron, the dish was named for him, and the name stuck even as it reached American shores a century after his death. In the 1950s, the dish enjoyed a minor vogue in fancy stateside restaurants; after a few decades in obscurity, it's seen a revival in recent years.

A RAKISH RUSSIAN COUNT
The namesake of a favorite noodle dish

Cheese Blintzes

Time to banish our memories of bad blintzes past.

by Cecelia Jenkins

BLAME IT ON bad luck, but for most of my life I didn't understand the appeal of blintzes. I'd only known them as eggy crêpes stuffed with gritty, sweetened cheese and topped with a cloying fruit sauce. But after a recent trip to New York City, our executive food editor Bryan Roof couldn't stop talking about the beautiful blintzes he'd eaten (see "Blintz Blitz").

The reasons so few people make blintzes were revealed by the existing recipes I found. They called for hard-to-find specialty pans and for flipping the giant crêpes halfway through cooking, which I found really tricky. And each recipe produced a gritty, not creamy, filling. I had work to do.

First I'd tackle the filling. I wanted it smooth, creamy, and just sweet enough. While blintzes are often made with farmer's cheese—a mild fresh cheese with a lovely flavor but a tendency toward grittiness—I found that ricotta made a much smoother filling. A little cream cheese added tanginess, and confectioners' sugar gave it just enough sweetness and body.

For the crêpes, I started with the test kitchen's favorite recipe, a simple batter that produces light, pliable crêpes about 6 inches in diameter. But because I'd eventually be folding these into rectangular packets stuffed with cheese filling, I needed them to be bigger than usual. I made a few alterations to the ingredient amounts and, rather than reach for a small crêpe pan, grabbed a 12-inch nonstick skillet. Scooping ⅓ cup of the batter into my hot, lightly buttered pan, I slowly swirled it to cover the surface and cooked it for about 1 minute, until it was lightly golden on the bottom.

While regular crêpes must be flipped at this point to achieve a lovely browned color on both sides, crêpes for blintzes need to cook through only long enough to firm up for filling and folding; after all, one side is invisible on the plate. I could simply remove the crêpes one by one as they cooked and pile them onto a plate. I was happy to find that they didn't stick to each other.

Once filled, these blintzes would make a second visit to the skillet to brown and warm through. To guard against any filling oozing out into the skillet, I had to fold them up very carefully. Here's how: After spooning the filling onto each crêpe, I folded over the bottom edge and then the sides. I

Our raspberry sauce couldn't be easier: frozen fruit, sugar, and salt simmered for 10 minutes.

finished rolling the crêpe around the filling to form a neat, tidy blintz. I could nestle six of these blintzes at a time into my skillet to finish off.

Bonus: I found that if I wrapped up the blintzes, I could hold them in the freezer overnight (or for up to a month) before browning them in the skillet, right from the freezer, when I was ready to serve.

A bright, quick-cooking sauce of tart raspberries balanced the rich, lightly sweetened blintz filling. My bad blintz memories were banished.

Blintz Blitz

A stroll through New York City's blintz district reveals a range of takes on this traditional Eastern European dish of tender crêpes wrapped around sweetened farmer's cheese, which can be breakfast or dessert. *by Bryan Roof*

ON THE ROAD

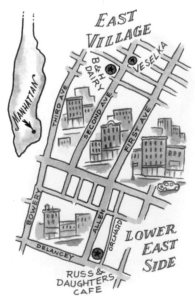

Veselka

At Veselka, a diner-style restaurant situated in New York City's East Village, the fare reflects the neighborhood's deeply rooted Ukrainian community—stuffed cabbage, goulash, and borscht are staples, along with blintzes. Here, the crêpes are folded into quarters, dusted with confectioners' sugar, and eaten with a bright berry compote. When it was founded in 1954, Veselka (the name means "rainbow" in Ukrainian) was simply a newsstand serving takeaway lunches; today, early-lunching old timers and late-night club kids keep the tables crowded 24 hours a day.

Blintz Construction

Add Filling
Spread 2 tablespoons of filling at the edge of each crêpe.

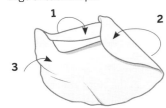

Fold in 3 Sides
Cover the filling, and then fold in the two sides that are perpendicular to the first.

Roll Gently
The crêpes enclose the filling and form tidy rectangles.

CHEESE BLINTZES WITH RASPBERRY SAUCE

Makes 12 blintzes, serves 4 to 6

Don't worry if you lose a few crêpes along the way; the batter makes about 15 to account for any mistakes. When making the crêpes, if the batter doesn't stick to the skillet when swirling, that means the skillet is too greased and/or not hot enough. Return the skillet to the heat and cook 10 seconds longer; then try again to swirl the batter. With the next try, use less butter to brush the skillet. If the filled and rolled blintzes split on the sides, be careful while searing them because the filling may sputter when it hits the hot skillet. You do not need to thaw the raspberries before making the sauce. Our favorite ricotta cheese is Belgioioso Ricotta con Latte Whole Milk Ricotta Cheese.

FILLING

- 11 ounces (1¼ cups plus 2 tablespoons) whole-milk ricotta cheese
- ½ cup (2 ounces) confectioners' sugar
- 1 ounce cream cheese, softened
- ¼ teaspoon salt

SAUCE

- 10 ounces (2 cups) frozen raspberries
- ¼ cup (1¾ ounces) granulated sugar
- ¼ teaspoon salt

CRÊPES

- 2 cups (10 ounces) all-purpose flour
- 2 teaspoons granulated sugar
- ½ teaspoon salt
- 3 cups whole milk
- 4 large eggs
- 4 tablespoons unsalted butter, melted and cooled, plus 4 tablespoons unsalted butter

1. FOR THE FILLING: Whisk all ingredients in bowl until no lumps of cream cheese remain. Refrigerate until ready to use. (Filling can be refrigerated for up to 2 days.)

2. FOR THE SAUCE: Combine raspberries, sugar, and salt in small saucepan. Cook over medium heat, stirring occasionally, until slightly thickened, 8 to 10 minutes. (Sauce can be refrigerated for up to 2 days.)

3. FOR THE CRÊPES: Whisk flour, sugar, and salt together in medium bowl. Whisk milk and eggs together in separate bowl. Add half of milk mixture to flour mixture and whisk until smooth. Whisk in 3 tablespoons melted butter until incorporated. Whisk in remaining milk mixture until smooth. (Batter can be refrigerated for up to 2 days before cooking. It will separate; rewhisk it before using.)

4. Brush bottom of 12-inch nonstick skillet lightly with some of remaining 1 tablespoon melted butter and heat skillet over medium heat until hot, about 2 minutes. Add ⅓ cup batter to center of skillet and simultaneously lift and rotate skillet in circular motion to swirl batter, allowing batter to run and fully cover bottom of skillet. Cook crêpe until edges look dry and start to curl and bottom of crêpe is light golden, about 1 minute. Using rubber spatula, lift edge of crêpe and slide it onto plate. Repeat with remaining batter, stacking crêpes and brushing skillet with melted butter every other time. (Adjust burner between medium-low and medium heat as needed toward end of crêpe-making process.)

5. Working with 1 crêpe at a time, spoon 2 tablespoons filling onto crêpe about 2 inches from bottom edge and spread into 4-inch line. Fold bottom edge of crêpe over filling, then fold sides of crêpe over filling. Gently roll crêpe into tidy package about 4 inches long and 2 inches wide. Repeat with remaining crêpes and filling. (Assembled blintzes can be transferred to plate, covered with plastic wrap, and refrigerated for up to 24 hours.)

6. Melt 2 tablespoons butter in now-empty skillet over medium heat. Add half of blintzes, seam sides down, and cook until golden brown, 2 to 4 minutes, gently moving blintzes in skillet as needed for even browning. Using spatula, gently flip blintzes and continue to cook until golden brown on second side, 2 to 4 minutes longer. Transfer blintzes to platter, seam sides down, and wipe skillet clean with paper towels. Repeat with remaining 2 tablespoons butter and remaining blintzes. Serve with raspberry sauce.

TO MAKE AHEAD

At end of step 5, transfer blintzes to rimmed baking sheet and freeze. Transfer frozen blintzes to zipper-lock bag and freeze for up to 1 month. When ready to cook, do not thaw blintzes. Reduce heat in step 6 to medium-low and cook blintzes, covered, until golden brown, 6 to 9 minutes per side.

B&H Dairy

Just down the street from Veselka, B&H Dairy is a kosher storefront that seems to be made for skinny people, because I can barely squeeze myself and my appetite through the room to a table that claims to seat four. A very tall man behind the counter shouts my order into the kitchen—four blintzes, please: cherry, blueberry, apple, and cheese. Here the fruit compote is rolled up with the cheese into the crêpe, which is then sautéed until lightly browned and crisped, a bit of filling oozing out of the ends in a beautiful mess. B&H Dairy opened more than 80 years ago; not even a gas explosion on the block in 2015 was able to shut it down.

Russ & Daughters Café

Sitting on Orchard Street in lower Manhattan, trendy Russ & Daughters Café is a polished 21st-century offshoot of the 100-year-old Russ & Daughters shop a few blocks away. I rub elbows with hip patrons perched on stationary stools at a marble-top counter to nosh on smoked fish served on wooden boards. Blintzes follow; at Russ & Daughters, they are about the size of an enchilada and are tightly wrapped, with their ends tucked in to contain the filling while they're browned on the griddle.

Rum Balls

Let's get ready to rum-ball...

by Morgan Bolling

We (hic) tested spiced and golden rums but settled on dark rum for the deepest flavor.

THE AMERICAN TABLE

The Rise of Rum Balls

Most cookies visit the oven before appearing in holiday spreads, but starting in the 1930s, no-bake recipes, including rum balls, took off in the United States. At the time, Americans craved sweets and wanted more homemade treats, but home ovens were often unreliable. Because rum balls relied on prebaked ingredients, home cooks were able to confidently produce these "cookies" at home. And when Prohibition ended in 1933, cooks could make boozy recipes without fear.

We Propose a Toast

Toasting nuts drives off some of their moisture, which crisps them and improves their texture. But more important, toasting activates some of the nuts' flavor compounds to make them taste better.

When we're toasting less than 1 cup of whole nuts, we do it in a skillet on the stovetop. But when we're toasting 1 cup or more (as for this recipe), we do it on a rimmed baking sheet in a 350-degree oven, shaking the sheet often to prevent scorching. The nuts are done when they're lightly browned and fragrant, which usually takes 5 to 10 minutes.

BOOZY, SWEET, AND a little mysterious—just what is a rum ball, anyway?—rum balls were originally made (or so the story goes) as a way for Depression-era bakeries to use up their leftover cake and cookie scraps. The bakers would mix their sweet debris with lots of rum and a binder (jam, corn syrup, or honey), roll it into balls, coat the balls with sugar, and sell them as adults-only trifles.

These delectable, no-bake confections soon became popular dinner-party treats (typically made with ground cookies) as people realized how easy they were to make. The appeal of rum balls is clear. They are direct delivery systems for two things many of us crave at holiday time: sugar and booze.

Wanting to breathe new life into this retro favorite, I stirred together a handful of recipes, many of them from the 1960s and '70s. One called for baking a whole sheet cake only to then crumble it and shape it into balls—way too much work for a simple dessert where not cooking is part of the appeal. Most recipes instead used store-bought bases: brownies from the bakery department, gingersnaps, vanilla wafer cookies, shortbread, or semisweet chocolate melted with cream. Our favorite recipe called for buzzing vanilla wafer cookies with pecans in the food processor and then stirring in extra sugar, rum, vanilla extract, and corn syrup. The mixture was shaped into balls and refrigerated to provide time for the flavors to meld and for the rum balls to firm up.

Right off the bat we found that toasting the pecans boosted their flavor and provided extra nutty depth (see "We Propose a Toast"). And a pinch of salt brought everything into focus. A quarter-cup of rum added a significant liquor accent to these treats—a rum ball should taste like rum, after all. But we found that the vanilla extract, which can taste boozy when raw, was adding a sharpness when coupled with the rum. Ditching the vanilla allowed us to increase the rum to 6 tablespoons for more flavor without needing a chaser.

Recipes were divided on the rum of choice, so we tasted golden, spiced, and dark rums in the recipe. The golden and spiced rums both had their merits, but we preferred the dark rum for its bold molasses-y kick. A quick roll in granulated sugar gave the rum balls enough glitz to make them worthy of being given as a gift. They were so good that I made variations including chocolate, coconut, and ginger, and I even made a nonalcoholic version so everyone could enjoy.

RUM BALLS

Makes about 48 balls

We developed this recipe using a 12-ounce box of vanilla wafers, but the cookies are also available in 11-ounce boxes. If all you can find is an 11-ounce box, there's no need to buy a second box to make up the extra ounce; just make the balls with 11 ounces of cookies. We prefer the bold flavor of dark rum here, but you can substitute golden or spiced rum, if desired.

- 1 cup granulated sugar
- 5 cups (12 ounces) vanilla wafer cookies
- 1¼ cups pecans, toasted
- 1 cup (4 ounces) confectioners' sugar
- 6 tablespoons dark rum
- ¼ cup light corn syrup
- ⅛ teaspoon salt

1. Place granulated sugar in shallow dish. Process cookies and pecans in food processor until finely ground, about 20 seconds. Transfer to large bowl. Stir in confectioners' sugar, rum, corn syrup, and salt until fully combined.
2. Working with 1 tablespoon at a time, shape mixture into balls. Transfer balls to dish with granulated sugar and roll to evenly coat; transfer to large plate. Refrigerate rum balls until firm, at least 1 hour. Serve. (Rum balls can be refrigerated for up to 1 week.)

CHOCOLATE RUM BALLS

Substitute 5 cups (12 ounces) chocolate wafer cookies for vanilla wafer cookies.

COCONUT RUM BALLS

Substitute ½ cup confectioners' sugar for granulated sugar, 1½ cups sweetened shredded coconut for pecans, and coconut rum for dark rum.

GINGER RUM BALLS

Process 6 tablespoons chopped crystallized ginger with vanilla wafer mixture.

NONALCOHOLIC RUM BALLS

Substitute ¼ cup root beer and 1 tablespoon vanilla extract for rum.

Spicy Fried Chicken Sandwiches

Pan-Seared Cod with Blistered Green Beans and Red Pepper Relish

Kielbasa with Hot Rice

Strip Steaks with Cauliflower and Roasted Garlic Butter

Pan-Seared Cod with Blistered Green Beans and Red Pepper Relish *Serves 4*

WHY THIS RECIPE WORKS: Draining and drying the peppers keeps the relish from becoming watery.

- 1 cup jarred roasted red peppers, patted dry and chopped fine
- ¼ cup whole almonds, toasted and chopped fine
- 3 tablespoons extra-virgin olive oil
- 1 tablespoon chopped fresh basil
- 1 teaspoon sherry vinegar
  Salt and pepper
- 1 pound green beans, trimmed
- 4 (6- to 8-ounce) skinless cod fillets, 1 inch thick
  Lemon wedges

1. Combine red peppers, almonds, 1 tablespoon oil, basil, vinegar, ½ teaspoon salt, and ⅛ teaspoon pepper in bowl; set aside.

2. Combine green beans, ¼ cup water, 1 tablespoon oil, 1 teaspoon salt, and ¼ teaspoon pepper in 12-inch nonstick skillet. Cover and cook over medium-high heat, shaking pan occasionally, until water has evaporated, 6 to 8 minutes. Uncover and continue to cook until green beans are blistered and browned, about 2 minutes longer. Transfer to serving platter.

3. Heat remaining 1 tablespoon oil in now-empty skillet over medium-high heat until shimmering. Add cod and cook until both sides are lightly browned and cod registers 140 degrees, about 6 minutes per side. Serve cod with green beans, relish, and lemon wedges.

TEST KITCHEN NOTE: Halibut or haddock can be substituted for the cod, if desired. Toast the almonds in a skillet over medium heat, stirring frequently, until browned and fragrant.

Spicy Fried Chicken Sandwiches *Serves 4*

WHY THIS RECIPE WORKS: Shallow-frying the chicken in a covered skillet makes quick and clean work of this crispy sandwich stuffer.

- 2 cups shredded red cabbage
- ⅓ cup jarred sliced jalapeños, plus 2 tablespoons brine
- ¼ cup mayonnaise
  Salt and pepper
- 1 tablespoon chipotle chile powder
- 6 (3-ounce) boneless, skinless chicken thighs, trimmed
- 1¼ cups all-purpose flour
- ½ cup cornstarch
- ½ cup vegetable oil
- 4 large sandwich rolls, split and toasted

1. Combine cabbage, jalapeños and 1 tablespoon brine, 2 tablespoons mayonnaise, ½ teaspoon salt, and ¼ teaspoon pepper in bowl; set aside.

2. Combine chile powder, remaining 2 tablespoons mayonnaise, remaining 1 tablespoon brine, and 1 teaspoon salt in large bowl. Add chicken and toss to coat. Combine flour and cornstarch in zipper-lock bag. Add chicken to bag, seal bag, and shake vigorously to coat.

3. Heat oil in 12-inch nonstick skillet over medium-high heat until shimmering. Add chicken to skillet, cover, and cook until chicken is deep golden brown and registers 175 degrees, 8 to 10 minutes, flipping chicken halfway through cooking. Transfer chicken to paper towel–lined plate. Cut each piece of chicken in half crosswise. Divide chicken and slaw evenly among rolls. Serve.

TEST KITCHEN NOTE: For a less spicy option, you can substitute dill pickle chips for the jalapeños and reduce or omit the chipotle powder, if desired.

Strip Steaks with Cauliflower and Roasted Garlic Butter *Serves 4*

WHY THIS RECIPE WORKS: Roasting whole garlic cloves alongside the cauliflower softens them just enough so that they mash easily into the softened butter.

- 1 large head cauliflower (3 pounds), cored and cut into 1½-inch florets
- 3 large shallots, peeled and quartered through root end
- 3 tablespoons vegetable oil
- 6 garlic cloves, peeled
  Salt and pepper
- 2 (1-pound) strip steaks, trimmed and halved crosswise
- 6 tablespoons unsalted butter, softened
- 1 tablespoon chopped fresh chives

1. Adjust oven rack to lowest position and heat oven to 425 degrees. Toss cauliflower, shallots, 2 tablespoons oil, garlic, ½ teaspoon salt, and ½ teaspoon pepper together on rimmed baking sheet. Roast until vegetables are tender and lightly browned, about 25 minutes, stirring halfway through roasting.

2. Meanwhile, pat steaks dry with paper towels and season with salt and pepper. Heat remaining 1 tablespoon oil in 12-inch nonstick skillet over medium-high heat until just smoking. Add steaks and cook, flipping them every 2 minutes, until exteriors are well browned and meat registers 125 degrees (for medium-rare), 10 to 12 minutes. Transfer to serving platter and tent with foil.

3. Combine butter, chives, roasted garlic, ¼ teaspoon salt, and ⅛ teaspoon pepper in bowl and mash with fork. Serve steaks with vegetables and garlic butter.

TEST KITCHEN NOTE: When quartering the shallots, keep the root ends intact to hold the petals together.

Kielbasa with Hot Rice *Serves 4*

WHY THIS RECIPE WORKS: The rice is done in just 12 minutes when cooked in lots of boiling water.

- ¼ cup sour cream
- 2 teaspoons lime juice
- 2 cups long-grain white rice
- 1¾ pounds kielbasa sausage, cut into 3-inch pieces
- ¼ cup extra-virgin olive oil
- 2 bell peppers (1 green and 1 red), stemmed, seeded, and cut into ¾-inch pieces
  Salt and pepper
- ½ cup jarred hot salsa
- 2 tablespoons tomato paste
- 2 tablespoons chopped fresh cilantro

1. Combine sour cream and lime juice in bowl; set aside. Bring 3 quarts water to boil in large saucepan over high heat. Add rice and cook, stirring occasionally, until just tender, about 12 minutes. Drain rice in fine-mesh strainer and rinse.

2. Meanwhile, cut ½-inch crosshatch pattern, ⅛ inch deep, on tops and bottoms of sausages. Heat oil in 12-inch nonstick skillet over medium-high heat until shimmering. Add sausages and cook until browned on both crosshatched sides, about 4 minutes. Transfer sausages to large plate and tent with foil.

3. Add bell peppers, 1 teaspoon salt, and ½ teaspoon pepper to now-empty skillet and cook over medium-high heat until browned, 5 to 7 minutes. Stir in salsa and tomato paste until combined, about 30 seconds. Add rice and cook, stirring frequently, until mixture is fully combined, about 3 minutes. Add sausages, cover, remove from heat, and let sit for 5 minutes. Drizzle sour cream mixture over top and sprinkle with cilantro. Serve.

Lemon Chicken and Orzo Soup

30-MINUTE SUPPER

Eggs with Sweet Potato and Swiss Chard Hash

30-MINUTE SUPPER

Steak and Potato Curry with Peas

30-MINUTE SUPPER

Luau Pizza

30-MINUTE SUPPER

Eggs with Sweet Potato and Swiss Chard Hash *Serves 4*

WHY THIS RECIPE WORKS: To speed things up, we microwave the potato mixture before adding it to the skillet.

- 1 pound Yukon Gold potatoes, unpeeled, cut into ½-inch pieces
- 1 pound sweet potatoes, peeled and cut into ½-inch pieces
- 1 onion, chopped
- 4 teaspoons Lawry's Seasoned Salt
- ¼ cup extra-virgin olive oil
- 12 ounces Swiss chard, stemmed and cut into 1-inch pieces
- 3 garlic cloves, sliced thin
- 2 teaspoons lemon juice
- 8 large eggs

1. Combine potatoes, sweet potatoes, onion, and 1 tablespoon seasoned salt in large bowl and microwave, covered, until potatoes are almost tender, about 10 minutes, stirring halfway through microwaving.

2. Meanwhile, heat 1 teaspoon oil in 12-inch nonstick skillet over medium heat until shimmering. Add chard, garlic, and ½ teaspoon seasoned salt and cook until tender, about 3 minutes. Transfer to bowl; stir in lemon juice.

3. Heat 3 tablespoons oil in now-empty skillet over medium-high heat until just smoking. Add potato mixture and cook until dark golden brown, about 10 minutes. Divide hash evenly among 4 plates and top with chard mixture.

4. Crack eggs into bowl. Heat remaining 2 teaspoons oil in now-empty skillet over medium-high heat until shimmering. Pour eggs into skillet and sprinkle with remaining ½ teaspoon seasoned salt. Cook until whites begin to set, about 1 minute. Remove from heat, cover, and let sit until egg whites are cooked through but yolks remain runny, about 2 minutes. Cut eggs into 4 portions and serve with hash.

Lemon Chicken and Orzo Soup *Serves 4*

WHY THIS RECIPE WORKS: Adding yolks to the hot broth thickens the soup and adds richness.

- 2 tablespoons unsalted butter
- 1 small onion, chopped fine
- 8 cups chicken broth
- 2 sprigs fresh thyme
  Salt and pepper
- 1 cup orzo
- 6 large egg yolks
- 6 tablespoons lemon juice (2 lemons)
- 2 cups shredded rotisserie chicken
- 2 tablespoons chopped fresh chives

1. Melt butter in large saucepan over medium heat. Add onion and cook until softened, about 4 minutes. Increase heat to medium-high; add broth, thyme sprigs, 1 teaspoon salt, and ½ teaspoon pepper; and bring to boil. Add orzo and cook until tender, 12 to 14 minutes. Remove from heat and discard thyme sprigs.

2. Whisk egg yolks and lemon juice in bowl until combined. Whisking constantly, slowly pour yolk mixture into hot soup. Stir in chicken, cover, and let sit for 10 minutes, until soup is thickened and chicken is warmed through. Sprinkle with chives. Serve.

TEST KITCHEN NOTE: You can substitute leftover poached or grilled chicken for the rotisserie chicken, if desired.

Luau Pizza *Serves 4*

WHY THIS RECIPE WORKS: Baking the pizza in a 500-degree oven ensures a crisp crust and spotty-brown mozzarella.

- 2 tablespoons extra-virgin olive oil
- 1 pound pizza dough
- ⅓ cup barbecue sauce
- 8 ounces mozzarella cheese, shredded (2 cups)
- 1 cup ½-inch pineapple pieces
- 6 slices cooked bacon, halved
- ½ cup thinly sliced red onion
- ¼ cup jarred banana pepper rings
- 2 scallions, sliced thin on bias
  Sriracha sauce

1. Adjust oven rack to upper-middle position and heat oven to 500 degrees. Brush rimmed baking sheet with 1 tablespoon oil.

2. Roll dough into 16 by 10-inch rectangle, about ¼ inch thick, on lightly floured counter. Transfer dough to prepared sheet and brush with remaining 1 tablespoon oil. Brush dough with barbecue sauce, leaving ½-inch border around edge, then sprinkle evenly with mozzarella, pineapple, bacon, and onion.

3. Bake until cheese is spotty brown and crust is golden, about 10 minutes, rotating sheet halfway through baking. Let pizza cool for 5 minutes. Sprinkle pizza with pepper rings and scallions, drizzle with Sriracha, and serve.

TEST KITCHEN NOTE: The test kitchen's winning barbecue sauce is Bulls-Eye Original BBQ Sauce.

Steak and Potato Curry with Peas *Serves 4*

WHY THIS RECIPE WORKS: Thinly sliced beef cooks more quickly than large chunks, making for a fast weeknight curry.

- 2 tablespoons vegetable oil
- 1½ pounds blade steak, trimmed and sliced thin
  Salt and pepper
- 1 pound Yukon Gold potatoes, unpeeled, cut into ½-inch pieces
- 3 garlic cloves, minced
- 1 tablespoon curry powder
- 1 teaspoon ground ginger
- 2 cups water
- 1 cup frozen peas, thawed
- ½ cup canned coconut milk
- 3 tablespoons chopped fresh mint

1. Heat oil in large Dutch oven over medium-high heat until just smoking. Add steak, 1 teaspoon salt, and ½ teaspoon pepper and cook until meat begins to brown, about 2 minutes. Stir in potatoes and cook until they start to absorb juices and begin to color, 6 to 8 minutes.

2. Stir in garlic, curry powder, and ginger and cook until fragrant, about 1 minute. Add water and scrape up any browned bits. Bring to boil and cook until potatoes are tender, 10 to 12 minutes. Off heat, stir in peas and coconut milk. Sprinkle with mint and serve.

TEST KITCHEN NOTE: We like to serve this dish with steamed white rice.

Chocolate

Passionate about chocolate?
Here's what you need to know to get cooking
with this miracle ingredient. *by Scott Kathan*

What Is Chocolate?

To make chocolate, the seeds of the tropically grown cacao bean are fermented, dried, roasted, and ground into a paste. The paste is called chocolate liquor, and it's the base of all the chocolate we eat. Chocolate liquor contains about 55 percent cocoa butter (which provides silky texture) and 45 percent cocoa solids (the source of chocolate flavor). The combination of cocoa butter and cocoa solids makes up the cocoa percentage in processed chocolate (ingredients such as sugar and milk make up the remaining percentage). Here are the types of chocolate we use most in the test kitchen, along with our carefully vetted taste test winners.

BITTERSWEET/SEMISWEET

Two words for the same thing: Federal regulations mandate that chocolates with these labels must contain at least 35 percent cacao. Note that semisweet chocolate chips have a similar cacao percentage but less cocoa butter, so they are cheaper to produce and melt less readily.

Test Kitchen's Pick
Ghirardelli 60% Cacao Bittersweet Chocolate Premium Baking Bar or **Ghirardelli 60% Cacao Bittersweet Chocolate Chips**

UNSWEETENED CHOCOLATE

This is usually pure chocolate liquor formed into bars. We like it in baking recipes because its lack of sugar means we can use different sweeteners.
Test Kitchen's Pick **Hershey's Unsweetened Baking Bar**
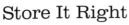

MILK CHOCOLATE

Mild, creamy milk chocolate needs to contain only 10 percent cacao. It's the star of our fantastic Milk Chocolate Cheesecake (**CooksCountry.com/ milkchocolatecheesecake**).
Test Kitchen's Pick
Dove Silky Smooth Milk Chocolate

COCOA POWDER

Simply dried, pulverized cocoa solids, Dutch-processed cocoa is less acidic than natural cocoa, but you can use the two interchangeably.
Test Kitchen's Pick
Hershey's Natural Cocoa Unsweetened

WHITE CHOCOLATE

Because white chocolate contains no cocoa solids (only cocoa butter, along with sugar, vanilla, milk solids, and often hydrogenated oil), it has zero chocolate flavor.

Store It Right

Unopened chocolate should be stored in a zipper-lock bag in a cool, dry place (such as a kitchen cabinet). Opened chocolate should be wrapped tightly in plastic wrap and given the same treatment. Improperly stored chocolate sometimes develops a white surface film called bloom; while harmless, bloom is unattractive. Luckily, it disappears when the chocolate is melted.

MAKE-AHEAD HOT CHOCOLATE
Makes 10 chocolate balls, enough for ten 1-cup servings

- 2 **cups (12 ounces) semisweet chocolate chips**
- 1 **cup heavy cream**
- ¼ **teaspoon salt**

1. Microwave chocolate chips, cream, and salt in large bowl, stirring occasionally, until smooth, about 2 minutes. Refrigerate until firm, about 2 hours.
2. Working with 3 tablespoons chilled chocolate mixture at a time, roll into 2-inch-diameter balls. Wrap balls individually in plastic wrap and transfer to zipper-lock bag. (Balls can be refrigerated for up to 5 days or frozen for up to 2 months.)

TO MAKE 1 CUP OF HOT CHOCOLATE:
Place 1 unwrapped chocolate ball and 1 cup milk in mug. Microwave, stirring occasionally, until smooth, about 2 minutes. Serve.

Our chocolate balls are easy to make and store.

Temper, Temper...

If you're melting chocolate to mix with other ingredients (as when making brownies), all you really need to do is melt it gently enough so that it doesn't burn or clump. But if you're melting it to frost a cake or to dip strawberries or cookies into, you need to temper it.

Good chocolate has a bright sheen and a snappy texture. But when it's melted and cooled, its chemical structure changes; if it is not tempered before it resolidifies, it will look dull and lack snap. The multistep tempering process usually involves a careful regimen of heating and cooling and then reheating the chocolate, taking its temperature along the way. But we developed an easier method.

1. Microwave Chocolate
Finely chop 3 ounces chocolate and place in microwave-safe bowl. Microwave at 50 percent power, stirring every 15 seconds, until just fully melted (chocolate will be slightly warmer than body temperature).
2. Add More Chocolate
Add 1 ounce finely grated chocolate (use small holes of box grater or rasp-style grater) and stir until smooth, returning bowl to microwave for no more than 5 seconds at a time if necessary until chocolate is fully smooth and incorporated.

Classic Roasted Beef Tenderloin

What's the best method for cooking this impressive holiday-time cut? We break it down for you.

by Morgan Bolling

BEEF TENDERLOIN'S MANY virtues are well-known: It looks impressive on the table, is luxuriously tender, and cooks relatively quickly. Plus, with its uniform shape and no bones, it's a breeze to carve. But it's an expensive cut, and there's not much leeway between just right and over-cooked. I set out to create a foolproof recipe that takes the anxiety and guess-work out of cooking this showstopping, crowd-pleasing roast.

You can buy a whole beef tender-loin either trimmed or untrimmed; untrimmed tenderloins are cheaper per pound, but the fatty side muscle called the chain, any exterior fat, and the silverskin must all be removed before roasting it (see "Six Steps to Prep a Tenderloin"). I started with a 5- to 6-pound trimmed whole beef tender-loin, which provides enough meat to feed a holiday crowd.

Salting the tenderloin overnight seasoned it throughout, giving it more intense flavor. After extensive testing, I opted to roast the meat gently in a low 250-degree oven to ensure that it cooked evenly. The relatively low heat also provided a comforting safety net—an extra 5 unplanned minutes at 250 degrees can do much less damage than those same 5 minutes at 450 de-grees. Pulling the roast when the center registered 125 degrees (and letting it rest for 30 minutes before carving) gave me perfectly moist, pink, medium-rare slices. But the outside of the roast was a pale gray—not exactly a festive (or appetizing) holiday color. I wanted a nicely browned, burnished crust that would add flavor and visual appeal.

I tried broiling the roast, but in the time it took to brown, the top third of the meat overcooked. I tested a few tricks to enhance browning during roasting, including coating the roast with butter, sugar, baking soda, or soy sauce. I even rubbed one tenderloin with mayonnaise. But none of these hacks really worked.

Gently cooking the beef in a 250-degree oven—and then searing it just before serving—ensures a perfectly rosy interior.

I wanted to sear the roast in a hot skillet on the stovetop to brown it after roasting, but a whole tenderloin doesn't fit in a skillet.

The solution? Slicing the roast in half before beginning the cooking pro-cess so I could later fit pieces together in a 12-inch skillet. This method also offered an additional advantage: With two pieces, I had more control over how each one was cooked—I could cook one piece to rare and the other to medium-rare, for instance. And cutting the tenderloin in half actually made it easier to bring it to the table but kept it looking impressive.

And there you have it: a simple yet highly refined and foolproof method for a tender and juicy holiday roast tender-loin. To take this roast over the top, we made a rich, glossy red wine sauce that takes a bit of work (and some extra meat if you bought a trimmed tenderloin) but is worth every minute you put into it.

CLASSIC ROAST BEEF TENDERLOIN
Serves 12 to 16

Plan ahead: The roast must be salted and refrigerated for at least 12 hours before cooking. If you're buying an untrimmed tenderloin, be sure it weighs 6 to 7 pounds. Serve with Red Wine Sauce (recipe follows), if desired.

- 1 (5-pound) trimmed whole beef tenderloin
   Kosher salt and pepper
- 2 tablespoons vegetable oil

1. Cut tenderloin crosswise at base of head to make 2 roasts. Using kitchen twine, tie head at 1-inch intervals. Tuck tail end of second roast underneath by 3 to 5 inches to create more even shape. Tie tucked portion with kitchen twine at 1-inch intervals to secure.

2. Place 1 roast on large sheet of plastic wrap and sprinkle all over with 1 tablespoon salt. Wrap tightly in double layer of plastic. Repeat with remaining roast and 1 tablespoon salt. Refrigerate roasts for at least 12 hours or up to 24 hours.

3. Adjust oven rack to middle position and heat oven to 250 degrees. Set wire rack in rimmed baking sheet. Season roasts with pepper and place on prepared wire rack. Roast until meat registers 125 degrees (for medium-rare) or 130 degrees (for medium), 1 hour 20 minutes to 1 hour 40 minutes for tail-end roast and 1 hour 40 minutes to 2 hours for head-end roast. Transfer roasts to carving board, tent with aluminum foil, and let rest for 20 minutes.

4. Pat roasts dry with paper towels. Heat oil in 12-inch nonstick skillet over medium-high heat until just smoking. Add both roasts and sear on all sides until well browned, 5 to 7 minutes. Transfer roasts to carving board, remove twine, and slice ½ inch thick. Serve.

Six Steps to Prep a Tenderloin (or Three If You Purchased a Trimmed Tenderloin)

Buying an untrimmed tenderloin can save you money, but it requires a little more prep work. Trimmed tenderloins are pricier and easier to prep. If you're using an untrimmed tenderloin, start with step 1; if you have a trimmed tenderloin, start with step 4.

Untrimmed

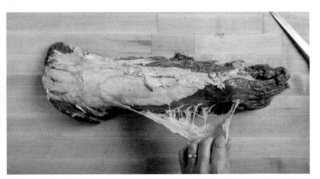

1. Trim Fat Place roast on cutting board with wider end (head) on left. Pat dry with paper towels, then pull away (cutting with boning knife as needed) and discard outer layer of fat.

2. Remove Chain Starting at thin end (tail) of roast, pull fatty chain away from side of roast, slicing through fat with boning knife as needed to detach it.

3. Remove Silverskin Insert boning knife under silverskin on tail end of roast. Angle knife slightly upward and use gentle sawing motion to remove silverskin.

Trimmed

4. Inspect Tenderloin With a trimmed tenderloin, it is easy to see how shape tapers from head (left) to tail (right). Look for and remove any excess fat or silverskin.

5. Cut in Two Slice tenderloin at base of head into 2 roasts. Tuck the end of tail piece under itself.

6. Tie Roasts Tie head and tail ends at even intervals with twine so that they cook evenly and retain their shapes.

RED WINE SAUCE *Makes about 2 cups*

Medium-bodied red wines, such as Côtes du Rhône or Pinot Noir, are best for this recipe. You can substitute chain meat trimmed from a beef tenderloin for the stew meat called for here.

- 5 tablespoons unsalted butter, cut into 5 pieces and chilled
- 12 ounces beef stew meat, cut into 1-inch pieces
- 2 tablespoons tomato paste
- 2 cups red wine
- 2 cups beef broth
- 1 shallot, sliced thin
- 2 tablespoons soy sauce
- 1½ tablespoons sugar
- 6 sprigs fresh thyme
- 2½ teaspoons cornstarch
- 1 tablespoon cold water
   Salt and pepper

1. Melt 1 tablespoon butter in large saucepan over medium-high heat. Add beef and cook, stirring occasionally, until well browned and fond forms on bottom of saucepan, 10 to 12 minutes.

2. Add tomato paste and cook until darkened in color and fragrant, about 1 minute. Stir in wine, broth, shallot, soy sauce, sugar, and thyme sprigs and bring to boil, scraping up any browned bits. Cook until reduced to 4 cups, 12 to 15 minutes.

3. Strain sauce through fine-mesh strainer set over bowl; discard solids. Return sauce to saucepan and bring to boil over medium-high heat. Dissolve cornstarch in cold water. Whisk cornstarch mixture into sauce and boil until slightly thickened, about 30 seconds. Reduce heat to low and whisk in remaining 4 tablespoons butter, 1 piece at a time. Season with salt and pepper to taste. Remove from heat and cover to keep warm.

Need a first course? Go to **CooksCountry.com/orangesalad** for our recipe for Orange-Ginger Salad.

Spice-Roasted Butternut Squash

We turned to the spice cabinet to find a counterpoint for the squash's natural sweetness.

by Ashley Moore

A shiny drizzle of flavored melted butter adds a festive holiday finish to the squash.

BUTTERNUT SQUASH IS a versatile underappreciated vegetable; its earthy sweetness is great when it's cut into cubes and roasted on its own, but it is also adept at taking on a variety of other flavors. I wanted to get out of my personal rut of roasting the squash with just salt, pepper, and oil and see how I could accent its flavor in a new way. The spice cabinet was a natural starting point.

I tried a handful of recipes for spice-roasted butternut squash and found a range of approaches, from composed salads featuring delicately spiced cubes to chile-coated wedges to simple preparations that looked a lot like home fries. While all were sprinkled with spices and roasted, some were dressed with vinaigrettes, others were sprinkled with chopped herbs, and a few had no further flourishes.

The first order of business was to establish a method for preparing and roasting the squash, one that would result in a tender texture and nice browning. After testing slices, cubes, chunks, and planks at a variety of temperatures, I settled on 1-inch pieces (easy to both prep and eat) and a 425-degree oven. To prevent messy sticking, I lined my chosen vessel, a rimmed baking sheet, with parchment paper.

We had taken a shine to a few recipes that used warm spices, so I proceeded down that same road. Cinnamon, which has a delicate sweetness of its own, complemented that same quality in the squash. To draw out the savory qualities of the vegetable, I added some ground cumin to the mix; the combination of these spices gave the dish a North African flair that my tasters loved. After tossing the squash with the spices and roasting it, I drizzled it with a flavored butter (with honey, lemon, and thyme) that I quickly made in the microwave just before serving. Truly amazing squash? Yes indeed.

My tasters were so happy with this recipe that I decided to make two flavor variations. The first one was based on a combination of allspice and cumin, with the lemon juice swapped out for lime juice. For the second variation I went with coriander instead of the cinnamon, orange juice in lieu of lemon, and fresh oregano in place of thyme. Knockouts, all three, with perfectly cooked, deeply seasoned squash and a drizzle of easy butter sauce.

SPICE-ROASTED BUTTERNUT SQUASH WITH HONEY-LEMON BUTTER
Serves 4
When peeling the squash, be sure to also remove the fibrous yellow flesh just beneath the skin.

- 3 tablespoons extra-virgin olive oil
  Salt and pepper
- 1 teaspoon ground cumin
- 1 teaspoon ground cinnamon
  Pinch cayenne pepper
- 3 pounds butternut squash, peeled, seeded, and cut into 1-inch pieces (7¾ cups)
- 2 tablespoons unsalted butter
- 1 tablespoon honey
- 1 teaspoon coarsely chopped fresh thyme
- 1 teaspoon lemon juice

1. Adjust oven rack to middle position and heat oven to 425 degrees. Line rimmed baking sheet with parchment paper.
2. Whisk oil, 1 teaspoon salt, 1 teaspoon pepper, cumin, cinnamon, and cayenne together in large bowl. Add squash and toss until evenly coated. Arrange squash in even layer on prepared sheet. Roast until squash is tender and browned on bottom, 30 to 35 minutes.
3. Microwave butter, honey, and ¼ teaspoon salt in small bowl until butter is melted, about 30 seconds. Stir in thyme and lemon juice. Using spatula, transfer squash to serving platter. Drizzle with butter mixture and serve.

SPICE-ROASTED BUTTERNUT SQUASH WITH HONEY-LIME BUTTER
Substitute ground allspice for cinnamon, 1 tablespoon minced fresh chives for thyme, and lime juice for lemon juice.

SPICE-ROASTED BUTTERNUT SQUASH WITH HONEY-ORANGE BUTTER
Substitute ground coriander for cinnamon, oregano for thyme, and orange juice for lemon juice.

How to Prep Butternut Squash

1. Lop ends off squash and use chef's knife to cut it into 2 pieces where bulb meets neck.

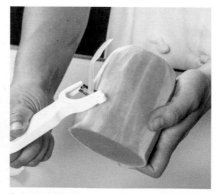

2. Use vegetable peeler to peel away skin and fibrous yellow flesh down to bright orange flesh.

3. Halve bulb end, then scoop out and discard seeds and pulp. Now you're ready to chop.

Foil-Roasted Potatoes

Tired of peeling and mashing? For a perfectly simple potato side dish, reach for the roll.

by Alli Berkey

IT'S EASY TO get passable roasted potatoes on the table with a minimum of effort: Just cut your potatoes into chunks, toss them in a roasting pan with some oil and salt and pepper, and slide the pan into a preheated oven. But there's a big difference between simply passable roasted potatoes and truly great ones. I had the latter in my sights, but I didn't want to jump through hoops for a simple side dish.

The best part of a roasted potato is its flavorful browned exterior, but cranking up the oven to achieve good browning often leaves the insides of the potatoes dry and grainy. I tried a few recipes that got around this problem by boiling the potatoes until they were almost done before quickly roasting them, or by covering the pan with foil for the first part of roasting and then uncovering it so the spuds could take on browning at the end. Both of these methods worked, but I sought a simpler way.

The recipe that called for covering the roasting pan with foil got me thinking about the French method of cooking foods *en papillote*, or in parchment-paper pouches. Foods cook very efficiently in these packets due to the trapped steam. I tried making a parchment packet for 2 pounds of potatoes (to serve six people), but it was tricky to handle such a large pouch made of delicate paper, and it took some finesse to crimp and seal the edges. Making the packet out of aluminum foil was far easier. I made three packets, one for each type of potato I wanted to test: russets, Yukon Golds, and red new potatoes, all cut into smallish chunks. I placed each pouch on a baking sheet and popped the sheets into the oven. After the potatoes had baked at 400 degrees for about 40 minutes, I cut into each packet (carefully, since a blast of hot steam can be dangerous) to find perfectly tender but barely browned potatoes; of the three samples, my tasters preferred the halved red potatoes for their beautifully creamy texture.

The potatoes needed more browning and a lot more seasoning. To increase the browning, I lowered the oven rack so the potatoes were closer to the heat source. I also added some butter to the packet, which helped with both browning and flavor. Fresh thyme and rosemary added a deeply fragrant herbal presence, and a good

bit of sliced garlic brought sweetness and depth. Finally, these potatoes hit all the marks: creamy interiors, nicely browned cut sides, and tons of flavor—all with an easy method that, as a bonus, made cleanup a breeze.

FOIL-ROASTED POTATOES *Serves 6*
Use potatoes that are no larger than 1½ inches in diameter.

- 2 **pounds small red potatoes, unpeeled, halved**
- 2 **teaspoons chopped fresh rosemary**
- 1¼ **teaspoons salt**
- 1 **teaspoon chopped fresh thyme**
- ½ **teaspoon pepper**
- 4 **tablespoons unsalted butter, cut into ½-inch pieces**
- 3 **garlic cloves, sliced thin**

1. Adjust oven rack to lowest position and heat oven to 400 degrees. Toss potatoes, rosemary, salt, thyme, and pepper in large bowl until potatoes are well coated.

2. Line baking sheet with 16 by 12-inch sheet of aluminum foil. Spread potato mixture evenly over foil, leaving 1½-inch border. Flip potatoes cut sides down. Scatter butter and garlic over potatoes. Place second 16 by 12-inch sheet of foil over potatoes. Beginning at 1 corner, fold foil inward in ½-inch increments 2 to 3 times to seal edge. Continue folding around perimeter of foil to create sealed packet.

3. Transfer sheet to oven and bake until potatoes are tender, about 40 minutes. Let potatoes cool for 5 minutes. Using tongs, tear away top sheet of foil, being careful of escaping steam. Serve.

Choose small red potatoes of similar size to ensure even cooking.

U.S. POSTAL SERVICE STATEMENT OF OWNERSHIP, MANAGEMENT, AND CIRCULATION

1. Publication Title: *Cook's Country*; 2. Publication No. 1552-1990; 3. Filing date: 10/01/17; 4. Issue frequency: Dec/Jan, Feb/Mar, Apr/May, Jun/Jul, Aug/Sept, Oct/Nov, 5. No. of issues published annually: 6; 6. Annual Subscription Price is $35.70; 7. Complete mailing address of known office of publication: 17 Station Street, Brookline, MA 02445; 8. Complete mailing address of headquarters or general business office of publisher: 17 Station Street, Brookline, MA 02445; 9. Full names and complete mailing addresses of publisher, editor, and managing editor: Publisher, David Nussbaum, 17 Station Street, Brookline, MA 02445, Editor, Jack Bishop, 17 Station Street, Brookline, MA 02445, Managing Editor, Todd Meier, 17 Station Street, Brookline, MA 02445; 10. Owner: America's Test Kitchen LP, 17 Station Street, Brookline, MA 02445; 11. Known bondholders, mortgages, and other securities: NONE; 12. Tax status: Has Not Changed During Preceding 12 Months; 13. Publication title: *Cook's Country*; 14. Issue date for circulation data below: August/September 2017; 15A. Total number of copies: Average number of copies each issue during preceding 12 months: 359,333 (Aug/Sep 2017: 348,579); B. Paid circulation: 1. Mailed outside-county paid subscriptions. Average number of copies each issue during preceding 12 months: 284,730 (Aug/Sep 2017: 274,004); 2. Mailed in-county paid subscriptions. Average number of copies each issue during preceding 12 months: 0 (Aug/Sep 2017: 0); 3. Sales through dealers and carriers, street vendors, and counter sales. Average number of copies each issue during preceding 12 months: 18,351 (Aug/Sep 2017: 19,429); 4. Paid distribution through other classes mailed through the USPS. Average number of copies each issue during preceding 12 months: 0 (Aug/Sep 2017: 0); C. Total paid distribution. Average number of copies each issue during preceding 12 months: 303,081 (Aug/Sep 2017: 293,433); D. Free or nominal rate distribution (by mail and outside mail); 1. Free or nominal Outside-County. Average number of copies each issue during preceding 12 months: 1,220 (Aug/Sep 2017: 1,126); 2. Free or nominal rate in-county copies. Average number of copies each issue during preceding 12 months: 0 (Aug/Sep 2017: 0); 3. Free or nominal rate copies mailed at other Classes through the USPS. Average number of copies each issue during preceding 12 months: 0 (Aug/Sep 2017: 0); 4. Free or nominal rate distribution outside the mail. Average number of copies each issue during preceding 12 months: 725 (Aug/Sep 2017: 725); E. Total free or nominal rate distribution. Average number of copies each issue during preceding 12 months: 1,945 (Aug/Sep 2017: 1,851); F. Total free distribution. Average number of copies each issue during preceding 12 months: 305,026 (Aug/Sep 2017: 295,284); G. Copies not Distributed. Average number of copies each issue during preceding 12 months: 54,307 (Aug/Sep 2017: 53,295); H. Total. Average number of copies each issue during preceding 12 months: 359,333 (Aug/Sep 2017: 348,579); I. Percent paid. Average percent of copies paid for preceding 12 months: 99.36% (Aug/Sep 2017: 99.37%)

Chocolate Chip Panettone

Dried fruit–studded panettone is a holiday favorite. But this year, we aimed to speed things up and sweeten the pot. *by Katie Leaird*

MY BIGGEST FAN, my mom, called to ask what I was working on in the test kitchen. When I told her "Panettone," the line went eerily quiet. Then my ever-honest mother responded, "Oh, that dry, boring Italian fruitcake? Good luck with that."

Why such disdain? Panettone is a beautiful sweetened and enriched bread (not a fruitcake) studded with dried and candied fruit or sometimes nuts. Traditionally, bakers let the dough rise for days, and it languidly develops its signature yeasty flavor and light, airy crumb. Rich with egg yolks and butter, fresh loaves of this large, domed bread have served as a favorite holiday gift for centuries in Italy. But as with most breads, fresher is better. Panettone loaves can voyage hundreds or thousands of miles to specialty grocery stores where they endure months on the shelves, stamped with astronomical price tags. By the time the panettone hits the table, it can be a stale, dry letdown.

I recently learned what a revelation fresh panettone can be when a test kitchen colleague developed a recipe for a lovely, tender classic panettone, one that reaches lofty heights thanks to its long proofing time and special panettone mold. Curious to see if I could replicate this success, I baked this version a few times with beautiful results. But I wanted something quicker (the holiday season is a busy time), and I didn't want to special-order any equipment. What's more, rather than rely on the traditional, grown-up additions of dried and candied fruit or nuts, I wanted to develop a recipe for a version that would please the whole family: chocolate chip panettone.

My first move was to lose the paper mold in favor of an 8-inch cake pan (a 9-inch pan made a loaf that was too squat). I knew that this switch might cost my panettone some height, but after a few experiments I found that my loaves were, if a little shorter, no less impressively domed.

Next, I focused on speeding up the dough's rising time. I was using instant yeast which, unlike active dry yeast, can be added directly to dough without being activated first. The instant yeast

 Go to **CooksCountry.com/jan18** to see which almond extract our tasters rated as their favorite.

Dried fruits are traditional add-ins for holiday panettone, but we chose a sweeter route—crowd-pleasing chocolate chips.

will do its thing when it meets room-temperature, or even cold, liquid, but it will work faster if things are warmer. So I microwaved the milk (the traditional liquid for panettone) before stirring it in to drive up the overall temperature of the dough. This trimmed a bit of time from the process.

An even more effective accelerator was hiding in the sweetener. Swapping corn syrup for sugar sped up the proofing significantly (see "A Vote for Corn Syrup"), shaving about an hour off each leg of the two-step rise. This switch had a happy effect on the texture, too; the panettone made with corn syrup retained its moisture over time, resulting in leftovers that remained fresh-tasting even several days after baking. Eggs and plenty of butter add richness to this bread; after experiments I settled on one egg plus two yolks and a stick of butter for the best balance.

I now had a light, tender, lofty loaf of panettone made in less than half the time required for a typical recipe. And while the chocolate chips were a hit, I found that a bit of candied orange peel kneaded into the dough with the chocolate chips, plus a bit of vanilla extract and almond extract, gave this loaf a fully realized, festive holiday flavor.

My freshly baked and sweetly studded panettone was certainly something to celebrate. Even my mom fell in love with this loaf.

Ever heard the one about the holiday fruitcake that never gets eaten but just travels from family to family in an endless loop of regifting? There may be one in your freezer right now. No one is keen on eating it, but throwing it away seems indelicate or unkind. It was a gift, after all!

THE AMERICAN TABLE

This "traveling fruitcake" story is similar to the holiday tradition of panettone. For more than a century, Italian American families around the United States have exchanged loaves of panettone at Christmas time. When you've got a lot of friends, that may mean a lot of loaves of panettone exchanged, with some families trading a dozen or more loaves back and forth. The tradition also calls for any extra loaves to be paid forward to a less fortunate neighbor.

But whether received as a gift or made from scratch at home, there's a good-luck legend baked into every loaf of panettone: After cutting it up, a slice is set aside and saved until next Christmas, ensuring good fortune all year.

3 Easy Steps to Shaping Panettone

Shaping panettone is easy if you follow these three simple steps.

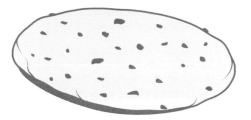

Pat Dough into Disk
After letting the dough rise, pat it into a 12-inch disk.

Fold Edges Inward
Working around the circumference, lift and fold the edges of the dough into the middle.

Flip Dough and Form into Ball
Invert the dough seam side down, cup the sides with your hands, and roll it in circles to form a smooth ball.

CHOCOLATE CHIP PANETTONE
Makes 1 loaf

Use an instant-read thermometer to make sure the milk is the correct temperature. If using a traditional 6 by 4-inch paper panettone mold, which you can find online or at kitchen supply stores, extend the baking time in step 6 by 10 minutes.

- ¾ cup warm milk (110 degrees)
- 2 large eggs plus 2 large yolks
- 3 tablespoons light corn syrup
- 1 teaspoon vanilla extract
- ½ teaspoon almond extract
- 2¾ cups (13¾ ounces) all-purpose flour
- 2¼ teaspoons instant or rapid-rise yeast
- 1 teaspoon salt
- 8 tablespoons unsalted butter, cut into 8 pieces and softened
- 1 cup (6 ounces) mini chocolate chips
- 3 ounces finely chopped candied orange peel

1. Whisk milk, 1 egg and yolks, corn syrup, vanilla, and almond extract in 2-cup liquid measuring cup until combined. Using stand mixer fitted with dough hook, mix flour, yeast, and salt on medium-low speed until combined, about 5 seconds. With mixer running, slowly add milk mixture and knead until cohesive dough forms and no dry flour remains, 3 to 5 minutes, scraping down bowl and dough hook as needed.

2. With mixer running, add butter 1 piece at a time until incorporated. Increase speed to medium-high and knead until dough pulls away from sides of bowl but still sticks to bottom, about 10 minutes. Reduce speed to low, add chocolate chips and orange peel, and knead until fully incorporated, about 2 minutes.

3. Turn out dough onto lightly floured counter and knead until smooth, about 1 minute. Form dough into tight ball and transfer to greased large bowl. Cover with plastic wrap and let rise at room temperature (about 70 degrees) until doubled in size, about 2 hours.

4. Grease 8-inch cake pan. Pat dough into 12-inch disk on lightly floured counter. Working around circumference of dough, fold edges of dough toward center to form rough square. Flip dough over and, applying gentle pressure, move your hands in small circular motions to form dough into smooth, taut ball. Transfer ball, seam side down, to prepared pan. Cover loosely with greased plastic and let rise at room temperature until center is about 2 inches above lip of pan, 2 to 2½ hours.

5. Adjust oven rack to middle position and heat oven to 350 degrees. Lightly beat remaining egg and brush over dough. Bake until golden brown, 15 to 20 minutes.

6. Rotate pan, tent with aluminum foil, and continue to bake until center of loaf registers 190 degrees, 30 to 40 minutes longer. Transfer pan to wire rack and let cool for 15 minutes. Remove loaf from pan and let cool completely on wire rack, about 3 hours. Serve.

ORANGE AND RAISIN PANETTONE

Omit chocolate chips. Combine ¾ cup golden raisins and 2 tablespoons orange juice in small bowl, cover, and microwave until steaming, about 1 minute. Let sit until raisins are softened, about 15 minutes. Add 2 teaspoons grated orange zest to milk mixture in step 1. Add raisins (plus any juice remaining in bowl) with candied orange peel in step 2.

The Shape of Things to Come

The cooking vessel has a big impact on the shape of your finished panettone. We tried baking our loaf in saucepans, empty coffee cans, and with a homemade aluminum foil collar, but we found that using an 8-inch cake pan made the bread that best approximated the tall shape of panettone baked in a specialty paper mold.

TRADITIONAL PAPER MOLD
Tall and cylindrical

8-INCH CAKE PAN
The perfect middle ground

9-INCH CAKE PAN
Too squat

A Vote for Corn Syrup

There are two reasons we use corn syrup instead of white sugar in our recipe. First, corn syrup behaves like an invert sugar, and invert sugars are easier for yeast to digest, meaning carbon dioxide is produced sooner and the dough rises faster. And second, baked goods made with invert sugars retain moisture—and thus stay fresh-tasting—longer than those made with sugar. This is because sugar is molecularly attracted to water and will draw moisture from the baked goods as they sit. Corn syrup is not attracted to water, so the moisture stays distributed throughout the baked bread longer.

Chewy Sugar Cookies

Our sweet, tender sugar cookies have a pleasant chew—and a few surprising ingredients.

by Katie Leaird

Texture Tips for Chewy Cookies

Three Fats Lead to a Chewy—Not Crumbly—Texture

Why do we need three different kinds of fat for these simple sugar cookies? To optimize chewy texture without sacrificing flavor.

You're likely familiar with the two basic types of fats, saturated and unsaturated. Saturated fats (such as butter) are solid at room temperature, while unsaturated fats (such as oil) are liquid at room temperature. When fats bake together, they reorganize themselves chemically. Once cooled, the fats form new crystal structures that ultimately determine the cookie's texture (chewy, crisp, crumbly, etc.). To create the specific chewy texture we wanted in these cookies, we learned that we needed a combination of saturated and unsaturated fats. That meant including vegetable oil, which doesn't add any flavor. To compensate for the bland oil, we replaced some of the butter with rich, tangy cream cheese to boost the flavor while keeping the chewy texture.

Melt the Butter

Many recipes for cakes and cookies call for creaming together softened butter and sugar, which beats air into the mixture and yields tall, light baked goods. But our goal with these cookies was good chew, so we melted the butter instead. Why does melted butter lead to more chew? Liquid butter encourages more gluten development in the cookie dough than solid butter does. Too much gluten would make the cookies tough, but melted butter boosts gluten formation just enough to promote chew.

Top Notch: Baking Soda Makes for Crackly Tops

Baking soda works by reacting with acidic ingredients in batters and doughs and releasing carbon dioxide, which causes expansion and rise. In this sugar cookie dough, the baking soda reacts with the acids naturally present in the cream cheese. Before the cookies can set in the oven, the carbon dioxide bubbles rise to the tops of the cookies and burst, creating fissures. These fissures set to form the lovely, crackly tops of these chewy sugar cookies.

Key Tools

Rimmed Baking Sheet

We use these pans for everything from cookies to one-pan dinners. Our favorite is the **Nordic Ware Baker's Half Sheet** ($14.97). We recommend having at least two in your kitchen.

Whisk

The best whisks feel balanced and work efficiently. Our favorite all-purpose whisk, the **OXO Good Grips 11" Balloon Whisk** ($9.99), makes whisking a pleasure.

Cookie Spatula

Small, agile cookie spatulas make it easy to maneuver between cookies on a crowded sheet. Our favorite is the **KitchenAid Cookie/Pastry Lifter** ($8.00).

Step by Step

1. Prep baking sheets
Line 2 rimmed baking sheets with parchment paper and heat oven to 350 degrees.
Why? Parchment keeps the cookies from sticking to the sheets and makes cleanup easier.

2. Combine dry ingredients
Whisk flour, baking powder, baking soda, and salt together in medium bowl. Set aside.
Why? Whisking distributes the leaveners and salt evenly in the dough. It also breaks up any clumps; sifting isn't necessary.

3. Combine sugar and dairy
In large bowl, pour melted butter over sugar and cream cheese and whisk to combine.
Why? Using melted butter enables you to whisk the ingredients together by hand. The cream cheese adds flavor.

4. Add oil
Whisk in vegetable oil until incorporated.
Why? Using oil—an unsaturated fat that is an unusual ingredient for sugar cookies—ensures optimal chew.

5. Add wet ingredients
Add egg, milk, and vanilla and whisk until smooth.
Why? Adding a little liquid, but not too much, helps smooth out the edges of the cookies.

CHEWY SUGAR COOKIES
Makes 24 cookies
The final dough will be slightly softer than most cookie doughs. For the best results, handle the dough as briefly and gently as possible when shaping the cookies. Overworking the dough will result in flatter cookies.

2¼ cups (11¼ ounces) all-purpose flour
1 teaspoon baking powder
½ teaspoon baking soda
½ teaspoon salt
1½ cups (10½ ounces) sugar, plus ⅓ cup for rolling
2 ounces cream cheese, cut into 8 pieces
6 tablespoons unsalted butter, melted
⅓ cup vegetable oil
1 large egg
1 tablespoon milk
2 teaspoons vanilla extract

1. Adjust oven rack to middle position and heat oven to 350 degrees. Line 2 rimmed baking sheets with parchment paper. Whisk flour, baking powder, baking soda, and salt together in medium bowl; set aside.

2. Place 1½ cups sugar and cream cheese in large bowl. Place remaining ⅓ cup sugar in shallow dish and set aside. Pour melted butter over sugar and cream cheese and whisk to combine (some small lumps of cream cheese will remain but will smooth out later). Whisk in oil until incorporated. Add egg, milk, and vanilla and whisk until smooth. Add flour mixture and mix with rubber spatula until soft, homogeneous dough forms.

3. Divide dough into 24 equal pieces, about 2 tablespoons each. Using your hands, roll dough into balls. Working in batches, roll balls in reserved sugar to coat and evenly space on prepared sheets, 12 balls per sheet. Using bottom of drinking glass, flatten balls to 2 inches in diameter. Sprinkle tops of cookies evenly with 4 teaspoons of sugar remaining in shallow dish (2 teaspoons per sheet); discard any remaining sugar.

4. Bake cookies 1 sheet at a time until edges are set and just beginning to brown, 11 to 13 minutes, rotating sheet halfway through baking. Let cookies cool on sheet for 5 minutes, then transfer to wire rack. Let cookies cool completely before serving.

CHEWY COCONUT-LIME SUGAR COOKIES
Whisk ½ cup sweetened shredded coconut, chopped fine, into flour mixture in step 1. Add 1 teaspoon grated lime zest to sugar–cream cheese mixture in step 2 and substitute 1 tablespoon lime juice for vanilla extract.

Go to **CooksCountry.com/vanilla** to read the results of our tasting of vanilla extracts.

6. Add flour mixture
Add flour mixture and mix with rubber spatula until soft, homogeneous dough forms.
Why? Since this dough is softer than most, you can easily mix it by hand.

7. Divide and shape dough
Divide dough into 24 equal pieces, about 2 tablespoons each. Using your hands, roll dough into balls.
Why? Rolling the dough, rather than dropping it in mounds from a spoon, will yield thick, even cookies.

8. Coat in sugar
Roll balls in sugar to coat and evenly space on prepared sheets. Using bottom of drinking glass, flatten balls to 2 inches in diameter. Sprinkle tops with sugar.
Why? This final layer of sugar creates the cookies' signature crunchy, sweet exteriors.

9. Bake and rotate
Bake cookies 1 sheet at a time until edges are set and just beginning to brown, 11 to 13 minutes, rotating sheet halfway through baking.
Why? Baking the cookies one sheet at a time and rotating the sheet ensure even baking.

10. Let cookies cool on sheet
Let cookies cool on sheet for 5 minutes, then transfer to wire rack.
Why? To prevent breakage, the cookies need to cool slightly before being transferred from the baking sheet to the wire rack.

Pork Tinga

Deeply flavored shredded pork? Sounds like a job for the slow cooker.

by Matthew Fairman

TINGA IS A Mexican dish of spicy shredded meat (in most cases, the meat of choice is pork). The meat is often served atop crisp tostada shells or is sometimes spooned into tacos. Imagine pork shoulder that's been gently braised with tomatoes and smoky chipotle chiles and then shredded and showered with all the fixings—chopped avocado, a squeeze of lime, crumbled cheese. So good.

But each time I make my favorite recipe for pork tinga in a Dutch oven, I start to lose steam halfway through the process. Sure, the recipe yields rich, spicy shredded pork balanced with concentrated sweet and savory tomato flavor. But it requires browning the pork pieces in batches, simmering them in water and aromatics for hours to make a pork broth, sautéing more aromatics for a tomato sauce that incorporates that pork broth, and finally cooking the pork with the sauce until it's soft enough to shred. Could I switch gears and lean on the slow cooker to do the heavy lifting? I wanted to find out.

It's always a good idea to test the easiest possible solution first, and that was simply to dump all the raw ingredients for this favored recipe into the slow cooker, throw on the cover, and let it rip. What I got was pork soup—and none of the browned bits of pork that my tasters craved. "Dump and run" was not going to cut it here.

I clearly had too much moisture for the closed environment of the slow cooker, so I tried a simple ingredient swap, ditching tomato sauce for tomato paste, which has far less moisture. The consistency of this batch was better but still too wet.

No sweat. I switched back to the tomato sauce and slow-cooked the pork mixture again. It was still too wet, but this time, after mashing the pork into the sauce, I transferred the resulting soupy mixture to a large nonstick skillet set over high heat. After about 10 minutes, the moisture had cooked off and the mixture began to sizzle and brown on the edges.

I stuck a fork in and tried a bite. It was good enough that I contemplated hiding it from my colleagues and taking it all home for myself. But the aromas were too enticing; coworkers soon closed in, waving tostada shells, to devour the tinga.

A collection of garnishes takes this supersavory slow-cooked pork over the top.

Boston Butt

Despite its name, this flavorful cut actually comes from the upper portion of the hog's shoulder. Also called pork butt, it is relatively fatty and tough and thus needs long, slow cooking to tenderize. It's our go-to cut for pork stews, pulled pork, and *tinga*.

PERFECT CUT FOR TINGA

SLOW-COOKER MEXICAN SHREDDED PORK TOSTADAS
Serves 4 to 6

Mexican *tinga* is traditionally served on tostadas (crisp fried corn tortillas), but it is also served in tacos or burritos or over rice. You can use store-bought tostada shells or make your own (recipe follows). Our favorite ready-made tostadas are Mission Tostadas Estilo Casero. Two teaspoons of minced canned chipotle chiles in adobo sauce can be substituted for the chipotle chile powder, if desired.

 2 **pounds boneless pork butt roast, trimmed and cut into 2-inch pieces**
 1 **(15-ounce) can tomato sauce**
 1 **onion, chopped fine**
 4 **garlic cloves, minced**
 1½ **teaspoons chipotle chile powder**
    Salt
 1 **teaspoon dried oregano**
 ½ **teaspoon dried thyme**
 2 **bay leaves**
 12 **tostada shells**
    Crumbled queso fresco
    Fresh cilantro leaves
    Sour cream
    Diced avocado
    Lime wedges

1. Combine pork, tomato sauce, onion, garlic, chile powder, 1 teaspoon salt, oregano, thyme, and bay leaves in slow cooker. Cook until pork is tender, 5 to 7 hours on high or 8 to 10 hours on low. Discard bay leaves. Using potato masher, mash pork in slow cooker until shredded into bite-size pieces.
2. Transfer contents of slow cooker to 12-inch nonstick skillet. Cook over high heat, stirring occasionally, until all liquid has evaporated and mixture begins to brown in spots, 10 to 12 minutes. Season with salt to taste. Spoon small amount of pork onto center of each tostada shell and serve, passing queso fresco, cilantro, sour cream, avocado, and lime wedges separately.

BAKED TOSTADAS
Makes 12 tostadas

Adjust oven racks to upper-middle and lower-middle positions and heat oven to 450 degrees. Arrange twelve 6-inch corn tortillas in single layer on 2 rimmed baking sheets. Brush both sides of each tortilla with vegetable oil (about 2 tablespoons per sheet). Place inverted wire rack on top of tortillas on each sheet to keep tortillas flat. Bake until tortillas are lightly browned and crisp, 15 to 18 minutes, switching and rotating sheets halfway through baking.

Chicken, Broccoli, and Rice

This back-of-the-can recipe was due for an update. *by Cecelia Jenkins*

IT'S COMFORT FOOD at its very best: a pot of creamy, cheesy rice emerging from the oven studded with emerald-green broccoli florets and topped with golden-brown, juicy chicken. Often baked in a casserole dish, it's a homey, happy supper.

Over the years, condensed soup has been the backbone of this classic casserole combo as a convenient base to flavor and bind the dish. The recipe is a breeze: You just stir the soup together with rice, cheese, and broccoli and perhaps some water; place boneless, skinless chicken breasts on top; and bake until the rice and chicken are done. But the one-note flavor and the saltiness of many condensed soups can overwhelm the dish. My goal was a refreshed one-pot recipe that maintained all the comfort but canned the can.

After experimenting with simply replacing the canned soup with chicken broth, I was able to identify my two main challenges. The first was achieving evenly cooked rice, which was dependent on having just enough liquid and just enough time. The second was building the kind of smooth, saucy base that canned soup creates.

Simply stirring everything together and baking it gave me pockets of crunchy, undercooked rice, so I decided to take a staggered approach, giving the rice a head start on the stove. This meant switching from a casserole dish to a Dutch oven. Over medium-high

heat, I stirred together rice, butter, chopped onion, and minced garlic; cooked the mixture for just a couple of minutes; and then added chicken broth and uncovered the pot. Once the rice absorbed nearly all the broth, I stirred in the cheese to create a creamy and cohesive mixture. I added some broccoli florets and topped it all with the chicken. I covered the pot to trap heat and cook everything through, but this approach gave me scorched rice, even over low heat. I tried again, this time sliding the pot into the oven, uncovered.

I was getting closer. The rice came out with tender, separate grains bound

by creamy cheese, but by the time the chicken cooked through, my broccoli had turned to mush. The solution? Browning the chicken on one side at the beginning to give it a head start. Once it was golden, I could set it aside while I started the rice; as a bonus, I stirred the flavorful browned bits the chicken left behind into the rice for even more savory flavor.

My casserole emerged from the oven with each component cooked just right. It was richly flavored and comforting to eat, just like the canned-soup version, but fresher, more flavorful, and as far as my tasters were concerned, much better.

What you can't see: extra-sharp cheddar cheese stirred into the rice for maximum flavor.

ONE-POT CHICKEN WITH BROCCOLI AND RICE *Serves 4*

Our favorite white rice is Lundberg Organic Long-Grain White Rice.

- 4 (6- to 8-ounce) boneless, skinless chicken breasts, trimmed
  Salt and pepper
- 4 tablespoons unsalted butter
- 1 onion, chopped
- 2 garlic cloves, minced
- 1½ cups long-grain white rice
- 4 cups chicken broth
- 12 ounces broccoli florets, cut into 1-inch pieces
- 6 ounces extra-sharp cheddar cheese, shredded (1½ cups)
- 1 ounce Parmesan cheese, grated (½ cup)

1. Adjust oven rack to middle position and heat oven to 400 degrees. Pat chicken dry with paper towels and season with salt and pepper.
2. Melt 2 tablespoons butter in Dutch oven over medium-high heat. Add chicken, skinned side down, and cook until browned, about 5 minutes. Transfer chicken to plate, browned side up.
3. Melt remaining 2 tablespoons butter in now-empty pot over medium-high heat. Add onion, garlic, ½ teaspoon pepper, and ¼ teaspoon salt and cook until onion is just softened, about 3 minutes, scraping up any browned bits. Stir in rice and cook until edges of rice begin to turn translucent, about 2 minutes.
4. Stir in broth and bring to boil. Reduce heat to medium-low and simmer, uncovered, until nearly all liquid is absorbed, about 12 minutes, stirring occasionally.
5. Off heat, stir in broccoli, cheddar, and Parmesan. Scrape down sides of pot with rubber spatula. Top rice mixture with chicken, browned side up, and add any accumulated chicken juices from plate. Transfer to oven and bake, uncovered, until chicken registers 160 degrees, about 20 minutes. Let cool for 10 minutes before serving.

Four Steps to One-Pot Chicken with Broccoli and Rice

1. Sear chicken in melted butter to create flavorful browning. Remove chicken.

2. Sauté onion and garlic, add rice, add broth, and cook until liquid is absorbed.

3. Off heat, stir broccoli and cheese into cooked rice.

4. Return browned chicken to pot and bake until chicken and broccoli are done.

Cheese Logs

A cheese log for every occasion—and no broken crackers.

by Matthew Fairman

PICTURE YOURSELF AT a holiday party. You've got your hands full: a long-stemmed wine glass in one and a tiny plastic plate in the other. You stack one on the other, grab a delicate cracker, and reach for the cheese log, hoping to scoop out a bite. No such luck: Your cracker shatters, and you get no cheese. We've all been there.

I set out to change this scenario by creating a cheese log that was firm enough to hold its shape but creamy enough to forestall broken crackers. And I wanted it to be easily adaptable into a suite of cheese logs that had surprising flavors and were suitable for any occasion.

For a reliable base, I settled on a simple ratio of half semisoft cheese (think cheddar or Jack cheese) and half cream cheese, which lends both tanginess and luscious texture. But these two ingredients alone created a cheese that was still too hard at room temperature. The addition of creamy mayonnaise gave the mixture a texture pliable enough to be easily shaped using plastic wrap: just firm enough to hold its shape when cool yet soft enough to easily drag a cracker through at room temperature.

With my base settled, I turned my attention to different flavor profiles. For a classic cheddar-with-chive cheese log, I combined extra-sharp cheddar with a touch of horseradish, Worcestershire, and garlic. Next, a bacon-covered pimento cheese log, because life is short. Then, I paired goat cheese with herbes de Provence

Equal parts cream cheese and cheddar produce a cheese log soft enough for scooping.

(a widely available herb mixture) for an extra-tangy log. For those occasions when my long-stemmed glass is holding a margarita, there's a green chile and chipotle cheese log coated in crushed tortilla chips. And finally, for the wine and cheese soirée, I coated a soft, mild blue cheese with walnuts, dates, and honey.

CHEDDAR CHEESE LOG WITH CHIVES
Serves 10 to 15

We chill the cheese log in the freezer because it's much easier to roll in the chives when firm. Once the cheese log has been garnished, it can be wrapped tightly in plastic wrap and refrigerated for up to two days. Buy refrigerated prepared horseradish, not the shelf-stable kind, which contains preservatives and additives.

- 6 ounces extra-sharp yellow cheddar cheese, shredded (1½ cups)
- 6 ounces cream cheese
- ¼ cup mayonnaise
- 1 tablespoon prepared horseradish, drained
- 2 teaspoons Worcestershire sauce
- 1 small garlic clove, minced
- ½ teaspoon pepper
- ½ cup minced fresh chives

1. Process cheddar, cream cheese, mayonnaise, horseradish, Worcestershire, garlic, and pepper in food processor until smooth, scraping down sides of bowl as needed, about 1 minute.
2. Lay 18 by 11-inch sheet of plastic wrap on counter with long side parallel to counter edge. Transfer cheese mixture to center of plastic and shape into approximate 9-inch log with long side

parallel to counter edge. Fold plastic over log and roll up. Pinch plastic at ends of log and roll log on counter to form tight cylinder. Tuck ends of plastic underneath. Freeze until completely firm, 1½ to 2 hours.
3. Spread chives on large plate. Unwrap cheese log and roll in chives to evenly coat. Transfer to serving dish and let sit at room temperature for 1 hour. Serve.

PIMENTO CHEESE LOG WITH BACON
Omit horseradish. Add 1 minced small shallot and ¼ teaspoon cayenne pepper to food processor with cheese. After processing, add ½ cup jarred chopped pimentos, patted dry, and pulse to combine, about 3 pulses. Substitute finely chopped cooked bacon for chives.

GOAT CHEESE LOG WITH HERBES DE PROVENCE
Omit mayonnaise and horseradish. Substitute 1½ cups crumbled goat cheese for cheddar and 2 tablespoons extra-virgin olive oil for Worcestershire sauce. Substitute 3 tablespoons herbes de Provence for chives. Drizzle cheese log with 2 tablespoons extra-virgin olive oil before serving.

CHILE CHEESE LOG WITH TORTILLA CHIPS
Substitute Monterey Jack cheese for cheddar, 2 tablespoons minced canned chipotle chile in adobo sauce for horseradish, and lime juice for Worcestershire sauce. After processing, add ⅓ cup drained canned chopped green chiles and pulse to combine, about 3 pulses. Substitute crushed blue corn tortilla chips for chives.

BLUE CHEESE LOG WITH WALNUTS AND HONEY
Omit mayonnaise, horseradish, Worcestershire, and garlic. Substitute 1½ cups soft, mild blue cheese for cheddar. Increase pepper to 1 teaspoon. Substitute ¼ cup walnuts, toasted and chopped fine, and ¼ cup chopped pitted dates for chives. Drizzle cheese log with 2 tablespoons honey before serving.

PIMENTO CHEESE LOG WITH BACON

GOAT CHEESE LOG WITH HERBES DE PROVENCE

CHILE CHEESE LOG WITH TORTILLA CHIPS

BLUE CHEESE LOG WITH WALNUTS AND HONEY

Chicken Chow Mein

Our goal: a flavorful, vibrant supper that comes together quickly.

by Alli Berkey

CHOW MEIN IS an adaptable concept. Translating roughly as "fried noodles," it consists of—you guessed it—noodles cooked quickly together with lightly browned vegetables, sometimes seared meat, and a flavorful sauce. Its flexibility means that over the years, cooks have made it with whatever ingredients are fresh and at hand; we've created many versions in the test kitchen. This time I wanted a simple version for two using ingredients available year-round.

I started by using quick-cooking Chinese egg noodles, which are found near the wonton wrappers in the produce section at my supermarket. Because they bring quite a bit of starchiness to the dish, I found that rinsing them after cooking them in boiling water (for just a few minutes to soften them) was a must to keep the resulting sauce from turning pasty and thick. Also, tossing the rinsed noodles with a bit of vegetable oil kept them from clumping together.

A key part of this dish is quick high-heat cooking, traditionally done in a wok. But we've found that skillets, with their flat bottoms, work better on American stoves, so I used a 12-inch nonstick skillet instead, which had enough surface area for me to keep the ingredients moving around the skillet without spilling out onto my range. It worked beautifully.

While chow mein can come with pork, beef, or even no meat at all, I wanted to use quick-cooking chicken breast, cut into ¼-inch-thick slices. After 2 minutes of cooking the chicken over high heat, I was ready to add my vegetables. Sliced shiitake mushrooms helped bulk up the dish with a meaty earthiness. Carrots provided a bit of sweetness, and celery added a crisp bite. I added minced garlic, ginger, and some chopped scallions (just the white parts for now) for vibrant flavor.

With such intense heat, burning and uneven cooking were clear and present dangers. My experiments proved that it was vital to keep everything moving constantly. For this nonstop movement, a nonstick-friendly wooden spoon or heatproof plastic spatula was essential. The good news? Everything cooks through in just a few short minutes. Off the heat, I tossed in the cooked noodles.

It was now time to bring everything together with a flavorful sauce. A sweet and salty combination of oyster sauce and soy sauce gave me a savory base; a bit of sugar provided just enough sweetness for balance. After a thorough toss, I added a final note of freshness with some chopped scallion greens and a few bean sprouts.

CHICKEN CHOW MEIN FOR TWO

Four ounces of dried angel hair pasta can be substituted for the Chinese egg noodles, if desired. Kikkoman Soy Sauce won the test kitchen's recent taste test of soy sauces. The best tool for grating ginger is a rasp-style grater.

- 4 ounces fresh Chinese egg noodles
- 2 tablespoons vegetable oil
- ¼ cup water
- 2 tablespoons oyster sauce
- 1 tablespoon soy sauce
- 1 teaspoon sugar
- ¼ teaspoon pepper
- 1 (6- to 8-ounce) boneless, skinless chicken breast, trimmed and sliced crosswise ¼ inch thick
- 4 ounces shiitake mushrooms, stemmed and sliced thin
- 1 small carrot, sliced thin on bias
- 1 celery rib, sliced thin on bias
- 3 scallions, green and white parts separated and sliced thin
- 2 garlic cloves, minced
- 2 teaspoons grated fresh ginger
- 2 ounces (1 cup) bean sprouts

1. Bring 3 quarts water to boil in large saucepan. Add noodles and cook until tender. Drain noodles in colander and rinse thoroughly with cold water. Toss noodles and 1 tablespoon oil together in bowl; set aside.
2. Whisk water, oyster sauce, soy sauce, sugar, and pepper together in separate bowl; set aside.
3. Heat remaining 1 tablespoon oil in 12-inch nonstick skillet over high heat until just smoking. Add chicken and cook until browned on both sides, about 2 minutes. Add mushrooms, carrot, and celery and cook, stirring frequently, until vegetables are tender and mushrooms begin to brown, about 4 minutes.
4. Add scallion whites, garlic, and ginger and cook until fragrant, about 30 seconds. Off heat, add bean sprouts, noodles, and sauce mixture and toss to combine. Serve, sprinkled with scallion greens.

Don't let the long ingredient list fool you: This dish comes together in minutes.

The Right Noodles for the Job

We call for fresh Chinese egg noodles here, which are sold in many supermarkets, usually packaged similarly to those pictured below on the left and found refrigerated in or near the produce section. The noodles come in various thicknesses; be sure to buy the thinnest you can find. If you can't find them, you can substitute 4 ounces of dried angel hair pasta. Do not use a thicker Italian pasta such as spaghetti, which will throw off the balance of the dish.

FRESH CHINESE EGG NOODLES
Our top choice for chow mein

ANGEL HAIR PASTA
An acceptable substitute

Inexpensive Blenders

Our winning midrange and high-end blenders are excellent—but pricey. Could we find a decent option for less than $100? *by Hannah Crowley*

7 Blenders 11 Tests

- Blend kale and pineapple smoothies
- Blend frozen strawberry margaritas
- Emulsify mayonnaise
- Puree tomato soup
- Crush ice
- Process chipotle peppers and garlic to check for odor retention and staining
- Make almond butter
- Wash 10 times by hand or in dishwasher
- Measure noise levels on lowest and highest speeds with decibel meter
- Measure lowest speed of each blender with tachometer
- Weigh and measure each blender's jar, base, and blade

OUR WINNING MID-RANGE and high-end blenders, The Breville Hemisphere Control ($199.95) and the Vitamix 5200 ($449.00), respectively, are capable and durable—and expensive. Could we find a good blender for less than $100.00 for those not wanting to spend more? To find out, we selected seven top sellers priced from $60.68 to $99.99 and conducted a taxing series of tests, assessing the quality of the food produced and each model's ease of use and durability.

Flash forward three weeks to our final test—almond butter—and its aftermath. One blender is dead, smoke wafting from its buttons. Two are playing dead. A massacre. And the four survivors have barely produced so-so results. This tough test shows that there is a correlation between price and performance. But not every home cook wants to make nut butter. Some folks just want a darn margarita, a smoothie, or some soup. For them, we found a very good blender.

But first, let's look back to when all seven blenders were still alive and kicking. Throughout testing we noticed that some blended their contents nicely, while others left large chunks of food behind. We compared power; blade shape, size, and positioning; and jar shape but found no blanket explanation for why some models blended better than others. Instead, small differences in blade shape and orientation, jar design, and power allowed some blenders to create better movement inside their jars so that all the food was drawn into the blades and propelled up again.

We noticed that food inside wider jars was bashed about, incorporating extra air; we had to scrape them down more, too. We preferred blenders with narrower jars, as they kept their contents more contained so that their blends were dense and smooth, not frothy, and they required fewer scrape-downs.

Our winner had the narrowest jar, plus three deep vertical ribs running up its sides. At the bottom of the jar, the ribs curved into little ramps designed to direct food from the bottom of the jar up, around, and down again. And they really worked. We could see the food traveling along them and down onto the blades quickly and efficiently.

We often use blenders to make sauces, dressings, and dips with pungent ingredients or in small volumes. To see if the jars would stain or retain odors, we processed chipotle peppers and garlic in each machine. We then tried to make mayonnaise to see how they fared with a small amount of ingredients. Some stained more than others, and four of seven couldn't make mayonnaise, which is especially tricky because it's a small-volume recipe that has to be combined slowly to emulsify properly. Two of the blenders' blades were set too high in relation to the shape of their jars, so they couldn't reach the ingredients underneath to combine them. And three blenders had low speeds that were simply too fast—between 10,000 and 20,000 revolutions per minute (rpm)—preventing the mixture from emulsifying. Blenders with slower low speeds, less than roughly 8,500 rpm, were more likely to be able to emulsify.

We also found major differences in how easy the blenders were to operate. We preferred control panels with easy-to-press, clearly labeled buttons; lighter plastic jars to heavier glass ones; and jars that were easy to attach, detach, and pour from.

Our top-rated model was simple to operate and blended exceptionally well. It couldn't make almond butter, but its overheat protection system stopped its motor so it wouldn't burn out while trying to. The Breville and the Vitamix are clearly superior, but for simple blending tasks, our winner, from Black + Decker, is an excellent choice.

 Go to **CooksCountry.com/jan18** to read the full testing results and see the complete results chart.

KEY **Good ★★★   Fair ★★   Poor ★**

RECOMMENDED

CRITERIA

Black + Decker
Performance FusionBlade Blender
Model: BL6010
Price: $80.26
Decibels: 84.5 (low), 95.3 (high)
Lowest rpm: 8,558
Jar Width: 4.25 in

Blending and Ice Crushing	★★★
Mayonnaise	★★★
Almond Butter	0
Cleaning and Handling	★★
Controls and Operations	★★★
Noise Level	★★★

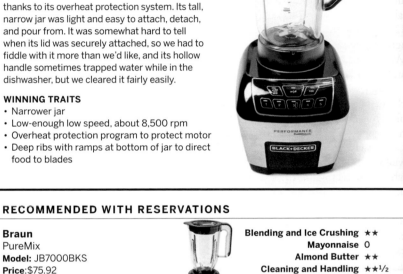

Comments: Our top-rated inexpensive blender made impressively silky smoothies, frozen margaritas, mayonnaise, and pureed soups that were on par with those produced by blenders costing five times as much. It was notably quiet and didn't stain or trap odors. It overheated during the almond butter test but recovered afterward thanks to its overheat protection system. Its tall, narrow jar was light and easy to attach, detach, and pour from. It was somewhat hard to tell when its lid was securely attached, so we had to fiddle with it more than we'd like, and its hollow handle sometimes trapped water while in the dishwasher, but we cleared it fairly easily.

WINNING TRAITS
- Narrower jar
- Low-enough low speed, about 8,500 rpm
- Overheat protection program to protect motor
- Deep ribs with ramps at bottom of jar to direct food to blades

RECOMMENDED WITH RESERVATIONS

Braun
PureMix
Model: JB7000BKS
Price: $75.92
Decibels: 89.4 (low), 95 (high)
Lowest rpm: 10,928
Jar Width: 4.5 in

Blending and Ice Crushing	★★
Mayonnaise	0
Almond Butter	★★
Cleaning and Handling	★★½
Controls and Operations	★★
Noise Level	★★★

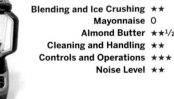

Ninja
Professional Blender
Model: BL610
Price: $64.89
Decibels: 93.6 (low), 97.3 (high)
Lowest rpm: 3,440
Jar Width: 6 in

Blending and Ice Crushing	★★
Mayonnaise	0
Almond Butter	★★½
Cleaning and Handling	★★
Controls and Operations	★★★
Noise Level	★★

Cuisinart
Velocity Ultra 7.5 1 HP Blender
Model: SPB-650
Price: $99.99
Decibels: 92.2 (low), 96.7 (high)
Lowest rpm: 3,411
Jar Width: 5.4 in

Blending and Ice Crushing	★★
Mayonnaise	0
Almond Butter	★★
Cleaning and Handling	★★½
Controls and Operations	★★
Noise Level	★★

NOT RECOMMENDED

Oster Pro
1200 PLUS Blend-n-Go Smoothie Cup & Food Processor Attachment
Model: BLSTMB-CBF-000
Price: $88.28

Hamilton Beach
Multiblend Blender with Built-in Travel Jar
Model: 53517
Price: $60.68

Omega
BL330R Blender
Model: BL330R
Price: $69.95

Supermarket Extra-Sharp Cheddar

The best extra-sharp cheddars are bold but balanced. Which cheese should you buy?

by Lauren Savoie

CHEDDAR COMES IN many styles—mild, sharp, extra-sharp, and more. These terms aren't regulated by the U.S. Food and Drug Administration, but they usually indicate how long a cheese has been aged. Typically, older cheeses are bolder, which is why we choose extra-sharp cheddar when we want stronger, punchier flavor.

Knowing that extra-sharp cheddars are never going to be top-notch melters, we sought a cheese that was fantastic to eat plain but that also held up decently in recipes where melting is required. We selected seven top-selling nationally available cheddars that were either labeled "extra-sharp" or were aged for 12 to 24 months, which most experts agree is typical for extra-sharp cheddars. We tried them plain, in grilled cheese, and in macaroni and cheese.

It was no surprise that some of the cheddars we loved plain for their complex, powerful flavor and crumbly texture were oily and grainy when melted. Conversely, some cheeses that melted well were soft, chewy, and a bit bland when sampled plain. A few struck the perfect balance.

Dean Sommer, cheese and food technologist at the University of Wisconsin's Center for Dairy Research, explained that the characteristics consumers like in a cheese-plate cheddar are at odds with the qualities prized for melting. The longer a cheese ages, the more time bacteria in the cheese have to break down the protein structure and form the flavor compounds responsible for the "sharp" flavor. This protein structure change causes an aged cheese to become more crumbly and drier and not great at melting.

In our lineup, the cheeses that didn't melt well were all aged for close to 24 months. Kraft, the manufacturer of the three best melters (including our winner), wouldn't tell us how long it ages its cheeses, but experts explained that their softer textures and slight give when squeezed meant that these cheeses were likely aged for about 12 months—a year less than some other cheddars.

But of the cheeses that we confirmed or suspected as being aged for about a year, some were flavorful while others were bland. To find out why, we sent all the cheeses to an independent lab to learn more about two key elements: moisture and fat. Aging usually has a direct impact on moisture in cheeses that are rinded or wrapped in porous materials, but supermarket cheddar blocks are wrapped in nonporous plastic and lose remarkably little moisture during aging (which takes place before they're cut into smaller blocks and packaged for purchase). So while aging doesn't affect moisture content much in supermarket cheddar, the amount of moisture in the cheese can affect flavor perception and melting—as can the amount of fat. If the fat or moisture level is too low, a cheese can taste too sharp or even bitter and won't melt well. Conversely, if a cheese has too much fat or moisture, it may melt well but will likely be bland because its flavor is diluted by the fat and water.

The cheddars in our lineup ranged from 32 to 36 percent fat and from 33 to 37 percent moisture. Sommer noted that a mere 1 percent difference in fat or moisture can make a cheese too firm to melt well or too soft for a cheese plate. Our winner contained a relatively high 35 percent fat and 36 percent moisture, which seems to be the ideal combination for a flavorful cheese that melts well.

We chose Cracker Barrel Extra Sharp White Cheddar Cheese as our winner. It not only melted beautifully but was also our favorite for snacking. But we wondered: Why was Cracker Barrel's orange cheddar lower in our ranking? In addition to using annatto, a natural food dye, this cheese was

The Age Conundrum

An older cheddar offers more intense flavor, but it loses the ability to melt perfectly as it ages. If you like bold flavor and aren't going to cook with it, select an older cheddar.

lower in fat and higher in moisture than our winner, so it's likely that it was engineered to be milder.

Manufacturers sometimes make their white and orange cheddars different to suit regional preferences, but Sommer told us there's another factor at play: *terroir*. Although Cracker Barrel wouldn't confirm, these two cheeses are likely produced in different parts of the country. Sommer explained that extra-sharp cheddar, perhaps more than any other cheese, reflects its terroir because aged cheddar picks up a lot of benevolent "contaminant" bacteria from the air, the milk used, and its environment, which impacts its flavor.

Cracker Barrel Extra Sharp White Cheddar Cheese is a great all-around cheese. If you're looking for a stronger flavor for eating plain (not for cooking), we suggest buying a cheese that's aged longer, such as Kerrygold Reserve Cheddar.

RECOMMENDED

Our Favorite

Cracker Barrel
Extra Sharp White Cheddar Cheese
Price: $3.99 for 8 oz ($0.50 per oz)
Color: White
Age: Proprietary
Fat: 35%
Moisture: 36%
Made in: Proprietary

Comments: Described by one taster as "sharp designed to please all palates," this white cheddar was "rich" and "easy to eat," with the "perfect balance of tang." Its moderate amounts of fat and moisture ensured a cheddar that was "crumbly" when sampled plain but still "creamy" when cooked.

Cabot
Vermont Extra Sharp Cheddar Cheese
Price: $3.59 for 8 oz ($0.45 per oz)
Color: White
Age: 12 months
Fat: 33%
Moisture: 37%
Made in: Vermont

Comments: This Vermont-made white cheddar had "great tang" and an "assertive" sharpness that tasters who like bolder cheeses loved. It melted decently, with a "creamy" smoothness and a "pleasant ooze factor," though a few tasters noted some "graininess." Sampled plain, it was "firmer" and was great on crackers.

Kerrygold
Reserve Cheddar
Price: $7.99 for 7 oz ($1.14 per oz)
Color: White
Age: 24 months
Fat: 32%
Moisture: 36%
Made in: Ireland

Comments: Thanks to its moderate moisture level, this Irish import was decently "melty," softening into a "pillowy," "creamy" layer in grilled cheese and coating the pasta nicely in mac and cheese. More polarizing was its "fragrant," "grassy" flavor, which reminded some tasters more of "Parmesan" or "Swiss" than of cheddar.

Cabot
Private Stock Cheddar Cheese
Price: $5.00 for 8 oz ($0.63 per oz)
Color: White
Age: 18 to 24 months
Fat: 34%
Moisture: 37%
Made in: Vermont

Comments: The premium option from Cabot, this aged cheddar was "punchy" and "slightly bitter." When melted, however, it was a bit "gritty," "grainy," and "overly pungent." Said one taster about its grilled cheese: "I would eat the heck out of that cheese on a cracker, but it's way too sharp for a sandwich."

Cracker Barrel
Extra Sharp Cheddar Cheese
Price: $3.99 for 8 oz ($0.50 per oz)
Color: Orange
Age: Proprietary
Fat: 34%
Moisture: 37%
Made in: Proprietary

Comments: This orange cheese was "milky" and "mild," with a "soft," almost "plasticky" texture. When melted, tasters deemed it "classic," "familiar," and "buttery," with the ideal "creamy" smoothness we expect from melted cheese. However, many thought it lacked enough sharpness for snacking plain.

RECOMMENDED WITH RESERVATIONS

Grafton Village Cheese
2 Year Aged Vermont Raw Milk Cheddar Cheese
Price: $5.50 for 8 oz ($0.69 per oz)
Color: White
Age: 24 months
Fat: 36%
Moisture: 33%
Made in: Vermont

Kraft Natural
Extra Sharp Cheddar Cheese
Price: $3.14 for 8 oz ($0.39 per oz)
Color: Orange
Age: Proprietary
Fat: 36%
Moisture: 37%
Made in: Proprietary

Go to **CooksCountry. com/jan18** to read the full tasting results and see the complete results chart.

Chestnut Soup

"As a little kid, I was traumatized by chestnuts in the form of a soufflé that my sister made for Christmas breakfast one year. 'Looks like chocolate,' my young brain calculated. A stolen bite revealed otherwise . . . Choke! I've come around, though, and now I'm a chestnut-obsessed adult."

—ADAM RIED
Cook's Country TV Equipment Corner

We're celebrating the tenth season of Cook's Country from America's Test Kitchen on PBS. Join hosts Julia Collin Davison and Bridget Lancaster, along with cast members Adam Ried (above), Bryan Roof, Christie Morrison, Ashley Moore, and Jack Bishop. Check your local listings or visit CooksCountry.com for more info.

COMING NEXT ISSUE

*We're in the mood for Italian food. To satisfy our cravings, we'll travel to Philadelphia for a big bowl of **Drop Meatballs** and to Brooklyn for a meaty loaf of **Prosciutto Bread**. In between, we'll feast on **Shrimp Tacos**, **Braised Short Ribs**, and our new favorite potato fry-up, **Bubble and Squeak**. We'll engage in a bit of tailgating with **Buffalo Chicken Dip** and finish with a visit to Indiana for a slice of sweet, creamy **Hoosier Pie**. Join us!*

CREAMY CHESTNUT SOUP *Serves 6*
If the soup seems too thick, add extra half-and-half to reach the desired consistency. We prefer homemade chicken stock here. If you use store-bought, choose a low-sodium chicken broth.

- 1 tablespoon unsalted butter
- 12 ounces leeks, white and light green parts only, halved lengthwise, sliced thin, and washed thoroughly
- 1 ripe Bartlett or Bosc pear, peeled, halved, cored, and chopped
- 1 celery rib, chopped
- 1 teaspoon minced fresh thyme
- 1 bay leaf
  Salt and pepper
- 4 cups chicken broth
- 3 cups (14 ounces) peeled cooked chestnuts, chopped
- ¾ cup half-and-half
- 2 tablespoons brandy or cognac
- ½ teaspoon sherry vinegar
  Pinch ground nutmeg
- ¼ cup minced fresh chives

1. Melt butter in large saucepan over medium heat. Add leeks, pear, celery, thyme, bay leaf, and ½ teaspoon salt and cook until leeks just begin to soften, about 3 minutes. Reduce heat to low, cover, and continue to cook, stirring occasionally, until leeks and pears are soft, about 8 minutes longer.
2. Stir in broth and chestnuts and bring to boil over high heat. Reduce heat to medium-low, cover, and simmer until chestnuts are very tender, about 20 minutes. Discard bay leaf.
3. Working in batches, process soup in blender until very smooth, 30 to 60 seconds per batch. (Alternatively, blend with immersion blender until smooth, about 2 minutes.)
4. Transfer soup to clean saucepan. Stir in half-and-half, brandy, vinegar, nutmeg, ½ teaspoon salt, and ¼ teaspoon pepper. Bring to simmer over medium heat. Season with salt and pepper to taste. Serve, sprinkled with chives.

RECIPE INDEX

FIND THE ROOSTER!

A tiny version of this rooster has been hidden in a photo in the pages of this issue. Write to us with its location, and we'll enter you in a random drawing. The first correct entry drawn will win our favorite inexpensive blender, and each of the next five will receive a free one-year subscription to Cook's Country. To enter, visit CooksCountry.com/rooster by December 27, 2017, or write to Rooster DJ18, Cook's Country, 21 Drydock Avenue, Suite 210E, Boston, MA 02210. Include your name and address. Aphton Check of Prairie du Chein, Wisconsin, found the rooster in the August/September 2017 issue on page 18 and won our favorite paper towels.

WEB EXTRAS

Free for four months at
CooksCountry.com

READ US ON IPAD

Download the Cook's Country app for iPad and start a free trial subscription or purchase a single issue of the magazine. All issues are enhanced with full-color Cooking Mode slide shows that provide step-by-step instructions for completing recipes, plus expanded reviews and ratings. Go to CooksCountry.com/iPad to download our app through iTunes.

CHOCOLATE-ALMOND COCONUT CAKE

This showstopper features a shiny chocolate glaze, crunchy almonds, and coconut both inside and out.

by Katie Leaird

TO MAKE THIS CAKE, YOU WILL NEED:

- ½ cup (1½ ounces) sweetened shredded coconut, toasted
- ½ cup sliced almonds, toasted
- 3 (8-inch) Coconut Layer Cake Rounds
- 1 recipe Coconut Cake Filling*
- 1 cup heavy cream
- ¼ cup light corn syrup
- 8 ounces semisweet chocolate, chopped fine
- ½ teaspoon vanilla extract

TO ASSEMBLE:

Combine coconut and almonds in small bowl; set aside. Place 1 cake layer on rimmed baking sheet. Spread half of filling evenly over cake. Top with second cake layer, then spread remaining filling evenly over top. Top with third cake layer. Smooth any filling that has been pushed out from between layers around sides of cake.

FOR THE GLAZE:

Combine cream and corn syrup in medium saucepan and bring to simmer over medium heat. Off heat, stir in chocolate and vanilla until smooth. Let sit until slightly thickened, about 10 minutes. Pour glaze evenly over top and sides of cake. Let sit until glaze is nearly set, about 20 minutes. Gently press coconut-almond mixture onto sides of cake. Refrigerate cake until glaze is fully set, about 30 minutes. Using 2 large spatulas, transfer cake to plate or pedestal. Serve.

COCONUT LAYER CAKE ROUNDS

*Makes three 8-inch layers
or two 9-inch layers*

Cream of coconut is often found in the soda and drink-mix aisle of the grocery store. One 15-ounce can is more than enough for the cake; make sure to stir it well before using because it separates as it stands.

- 1 large egg plus 5 large whites
- ¾ cup cream of coconut
- ¼ cup water
- 1 teaspoon vanilla extract
- 1 teaspoon coconut extract
- 2¼ cups (9 ounces) cake flour
- 1 cup (7 ounces) sugar
- 1 tablespoon baking powder
- ¾ teaspoon salt
- 12 tablespoons unsalted butter, cut into 12 pieces and softened

1. Adjust oven rack to middle position and heat oven to 325 degrees. Grease three 8-inch round cake pans and line with parchment paper.

2. Whisk egg and whites, cream of coconut, water, vanilla, and coconut extract together in 2-cup liquid measuring cup. Using stand mixer fitted with paddle, mix flour, sugar, baking powder, and salt on low speed until combined, about 5 seconds. Add butter, 1 piece at a time, and mix until only pea-size pieces remain, about 1 minute.

3. Add half of egg mixture, increase speed to medium-high, and beat until light and fluffy, about 1 minute. Reduce speed to medium-low, add remaining egg mixture, and beat until incorporated, about 30 seconds. Give batter final stir by hand.

4. Divide batter evenly among prepared pans and smooth tops with rubber spatula. Bake until tops are light golden and toothpick inserted in centers comes out clean, 22 to 24 minutes, rotating pans halfway through baking. Let cakes cool in pans on wire rack for 10 minutes. Remove cakes from pans, discarding parchment, and let cool completely on rack, about 2 hours.

 *Go to CooksCountry.com/jan18 for our Coconut Cake Filling recipe, or use your own recipe.

INSIDE THIS ISSUE